ENGLAND'S NORTHERN FRONTIER

The three counties of England's northern borderlands have long had a reputation as an exceptional and peripheral region within the medieval kingdom, preoccupied with local turbulence as a result of the proximity of a hostile frontier with Scotland. Yet, in the fifteenth century, open war was an infrequent occurrence in a region which is much better understood by historians of fourteenth-century Anglo-Scottish conflict, or of Tudor responses to the so-called border reivers. This first book-length study of England's far north in the fifteenth century addresses conflict, kinship, lordship, law, justice and governance in this dynamic region. It traces the norms and behaviours by which local society sought to manage conflict, arguing that common law and march law were only parts of a mixed framework which included aspects of 'feud' as it is understood in a wider European context. Addressing the counties of Northumberland, Cumberland and Westmorland together, Jackson W. Armstrong transcends an east–west division in the region's historiography and challenges the prevailing understanding of conflict in late medieval England, setting the region within a wider comparative framework.

JACKSON W. ARMSTRONG is Senior Lecturer in History at the University of Aberdeen, where he specialises in late medieval Scottish and English history. He has led two major funded projects concerned with Scotland's earliest and most complete body of legal and town records, the UNESCO-designated Aberdeen council registers. Armstrong has previously served as book reviews editor for the *Scottish Historical Review* and as a trustee of the Society of Antiquaries of Scotland.

Cambridge Studies in Medieval Life and Thought
Fourth Series

General Editor:
JOHN ARNOLD
Professor of Medieval History, University of Cambridge, and Fellow of King's College

Advisory Editors:
CHRISTOPHER BRIGGS
Senior Lecturer in Medieval British Social and Economic History, University of Cambridge,
and Fellow of Selwyn College

ADAM J. KOSTO
Professor of History, Columbia University

ALICE RIO
Professor of Medieval History, King's College London

MAGNUS RYAN
Senior Lecturer in History, University of Cambridge, and Fellow of Peterhouse

The series *Cambridge Studies in Medieval Life and Thought* was inaugurated by G.G. Coulton in 1921; Professor John Arnold now acts as General Editor of the Fourth Series, with Dr Christopher Briggs, Professor Adam J. Kosto, Professor Alice Rio and Dr Magnus Ryan as Advisory Editors. The series brings together outstanding work by medieval scholars over a wide range of human endeavour extending from political economy to the history of ideas.

This is book 118 in the series, and a full list of titles in the series can be found at:
www.cambridge.org/medievallifeandthought

ENGLAND'S NORTHERN FRONTIER

Conflict and Local Society in the Fifteenth-Century Scottish Marches

JACKSON W. ARMSTRONG
University of Aberdeen

CAMBRIDGE
UNIVERSITY PRESS

University Printing House, Cambridge CB2 8BS, United Kingdom

One Liberty Plaza, 20th Floor, New York, NY 10006, USA

477 Williamstown Road, Port Melbourne, VIC 3207, Australia

314–321, 3rd Floor, Plot 3, Splendor Forum, Jasola District Centre, New Delhi – 110025, India

79 Anson Road, #06–04/06, Singapore 079906

Cambridge University Press is part of the University of Cambridge.

It furthers the University's mission by disseminating knowledge in the pursuit of
education, learning, and research at the highest international levels of excellence.

www.cambridge.org
Information on this title: www.cambridge.org/9781108472999
DOI: 10.1017/9781108561686

© Jackson W. Armstrong 2020

This publication is in copyright. Subject to statutory exception
and to the provisions of relevant collective licensing agreements,
no reproduction of any part may take place without the written
permission of Cambridge University Press.

First published 2020

A catalogue record for this publication is available from the British Library.

Library of Congress Cataloging-in-Publication Data
NAMES: Armstrong, Jackson W. (Jackson Webster), 1978– author.
TITLE: England's northern frontier : conflict and local society in the fifteenth-century
Scottish marches / Jackson W. Armstrong, University of Aberdeen.
OTHER TITLES: Conflict and local society in the fifteenth-century Scottish marches
DESCRIPTION: Cambridge, United Kingdom ; New York, NY : Cambridge University Press, 2020.
| Series: Cambridge studies in medieval life and thought: fourth series ; 118 |
Includes bibliographical references and index.
IDENTIFIERS: LCCN 2020012376 (print) | LCCN 2020012377 (ebook) | ISBN 9781108472999
(hardback) | ISBN 9781108460859 (paperback) | ISBN 9781108561686 (epub)
SUBJECTS: LCSH: England, Northern–History–To 1500. | Scottish Borders (England and Scotland)–
History, Military. | Scotland–History, Military–To 1500. | England–Foreign relations–Scotland.
| Scotland–Foreign relations–England. | Great Britain–Politics and government–1399–1485.
| Great Britain–History–Lancaster and York, 1399-1485. | Conflict management–Great Britain–
History–To 1500. | Local government–Great Britain–History–To 1500.
CLASSIFICATION: LCC DA670.N73 A76 2020 (print) | LCC DA670.N73 (ebook) |
DDC 942.7/04–dc23
LC record available at https://lccn.loc.gov/2020012376
LC ebook record available at https://lccn.loc.gov/2020012377

ISBN 978-1-108-47299-9 Hardback

Cambridge University Press has no responsibility for the persistence or accuracy
of URLs for external or third-party internet websites referred to in this publication
and does not guarantee that any content on such websites is, or will remain,
accurate or appropriate.

For Vicky, Findlay and Innes

CONTENTS

List of Figures	*page* ix
List of Maps	x
Acknowledgements	xi
List of Abbreviations	xiv

I	INTRODUCTION	I
	Overview	I
	The Far North, Conflict and Governance	4
	The Problem of Conflict	22
	The Governance of the 'contreis . . . in euery partie off the lande'	36
	Sources and Outline	44

	Part I	47
2	FRONTIERS AND BORDERLANDS	49
	Frontiers and Borderlands	49
	Boundary and Gateway	57
	Writing the Marches	65
3	EARTH AND STONE	74
	Towers and Castles	75
	Landscape and Settlement	93
	Conclusion at Part I	105

	Part II	107
4	THE NOBILITY, GENTRY AND RELIGIOUS HOUSES	109
5	LORDSHIP, KINSHIP AND THE SURNAMES	119
	Lords and Men	120
	Kinship and Landed Society	124
	Naming Customs and Practices	130
	The Surnames	136
	The Surnames of 1498	139

vii

Contents

English Surnames with Scottish Dimensions	145
Models and Indications of Leadership among the Surnames	155
Conclusion at Part II	163

Part III
165

6	THE ADMINISTRATION OF JUSTICE	167
	Justice in England and Europe	168
	Royal Justice and English Common Law	172
	Border Justice and March Law	181
	Conclusion at Chapter 6	197
7	PATTERNS OF CONFLICT	199
	Court Records and Figures: The Evidence Assembled	201
	Conflict and Court Activity	210
	Conflict, War and Truce	224
	Violent Offences	232
	The Border Liberties	236
8	CROSS-BORDER CONFLICT	242
	Lesser Illicit Activity	246
	Aeneas Sylvius Piccolomini's Report	259
	A 'Raiding Culture'	264
	Conclusion at Chapters 7 and 8	268
9	DISCORD	270
	Language and Social Emotion	273
	The Support Group	291
	The Nature of Violence	297
10	CONCORD	308
	Love and Law	309
	The Objectives of Peacemaking	315
	Reconciliation Ceremonies	320
	Compensation	328
	Contracts of Lordship and Kinship	331
11	CONCLUSIONS	337

Bibliography	346
Index	387

viii

FIGURES

1	National upheaval and new KB (total), 1400–50	*page* 202
2	National upheaval and all KB (total), 1400–50	202
3	National upheaval and new KB (total), 1450–1500	203
4	National upheaval and all KB (total), 1450–1500	203
5	National upheaval and new KB (by county), 1400–50	204
6	National upheaval and all KB (by county), 1400–50	205
7	National upheaval and new KB (by county), 1450–1500	206
8	National upheaval and all KB (by county), 1450–1500	207
9	JUST 3 (gaol delivery) offences (total), 1395–1460	208
10	JUST 3 (gaol delivery) offences (by county), 1395–1460	209
11	Truces and new KB (total), 1400–50	225
12	Truces and all KB (total), 1400–50	225
13	Truces and new KB (total), 1450–1500	226
14	Truces and all KB (total), 1450–1500	226
15	Truces and JUST 3 (gaol delivery) offences (total), 1395–1460	227
16	Redesdale, Tynedale and Hexhamshire mentioned in KB, C 1, JUST 3, DURH 3, DURH 19 (offence date used where possible) (total), 1395–1495	228

ix

MAPS

1	The Far North and cellular 'Country-Provinces'	*page* 43
2	The Anglo-Scottish Borderlands	52
3	Cumberland, Westmorland, Furness and parts of Scotland	62
4	Northumberland and parts of Scotland	70
5	Towers in Ireland and Britain	90
6	Rural 'Settlement Provinces' (after Roberts and Wrathmell)	101

ACKNOWLEDGEMENTS

No piece of sustained scholarship would be possible without the generosity and support of others. That is especially so in a work of long gestation, and it is a pleasure to acknowledge the most important debts of gratitude that I have incurred on the long the path of researching and writing this book. My first thanks are to the institutions and people that have given their financial and organisational support for the work that has contributed towards this project. This includes my old college, Trinity Hall, where during 2001–2 and 2003–7 at various times I held funding from the ORS Awards Scheme, a Canadian Social Sciences and Humanities Research Council doctoral fellowship, and funding administered by the Cambridge Commonwealth Trust, the Faculty of History, and the Master and Fellows of Trinity Hall. More recently the University of Aberdeen has supported me with funding for archival research trips, and semesters of research leave in 2013 (when I composed much of Chapter 1 and the broad frame of argument) and 2015 (when Chapters 2 and 3 were written). I owe thanks to the editors and everyone concerned in the production of the book at Cambridge University Press, especially Liz Friend-Smith and Professor Rosamond McKitterick, for their patience and support since this work was first proposed. I am grateful to the series editors and anonymous readers for their reports on draft chapters, and to Stephanie Sakson, who copy-edited the text, and Kate McIntosh, who created the index.

Some acknowledgements are necessary regarding source collections. All materials in the National Archives of the UK and in other repositories have been consulted directly unless stated otherwise. *The Anglo-American Legal Tradition,* the digital image archive assembled by R.C. Palmer, E.K. Palmer and S. Jenks (aalt.law.uh.edu/aalt.html) has been used to check various references. I also register my thanks to those highly skilled archivists and librarians at a number of institutions who have given their expert and invaluable guidance to me on so many occasions when

Acknowledgements

consulting collections in their care. Some of those collections have been in private hands, and I appreciate the permission of the duke of Northumberland to consult archives held at Alnwick Castle and microfilms held in the British Library. Some materials were made accessible to me by other scholars: I remain indebted to Dr Rosemary Milligan-Hayes and Professor Richard Hoyle for, some time ago, generously allowing me access to unpublished transcripts of king's bench indictments after 1460.

We learn from people most of all, and a great number of people have helped advance my understanding of the past in various connections with this book. That includes my colleagues, students and friends in Aberdeen since 2008, particularly those whose conversation has enriched my perspective on England and its neighbours: Mr David Gibbons-Wood; Drs Andrew Dilley, Edda Frankot, Claire Hawes, William Hepburn, Dan MacCannell, Aly Macdonald, Andrew Mackillop, Andrew Simpson, Paula Sweeney, Adelyn Wilson; and Professors Michael P. Brown, Peter Davidson, Karin Friedrich, Robert Frost (and his Pennington kinsfolk), Jane Geddes, Michael Gelting, Bill Naphy, Ralph O'Connor and Jane Stevenson. I should also like to thank my academic colleagues elsewhere whose intellectual stimulation and conversation has helped in the development of this project in different ways, and at different times. This includes the two examiners of my PhD, who were Professor John Watts and the late Dr Jenny Wormald; Dr Amy Blakeway and Dr Peter Crooks (both of whom generously read and commented on portions of the book in draft), Professor Steve Boardman, Professor Michael H. Brown, Dr Caroline Burt, Dr Ali Cathcart, Dr Paul Cavill, Dr Neil Coates, Professor Chris Given-Wilson, Professor Julian Goodare, the late Professor Tony Goodman, Dr Sandy Grant, Dr Andy King, Professor Christian Liddy, Dr Iain MacInnes, Dr Tony Moore, Professor Cynthia Neville, Mr Richard Partington, Professor A.J. Pollard, Dr Sandra Raban, Dr Gianluca Raccagni, Professor Christine Reinle, Professor Jörg Rogge, Dr James Ross, Dr Andrea Ruddick, Dr Benjamin Thompson, Dr Carl Watkins, Dr Paul Webster, and Mr Gunnar Welle are some who stand out. Several others are recognised with specific thanks in the footnotes, and more still unnamed here will know who they are. In many ways this project first began when I was an undergraduate visiting at the University of Edinburgh in 1999–2000. I benefitted from the encouragement of the academic faculty there, a number of whom are named above. That year I also had the pleasure of finding a welcoming network of historically minded friends in and around Carlisle, whose warmth and hospitality were so important to me, and to this project, that year and during subsequent research trips: Stuart Hepburn, Diana Armstrong, and Fiona Armstrong. At Queen's University at Kingston, Professor Monica Sandor

Acknowledgements

faithfully supervised my Honours dissertation (comparing John of Lancaster's letters with Robert Carey's memoirs), and while at Queen's and in subsequent years I remain grateful to Professor Bob Malcolmson for his counsel and wisdom.

My chief academic debt is to Professor Christine Carpenter, who supervised the postgraduate dissertations from which this book has grown. When we first corresponded about my MPhil application well before we met, we bonded over the fact that we were both descended from disreputable border Surnames. Christine mentioned her delight when, many years ago while still a Johnston (her maiden name), she saw a production of John Arden's great play *Armstrong's Last Goodnight* at the National Theatre, and in the opening scenes the plot was set in motion by the killing of Johnston(e) of Wamphray by Johnnie Armstrong of Gilnockie's relations. Since that first exchange and long after her official duties as supervisor concluded, Christine has been an inspiration, teacher and friend of the highest order. In her capacity as the book's progress editor for the Cambridge University Press series she also read the entire manuscript, providing an unstinting critique. We may disagree on various points of interpretation, but her support has always been full and so is my gratitude. It should go without saying that any errors of fact or judgement that remain in this work are my own.

My final thanks are for my family: For my parents Andy and Wynne, whose encouragement and support first enabled me to embark on the journeys that have led to this book. For my parents-in-law Jane and Neil, who have supported me in so many ways, including steady supply of coffee and cheese during writing spells at Greenbank. For my children Findlay and Innes, both always in their ways understanding and wonderfully diverting. My greatest thanks are to my wife Vicky for her patience, love and intellectual companionship. In a sense, I also owe this book thanks for helping me to find her: it was during a research stay in Edinburgh as a postgraduate student that we first met. I have no doubt that her relief at publication will exceed my own. With love this book is dedicated to Vicky, Findlay and Innes.

xiii

ABBREVIATIONS

Note: All references to archival documents in the notes begin with an abbreviation denoting the name of the repository, except for references to documents in The National Archives of the United Kingdom (Public Record Office), Kew.

ADA	*The Acts of the Lords Auditors of Causes and Complaints, 1466–1494*, ed. T. Thomson, (Edinburgh, 1839)
ADC, I	*The Acts of the Lords of Council in Civil Causes, 1478–1495*, ed. T. Thomson (Edinburgh, 1839)
BIHR	*Bulletin of the Institute of Historical Research*
BJRL	*Bulletin of the John Rylands Library*
BL	British Library
CAC	Cumbria Archive Centre
Cal. Deeds	*Calendar of Ancient Deeds*
Cal. Papal Reg.	*Calendar of Entries in the Papal Registers*
Cata. Deeds	*Catalogue of Ancient Deeds*
Cbl.	Cumberland
CChR	*Calendar of the Charter Rolls*
CCR	*Calendar of Close Rolls*
CDS	*Calendar of Documents Relating to Scotland*
CFR	*Calendar of Fine Rolls*
Chron. Hardyng	John Hardyng, *The Chronicle of Iohn Hardyng*, ed. H. Ellis (London, 1812)
CIM	*Calendar of Inquisitions Miscellaneous*
CIPM	*Calendar of Inquisitions Post Mortem*
Coldingham	*Coldingham Correspondence. The Correspondence, Inventories, Account Rolls and Law Proceedings of the Priory of Coldingham*, ed. J. Raine, Surtees Society, 12 (London, 1841)
CPR	*Calendar of Patent Rolls*

xiv

List of Abbreviations

CSL	*Calendar of Signet Letters of Henry IV and Henry V (1399–1422)*, ed. J.L. Kirby (London, 1978)
CWAAS	Cumberland and Westmorland Antiquarian and Archaeological Society
DCM	Durham Cathedral Muniments
DSL	*Dictionary of the Scots Language*, Scottish Language Dictionaries (2001–), http://www.dsl.ac.uk/
DUL	University of Durham Library
EHR	*English Historical Review*
English Chron.	*An English Chronicle, 1377–1461*, ed. W. Marx (Woodbridge, 2003)
English Suits	*English Suits before the Parlement of Paris, 1420–1436*, ed. C.T. Allmand and C.A.J. Armstrong, Camden, 4th ser., 26 (Cambridge, 1982)
ER	*The Exchequer Rolls of Scotland*, ed. J. Stuart et al., 23 vols (Edinburgh, 1878–1908)
Foedera	*Foedera, Conventiones, Litterae etc.*, ed. T. Rymer, 10 vols (Hagae Comitis, 1745; reprint, Farnborough, 1967)
Fox's Register	*The Register of Richard Fox, Lord Bishop of Durham, 1494–1501*, ed. M.P. Howden, Surtees Society, 147 (London, 1932)
GEC	G.E. Cokayne, *The Complete Peerage*, ed. H.V. Gibbs et al., 14 vols (London, 1910–98)
HMC	*Historical Manuscripts Commission*
HNP	Howard of Naworth Papers (in DUL)
HOP	*History of Parliament: The House of Commons 1386–1421*, 4 vols, ed. J.S. Roskell, L. Clark and C. Rawcliffe (Stroud, 1992)
Incerti	*Incerti Scriptoris Chronicon Angliae ...*, ed. J.A. Giles (London, 1848)
JLH	*Journal of Legal History*
JUST	Justices Itinerant
KB	King's Bench
LHR	*Law and History Review*
Liber Pluscardensis	*Liber Pluscardensis*, ed. F.J.H. Skene, 2 vols (Edinburgh, 1877–80)
LOE	*List of Escheators for England and Wales,* ed. A.C. Wood, List and Index Society, 72 (London, 1971)
LOS	*List of Sheriffs for England and Wales*, ed. A. Hughes, Lists and Indexes, Public Record Office, 9 (London, 1898; reprint, New York, 1963)

List of Abbreviations

MED	*The Middle English Compendium* (including *Middle English Dictionary*), ed. F. McSparran et al., University of Michigan (2006–), at https://quod.lib.umich.edu/m/mec/index.html
NA	Northumberland Archives
Nbl.	Northumberland
NCH	*A History of Northumberland. Issued under the Direction of the Northumberland County History Committee*, 15 vols (Newcastle, 1893–1940)
Northern Petitions	*Northern Petitions Illustrative of Life in Berwick, Cumbria and Durham in the Fourteenth Century*, ed. C.M. Fraser (Durham, 1981)
Northumb. Petitions	*Ancient Petitions Relating to Northumberland*, ed. C.M. Fraser, Surtees Society, 176 (Durham and London, 1966)
NRS	National Records of Scotland
NUL	Newcastle University, Philip Robinson Library
OED	*The Oxford English Dictionary* (2nd edn, 1989, and Additions series, 1993–), consulted at *OED Online*, http://dictionary.oed.com
Oxford DNB	*Oxford Dictionary of National Biography*, ed. H.C.G. Matthew and B.H. Harrison (Oxford, 2004)
Pèlerinage	*Le pèlerinage de l'âme de Guillaume de Deguileville*, ed. J. J. Stürzinger, Roxburghe Club (London, 1895)
Plumpton Letters	*The Plumpton Letters and Papers*, ed. J. Kirby, Camden Society, 5th Ser., 8 (Cambridge, 1996)
PPC	*Proceedings and Ordinances of the Privy Council of England*, ed. H. Nicolas, 7 vols (London, 1834–7)
PROME	*The Parliament Rolls of Medieval England, 1275–1504*, ed. C. Given-Wilson, 16 vols (Woodbridge, 2005)
Pylgremage	*The Pylgremage of the Sowle*, ed. F. van Vorsselen (s.d.), consulted at http://pilgrim.grozny.nl
REM	*Return of the Names of Every Member . . ., Part I: Parliaments of England, 1213–1702* (London, 1878)
RMS	*Registrum Magni Sigilli Regum Scotorum. Register of the Great Seal of Scotland*, ed. J.M Thomson et al., 11 vols (Edinburgh, 1882–1914). Scottish Record Society, reprint (Edinburgh, 1984)
Rot. Scot.	*Rotuli Scotiae in Turri Londinensi . . .*, ed. D. Macpherson et al., Record Commission, 2 vols (London, 1814–19)

xvi

List of Abbreviations

RP	*Rotuli Parliamentorum . . .*, ed. J. Strachey et al., Record Commission, 6 vols (London, 1767–7)
RPS	*The Records of the Parliaments of Scotland to 1707*, ed. K. M. Brown et al. (St Andrews, 2007–), www.rps.ac.uk
Scotichronicon	*Scotichronicon by Walter Bower in Latin and English*, ed. D.E.R. Watt, 9 vols (Aberdeen, 1987–98)
SHR	*Scottish Historical Review*
Smyth, *Berkeleys*	John Smyth, *The Lives of the Berkeleys . . . and Description of the Hundred of Berkeley*, ed. J. Maclean, 3 vols (Gloucester, 1883–5)
SR	*Statutes of the Realm*, ed. A. Luders et al., 11 vols in 12, Record Commission (London, 1810–28; republ., London, 1963)
Statuta Ecclesia Scoticanae	*Concilia Scotiae: Ecclesiae Scoticanae Statuta tam Provincilia quam Synodalia quae Supersunt MCCXXV– MDLIX*, ed. J. Robertson, Bannatyne Club, 2 vols (Edinburgh, 1866)
Stonor Letters	*Kingsford's Stonor Letters and Papers, 1290–1483*, ed. M. C. Carpenter (Cambridge, 1996)
TA	*Accounts of the Lord High Treasurer of Scotland, 1473–1498*, ed. T. Dickson and J.B. Paul et al., 13 vols (Edinburgh, 1877–1978)
TCWAAS	*Transactions of the Cumberland and Westmorland Antiquarian and Archaeological Society*
TDGNHAS	*Transactions of the Dumfriesshire and Galloway Natural History and Antiquarian Society*
TRHS	*Transactions of the Royal Historical Society*
Wml.	Westmorland
York Civic Records	*York Civic Records*, ed. A. Raine and D. Sutton, 9 vols, Yorkshire Archaeological Society, Record Ser., 98–138 (Wakefield, York and Leeds, 1939–78)

1

INTRODUCTION

OVERVIEW

This book has two main aims. Its subject is the far north in the fifteenth century, in a time period significant for the region in being much less well understood than either the preceding century (dominated by Anglo-Scottish warfare) or the following one (in which the so-called border reivers were so well documented by Tudor administrators and their Scottish counterparts). The first aim is to investigate the far north in light of its prevailing reputation as different from the rest of England: an alien, turbulent and exceptional 'periphery' distant from the realm's heartland. The question to be pursued is how local society governed itself, in particular, how it sought to manage conflict, in the northern marches. The second aim is the more ambitious. While drawing local, national and international comparisons where relevant and helpful, it is to raise questions from this example about the geography of power and the nature of conflict in the English kingdom as a whole.[1]

Our knowledge of these matters concerning late medieval England is well established. The present state of the field owes its foundation to the work of K.B. McFarlane. In the middle decades of the last century McFarlane rewrote the agenda for the study of politics and political society, demolishing the Whig approach which had dominated for a hundred years. The older interpretation, set by William Stubbs and Charles Plummer, was concentrated on criticism of 'overmighty subjects' and their use of 'bastard feudalism' to secure personal interests, and on seeking to understand England's past chiefly in order to explain the institutional development of parliament as the pillar of Victorian

---

[1] Footnotes in this overview section are kept to a minimum; subsequent notes in this chapter contain full references.

I

Introduction

English liberty.[2] Since the McFarlane reformation, a great deal of work has been done on late medieval England's rich array of archives, which lend themselves well to the study of landowners in the localities. From this has emerged a patchwork of local studies, many of them focused on particular counties; the landmark statement of this type is Christine Carpenter's *Locality and Polity: A Study of Warwickshire Landed Society, 1401–1499*. A number of other works have explicitly used evidence drawn from case studies in certain areas to illuminate national issues. The best examples of this work, such as Edward Powell's *Kingship, Law and Society: Criminal Justice in the Reign of Henry V* and Helen Castor's *The King, the Crown, and the Duchy of Lancaster*, have tended to focus on localities no further north than the midlands. All this has achieved a present understanding of the late medieval (and in particular of the fifteenth-century) kingdom which was defined by a precociously centralised monarchical government, requiring effective rulership exercised by capable kings (and prone to drift towards disaster if kings were unable to provide this). The governance of the realm required cooperation between kings and nobility, and, in turn, collaboration between the nobility and the gentry. In this way private power and public authority were fused together. The private power of all landowners and the ability to command men was derived from land, and the king's law guaranteed rights in land; effective kingship was thus especially about making the law work. The gentry gave their support to the nobility by participating in a nobleman's following or affinity; in return, gentlemen, esquires and knights received their lord's backing in the protection of their landed interests. All landowners shared in a fundamental consensus about the acceptable limits of occasional violence and the preference for swift, informal and peaceful resolution of disputes.[3]

If such is the current understanding of the late medieval kingdom as a whole, the place of the English far north in this framework remains unresolved. 'In a society so disorderly, so physically remote from the king and the central courts at Westminster, bastard feudalism provided the squirearchy with its only hope of some kind of security.'[4] This is one view of the region expressed some time ago by R.L. Storey and it is a perspective which if problematic in some regards has proved

---

[2] M.C. Carpenter, 'Political and Constitutional History: Before and After McFarlane', in R.H. Britnell and A.J. Pollard (eds), *The McFarlane Legacy: Studies in Late Medieval Politics and Society* (New York, 1995), 175–206.

[3] G.L. Harriss, 'Introduction', in K.B. McFarlane (ed.), *England in the Fifteenth Century: Collected Essays* (London, 1981), xx–xxv. For Carpenter, Powell and Castor, see below, notes 31, 43, 82.

[4] R.L. Storey, 'The North of England', in S.B. Chrimes, C.D. Ross and R.A. Griffiths (eds), *Fifteenth-Century England 1399–1509* (Manchester, 1972), 132.

Introduction

remarkably durable.[5] We have come to know a great deal about the late medieval English north generally, or, rather, to know a great deal about the careers of the northern nobility, especially the magnates, and about many of the more prominent knights and barons. Much less is clearly known about the lesser rungs of political society in the region, the lower gentry and upper peasantry, and about the deep assumptions which shaped their choices and actions in local affairs. As it presents the conceptual framework for what is to follow, the second section of this introductory chapter will review the relevant historiography of the north. All the same it is worth noting here at the very outset that the English 'north' is amorphous. The 'north' of course refers to a cardinal direction, an idea, not a place. It took on a particular modern sense as a consequence of industrialisation, but it has a deeper past too, for the 'north' as an idea has always had a mythical status in European culture.[6] For the purposes of this book, the focus is on a defined area, identified in our period as the marches towards Scotland. That consisted of the three counties of Westmorland, Cumberland and Northumberland and the liberties within them. This, as we shall see, has long been understood as a disturbed upland zone with atypical social structures, shaken further by the effects of late medieval Anglo-Scottish border war.

Much of the archival research for this study was completed during the years when the US and NATO-led war in Afghanistan was at its most intense. Journalists at the time regularly reported on 'remote rural' Afghanistan and its 'often violent culture of blood feud and local justice where the reach of central government is weak or non-existent'.[7] The mountainous valleys of the Afghan–Pakistan border were described as 'tribal frontiers'.[8] Influential in shaping such thinking about the region by journalists and Western generals was Sir Winston Churchill's quasi-ethnographical account of his experience there in another conflict, *The Story of the Malakand Field Force: An Episode of Frontier War.*[9] Then Churchill wrote of a world in 'a state of continual tumult' which led the border clans to dwell in fortified towers, possess an 'absolute lack of reverence for all forms of law and authority' and engage in 'family vendettas and private blood feuds' instructed by an honour code

---

[5] For example, see S.G. Ellis, *Defending English Ground: War and Peace in Meath and Northumberland, 1460–1542* (Oxford, 2015), 84. For the development of this theme in the historiography see below, p. 7.

[6] P. Davidson, *The Idea of North* (London, 2005).

[7] 'Afghanistan's Feared Woman Warlord', *BBC News Online,* 16 March 2006.

[8] 'Analysis: Pakistan's Tribal Frontiers', *BBC News Online,* 14 December 2001.

[9] 'Dinner Date with the Presidents', *BBC News Online,* 30 September 2006.

Introduction

'incomprehensible to a logical' and 'civilised' mind.[10] The present study has nothing to do with Afghanistan, but it does have much to do with the ideas expressed here which parallel the range of assumptions at work in enduring interpretations of England's northern frontier in the late middle ages: that it was also a remote and hilly landscape inhabited by feuding clansmen who, in response to incessant tumult, built fortified houses and lived by raiding and feud.[11] One of the chief contentions of this book is that otherwise poorly understood patterns (both violent and peaceful) of local conflict and social organisation are detectable in the northern marches, but that such behaviours and structures were not primarily a consequence of a hostile border or of life in a sub-mountainous landscape. Rather, it will be argued that something like 'feud' may be identified here and explained as a function of a culture of conflict which is best understood in a European context. Of England it has been said that 'if blood-feuds did arise they were rare'.[12] Such was the view expressed by McFarlane on the nature of conflict among the nobility in a foundational essay on the War of the Roses. It is the second aim of this book which is the more daunting: to bring the far north more satisfactorily into a framework of understanding applicable to the whole kingdom. This is to prompt questions about conflict throughout England and, in relation to this, about our understanding of some of the rules, and the geography, of power in the kingdom.

THE FAR NORTH, CONFLICT AND GOVERNANCE

In 1419 the castle of Wark [castrum de Werk] was captured at night by William Haliburton of Fast Castle, who was then tricked [deceptus] by Sir Robert Ogle and killed [interfectus] treacherously [proditorie] along with twenty-three very gallant Scots [Scoti viri fortissimi]. After they had taken the castle, Sir Robert Ogle was there at once, parleying [tractatum] with them and making many promises in connection with handing over the building [deliberacione domus]. But meanwhile the English ascended the rope ladders which the Scots had left hanging from the walls, climbed over and threw the headless corpses [decapitatorum cadavera] of all the Scots over the walls.

—Walter Bower, *Scotichronicon*[13]

---

[10] W.S. Churchill, *The Story of the Malakand Field Force* (2nd edn, London, 1899), 7–8.

[11] See comment on Sir Walter Scott below at note 26.

[12] McFarlane, *England in the Fifteenth Century*, 243.

[13] *Scotichronicon*, viii, 112–13. Wark's description as a '*castrum*' suggests that Wark-on-Tweed is intended, not the tower of Wark-in-Tynedale. See also *Liber Pluscardensis*, i, 353 (Latin); ii, 265 (translation).

Introduction

Thus the chronicler Walter Bower recounted in the 1440s a particularly gruesome, calculated and exhibitory episode of border violence. The Scottish abbot's matter-of-fact prose touches a number of themes pertinent to England's far north, not least that of Anglo-Scottish conflict, which had oscillated fitfully between war and truce since 1296; the most recent interjection of formal peace was that of 1328, quickly abandoned.[14] There is savagery and deceit too: by the fifteenth century the inhabitants of the English northern counties, and especially of those counties within the frontier jurisdiction known as the marches towards Scotland, had a well-established reputation for fierceness and unrest that was observed by English writers.[15] This was not just martial belligerence directed towards the Scottish foe. The experience of border raiding and defence, so the familiar assertion goes, generated a militarised society in a region where violent assault and plunder were accepted and normalised facts of life.[16] Chronicle accounts of the Wars of the Roses that noted 'the malyce of the northermen' are well known to historians, as are the colourful verses on the perfidious and alien nature of the '*Gens Boreae*' penned by Abbot John Whethamstede of St Albans.[17] Malory's Sir Balin 'le saveage' arises from sepentrional stock; 'borne in Northehumbir-londe', without hesitation he decapitates the Lady of the Lake in revenge for the slaughter of his mother.[18] Even if such a perception of English northerners was nothing new, the case has been made that the civil convulsions of the fifteenth century – and the role therein of militarised northerners – was of particular significance in the development of attitudes towards the English north, and of a 'northern consciousness'.[19] In this vein Clement Paston informed his brother by letter following the battle of Wakefield that the 'pepill in the northe robbe and styll and ben

---

[14] I.A. MacInnes, *Scotland's Second War of Independence, 1332–1357* (Woodbridge, 2016), 1.

[15] *Plumpton Letters*, 1; A. Goodman, *The Wars of the Roses: Military Activity and English Society, 1452–97* (London, 2002), 225–6; A.J. Pollard, *North-Eastern England during the Wars of the Roses* (Oxford, 1990), 25–7; H.M. Jewell, *The North-South Divide: The Origins of Northern Consciousness in England* (Manchester, 1994); M.C. Carpenter, *The Wars of the Roses: Politics and the Constitution in England, c. 1437–1509* (Cambridge, 1997), 55–6, 184, 259; A. King, 'The Anglo-Scottish Marches and the Perception of "the North" in Fifteenth-Century England', *Northern History*, 49 (2012), 37–50, esp. 44.

[16] The traditional view is rehearsed in S.G. Ellis, 'Region and Frontier in the English State: The English Far North, 1296–1603', in S.G. Ellis and R. Esser (eds), *Frontiers, Regions and Identities in Europe* (Pisa, 2009), 77–100, at 88; Ellis, *Defending English Ground*, 84.

[17] *English Chron.*, 97; *Political Poems and Songs*, ed. T. Wright, 2 vols, Rolls Ser. (1859–61), ii, 262. Elsewhere Whethamstede wrote affectionately of his kinsmen who served Tynemouth Priory: John Amundesham, *Annales Monasterii S. Albani*, ed. H.T. Riley, 2 vols (London, 1870–1), i, 220.

[18] Thomas Malory, *Malory, Works*, ed. E. Vinaver (2nd edn, Oxford, 1971), 37, 39, 41.

[19] H.M. Jewell, 'North and South: The Antiquity of the Great Divide', *Northern History*, 27 (1991), 1–25, at 19 (discussing William of Malmesbury); Jewell, *North-South Divide*, esp. 42–52, 57–63, 130, 133–4.

Introduction

apoyntyd to pill ... and gyffe a-way menys goodys and lyfflodys in all the sowthe cwntré'.[20] It is telling that the soldier and chronicler John Hardyng, who relished narrating skirmish and war with the Scots, was careful in the 1460s to remind his addressee, Edward IV, of the loyalty of 'the north parte', and to suggest that the oracle of Jeremiah 1:14 referred in fact to the true north: to Scotland.[21] Two decades later the Crowland continuator readily applied the same piece of scripture to the insurrection of the king's northern lieges.[22] Of course, reading such material requires sensitivity to the universal *topos* of northern barbarity and incivility cultivated since classical antiquity, and which is more often to the fore in studies of periods preceding and following the later middle ages.[23] Indeed, historians of Scotland have also become alert to the 'portfolio of developed motifs' upon which late medieval authors drew as they wrote about the peoples of their own realm.[24] Walter Bower himself turned to passages from Vegetius on the *sepentrionales populi* in order to explain the headstrong pugnacity of his co-lieges, the *Scoti transmontani*, those dwelling beyond the Mounth.[25]

This book is about how local society was governed, and governed itself, in particular, how conflict was managed, in England's fifteenth-century far north. These 'remote provinces', wrote Sir Walter Scott in 1814, 'were inhabited by wild clans as lawless as their northern neighbours, resembling them in manners and customs, inhabiting similar

---

[20] *Paston Letters and Papers of the Fifteenth Century,* ed. N. Davis, 2 vols. (Oxford, 1971–6), i, no. 114, p. 198.

[21] *Chron. Hardyng,* 380, 420.

[22] *The Crowland Chronicle Continuations 1459–1486,* ed. N. Pronay and J. Cox (London, 1986), 191, noted by Pollard, *North-Eastern England,* 26n 66.

[23] W.R. Jones, 'The Image of the Barbarian in Medieval Europe', *Comparative Studies in Society and History,* 13 (1971), 376–407; K. Lavezzo, *Angels on the Edge of the World: Geography, Literature and English Community, 1000–1534* (Ithaca, 2006), 65–70. See comment on Jean Bodin in S. Carroll, 'Introduction', in S. Carroll (ed.), *Cultures of Violence: Interpersonal Violence in Historical Perspective* (Basingstoke, 2007), 36. This *topos* later came to be developed and, to an extent, reversed: Montesquieu, *The Spirit of the Laws,* trans. T. Nugent, rev. J. V. Prichard (London, 1914), 241. On perceptions of the Tudor north, see Jewell, *North-South Divide,* 56–76, esp. 63; S.G. Ellis, *Tudor Frontiers and Noble Power: The Making of the British State* (Oxford, 1995), 67–77; S.G. Ellis, 'Civilizing Northumberland: Representations of Englishness in the Tudor State', *Journal of Historical Sociology,* 12 (1999), 103–27; 'Civilizing the Natives: State Formation and the Tudor Monarchy, c. 1400–1603', in S.G. Ellis and L. Klusáková (eds), *Imagining Frontiers, Contesting Identities* (Pisa, 2007), 77–92; Storey, *The End of the House of Lancaster* (London, 1966; rev. 2nd edn, 1999), 105 (on the fifteenth century).

[24] M. MacGregor, 'Gaelic Barbarity and Scottish Identity in the Later Middle Ages', in D. Broun and M. MacGregor (eds), *Mìorun Mòr nan Gall, 'The Great Ill-Will of the Lowlander'? Lowland Perceptions of the Highlands, Medieval and Modern* (Glasgow, 2009), 11; T. Brochard, 'The 'Civilizing' of the Far North of Scotland, 1560–1640', PhD thesis, University of Aberdeen (2010).

[25] MacGregor, 'Gaelic Barbarity', 19; *Scotichronicon,* viii, 266–7.

Introduction

strong-holds, and subsisting, like them, by rapine'.[26] As suggested above, this view has held considerable sway over historians. Even in works of high calibre they have long been satisfied to make colourful throw-away remarks about society in the northern English marches: that it was riddled with 'endemic violence'[27] and a 'characteristic northern indifference to the authority of the law'.[28] Another historian describes the borderlands as 'traditionally lawless and including some of [England's] wildest terrain', a 'sensitive area' where 'problems of maintaining order and administrative machinery were endemic'.[29] In more recent work comparable claims are still to be found about 'a taste for violence and "private" warfare',[30] a 'culture of an unstable march society' in the 'isolated and fragmented world' of the 'rugged border valleys'.[31] Further comment on this 'remote region' has described the far north as 'set apart from the main currents of English society by virtue of the dictates of border warfare and its close proximity to England's perennial enemy'.[32] And other work using evidence drawn from the area points to the role of the 'armed frontier' in fostering 'the social and the legal conditions that [allowed] feuding to continue' in the marches up to the regal union of 1603.[33] There is no question that the late medieval far north was among those parts of the

---

[26] W. Scott, *The Border Antiquities of England and Scotland*, 2 vols (London, 1814), ii, p. lxv.

[27] M.E. James, *Change and Continuity in the Tudor North: The Rise of Thomas, First Lord Wharton* (York, 1965), 7. See also G.M. Trevelyan, *English Social History* (London, 1994), 153.

[28] C.D. Ross, *Edward IV* (London, 1983), 202 (and similar comment at 194 on Wales and the Welsh Marches). For 'endemic' criminality elsewhere, see A. Herbert, 'Herefordshire, 1413–61: Some Aspects of Society and Public Order', in R.A. Griffiths (ed.), *Patronage, The Crown and the Provinces in Later Medieval England* (Gloucester, 1981), 103–22.

[29] J.S. Cockburn, 'The Northern Assize Circuit', *Northern History*, 3 (1968), 118–30, at 122. See also Storey, 'The North of England', 131; G.W. Bernard, *The Power of the Early Tudor Nobility: A Study of the Fourth and Fifth Earls of Shrewsbury* (Brighton, 1985), 109–12.

[30] M.L. Holford and K.J. Stringer, *Border Liberties and Loyalties in North-East England, c. 1200–c. 1400* (Edinburgh, 2010), 322. This important book is discussed below with regard to liberties and franchises.

[31] Ibid., 332. See also M.C. Carpenter, *Locality and Polity: A Study in Warwickshire Landed Society, 1401–1499* (Cambridge, 1992), 484, 641.

[32] M. Arvanigian, 'Henry V, Lancastrian Kingship and the Far North of England', in G. Dodd (ed.), *Henry V: New Interpretations* (Woodbridge, 2013), 77–101, at 77 (quote), 78, 80. See also G. McKelvie, 'Henry VII's Letter to Carlisle in 1498: His Concerns about Retaining in a Border Fortress', *Northern History*, 54 (2017), 149–66, at 151–2; M. Arvanigian, 'A County Community or the Politics of the Nation? Border Service and Baronial Influence in the Palatinate of Durham, 1377–1413', *Historical Research*, 82 (2009), 41–61.

[33] K.J. Kesselring, *Making Murder Public: Homicide in Early Modern England, 1480–1680* (Oxford, 2019), 75 (quote), 83–4. For similar examples, see J.M. Schultz, *National Identity and the Anglo-Scottish Borderlands, 1552–1652* (Woodbridge, 2019), 92, 117; E.M. Jamroziak, *Survival and Success on Medieval Borders: Cistercian Houses in Medieval Scotland and Pomerania from the Twelfth to the Late Fourteenth Century* (Turnhout, 2011), 17–18; D.E. Thiery, 'Plowshares and Swords: Clerical Involvement in Acts of Violence and Peacemaking in Late Medieval England, c. 1400–1536', *Albion*, 36 (2004), 201–22, at 22n 5, 109n 8; J. Gray, 'Lawlessness on the Frontier: The Anglo-Scottish Borderlands in the Fourteenth to Sixteenth Century', *History and Anthropology*, 12 (2001), 381–408.

Introduction

kingdom with the lowest distribution of population and lay wealth.[34] Yet hand in hand with the actuality of a relatively sparsely inhabited and impoverished territory is another old chestnut, that the far north was in consequence isolated and distant, a socially and culturally backward 'dark corner of the land', contrasted with the more populous, prosperous, cultivated and unified south-east.[35]

Linked directly to the view of a remote, violent and hopelessly 'lawless' English far north is an issue that has been fundamental to the historiography of fifteenth-century England as a whole: the role of lordship, both its exercise in the locality and its effects in the wider kingdom. Here most attention has been directed to the greater nobility, in an older school of thought in the guise of the 'overmighty subject'. Not least among these medieval megafauna were the great northern magnates, the Percys and the Nevilles, who, so the older formulation went, flouted royal authority and led their unruly followers in private quarrels, ultimately leading to civil war and the collapse of the Lancastrian regime in the later 1450s.[36] Of course, that regime itself was founded by a vastly 'overmighty subject', and much scholarship concerning the north in the reigns of Richard II and Henry IV has focused on the relationship between the crown and the Percys and Nevilles, who were so important to the Lancastrian usurpation.[37] Arising from this theme is

[34] R.S. Schofield, 'The Geographical Distribution of Wealth in England, 1334–1649', *Economic History Review*, 18 (1965), 483–510, at 506; Jewell, *North-South Divide*, 90–5; G.L. Harriss, *Shaping the Nation: England 1360–1461* (Oxford, 2005), 210. See also *The Poll Taxes of 1377, 1379, and 1381*, ed. C.C. Fenwick, 3 vols (Oxford, 1998–2005).

[35] S.G. Ellis, 'Crown, Community and Government in the English Territories, 1450–1575', *History*, 71 (1986), 187–204; S.G. Ellis, 'The English State and Its Frontiers in the British Isles, 1300–1600', in D.J. Power and N. Standen (eds), *Frontiers in Question: Eurasian Borderlands, 700–1700* (Basingstoke, 1999), 153–81; and M.J. Bennett, *Community, Class and Careerism: Cheshire and Lancashire Society in the Age of 'Sir Gawain and the Green Knight'* (Cambridge, 1983), 8. For a summary, see J. Le Patourel, 'Is Northern History a Subject?', *Northern History*, 12 (1976), 1–15, at 11–13. See also T. Thornton, *Cheshire and the Tudor State 1480–1560* (Woodbridge, 2000), 251; A.J.L. Winchester, *Landscape and Society in Medieval Cumbria* (Edinburgh, 1987), 2; Pollard, *North-Eastern England*, 1–2. On early modern 'dark corners' and an east–west divide, see D. MacCannell, '"Dark Corners of the Land"? A New Approach to Regional Factors in the Civil Wars of England and Wales', *Cultural and Social History*, 7 (2010), 171–89, esp. 174, 185n 23.

[36] An influential interpretation adopted by Storey, *House of Lancaster*, 27; Storey, 'The North of England', 137.

[37] For example, J.M.W. Bean, *The Estates of the Percy Family, 1416–1537* (Oxford, 1958); J.M.W. Bean, 'Henry IV and the Percies', *History*, 44 (1959), 212–27; P. McNiven, 'The Scottish Policy of the Percies and the Strategy of the Rebellion of 1403', *BJRL*, 62 (1979), 498–530; J.A. Tuck, 'Richard II and the Border Magnates', *Northern History*, 3 (1968), 27–52; J.A. Tuck, 'Northumbrian Society in the Fourteenth Century', *Northern History*, 6 (1971), 22–39; J.A. Tuck, 'The Emergence of a Northern Nobility, 1250–1400', *Northern History*, 22 (1986), 1–17; J.A. Tuck, 'The Percies and the Community of Northumberland in the Later Fourteenth Century', in J.A. Tuck and A. Goodman (eds), *War and Border Societies in the Middle Ages* (London, 1992), 178–95.

Introduction

the long-standing notion of a governmental 'problem of the north' generally – not just of the three marcher counties – in which English rulers, on the one hand, needed powerful nobles to defend the border but, on the other, faced a potential threat from these same men.[38] Historians have been less clear as to what areas constituted the region of 'north' which presented this dilemma; certainly, magnates with power bases firmly established in Yorkshire served the crown as wardens of the march, the crown officers who supervised border defence and border law.[39] Older work viewed the wardens as avaricious lords, recruiting from among the gentry 'private armies at the king's expense' and posing a 'formidable a threat to the peace of England'.[40] Certainly, some magnates who served as wardens caused serious trouble. The Percys between 1403 and 1408, and again in 1442–3, the Middleham Nevilles in 1469, and both families in 1453 fit this profile of behaviour,[41] but the role of the wardens and the courts of march law which they administered has come to be viewed as integral to the system not only of local defence but also of peacekeeping in northern England.[42] More generally, historians came to view the gentry followings of late medieval English nobles in a constructive light, no longer simply the unruly consequence of corrupt 'bastard feudal' recruiting, committing depredations at their lord's whim. As already noted, through work inspired by McFarlane, historians' understanding of magnate affinities moved towards appreciating their political complexity. Although sometimes difficult to control (and, so

---

[38] G.T. Lapsley, 'The Problem of the North: A Study in English Border History', *American Historical Review*, 5 (1900), 440–66, at 452; M.L. Bush, 'The Problem of the Far North: A Study of the Crisis of 1537 and Its Consequences', *Northern History*, 6 (1971), 40–63. Reframing this as a wider 'problem of the borders' linking the 'outlying parts' towards Wales, Ireland and Scotland, see Ellis, 'Crown, Community and Government', 193; Ellis, *Tudor Frontiers*, 33, 40–5, 48.

[39] For example, Lapsley, 'Problem of the North', 441; Storey, 'The North of England', 129–31. For comment, Pollard, *North-Eastern England*, 150–3; Jewell, *North-South Divide*, ch. 1; Macdonald, *Border Bloodshed: Scotland, England and France at War 1369–1403* (East Linton, 2000), 202.

[40] R.L. Storey, 'The Wardens of the Marches of England towards Scotland 1377–1489', *EHR*, 72 (1957), 593–615, quotations from 607, 609. See also Tuck, 'Richard II', 27–30, 48. On the wardens, see also T. Hodgkin, *The Wardens of the Northern Marches* (London, 1908); H. Pease, *The Lord Wardens of the Marches of England and Scotland* (London, 1913); R.R. Reid, 'The Office of Warden of the Marches: Its Origin and Early History', *EHR*, 32 (1917), 479–96; S.B. Chrimes, 'Some Letters of John of Lancaster as Warden of the East Marches towards Scotland', *Speculum*, 14 (1939), 3–27; C.H. Hunter Blair, 'The Wardens and Deputy Wardens of the Marches of England towards Scotland in Northumberland', *Archaeologia Aeliana*, 4th ser., 28 (1950), 18–95.

[41] Pollard, *North-Eastern England*, 246–7, 255–7, 304–7; Harriss, *Shaping the Nation*, 496–7, 521–2, 532–3, 607, 627.

[42] C.J. Neville, 'Border Law in Late Medieval England', *JLH*, 9 (1988), 335–56; C.J. Neville, 'Keeping the Peace on the Northern Marches in the Later Middle Ages', *EHR*, 109 (1994), 461–78; C.J. Neville, *Violence, Custom and Law: The Anglo-Scottish Border Lands in the Later Middle Ages* (Edinburgh, 1998). For 1442–3, see R.A. Griffiths, *The Reign of King Henry VI* (Berkeley, 1981), 578–9.

Introduction

the historiography suggests, perhaps especially so in areas distant from Westminster), they could facilitate effective local governance when managed aptly by a powerful lord.[43] The present study is indebted to the work of others who have explored the structures of landed society in the English north and the role of northern magnates in local and national politics. Such work, especially studies of the north-east published in the 1970s–1990s, found that the Percy and Neville of Middleham affinities tended to provide a measure of continuity and a 'stabilising bond' among local nobility and gentry.[44] By contrast, regarding Cumberland and Westmorland, one researcher has argued for the strength of gentry localism triumphing over noble politics, and a similar point has been made about the limits of Percy influence in Northumberland.[45] The period after 1471, however, has produced contradictory interpretations. Whereas earlier scholars argued for continuing crown reliance on powerful northern magnates, like Richard, duke of Gloucester, and Henry Percy, fourth earl of Northumberland, newer work questions the influence these men actually wielded and the extent of the resources put at their disposal by the crown. While Gloucester's influence in Yorkshire has long been understood to have been dependent upon Percy support, research now suggests that his dominance in the north-west was also far from complete.[46] On the other hand, according to one writer, it was

[43] The seminal statement is K.B. McFarlane, 'Bastard Feudalism', in K.B. McFarlane, *England in the Fifteenth Century: Collected Essays* (London, 1981), 23–43. The landmark study is Carpenter, *Locality and Polity,* and indispensable contributions are S. Walker, *The Lancastrian Affinity 1361–1399* (Oxford, 1990); and H.R. Castor, *The King, the Crown, and the Duchy of Lancaster* (Oxford, 2000). See also Carpenter, *Wars of the Roses,* chs 1–3; Harriss, *Shaping the Nation,* 6; M.C. Carpenter, 'Bastard Feudalism in Fourteenth-Century Warwickshire', Dugdale Society Occasional Papers, 52 (2016), esp. 3–5.

[44] Pollard, *North-Eastern England,* 401; P. Jalland, 'The Influence of the Aristocracy on Shire Elections in the North of England, 1450–70', *Speculum,* 47 (1972), 483–507; A.J. Pollard, 'The Northern Retainers of Richard Nevill, Earl of Salisbury', *Northern History,* 11 (1975), 52–69; A.J. Pollard (ed.), *The North of England in the Age of Richard III* (Stroud, 1996); R.A. Griffiths, 'Local Rivalries and National Politics: The Percies, the Nevilles, and the Duke of Exeter, 1452–55', in R.A. Griffiths (ed.), *King and Country: England and Wales in the Fifteenth Century* (London, 1989), 321–64.

[45] (For further comment on more recent work see the following paragraph.) P.W.N. Booth, 'Landed Society in Cumberland and Westmorland, c. 1440–1485: The Politics of the Wars of the Roses', PhD thesis, University of Leicester (1998); P.W.N. Booth, 'Richard Duke of Gloucester and the West March towards Scotland, 1470–1483', *Northern History,* 36 (2000), 233–46, at 237, 239, 241; P.W.N. Booth, 'Men Behaving Badly? The West March towards Scotland and the Percy-Neville Feud', in L. Clark (ed.), *The Fifteenth Century III: Authority and Subversion* (Woodbridge, 2003), 95–116; A. King, '"They have the Hertes of the People by North": Northumberland, the Percies and Henry IV, 1399–1408', in G. Dodd and D. Biggs (eds), *Henry IV: The Establishment of the Regime, 1399–1406* (Woodbridge, 2003), 139–59.

[46] James, *Change and Continuity,* 4–5; M. Weiss, 'A Power in the North? The Percies in the Fifteenth Century', *Historical Journal,* 19 (1976), 501–9; M. Hicks, 'Dynastic Change and Northern Society: The Career of the Fourth Earl of Northumberland, 1470–89', *Northern History,* 14 (1978), 78–107;

Introduction

during the period when Richard himself was king that there occurred 'the revival of royal authority' in the north which, from the 1450s, the crown had relinquished to the Middleham Nevilles and Gloucester as their successor, commanding the largest northern affinity.[47] This has been compared with similar consolidations at this time in the Welsh and Irish marches. The early Tudor period from 1485 is generally understood to have involved new and direct royal intrusion into networks of lordship in the far north. The 1490s is the decade from which source materials relating directly to the marches begin to survive in greater number. They consequently give an impression of escalating unrest, even as other parts of the kingdom experienced relative stability.[48] In contrast to older views on the failings of the nobility, a consensus now exists that governmental policy under the early Tudors at best caused new problems in place of old ones and, at worst, may have been fundamentally destabilising.[49]

The emphasis of the last half-century of scholarship on the north has generally been on tracing forces for continuity and stability in what had conventionally been seen as a turbulent and widely disturbed region.[50] This includes significant attention (by no means limited to the marcher

C.D. Ross, *Richard III* (London, 1981), 168; Ross, *Edward IV*, 200–3, 339–40; R. Horrox (ed.), *Richard III and the North* (Hull, 1986); K. Dockray, 'Richard III and the Yorkshire Gentry, c. 1471–1485', in P.W. Hammond (ed.), *Richard III: Loyalty, Lordship and Law* (London, 1986), 38–57; Ellis, *Tudor Frontiers*, 40–4, 48. For Carlisle's relations with local landowners, see H.R.T. Summerson, *Medieval Carlisle*, 2 vols (Kendal, 1993); H.R.T. Summerson, 'Carlisle and the English West March in the Later Middle Ages', in A.J. Pollard (ed.), *The North of England in the Age of Richard III* (Stroud, 1996), 89–113.

[47] On Gloucester, see R. Horrox, *Richard III: A Study of Service* (Cambridge, 1989), ch. 1. A.J. Pollard, 'Introduction', in Pollard (ed.), *Age of Richard III*, xvi, quotation from xix–xx.

[48] Pollard, *North-Eastern England*, 403–4; Ross, *Richard III*, 193–204; James, *Change and Continuity*; M.E. James, *A Tudor Magnate and the Tudor State: Henry Fifth Earl of Northumberland* (York, 1966); M.E. James, 'The First Earl of Cumberland (1493–1542) and the Decline of Northern Feudalism', *Northern History*, 1 (1966), 43–69, at 48–9; S.G. Ellis, *Reform and Revival: English Government in Ireland, 1470–1534* (Woodbridge, 1986); S.G. Ellis, 'A Border Baron and the Tudor State: The Rise and Fall of Lord Dacre of the North', *Historical Journal*, 35 (1992), 253–77; Ellis, *Tudor Frontiers*, 260–2.

[49] Ellis, *Tudor Frontiers*; S.J. Gunn, *Early Tudor Government, 1485–1558* (Basingstoke, 1995), 62–70; R.B. Dobson, 'Politics and the Church in the Fifteenth-Century North', in Pollard (ed.), *Age of Richard III*, 1–17, at 6; Pollard, 'Introduction', in ibid., xii–xiii; Carpenter, *Wars of the Roses*, 23, 25; C. Etty, 'A Tudor Solution to the "Problem of the North"? Government and the Marches towards Scotland, 1509–1529', *Northern History*, 39 (2002), 209–26.

[50] Pollard, *North-Eastern England*, 5, and ch. 1; A.J. Pollard, 'The Crown and the County Palatine of Durham, 1437–94', in Pollard (ed.), *Age of Richard III*, 67–88; Dobson, 'Politics and the Church'; A.J. Pollard, 'The Characteristics of the Fifteenth-Century North', in J.C. Appleby and P. Dalton (eds), *Government, Religion and Society in Northern England, 1000–1700* (Stroud, 1997), 131–43; R.H. Britnell and C.D. Liddy (eds), *North-East England in the Later Middle Ages* (Woodbridge, 2005); A. King and M.A. Penman (eds), *England and Scotland in the Fourteenth Century: New Perspectives* (Woodbridge, 2007).

Introduction

counties) directed towards the political and social roles of ecclesiastical institutions, chiefly those based at York, Durham and Carlisle, in promoting good order.[51] With reference to the north-east generally and especially the work of Pollard, the trend has been to normalise local society, to minimise the extent of the area that can be characterised as a 'true frontier zone',[52] to acknowledge that the effects of war with Scotland were restricted to northern Northumberland[53] and to come to see the gentry of the north-east as 'in almost all respects like gentry societies elsewhere in late medieval England'.[54] There are dissenting voices. Ellis's focus on the north-west continues to highlight the turbulent 'otherness' of that part of the realm: relatively impoverished, violent and militarised. His arguments in this regard, and recently extended to the north-east, are ultimately in pursuit of the sixteenth-century origins of the British state (a matter to which we shall return in a moment) and rely on a dynamic between English heartland and borderland in which the latter was exceptional in its lack of uniformity and in its vast territorial scope.[55] Indeed, the notion that within this northern borderland one corner was wilder than the other is not a new one.[56] The line of interpretation in some ways reflects the tendency of researchers to approach the late medieval and early modern marches from one side of the Pennines or the other. To such an extent the north-east and the north-west seem to occupy their own intellectual 'provinces' and have tended to generate their own subregional historiographies, following a pattern established by antiquarians like William Nicolson and Richard Burn, for Westmorland and Cumberland, and James Raine and John Hodgson for Northumberland; indeed, each produced its own

---

[51] R.B. Dobson, 'Richard Bell, Prior of Durham (1464–78) and Bishop of Carlisle (1478–95)', *TCWAAS*, n.s., 65 (1965), 182–221; R.B. Dobson, *Durham Priory 1400–1450* (London, 1973); R.B. Dobson, 'Cathedral Chapters and Cathedral Cities: York, Durham and Carlisle in the Fifteenth Century', *Northern History*, 19 (1983), 15–44; R.B. Dobson, 'The Northern Province in the Later Middle Ages', *Northern History*, 42 (2005), 49–60; C.D. Liddy, *The Bishopric of Durham in the Late Middle Ages* (Woodbridge, 2008); Holford and Stringer, *Border Liberties and Loyalties*.

[52] Pollard, *North-Eastern England*, 20. See also B.W. Beckingsale, 'The Characteristics of the Tudor North', *Northern History*, 4 (1969), 67–83.

[53] Pollard, *North-Eastern England*, 46. See also Liddy, *Bishopric of Durham*, 14. See below, p. 92.

[54] A.J. Pollard, 'Use and Ornament: Late-Twentieth-Century Historians on the Late Medieval North-East', *Northern History*, 42 (2005), 61–74, at 66.

[55] See below, p. 20. Ellis, *Tudor Frontiers*, esp. ch. 2; Ellis, 'The English State', 155, 163; Ellis, *Defending English Ground*, 12–14, 40. Ellis emphasises the 'turbulent lineage society' of the far north (e.g., 'A Crisis of the Aristocracy? Frontiers and Noble Power in the Early Tudor State', in J.A. Guy (ed.), *The Tudor Monarchy* (London, 1997), 330–40, at 331, echoing James, *Change and Continuity*, 6.

[56] The East March's reputation for relative tranquillity was noted by Scott, *The Border Antiquities*, ii, p. lxv; *Statuta Ecclesiae Scoticanae*, i, p. xcvi, n 2.

Introduction

assortment of antiquarian societies.[57] Although historians of the far north of course remain in dialogue, the partition has tended to be reinforced by present-day concentrations of research and funding.[58]

Taking the English far north as a whole, as this book does now, there are further issues that relate to its long-standing reputation for disorder and tumult, and current refinements or reassessments of that view. In recent years a major study of the north-east has offered detailed local analyses of several franchise lordships north of the Tees before 1400.[59] In doing so it addresses a vital concern linked to the historiographical 'problem of the north': the presence of special liberties that, at worst, were lawless enclaves whose presence ensured the area was not governed like the rest of the kingdom.[60] That study finds significant variation between these franchises not only in the degree of jurisdictional autonomy they asserted but also in their ability to act as cohesive focal points for local landowners. With reference to the liberties of Northumberland in the fourteenth century, it finds that, partly as a consequence of the pressures of warfare, these were highly adaptable structures 'layered' into the governmental landscape of the kingdom and that their gentry inhabitants were active participants in society beyond each lordship.[61] All the same, for the liberty of Tynedale in particular, the authors find 'fluctuating allegiances ... and assaults on enemy and neighbour alike'

---

[57] W. Nicolson and R. Burn, *The History and Antiquities of the Counties of Westmorland and Cumberland*, 2 vols (London, 1777); J. Hodgson, *A History of Northumberland*, 3 vols in 7 (Newcastle, 1820–58); *The Priory of Hexham*, ed. J. Raine (Durham, 1864–65); *The History and Antiquities of North Durham*, ed. J. Raine (London, 1852).

[58] Exemplary for the north-west is the work of Ellis and of Summerson, noted above. See also Winchester, *Landscape and Society*; A.J.L. Winchester, *The Harvest of the Hills: Rural Life in Northern England and the Scottish Borders 1400–1700* (Edinburgh, 2000); Booth, 'Landed Society'; Booth, 'Richard, Duke of Gloucester'; Booth, 'Men Behaving Badly?'; J.P. Marsh, 'Landed Society in the Far North-West of England, 1332–1461', PhD thesis, University of Lancaster (2001). Exemplary for the north-east are Pollard, *North-Eastern England*; R.A. Lomas, *North-East England in the Middle Ages* (Edinburgh, 1992); M.M. Meikle, *A British Frontier? Lairds and Gentlemen in the Eastern Borders, 1540–1603* (East Linton, 2004); Britnell and Liddy (eds), *North-East England*; and A. King, 'Englishmen, Scots and Marchers: National and Local Identities in Thomas Gray's *Scalacronica*', *Northern History*, 36 (2000), 217–32; A. King, 'Best of Enemies: Were the Fourteenth-Century Anglo-Scottish Marches a "Frontier Society"?', in A. King and M.A. Penman (eds), *England and Scotland in the Fourteenth Century: New Perspectives* (Woodbridge, 2007), 116–35; King, 'The Anglo-Scottish Marches'. The establishment of the North-East England History Institute (NEEHI) and its associated book series underscored these concentrations, even as the journal *Northern History* has continued a wider dialogue.

[59] Holford and Stringer, *Border Liberties*.

[60] Lapsley, 'Problem of the North', 452. See also Ellis, 'Crown, Community and Government', 192–3.

[61] Holford and Stringer, *Border Liberties*, esp. 413–32, at 419 and 430–1. Their analysis generally follows in the path set by Pollard, *North-Eastern England*.

Introduction

resulting from the shock of fourteenth-century war.[62] Of course, England's far north was not alone in accommodating privileged jurisdictions. The historiography of Cheshire has tended to rely upon an understanding of a highly militarised local society, given to violence and disorder, and reinforced by palatinate privilege.[63] Cheshire's geographical location situates it conceptually as partly northern (with strong links to Lancashire, another palatine county, a point to which we shall return below), but it is Cheshire's orientation towards Wales that has more often underpinned historical interpretations of the palatinate.[64] Work directly concerned with the late medieval Principality and March of Wales reveals a similar outlook on franchises and their potential to shelter lawbreakers and encourage unrest.[65] Looking over the sea, the English lordship in late medieval Ireland has undergone fresh scrutiny, but the theme of disorder has long been a staple in the historical study of that territory too.[66] All these places were situated on or adjacent to frontiers which were at times sites of military conflict; to varying degrees they were marcher territories. Particularistic arrangements for immunity have sometimes been explained as a consequence of the need for delegated royal authority in districts requiring special strategic consideration; more generally, they may be seen as an attribute of a wider pattern of large and coherent lordships existing beyond southern and midland England where a more fragmented organisation of landholding was common.[67] Yet the problem of franchise liberties remains unresolved. Led by recent studies of

---

[62] Holford and Stringer, *Border Liberties*, 322 (cf. 396 for Redesdale).

[63] See the historiographical survey in Thornton, *Cheshire*, esp. 8–10, and 189–91; also Bennett, *Community, Class and Careerism*, 11, 243–4, tending to emphasise the importance of military service rather than local conflict.

[64] P. Morgan, *War and Society in Medieval Cheshire, 1277–1403* (Manchester, 1987). See also Harriss, *Shaping the Nation*, 177; Thornton, *Cheshire*, 252.

[65] R.R. Davies, *Lordship and Society in the March of Wales, 1282–1400* (Oxford, 1978), 277; G. Williams, *Renewal and Reformation: Wales c. 1415–1642* (Oxford, 1993), 46–54; R.A. Griffiths, 'Wales and the Marches in the Fifteenth Century', in Chrimes, Ross and Griffiths (eds), *Fifteenth-Century England*, 145–72; R.A. Griffiths, 'Patronage, Politics and the Principality of Wales, 1413–1461', in Hearder and Loyn (eds), *British Government and Administration*, 69–86; see also R.A. Griffiths, T. Hopkins and R. Howell (eds), *Gwent County History, Volume II: The Age of the Marcher Lords, c. 1070–1536* (Cardiff, 2008), ch. 10.

[66] J.F. Lydon, 'The Problem of the Frontier in Medieval Ireland', *Topic*, 13 (1967), 5–22; R. Frame, *Ireland and Britain, 1170–1450* (London, 1998), 206–9; Ellis, *Ireland in the Age of the Tudors, 1447–1603* (London, 1998), 20; P. Crooks, 'Factions, Feuds and Noble Power in Late Medieval Ireland, c. 1356–1496', *Irish Historical Studies*, 35 (2007), 425–54, at 427; B. Smith, *Crisis and Survival in Late Medieval Ireland: The English of Louth and Their Neighbours, 1330–1450* (Oxford, 2013), 183; Ellis, *Defending English Ground*, 37–45, 52.

[67] An important summary is given by R. Frame, *The Political Development of the British Isles, 1100–1400* (Oxford, 1990), 64–5, 68–9. See also Ellis, *Tudor Frontiers*, 33–6, 40–4; Bennett, *Community, Class and Careerism*, 11; R.L. Storey, *Thomas Langley and the Bishopric of Durham 1406–1437* (London, 1961), 144; Storey, 'The North of England', 138–42.

Introduction

Cheshire and Durham, significant complexity has been shown to be at work in the vigorous longevity of such autonomous jurisdictions, and variegation and pluralism rather than national uniformity have been the keynotes in understandings of the wider English polity formulated through such work.[68] In reviewing all this it is important to observe that the liberties near to England's border with Scotland were situated in a region that was distinctive for being the only part of the English realm which bounded another sovereign kingdom, of the kind that Reynolds describes as a regnal community.[69]

The English far north, and the Anglo-Scottish marches generally, have long been understood to be an area 'strongly and uniquely influenced' by war.[70] This view is indeed repeated over and over in late medieval petitions from the marcher counties pleading exemptions in light of raiding and burning by Scottish 'enemies', and it has shaped assumptions about an intrinsic violent pathology in the region, highlighted in the remarks noted above.[71] Yet all the same, in 1584 it was to be *long peace* with Scotland that was among the causes attributed by Elizabethan officials to 'decay' in the marches.[72] War (or its absence) is not alone in being held up as shaping the distinctive character of the marches. Given a reputation for 'lawlessness', it is not without irony that another characteristic feature of the borderlands is its legal framework – the law of the march administered by the wardens in their judicial capacity. The work of two historians illustrates directions of scholarship on the two themes of border war and border law. One is Macdonald, who considers the military history of the fourteenth-century Anglo-Scottish marches, a

---

[68] Thornton, *Cheshire*, 250, 252; T. Thornton, 'Fifteenth-Century Durham and the Problem of Provincial Liberties in England and the Wider Territories of the English Crown', *TRHS*, 6th ser., 11 (2001), 83–100; Liddy, *Bishopric of Durham*, 6, 9, 12; Holford and Stringer, *Border Liberties*, 365, 398, 410–11 (discussing Redesdale); T. Johnson, 'Law, Space, and Local Knowledge in Late-Medieval England', PhD thesis, Birkbeck, University of London (2014), 197–202.

[69] S. Reynolds, *Kingdoms and Communities in Western Europe, 900–1300* (Oxford, 1984), 254, 262, 274. See below, p. 51.

[70] Macdonald, *Border Bloodshed*, 6 (quote); see also MacInnes, *Scotland's Second War of Independence*, 157–97; Pollard, *North-Eastern England*, 207–16, 219; J.A. Tuck, 'War and Society in the Medieval North', *Northern History*, 11 (1985), 33–52; P.C. Maddern, *Violence and Social Order: East Anglia 1422–1442* (Oxford, 1992), 17–18; M.C. Carpenter, 'Law, Justice and Landowners in Late Medieval England', *LHR*, 1 (1983), 205–37, at 229. A classic statement is Nicolson and Burn, *History and Antiquities*, i, pp. vii–cxxiv, esp. vii.

[71] R.T. Spence, 'The Pacification of the Cumberland Borders, 1593–1628', *Northern History*, 13 (1977), 59–160, at 156: The Borders were 'an essentially closed society whose endemic violence was partly absorbed internally'.

[72] R. Newton, 'The Decay of the Borders: Tudor Northumberland in Transition', in C.W. Chalklin and M.A. Havinden (eds), *Rural Change and Urban Growth, 1500–1800* (London, 1974), 2–31, at 16–17.

Introduction

subject that continues to draw the bulk of scholarly attention on the late medieval borders.[73] He challenges the application back into the later middle ages of a sixteenth-century model of the borderlands based on expectations of an illicit culture of kin-based feuding and livestock raiding (a model that has influenced ideas about the social retardation of both sides of the border).[74] He studies warfare from a Scottish governmental perspective, providing an explanation for Anglo-Scottish conflict which helpfully goes beyond untested assumptions about endemic border violence.[75] The other historian is Neville, who can be counted among those who have taken a long view to look fruitfully across the period from the thirteenth century to the sixteenth.[76] Her work in this area (which concludes in 1502) concerns the legal history of the marches. Neville examines the development of march law and the march wardens who, by the fifteenth century, had a dual role in supervising border defence and border justice, the latter according to march law in both domestic and international courts.[77] Neville also addresses certain common law courts and the operation of the judicial apparatus

[73] A significant portion of this vast historiography is captured in the work referenced throughout King and Penman (eds), *England and Scotland*; A. King and D. Simpkin (eds), *England and Scotland at War, c. 1296–c. 1513* (Leiden, 2012); A.J. Macdonald, 'Courage, Fear and the Experience of the Later Medieval Scottish Soldier', *SHR* 92 (2013), 179–206; A.J. Macdonald, 'Trickery, Mockery and the Scottish Way of War', *Proceedings of the Society of Antiquaries of Scotland* 143 (2013), 319–37; MacInnes, *Scotland's Second War of Independence*.

[74] A classic statement of the sixteenth-century model is D.L.W. Tough, *The Last Years of a Frontier* (Oxford, 1928), and, of course, *The Memoirs of Robert Carey*, ed. F.H. Mares (Oxford, 1972). Aspects of the border ballad tradition have been examined in J. Reed (ed.) *The Border Ballads* (London, 1973); J. Reed, 'The Ballad and the Source: Some Literary Reflections on the Battle of Otterburn', in J.A. Tuck and A. Goodman (eds), *War and Border Societies in the Middle Ages* (London, 1992), 94–123.

[75] Macdonald, *Border Bloodshed*, 6–7, 198–202; A.J. Macdonald, 'Approaches to Conflict on the Anglo-Scottish Borders in the Late Fourteenth Century', in A.I. Macinnes et al. (eds), *Ships, Guns and Bibles in the North Sea and Baltic States, c. 1350–c. 1700* (East Linton, 2000), 47–64. Tuck, 'War and Society', is an example of the approach that Macdonald scrutinises.

[76] Others include A. Goodman, 'Religion and Warfare in the Anglo-Scottish Marches', in R.J. Bartlett and A. MacKay (eds), *Medieval Frontier Societies* (Oxford, 1989), 245–66; R.A. Lomas, 'The Impact of Border Warfare: The Scots and South Tweedside, c. 1290–c. 1520', *SHR*, 75 (1996), 143–67; H.R.T. Summerson, 'Peacekeepers and Lawbreakers in Medieval Northumberland, c. 1200–c. 1500', in M. Prestwich (ed.), *Liberties and Identities in the Medieval British Isles* (Woodbridge, 2008), 56–76. A literary overview is offered in M.P. Bruce and K.H. Terrell (eds), *The Anglo-Scottish Border and the Shaping of Identity, 1300–1600* (New York, 2012).

[77] Neville, 'Border Law'; Neville, 'Keeping the Peace'; Neville, *Violence, Custom and Law*; C.J. Neville, 'The Law of Treason in the English Border Counties in the Later Middle Ages', *LHR*, 9 (1991), 1–30; C.J. Neville, 'Scottish Influences on the Medieval Laws of the Anglo-Scottish Marches,' *SHR*, 81 (2002), 161–85; C.J. Neville, 'Remembering the Legal Past: Anglo-Scottish Border Law and Practice in the Later Middle Ages', in Britnell and Liddy (eds), *North-East England*, 43–56; C.J. Neville, 'Arbitration and Anglo-Scottish Border Law in the Later Middle Ages', in Prestwich (ed.), *Liberties and Identities*, 37–55.

Introduction

available to the English royal administration in the marches.[78] Although both writers in some measure offer a cross-border study, Neville generally adopts the perspective of the English government, a view which is comparable to Macdonald's emphasis on a Scottish governmental perspective.

Whereas medieval Anglo-Scottish relations and diplomacy have a substantial historiography,[79] dedicated cross-border studies are uncommon, and those for the fifteenth century are even more rare.[80] A signal reason for this is the disparity of source materials, something which makes a comparative study problematic. A doctoral thesis by Cardew in 1974 first attempted this through 'a detailed descriptive survey of the society of the Anglo-Scottish borders in the second half of the fifteenth century'.[81] That thesis does what it sets out to do and concentrates heavily on the relatively source-rich 1490s. It is a creation of its time, predating the major reassessments of law and governance that emerged in the 1980s.[82] The only published cross-border study of the fifteenth century is Goodman's article of 1987 that focused on ties of economy and kinship. There he argues that the marches, divided by a precariously

---

[78] C.J. Neville, 'Gaol Delivery in the Border Counties, 1439–1459', *Northern History*, 19 (1983), 45–60; C.J. Neville, 'War, Crime and Local Communities in the North of England in the Later Middle Ages', in J. Drendel (ed.), *La Société Rurale et les Institutions Gouvernementales au Moyen Âge* (Montreal, 1995), 189–201.

[79] P.J. Bradley, 'Henry V's Scottish Policy: A Study in Realpolitik', in P.J. Bradley and J.S. Hamilton (eds), *Documenting the Past* (Woodbridge, 1989), 177–95; D. Dunlop, 'The "Redresses and Reparacons of Attemptates": Alexander Legh's Instructions from Edward IV, March–April 1475', *Historical Research*, 63 (1990), 340–53; A. Young, 'The North and Anglo-Scottish Relations in the Thirteenth Century', in J. C. Appleby and P. Dalton (eds), *Government, Religion and Society in Northern England, 1000–1700* (Stroud, 1997), 77–89; M.H. Brown, 'French Alliance or English Peace? Scotland and the Last Phase of the Hundred Years War, 1415–53', in L. Clark (ed.), *The Fifteenth Century VII: Conflicts, Consequences and the Crown in the Late Middle Ages* (Woodbridge, 2007), 81–99; J.-P. Genet, 'Scotland in the Later Middle Ages: A Province or a Foreign Kingdom of the English?', in H. Skoda, P. Lantschner and R.L.J. Shaw (eds), *Contact and Exchange in Later Medieval Europe: Essays in Honour of Malcolm Vale* (Woodbridge, 2012), 127–43.

[80] The substantial published cross-border studies concerning the sixteenth century are Meikle, *A British Frontier*; and Schultz, *National Identity and the Anglo-Scottish Borderlands*. For the central middle ages, see most recently the essays collected in K.J. Stringer and A.J.L. Winchester (eds), *Northern England and Southern Scotland in the Central Middle Ages* (Woodbridge, 2017); for earlier treatments, see G.W.S. Barrow, 'The Anglo-Scottish Border', *Northern History*, 1 (1966), 21–42; G.W.S. Barrow, 'Frontier and Settlement: Which Influenced Which? England and Scotland, 1100–1300', in Bartlett and MacKay (eds), *Medieval Frontier Societies*, 3–21; G.W.S. Barrow, 'The Anglo-Scottish Border: Growth and Structure in the Middle Ages', in W. Haubrichs and R. Schneider (eds), *Grenzen und Grenzregionen, Frontières et régions frontalières, Borders and Border Regions* (Saarbrücken, 1993), 197–212; K.J. Stringer, 'North-East England and Scotland in the Middle Ages', *Innes Review*, 44 (1993), 88–99.

[81] A. Cardew, 'A Study of Society on the Anglo-Scottish Border 1455–1502', PhD thesis, University of St Andrews (1974), iii.

[82] Exemplified in E. Powell, *Kingship, Law, and Society: Criminal Justice in the Reign of Henry V* (Oxford, 1989).

Introduction

restored boundary following the upheavals of the fourteenth century, comprised a singular 'frontier society' in two halves, in which cross-border contacts may have been more frequent and significant for common borderers than for their social superiors. Goodman pointed to indications of low population levels, coinciding with the abandonment of cultivated settlement in favour of pastoralism. Goodman raised for investigation the topic of acculturation – in the sense of cross-border recognition of shared cultural values, habits and pursuits, not least with reference to martial behaviour.[83] Unlike the more developed discussion of acculturation in an Anglo-Irish context (recently advanced even further by Booker),[84] debate on this topic in the Anglo-Scottish marches has usually been concerned with how far the mutual experience of war and chivalric interchanges might foster cross-border sympathies strong enough to outweigh countervailing expressions of national allegiance or sentiment.[85] King has revisited the topic with reference to fourteenth-century landowners: while underscoring that, by 1296, gentry on both sides of the Anglo-Scottish marches were 'thoroughly and comprehensively acculturised', he argues that any shared marcher identity was decidedly secondary to English and Scottish national sentiment.[86] Yet the question of acculturation is important because it goes beyond matters of identity and cross-border amity and animosity. It can be concerned with a complex and subtle range of shared cultural norms relating, for example, to social structures and the management of conflict. Acculturation is also an important aspect of the interpretative framework adopted

---

[83] A. Goodman, 'The Anglo-Scottish Marches in the Fifteenth Century: A Frontier Society?', in R.A. Mason (ed.), *Scotland and England, 1286–1815* (Edinburgh, 1987), 18–33, at 18–19, 28–30; A. Goodman, 'Introduction', in J.A. Tuck and A. Goodman (eds), *War and Border Societies in the Middle Ages* (London, 1992), 1–29, at 2, 8–13, 20–4.

[84] S. Booker, *Cultural Exchange and Identity in Late Medieval Ireland: The English and Irish of the Four Obedient Shires* (Cambridge, 2018), esp. 2, 45–96. The anxious contemporary term for the phenomenon in the lordship of Ireland was 'degeneracy'. See Frame, *Ireland and Britain*, 211; R.R. Davies, 'The Peoples of Britain and Ireland 1100–1400 III. Laws and Customs', *TRHS*, 6th ser., 6 (1996), 1–23, at 12; A. Ruddick, *English Identity and Political Culture in the Fourteenth Century* (Cambridge, 2013), 152–5.

[85] On the subject of identities in the borderlands, see C.J. Neville, 'Local Sentiment and the "National" Enemy in Northern England in the Later Middle Ages', *Journal of British Studies,* 35 (1996), 419–37; T. Thornton, '"The Enemy or Stranger, That Shall Invade Their Countrey": Identity and Community in the English North', in B. Taithe and T. Thornton (eds), *War: Identities in Conflict 1300–2000* (Stroud, 1998), 57–70; King, 'Englishmen, Scots and Marchers'; Macdonald, *Border Bloodshed*, 161, 183, 207, 216, 227–8, 235–41; A.J. Macdonald, 'John Hardyng, Northumbrian Identity and the Scots', in Britnell and Liddy (eds), *North-East England*, 29–42; A. Goodman, 'Anglo-Scottish Relations in the Later Fourteenth Century: Alienation or Acculturation?', in King and Penman (eds), *England and Scotland,* 236–53.

[86] King, 'Best of Enemies', 131. Cf. Goodman, 'Introduction', in Tuck and Goodman (eds), *War and Border Societies,* 2 ('acculturation was the norm across the frontier before the later medieval attempts to transform it into a sharply defined political and military barrier').

Introduction

by Goodman, which is to ask whether and when the Anglo-Scottish marches constituted a 'frontier society'. In his work he introduced the wide field of frontier studies to this borderland, the 'frontier' as an analytical concept having been first articulated with regard to American history by Turner in the nineteenth century, and to European history by Febvre and Asian history by Lattimore in the twentieth century.[87] The investigation of frontiers, borders and boundaries of all conceivable types has generated an immense literature, and historical approaches to the topic have generally adopted a comparative emphasis.[88] For the middle ages, such work has highlighted the recurring phenomenon of marcher jurisdictions, memorably characterised by Lourie as societies 'organised for war'.[89] This was at about the same time that scholars of other historical contexts gave prominence to the idea that 'social militarisation' could be a means of governmental and political integration, an idea suggestive of the potential for a positive consolidating experience in marcher districts, rather than one of fragmentation or alienation.[90]

The nature of the Anglo-Scottish marches as a frontier, particularly of a military character, will be developed in a subsequent chapter. Here it should be noted that one aim of this book is to assess the significance of that frontier from the English side. The doctoral thesis from which this book emerges heeded the observation that 'borders defined in linear fashion need to be viewed in the context of the regions they bisect'.[91]

---

[87] F.J. Turner, 'The Significance of the Frontier in American History', in F.J. Turner (ed.), *The Frontier in American History* (New York, 1920), 1–38; L. Febvre, 'The Problem of Frontiers and the Natural Bounds of States', in L. Febvre, *A Geographical Introduction to History*, trans. E.G. Mountford and J.H. Paxton (London, 1932), 296–314; L. Febvre, '*Frontière*: The Word and the Concept', in L. Febvre, *A New Kind of History: From the Writings of Lucien Febvre*, trans. K. Folca, ed. P. Burke (London, 1973), 208–18; O. Lattimore, *Studies in Frontier History: Collected Papers, 1928–58* (Paris, 1962), esp. 'The Frontier in History' at 469–91. Bennett, *Community, Class and Careerism*, 66, 248, describes Lancashire and Cheshire (1375–1425) as a 'frontier society', in the Turnerian sense. J. Thirsk (ed.), *The Agrarian History of England and Wales, Volume IV: 1500–1640* (Cambridge, 1967), 16, describes Cbl., Wml., Furness, Durham and Nbl. together as a 'frontier province, harbouring a characteristic frontier society', but without further conceptualisation.

[88] The indispensable conceptual starting point is Power and Standen (eds), *Frontiers in Question*. See also A. Abulafia and N. Berend (eds), *Medieval Frontiers: Concepts and Practices* (Aldershot, 2002); F. Curta (ed.), *Borders, Barriers, and Ethnogenesis. Frontiers in Late Antiquity and the Middle Ages* (Turnhout, 2005).

[89] E. Lourie, 'A Society Organised for War: Medieval Spain', *Past & Present*, 35 (1966), 54–76, esp. 58–9; Goodman, 'The Anglo-Scottish Marches', 18; Ellis, 'The English State', 163–4. On 'march' applied to Wales, see M. Lieberman, *The Medieval March of Wales: The Creation and Perception of a Frontier, 1066–1283* (Cambridge, 2010), 5–19. See also B. Holden, *Lords of the Central Marches: English Aristocracy and Frontier Society, 1087–1265* (Oxford, 2008).

[90] P.H. Wilson, 'Social Militarization in Eighteenth Century Germany', *German History*, 18 (2000), 1–39. On the topic of war, periphery and integration, see King, 'Best of Enemies', 134.

[91] D.J. Power, 'French and Norman Frontiers in the Central Middle Ages', in Power and Standen (eds), *Frontiers in Question*, 105–27, at 114. Cf. D. Hay, 'England, Scotland and Europe: The

Introduction

That thesis was explicitly comparative; it examined local society on both sides of the border in the fifteenth century. Concentrating on the gentry and the lower orders, it found significant cross-border commonalities in patterns of kinship structures and in disputing processes and argued that such features resembled more the rest of Scotland than the rest of England.[92] Although the focus of this book is the English side of the border, and it is addressed predominantly to historians of England and seeks to develop its findings with relevance to England as a whole, the work does not abandon the wider framework with which it began, even as it frees itself from replicating a comparative mode of writing. Against the general conclusion of prevailing cross-border similarities, the aim here is to explore in greater depth what such similarities reveal about apparent differences with other parts of England, as opposed to comparisons with Scotland. Those Anglo-Scottish similarities will be reviewed where appropriate in the chapters that follow. A significant reason behind this choice for the road ahead is that the marches straddle not just a historical frontier but also a historiographical one.

Studies of borders in this island archipelago by necessity draw on the framework of the 'New British History', first outlined by Pocock. One of the aims of this approach has been the integration of the historiographies of the four nations of England, Scotland, Wales and Ireland.[93] The archipelagic approach has found particular traction (and reaction), on the one hand, in the period of unions after 1603 and, on the other, in the period from the late eleventh to the early fourteenth century. To this extent it has generally focused on the expansion of, and response to, English influence in these islands during both periods, especially with regard to political development and 'state formation', an issue already raised above with regard to Ellis's work.[94] Pocock's agenda has most

---

Problem of the Frontier', *TRHS*, 5th ser., 25 (1975), 77–91, at 87: 'the Borders were a region and remain a region'.

[92] J.W. Armstrong, 'Local Conflict in the Anglo-Scottish Borderlands, c. 1399–1488', PhD thesis, University of Cambridge (2007).

[93] J.G.A. Pocock, 'British History: A Plea for a New Subject', *Journal of Modern History*, 47 (1975), 601–28; A. Grant and K.J. Stringer (eds), *Uniting the Kingdom? The Making of British History* (London, 1996).

[94] See above, p. 12. Frame, *Political Development*; Frame, *Ireland and Britain*; R.R. Davies, *Domination and Conquest: The Experience of Ireland, Scotland and Wales, 1100–1300* (Cambridge, 1990); R.R. Davies (ed.), *The British Isles, 1100-1500: Comparisons, Contrasts, and Connections* (Edinburgh, 1988); B. Bradshaw and J.S. Morrill (eds), *The British Problem, c. 1534–1707* (London, 1996); G. Burgess (ed.), *The New British History: Founding a Modern State 1603–1715* (London, 1999); R.R. Davies, *The First English Empire: Power and Identities in the British Isles 1093–1343* (Oxford, 2000), esp. at 57, 61, 192; A.I. Macinnes and J. Ohlmeyer (eds), *The Stuart Kingdoms in the Seventeenth Century: Awkward Neighbours* (Dublin, 2002); P. Crooks, 'State of the Union: Perspectives on English Imperialism in the Late Middle Ages', *Past & Present*, 212 (2011), 3–42.

Introduction

readily been taken up in a comparative framework, but too often this has proven to be a cumbersome or even awkward ideal to pursue within the scope of a single work.[95] Its best results have tended either to take the guise of comparatively informed studies of particular nations – 'British histories' – or to produce macro-level works of synthesis.[96] Latterly, and in concert with modern imperial historiography's search for 'British world(s)', it has generated a perspective dubbed the 'English world' approach, which concentrates on the fluidity of Englishness and English political culture in the these islands and across the English Channel in the later middle ages.[97] Work that achieves a genuinely integrated British history, in pursuit of a finite topic across these islands, is a rarity.[98] The 'British Isles' approach or method seems to work best as an assembly of independent investigations, themselves later to be marshalled as case studies for comparison. With all this in mind, the present book does not attempt a 'British Isles' history in itself. All the same, as I have just made clear, such a comparative framework and interest remains implicit in the questions which inform the wider study from which the book emerges.[99] My present purpose is not to trace (as others have done in earnest) the telos of the British state in the disturbed peripheries subject to English rule in the period before the regal union.[100] To view England's far north as an exception deviating from the norms of the metropolitan

---

[95] Useful comment is found in A.I. Macinnes, 'Making the Plantations British, 1603–38', in S.G. Ellis and R. Esser (eds), *Frontiers and the Writing of History, 1500–1850* (Hannover-Laatzen, 2006), 95–125, at 96–7.

[96] For the former, see M.H. Brown, *Bannockburn: The Scottish War and the British Isles, 1307–1323* (Edinburgh, 2008). For the latter, see H. Kearney, *The British Isles: A History of Four Nations* (Cambridge, 1989); and M.H. Brown, *Disunited Kingdoms: Peoples and Politics in the British Isles, 1280–1460* (Harlow, 2013).

[97] For recent comment, see B. Smith, 'Late Medieval Ireland and the English Connection: Waterford and Bristol, c. 1360–1460', *Journal of British Studies,* 50 (2011), 546–65, at 546; Smith, *Crisis and Survival,* 4, 167. Signal contributions include Frame, *Political Development*; R.A. Griffiths, 'Crossing the Frontiers of the English Realm in the Fifteenth Century', in H. Pryce and J. Watts (eds), *Power and Identity in the Middle Ages: Essays in Memory of Rees Davies* (Oxford, 2007), 211–25; B. Smith (ed.), *Ireland and the English World in the Late Middle Ages: Essays in Honour of Robin Frame* (Basingstoke, 2009), 1–6; S. Duffy and S. Foran (eds), *The English Isles: Cultural Transmission and Political Conflict in Britain and Ireland, 1100–1500* (Dublin, 2013); Ruddick, *English Identity*; Booker, *Cultural Exchange and Identity.*

[98] R.R. Davies, *Lords and Lordship in the British Isles in the Late Middle Ages,* ed. B. Smith (Oxford, 2009), is an exception, as is O.H. Creighton, *Designs Upon the Land: elite Landscapes of the Middle Ages* (Woodbridge, 2009).

[99] Particular case study statements are pursued in J.W. Armstrong, 'Violence and Peacemaking in the English Marches towards Scotland, c. 1425–1440', in L. Clark (ed.), *The Fifteenth Century VI: Identity and Insurgency in the Late Middle Ages* (Woodbridge, 2006), 53–71; J.W. Armstrong, 'The "Fyre of Ire Kyndild" in the Fifteenth-Century Scottish Marches', in S.A. Throop and P.R. Hyams (eds), *Vengeance in the Middle Ages: Emotion, Religion and Feud* (Farnham, 2010), 51–84.

[100] Ellis, 'The English State', 176; Ellis, 'Tudor Frontiers in History and Historiography', in S.G. Ellis and R. Esser (eds), *Frontiers and the Writing of History, 1500–1850* (Hannover-Laatzen, 2006),

Introduction

'centre' or 'core' of the realm because it was a 'periphery' risks circularity of argument. It also risks oversimplifying the late medieval kingdom, washing out the nuance of a dynamic period in order to explain later processes of territorial and governmental integration. The far north, it will be argued, was in some ways distinctive and in some places disturbed. How and why this was so are the essential problems to be pursued here.

THE PROBLEM OF CONFLICT

As has been observed, whether involving external warfare, national strife, the marauding of reivers or local feuding, violent conflict is emblematic of the northern marches. Above all, this has been associated with the 'Surnames', those clannish groups the membership of which was heavily drawn from among the lower orders. Conflict is an essential aspect of the borderland's character, chiefly the retaliatory feuding and illicit kin-based raiding culture which have been so important in conventional portrayals of the marches. Mervyn James, writing about the early sixteenth century, colourfully expressed this view: 'the "deadly feude" whereby the violence done to any member of the clan was implacably avenged by the kin was the natural outcome of the close identification of individual and family'.[101] The history of kinship is a vast subject area.[102] Yet in the marches it is a topic closely intertwined with conflict, and in explaining this link, a major question concerns the origins of the Surnames, for which the routine answer is that these local kindreds emerged as a consequence of the Anglo-Scottish warfare that was 'endemic' from 1296.[103] Yet, if the origins of the Surnames lie in the military strife of

---

73–93, at 93; Ellis, *Defending English Ground*, 1–4, 8–9. By contrast, see Crooks, 'Factions, Feuds', 429, on the English lordship in Ireland.

[101] James, *Change and Continuity*, 6–9. For a rather blunt approach to feud in this period: M.M. Meikle, 'Northumberland Divided: Anatomy of a Sixteenth-Century Bloodfeud', *Archaeologia Aeliana*, 5th ser., 20 (1992), 79–89; Meikle, *A British Frontier*, ch. 7.

[102] For indicative approaches to kin and family, see R.M. Smith (ed.), *Land, Kinship and Life-Cycle* (Cambridge, 1984); R.A. Houlbrooke, *The English Family 1450–1700* (Harlow, 1984); D. Cressy, 'Kinship and Kin Interaction in Early Modern England', *Past & Present*, 113 (1986), 38–69; W. Coster, *Family and Kinship in England, 1450–1800* (New York, 2001); P. Fleming, *Family and Household in Medieval England* (Basingstoke, 2001); G.T. Beech, M. Bourin and P. Chareille (eds), *Personal Names Studies of Medieval Europe: Social Identity and Familial Structures* (Kalamazoo, MI, 2002); D.W. Sabean, S. Teuscher and J. Mathieu (eds), *Kinship in Europe: Approaches to Long-Term Development (1300–1900)* (New York and Oxford, 2007).

[103] Tuck, 'Richard II', 27–30; Ellis, *Tudor Frontiers*, 60–76; Holford and Stringer, *Border Liberties*, 322, 396; Brown, *Disunited Kingdoms*, 185; Schultz, *National Identity and the Anglo-Scottish Borderlands*, 92–4. The peasant 'brigands' of Normandy after 1417 bear some comparison: V. Challet, 'Tuchins and "Brigands de Bois": Peasant Communities and Self-Defence

Introduction

the fourteenth century, the first recorded use of the term occurs as late as 1498. As for border turbulence generally, it has been suggested that early Tudor policy consolidated or even exacerbated this phenomenon. Still, there has been little interrogation of the structures of fifteenth-century local society in pursuit of the question of when (and why) the Surnames first arose.[104]

The problem of the origins of the Surnames, of particular social structures and the conflict associated with them on a local level, is usually answered by turning the question into one about the strength of governmental structures. The familiar conjecture is that a kin-based society or, equally, a society in which the 'spirit or the practice' of feud is strong, has a correspondingly weak system of government. Thus, if men acted out of vengeance, they did so for mutual protection because the crown and its government failed to offer them security.[105] Equally, if men identified readily with an extended kin group, they did so because governmental organisation was underdeveloped.[106] Such claims have been made for the English marches towards Scotland and Wales and in Ireland.[107] All this leads quickly to questions of the role of authority, law and the 'state', and anthropological studies of 'stateless' societies have been influential in

---

Movements in Normandy during the Hundred Years War', in L. Clark (ed.), *The Fifteenth Century IX: English and Continental Perspectives* (Woodbridge, 2010), 85–99.

[104] *CPR 1494–1509*, 160 (1498). Houlbrooke, *English Family*, 50–1; Tuck, 'War and Society', 51–2; Ellis, *Tudor Frontiers*, 61–2; Etty, 'A Tudor Soluttion'; C. Etty, 'Neighbours from Hell? Living with Tynedale and Redesdale, 1489–1547', in Prestwich (ed.), *Liberties and Identities*, 120–40. For common thieves, see James, *A Tudor Magnate*, 10–11, 30. For related studies of naming customs, and 'northern-ness', see D. Postles, 'Defining the "North": Some Linguistic Evidence', *Northern History*, 38 (2001), 27–46.

[105] D.L. Smail, 'Faction and Feud in Fourteenth-Century Marseille', in J.B. Netterstrøm and B. Poulsen (eds), *Feud in Medieval and Early Modern Europe* (Aarhus, 2007), 113–33, at 114 (quotation), discussing B. Guenée, *Tribunaux et Gens de Justice dans le Bailliage de Senlis à la fin du Moyen Âge* (Paris, 1963), 293–5, on 'la justice impuissante'. For parallels with older views of arbitration, see Powell, *Kingship, Law, and Society*, 98; T. Kuehn, *Law, Family, and Women: Toward a Legal Anthropology of Renaissance Italy* (London, 1991), 19.

[106] Sabean, Teuscher and Mathieu (eds), *Kinship in Europe*, 1–3, 4, 12, 13, 15, 20, 24; S. Teuscher, 'Politics of Kinship in the City of Bern at the End of the Middle Ages', in ibid., 76–90, at 76–7 (noting the influence of Burckhardt), 85–7. Conventional statements are found in L. Stone, *The Family, Sex and Marriage in England, 1500–1800* (London, 1977), 133; J. Heers, *Family Clans in the Middle Ages* (Amsterdam, 1977), 251–2.

[107] G. Ridpath, *The Border History of England and Scotland* (London, 1776), 173; Tuck, 'Richard II', 27–30; Tuck, 'Northumbrian Society', 26–8; R.R. Davies, 'The Survival of the Bloodfeud in Medieval Wales', *History*, 54 (1969), 338–57, at 341, 350; Frame, *Ireland and Britain*, 207–9; C. Maginn, 'English Marcher Lineages in South Dublin in the Late Middle Ages', *Irish Historical Studies*, 34 (2004), 113–36, at 114, 117; K.A. Waters, 'The Earls of Desmond and the Irish of South-Western Munster', *Journal of Medieval History*, 32 (2006), 54–68, at 56, 67–8. On feud and kinship throughout Scotland, see K.M. Brown, *Bloodfeud in Scotland 1573–1625: Violence, Justice and Politics in an Early Modern Society* (Glasgow, 1986), 6–7, 277; Macdonald, *Border Bloodshed*, 3, 199, 227–34, esp. 228.

Introduction

shaping historical understandings.[108] Although historians of European statehood have long been concerned with the development of administrative and commercial capacity, of financial and representative mechanisms, as well as judicial and military developments,[109] Max Weber's influential conception of a strong modern state claiming monopoly over the legitimate use of force and the apparatus of coercion has remained influential, even when evaluating the ambitions of pre-modern rulers.[110] And for late medieval England, the Weberian formulation has explained the clout of the nobility: landownership (and the law which guaranteed the peaceful possession of land) has been identified as the basis of the private power that underwrote public governmental authority. That private power was ultimately expressed in the ability to call tenants to arms, and for this reason, it is argued, late medieval kings were required to heed a measure of consensus within political society, and those who did not struggled to rule.[111] In addition, the strength of horizontal linkages amongst landowners has been emphasised, in the form of gentry networks that tended to reinforce stability on the local level.[112] So the

[108] Carroll (ed.), *Cultures of Violence*, 4, 16, 24; D.L. Smail, 'Violence and Predation in Late Medieval Mediterranean Europe', *Comparative Studies in Society and History*, 54 (2012), 7–34; H. Zmora, *The Feud in Early Modern Germany* (Cambridge, 2011), 13, 21, 80, 128. See also M. Mann, *The Sources of Social Power*, 3 vols (Cambridge, 1986–2012), i, ch. 1, esp. 11, 22–7.

[109] J.L. Watts, *The Making of Polities: Europe 1300–1500* (Cambridge, 2009), 23–34; R.R. Davies, 'The Medieval State: The Tyranny of a Concept?', *Journal of Historical Sociology*, 16 (2003), 280–300, at 289–91. See also M.J. Braddick, 'State Formation and Social Change in Early Modern England: A Problem Stated and Approaches Suggested', *Social History*, 16 (1991), 1–17, at 2, 6–7; A. Harding, *Medieval Law and the Foundations of the State* (Oxford, 2002), chs 8 and 9; J.J. Sheehan, 'The Problem of Sovereignty in European History', *American Historical Review*, 111 (2006), 1–15.

[110] W.C. Brown, *Violence in Medieval Europe* (London, 2014), 2, 291–5; R.W. Kaeuper, *War, Justice and Public Order: England and France in the Later Middle Ages* (Oxford, 1988), 12, 140, 381, 392. But see A. Black, *Political Thought in Europe, 1250–1450* (Cambridge, 1992), 186–7; Smail, 'Violence and Predation', 34; N. Rouland, *Legal Anthropology* (London, 1994), 257–8, 279, 283; H. Kaminsky, 'The Noble Feud in the Later Middle Ages', *Past & Present*, 177 (2002), 55–83, at 79.

[111] The most explicit discussion is Carpenter, *Locality and Polity*, 283–4 (and literature cited there), 349, 354, 592, 628. Elsewhere see Carpenter, 'Law, Justice and Landowners', 213–16; Powell, *Kingship, Law, and Society*, 271–2; M.C. Carpenter, 'Gentry and Community in Medieval England', *Journal of British Studies*, 33 (1994), 340–80, at 358–9; G.L. Harriss, 'Political Society and the Growth of Government in Late Medieval England', *Past & Present*, 138 (1993), 28–57, at 32. Most recently (and implicitly) Harriss, *Shaping the Nation*, 163–4, 193, 206; M.C. Carpenter, 'Political and Geographical Space: The Geopolitics of Medieval England', in B.A. Kümin (ed.), *Political Space in Pre-industrial Europe* (Farnham, 2009), 117–133, at 118; Liddy, *Bishopric of Durham*, 16; C. Burt, *Edward I and the Governance of England, 1272–1307* (Cambridge, 2013), 10–11, 32–4, and 229. A different emphasis is taken in Maddern, *Violence and Social Order*, 11–12, 66, 71, 110, 133, 218, concerning the ways in which the public performance of righteous violence reinforced the moral and social order.

[112] Especially so by S. Payling, *Political Society in Lancastrian England: The Greater Gentry of Nottinghamshire* (Oxford, 1991), 108, 218–20. Carpenter (*Locality and Polity*, 296 and chs 9 and 16) places relatively less emphasis on horizontal ties but still notes their significance. See also Carpenter,

Introduction

relationship between public and private power has been understood against the measuring bar of a state with a monopoly on force – there was no such monopoly, but an effective king commanding the respect of the nobility could put their private power at his disposal to achieve something approaching it.[113] There is no difficulty in viewing landed power as a vital tool for governance, but the commonplace of a precocious England, 'perhaps Europe's most highly centralised medieval state' risks anachronism.[114] If it is the Weberian state that this sentiment invokes, then any social fabric featuring kin-based raiding and local conflict becomes an irregularity: either a vestigial organ or an emergent tumour. Assessments of the Surnames that are based on assumptions about kin-based organisation and violence as archaic or malignant phenomena which should disintegrate in the face of forceful governmental structures must be handled with caution.[115]

All this opens up the question of conflict as an analytical category in its own right. Once thought of as synonymous with destructive disorder or lawlessness, conflict has been reframed in much broader terms. By one account, conflict encompasses 'several kinds of inter-personal or inter-group tension', which include 'threats, promises, negotiation, ritual, use of force', related emotions and disputing. The latter phenomenon, dispute, carries its own extensive scholarship, and it has been construed as a particular 'phase' of conflict, one that is 'articulated as a claim, between two or more parties, concerning some specific subject matter'.[116] Within this schema, researchers have sought to discern the regular forms and patterns by which societies manage conflict. They have looked for frameworks of norms expressed both formally through law and institutions and informally through custom and usage. If 'politics is about making claims', it should come as no surprise that a discussion of

---

'Gentry and Community in Medieval England'; M.C. Carpenter, 'The Stonors and Their Circle in the Fifteenth Century', in R.E. Archer and S. Walker (eds), *Rulers and Ruled in Late Medieval England* (London, 1995), 175–200, at 195–6.

[113] See below, p. 39.

[114] Burt, *Edward I*, 11 (quote). See also Davies, *First English Empire*, 195, 201. However, see the vigorous interrogation by Davies, 'The Medieval State', 286–90.

[115] For example, see James, *A Tudor Magnate*; Tuck, 'War and Society'; Ellis, *Tudor Frontiers*; Etty, 'Neighbours from Hell'. By contrast, other work has found late medieval 'state organisation systematically had recourse to normative concepts of kinship and reinforced their significance': Sabean, Teuscher and Mathieu (eds), *Kinship in Europe,* 13. See also Teuscher, 'Politics of Kinship', 85–7.

[116] W.C. Brown and P. Górecki (eds), *Conflict in Medieval Europe: Changing Perspectives on Society and Culture* (Aldershot, 2003), 1–2. A valuable overview may be found in J. Jordan, 'Rethinking Disputes and Settlements: How Historians Can Use Legal Anthropology', in S. Cummins and L. Kounine (eds), *Cultures of Conflict Resolution in Early Modern Europe* (London, 2016), 17–50.

Introduction

conflict is really an appraisal of political patterns and configurations.[117] Such a discussion builds on an understanding of dispute whereby parties have an array of options to choose from in pursuing their objectives.[118] These include not only the use of violence but also adjudication by law in court and a range of avenues for compromise, covering negotiation, mediation and arbitration. The characteristics of a disputant's society determine the availability of, and emphasis placed upon, these different methods. One major variable is the quality and effectiveness of political structures and governmental institutions.[119] Yet even in societies with robust governmental machinery, a judicial system might still serve as only one set of resources for disputants relying primarily on other means of disputing. Moreover, different disputing strategies might overlap and be used in combination by contending parties.[120] Conflict's scope for being a socially constructive phenomenon has been explored in work that showcases how conflict defined and created groups and even constituted a social structure itself in medieval France.[121] In a world where frequent contact with one's friends and enemies was unavoidable, so was the need for a disputant's associates to take sides in processes which created not

---

[117] Sheehan, 'Problem of Sovereignty', 3 (citing Keith Baker's phrase). On 'frames, forms and patterns', see Watts, *Making of Polities*, 35.

[118] S. Roberts, 'The Study of Dispute: Anthropological Perspectives', in J. Bossy (ed.), *Disputes and Settlements: Law and Human Relations in the West* (Cambridge, 1980), 1–24, at 3–4, 7, 15; C. Rawcliffe, 'The Great Lord as Peacekeeper: Arbitration by English Noblemen and Their Councils in the Later Middle Ages', in J.A. Guy and H.G. Beale (eds), *Law and Social Change in British Society* (London, 1984), 34–54; C. Rawcliffe, 'Parliament and the Settlement of Disputes by Arbitration in the Later Middle Ages', *Parliamentary History*, 9 (1990), 316–42; E. Powell, 'Arbitration and the Law in England in the Late Middle Ages', *TRHS*, 5th ser., 33 (1983), 49–68, at 52–3; E. Powell, 'Settlement of Disputes by Arbitration in Fifteenth-Century England', *Law and History Review*, 2 (1984), 21–43; Powell, *Kingship, Law, and Society*, 91–7, 243–4; L.B. Smith, 'Disputes and Settlements in Medieval Wales: The Role of Arbitration', *EHR*, 106 (1991), 835–60; Maddern, *Violence and Social Order*, 15–16; Brown and Górecki (eds), *Conflict in Medieval Europe*, 7. The essential introduction is S. Roberts, *Order and Dispute: An Introduction to Legal Anthropology* (Oxford, 1979).

[119] More straightforward options included flight or acquiescence: L. Nader and H.F. Todd (eds), *The Disputing Process* (New York, 1978), 4–5, 8–12, 15–31, 34–5. See also Powell, 'Arbitration and the Law', 51.

[120] Brown and Górecki (eds), *Conflict in Medieval Europe*, 23–5, 279–82; P.R. Hyams, *Rancor and Reconciliation in Medieval England* (Ithaca, 2003), 5–6, 8; G. Halsall, 'Violence and Society in the Early Medieval West: An Introductory Survey', in G. Halsall (ed.), *Violence and Society in the Early Medieval West* (Woodbridge, 1998), 1–45, at 11, 16, 21, 32–3.

[121] P.J. Geary, 'Living with Conflicts in Stateless France: A Typology of Conflict Management Mechanisms, 1050–1200', in P.J. Geary, *Living with the Dead in the Middle Ages* (Ithaca, 1994), 125–60, at 138–40. On conflict as structure, see also W.I. Miller, *Bloodtaking and Peacemaking: Feud, Law and Society in Saga Iceland* (Chicago, 1990), 262; S.D. White, '"Pactum . . . Legem Vincit et Amor Judicium": The Settlement of Disputes by Compromise in Eleventh-Century Western France', *American Journal of Legal History*, 22 (1978), 281–308, at 303–5, 308; Roberts, *Order and Dispute*, 45–8.

Introduction

only antagonism but also cohesion.[122] Conflict created new social bonds and tested existing ones, causing them to be either reaffirmed or denied. It can be understood not as consisting of discrete events, each with a beginning, middle and end, but rather as long-term, often inherited, relationships which give meaning to social groups. Episodes or incidents of dispute are moments when such deeper conflictual relationships 'break into the open, are used for certain social purposes, and then seem to disappear, only to re-emerge still later'.[123] This approach acknowledges that finite settlement was frequently not an objective of disputing. In such a way, parties might have sought among other goals an opportunity to gain temporary advantage, to assert rights or defend reputation, to attract allies, or to deter opponents.[124] Even attempted compromise might only perpetuate a dispute. Still, some resolutions could be more enduring than others and might look a great deal like settlements. Such a 'successful' resolution makes peace by transforming the deeper relationships just mentioned, altering the bonds defining social relationships. At the same time, disputants' support groups rely on those very bonds for cohesion, so an enduring compromise calls for new, positive relationships to be created between opposing groups, in other words, for amity to replace enmity.[125] Conflict is thus not simply destruction and disorder. Conflict management is a generative process, a creative means of social problem-solving. In a fundamentally positive view of human society, conflict may build, reinforce and renovate social bonds – and the very norms by which conflict itself is managed.

Violence, crime and war are subjects intimately linked to ideas about conflict, and each has developed its own specialist literature. As a universal human experience, violence has been the subject of considerable scholarly attention, often through studies which privilege cultural interpretations.[126] Violence answers to a range of definitions, but that to

---

[122] For a comparable discussion of what he calls 'inimical intimacy', see Zmora, *The Feud,* 49–76, 77, 98.

[123] Geary, 'Living with Conflicts', 138–40. On an episodic model of conflict, see J.M. Wallace-Hadrill, 'The Bloodfeud of the Franks', *BJRL,* 41 (1959), 459–87, at 483, 486–7; J. Black-Michaud, *Cohesive Force: Feud in the Mediterranean and the Middle East* (Oxford, 1975), 15–19, 68, 74–8, 85; S.D. White, 'Clothild's Revenge: Politics, Kinship and Ideology in the Merovingian Bloodfeud', in S.K. Cohn and S.A. Epstein (eds), *Portraits of Medieval and Renaissance Living, Essays in Memory of David Herlihy* (Michigan, 1996), 107–30, at 120–5.

[124] H. Zmora, *State and Nobility in Early Modern Germany: The Knightly Feud in Franconia, 1440–1567* (Cambridge, 1997), 109; Zmora, *The Feud,* 60, 63, 72; Harris, *Shaping the Nation,* 197.

[125] Geary, 'Living with Conflicts', 148, 150, 154–5, 159; S.M. Wright, *The Derbyshire Gentry in the Fifteenth Century* (Chesterfield, 1983), 126; Powell, *Kingship, Law, and Society,* 102 and 107; Hyams, *Rancor and Reconciliation,* 11–14, 16.

[126] For a recent summation, see Carroll (ed.), *Cultures of Violence,* 1–43; S. Carroll, *Blood and Violence in Early Modern France* (Oxford, 2006), 5; H. Skoda, *Medieval Violence: Physical Brutality in Northern*

Introduction

which this book confines itself is the rather conventional understanding of physical force exercised against persons or property.[127] The image with which this section began, of headless corpses thrown down from the walls of Wark Castle, suggests a meaning communicated through an overt physical act, a message rendered in the 'language of social order'.[128] Even given the general pugnacious and hot-tempered repute of late medieval Englishmen, this highlights violence's symbolic and ritual potential, sometimes viewed as a mechanism for the constraint and canalisation of aggressive behaviour. Perhaps more apt is the observation that ritual allows violent acts a measure of formula and predictability, even where hot-blooded passion is mixed with rational calibration.[129] In no small part it is from attempts to legitimate, regulate and categorise violence that the notions of crime and war emerge. Early modernists have favoured crime and the records of criminal justice for the investigation of social order and discipline as negotiated through everyday life.[130] Similar agendas have been applied to the later middle ages, although with varied emphasis on political considerations.[131] The

---

France 1270–1330 (Oxford, 2013), 1–8, 18–49. See also the reservations about cultural explanations of J.C. Wood, 'Conceptualizing Cultures of Violence and Cultural Change', in Carroll (ed.), *Cultures of Violence*, 79–96, at 92–3. For the early middle ages, see Halsall, 'Violence and Society', esp. 7–19. For England, see Maddern, *Violence and Social Order*, ch. 1, 234; S.D. Amussen, 'Punishment, Discipline and Power: The Social Meanings of Violence in Early Modern England', *Journal of British Studies*, 34 (1995), 1–34, at 1–2; R.W. Kaeuper, *Chivalry and Violence in Medieval Europe* (Oxford, 1999).

[127] As per Carroll (ed.), *Cultures of Violence*, 8.

[128] Maddern, *Violence and Social Order*, 234 (quotation); Amussen, 'Punishment, Discipline and Power', 6–7; Halsall, 'Violence and Society', 11, 16, 32–3; P. Palmer, 'At the Sign of the Head: The Currency of Beheading in Early Modern Ireland', in Carroll (ed.), *Cultures of Violence*, 129–55.

[129] C. Phythian-Adams, 'Rituals of Personal Confrontation in Late Medieval England', *BJRL*, 73 (1991), 65–90, at 68 (on pugnacity), and 72–3, 77, 90, on confrontational rituals in England; Kaeuper, *War, Justice and Public Order*, 136–7. For predictability: Carroll (ed.), *Cultures of Violence*, 5, 12, 29, and 21.

[130] For instance, C.B. Herrup, *The Common Peace: Participation and the Criminal Law in Seventeenth-Century England* (Cambridge, 1987); M. Gaskill, *Crime and Mentalities in Early Modern England* (Cambridge, 2000); J.A. Sharpe, *Crime in Early Modern England 1550–1800* (2nd edn, London, 1999); S. Hindle, *The State and Social Change in Early Modern England, 1550–1640* (Basingstoke, 2000), 116–45; G. Walter, *Crime, Gender and Social Order in Early Modern England* (Cambridge, 2003); V.A.C. Gatrell, B. Lenman and G. Parker (eds), *Crime and the Law: The Social History of Crime in Western Europe since 1500* (London, 1980).

[131] For France, see C. Gauvard, *'De Grace Especial': Crime, État et Société en France à la fin du Moyen Âge*, 2 vols (Paris, 1991). For England, the most politically attuned assessments are Powell, *Kingship, Law, and Society*, 9–20, 50; Carpenter, *Locality and Polity*, 615–44; Payling, *Political Society*, esp. ch. 7; Maddern, *Violence and Social Order*. Less alert to political contexts is work including J.G. Bellamy, *Crime and Public Order in England in the Later Middle Ages* (London, 1973); J.G. Bellamy, *Criminal Law and Society in Late Medieval and Tudor England* (Gloucester, 1984); J.G. Bellamy, *The Criminal Trial in Later Medieval England* (Stroud, 1998); B.A. Hanawalt, *Crime and Conflict in English Communities, 1300–1348* (Cambridge, MA, 1979); M.K. McIntosh, *Controlling*

Introduction

terminology adopted for this subject is telling. 'Crime' is of course freighted with the unambiguous modern-day separation between criminal and civil law (or crime and tort). It is widely accepted that public criminal justice, akin to our modern understanding of the idea, was administered in late medieval England, and this presupposes a neat association of crime with 'public order' and trespass with 'private redress'.[132] On the one hand, this is a helpful and constructive way to make sense of legal records. On the other, it projects deceptively finite categories onto an indefinite reality – categories that may be clearer to historians than to the medieval offenders, victims and litigants. Altogether, it seems preferable to avoid speaking of 'crime' wherever possible in favour of a less loaded terminology of offences (whether classified as felony, trespass or lesser wrongdoings), reflecting situations and allegations of fact which could and did enter the courts in a number of ways.[133] Circumventing the word 'crime' in our analytical terminology (even if it can be found as a historical term in the middle ages) may assist us to understand better the nature of conflict and its official regulation.[134] The third subject, war, the context of the Wark vignette, is perhaps even more multifarious. Whereas its anthropological definition turns on questions of organisation and social sanction, its historiographical legacy is to be both cause and symptom of apparent disorder in the

---

Misbehavior in England, 1370–1600 (Cambridge, 1998). Useful overviews include M.T. Clanchy, 'Law, Government and Society in Medieval England', *History*, 59 (1974), 73–8; J.A. Sharpe, 'The History of Crime in Late Medieval and Early Modern England: A Review of the Field', *Social History*, 7 (1982), 187–203; J.B. Post, 'Crime in Later Medieval England: Some Historiographical Limitations', *Continuity and Change*, 2 (1987), 211–24; M. Gaskill, 'New Directions in the History of Crime and the Law in Early Modern England', *Criminal Justice History*, 17 (2002), 147–69.

[132] J.H. Baker, *An Introduction to English Legal History* (3rd edn, London, 1990), 571.

[133] See Sharpe, 'The History of Crime', 188–9; M.L. Bohna, 'Political and Criminal Violence in Fifteenth-Century England', in R. W. Kaeuper (ed.), *Violence in Medieval Society* (Woodbridge, 2000), 91–104; Dean, *Crime in Medieval Europe, 1200–1550* (London, 2001), 96–108; Harding, *Medieval Law*, 60, 240, 242–6; E.M. Peters, 'Introduction: The Reordering of Law and the Illicit', in R.M. Karras, J. Kaye and E.A. Matter (eds), *Law and the Illicit in Medieval Europe* (Philadelphia, 2008), 1–14, at 7. For Maddern, *Violence and Social Order*, 49, 'crime' is a label partly dependent on an offender's relative social status. M.K. McIntosh, 'Finding Language for Misconduct: Jurors in Fifteenth-Century Local Courts', in B.A. Hanawalt and D. Wallace (eds), *Bodies and Disciplines: Intersections of Literature and History in Fifteenth-Century England* (Minneapolis, 1996), 87–122; and McIntosh, *Controlling Misbehavior*, uses 'misconduct' or 'misbehaviour' in reference to nonfelonious offences entertained at lower jurisdictions. For indispensable caution on the use of legal records, see Carpenter, *Locality and Polity*, 705–9. For an earlier period, see Hyams, *Rancor and Reconciliation*, 13, 80 (using 'downward justice'), 220–4, 226–30, 234–41.

[134] John Fortescue writes of *criminis* and *causis criminalibus* with reference to felony and treason: *The Governance of England*, ed. C. Plummer (Oxford, 1885), 141; John Fortescue, *De Laudibus Legum Angliae*, ed. S. Chrimes (Cambridge, 1942), 62–5. See also *Paston Letters*, ed. Davis, ii, no. 881, p. 529 ('to answere of swich crymes').

Introduction

later middle ages.[135] For the medievalist, the categorisation of war (with its accompanying complexity of related legal and customary issues) is a problem that concerns both scale and authority.[136] Interpretations of war in late medieval France and Germany have come to avoid the familiar binary distinction between 'public' and 'private' war, loaded with assumptions derived from the modern state.[137] Indeed, linking violence, crime and war is the view that sole legitimate authority over these matters (all involving physical force) is the test of the modern Weberian state.[138] Narratives of the 'rise' of the state often rely on ideas about the transition from the primitive to the developed, from the archaism of medieval decline to the sophistication of modern progress.[139] With reference to violence in particular, a narrative of this ilk is Norbert Elias's influential 'civilising process' – a view of the slow domestication of the early modern European nobility which transformed vengeful medieval warriors into tame Baroque courtiers.[140] Despite its devotees, Elias's theory has been challenged by those who point to the regulation of aggressive behaviour in earlier periods or who contest the claim that violence ever came to be repressed.[141] With reference to Tudor and

---

[135] J. Haas, *The Anthropology of War* (Cambridge, 1990), 1–2. On the historiography of 'war and disorder', see Watts, *Making of Polities,* 19–23.

[136] M.H. Keen, *The Laws of War in the Late Middle Ages* (London, 1965), 104–5, 108–9; Maddern, *Violence and Social Order,* 17–18, 86–7; Halsall, 'Violence and Society', 27–9; R.W. Kaeuper, 'Debating Law, Justice and Constitutionalism', in R.W. Kaeuper (ed.), *Law, Governance and Justice: New Views on Medieval Constitutionalism* (Leiden, 2013), 1–14, at 7, 12.

[137] G. Algazi, 'The Social Use of Private War: Some Late Medieval Views Reviewed', *Tel Aviver Jahrbuch für deutsche Geschichte,* 22 (1993), 253–73; Kaminsky, 'The Noble Feud', 55–6, 74; Zmora, *The Feud,* 15, 47–9. See also J. Firnhaber-Baker, *'Jura in medio:* The Settlement of Seigneurial Disputes in Later Medieval Languedoc', *French History,* 26 (2012), 441–59, at 445–7; J. Firnhaber-Baker, *Violence and the State in Languedoc, 1250–1400* (Cambridge, 2014), 6–7.

[138] C. Tilly, 'Reflections on the History of European State-Making', in C. Tilly (ed.), *The Formation of National States in Western Europe* (Princeton, 1975), 3–83, at 42; Sheehan, 'Problem of Sovereignty', 3–4, 6; Amussen, 'Punishment, Discipline and Power', 2; J. Firnhaber-Baker, 'Seigneurial War and Royal Power in Later Medieval Southern France', *Past & Present,* 208 (2010), 37–76, at 37; J. Firnhaber-Baker, 'Techniques of Seigneurial War in the Fourteenth Century', *Journal of Medieval History,* 36 (2010), 90–103, at 91; B. Donagan, 'Codes and Conduct in the English Civil War', *Past & Present,* 118 (1988), 65–95, at 75–6, 78–80.

[139] On narratives of transition, see Watts, *Making of Polities,* 11–12, 25. On violence and the transition from the ancient world to the medieval, see Halsall, 'Violence and Society', 4.

[140] Neatly summarised in Carroll, *Blood and Violence,* 2–4. See N. Elias, *The Court Society,* trans. E. Jephcott (Oxford, 1983); N. Elias, *The Civilizing Process,* trans. E. Jephcott, 2 vols (Oxford, 1994); J. Fletcher, *Violence and Civilization: An Introduction to the Work of Norbert Elias* (Cambridge, 1997). See also J. Burckhardt, *The Civilization of the Renaissance in Italy,* trans. S.G.C. Middlemore (5th edn, London, 1904), 446–50; J. Huizinga, *The Autumn of the Middle Ages,* trans. R.J. Payton and U. Mammitzsch (Chicago, 1996), ch. 1, esp. 17.

[141] For comment, see G. Schwerhoff, 'Criminalized Violence and the Process of Civilization: A Reappraisal', *Crime, Histoire & Sociétés/Crime, History & Societies,* 6 (2002), 103–26; N. Mears, 'Courts, Courtiers and Culture in Tudor England', *Historical Journal,* 46 (2003),

Introduction

Stuart England and the north in particular, it seems apparent that Elias informed, in general terms at least, aspects of Mervyn James's interpretations. James's eloquent analysis of changing conceptions of order, honour and nobility led to his view that landowners, especially in peripheral areas harbouring a turbulent 'lineage society', succumbed to homogenising market forces and assimilated the peaceful values of a metropolitan 'civil society' before 1640.[142] While James's view has been influential, particularly for those who have followed his interest in the Tudor north,[143] his narrative of decline and transition, and of a 'lineage society' reaching back into the fifteenth century and earlier, must be treated with caution.[144] And finally, looking again to a wider European perspective, legislative efforts to 'criminalise' the use of violence in the form of 'private' (or seigneurial, or sub-princely) war – through restrictions enacted in France in the thirteenth and fourteenth centuries, in England through the Great Statute of Treasons of 1352 and in Germany at the Imperial Diet of 1495 – may seem blunt measures but significant milestones achieved by maturing 'states'.[145] For England, related to all this are questions about the governance of the kingdom and changing relationships within political society, especially between the gentry, the nobility and the crown (the statute of 1352 restricted the scope of treason by keeping the levying of war against the king a treasonous offence, but making riding in arms against another subject a felony or trespass, according to the circumstances). What these French, English and German enactments have in common is that they are attempts by rulers and assemblies to regulate aspects of a culture of conflict at the point where violence, crime and war intersect.

703–22, at 720–1; Carroll, *Blood and Violence*, 3–4, 307–11; Carroll (ed.), *Cultures of Violence*, 5 (on Elias, Burckhardt, Huizinga and Freud). See also G. Algazi, 'Pruning Peasants: Private War and Maintaining the Lords' Peace in Late Medieval Germany', in E. Cohen and M.B. de Jong (eds), *Medieval Transformations: Texts, Power and Gifts in Context* (Leiden, 2001), 245–74, at 264–5, on 'wild' and 'garden' cultures.

[142] M.E. James, *Family, Lineage and Civil Society: A Study of Society, Politics and Mentality in the Durham Region, 1500–1640* (Oxford, 1974), 19–40, 177–98, esp. 178, 186; M.E. James, *Society, Politics and Culture: Studies in Early Modern England* (Cambridge, 1986), 4–10, 270–6, 314–23. For comment on James, see Liddy, *Bishopric of Durham*, 11; J.A. Sharpe and J.R. Dickinson, 'Revisiting the "Violence We Have Lost"', *EHR*, 131 (2016), 293–323, at 314.

[143] Noted above with reference to Surnames and feud, p. 22.

[144] For 'lineage society' applied in Devonshire, see M. Cherry, 'The Courtenay Earls of Devon: The Formation and Disintegration of a Late-Medieval Aristocratic Affinity', *Southern History*, 1 (1979), 71–97, at 71, 97.

[145] J. Dewald, *The European Nobility, 1400–1800* (Cambridge, 1996), 112; Harding, *Medieval Law*, 240; Zmora, *The Feud*, 128; Kaminsky, 'The Noble Feud', 66, 68, 75–6; Maddern, *Violence and Social Order*, 90, 145; Kaeuper, *War, Justice and Public Order*, 225–67; J.G. Bellamy, *The Law of Treason in England in the Later Middle Ages* (Cambridge, 1970), 14, 62–3, 90–2, 201.

Introduction

Late medieval attempts through governmental structures to regulate conflict draw our attention back to the subject of feud.[146] The elusive concept of feud and its processes of public, customary violence and peacemaking are well known. Just as conflict was once understood as destructive disorder, so feud has carried a negative reputation. The two seminal statements on the subject were to turn this reputation on its head. Familiar to historians working in the English language is Max Gluckman's anthropological treatment of feud as a functionalist mechanism for peaceful equilibrium in 'stateless' societies, first published in 1955.[147] For scholars working in German, the major interpretative advance came from Otto Brunner in his 1939 study of the feud in late medieval Austria.[148] Brunner's understanding of feud emphasised its legal, political and constitutional dimensions. In his conception it was a legitimate mechanism for the assertion and defence of noble rights, a modality of justice that had its own formulas and rules.[149] In the words of his translator, Brunner's feud had a 'constitutionally creative role', which has stood in stark contrast to the monarchist emphasis of French historiography and the story of the advancing common law in the English tradition.[150] Feud is a sprawling and fascinating subject, and scarcely more can be done here than to highlight some significant elements of the topic which inform the present study.[151] First, it bears reiteration that feud is as

[146] As this paragraph shows, feud is a part of the wider concept of conflict. See above, p. 25, and full treatment below at p. 270–3.

[147] M. Gluckman, 'The Peace in the Feud', *Past & Present*, 7 (1955), 1–14. Gluckman built upon the anthropological work of E.E. Evans-Pritchard, *The Nuer* (Oxford, 1940), and E. Colson, 'Social Control and Vengeance in Plateau Tonga Society', *Africa*, 23 (1953), 199–212, and he in turn inspired Wallace-Hadrill, 'Bloodfeud of the Franks'. See also F.L. Cheyette, '*Suum cuique tribuere*', *French Historical Studies*, 6 (1970), 287–99; S.D. White, 'Feuding and Peace-Making in the Touraine around the Year 1100', *Traditio*, 42 (1986), 195–263; J.B. Netterstrøm, 'Introduction: The Study of Feud in Medieval and Early Modern History', in Netterstrøm and Poulsen (eds), *Feud in Medieval and Early Modern Europe*, 9–67, at 9–12.

[148] O. Brunner, *Land and Lordship: Structures of Governance in Medieval Austria*, trans. H. Kaminsky and J.V.H. Melton (Philadelphia, 1992). C. Petit-Dutaillis, *Documents nouveaux sur les moeurs populaires et le droit de vengeance dans les Pays-Bas* (Paris, 1908), illustrated '*guerres familiales*' in the Burgundian Low Countries, but he remained firmly within a French monarchist historical tradition.

[149] On Brunner, see, for example, Zmora, *State and Nobility*, 4–8; Kaminsky, 'The Noble Feud', 55–9; Netterstrøm, 'Introduction: The Study of Feud', 20–3.

[150] Kaminsky, 'The Noble Feud', 58. See also Zmora, *The Feud*, 7–8; J.B. Netterstrøm, 'Feud in Late Medieval and Early Modern Denmark', in Netterstrøm and Poulsen (eds), *Feud in Medieval and Early Modern Europe*, 175–87, commenting on the work of Ole Fenger and his inspiration derived from both Gluckman and Brunner.

[151] For a masterly overview of the subject, see Netterstrøm, 'Introduction: The Study of Feud', 9–67, and, more succinctly, Dean, *Crime in Medieval Europe*, 98–108. For German historiography, see Zmora, *The Feud*, 1–28. Recent volumes include Throop and Hyams (eds), *Vengeance in the Middle Ages*; B.S. Tuten and T.L. Billado (eds), *Feud, Violence and Practice: Essays in Medieval Studies in Honor of Stephen D. White* (Farnham, 2010).

Introduction

much a tool for peace and the binding of the social fabric as it is a pretext for violence. Second, feuding was integrated – however problematically and with mixed results – into processes of governmental growth in the middle ages and later. In Germany, this was through the assertion of rights and jurisdictions, even by princely 'state-builders'.[152] In France (and indeed in Scotland and the Burgundian Low Countries), this was through pardon as a mechanism of royal grace, whereby rulers aspired to harness and regulate peacemaking processes.[153] Third, it should be observed that feud is a category of analysis which refers to a contested array of words describing historical behaviours. Writers have assigned various distinctions between feud words (the English term 'blood feud' is one such variant) to describe underlying behaviour. These distinctions have hinged on questions of social status, of individual or group action and liability or of whether what is described in the record is a single hostile episode or an interminable chain of retaliatory acts.[154] One durable view, first expressed by Brunner, has been of the essential difference between knightly feud (*Fehde*, as the prerogative of the nobility) and all the rest.[155] Even so, recent work on Germany, France and Denmark has challenged this idea, breaking down the distinction between the knightly or noble feud and similar customary practices found among the lower orders, notably, among townspeople and peasants.[156] The result of all this is a cacophony of interpretation, which

---

[152] Zmora, *The Feud*, 21, 80, 128, 137, 144, 164.

[153] S. Carroll, 'The Peace in the Feud in Sixteenth- and Seventeenth-Century France', *Past & Present*, 178 (2003), 74–115, at 109–10, 115. On vengeance and pardon, see C. Gauvard, 'La justice pénale du roi de France à la fin du Moyen Âge', in X. Rousseau and R. Lévy (eds), *Le pénal dans tous ses états: justice, états et sociétés en Europe: XIIe–XXe siècles* (Brussels, 1997), 81–112. For the Burgundian Netherlands, see W. Prevenier, 'The Two Faces of Pardon Jurisdiction in the Burgundian Netherlands: A Royal Road to Social Cohesion and an Effectual Instrument of Princely Clientelism', in P. Hoppenbrouwers, A. Janse and R. Stein (eds), *Power and Persuasion: Essays on the Art of State Building in Honour of W.P. Blockmans* (Turnhout, 2010), 177–95. For Scotland: J.W. Armstrong, 'The Justice Ayre in the Border Sheriffdoms, 1493–1498', *SHR*, 92 (2013), 1–37, at 30–7. Fortescue himself commented on the relative frequencies of hanging for larceny in England, France and Scotland: *Governance of England*, 141–2.

[154] A non-exhaustive list would include, in Latin, *faida*, *guerra*, *odium* and *inimicitia* (sometimes *inimicitia mortalis* or *capitalis*); in French, *guerre*; in Italian, *vendetta* and *faide*; and in German, *Fehde*, *Totschlagsfehde* and *Blutrache*. See Netterstrøm, 'Introduction: The Study of Feud', 21, 45, 39–40; E. Muir, *Mad Blood Stirring: Vendetta in Renaissance Italy* (Baltimore, 1993), xxiv.

[155] Kaminsky, 'The Noble Feud', 55–6.

[156] Kuehn, *Law, Family, and Women*, esp. ch. 2; T. Dean, 'Marriage and Mutilation: Vendetta in Late Medieval Italy', *Past & Present*, 157 (1997), 3–36; T. Dean, 'Violence, Vendetta and Peacemaking in Late Medieval Bologna', *Criminal Justice History*, 17 (2002), 1–17; C. Reinle, 'Peasants' Feuds in Late Medieval Bavaria (Fourteenth–Fifteenth Century)', in Netterstrøm and Poulsen (eds), *Feud in Medieval and Early Modern Europe*, 161–74; D.L. Smail, 'Hatred as a Social Institution in Medieval Society', *Speculum*, 76 (2001), 90–126; D.L. Smail, *The Consumption of Justice: Emotions, Publicity, and Legal Culture in Marseille, 1264–1423* (Ithaca, 2003); J.B. Netterstrøm, 'Feud,

Introduction

leads to a fourth point, that a broadly agreed definition of feud has long eluded scholars.[157] Early medievalists have been the most severely sceptical, suggesting that feud was more fiction than fact or that it should be dispensed with altogether in favour of more precise terminology.[158] With these challenges in mind, it is useful to think in terms of a descriptive concept of feud, rather than a restrictive definition.[159] Scholars working along these lines have tended to give feud a 'light' working definition, and from there identify and look for what may be termed feud-like elements in source materials.[160] Feud as an analytical category for our purposes will be developed in a subsequent chapter,[161] but such a working definition requires a clearer understanding of the differences (and overlaps) between words and concepts. For instance, historians of another field have considered concepts not as single entities but as 'a network of value-laden terms that constitute a conceptual field', a concept being 'a network that is constantly changing both in the composition of terms and in the meanings of some of those terms'.[162] Medieval historians have in such a way focused on French *guerre*.[163] Other words that have drawn attention in a comparable lexicographical approach include 'enmity' or 'hatred', related words like 'malice' or 'anger' or *odium*, the Latin antonyms *amicus/inimicus* and *amicitia/inimicita* and their vernacular equivalents, and those to do with love and friendship.[164] A maturing history of emotions has assisted some of this

---

Protection and Serfdom in Late Medieval and Early Modern Denmark (c. 1400–1600)', in P. Freedman and M. Bourin (eds), *Forms of Servitude in Northern and Central Europe: Decline, Resistance and Expansion* (Turnhout, 2005), 369–84.

[157] This is despite numerous attempts at an overall definition, including Evans-Pritchard, *The Nuer*, 150; Black-Michaud, *Cohesive Force*, 121–3, 126–8, 162–7, 191–204; C. Boehm, *Blood Revenge: The Anthropology of Feuding in Montenegro and Other Tribal Societies* (Lawrence, KS, 1984), 218–20.

[158] P. Sawyer, 'The Bloodfeud in Fact and Fiction', *Acta Jutlandica*, 63 (1987), 27–38; Halsall, 'Violence and Society', 19, 22, 24–5, proposes 'customary vengeance'. For similar scepticism about feud and violence in late medieval Normandy (with comment on England), see A.J. Finch, 'The Nature of Violence in the Middle Ages: An Alternative Perspective', *Historical Research*, 70 (1997), 249–68.

[159] On the trend towards description over definition, see Netterstrøm, 'Introduction: The Study of Feud', 49–59. An astronomer reminds us that scientists work by concepts rather than by definitions: M. Brown, *How I Killed Pluto and Why It Had It Coming* (New York, 2010), 272.

[160] Notably, Brown, *Bloodfeud in Scotland*, 4–5; Hyams, *Rancor and Reconciliation*, xvi, 8–9, 12, 32–3, 210–15. On 'feud-like hostilities', which he excludes from his model, see Black-Michaud, *Cohesive Force*, 129.

[161] See below, pp. 271 and 308–9.

[162] M. Knights et al., 'Commonwealth: The Social, Cultural and Conceptual Contexts of an Early Modern Keyword', *Historical Journal*, 54 (2011), 659–87, at 661.

[163] Firnhaber-Baker, 'Techniques of Seigneurial War', 91, 97 (although distancing the point from notions of feud).

[164] R.J. Bartlett, '"Mortal Enmities": The Legal Aspect of Hostility in the Middle Ages', in Tuten and Billado (eds), *Feud, Violence and Practice*, 197–212; Smail, 'Hatred as a Social Institution'. See

Introduction

work, putting the focus onto the patterns of emotion shaping feud-like behaviours, including the seeking of vengeance to right a wrong. This work recognises that emotion is a richly useful and instrumental aspect of human behaviour. With social emotions at the core of his argument, Hyams has traced a vibrant 'vengeance culture' in England up to the end of the thirteenth century.[165]

Did such a culture of vengeance or enmity exist in late medieval England? An interesting preliminary answer in the affirmative has been offered by Reinle, who has examined some well-known violent episodes among landowners in the fifteenth century. She has claimed feud in England as a 'cultural phenomenon'.[166] Kaminsky has put forward a Brunnerian understanding of 'noble feud' as a tool with which to challenge 'state-centred constructions' of the later middle ages and has asked a provocative question about the implications of McFarlane-inspired study of the norms which shaped the attitudes and behaviours of landowners.[167] By contrast, historians of England in the last several decades have freely wielded 'feud', 'vendetta' and sometimes 'private war', as general terms of analysis to describe violent 'disorders' within landed society, reinforcing the idea of local conflict as self-evidently contradictory to good order and the peace of the realm.[168] While dispute over the possession of land and property rights was pervasive among

---

also M.T. Clanchy, 'Law and Love in the Middle Ages', in Bossy (ed.), *Disputes and Settlements,* 47–67.

[165] Hyams, *Rancor and Reconciliation,* 67 (quote), also 246–55. B.H. Rosenwein (ed.), *Anger's Past: The Social Uses of an Emotion in the Middle Ages* (Ithaca, NY, 1998) esp. 3; S.D. White, 'The Politics of Anger', in ibid., 127–52; L.A. Pollock, 'Anger and the Negotiation of Relationships in Early Modern England', *Historical Journal,* 47 (2004), 567–90. See also the cautious assessment in J.G.H. Hudson, 'Feud, Vengeance and Violence in England from the Tenth to the Twelfth Centuries', in Tuten and Billado (eds), *Feud, Violence and Practice,* 29–53.

[166] C. Reinle, '"Fehde" und gewaltsame Selbsthilfe in England und im römisch-deutschen Reich', in R. Lieberwirth and H. Lück (eds), *Akten des 36. Deutschen Rechtshistorikertages* (Baden-Baden, 2008), 1–34, at 33.

[167] Kaminsky, 'The Noble Feud', 81.

[168] Storey, *House of Lancaster,* 155 (and see further 191–3); R.L. Storey, 'Disorders in Lancastrian Westmorland: Some Early Chancery Proceedings', *TCWAAS,* n.s., 53 (1953), 69–80. Wright, *Derbyshire Gentry,* 126, proceeds more carefully but accepts Storey's sentiment. On private war, see J. Blow, 'Nibley Green 1470: The Last Private Battle Fought in England', in C.M.D. Crowder (ed.), *English Society and Government in the Fifteenth Century* (Edinburgh, 1967), 87–111. Examples of the term 'feud' used haphazardly include N. Saul, *Scenes from Provincial Life: Knightly Families in Sussex 1280–1400* (Oxford, 1986), 73; J.G. Bellamy, *Bastard Feudalism and the Law* (London, 1989), 4–5, 76–7, 120; Powell, *Kingship, Law, and Society,* 175 (although more precision is used at 71); Walker, *The Lancastrian Affinity,* 258; Carpenter, *Locality and Polity,* 185, 379, 426, 461; Harriss, *Shaping the Nation,* 195, 199, 200, 202, 206; A.J. Pollard, 'Provincial Politics in Lancastrian England: The Challenge to Bishop Langley's Liberty in 1433', in K. Dockray and P. Fleming (eds), *People, Places and Perspectives* (Stroud, 2005), 69–78, at 72, 76; Genet, 'Scotland in the Later Middle Ages', 133.

Introduction

landowners, it is also clear that less tangible matters caused tensions, such as the recognition of social status and the defence of one's 'name state honour dignite and preemynence'.[169] Yet the precise vocabulary selected by medieval observers to describe and explain certain violent confrontations merits close scrutiny. Should the behaviour of men in Westmorland in 1388 who led an assault at Selside and then at Kendal, described as 'modo guerre et modo Scottorum', be understood *solely* as a reference to methods of border raiding, or did this carry other layers of meaning?[170] London's *Great Chronicle* recounted the death of the fourth earl of Northumberland in the Yorkshire rising of 1489, noting that the earl had been slain by men 'owyng unto hym dedly malyce ffor the dysapoyntyng of kyng Rychard at Bosworth ffeeld'.[171] As an indication of ascribed motivations for lethal violence (all the more notable as a Londoner's explanation for the behaviour of dissident northerners), how far is the use of terms such as 'deadly malice' suggestive of a generally acknowledged culture of enmity or of a particular category of dispute that might have been recognised by the chronicler and his readers? In what follows my intention is to assess local conflict in England's far north with due attention to the role of 'the king's law in the king's courts' and to arbitration process out of court but also to the potential involvement and interplay of alternative modes, practices and frameworks for the management of conflict in local society.[172] Such frameworks need not be mutually exclusive.[173]

THE GOVERNANCE OF THE 'CONTREIS ... IN EUERY PARTIE OFF THE LANDE'

Continental comparisons, especially with the 'polycentric realm' of Germany, may be all very well, but the precociously developed 'unitary

---

[169] M.W. Warner and K. Lacey, 'Neville vs. Percy: A Precedence Dispute circa 1442', *Historical Research,* 69 (1996), 211–17, at 216.

[170] See the discussion below, at p. 275. For this reference, see Storey, 'The North of England', 131, citing KB 27/518 *rex* rot. 17. The court record, and the related petition (SC 8/222/11076–7) indicate the attackers' intent to kill certain members of the de Burgh family.

[171] *The Great Chronicle of London,* ed. A.H. Thomas (London, 1938), 242.

[172] Quotation from W.M. Ormrod, *The Reign of Edward III: Crown and Political Society in England 1327–1377* (London, 1990), 160. For a 'particular mental category of dispute', see Hudson, 'Feud, Vengeance and Violence', 48. J.L. Watts, *Henry VI and the Politics of Kingship* (Cambridge, 1996), 32, asks whether chivalry offered landowners, 'as knights, a code for independent action' and argues that, rather than serving as an 'incitement to self-assertion and violence' (ibid., 33), chivalry's communitarian emphasis united landowners in service of 'king and common weal' (ibid., 36).

[173] This point is developed further below, at pp. 188 and 197 and in Chapters 9 and 10. On 'coexistence', see Dean, *Crime in Medieval Europe,* 104, 163; C. van Dijk, *John Gower and the Limits of the Law* (Woodbridge, 2013), 189–90.

Introduction

kingdom' of England was surely different, or so it might be argued.[174] Indeed, the early 'universal pretentions' of England's royal legal system and its common law are widely accepted as having been realised by the reign of Edward I,[175] the king to whom the 'Irish of Ireland' offered en masse to purchase English common law for 10,000 marks.[176] Whether it was a sudden or slow transition, the conventional claim is that by the later middle ages the 'triumph' of English royal government had overseen the replacement of vengeance and private war with an overarching system of conflict management provided by the king through his sovereign duty to provide peace, justice and good rule with the support of political society.[177] Yet if there was a triumph, it was a precarious one, for glances ahead in time suggest natural ebb and flow.[178] To some extent the acceptance of the 'monotheism' of the common law as against codes and practices of duelling remained contested as late as 1804.[179] This is not to deny that in the later middle ages royal justice was held up in political discourse as the supreme means for the punishment of offenders and the remedy of wrong, but there are qualifications.[180] Liberties and franchises have already been discussed. In the 'palimpsest of jurisdictions' throughout England, inferior courts administered justice according to rules shaped by common law norms and governed by royal charter and parliamentary statute, but also derived to a significant extent from local

---

[174] Davies, 'The Medieval State', 288, 295.

[175] Hyams, *Rancor and Reconciliation*, 242, 246 (first quote); M.C. Carpenter, 'War, Government and Governance in England in the Later Middle Ages', in L. Clark (ed.), *The Fifteenth Century VII: Conflicts, Consequences and the Crown in the Late Middle Ages* (Woodbridge, 2007), 1–22, at 1. See also Burt, *Edward I*, 15–16, 27–28, 236–41; Davies, *Domination and Conquest*, 121, 127.

[176] J. Otway-Ruthven, 'The Request of the Irish for English Law, 1277–80', *Irish Historical Studies*, 6 (1949), 261–70, at 267 (second quote); Davies, *First English Empire*, 159–60 (and works cited at 160n 68).

[177] See comments in the following paragraphs on 'new constitutional history'. For comment on the traditional view of the 'triumph of royal government', see Kaminsky, 'The Noble Feud', 59; Davies, *First English Empire*, 54, 195, 201. This is well captured in Harding, *Medieval Law*, 22, 33, 37, 93–4, 97, 105–6, 198, 240–1, and most clearly at 245. See also K.B. McFarlane, 'Service, Maintenance, and Politics', in K.B. McFarlane, *The Nobility of Later Medieval England: The Ford Lectures for 1953 and Related Studies*, ed. J.P. Cooper (Oxford, 1973), 102–21, at 115 (and see McFarlane, *England in the Fifteenth Century*, 243); Bernard, *Power of the Early Tudor Nobility*, 201–4; Powell, *Kingship, Law, and Society*, 113, 274; Ormrod, *Edward III*, 160; Castor, *Duchy of Lancaster*, 3–21, esp. 5. For a more 'sudden transition', see Dean, *Crime in Medieval Europe*, 104.

[178] L. Anderson, *A Kind of Wild Justice: Revenge in Shakespeare's Comedies* (Newark, 1987), 13–15, discussing Francis Bacon's essay 'Of Revenge' (1597); Kesselring, *Making Murder Public*, 1–19, 68–93.

[179] D.T. Andrew, 'The Code of Honour and Its Critics: The Opposition to Duelling in England, 1700–1850', *Social History*, 5 (1980), 409–34, at 421.

[180] Fortescue, *Governance of England*, 116; C.J. Nederman (ed.), *Political Thought in Early Fourteenth-Century England: Treatises by Walter of Milemete, William of Pagula, and William of Ockham* (Turnhout, 2002), 51.

Introduction

custom (that of the manorial courts being best known).[181] On the other end of the spectrum from local particularism, the foreign interests of urban merchants required engagement with the international frameworks of maritime and merchant laws and customs, just as English kings, nobles and gentry engaged with international codes of chivalry and the laws of war.[182] Similarly, the spiritual jurisdiction of the church offered an international legal framework to address, especially, defamatory, testamentary and matrimonial matters.[183] The widespread influence of the learned laws has been observed, notably of the canon law on the formulae of arbitration, and of course the church's reach also extended to felony, at least with regard to claims of sanctuary and benefit of clergy.[184] All this was so throughout the realm,[185] but as we have seen the far north accommodated yet another legal cohabitant. Whereas march law applied strictly beyond the kingdom's bounds in the March of Wales, in the far north march law operated throughout the three northern counties of the realm.[186]

Through all of these channels different legal waters flowed into the kingdom and fed the wells from which ideas and practices of social order and justice were drawn. But our understanding of how these influences mixed with the law of Westminster in the minds of landowners is relatively weak. Among historians who have investigated self-regulatory processes in the local societies of late medieval England, one summation underlines the point that 'it was not primarily the king's law that kept the

---

[181] A. Musson and W.M. Ormrod, *The Evolution of English Justice: Law, Politics and Society in the Fourteenth Century* (Basingstoke, 1999), 8–10 (quotation from 8); D. Ibbetson, 'Custom in Medieval Law', in A. Perreau-Saussine and J.B. Murphy (eds), *The Nature of Customary Law: Legal, Historical and Philosophical Perspectives* (Cambridge, 2007), 151–75, at 167–75; J.G.H. Hudson, 'Introduction: Customs, Laws, and the Interpretation of Medieval Law', in P. Andersen and M. Münster-Swendsen (eds), *Custom: The Development and Use of a Legal Concept in the Middle Ages* (Copenhagen, 2009), 1–16, at 10. On 'accustomed practices', see below, pp. 188 and 197.

[182] Kadens, E., 'Order within Law, Variety within Custom: The Character of the Medieval Merchant Law', *Chicago Journal of International Law*, 5 (2004), 39–65, at 56; R. Ward, *The World of the Medieval Shipmaster: Law, Business and the Sea, c. 1350–c. 1450* (Woodbridge, 2009), 9–10.

[183] Baker, *Introduction to English Legal History*, 148–50; *Lower Ecclesiastical Jurisdiction in Late-Medieval England*, ed. L.R. Poos (Oxford, 2001), xlvii–lii. On provincial legislation and legal culture, see I. Forrest, 'English Provincial Constitutions and Inquisition into Lollardy', in M.C. Flannery and K.L. Walter (eds), *The Culture of Inquisition in Medieval England* (Woodbridge, 2013), 45–59, at 50–2, 59.

[184] Van Dijk, *John Gower*, 4; Powell, *Kingship, Law, and Society*, 106. For compurgation by clergymen, see *The Register of Thomas Langley, Bishop of Durham, 1406–1437*, ed. R.L. Storey, 6 vols (Durham, 1949–67), v, p. 125.

[185] See also Johnson, 'Law, Space, and Local Knowledge in Late-Medieval England', 22–3.

[186] On Wales, see Davies, *Lordship and Society*; on Wales and Ireland, see R.A. Griffiths, 'The English Realm and Dominions and the King's Subjects in the Later Middle Ages', in R.A. Griffiths (ed.), *King and Country: England and Wales in the Fifteenth Century* (London, 1989), 33–54, at 34.

Introduction

peace amongst landowners' before the end of the fifteenth century.[187] Rather, as another writer has it, royal justice was a relative newcomer, fairly recently 'superimposed on local community justice', in other words on the 'infrastructure of family, kinsmen, neighbours and social equals' which provided an older context of processes for coping with local disputes.[188] Thus local society remained firmly self-policing even as it embraced and propagated the common law which the king guaranteed, and which swelled during the later middle ages to become the paramount framework shaping the behaviour of landowners, especially towards the defence and pursuit of property and its associated responsibilities and privileges. The best-known expression of such modes of disputing is that of extra-judicial arbitration, ostensibly aimed at conciliation and compromise, and almost always intertwined with litigation.[189]

All of this is fundamental to the approach taken by a number of historians in recent decades to write a 'new constitutional history' of governance, taking institutions together with the ideas and norms that informed and constrained the actions of kings and landowners, both in formal public life and through informal networks of power. The crown, the common weal and, as just mentioned, the king's common law have been put to the fore in understanding the principles which shaped politics, concentrating especially on the language and values of justice which underpinned the security of property and, by extension, of political power. The thrust of this work has been neither 'top-down' nor 'bottom-up', but rather to emphasise the inherent reciprocity between king, nobility and gentry that was required to make this participatory system function.[190] This approach to the ideas, norms and structures of governance, interpreted as far as possible from the perspective of landowners themselves, represents a vital advance in our understanding of the

---

[187] Carpenter, 'Law, Justice and Landowners'; Carpenter, *Wars of the Roses*, 53–4, 60; Carpenter, *Locality and Polity*, 282, 637 (arguing that the 'predominance of a centralised public authority' was realised by c. 1500).

[188] Wright, *Derbyshire Gentry*, 119, 142 (quotations); Maddern, *Violence and Social Order*, 16; Carpenter, *Locality and Polity*, 282–3 ('this legal system was only a very recent intruder into a web of private relationships'), 354, 628. Kaeuper, *War, Justice and Public Order*, 134–5, 142, 182, assumes less cautiously the existence of an 'ancient' code and impulse towards vengeance and 'brutal self-help'.

[189] See below, pp. 169 and 309. Powell, *Kingship, Law, and Society*, 106, 269–75, esp. 273; Powell, 'Settlement of Disputes'; Powell, 'Arbitration and the Law'; Carpenter, 'Law, Justice and Landowners', 225, 236.

[190] See 'Overview' above, and pp. 25 and 342. The fullest statements are Powell, *Kingship, Law, and Society*; Carpenter, *Locality and Polity*; Carpenter, *Wars of the Roses*; Watts, *Henry VI*. Sceptical comment includes W.M. Ormrod, 'Parliament, Political Economy and State Formation in Later Medieval England', in Hoppenbrouwers, Janse and Stein (eds), *Power and Persuasion*, 123–39.

Introduction

late medieval polity, and certain ideas (e.g., that of 'the crown') have been very carefully examined in this regard.[191] Studies of gentry violence have come to rest intuitively on the view that a consensus existed among landowners about the tolerable limits of violence, amounting to a shared but unwritten agreement as to the acceptable conventions of disputing.[192] The shape and scope of this gentry consensus has been expressed in reasonably general terms, although the conceptual thrust of all this work has been more restrained and nuanced than the summary offered here might imply. Still, other than in discussion of the learned and common law influences on arbitration, the potential variety and sources of norms that shaped or prescribed English landowners' attitudes towards violence and peacemaking, and self-regulatory processes in local society more generally, remain relatively underdeveloped.[193] Even at a more descriptive level, the patterns and regularities of such behaviours stand to be examined closely and in their own right, informed by the literature on conflict just surveyed.[194] Perhaps especially in England's far north, deeply associated as it long has been with violent turbulence and strength of kinship, the potential is tremendous for such an exploration of how local society managed conflict as it governed itself. What norms, customs and practices, in addition to those of royal justice, may have shaped conflict in this part of the kingdom? The significance of such an exploration, moreover, is greater than merely a further enrichment of the history of conflict and dispute (valuable as that should be in its own right); the questions to be pursued here go to a fundamental understanding of the governance of late medieval England.

It would be relatively straightforward to write a book that confirmed existing perceptions of the far north as a periphery, different from the central core of the realm due to its remoteness and special circumstances. As will already be clear, in pursuing what follows I wish to avoid explaining whatever patterns may be found at the northern marches as aberrations only to be expected in a marginal area, distant from the kingdom's 'heartland' and destabilised by a hostile border and by a

---

[191] Watts, *Henry VI*; Castor, *Duchy of Lancaster*.

[192] Maddern, *Violence and Social Order*, 34; Carpenter, 'Law, Justice and Landowners', 235; Carpenter, *Locality and Polity*, 358–9, 397, 433, 561, 572, 581, 610, 612, 620, 622; Harriss, 'Political Society', 51.

[193] See below, pp. 314 and 335.

[194] For explicit focus on the patterns of confrontation, see Phythian-Adams, 'Rituals of Personal Confrontation'; Reinle, '"Fehde" und gewaltsame Selbsthilfe'. Work on gentry *mentalités* tends to skirt around conflict. For example, P.C. Maddern, '"Best Trusted Friends": Concepts and Practices of Friendship among Fifteenth Century Norfolk Gentry', in N. Rogers (ed.), *England in the Fifteenth Century: Proceedings of the 1992 Harlaxton Symposium* (Stamford, 1994), 100–17.

Introduction

relatively independent nobility.[195] This approach calls for some schematic discussion. Problematic ideas of the precociously centralised English medieval state, and of the path to a post-1603 British state, have been touched on above. As others have noted, centralisation is a predominant theme in the historiography of government and governance in the territories ruled by English monarchs, especially from the reign of Edward I to that of Elizabeth I. This keynote of English political history has concentrated on a parallel story of institutional uniformity, on the one hand, and bureaucratic centralisation, on the other.[196] Whereas medievalists have come to think of English government as something undertaken in reciprocal dialogue with the crown by landowners in self-policing localities (as we have just observed),[197] a comparably participatory model of governance has also emerged for the early modern period, reframing the state as 'a dispersed and de-centred authority', with institutions not sited in Westminster but 'locally, in the parishes, boroughs and counties'.[198] The approach of early modernists to centralisation tends to emphasise standardisation and uniformity of ways of doing things, a process of homogenisation overriding local particularities. In this configuration, state formation becomes a process; the 'centre' becomes less an institutional or geographical entity and more a shared conception in the minds of those who governed. All the same, the early modern emphasis on centralisation as 'homogenisation' was reinforced by institutional and geographical ideas. The process of the English Reformation, and in no small part through the acts of supremacy and uniformity of the 1530s–1550s subordinating canon law to common law and asserting conformity of religious worship, surely influenced (and reflected) expectations of homogeneity.[199]

---

[195] The summary given by Frame, *Political Development*, 222, remains pertinent. For recent statements of the scholarly status quo, see Jamroziak, *Survival and Success on Medieval Borders*, 17–18; Arvanigian, 'Henry V, Lancastrian Kingship and the Far North of England', 77–8.

[196] Thornton, *Cheshire*, 5–8, 13, 243, 245, 248–9. See also Ellis, 'Crown, Community and Government', 187.

[197] Harriss, 'Political Society', 33; Carpenter, *Locality and Polity*, 282, 354, 628; Carpenter, *Wars of the Roses*, 62–3; P.R. Coss, 'Hilton, Lordship and the Culture of the Gentry', in C. Dyer, P.R. Coss and C. Wickham (eds), *Rodney Hilton's Middle Ages: An Exploration of Historical Themes* (Oxford, 2007), 34–52, at 48.

[198] M. Knights et al., 'Towards a Social and Cultural History of Keywords and Concepts', *History of Political Thought*, 31 (2010), 427–48, at 430, commenting especially on M.J. Braddick, *State Formation in Early Modern England, c. 1550–1700* (Cambridge, 2000); Hindle, *The State and Social Change*. For similar approaches to early modern Italy, see E.F. Guarini, 'Center and Periphery', in J. Kirshner (ed.), *The Origins of the State in Italy: 1300–1600* (Chicago, 1996), 74–96.

[199] Similarly, early modern cartography came to define 'political authority as linear, geometric, and homogeneous': J. Branch, *The Cartographic State: Maps, Territory and the Origins of Sovereignty* (Cambridge, 2014), 86.

Introduction

In examining notions of 'centre', 'periphery' and 'locality' as applied to the late medieval English kingdom, I have already devoted some consideration to these matters,[200] recognising centre–periphery as a twentieth-century variation upon a much older conceptual apparatus, that of centre–locality. The Victorian (and Prussian) legacy of thought about government and its 'machinery' is traced and the idea of a 'centre' (or 'core') and 'central' government is challenged as an anachronistic distortion which necessitates a view of the northern marches as remote, exceptional and peripheral. That investigation need not be rehearsed here other than to underline the present concern to ask how the collection of localities in England's late medieval far north might be most fruitfully conceptualised, without reference to 'centre' and 'periphery'. In response, inspiration is taken from others (especially local, landscape and urban historians) to propose an alternative view of the kingdom, a composite, cellular England which royal – not 'central' – government sought to harness.[201] This is to see England as an agglomeration of porous cells, each one defined by watersheds and urban hinterlands, each one outward-looking and integrated with its neighbours into a wider whole. I speculate that such cellular units may be the 'contreis' of which Sir John Fortescue writes in the quotation in the heading above,[202] 'country' being a thorny and fluid medieval and early modern term but one which approximately expressed the intermediary milieu in which the local and national interacted. In that essay the divisions proposed with which to understand the far north and some of its neighbouring territories are the cells (or 'country-provinces') of *Newcastle-Durham*, *Carlisle-Solway*, and *Chester-Lancaster-Furness*, identified in Map 1.[203] The purpose of such an exercise is not to erase county boundaries, for county units are vital if we are to understand and use the records of royal government. This was the crucial unit of administration throughout the kingdom (excluding

---

[200] J.W. Armstrong, 'Centre, Periphery, Locality, Province: England and Its Far North in the Fifteenth Century', in P. Crooks, D. Green and W.M. Ormrod (eds), *The Plantagenet Empire, 1259–1453: Proceedings of the 2014 Harlaxton Symposium* (Donington, 2016), 248–72.

[201] I draw especially upon the framework of 'cultural provinces' as proposed by C. Phythian-Adams, *Societies, Cultures and Kinship, 1580–1850: Cultural Provinces and English Local History* (Leicester, 1993), 2–10; C. Phythian-Adams, 'Frontier Valleys', in J. Thirsk (ed.), *The English Rural Landscape* (Oxford, 2000), 236–62. I also draw on B.K. Roberts and S. Wrathmell, *Region and Place: A Study of English Rural Settlement* (London, 2002), 6–12; J. Kermode, 'Northern Towns', in D. Palliser (ed.), *The Cambridge Urban History of Britain, Volume I: 600–1540* (Cambridge, 2000), 657–79; D.M. Palliser, *Towns and Local Communities in Medieval and Early Modern England* (Aldershot, 2006), c. II, c. III, c. VI. See further discussion below, p. 100.

[202] Discussing magnates and royal offices, Fortescue (*Governance of England*, 151) writes: 'Ffor thai mowe best rule the contreis wheras ther offices ben, wich is in euery partie off the lande'.

[203] Armstrong, 'Centre, Periphery, Locality, Province', 267–70; this essay also reviews literature on the 'country'.

Introduction

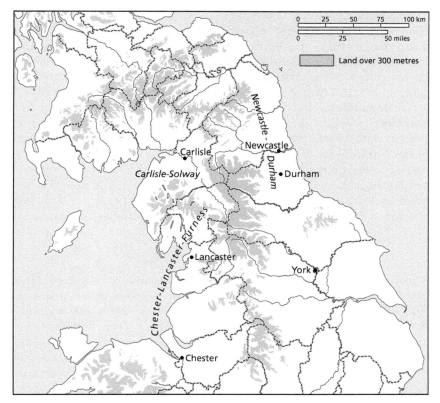

Map 1   The Far North and cellular 'Country-Provinces'

palatinates and lesser franchises, of course) and the unit by which official records were organised. It is, however, to offer a means to explore the ways in which we might think about the far north, the English realm and indeed the wider territories subject to the English crown without any necessity that they should be understood through processes of centralisation, a centre–periphery perspective, or its close relative, that of centre–locality. A recent comment on European comparative legal history has challenged the utility of a centre–periphery model and observed that the idea of a standard and exceptions or deviations from it is often more beneficial to study of 'peripheries' than of 'centres'.[204]

[204] H. Pihlajamäki, 'Comparative Contexts in Legal History: Are We All Comparatists Now?', in M. Adams and D. Heirbaut (eds), *The Method and Culture of Comparative Law* (Oxford, 2014), 121–32, at 126–7.

43

Introduction

The present effort notes the work observed earlier on the various liberties of the north-east which has emphasised 'alternative institutional frameworks' to those dominated by the king, and pointed towards a pluralist – even polyfocal – polity, a far more heterogeneous, agglomerated and sometimes tentative kingdom than the unitary and centralised realm of conventional understanding.[205] Through a study of social organisation and local conflict, the deeper task exercising the chapters that follow is to contest the view of the precocious medieval English state, chiefly in terms of assumptions about universal authority of the common law in regulating local conflict. That task is assisted by leaving aside interpretations about centralisation and centre–periphery relationships, however entrenched they may be. It is hoped that we stand to learn something new about the late medieval polity as we consider a collection of localities on England's northern frontier.

SOURCES AND OUTLINE

The corpus of source materials for this investigation of three counties may be summarised very briefly and placed into four main categories. The first is evidence produced by the English governmental administration, and fortunately much of this material has been published, for example, the rolls of parliament and chancery, and records of diplomatic relations. Further attention has been given to unpublished official documents, such as those of the exchequer. Scottish governmental records have also been examined where available and deployed here where relevant for the light they cast on England. The second category, also emanating from royal government, is that of the law courts, which encompassed relevant gaol delivery rolls (which survive up to 1459), chancery petitions, and king's bench indictments and plea rolls. The third category is published narrative and literary sources, consisting primarily of contemporary chronicles. The final category of sources consists of charters, indentures and other family and civic or corporate material surviving in national or county record offices or private collections. Only some of this material is published.

The plan of the book is as follows. Part I includes Chapter 1, on 'frontiers and borderlands', addressing the conceptual and historical understandings of our region of study, and Chapter 2, on 'earth and stone' which investigates the towers and castles of the marches and the

---

[205] Holford and Stringer, *Border Liberties,* 4, 5, 7 (quotation), 8. See also Thornton, *Cheshire,* 252; Bennett, *Community, Class and Careerism,* 7 (on a 'core' region). See Lavezzo, *Angels on the Edge,* 73–6, 84 –5, on Cheshire and England in Higden's *Polychronicon.*

Introduction

region's landscape and patterns of habitation and agriculture. Part II is comprised of Chapter 4, which identifies the important landowners of the border counties, and Chapter 5, which addresses sociopolitical structures, investigating patterns of lordship and kinship. Particular regard is given to the subject of the so-called border Surnames and the question of whether they are traceable in the fifteenth century. Part III then turns our attention to aspects of conflict. Chapter 6 examines the administration of justice, considering what is known about England and some other relevant jurisdictions, before assessing royal justice and common law, and border justice and march law, in the far north. Chapter 7 offers, as far as sources allow, a quantitative analysis of the relationship between national politics and local conflict. It presents a chronology of conflict derived mostly from legal records and assesses the level and nature of recorded violence. Chapter 8 focuses on the Anglo-Scottish dimension of conflict in the marches, pursuing the question of whether a cross-border 'raiding culture' obtained in the fifteenth century. Chapters 9 and 10 are concerned with what will be called the 'accustomed practices' of conflict which shaped processes of discord and concord in the phenomenon of what might be described as 'feud'. This analysis focuses on language, supporters, types of violence and the use of violence, and the role of vengeance. It also looks beyond the already considerable sophistication of what is known about informal dispute resolution and arbitration to consider more widely the making of peace by compromise and the range of practices which this involved. These two chapters are focused on developing a full understanding of the culture of conflict which obtained in the far north and, where relevant, on raising questions about our understanding of conflict in the rest of the kingdom.

★★★

The red sandstone wall of the passage outside the oratory in Carlisle Castle is etched with a series of images datable to c. 1480. This artwork, on the second floor of the keep, partly comprises a menagerie of fantastical fauna; in a way it is reminiscent of the Gundestrup cauldron of a much earlier age. There is an unrefined informality in the carvings, and palpable personality in the figures among them. Many of these creatures are heraldic beasts, accompanied by other devices associated with the families of Dacre, Greystoke and Percy and with Richard, duke of Gloucester. There are also helms and suits of armour, but, perhaps chiefly, the carvings include the iconography of Christian devotion: the IHS monogram of the holy name, the crucifixion, lilies, St George and

Introduction

the dragon, St Catherine and her wheel. There are numerous less identifiable figures among the carvings: stags and a horned man, mermaids and mirrors. A sinister quality, too, harbours here. Some scenes exude a violent intensity (over and above the conventional religious imagery), such as that of two men engaged in armed combat. Elsewhere, a figure (St Edmund?) is pinned with arrows or spears, his genital area gouged out of the stone. This artwork falls into the category of so-called medieval graffiti and to that extent it illustrates the wider genre, with a visual repertoire shaped by themes of pious devotion, chivalry and fantasy.[206] It is set within a layered frame of reference that is at once Cumbrian, English and European; at once sacred and secular; at once destructive and creative. Contemplation of this visual assemblage quickly prompts questions about the meanings intended by the person or, more likely, persons who made these carvings. What did they intend to record in the stone, and for what purposes? One can readily imagine medieval viewers, perhaps wielding candlelight on a dark winter afternoon; what did they read in these figures and symbols? To ask questions of this nature involves interpretation of frameworks of understanding. Our present task is not so very different. It is to understand, even if only indirectly, a part of the changing cultural 'grammar' of society, and to come to know better an important part of England's past.

---

[206] M. Champion, *Medieval Graffiti: The Lost Voices of England's Churches* (London, 2015).

PART I

2

FRONTIERS AND BORDERLANDS

> Item it is ordanit at na man na woman passe in Inglande no speke with Inglismen without speciale leif of the wardane or of his lowtenande or of thaim hafand powere direct to thaim be lettir to gewe leif at has thare lettir of powere to schwa.... And quhasa passis without leif in illing of thare nichtbouris and maner as is forsade, he salbe at the wardane court of tressoune and his lif and his gud in the wardanis will.[1]
>
> —Scottish Parliament, 'Statutis ordanit for the marchis' (1430)

The purpose of this chapter is twofold: to address the concept of England's far north as a frontier and to examine corresponding ideas about the spatial environment of the region. On the one hand, the problem is to address what this means for our historical understandings today; on the other, it demands also that we explore what this meant for the later middle ages. If militarisation is often understood to be a feature of medieval frontier societies generally, then it is a matter which we shall touch on only briefly here; the topic will be picked up again in subsequent chapters.[2] To the forefront of the agenda now comes a scrutiny of the ideas we bring to the subject and an examination of the ways in which the medieval frontier could be ambivalent: both clear and ambiguous, and at once static and dynamic.

FRONTIERS AND BORDERLANDS

Over the past century and more, frontiers and borderlands have sustained a vast and thriving literature, often concerned with nomenclature and taxonomy.[3] The present study, in choosing 'frontier' as a leading

---

[1] *RPS*, 1430/41.

[2] Goodman, 'Introduction', in Tuck and Goodman (eds), *War and Border Societies*, 1.

[3] See above, p. 19, and the works cited there. For an effective summary see Power and Standen (eds), *Frontiers in Question*, 1–31; R.I. Burns, 'The Significance of the Frontier in Middle Ages', in Bartlett and MacKay (eds), *Medieval Frontier Societies*, 307–30. See also Lattimore, *Studies in Frontier*

49

Part I

category of analysis, does so with the intention to recognise its advantages and limitations as 'a convenient tool for historical interpretation'.[4] The preceding chapter commented briefly on the historiography of frontier studies applied to the Anglo-Scottish marches led by Goodman, and the wider comparative emphasis which has driven so much work on the topic. Pre-modern frontiers have attracted abiding attention from historians. Three leading overviews have been offered in English-language collections edited by Bartlett and MacKay, Power and Standen, and Abulafia and Berend.[5] The first two collections place military dimensions at the foreground of discussion, in some ways reflecting Lourie's emphasis on medieval marches as societies 'organised for war'. Abulafia and Berend give much less consideration to military frameworks, and instead encourage us to think of medieval frontiers as states of mind.[6] The introduction offered by Power and Standen sets out a helpful discussion of two widely used classifications of frontiers, those which are linear, and those which are zonal. For political scientists and geographers *zonal frontiers* are understood to be ambiguous spaces, sometimes no-man's lands 'between' different political powers, and sometimes wildernesses 'beyond' more definitely controlled territory. By contrast, *linear frontiers* tend to describe artificial lines of separation, as between sovereign territories. However, pre-modern frontiers have been shown to have exhibited features of both, such that a hybrid 'linear zonal boundary sense' may be useful.[7] Work on medieval frontiers has often tended towards the identification of so-called frontier societies. In the Anglo-Scottish case, this has turned upon the topics of cross-border acculturation, and the

---

  History, 469–91. On Herbert Bolton and Frederick Jackson Turner, see A.L. Hurtado, 'Parkmanizing the Spanish Borderlands: Bolton, Turner, and the Historians' World', *Western Historical Quarterly*, 26 (1995), 149–67.

[4] E.M. Moreno, 'The Creation of a Medieval Frontier: Islam and Christianity in the Iberian Peninsula, Eighth to Eleventh Centuries', in Power and Standen (eds), *Frontiers in Question*, 32–54, at 37.

[5] Bartlett and MacKay (eds), *Medieval Frontier Societies*; Power and Standen (eds), *Frontiers in Question*; Abulafia and Berend (eds), *Medieval Frontiers*. In addition, see Ellis and Esser (eds), *Frontiers and the Writing of History*; Ellis and Esser (eds), *Frontiers, Regions and Identities*; Ellis and Klusáková (eds), *Imagining Frontiers*; E. O'Byrne and J. Ní Ghradaigh (eds), *The March in the Islands of the Medieval West* (Leiden, 2012).

[6] Lourie is cited above, p. 19, and below, p. 63. N. Berend, 'Medievalists and the Notion of the Frontier', *The Medieval History Journal*, 2 (1999), 55–72, at 60–1, touches on militarisation and warfare.

[7] P. Sahlins, *Boundaries: The Making of France and Spain in the Pyrenees* (Berkeley, 1989), 4; Power and Standen (eds), *Frontiers in Question*, 2–3, 5, 9, 13 (and 10, 12, 27 on hybridity); Berend, 'Medievalists and the Notion of the Frontier', 68, 69 (quote). On the related field of 'borderlands history', see P. Hämäläinen and S. Truett, 'On Borderlands', *Journal of American History*, 98 (2011), 338–61, at 340 (quote), 341, 347.

Frontiers and Borderlands

complex subject of identities, local and national.[8] Yet the usefulness of 'frontier society' as a category of analysis has been challenged with demands for greater precision.[9] The late medieval Anglo-Scottish frontier was both linear (insofar as it formed an agreed boundary separating two sovereign jurisdictions) and zonal (in that it applied the framework of the march, on both sides of the border, to denote areas of special jurisdiction arising as a result of proximity to the border). In this way, the Tweed–Solway borderline was principally a political and jurisdictional boundary rather than a religious, linguistic or cultural divide. The present study is not concerned with whether it should be classified as a frontier society of any particular type; rather, the focus is on a better understanding of society at the frontier, and what it may suggest about the rest of England.

As has already been observed, the Anglo-Scottish frontier was unique in the insular world for being the only land boundary between two fully realised sovereign kingdoms (see Map 2).[10] Unlike the Welsh or Irish marches of the later middle ages, the frontier between England and Scotland was not an advancing or contracting district of conquest and clientage; from the twelfth century onwards, and certainly from the demarcation agreed in 1237, it was subject to a remarkably clear and static geographical definition, even if control over that well-defined area could itself be fluid and dynamic.[11] Relevant to the discussion of the frontiers of the English realm is that frontiers generally have been closely related to assumptions about centre and periphery, where the periphery itself is equated with the frontier.[12] Frontiers which came to be visually represented as coloured boundaries on early modern maps understood to be the creations of territorial and 'centralising' states also speak to such ideas.[13] There is a moral dimension which has accrued here as well, captured in

---

[8] As per Goodman, 'Anglo-Scottish Marches'; King, 'Best of Enemies'; see above, p. 18. L. Dauphant, *Le Royaume des Quatre Rivières: l'espace politique français (1380–1515)* (Seyssel, 2012), 233–72, considers the question of frontier societies in late medieval France, and emphasises not their exceptionality but the realm's frontiers as *containers* of the royal *État* (at 262).

[9] Berend, 'Medievalists and the Notion of the Frontier', 68–71. For the monastic experience around frontiers of different types, see E.M. Jamroziak and K. Stöber (eds), *Monasteries on the Borders of Medieval Europe: Conflict and Cultural Interaction* (Turnhout, 2013).

[10] See above, p. 15, and below, p. 63. For the Northern Isles, see I.P. Grohse, *Frontiers for Peace in the Medieval North: The Norwegian-Scottish Frontier c. 1260–1470* (Leiden, 2017).

[11] Barrow, 'Frontier and Settlement'; Power and Standen (eds), *Frontiers in Question*, 7; Lieberman, *Medieval March of Wales*, 11.

[12] See Berend, 'Medievalists and the Notion of the Frontier', 68, on 'peripheral zones'.

[13] Branch, *Cartographic State*, 21, 80, 83–8, 86, 87, 97–8. See also S. Rokkan, 'Territories, Centres and Peripheries: Towards a Geoethnic-Geoeconomic-Geopolitical Model of Differentiation within Western Europe', in J. Gottmann (ed.), *Centre and Periphery: Spatial Variation in Politics* (London, 1980), 163–204, at 174–8, 198, on 'external' and 'interface' peripheries, which look rather like North American frontiers of expansion and settlement (external), and European frontiers as boundaries between governing authorities (interface).

Part I

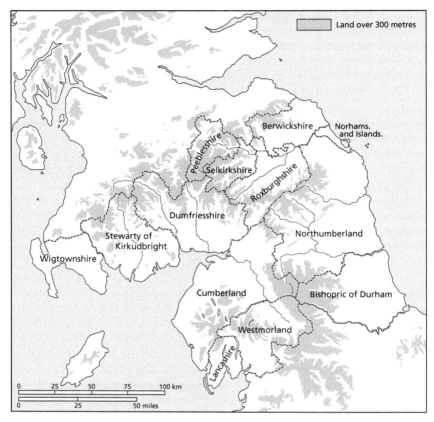

Map 2 The Anglo-Scottish Borderlands

Frederick Jackson Turner's description of the advancing American frontier as 'the meeting point between savagery and civilisation'.[14] These connotations have long been part of the conceptual baggage carried by frontiers, even as scholars have come to emphasise their porousness and diversity. Indeed one of the most helpful contributions of more recent early modern-focused 'borderlands history' to this wider scholarship has been a willingness to break free from such assumptions. That work underscores the ambiguity of frontiers as places 'where boundaries are also crossroads, peripheries are also central places, homelands are also passing-through places, and the end points of empire are also forks in the road'.[15]

[14] Quoted in Power and Standen (eds), *Frontiers in Question*, 9.
[15] Hämäläinen and Truett, 'On Borderlands', 338.

Frontiers and Borderlands

The present book adopts 'frontier' primarily to refer to a political boundary and the territory (or zone) adjacent to that boundary. The most prevalent term in our source material is 'march', although sometimes chosen were other words, including 'border' and 'frontier' (of which more below). In this study 'march' and 'marches' are used especially in a jurisdictional sense, to convey that area which was subject to special administrative arrangements under the direction of the wardens of the march. By our period the march was normally divided into the east, middle and west marches, each with its own warden.[16] The marches were a territory not only under a particular jurisdiction but under a jurisdiction which was orientated *outwards*. In this case the three English marches towards Scotland faced the three Scottish marches towards England, and vice versa, so that at its fullest extent the late medieval Anglo-Scottish frontier comprised six distinct marches. Thus England's northern marches were again unlike the marches in Ireland, a zone which fluctuated geographically, or those in Wales, a collection of lordships which were external to the English kingdom.[17] Here my discussion generally uses 'frontier' as a broad-shouldered concept, carrying with it three main subcategories. Although I make no claims to absolute precision of usage, this book speaks of these subcategories of frontier in the following ways: (1) a cross-border, Anglo-Scottish zonal sense; (2) a sense which refers to either the English or the Scottish portions of this zone; and (3) a linear or boundary sense.

Examining how fifteenth-century writers and officials described frontiers is a way to approach how they understood the concept. The first known occurrence in Middle English of the word 'frontier' in the sense of a boundary comes from an early fifteenth-century translation of the French dream poem, *Le Pèlerinage de l'Âme*. In that work 'frontiers of the realm' and 'borders of the realm' were interchangeable expressions,

---

[16] Reid, 'The Office of Warden'; Hunter Blair, 'The Wardens'; Storey, 'Wardens of the Marches'; Barrow, 'Anglo-Scottish Border'; G. Neilson, 'The March Laws', ed. T.I. Rae, in *Miscellany I* (Stair Soc., 1971); H.R.T. Summerson, 'The Early Development of the Laws of the Anglo-Scottish Marches, 1249–1448', in W.M. Gordon and T.D. Fergus (eds), *Legal History in the Making: Proceedings of the Ninth British Legal History Conference* (London, 1991), 29–42; Neville, *Violence, Custom and Law*, 2–11, 185; M.H. Brown, 'War, Allegiance, and Community in the Anglo-Scottish Marches: Teviotdale in the Fourteenth Century', *Northern History*, 41 (2004), 219–38.

[17] E.g., see P.M. Duffy, 'The Nature of the Medieval Frontier in Ireland', *Studia Hibernica*, 22–3 (1982–3), 21–38; Smith, *Crisis and Survival*, 201–2; Davies, *Lordship and Society*. The powers of the Welsh marcher lords were inherited regalities affixed to the possession of property. See R.R. Davies, 'Kings, Lords and Liberties in the March of Wales, 1066–1272', *TRHS*, 5th ser., 29 (1979), 41–61, at 42. In Scottish historiography and usage, the plural 'borders' is normally the equivalent of 'marches'. The 'Scottish Borders' local authority of today thus preserves in its name a sense of the ancient term 'marches'. The subtitle of this book uses 'Scottish Marches' as shorthand for what more strictly should be described as the English marches towards Scotland.

Part I

the latter apparently introduced by the English translator. The poem speaks of an area externally threatened by 'perille of enemyes', in which 'tounes and castels' were to be kept by worthy commanders.[18] Comparable usage in the fifteenth century may be found elsewhere, as in a suit between Englishmen in northern France in 1426. This case recorded that one party held the castle of Clinchamps in Maine comté, 'et tient frontiere contre les ennemis'.[19] Language also allowed the idea of frontiers or borders internal to England to be expressed, as it was in Lord Berkeley's reply to Lord Talbot's challenge prior to the battle of Nibley Green in 1470. This location, it was asserted, had been selected as the place for their contest of 'knighthood and manhood' because it 'standeth in the borders' of the manors that were in dispute between the parties.[20]

With regard to the English frontier towards Scotland, a petition of 1415 on behalf of the 'poueres liges' of the counties of Northumberland, Cumberland and Westmorland is instructive. In its bid for exemption from payment of the fifteenth and tenth granted in parliament, this document foregrounded the local population's efforts in resisting 'la malice des enemys'. In doing so it asked the king to consider that the 'said counties are the frontiers on the marches of Scotland'.[21] This usage suggests a contemporary sense in which 'frontiers' and 'marches' were broadly interchangeable terms, placed together here for greater effect. However, the phrasing also points to some more subtle distinctions. Whereas counties could themselves *be* the frontiers (of the realm), the marches were a territory which one stood *upon*, or *within*. A petitioner from Westmorland in 1421 wrote of the barony of Gilsland, situated 'en la marche' of Scotland, in the county of Cumberland.[22] Here is a sense of the march as a space to be entered, which is also reflected in late medieval literary usage. Mandeville wrote of 'going into the marches'.[23] Malory's heroes are frequently found 'in [these] marches' (and the territory of his kings comprised both marches *and* lands).[24] For Malory, marches were

---

[18] *OED*, s.v. 'frontier, n. and adj.'; ibid., 'border, n.' (giving a quotation from 1489 as the earliest in the comparable sense). *Pèlerinage*, 248; *Pylgremage*, bk. IV, c. xxx, http://pilgrim.grozny.nl/0430 .htm, accessed 9 June 2013. This point is observed indirectly by Power and Standen (eds), *Frontiers in Question*, 29n 22.

[19] *English Suits*, 116.   [20] Smyth, *Berkeleys*, ii, p. 111. See also Blow, 'Nibley Green', 106.

[21] *Northern Petitions*, no. 120, p. 156: '*ditz Countes sont les frountures sur les Marches descoce*'.

[22] SC 8/24/1174: '*Gillesland qest en la marche de Scotteland deuant le counte de [Cumberland]*'. See also *CPR 1377–81*, 447: licence to crenellate a house at the manor of Workington (Cbl.), 'by the march of Scotland'.

[23] K. Sisam, *Fourteenth Century Verse and Prose* (Oxford, 1970), 104.

[24] *Malory, Works*, ed. Vinaver, 130 'in this marchis', 502 'how cam he into thys marchys', 254 'in your marchys and landys'. Arthur's England is circumscribed by the 'marchis of Cornuwayle, of Walis, and of the Northe': 27.

Frontiers and Borderlands

threshold spaces in which friendly travellers ought to be greeted with 'chere' and from which enemies were to be repelled. This literary understanding of marches accords well with the evidence from the far north.[25] The duke of Gloucester warned the City of York in 1480 of intelligence that the Scottish host intended 'to entre into the ... marches of these north partyes' and that the earl of Northumberland understood 'they entende to entre into hys marches'.[26] Marches were also territory in which people dwelled and which, as a consequence, could convey attributions of personal identity. For example, the archbishop of York brought 'marchmen' from Tynedale and Hexhamshire to strong-arm his opponents in Yorkshire in 1441, and Sir Robert Ogle's retinue of 600 men, brought south from Northumberland to fight at St Albans in 1455, were called 'men of the marches'.[27] Yet, within the march itself, finer distinctions may be detected. For example, in the late 1390s, Thomas Sandes, a Cumberland JP, was accused of leading 'certain marchers dwelling on the border of the west march of England' in an armed assault on the tenants of Bridekirk, near Cockermouth.[28] Likewise, at a trial in Cumberland in 1421, a clerk recorded the occupation of two locals as 'marcheman'.[29] Similarly, the clerk enrolling the names of five English soldiers garrisoned at Roxburgh in 1400 described them as being 'de marchia'.[30] It would appear that, while outsiders might group all inhabitants of the three march counties together, terms of reference within the region itself were more fluid and relative.[31] It may be unsurprising that places (e.g., Gilsland) and people (e.g., 'certain marchers') placed close to the borderline itself were more readily defined as being of the march than, say, their counterparts in Westmorland or western Cumberland. More interesting, perhaps, is the fact that the term 'march' carried at once a strict jurisdictional sense *and* such a potential for ambiguity.

---

[25] *Malory, Works,* ed. Vinaver, 14, 162. Lieberman has shown, with reference to the march of Wales before 1283, that the term 'march' denoted a malleable idea, 'conceptualised and demarcated in quite different ways at different times'. Lieberman, *Medieval March of Wales,* 5–19, 19–22, quote from 20.

[26] *York Civic Records,* i, 34.

[27] *Plumpton Correspondence,* ed. T. Stapleton (London, 1839), liv–lv; Goodman, *Wars of the Roses,* 23.

[28] '*certeinz marchers demaunr' sur la bordure de la westmarche Dengleteere*' (C 1/7/213). This undated incident was probably related to the Sandes-Brisco dispute (*CCR 1396–99,* 220, 233; *CCR 1399–1402,* 100, 105). See also Summerson, *Medieval Carlisle,* ii, 399.

[29] JUST 3/199 rot. 30 (John Stodherd of Cumrew), 30d (James Raa of Arthuret).

[30] E 101/42/40; *CDS,* IV, no. 567, p. 118: others were listed as '*de Tevedale*', '*de Ridesdale*' or '*de Northumb[e]r[land]*'.

[31] *York Civic Records,* i, 24: a proof of English birth registered in York in 1477 recorded that the subject, born in Nbl., brought men to vouch for him who were 'ful notable and discreit personez born within the Counties of Northumbreland, Westmerland and Cumberland'.

55

Part I

It may have been with such possible ambiguity in mind that the legal-diplomatic language of the period used a range of frontier terminology that aimed to be both comprehensive and precise. In 1399 Henry 'Hotspur' Percy, warden of the marches of England towards Scotland 'in partibus de la Est Marche', was instructed by Richard II to see to the conservation of the Anglo-Scottish truce 'infra fines et limites Marchiarum' of the east march.[32] The armistice of the preceding year had made references to 'the bownds of the Marches' and to the responsibilities of each warden to redress breaches of truce '[be]langand to his Bownds'.[33] More particular attention was at times given to the 'fines limites terminos et bundas' around the English-held castles of Berwick, Roxburgh and Jedburgh, which were acknowledged in 1405 to be among those places situated 'on and in the marches shared among [*inter*] the English and Scottish realms and also [*ac*] in the realm of Scotland'.[34] Such contested areas, known as 'debatable lands', were a recurring theme of Anglo-Scottish truce indentures. Most notably, this included the stretch of land in the west march between the rivers Sark and Esk (about four miles wide by twelve miles deep) called the 'Batable Landez or Threpe Landez'. These were first addressed in the truce of 1449.[35] In 1474 and 1475 English truce commissioners were instructed to treat with their Scottish counterparts by inquiry and perambulation so as to determine the disputed fishery on the River Esk, and this resumed in the 1480s and 1490s with the additional question of the 'metis finibus limitibus et bundis' of the debatable lands (*terrarum batabilium*) in the west marches. They were also to investigate the 'metibus finibus limitibus et bundis' of the west marches themselves.[36] In summary, late medieval terminology suggests that the Anglo-Scottish borderlands were understood with a number of words (including the French vernacular *bordure* and *frounture*), but in all this the idea of the march was paramount. It described a threshold territory, facing outwards from the realm to the adjacent lands beyond. The march conferred a territorial jurisdiction, which was normally subdivided, but which also carried a sense of ambiguity which decreased with closer proximity to the borderline. The precise demarcation of that international boundary tended to introduce the widest

---

[32] *Rot. Scot.*, ii, 147.   [33] *Foedera*, III, iv, 153 (1398).

[34] *Rot. Scot.*, ii, 173–4 (1405); *Foedera*, V, i, 50 (1438). Berwick was specifically identified as '*extra bundas et limites dicti regni nostri*' in 1383 (*Rot. Scot.*, ii, 48).

[35] *CDS*, IV, no. 1221, p. 247; *Foedera*, V, ii, 15–16 (1449). T.H.B. Graham, 'The Debatable Land', *TCWAAS*, n.s., 12 (1912), 33–58; T.H.B. Graham, 'The Debatable Land, Part II', *TCWAAS*, n. s., 14 (1914), 132–57; W.M. MacKenzie, 'The Debateable Land', *SHR*, 30 (1951), 109–25; Neville, *Violence, Custom and Law*, 5, 69, 81, 127–8, 141–2.

[36] *Rot. Scot.*, ii, 450 (1474), 452 (1475), 479 (1487), 491 (1489, quotations), 498 (1491), 513–14 (1494).

Frontiers and Borderlands

range of terms into the record, reflecting the expansive tendencies of late medieval legal phraseology more generally.

BOUNDARY AND GATEWAY

Setting aside the minutiae of terminology, we now turn to take stock of the outline of events which shaped the Anglo-Scottish frontier in the later middle ages. The border came to be clearly defined in a form which proved durable through the Treaty of York in 1237.[37] This settled in writing the Anglo-Scottish boundary by means of the Scottish king's resignation of all claims to the counties of Northumberland, Cumberland and Westmorland and confirmation of his personal possession of the lordships of Tynedale and Penrith to be held of the English crown. Thus in the later middle ages the international boundary was to overlay an established administrative structure of Scottish sheriffdoms and English counties. By European standards it was an unusually clear-cut demarcation. And it was as a corollary to this demarcation that the border and its adjacent marches came to be defined by the well-articulated legal framework of march law, first codified in 1249 as the *Leges Marchiarum*.

From 1296, and throughout most of the fourteenth century, periods of open war meant that the frontier region was marked by shifting areas of control, predominantly favourable to England. But still the overall division of Scottish and English territory as agreed in 1237 persisted, and the counties and sheriffdoms of the borderlands remained well defined beneath the ebb and flow of conquest and reconquest. Whereas English forces occupied portions of southern Scotland for much of this period, the fundamental jurisdictional boundary remained intact. The goal of that occupation was the subordination of the whole Scottish kingdom, not a piecemeal expansion of the English one.[38] The terms arranged for Edward Balliol's concession of 2,000 librates of Scottish territory to his sponsor Edward III in June 1334 are telling. This was perhaps the only occasion on which an enlargement of the English realm was promised. The settlement identified the several sheriffdoms 'on the marches of Scotland adjacent to England' to be separated from the Scottish crown and 'annexed, united, and incorporated' into the English crown

---

[37] *Anglo-Scottish Relations, 1174–1328; Some Selected Documents*, ed. E.L.G. Stones (London, 1965), 38–53.

[38] G.W.S. Barrow, 'Lothian in the First War of Independence', *SHR*, 55 (1976), 151–71; Brown, 'Teviotdale in the Fourteenth Century'.

Part I

and realm.[39] However, in practice, these 'lands, tenements and lordships' were identified as territory of the English crown in Scotland, to be administered by English officials but according to Scottish custom and law.[40] Moreover, this apparatus was not to be sustained, and by 1341 the extent of territory under English control was drastically reduced in the face of advances by Scottish forces loyal to David II.

The conflict sprung of the fourteenth century created new complexity for the administrative framework of the march itself. On the English side of the border a single unitary march first came to be divided into eastern and western parts in 1345. This was a function of the expanding military and judicial roles of the border officials, chiefly the wardens, in this period.[41] The division followed the Pennines, so that the west march comprised Cumberland and Westmorland, and the east march covered Northumberland. Although the middle march was first carved out of the east march in 1381, it was not until 1470 that reference to the middle march appears regularly in English documents.[42] The authority granted to the wardens in their marches did not exclude them from exercising jurisdiction within liberties, using the formula '*tam infra libertates quam extra*'.[43] As we have noted above, potential ambiguity increased with distance from the borderline, and so was more pronounced at the southern reaches of march jurisdiction. In the reign of Edward II a Lancashire jury had accepted that the law of the march applied at Hornby Moor (in Lonsdale),[44] but in the fifteenth century no evidence suggests march law was ever applied in the county palatine of Lancaster nor within the bishopric of Durham between Tyne and Tees.[45] Yet in 1453 complaint was made by the Yorkshire commons of the oppression

[39] *Foedera*, II, iii, 115: '*terrae … super marchiam regni nostri Scotiae, regno angliae adjacentibus … separata a regali dignitate & corona Scotiae imperpetuum, & regali dignitati, & coronae, ac regno Angliae, perpetuis temporibus annexa, unita, & incorporata*'. See R.G. Nicholson, *Edward III and the Scots: The Formative Years of a Military Career, 1327–1335* (Oxford, 1965), 160.

[40] For example, see *Rot. Scot.*, i, 276; *Foedera*, II, iii, 116; and comment in I.A. MacInnes, '"To Be Annexed Forever to the English Crown": The English Occupation of Southern Scotland c. 1334–1337', in King and Simpkin (eds), *England and Scotland at War*, 183–202, at 183.

[41] Neville, *Violence, Custom and Law*, 15–64, esp. p. 37.

[42] Reid, 'The Office of Warden', 486–7; Storey, 'Wardens of the Marches', 596n 4; Tuck, 'Richard II', 41–2.

[43] As per commissions granted in 1453 and 1470 (*Rot. Scot.*, ii, 372, 422–3). See also Holford and Stringer, *Border Liberties*, 390; M. Prestwich, '"*Tam infra libertates quam extra*": Liberties and Military Recruitment', in M. Prestwich (ed.), *Liberties and Identities in the Medieval British Isles* (Woodbridge, 2008), 111–19.

[44] King, 'Englishmen, Scots and Marchers', 23.

[45] Assertions (by Ellis, *Defending English Ground*, 18; citing Storey, *House of Lancaster*, 109) that the English west march somehow excluded the barony of Kendale, or Cumberland south of Derwent, are mistaken. See also Reid, 'The Office of Warden'; Storey, 'Wardens of the Marches'.

Frontiers and Borderlands

and extortion of the warden courts, and as a result parliament confirmed that jurisdiction of these courts was to be confined to the three march counties and Newcastle-upon-Tyne.[46] All the same, a command to summon fighting men northwards to resist invasion in 1480, sent from the earl of Northumberland to the mayor of York on the king's behalf 'and also on myn as Warden', suggests that the wardens themselves continued to harbour a generous interpretation of their remit.[47]

The annealing process of military conflict in the fourteenth century was followed by a cooling in the fifteenth century. The general trend in our main period of interest was a gradual subsiding of extended areas of control back along the static lines agreed in the thirteenth century. Warfare itself became confined to sporadic outbursts. Particularly destructive clashes occurred at Humbleton in 1402 (a defeat for Scotland) and at the Sark in 1448 (a defeat for England), but no major battlefield engagement would follow until Flodden in 1513. In this period Anglo-Scottish diplomacy returned to an interest in pursuing a precise definition of the *limites* noted above. The understanding of the clear boundary of 1237 dividing the land of both realms endured into the later fifteenth century, when the correspondence of the city of York remarked on English wardens preparing 'to entre the ground of Scotland', and on expeditionary expenses to be incurred 'as wele in Skotland ground as in Yngland ground'.[48] There was no middle space, no null territory or no-man's-land. Areas of 'debatable land' were exceptions to a prevailing view of the frontier as a zone shaped by a clear division. Still, in the early fifteenth century, England projected its control into Scottish territory, concentrated in the Tweed–Teviot watershed. A string of English-held towns marked out this provincial axis in the reign of Henry IV. Furthest inland was Jedburgh on the Teviot Water, then Roxburgh at the Teviot–Tweed confluence, and Berwick at the mouth of the Tweed. These three towns were 'little more than isolated garrison-posts in hostile territory'.[49] But gradually this ground was lost to Scottish advances. In 1409 Jedburgh was captured, after which time Roxburgh became the anchor point for English influence over the lower Tweed.[50] Then

---

[46] *PROME*, March 1453, item 66; *SR*, II, 363 (c. iii). See also Reid, 'The Office of Warden', 485; Neville, *Violence, Custom and Law*, 145.

[47] *York Civic Records*, i, 36.   [48] *York Civic Records*, i, 55, 64 (both 1482).

[49] R.D. Oram, 'Dividing the Spoils: War, Schism and Religious Patronage on the Anglo-Scottish Border, c. 1332–c. 1400', in King and Penman (eds), *England and Scotland*, 136–56, at 156.

[50] Lochmaben Castle in Annandale, Fast Castle and Cockburnspath Tower in Berwickshire temporarily came into English possession when their Scottish lord, George Dunbar, earl of March, switched allegiance between 1400 and 1409 (see A.J. Macdonald, 'Kings of the Wild Frontier? The Earls of Dunbar or March, c. 1070–1435', in S.I. Boardman and A. Ross (eds), *The Exercise of Power in Medieval Scotland* [Dublin, 2003], 139–58, 155, 225).

Part I

Roxburgh too fell in 1460, and in 1461 Lancastrian forces handed Berwick to the Scots. With Berwick lost, the projection of English power into the Merse (the northern part of the Tweed watershed) became unsustainable, and by 1462 the last Durham monks resident at Coldingham Priory were expelled to England.[51] At about the same time the Scottish abbot of Kelso suffered accusations of his English adherence and assistance, and by 1464 he too was forced out of his abbacy.[52] The extent of Scottish control had advanced, and now the muddy waters of allegiance could be clarified behind it. It was the duke of Gloucester's seizure of Berwick in 1482 that reinstated England's only foothold north of the border, a sort of Scottish Calais.[53] Although leadership in war against England was a conceit of Scottish border magnates (such as the Dunbars of March and the Black and Red Douglases) and of all the Scottish kings of our period, in truth war became a less important characteristic of the marches as the century progressed. Once the old extent of Scottish territory had been reclaimed, with the exception of Berwick, the impetus for military confrontation from both sides receded accordingly. It would not reappear at scale before the 1540s.

If the tendency overall was a steady setting of the frontier back along its thirteenth-century lines, then this was undermined at points by a certain counter-trend of fluidity. The first such occasion arose very overtly in the first reign of Edward IV. From 1461 to 1464, Lancastrian forces obtained Scottish and French support in a series of invasions and sieges in the English far north. This was foreign interference in an English civil war, rather than any extension of sustained Scottish control in Cumberland or Northumberland. However, it resembled the manner in which English forces had before, and would again in the future, take advantage of internal Scottish strife to project military power across the border. Further signs of fluidity later in the fifteenth century are more

---

[51] On Coldingham Priory, see R. B. Dobson, 'The Last English Monks on Scottish Soil: The Severance of Coldingham Priory from the Monastery of Durham, 1461–78', *SHR*, 46 (1967), 1–25.

[52] *Calendar of Scottish Supplications to Rome*, ed. A.I. Dunlop et al., *V (1447–71)*, no. 809, p. 234; no. 859, pp. 249–50; no. 865, p. 252; no. 905, p. 266; no. 996, pp. 296–7; no. 999, p. 298; no. 1026, p. 306. Abbot Richard Robson may have been a relation of the Robsons of Hownam (NRS: GD 98/Box 2/108.12, p. 1).

[53] J.A. Tuck, 'A Medieval Tax Haven: Berwick upon Tweed and the English Crown, 1333–1461', in R.H. Britnell and J. Hatcher (eds), *Progress and Problems in Medieval England: Essays in Honour of Edward Miller* (Cambridge, 1996), 148–67; J. Donnelly, 'An Open Port: The Berwick Export Trade, 1311–1373', *SHR*, 78 (1999), 145–69. Berwick did not send MPs before 1461. This continued after 1482 (none were sent in 1491), but it was listed as a parliamentary constituency in 1512: *History of Parliament: The House of Commons 1509–1558*, 3 vols, ed. S.T. Bindoff (London, 1982), i, 161. For the interactions of Berwick burgesses with Nbl. gentry, see A. Macdonald, 'Calendar of Deeds in the Laing Charters Relating to Northumberland', *Archaeologia Aeliana*, 4th ser., 28 (1950), 105–31, no. 56, p. 127 (1449); nos 64–8, pp. 129–30 (1491–2).

60

Frontiers and Borderlands

suggestive in nature, and they come in relation to the history of the debatable land of the west marches. As we have noted, this territory was first mentioned in the truce of 1449 (in all probability brought to the fore by the battle of the Sark the preceding year). Todd has advanced the argument that the debatable land arose on the diplomatic agenda because of English claims to a twelfth-century cross-border landholding, which subsequently passed to the English crown in the fourteenth century. That ancient lordship had comprised the three parishes of Arthuret, Kirkandrews and Canonbie, the latter two situated on the western side of the River Esk (extending to the River Sark in Kirkandrews, and with the Esk dividing Canonbie further inland), and the first, Arthuret, situated on the eastern side and extending to the River Lyne (see Map 3). England possessed Arthuret entire but also claimed Canonbie and Kirkandrews, and it was these latter two parishes which comprised the debatable land. No comparable Scottish claim to Arthuret parish survives, despite the fact that Scotland had an equal or better claim to make (given that the entire lordship had been established under David I of Scotland when he held Cumberland).[54] If the appearance of the western debatable land in 1449 marked an agreement to disagree over the finer grain of the borderline, then the diplomatic attention given to the Esk fishery (from the 1470s) and the boundaries of the debatable land in the 1480s and 1490s, noted above, suggests an escalation of contested claims to this territory.[55] Some further illumination may come from Scottish court records of the 1490s in which numerous references are made to offenders in Scotland's southern marches acting in league with the rebels or traitors of 'Levyn', sometimes in cooperation with Englishmen.[56] Although scholars have noted the Levyn rebels, the significance of this group has never been explained.[57] It is an instructive fact that Levyn is an old form of the name for the River Lyne.[58] Such references to the Levyn traitors make better sense if we consider the possibility that the identification of certain malefactors as 'rebels of Levyn' represents a strand of a Scottish claim to the parish of Arthuret between the Esk and the Lyne. What this may suggest is that the Scottish crown had come to view the inhabitants

---

[54] J.M. Todd, 'The West March on the Anglo-Scottish Border in the Twelfth Century, and the Origins of the Western Debatable Land', *Northern History*, 43 (2006), 11–19, at 17–19 (postulating a lordship created for William de Rosedale c. 1136 × 1157).

[55] In the truce of 1398, Kirkandrews[-on-Esk] had been listed as one border meeting place among many: *Foedera*, III, iv, 153.

[56] NRS: JC 1/1, fols 8v, 10v, 12v, 13r, 14r–v, 15r–v, 21v, 22v, 23r–v, 24r–v, 25r, 29v, 30r–v, 31r–v, 32r.

[57] R.B. Armstrong, *The History of Liddesdale, Eskdale, Ewesdale, Wauchopedale and the Debatable Land, Part 1* (Edinburgh, 1883), 188; Cardew, 'Anglo-Scottish Border', 314, 319, 337, 353.

[58] *The Place-Names of Cumberland*, ed. A.M. Armstrong et al., 3 vols (Cambridge, 1950–2), iii, 21, *sub* 'Lyne, R'.

Part I

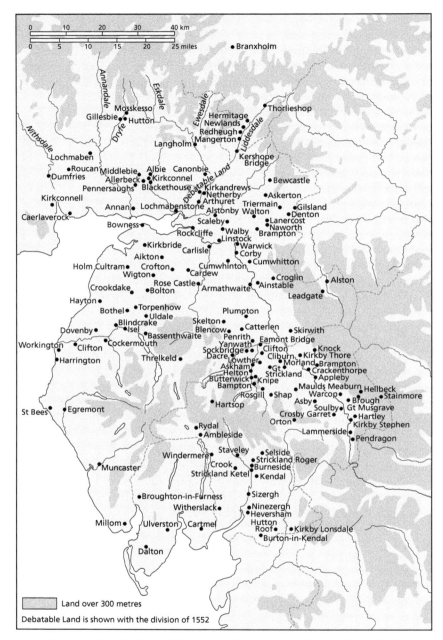

Map 3   Cumberland, Westmorland, Furness and parts of Scotland

Frontiers and Borderlands

of Arthuret not as English subjects but rather as native Scots treasonably in rebellion for open allegiance to England. It may also be possible that the otherwise obscure reference to the rebels of 'Esdale' (*sic*) and 'the Inglismen that come with them' in the truce of 1473 results from an earlier assertion of such a Scottish claim extending from the Esk to the Lyne. The item agreed in the truce provides that these rebels are to make redress for offences according to the 'Law of the Bordour', a measure which would have postponed the question of whether they should also be subject to the law of Scotland or of England. This provision was made one year before the negotiations commenced over the Esk fishery, noted above, and at the very least it indicates an increasing level of scrutiny by both governments of this corner of the borderland.[59] All of this speaks to a certain contrary flow against the main trend of the fifteenth century, which was the reversion of the border line of control back to the boundary agreed in 1237. In itself it does little to suggest a view of the marches overall as an empty no-man's-land, or some undefined middle space. The debatable land in the west was an exception, arising from a specific dispute. Contrary to conventional wisdom, it should be understood as an illustration of the expectation that the precise boundary between England and Scotland *ought* to be known and accepted.[60]

This brings us to a deeper point about the Anglo-Scottish marches in the fifteenth century. Whereas Lourie's description of medieval frontiers as societies 'given to war as a way of life' has so often prevailed in historical approaches to this medieval borderland, the march was much more than this.[61] It was defined by a boundary that demarcated English and Scottish territory. But the march was also, and more importantly, a threshold or gateway, an interface between the realms. In this way the march encompassed a society organised for law, diplomacy and trade, as much as for defence.[62] Furthermore, unlike a recent analysis of late medieval France's frontiers, England's northern marches were not primarily a means to 'contain' the realm.[63] England's northern frontier was orientated outwards, primarily by land towards Scotland. The point about law and diplomacy will be developed elsewhere, but as for trade Carlisle and Berwick were

---

[59] E 39/52; *Foedera*, V, iii, 35. 'The Rebell of Esdale, the tyme of thair being Rebell to the King, and at his Horn . . .': to be 'at the horn' in Scotland was to be outlawed.

[60] S.M. Jack, 'The "Debatable Lands", Terra Nullius, and Natural Law in the Sixteenth Century', *Northern History*, 41 (2004), 289–300, advances claims strongly influenced by 'no-man's-land' assumptions. See the discussion of frontier rhetoric, and particularly of barrenness below, p. 92.

[61] Lourie, 'A Society Organised for War', 59.   [62] See above, pp. 15 and 51.

[63] Dauphant, *Royaume des Quatre Rivières*, 262, 272, on France's frontiers more as containers than as barriers against external enemies. On the sense of frontier as gateway, see Power and Standen (eds), *Frontiers in Question*, 46, 58–9.

Part I

the foremost northern gateways in this regard – that latter's exterior position allowing it an exceptional tax status which made it an attractive haven for export, legal and illegal, to the detriment of the merchants of Newcastle-upon-Tyne.[64] Carlisle, firmly within the English realm and without extraordinary trading privileges, nevertheless persevered and at times prospered in part through its continuous trade with Scotland.[65] In 1483 parliament legislated that all Scottish commerce was to be directed into England through the town Berwick, excepting the city of Carlisle 'and the portes or crekys perteynyng to the westmerche' which were to be directed there.[66] The act recognised the importance of these two urban sites as the pre-eminent portals for commercial intercourse with Scotland in the northern marches. Moreover, the extent to which the march accommodated an inward flow not just of goods and produce but also of people and services is apparent in the extent to which Scottish aliens were resident in the northern counties in the mid-fifteenth century.[67]

The gateway of the marches faced outwards not just over land but over water. The nature of the march at sea is a relatively underexplored topic despite Anglo-Scottish truces regularly including provision for maritime interactions.[68] All the same, that the 'high seas' between Britain and Ireland were a space 'outside the bounds and limits of the truce' was expressed in one English licence of 1388, issued to a merchant of Liverpool seeking to redeem his ship, sailors and cargo, all of which had been captured at sea by Scots and taken to Galloway.[69] Piratical activities of this nature were one aspect of diplomatic relations with Scotland and its allies.[70] Another recurrent issue was the plunder of Scottish ships (and Scottish cargoes carried by foreign ships) wrecked or run aground on the English coast, and ensuing claims for restitution.[71] John Hardyng keenly observed the extent to which raiding was an activity conducted by sea as well as by land. His own ambitious plan for the full invasion of Scotland in the fifteenth century was an expedition by land supported throughout by an English fleet at sea. He

---

[64] Tuck, 'A Medieval Tax Haven'; Donnelly, 'An Open Port'; C.M. Fraser, 'The Economic Growth of Newcastle upon Tyne, 1150–1536', in D. Newton and A.J. Pollard (eds), *Newcastle and Gateshead before 1700* (Chichester, 2009), 41–64.

[65] Summerson, *Medieval Carlisle*, i, 344 – 50; ii, 551, 571.　　[66] *PROME*, January 1483, item 32.

[67] Most recently, see J. M. Bennett, 'Women (and Men) on the Move: Scots in the English North c. 1440', *Journal of British Studies*, 57 (2018), 1–28, and the sources cited therein.

[68] Dunlop, 'Redresses and Reparacons'; Neville, *Violence, Custom and Law*, 36, 131, 134, 139, 159.

[69] *Rot. Scot.*, ii, 91 (*in alto mari extra bundas [et] limites treugarum*). The captors were apparently men of William Douglas of Nithsdale, son of Archibald, third earl of Douglas.

[70] C.J. Ford, 'Piracy or Policy: The Crisis in the Channel, 1400–1403', *TRHS*, 5th ser., 29 (1979), 63–78. See also an incident of 1470 involving a Northumbrian knight and esquire: *CPR 1467–77*, 197.

[71] *CPR 1408–13*, 173; *CDS*, iv, 159 (1409). See also *CPR 1429–36*, 105 (1431); *CPR 1446–52*, 532 (1451).

Frontiers and Borderlands

comments in particular detail on the ports and havens along the eastern Scottish coast which could offer a supply fleet sufficient harbour.[72] To the western coast, a provision which appeared in the Anglo-Scottish truces of 1484, 1488 and 1497 was to exclude the Scottish lordship of Lorn and the English island of Lundy from the terms of the agreement.[73] There are various possible interpretations of the purpose of this exclusion. One tentative scenario is that this was related to the earl of Northumberland's contested claim to Lundy island (with its associated status distinct from the mainland territory of the kingdom) in the 1480s, which was ultimately unsuccessful. The truces of 1484 and 1488 may possibly have been occasions on which the earl as warden experimented with ensuring the Anglo-Scottish indentures conveniently served as supporting documents for his personal claim.[74] Perhaps more persuasive, however, is that the exemption of Lorn and Lundy was a means by which both sovereign powers could avoid taking responsibility for Irish Sea piracy.[75] The marches overlooked the sea, and in this way served as much as a water-gate as they did a landward interface.

WRITING THE MARCHES

The Anglo-Scottish frontier may be examined from another angle, namely, that of how this spatial environment was perceived in late medieval minds. One way into this question is suggested by the account of Ghillebert de Lannoy, a visitor to the marches who recorded his peregrination of England, Scotland and Ireland in 1430. Travelling northwards by what must have been a vessel plying the coastline, Lannoy noted only the towns through (or by) which he passed. From Newcastle-upon-Tyne, he went to Bamburgh, and then Berwick. From there he continued into Scotland, reaching Dunbar, and then north as far as the Tay. From there he passed inland to Stirling and thence southwards again to Dumfries and Carlisle. From Carlisle his next stop was Lancaster, and then on to Cockersand Abbey, from where he crossed the Irish Sea to Drogheda. This traveller preferred the sea road, which brought a natural focus to the harbours and port towns into which he called.[76]

---

[72] *Chron. Hardyng*, 364–6, 424, 426, 428.   [73] *Foedera*, V, iii, 150–3; *Rot. Scot.*, ii, 488–90, 536–30.

[74] *CCR 1485–1500*, nos 403, 410, pp. 111–12, 114–15.

[75] Cardew, 'Anglo-Scottish Border', 280; S.I. Boardman, *The Campbells, 1250–1500* (Edinburgh, 2006), 228.

[76] Ghillebert Lannoy, *Oeuvres de Ghillebert de Lannoy*, ed. C. Potvin and J.C. Houzeau (Louvain, 1878), 167–9. The importance of the harbour in early fourteenth-century designs at Dunstanburgh Castle is discussed in W.D. Simpson, *Further Notes on Dunstanburgh Castle* (Gateshead, 1949), 8–13.

Part I

Lannoy recounted his journey as a series of places encountered. At first thought this may seem a banal comment, but further reflection on his itinerant view of the space through which he passed suggests it does not easily satisfy our modern expectations. Recent work has brought together investigations of space in the pre-modern world, and such studies have tended to draw out an emphasis on the heterogeneity and relativity of medieval spatial understandings, by contrast to more uniform and monological modern views.[77] As for the Anglo-Scottish borderlands in the fifteenth century, we have already noted a prevailing trend in the reversion of the border in our period to its old extent. We have noted the mutual acknowledgement of the debatable land in the fifteenth century. It is revealing that the eventual imposition of a boundary through that territory was a project not of this century but of the following one. This period experienced technological changes in mapmaking resulting from the renaissance revolution in cartography. Such changes came to be intimately linked with long-term trends towards a modern governmental 'territoriality', based upon a geometrical view of space.[78] By the mid-sixteenth century the use of sophisticated maps was so pervasive as to underpin the international process by which French representatives adjudicated a final division of the debatable land. The maps drawn up for the purpose in 1552 were a technological solution to a long-standing problem of how to describe the border.[79] A further novelty for the Anglo-Scottish border that came with the final division of the debatable land was the construction of the Scots' Dyke.[80] This was no reinvention of the Roman walls or Offa's Dyke as colossal landscaping projects from Britain's deeper past. The labourers of 1552 excavated a bank in the ground along the parish boundary between Canonbie and Kirkandrews-on-Esk. It represented a new national boundary, marking out in the ground the line which had been drawn on the map. The point to make here is that any expectation or assumption that the late medieval marches were appreciated in similar terms – that is, with a need for space to be precisely demarcated in a drawn spatial record – is anachronistic.

Such renaissance cartographic efforts were a very different enterprise to the border perambulations of the thirteenth century. Not long after the

---

[77] M. Cohen and F. Madeline (eds), *Space in the Medieval West: Places, Territories and Imagined Geographies* (Farnham, 2013), 1–9; B. Kümin (ed.), *Political Space in Pre-industrial Europe* (Farnham, 2009).

[78] Branch, *Cartographic State*, 21; P. Barber and T. Harper, *Magnificent Maps: Power, Propaganda and Art* (London, 2010), 14.

[79] MPF 1/257. I am indebted to Amy Blakeway for first bringing these plans to my attention.

[80] J.L. Mack, *The Border Line* (Edinburgh, 1926), 85–8; MacKenzie, 'The Debateable Land', 113, 127–8.

Frontiers and Borderlands

treaty of 1237 settling the border line in general terms, in 1245 and again in 1246 six English and six Scottish knights assembled at Reddenburn on the south side of the Tweed to determine the local boundary between the English lands of Carham and the Scottish lands of Hadden. Both meetings failed to establish agreement.[81] These fresh-air assembly practices were alive and well in the fifteenth century, as one richly detailed narrative attests. On 17 October 1401, representatives of the English and Scottish kings met in a field near Kirk Yetholm, where they spent the first day of their gathering going through the ceremonial formalities of exchanging and collating their diplomatic credentials. At night they retired to their own separate camps (doubtless for food, drink and entertainment). They met again in the same place the following day. On the third day, they had agreed to assemble at the church of Carham, some ten miles distant, each side with an entourage of fifty spearmen and fifty attendants. On the day, their encounter actually occurred on the top of a nearby hill, where the English side found their Scottish colleagues arrayed in a line '*ad bellum*', but willing to talk nonetheless. On the fourth and final day they met in a field near Carham church. Following the departure of both parties at the completion of proceedings, the English commissioners retired southwards to Alnwick Castle. The size of these gatherings must have been impressive, and with trains of tents, supplies and followers must have resembled hostings for war.[82] Locations like Reddenburn and Haddenstank in the east marches; Gamelspath, Lilliot Cross and Rulehaugh in the middle marches; and the Lochmabenstone in the west marches have long been noted as traditional locations for border meetings. They predate the compilation of the *Leges Marchiarum* of 1249 and continued in use throughout the fifteenth century, being frequently specified in truce indentures for this purpose.[83] The Lochmabenstone by Gretna village is remarkable for the use of a large granite boulder, probably the remains of a stone circle, to identify a customary outdoor venue for Anglo-Scottish assemblies.[84] When representatives of either side convened in these fields, churches, hilltops and burn-sides, the

---

[81] Neville, *Violence, Custom and Law*, 5.

[82] *Anglo-Scottish Relations*, ed. Stones, 172–82 (quote from 178). This document takes the form of a notarial instrument drawn up at Alnwick Castle on 23 October 1401.

[83] As per *Foedera*, III, iv, 151, 153 (for 1398), which also specified meetings at Kershope Bridge and Kirkandrews[-on-Esk] in the west. Neilson, 'March Laws', 16–17; Barrow, 'Anglo-Scottish Border', 39–40; G.W.S. Barrow, *The Kingdom of the Scots: Government, Church and Society from the Eleventh to the Fourteenth Century* (Edinburgh, 2003),127; H.R.T. Summerson, 'The Early Development', 32–3; Neville, *Violence, Custom and Law*, 5, 82, 128, 131, 137, 163–4, 188.

[84] O.J.T. O'Grady, 'The Setting and Practice of Open-Air Judicial Assemblies in Medieval Scotland: A Multidisciplinary Study', PhD thesis, University of Glasgow (2008), 297, 305–11. The Lochmabenstone is also known as the Clochmabenstane.

Part I

border was not so much marked out in the ground as enacted in the process of assembly. There is similarity in all this (and especially the inconclusive meetings of the 1240s) with the normal medieval practice of processions and perambulations of the boundaries of parishes, towns or private parcels of land, which might be accompanied by the erection and maintenance of physical markers in the landscape.[85] But there is also difference, for these Anglo-Scottish assemblies typically did not occur at the jurisdictional boundary. They were held at meeting places, sites of interaction enrobed with the familiarity of custom, where the border was *performed* with a show of ceremonious pageantry, as much as force in numbers.

If the late medieval border itself was enacted through assembly, it was in writing that these sites were recorded in truce agreements. In a similar fashion, the northern marches more broadly were discerned on paper and parchment through textual description, not visual depiction.[86] An inventory of 1415 entitled '*Nomina castrorum et fortaliciorum infra comitatum Northumbriae*' was drawn up presumably to assess the defensibility of Northumberland prior to the Agincourt expedition of that year.[87] This source (to which we shall return later) offers a helpful window onto the spatial understanding of the marches in our period of interest. In 1891 Cadwallader John Bates represented this survey visually, creating a modern map to identify the places named. His map is attractive and instructive, but it speaks more to the Victorian mind-set than the medieval one, and to that extent it is an anachronism.[88] The inventory of 1415 was drawn up at much the same time as Claudius Ptolemy's *Geographia* was first being translated into Latin in Italy. The changes in cartographical practice originating with the Ptolemaic coordinate grid system were not to have their effects in England for some time: Christopher Saxton's national mapping project was still some sixteen decades in the future. Medieval visual representations of space were of a very different nature. The *mappaemundi* of the middle ages were concerned with portraying a cosmological framework, rather than a geometrical depiction of landforms, and itinerary maps and portolan charts depicted

---

[85] On perambulations generally, see S. Justice, *Writing and Rebellion: England in 1381* (Berkeley, 1994), 165–7, 171. Winchester, *Harvest of the Hills*, 29, illustrates the bank and ditch running along the crest of the fells between Rydal and Grasmere in Kendale barony. See also *York Civic Records*, ii, 164 (for the city's bounds in 1500).

[86] Branch, *Cartographic State*, 46.

[87] From BL: Harleian MS 309; printed in C.J. Bates, *The Border Holds of Northumberland* (Newcastle, 1891), 12–20.

[88] Bates, *Border Holds*, facing p. 14. On the location of towers, see also A. Goodman, 'The Defence of Northumberland: A Preliminary Survey', in M. Strickland (ed.), *Armies, Chivalry and Warfare in Medieval Britain and France* (Stamford, 1998), 161–72, at 169.

Frontiers and Borderlands

routes of travel between a series of places.[89] Of course, cosmology was not the purpose of the list of 1415; it was a detailed descriptive effort which was undertaken in the format most appropriate for the task at hand: written text. This inventory enumerated 115 sites in two sections, '*Nomina castrorum et fortaliciorum*' (37 sites), followed by '*Nomina fortaliciorum*' (78 sites). The list was not random but followed a pattern. The compiler did not use or require a visual framework, although his thinking becomes clearer to our modern perceptions when we consider it with a map in mind.[90] A certain geographical clustering is apparent in the listing, which generally proceeds in the order of an anti-clockwise circuit around Northumberland (see Map 4). The first section (*Nomina castrorum*) starts with the royal castle and county seat at Newcastle-upon-Tyne, then nearby Tynemouth, then Ogle on the River Blyth, and Morpeth and Mitford on the River Wansbeck, all of which are in the south-east of the county. It then gives the Percy residences of Warkworth and Alnwick, and the three royal sites of Dunstanburgh, Bamburgh and Berwick. The list then identifies several fortresses and habitations on the Tweed and in the valley of the River Till, and then moves further south into upper Coquetdale and its tributaries. Attention continues southwards still to several buildings in South Tynedale. Breaking from this pattern the major castle of Roxburgh is then named, followed by six places which are scattered around the county – as if to tidy up what may have been omitted by mistake in the first pass. The second section (*Nomina fortaliciorum*) similarly begins in the south-east corner of the county, between the rivers Tyne and Blyth. It then circuits northwards, to sites between the Blyth and the Wansbeck. The view moves further north to give several dwelling places in the vicinity of Dunstanburgh, Bamburgh and Berwick. Next it turns westwards to the Tweed, and Glendale, then south through the Breamish valley, the upper Aln, and the upper Coquet and their tributaries. From there it gives habitations in Redesdale and then the South Tyne, finally moving eastwards towards Corbridge and from there to Belsay in the Blyth valley again. This circuit completed, there follows a more disorganised enumeration of some twenty-three buildings before the list concludes. However, a sizeable portion (14 of 23) of this final enumeration are places north of the Aln, so it would seem that the compiler of the list was again filling in apparent gaps, here with

---

[89] A. Scafi, 'Defining Mappaemundi', in P.D.A. Harvey (ed.), *The Hereford World Map: Medieval World Maps and Their Context* (London, 2006), 345–54, at 349; Branch, *Cartographic State*, 48–55, noting also that medieval space was perceived as much in terms of time as in terms of distance. On map use in fifteenth-century France, see Dauphant, *Royaume des Quatre Rivières*, 185–6.

[90] Branch, *Cartographic State*, 66: 'once the Ptloemaic grid has been imposed on the world, other understandings of space are made untenable'.

Part I

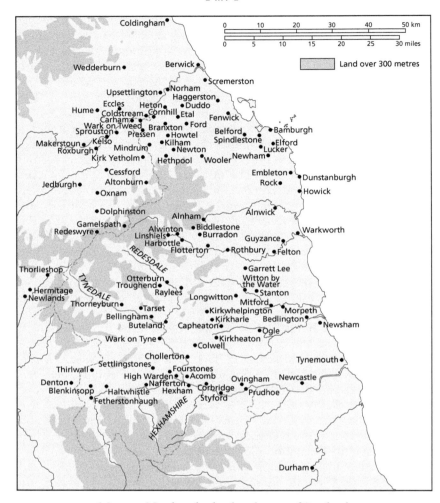

Map 4   Northumberland and parts of Scotland

information from informants familiar with that part of the county. What is more, in this section four of the six so-called vicar's peles appear, perhaps an indication that the compiler had indeed exhausted his knowledge of landowners' residences.[91] The interpretation of the compilation

---

[91] It does not appear that sites were grouped according to wards within the county.

Frontiers and Borderlands

process proposed here points to the importance of both writing and orality in the inventory's assembly. It was a product not of visual portrayal but of textual representation.

A comparable pattern may be found nearly a century later. In 1509 a list of Northumberland 'holdis and towneshyppes' was drawn up.[92] This list enumerates thirty sites within the shadow of the Cheviot. It estimates garrison capacity and specifies distances from Teviotdale (Roxburghshire) and from the Merse (Berwickshire), the adjacent Scottish sheriffdoms. The list begins in the vicinity of Bamburgh in the north of the county, giving five buildings around and including Belford, all of which are north of the Waren Burn. It then shifts to Heton and Etal on the River Till, and moves southwards up that valley, to Bewick where the Till meets the River Breamish. Next the survey back-tracks up the valley and its tributaries not to miss Lilburn, Wooler and Ford, before returning to Ingram on the Breamish. After this, the major fortresses at Norham and Berwick are given. The remainder of the list focuses on 'holdis' in the upper valleys of the Aln and Coquet, and their tributaries. There are certain commonalities in both the Northumbrian inventories of 1415 and 1509: both list buildings as well as the people who kept them; neither shows concern for the internal boundaries of seigneurial liberties; and, most importantly for the present discussion, they testify to an understanding of geographical space achieved not through a visual medium but through a written one. Such an approach to geographical knowledge through text, in the form of a list, described places in the landscape as a traveller would encounter them. This was description by itineration, albeit an itineration expressed by mouth and recorded by pen. That route followed, in broad terms at least, an overall circuit pattern starting from near the mouth of the Tyne and moving anti-clockwise around the county. At a finer-grained level that circuit followed the coast and the dales, glens and valleys which inscribed the landscape itself, all of which should remind us of the natural arteries of communication by which the marches were travelled, remembered and perceived. An itinerant sense of space was not peculiar to the English far north. Itineration was of course the exercise undertaken regularly by the assize justices throughout the kingdom, and the justices' perambulations of the realm generated copious legal records (such as those of the northern circuit, which will be integral to analysis in subsequent chapters), marking those places and times at which royal justice was enacted.

---

[92] Entitled: 'Holdis and Towneshyppes too lay in Garnysons of horsemen And how fer they bee from Tevedale & the Mars & who be the owners & inabytaunttes in the howses'. Formerly among the PRO series 'chapter house books' (B 1/24); printed in Bates, *Border Holds*, 23–4.

Part I

Perhaps no fifteenth-century marcher expressed this perambulatory understanding of space better than John Hardyng. His *Chronicle* relates historical and contemporary events and set forth a detailed schedule for an English invasion and conquest of Scotland. His style of writing frequently adapted the use of place lists:

> Thest marche hole of Scotlande then he brent
> And market townes echeone or that he stente
> Howyk, Selkirke, Iedworth, & all Dunbarre
> Laudre also with all Laudre dale.[93]

His plan for invasion was set out as a detailed itinerary. He specified the distances in miles between the villages and towns which were to be the objectives of his proposed campaign, and in his verse passages he gave brief descriptions of the places identified, in effect offering a written survey of the northern kingdom. Hardyng also ensured that his itinerary-style description was accompanied by a visual supplement, in the form of attractive and richly coloured maps which appeared in the 'Lancastrian' and 'Yorkist' versions his text.[94] But these drawings of Scotland and of England's northern extremities were no exercise in Ptolemaic grid-coordinate accuracy. In the broadest terms they correctly place major towns and rivers in relation to each other, but they are essentially non-geometrical in nature. Hardyng's maps offer a schematic representation designed to capture the imagination, and towns and castles are drawn with fantastical whimsy. Their deeply medieval heritage is confirmed by the depiction, on the map included in the version intended for Edward IV, of 'the palais of Pluto, king of Hel, neighbore to Scottz', surrounded by the four rivers of the underworld.[95] For the inhabitants of the English far north in the age of Hardyng, the conception of the marches and the lands beyond were shaped by an itinerant sense of space. This was a fluid, flexible and functional way of thinking about and recording geographical information. It did not anticipate the cartographical spatial logic that would begin to take hold in the middle decades of the sixteenth century.

---

[93] *Chron. Hardyng,* 383.

[94] *Chron. Hardyng,* 414–20, 422–9 (the invasion plan). Hardyng's map has been reproduced in a number of places (most often from BL: Lansdowne 204, fols 226v–227r). Note also Branch, *Cartographic State,* 59, 'in order to claim territory one had to describe it in terms of place-specific characteristics'.

[95] *Chron. Hardyng,* 419. For comment on Pluto's palace (shown on BL: Harley 661 fol. 188), see S. Peverley, 'Anglo-Scottish Relations in John Hardyng's Chronicle', in M. Bruce and K.H. Terrell (eds), *The Anglo-Scottish Border and the Shaping of Identity, 1300–1600* (New York, 2012), 69–86, at 79–80.

Frontiers and Borderlands

Indeed, it is a way of understanding territory which deserves much closer attention in its own right.[96]

Identities (especially national identities) have not featured prominently in this discussion of frontiers and space. That choice has been deliberate. The concern advanced here is more with orientations, that is to say, with the outlooks towards the frontier and what existed beyond, towards other parts of the marches themselves or to the frames of experience which textured society. It is no anomaly that when the envelope of English control in southern Scotland in the fifteenth century receded, it did so down the Tweed valley: this was a natural landscape cell which focused on the town of Berwick and the Tweed watershed. Furthermore, what the preceding discussion offers is a comment on the frontier that eschews centre–periphery thinking.[97] England's northern marches were not a marginal world; they were a conceptual apparatus which took shape around the local societies of the far north, inter-layered with counties and liberties and lordships. Certain ways in which these societies were robust in their own social and cultural patterns are the subject of the following chapter. We should avoid explaining such patterns away as 'peripheral' exceptions to norms more familiar at the 'centre'.

---

[96] Dauphant, *Royaume des Quatre Rivières*, 151–74, offers a provocative discussion of space and territorial representation in fifteenth-century France, before the emergence of a chorographical genre.

[97] These wider issues are addressed above, at p. 42.

3

EARTH AND STONE

[T]he king oure sovereign lord conceiveth well that the sure keeping of the towne and castell of Berwik is a grete diffence ayemst the Scottis and a grete wele suerte and ease unto all his realme and especiall to the northe parties of the same.[1]

—*Rotuli Scotiae in Turri Londinensi*

If the preceding chapter set out a conceptual apparatus with which to understand the northern marches, then this chapter examines two topics which have been salient in historical interpretations of the region. The first relates to the view of the far north as an 'embattled frontier society', defended by strings of garrisoned fortresses.[2] It is this particular emblem of the supposed exceptional militarisation of the region, its towers and castles, which shall be investigated. The second topic concerns the landscape of the 'northe parties' and its corresponding patterns of human activity and settlement. In both popular and academic accounts, the far north is often a wild country, remote, mountainous, dominated by difficult hill farming and rugged hill tribes. Such interpretations are shaped in part by modern assumptions about human geography; they are also partly informed by the rhetorical efforts of medieval borderers themselves. Marchers crafted petitions and turns of phrase in their dealings with the hierarchy of the king's government and with that of the church which (as should be no occasion for surprise) emphasised aspects of border life which played to their advantage and benefit. If what follows tends to offer an appraisal of existing work in a range of specialisms (including especially architectural and landscape history) more than a digestion of raw historical evidence, it does so seeking to engage the current historiography of the Anglo-Scottish marches with a view to provoking some critical debate and to opening up to scrutiny some of the

---

[1] *Rot. Scot.*, ii, 483 (1488).   [2] Arvanigian, 'Henry V', 77–81, at 80.

74

Earth and Stone

prevailing assumptions about the exceptional character of this area. The argument to be advanced here is that the towers and castles of the marches should not be understood solely, or even primarily, as a symptom of war and a pressing need for security. The point will also be pursued that the landscapes of the medieval far north cannot be reduced in any satisfactory way to a single category of 'upland' terrain, and so the diversity of farming practices and corresponding patterns of human habitation in the region require more nuanced appreciation if they are to be understood meaningfully.

TOWERS AND CASTLES

The English far north and the Anglo-Scottish borderlands more generally have long been identified with the architectural phenomenon of the tower, the so-called 'lesser castles of lesser men'.[3] To these buildings (often referred to as 'tower-houses') has generally been attributed an essentially military function and impetus in their design, emerging as a response to general late medieval war, violence and disorder.[4] For architectural historians, at least, this is an important and fluid subject area, facing a number of intellectual challenges and undergoing sweeping interpretative modifications. Indeed, it is now usual to note the sea change in the closely related field of castle studies which has taken place over the last three decades.[5] This reconsideration has brought to the fore attention to the non-military importance of castles, often with an emphasis on their architectural symbolism, and this work has generated fresh discussion of castles' economic functions, their roles as administrative nuclei and lordly residences, their setting in the landscape, and a reappraisal of their military and defensive significance. In this process a strong case has been made against the very idea of 'the castle' as a useful category, and writers tend now to be more comfortable discussing a continuum of 'noble buildings', or elite architecture, including the 'castle-homes of the higher nobility' and their imitators.[6] 'Fortress', for

---

[3] R.A. Brown, *English Castles* (London, 1976), 131 (a classic view of towers built out of the necessity of war).

[4] P. Dixon, 'Towerhouses, Pelehouses and Border Society', *Archaeological Journal*, 136 (1979), 240–52; P. Dixon, 'Border Towers: A Cartographic Approach', in J. Ashbee and J. M Luxford (eds), *Newcastle and Northumberland: Roman and Medieval Architecture and Art* (Leeds, 2013), 248–65. See comment in R.D. Oram, 'Introduction: Houses That Thieves Might Knock At', in R. Oram (ed.), *A House That Thieves Might Knock At* (Donington, 2015), ix–xv, at x–xi.

[5] J. Goodall, *The English Castle, 1066–1650* (New Haven, 2011), xvii (quote).

[6] C. Coulson, 'Freedom to Crenellate by Licence: An Historiographical Revision', *Nottingham Medieval Studies*, 38 (1994), 86–137, at 137 (quote); A. Wheatley, *The Idea of the Castle in Medieval England* (Woodbridge, 2004), 10–11. See also C. Coulson, *Castles in Medieval Society: Fortresses in*

Part I

example, has been ventured as one alternative term, but that is not without its own difficulties.[7] If the classification of elite architecture is a problem for castellology generally, then it is a pertinent issue when looking at towers. They have typically been interpreted as a by-product of the so-called 'decline of the castle' in the later middle ages.[8] All the same, 'tower-houses' have been called out more recently as a false subcategory of castles.[9] What is more, the decline of the castle thesis is now understood to be 'an essentially imaginary scenario' which has come under vigorous attack.[10] A recent series of 'tower studies' conferences and their published proceedings have sought to examine towers as a subject in their own right and have made considerable efforts at European comparisons, including towers built in the late thirteenth century and early fourteenth century in the Low Countries for no particular reason of defence.[11]

How should borderland towers be classified? There is no straightforward answer. They are sometimes called *pele* or *peel* towers, but this is now widely understood to be a perverse usage and, like 'tower-house' more generally, an unhelpful modern category conflated with historical terminology, too slippery and imprecise in how it is applied, especially in the Anglo-Scottish marches.[12] Pevsner's architectural guide for Northumberland provides a helpful chronological discussion of the medieval buildings that may be considered under the blanket term 'towers' and may be applied to the far north more generally.[13] One group of such buildings is sometimes known as 'hall houses', consisting of ground-floor or first-floor *aula,* dating especially from the thirteenth century. West of

---

    England, France, and Ireland in the Central Middle Ages (Oxford, 2003), 1–14, and 225, 229, on castles and estate administration.

[7] Coulson, *Castles in Medieval Society,* esp. 1–14, 29–63.

[8] M.W. Thompson, *The Decline of the Castle* (Cambridge, 1987), 2, 22–6.

[9] Oram, 'Introduction: Houses That Thieves Might Knock At', xi. On the invention of the term 'tower house' in 1860, see R. Sherlock, 'The Evolution of the Irish Tower House, 1400–1650', in Oram (ed.), *A House That Thieves Might Knock At,* 258–69, at 260–1.

[10] A. Emery, *Greater Medieval Houses of England and Wales: 1300–1500, Volume 1: Northern England* (Cambridge, 1996), 19.

[11] Oram (ed.), *A House That Thieves Might Knock At,* presenting essays from conferences in 2010 and 2011, including T. Hermans, 'Tower Houses in the Netherlands', in ibid., 47–61, at 60–1.

[12] *Chron. Hardyng,* 415n writes of Scottish 'toures & piles'. But see Emery, *Greater Medieval Houses,* 27; P.F. Ryder and J. Birch, 'Hellifield Peel: A North Yorkshire Tower House', *Yorkshire Archaeological Society Transactions,* 55 (1983), 73–94, at 82–4; C. McKean, 'A Taxonomy of Towers: A Reconnaissance of the Difficulties in Scotland', in Oram (ed.), *A House That Thieves Might Knock At,* 92–114, at 99.

[13] J. Grundy et al., *Northumberland* (Harmondsworth, 1992), 61–3. See Emery, *Greater Medieval Houses,* 21– 9 (discussion of 'Northumbria'), 163–70 ('Cumbria'); M. Hyde and N. Pevsner, *Cumbria: Cumberland, Westmorland and Furness* (New Haven, 2010), 26–8; N. Pevsner, *Cumberland and Westmorland* (London, 1967; repr., 1973).

Earth and Stone

the Pennines, the equivalent is the 'hall-and-cross-wing house', of a style familiar elsewhere in England.[14] A second group are the 'hall towers', generally erected in the decades c. 1300, consisting of a rectangular block with a hall on the first or second floor. A third group are what may be described as the 'solar towers' (another modern term), built around the middle decades of the fourteenth century as additions to existing complexes, typically at one end of an older hall. A fourth group comprises apparently solitary towers, built in the fifteenth and sixteenth centuries, reflecting an architectural trend prevailing north of the border. In the later sixteenth and early seventeenth centuries, further variations emerged as towers were converted into larger houses and defensible features were adopted in sub-manorial buildings. This was the era in which emerged the 'bastles', 'pelehouses' and 'stonehouses' so often identified in popular accounts of border life. Then, so it has been argued, did the prosperous Northumbrian peasants of the seventeenth century build in stone on their farms in imitation of their gentry landlords.[15] An important aspect of this classification is its emphasis on the *solitary* nature of the towers in the second and fourth groupings. This strongly resembles what was once thought to be a feature of towers in Scotland (which were built all over the country, not just in the southern marches) – that towers were free-standing buildings, isolated stone structures in the landscape. Such a view of Scottish towers has now been upended by archaeological investigation. Indeed, Scotland's towers are now accepted *normally* to have been part of complex sites, with external buildings and walls in wood and stone, even though all that may have survived the long centuries is the tower itself.[16] One suspects that similar conclusions may, in future, come to be drawn about the solitary towers of the English far north.

This overview encourages us to think of the historical buildings of the marches as multifarious and subject to changing styles of architecture. Something, too, may be learned from contemporary usage, as when late medieval writers mentioned towers, castles and other forms of housing.

---

[14] See also Emery, *Greater Medieval Houses*, 21 (and 28n), 167–9.

[15] Grundy et al., *Northumberland*, 63–5; Dixon, 'Border Towers', 254–5. See also G. Stell, 'Foundations of a Castle Culture: Pre-1603', in A. Dakin, M. Glendinning and A. MacKechnie (eds), *Scotland's Castle Culture* (Edinburgh, 2011), 3–34, at 12–14; R. Suggett, 'Living like a Lord: Greater Houses and Social Emulation in Late-Medieval Wales', in M. Airs and P.S. Barnwell (eds), *The Medieval Great House* (Donington, 2011), 81–95.

[16] C. McKean, 'A Suggested Chronology for the Scottish Medieval Country Seat', in Airs and Barnwell (eds), *Medieval Great House*, 61–80, at 68; R.D. Oram, 'The Greater House in Late Medieval Scotland: Courtyards and Towers c. 1300–c. 1400' in ibid., 43–60, at 45, 48–9; G. Eadie, 'Identifying Functions in Castles: A Study of Tower Houses in Ireland', in Oram (ed.), *A House That Thieves Might Knock At*, 2–18, at 16; McKean, 'A Taxonomy of Towers', 99, 104.

Part I

We should not expect the building terminology of the past to be any less fluid than our own. In Friesland, far away from the Anglo-Scottish marches, a study of medieval stone houses of humble dimensions (no larger than 12 m × 12 m) has found a range of terms used to describe such buildings: *castella, castra, domus lapidae, stins, stenen huus*.[17] Discussing buildings of a larger scale, Coulson points out that the term *fortalicium* was in some cases synonymous with *castellum* or *castrum* – and the use of one or the other might depend less on the quality of the residence than on the social rank of the proprietor.[18] Anglo-Scottish truces of our period frequently included an item on rules in the event of the capture of a 'castell or forteresce'.[19] In Latin this same item often referred to the capture of a *fortalitium* or to sieges of '*villarum aut castrorum aut fortalitiorum*'.[20] This suggests a desire to address a spectrum of buildings. The fourth earl of Northumberland used the style 'in my castell of Warkworth' to date his letters written from that base, but in other letters sent from his residence of Leconfield, Yorkshire, the same earl chose to date as written 'in my mannor of Lekingfeild'.[21] Clearly, a difference existed in his view of these two sites; the detail notwithstanding that Leconfield consisted of multiple towers within a quadrangular moat.[22] When Prince John, the future duke of Bedford, wrote to Henry IV as warden from the '*Chastell de Werkeworth*' in 1405, he spoke of the *chastelx* of Berwick, Jedburgh and Fast Castle (on the Berwickshire coast) and later more generally of the '*Chastelx garnysons et fortallessez*' in the east march.[23] John Hardyng only bothered to identify buildings in the marches at major sites, commenting on 'castelles' at Alnwick, Roxburgh, Bamburgh and Dunstanburgh.[24] The Scottish chronicler Walter Bower shows more flexibility of terminology when writing of fortresses that came in and out of English possession: Jedburgh and Lochmaben are *castra*, whereas Fast Castle is a *fortalicium*.[25] Similarly, when narrating the

---

[17] P.N. Noomen, *De stinzen in middeleeuws Friesland en hun bewoners* (Hilversum, 2009), introduction and 64–5. I am most grateful to Matthijs Gerrits for discussion and a summary of this book. See a review in English by T. Coomans, in *Speculum*, 86 (2011), 1105–6.

[18] Coulson, *Castles in Medieval Society*, 59–61.   [19] *Foedera* III, iv, 151 (1398).

[20] *Foedera* IV, iv, 110 (1424); *Foedera* V, i, 49 (1438).

[21] *Plumpton Letters,* nos. 65, 67, pp. 78, 80 (for Warkworth). John Neville, earl of Northumberland, wrote from 'my castle att Warkworth' in the 1460s: ibid., no. 19, p. 44. For dating at Leconfield, see, e.g., ibid. no. 63, p. 77.

[22] On Leconfield, see Emery, *Greater Medieval Houses*, 362–3. It was included in a licence for crenellation in 1308.

[23] Chrimes, 'Letters of John of Lancaster', 18 (1405), 26 (1411–12).

[24] *Chron. Hardyng*, 363–4, 373, 407–8.

[25] *Scotichronicon*, viii, 72–5. See quotation from ibid. (viii, 112–13) given earlier in Chapter 1 for Wark (on Tweed), as *castrum* and *domus*. Fast Castle is a 'fort' in *CPR 1401–5*, 428 (original roll not consulted).

Earth and Stone

Percy siege of Cocklaw (Roxburghshire) in 1403, Bower variously describes the beleaguered building as *castrum, turris periculo* and *municipium*.[26] Elsewhere he refers more generally to *municiones* (strongholds) in the marches.[27] The trend in sources like these was for large sites of royal or comital status generally to be called castles, but not without exception. For buildings of lesser size and status there was greater variability of terminology.

Similar patterns may be found in other sources. It is notable that the records of the English royal courts, which are so rich with the details of local events and replete with mentions of place names, do not offer much information about buildings. Still, and as might be expected, in these sources large sites such as Bamburgh, Prudhoe, Cockermouth, Egremont and Brougham were regularly identified as *castra*.[28] Buildings on a smaller scale tended to be called simply a 'house' if they were described at all – usually when a site was assailed or used for imprisonment. In cases arising in Westmorland, Burton (by Warcop) and Brampton (by Appleby) were identified as *meason* in French-language chancery petitions; these were manor houses without towers. If that should cause no surprise, more curiously the sites at Burneside and Cliburn, both of which consisted of hall complexes *with* a tower, were similarly described as houses.[29] All four of these sites belonged to gentry families. Across the whole century no references to *fortalitii* have been found in such legal proceedings, and just one example of a building described as a *turris*, which is in reference to a break-in to Alnham Tower in Northumberland.[30] Only two sites owned by knightly families (the Leghs of Isel and the Tilliols of Scaleby, both in Cumberland) were identified as *castra* in legal proceedings. Isel consisted of a tower, and Scaleby of a tower and courtyard complex within a circular moat.[31] To these may be added reference in the parliament rolls to Bothal Castle in Northumberland, subjected to a four-day assault in an

---

[26] *Scotichronicon*, viii, 48–57 (*municipium* at 54, line 19, and *turris periculo* on the following line).

[27] *Scotichronicon*, viii, 50.

[28] KB 9/245 m. 99 (Bamburgh); KB 27/706 *rex* rot. 1d, 710 *rex* rot. 8d, 714 *rex* rot. 5d (Prudhoe); KB 9/149/1/4 m. 25 (Cockermouth); KB 27/917 rot. 56, 929 rot. 37 (Egremont); JUST 3/199 m. 33 (Brougham). Grundy et al., *Northumberland*, 154–7 (Bamburgh), 545–6 (Prudhoe). Hyde and Pevsner, *Cumbria*, 192–5 (Brougham), 283–4 (Cockermouth), 340 (Egremont).

[29] C 1/6/282 (Burton); C 1/7/256: (Brampton); C 1/10/83 (Burneside); C 1/24/227 (Cliburn). For discussion of some examples noted here, see Marsh, 'Landed Society', 277–80. Hyde and Pevsner, *Cumbria*, 206–7 (Burneside), 280 (Cliburn).

[30] JUST 3/208 rot. 24. The tower belonged to the earl of Northumberland. See Grundy et al., *Northumberland*, 129.

[31] For Isel: KB 9/149/1/4 m. 25; Hyde and Pevsner, *Cumbria*, 424–5. For Scaleby: KB 9/288 mm. 2, 5; KB 27/798 *rex* rot. 35d; M.J. Jackson, *Castles of Cumbria* (Carlisle, 1990), 85–7; Hyde and Pevsner, *Cumbria*, 604–7.

Part I

inheritance dispute between two knightly brothers in 1409.[32] For sites of a scale lesser than that of the largest of fortresses, there was little consistency in the terminology used to describe the homes of landowners in legal records.

Instructive evidence also comes from the '*Nomina castrorum et fortaliciorum*' of 1415, which was introduced in the preceding chapter. Three terms are used in the list which covers 113 sites in Northumberland: *castrum*, *fortalicium* and *turris*.[33] The most recent discussion of this source suggests that *castrum* identified a site with an enclosing wall and, furthermore, that some of the marginal corrections and annotations on the survey indicate that this was perhaps an aspirational designation for a landowner's residence.[34] However, it is clear that in the view of the compilers and their informants there were just two broad categories that mattered in the inventory: *castrum* and *turris*. By contrast, only eight sites are identified as *fortalicii* – these include Horton by the Sea, Blenkinsop, Swinburne, Detchant and Capheaton, which appear in the first section of the survey as *castra* but are changed (demoted?) to *fortalicii* by marginal corrections. The three others are Harnham Hall, Shortflatt and Flotterton, which appear in the second section among the towers but are clearly identified there as '*fortalicii*'. An attempt may be made at tracing how some of these sites in the 1415 list were identified elsewhere in fifteenth-century sources, chiefly the records of inquisitions post mortem. In some examples we find straightforward consistency: Chillingham was described as a *castrum* in 1415, and indeed it had been identified as such in an inquisition of 1400.[35] Other cases are less consistent. The inquisition for Sir John Widdrington's lands taken in 1444 mentions only a capital messuage at Capheaton, the manor and vill of Great Swinburne and at Widdrington (which in 1415 was listed as possessing a tower, annotated to *castrum*) only the manor and vill.[36] The inquisition into Robert Raymes's holdings in 1490 identified no building at Shortflatt, only that the manor was held in chief.[37] Belford was among the *castra* enumerated in 1415. But an inquisition of 1438 for its owner, Thomas Lilburn, esq., identified it as a capital messuage called the 'fortilag' of Belford.[38] It had not been identified as a building in inquisitions for his ancestors in

---

[32] *RP*, iii, 629–30; *PROME*, January 1410, item 36. The brothers were Sir Robert Ogle and Sir John Bertram.

[33] Bates, *Border Holds*, 12–20.

[34] For discussion, see A. King, 'Fortresses and Fashion Statements: Gentry Castles in Fourteenth-Century Northumberland', *Journal of Medieval History*, 33 (2007), 372–97, at 372–3nn, 396–7. See also Emery, *Greater Medieval Houses*, 29n 8.

[35] *CIPM XVIII 1399–1405*, nos 4–5, p. 2.   [36] *CIPM XXVI 1442–7*, no. 223, pp. 131–3.

[37] *CIPM 1–12 Henry VII*, no. 565, p. 235.   [38] *CIPM XXV 1437–42*, no. 188, pp. 121–2.

Earth and Stone

1400 or in 1410, and neither was the building at Shawdon (another *castrum* in 1415).[39] Some properties possessing '*turri*' in 1415 may be shown simply to have been described as manors in inquisitions from 1422 (Belsay) and 1424 (Howick and Bavington).[40] All of this discussion of terminology is to show that fifteenth-century records display little consistency in how the so-called 'militarised architecture' of the marches was identified by contemporaries.[41] There was a considerable fluidity in terms used to describe elite buildings. Furthermore, such a variety of terminology used, even for the same site at different times, may suggest a variety of function expected and actually achieved. The impression given is of residences whose potential as defensible buildings (or even as suitable dwellings) fluctuated over time, as reflected in how, and even whether, they were described in writing.

The question of the function of landowners' castellated habitations in the marches is not a straightforward matter. All the same, a traditional view of towers and castles in the borderlands as built for the 'needs of defence' against Scottish forces in a 'heavily defended march' continues to flourish.[42] Despite an apparent proliferation of fortification in the fourteenth century, the effectiveness of such buildings in time of war is open to question. An ordinance of 1380 does indeed show concern with adequate repair, manning and supply of 'all castles and fortalices' within approximately twelve miles of the border. However, perhaps more revealing is a chronicle account of dissension among English *boreales dominos* which arose in 1389 when adequate support in men and money was refused to them to aid the defence of the east marches. According to the chronicler, the northern lords' response was to repair to their own *castella* and keep their heads below the parapet. Consequently, the whole *patria* with the exception of the fortresses was left unprotected ('*incustodia manebat*'), and so suffered from the destruction of Scottish raiders.[43] In the fifteenth century, major assaults and sieges of fortresses in English possession were relatively rare. A rough-and-ready list would include Alnwick (1405, various 1461–3), Berwick (1405, 1482), Warkworth (1405), Roxburgh (1436, 1460), Carlisle (1461), Bamburgh (various 1461–4),

---

[39] *CIPM XVIII 1399–1405*, no. 3, p. 1–2; *CIPM XIX 1405–1413*, no. 896, p. 320.

[40] *CIPM XXI 1418–1422*, no. 828, p. 287; *CIPM XXII 1422–7*, no. 390, pp. 348–9.

[41] Phrase taken from Oram, 'Introduction: Houses That Thieves Might Knock At', xi.

[42] Ellis, 'Region and Frontier', 82 (quotes, repeated in Ellis, *Defending English Ground*, 16); Dixon, 'Border Towers'; Winchester, *Landscape and Society*, 44–5. My own work (J.W. Armstrong, 'Local Society and the Defence of the English Frontier in Fifteenth-Century Scotland: The War Measures of 1482', *Florilegium*, 25 (2008), 127–49) has assessed Scottish fortifications in a similar light.

[43] *CPR 1377–81*, 455; *The Westminster Chronicle, 1381–1394*, ed. L.C. Hector and B.F. Harvey (Oxford, 1982), 396–7.

Part I

Dunstanburgh (various 1461–3), and Norham (1463, 1496–7). Many of these attacks, especially those of 1405 and the early 1460s, were suffered at the hands not of Scottish invaders but of English forces in the course of English civil strife. Such was the case when the earl of Warwick landed from the sea three great cannons to pummel the walls of Bamburgh in 1464. Prior to unleashing his bombardment, Warwick conveyed to the occupants the king's desire 'to have this jewel whole and unbroken'.[44] Scottish policy upon the seizure of the major English-held sites of Jedburgh (1409) and Roxburgh (1460) was to raze those castles to the ground. A similar approach was taken to several smaller towers near Norham in 1496.[45] In such language and action, the emblematic potential of architecture is clear: on the one hand, as a 'jewel' of royal possession; on the other, as an object fit for the overt demonstration of destructive power.[46]

In moving away from Victorian assumptions about the stern military architecture of the middle ages, towards understanding castellation 'in the inclusive medieval fashion to signify the emblems as well as the occasional reality of physical defence', fresh perspectives have been offered on the symbolic and cultural functions of noble architecture.[47] While such work has emphasised the drive for outward display of status and aspiration in the design of elite buildings, and the use of military insignia (crenellations, gatehouses, drawbridges and the like) as statements of lordship and rank in similar fashion to heraldic devices,[48] all the same there has been a tendency for academic discussion of these matters to stagnate into a debate over whether castles were 'really' about war or about status.[49] A parallel may be seen in the way in which historians, led by McFarlane, challenged the crude Victorian invention of 'bastard feudalism' in the mid-twentieth century and produced a much more nuanced understanding of late medieval political society – an

---

[44] 'This Juelle ... to have it, hoole, unbroken': John Warkworth, *A Chronicle of the First Thirteen Years of the Reign of King Edward the Fourth*, ed. J.O. Halliwell (1839), 37; Ross, *Edward IV*, 61.

[45] This continued a strategy from earlier centuries: R. Nicholson, *Scotland: The Later Middle Ages* (Edinburgh, 1974), 85, 131, 252, 549–50; Bates, *Border Holds*, 22; Armstrong, 'Local Society', 135n 37.

[46] On castles destroyed simply as a display of victory, see Firnhaber-Baker, 'Techniques of Seigneurial War', 92–4.

[47] Coulson, 'Freedom to Crenellate', 91 (quote), 92, 110–11. Coulson also observes (at 112) the 'centrist' notions from which sprang the Victorian 'restrictive theory' of licensing to crenellate.

[48] A. Emery, 'Late-Medieval Houses as an Expression of Social Status', *Historical Research*, 78 (2005), 140–61, at 159; Coulson, *Castles in Medieval Society*, 64; Emery, *Greater Medieval Houses*, 174–80.

[49] For thoughtful comment, see O.H. Creighton and R. Liddiard, 'Fighting Yesterday's Battle: Beyond War or Status in Castle Studies', *Medieval Archaeology*, 52 (2008), 161–9.

Earth and Stone

understanding in which the role of patronage has been ardently debated.[50] Integral to the militaristic Victorian 'doctrine about castles' are assumptions that the private power of landowners (exemplified in their personal followings as much as their fortified residences) was naturally opposed to public good order.[51] In parting from these assumptions, scholarly understanding of castles has only recently caught up with that of late medieval political society more generally, and it would seem important to heed these revisions when considering the elite architecture of the far north. For our purposes, what seems necessary is an appreciation of a range of purposes behind such buildings, a range which was shaped by softer cultural attitudes as much as harder considerations of defence and security. Towers in the marches surely combined practical functions in serving as residences, places for ceremony and entertainment, facilities for storage and administration, and fixed defensive sites that could double as short-range offensive bases. But they were also opportunities for the architectural display of the status and power of the builder and his successors – 'fortresses and fashion statements' in the words of one comment on fourteenth-century Northumberland.[52] In a similar way, an analysis of Irish towers has identified the threefold functions of security, domesticity and ostentation, allowing for 'defensive display and show of force'.[53] (This helps to elucidate the local £10 subsidy arranged in 1429 for those dwelling in the counties around Dublin who would undertake to build 'vn chastell ou vn tour sufficientment kernele', because the king's lieges there had suffered from the Irish enemies and English rebels for 'le defaut des chastelx et tours'.[54]) If we return to the 1415 and 1509 inventories of Northumberland, we should see in those lists not only an enumeration of defensive buildings

---

[50] An insightful appraisal may be found in E. Powell, 'After "After McFarlane": The Poverty of Patronage and the Case for Constitutional History', in D.J. Clayton, R.G. Davies and P. McNiven (eds), *Trade, Devotion and Governance: Papers in Later Medieval History* (Stroud, 1994), 1–16, esp. at 12.

[51] Coulson, 'Freedom to Crenellate', 86–9, 137 (quote). See an example of the older view enduring in M. Wood, *The English Medieval House* (London, 1983), 169. All this relates to wider assumptions about the transition of the medieval nobility into early modern courtiers. On early modern 'privacy', see Dewald, *European Nobility*, 44, 89–90.

[52] King, 'Fortresses and Fashion Statements'. Goodman, 'Defence of Northumberland', 169, suggests that residence in 'fortified dwellings was a common feature of "gentle living"'. See also Marsh, 'Landed Society', on Cbl. and Wml. before 1460.

[53] Eadie, 'Identifying Functions', 4, 8–10 (quote). This interpretation is in marked contrast to that offered by T.B Barry, 'The Last Frontier: Defence and Settlement in Late Medieval Ireland', in T.B. Barry, R. Frame and K. Simms (eds), *Colony and Frontier in Medieval Ireland: Essays Presented to J.F. Lydon* (London, 1995), 217–28, at 220–1.

[54] *Statute Rolls of the Parliament of Ireland, Reign of King Henry the Sixth*, ed. H.F. Berry (Dublin, 1910), 32–5.

Part I

but also an identification of each building's proprietor. These were registers of landowners as much as surveys of stone and mortar. Just as carrying a sword in public signalled gentility, so the possession of a castellated residence with defensive panoply signalled the 'official' capacity of lordship.[55]

Late medieval building works in the marches should be seen as signs not of peril but of relative prosperity. It was in order to celebrate the assembly of his great northern estates that the first earl of Northumberland undertook the construction of a great tower at Warkworth Castle on the Coquet; powerful families like the Percys 'encouraged a series of castle-building projects of outstanding grandeur and sophistication' in the reign of Richard II.[56] Similar developments at Alnwick Castle have been examined in this way.[57] As much as at such great fortresses, new builds and improvements in smaller residences were driven by optimism and self-confidence, rather than by insecurity and paranoia.[58] The fifteenth century may have been a period of economic deterioration, yet all the same this era in Northumberland's architectural history was marked by significant building work, and in general the focus was on improvements to and extension of existing accommodation, rather than on an increase in 'military strength'.[59] Despite the tribulations of the economy, landowners continued to take advantage of the opportunity for chivalric architecture which was offered by situation in the march. John Cartington's rebuild and expansion at Cartington Castle (licenced 1442) represents a major investment by a Northumbrian gentry family in the period.[60] Numerous other examples have been identified in the residences of gentry and nobility.[61] As for trends west of the Pennines,

---

[55] Coulson, *Castles in Medieval Society,* 20; Maddern, *Violence and Social Order,* 18–20, 84–7.

[56] Goodall, *The English Castle,* 323–4, noting the mason John Lewyn of Durham's work for the Percys at Warkworth, and for the crown at Carlisle (the castle's De Ireby Tower, consisting of a new outer gate with a barbican) and Roxburgh (a wall with three towers). See also Emery, *Greater Medieval Houses,* 199.

[57] J. Goodall, 'The Early Development of Alnwick Castle, c. 1100–1400', in Ashbee and Luxford (eds), *Newcastle and Northumberland,* 232–47, at 240–1.

[58] Emery, *Greater Medieval Houses,* 27; Oram, 'The Greater House', 60; Eadie, 'Identifying Functions', 5.

[59] Grundy et al., *Northumberland,* 60. On economic conditions, see Pollard, *North-Eastern England,* 52; Winchester, *Landscape and Society,* 45–55; Dobson, *Durham Priory,* 250–96; Tuck, 'War and Society', 42–3.

[60] Emery, *Greater Medieval Houses,* 63–5; CChR 1427–1516, 35.

[61] In Nbl.: Emery, *Greater Medieval Houses:* Belsay (49–50), Bywell (62), Cartington (63–5), Chillingham (65–7), Cocklaw (70–1), Cockle Park (71–2), Elsdon (90–1), Featherstone (93), Hefferlaw (104), Morpeth (121–2), Warkworth (144–50), Welton Hall (151), Wilmoteswick (154–5). See also Grundy et al., *Northumberland:* Edlingham (63, 263–4) and Shortflatt (596). Bates, *Border Holds,* 20–2, also notes towers at Fowberry, Hezelrigg, Hebburn, Bewick, Wooler, Ingram and Screenwood, before 1509.

Earth and Stone

Lott has identified two main periods of building in late medieval Westmorland, one in the 1370s and 1380s, and another during the middle decades of the fifteenth century. This is a pattern which Marsh suggests is broadly applicable to Cumberland too.[62] Various examples of fifteenth-century improvements and enhancements may be identified for Cumberland, such as the new tower at Millom built inside an existing fourteenth-century complex,[63] and similar work undertaken by secular landowners in Westmorland, such as at Kentmere, with a hall and lower wing added to an existing tower.[64] In those two western counties we find a number of hall-and-cross-wing houses, many with one or two towered cross-wings, continuing in use and undergoing embellishment in the fifteenth century.[65] To all this may be added numerous new works at ecclesiastical sites (such as the gatehouses at Tynemouth and Wetheral priories, and Alnwick Abbey) or at episcopal residences (such as Rose and Linstock by Carlisle).[66] By contrast, the castellated vicarages, rectories and parish church towers of the marches (the so-called vicar's peles) had been built generally in an earlier period.[67] Such buildings proclaimed the status of the vicar and enhanced the 'worship' of the lord of the manor.

---

[62] B. Lott, 'Seigneurial Hierarchy and Medieval Buildings in Westmorland', in G. Meirion-Jones, E. Impey and M. C. E. Jones, (eds), *The Seigneurial Residence in Western Europe AD c. 800–1600* (Oxford, 2002), 101–11, at 103–4. See also B. Lott, 'Medieval Buildings in Westmorland', PhD thesis, University of Nottingham (1995), 172; and discussion in Marsh, 'Landed Society', 282, 290–1.

[63] In Cbl.: Bewcastle (Jackson, *Castles of Cumbria*, 107), Catterlen (Emery, *Greater Medieval Houses*, 200–1), Cockermouth (Jackson, *Castles of Cumbria*, 46–7), Dalston (Emery, *Greater Medieval Houses*, 206), Derwentwater, Lord's Isle (Jackson, *Castles of Cumbria*, 53), Hayton (Jackson, *Castles of Cumbria*, 60; Pevsner, *Cumberland and Westmorland*, 136), Kirkoswald (Jackson, *Castles of Cumbria*, 67), Millom (Jackson, *Castles of Cumbria*, 74; Emery, *Greater Medieval Houses*, 229–31; Pevsner, *Cumberland and Westmorland*, 163), Scaleby (Jackson, *Castles of Cumbria*, 85–6; Emery, *Greater Medieval Houses*, 246–7).

[64] In Wml.: Emery, *Greater Medieval Houses*, for Appleby (262), Arnside (183–4), Clifton Hall (201), Kentmere Hall (216), Killington Hall (217), Middleton Hall (227–9), Preston Patrick Hall (241–3), Wharton Hall (255–6), Yanwath Hall (259). See also Jackson, *Castles of Cumbria*, for Appleby (29) and Howgill (62–3); Pevsner, *Cumberland and Westmorland*, for Howgill (277) and Yanwath Hall (299).

[65] Emery, *Greater Medieval Houses*, 167–9, and fig. 40.

[66] In Nbl.: Tynemouth gatehouse (Grundy et al., *Northumberland*, 589; Emery, *Greater Medieval Houses*, 141–2), Alnwick Abbey (Grundy et al., *Northumberland*, 104, 134–5), Hexham Tower (Emery, *Greater Medieval Houses*, 102), Hulne Priory (Emery, *Greater Medieval Houses*, 104); Newminster Abbey added a tower to the chapel at South Charlton, and a tower at Rothley (Bates, *Border Holds*, 21–2). In Cbl.: Bewley (Jackson, *Castles of Cumbria*, 33; Emery, *Greater Medieval Houses*, 191–2), Rose (Emery, *Greater Medieval Houses*, 244–6), Wetheral (Emery, *Greater Medieval Houses*, 203), Linstock (Jackson, *Castles of Cumbria*, 72; Pevsner, *Cumberland and Westmorland*, 175).

[67] Most were built in the thirteenth century (such as Ancroft church tower built over the nave) and the fourteenth century (Grundy et al., *Northumberland*, 63, 146; Emery, *Greater Medieval Houses*, 25, 29n 14; Hyde and Pevsner, *Cumbria*, 28–9).

Part I

These too required ongoing maintenance. In 1464 the diocesan registrar of Carlisle noted a fine levied against the rector of Bowness on Solway for not replying to a letter enquiring into repairs made at the *domus defensionis* there.[68]

It may be tempting to interpret efforts by religious houses to erect fortifying structures as a tell-tale evidence of a hostile frontier and its effect on local patterns of life. This is how the castle within and curtain wall surrounding Tynemouth Priory's site have been understood.[69] Yet some perspective is called for. A monastic house like Tynemouth was hardly alone in keeping an enclosed precinct. Thornton Abbey in Lincolnshire is a comparable example,[70] and, in deepest Suffolk, the great abbey of Bury St Edmunds maintained an extensive precinct wall – much of what still stands today exceeding four metres in height. Indeed in the thirteenth century Bury's wall was extended across the River Lark with a substantial three-arched 'abbot's bridge' to control river-borne traffic. All this did not stop the rioting townspeople of Bury from destroying the abbey's gatehouse in 1327, but the abbey's enclosure certainly marked out this important complex in the locality.[71] In Northumberland, it seems plausible that Tynemouth Priory's request for licence to crenellate in 1296 aimed both to reinforce the house's authority in a period when its liberty had been confiscated by the crown and to gain royal approval of physical enhancements against the backdrop of very recent, if intense, Anglo-Scottish conflict. That such improvements would have the benefit of increasing the priory's ability to provide refuge for its tenants in the event of future Scottish incursions was, perhaps, a secondary consideration.[72] Property held by Tynemouth suffered in the course of the fourteenth century. During a visitation in 1426, the abbot of St Albans praised the work done by his kinsman, a prior of Tynemouth, to restore the monastic hall at Wylam on the Tyne, whose 'defences had been worn down by the Scots'.[73] All the same, other religious houses situated closer to the Scottish border, including

---

[68] J. Wilson, (ed.), *The Victoria History of the County of Cumberland*, 2 vols (Westminster, 1901–5), ii, 257n 3.

[69] Grundy et al., *Northumberland*, 589; Holford and Stringer, *Border Liberties*, 216.

[70] On monastic and episcopal crenellation licences and Thornton Abbey (1382 and 1389), see Emery, *Greater Medieval Houses*, 175.

[71] A.B. Whittingham, *Bury St Edmunds Abbey, Suffolk* (London, 2012), 9, 22–4.

[72] Coulson, *Castles in Medieval Society*, 255, 259, on 'refuge'. For the licence of 1296, see *CPR 1292–1301*, 197. On the deprivation of the liberty between 1291 and 1299, see Holford and Stringer, *Border Liberties*, 207, 219.

[73] J. Amundesham, *Annales Monasterii S. Albani*, ed. H.T. Riley, 2 vols (London, 1870–1), i, 220. See also *NCH*, viii, 101.

Earth and Stone

Holm Cultram Abbey and Lanercost Priory, did not make special efforts at fortifying their precincts.[74]

If the late medieval bishops of Carlisle served from time to time as wardens of the west march, as did Bishop Marmaduke Lumley (d. 1450), their cathedral was no fortress-bastion. Had Bishop Lumley sailed in 1436 to Saint-Brieuc on Brittany's northern coast, he would have found the cathedral there just completing its second, south tower (the Tour Marie) – presumably, an architectural response to the sieges endured by the building in 1375 and 1394, enabling simultaneously a degree of practical protection and a statement of strength.[75] This is an imposing structure of impressive height, commanding the south-western approach to the building, within Saint-Brieuc itself. It may be worth comparing this with the squat cathedral crossing tower erected at Carlisle, in the course of repairs led by Bishop William Strickland (d. 1419) following the city's great fire of 1391.[76] Should the intensity of Anglo-Scottish conflict (not least in the 1330s) be thought to have driven such considerations of design, one must reflect on the fact that square castellated crossing towers on English cathedrals and abbeys in the late middle ages were by no means rare, and recall that the construction of Carlisle's gothic choir in the thirteenth and fourteenth centuries, with its Great East Window 'a work of mesmerizing beauty, not at all the kind of vulnerable masterpiece you would expect to find in an active garrison-town', was completed in 1340.[77] Clearly, more than the necessities of defence shaped ecclesiastical architecture in the marches towards Scotland.[78]

Building works in the marches should not be carelessly interpreted *primarily* as a sign of the exceptional pressure of the military frontier. There is no comparable inclination among historians to view the southern coast of England as a militarised zone, despite its elaborate system of defence against French seaborne raids across the Channel in the later middle ages. (Within the *terra maritima*, 'a belt of land running parallel to the coast and extending several miles inland', were found the beacons,

---

[74] The statement in Jamroziak, *Survival and Success,* 184, about a licence of 1304 to Holm Cultram Abbey to fortify its precinct is mistaken. The author cites Goodman, 'Religion and Warfare', 258 (citing a document printed in Wilson, (ed.), *Cumberland,* ii, 257n 1), discussing an episcopal licence for building a new chapel at Newton Arlosh.

[75] C. Leroy and D. de La Rivière, *Cathédrales et basiliques de Bretagne* (Paris, 2009), 134.

[76] Pevsner, *Cumberland and Westmorland,* 89; Summerson, *Medieval Carlisle,* ii, 402, 415.

[77] P. Johnson, *Cathedrals of England, Scotland and Wales* (London, 1990), 71.

[78] Carlisle was besieged in 1173–4, 1216 and 1315 and suffered a threatened attack by a Franco-Scottish force in 1385. It was an English civil war which led to the siege of 1461 (Summerson, *Medieval Carlisle,* i, 80–2, 96–7, 215–19, 319; ii, 446–8; Macdonald, *Border Bloodshed,* 90–1).

Part I

towns and castles which supported the *garde de la mer.*[79]) Northern evidence tends to relate to larger sites, but it is instructive of wider patterns. The Scottish incursions as far as Alnwick in 1433 were a factor cited in the supplication of the second earl of Northumberland, and the burgesses of the town, to obtain a licence in 1434 to 'enclose the whole town with a wall and to machicolate and otherwise fortify the said wall'.[80] It is worth speculating how much of this represented an exercise in opportunism on behalf of the earl and his manorial burgesses. The erection of a wall was as much a defensive measure as a gesture of economic control and a statement of urban prestige. In effect, its construction would bring the town of Alnwick into the wider defensive complex headed by the comital castle, and it would represent a significant economic investment during the period of construction, which included building of the town's Bondgate *turris*. This should be read as an expression of Alnwick's pretensions to an urban status similar to that of Berwick, Carlisle or Newcastle. Whatever may have been completed under the blessing of this licence before its completion in 1450, it was insufficient in the preceding year to repel a Scottish assault on Alnwick.[81] There are indications elsewhere of the extent to which such building operations (much like road-works today) were not one-off endeavours but ongoing projects. Walls, towers, halls and ancillary buildings required maintenance and underwent bursts of renovation when resources allowed.[82] At Norham Castle, the receiver's accounts of 1408 describe the stone and wood brought by land (oak beams from Lowick), river and sea (via the port of Berwick) for work on the castle's 'Westgate' tower. Details of the names of more than thirty-six masons, mortarers, stone-carters, and other labourers are given, almost all of a local character (such as Bank, Bell, Broun, Richardson, Rothirforth, Watson, Wodman,

---

[79] J.R. Alban, 'English Coastal Defence: Some Fourteenth-Century Modifications within the System', in R.A. Griffiths (ed.), *Patronage, the Crown and the Provinces in Later Medieval England* (Gloucester, 1981), 57–78, at 69–72; D. Spencer, 'Royal Castles and Coastal Defence in the Late Fourteenth Century', *Nottingham Medieval Studies*, 61 (2017), 147–70. See also Fortescue, *Governance of England*, 200, 234. In the reign of Richard II, 'gentz' dwelling 'sur les costs du meer' and 'sur les marches d'Escoce et autres marches' were identified as having armed themselves beyond the restrictions of sumptuary legislation: *PROME*, January1380, item 11.

[80] *CPR 1429–36*, 345; *PPC*, iv, 217.

[81] Bates, *Border Holds*, 21; M.R.G. Conzen, 'Alnwick, Northumberland: A Study in Town-Plan Analysis', *Transactions and Papers (Institute of British Geographers)*, 27 (London, 1960), 27, 30, 39. See 'Auchinleck Chronicle', in C. McGladdery, *James II* (rev. edn, Edinburgh, 2015), 276.

[82] J.F. Curwen, 'Penrith Castle. Some Suggestions and Notes from the Patent Rolls …', *TCWAAS*, 18 (1918), 174–88, at 175–6; *CPR 1389–92*, 499 (murage grant); *CPR 1396–9*, 524 (licence to Bishop Strickland of Carlisle to build a mantlet upon his crenellated 'chamber' in the town). On Penrith Castle's fifteenth-century works, especially under Richard, duke of Gloucester in the 1470s and 1480s, see Emery, *Greater Medieval Houses*, 178, 237–9, 262.

Earth and Stone

Witton). Similar work is recorded in a surviving account from 1428–9.[83] Here is a clear view of the way in which castles and towers served as works in progress and in time, almost perpetual projects by which the lord and his administrators were able to exercise economic command of the local population and control of local resources.

It is sometimes suggested that 'tower-houses' were peculiar to the borderlands, and 'in the English lowlands were unknown'.[84] Again, context is called for. Such a view neglects to appreciate the fact that towers were built not in the Anglo-Scottish marches alone but all over Scotland and Ireland too (see Map 5). It is also true that this style of building was adopted with some gusto in Lancashire, Durham and Yorkshire.[85] One might even be tempted to speak of a 'tower culture' expressed through this form of landowner's residence in the north and west of these islands – with the notable exception of Wales.[86] It will hardly do to suggest that all of Scotland and Ireland were in fact borderlands which required defensive dwellings.[87] When thinking about the material culture of buildings, and their distributions in the landscape, it is worth noting the distribution patterns of other forms of architecture, such as the cruck houses built by prosperous peasant householders in the later middle ages. These buildings are distributed across England with the exclusion of the eastern counties south of Yorkshire – a phenomenon which has proved difficult to explain.[88] This is a useful reminder that historical styles of building are shaped by a complicated range of factors, which should encourage caution towards simple explanations. What is more, Emery has observed the building of residential towers in southern English counties in the fifteenth century and noted the style's positive encouragement by Henry V.[89]

Perspective is required in other ways too. Just as the extent to which the earl of Northumberland and the burgesses of Alnwick might reasonably be expected of having multiple motivations in the building of their

---

[83] DUL, CCB B/72/3 (1428–9); CCB B/72/4 (1408).

[84] Ellis, 'Region and Frontier', 82 (quote, repeated in Ellis, *Defending English Ground,* 16).

[85] Pollard, *North-Eastern England,* 14–15; Marsh, 'Landed Society', 303–4.

[86] Oram, 'Introduction: Houses That Thieves Might Knock At'; Smith, *Crisis and Survival,* 191; Sherlock, 'The Evolution of the Irish Tower House'; Suggett, 'Living like a Lord', 84 (on an absence of towers in Wales). On Scotland, see also Meikle, *A British Frontier,* 150–1, 279. On the diversity of Scottish towers within a 'castle culture', see Stell, 'Foundations of a Castle Culture', 20–32.

[87] This is, in effect, the argument about 'a multiplicity of regional frontiers' in Ireland made by Barry, 'The Last Frontier', 227.

[88] N. Alcock and D. Miles, *The Medieval Peasant House in Midland England* (Oxford, 2013), 7–8. See also Suggett, 'Living like a Lord', on 'cruck-trussed houses' in Wales.

[89] Emery, *Greater Medieval Houses,* 27; Emery, 'Late-Medieval Houses', 152–7; Emery, 'Introductory Reflections after Greater Medieval Houses of England and Wales', in Airs and Barnwell (eds), *Medieval Great House,* 1–30, 13.

Part I

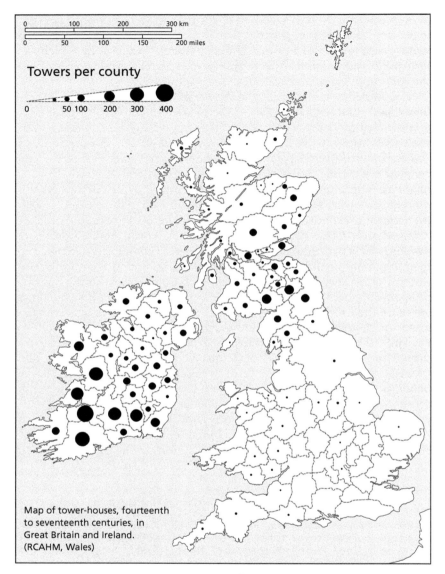

Map 5   Towers in Ireland and Britain

town wall, even as they faced a real threat from Scottish attack, we should be attuned to the natural inclination of those resident in the marches to take full advantage of their circumstances. With regard to Ireland in our period, one writer has pointed to the 'rhetoric of the

Earth and Stone

frontier' as it shaped dealings between local inhabitants and royal government.[90] Similar stylistic conventions in the northern marches are to be found in the petition by the *'poures liges'* of Cumberland, Westmorland and Northumberland in 1415 seeking exemption from parliamentary taxation, on the grounds of the great losses they had suffered and continued to endure at the hands of *'des enemys descoce'*.[91] Comparable language coloured Bishop Lumley of Carlisle's licence of 1443 for the appropriation of two churches 'in augmentation of his poor estates on the frontier of the west marches towards Scotland, which have been ruined by burnings and dilapidations done by the Scots in times of war'.[92] If 'danger was the currency of petition-speak', then it was a currency mastered by the inhabitants of the late medieval far north.[93] Even if it reflected aspects of real life in the borderlands, it was surely a magnification of reality and must be treated with caution. In 1441 the monks of Holm Cultram successfully petitioned the crown for a grant of view of frankpledge and a return of writs in their lands. They reminded their audience that their abbey was 'situated on the extreme march of England and exposed to the incursions of the Scots, who have frequently plundered and burned it and daily cause other damages'. The king's grant acknowledged that the abbot and convent were indeed 'put to continual expense in guarding the marches'.[94] The walls and castles of Berwick and Carlisle were always on the point of collapse; the Scottish enemies had always recently burned houses and crops; and the expenses of defence and repair were always pressing and burdensome. This was an alarmist language which Prince John of Lancaster learned to use from an early age in his letters to his father's council.[95] It was sometimes applied to castellated buildings, too. Sir Gilbert Curwen's crenellation of Workington in 1380 was justified as his manor was situated 'by the march of Scotland'. Bishop Strickland's licence to build a mantlet upon his house in Penrith 'on the march of Scotland' in 1399 was sought 'in aid and

---

[90] Smith, *Crisis and Survival*, 183 (quote), 204–5.
[91] *Northern Petitions*, p. 156, no. 120. For similar petitions, see *CPR 1388–92*, 203–4; *CPR 1401–5*, 181–2. For tax-shyness, see C. Briggs, 'Taxation, Warfare, and the Early Fourteenth Century 'Crisis' in the North: Cumberland Lay Subsidies, 1332–1348', *Economic History Review*, 58 (2005), 639–72, 669.
[92] *CPR 1441–6*, 183.
[93] Coulson, *Castles in Medieval Society*, 232 (quote), and 259–60. See also Tuck, 'A Medieval Tax Haven', 165.
[94] *CChR 1427–1516*, 12.
[95] Chrimes, 'Letters of John of Lancaster', 11, 27. In 1412 even John himself pleaded poverty, having coined his silver plate and gone into debt in order to pay the Berwick garrison's wages. See also *CPR 1446–52*, 508; *CPR 1452–61*, 498. For the walls of Carlisle, see *CPR 1408–13*, 40; *CPR 1416–22*, 408; *CPR 1422–9*, 538.

Part I

succour of the said town and adjacent country'. But it was not obligatory. Both these places were more distant from the border than the manor of Cartington in Northumberland, for which the owner's crenellation licence of 1442 made no mention of such borderland hazards.[96] At any rate, it has been observed that Scottish incursions in Norhamshire and Islandshire were normally limited to a 'very shallow strip of territory' along this part of the frontier, a strip of the marches often no more than four or four and a half miles in depth.[97]

If exaggerated destruction by the Scots was one strand of this frontier rhetoric, the other was the desolation of the land in the far north. Both can be found in the inquisitions post mortem of the period – a process ripe with opportunities for exaggeration and outright fiction, and clear financial incentives for bending reality so as to under-report property values. An inquisition of 1422 appraised the manor of Belsay as worth 20 marks annually only 'because of the barren nature of the land', and this is typical of valuations in the marches in the period.[98] Sometimes these strands were combined for good measure, as for the manor of Shawdon (by Alnwick) in an inquisition of 1438 which assessed the property as worth 20s only 'and no more these days because of the destruction of the Scots *and* the barrenness of the land'.[99] Six years later at Shotton, right beside Kirk Yetholm on the border with Roxburgh-shire, two waste husbandlands were of no value because of *both* the desolation of the country and the destruction of the Scots. It was not specified whether these circumstances at Shotton arose from the flight of tenants or to direct war damage.[100] In 1412, 'a great waste called the forest of Cheviot' was of no value because it was wasted by the Scots.[101] The rhetoric of barrenness and the dangers posed by a hostile enemy were no novelty arising from the wars of the fourteenth century.

---

[96] *CPR 1377–81*, 447; *CPR 1396–9*, 66, 480, 524; *CChR 1427–1516*, 35. See C. Coulson, 'Structural Symbolism in Medieval Castle Architecture', *Journal of the British Archaeological Association*, 132 (1979), 73–90, at 86 on 'justificatory phrases'. It is worth noting that an exemption for York in 1442 made much more of exposure to the Scots than did a comparable exemption for Newcastle in 1444 (*CChR 1427–1516*, 31, 39).

[97] Lomas, 'The Impact of Border Warfare', 149, 159, 163–4, 167. See above, p. 12, and further discussion below (pp. 264–8).

[98] *CIPM XXI 1418–22*, no. 828, p. 287. See Carpenter, 'General Introduction', in *CIPM 1422–7* (Woodbridge, 2003), 1–42, at 31 and, more generally, M. Hicks (ed.), *The Fifteenth-Century Inquisitions Post Mortem: A Companion* (Woodbridge, 2012).

[99] *CIPM XXV 1437–42*, no. 188, pp. 121–2.

[100] *CIPM XXVI 1442–7*, no. 223, pp. 131–3. Here also lands in Newton-on-the-Moor were called 'waste' and of low value due to the 'desolation of the country'.

[101] *CIPM XIX 1405–13*, nos 973, 979, pp. 348, 350. See also Coulson, *Castles in Medieval Society*, 355, for similar examples from fourteenth-century Cbl.. See I.A. MacInnes, 'To Be Annexed Forever', 185–91, on the term 'waste'.

Earth and Stone

In 1220 Richard Umfraville had asserted that Harbottle Castle was sited 'in the marches and necessary to defend the great waste towards Scotland'.[102] Here we find a loose sense of the frontier not as a clearly bounded set of territories but rather as an uncultivated wasteland, a more undefined expanse of hills, typically classified as forest, which were both of low value in terms of natural resources and kept that way by the regular devastation inflicted by the Scots.[103] As we have seen, this does not accord well with the prevailing trend of the fifteenth century, which was the setting of the border along its thirteenth-century lines.

To summarise, the view of towers and castles in the northern marches advanced here is that these buildings should be seen more as material cultural expressions of status and local power than as about the practicalities of defence. To be sure, a greater house was a residence and a fortress: a dwelling befitting a landholder's social status with the added advantage of 'some genuine protection for the builder and his family', and indeed an illustration of this will be noted in a later chapter.[104] Yes, local patterns are distinctive; there are many towers in the far north. Yet this needs to be understood in context, that this reflects a culture of elite building that reached far beyond the marches and across Scotland and Ireland. There were towers elsewhere in England too and, as we have seen, signs that towers in the marches served a range of functions, of which security was only one among many.

LANDSCAPE AND SETTLEMENT

We have already considered perceptions of the far north generally, and in relation to the idea of the frontier.[105] Now we turn to examine it with regard to landscape and settlement. To late medieval writers the English far north offered a complex landscape. In the fourteenth century, to Jean le Bel (an eyewitness to the campaign of 1327) Northumberland was '*sauvage paÿs, plains de desers et de grandes montagnes, et durement pouvres paÿs de toutes choses fors que de bestes*'. Lord Berners translated this passage in the 1520s as 'a savage and wylde countrey, full of desartis and mountaignes, and a right pore countrey of every thing, saving of beastis'.[106] Such a

---

[102] '*situm est in marchia Scotiae versus Magnam Wastinam ad magnam utilitatem regni, tam tempore pacis quam guerrae*': discussed in Coulson, *Castles in Medieval Society*, 221–3; Holford and Stringer, *Border Liberties*, 366.

[103] This strand fits with an early sense of the term 'march' as an entrance to a forest (c. 1200). See Power and Standen (eds), *Frontiers in Question*, 8, and see also 10, 24, on 'frontier wasteland'.

[104] Emery, 'Introductory Reflections', 19. See below, p. 260.   [105] See above, pp. 5–6 and 55.

[106] Jean Le Bel, *Chronique de Jean le Bel*, ed. J. Viard and E. Déprez, 2 vols (Paris, 1904–5), i, 49. Jean Froissart, *The Online Froissart*, ed. P. Ainsworth and G. Croenen, version 1.5 (Sheffield: HRIOnline,

Part I

conventional description of a difficult-to-govern region will be familiar to readers of the Western media of the early twenty-first century, appearing (as was noted in Chapter 1) with almost obligatory regularity in reports on the conflict in Afghanistan. These descriptions have a long pedigree, and we have already commented on the portfolio of motifs adapted from the classical world to demarcate civility and barbarity in the middle ages.[107] Moving from the medieval into the modern era, literary constructions continued to frame background assumptions. The wild and weathered Pennine moorland, permanently projected into cultural consciousness by the Brontës (most exultantly in *Wuthering Heights*), reinforced the perceptions of northern England's upland terrain already cultivated by Scott with regard to both sides of the Anglo-Scottish border. The writing of Wordsworth and Coleridge celebrated this natural scenery in the Lakeland fells.[108] In this way, over time, layers of cultural meaning have been projected onto the northern landscape, and particularly its higher ground. In the middle ages, Le Bel's '*grandes montagnes*' view of the far north was not the only image in currency. His '*sauvage paÿs*' could stand in other writing of its period for all England: both Gower and Chaucer narrate the journey of the rudderless ship carrying an exiled queen in the *Tale of Constance*. Her vessel is tossed by the waves from the Mediterranean Sea into the Atlantic, and eventually onto the far sands of pagan Northumberland's coast where she finds and marries King Alla. In this story Northumberland's perceived remoteness underlines England's historical 'otherworldliness', thus marking out an exceptional status for the realm and its place within Latin Christendom.[109]

We have already noted aspects of a frontier rhetoric put to use in our period. A related rhetoric of isolation and remoteness was harnessed in the far north, not least colourfully by the Cistercian abbey of Furness (situated on the peninsula of the same name, within the county of Lancashire north of Sands). In 1419 a mandate from the archbishop of

---

2013), www.hrionline.ac.uk/onlinefroissart; accessed 1 July 2014 (reproducing Toulouse, Bibliothèque municipale, MS 511, fol. 17r; and Besançon, Bibliothèque municipale, MS 864, fol. 14r). *The Chronicle of Froissart*, translated by J. Bourchier, Lord Berners, ed. W.E. Henley, 6 vols (London, 1901–3), i, p. 48. For comment, see Reed, 'The Ballad and the Source', 104; King, 'Anglo-Scottish Marches', 38.

[107] See above, p. 6. On early Tudor perceptions of civility and savagery, see Ellis, *Tudor Frontiers*, 46–77.

[108] See P. Morgan, 'Wild Wales: Civilizing the Welsh from the Sixteenth to the Nineteenth Centuries', in P. Burke, B. Harrison and P. Slack (eds), *Civil Histories: Essays Presented to Sir Keith Thomas* (Oxford, 2000), 265–83, at 270, 275–7, on shifting portrayals of the Welsh people and landscape.

[109] Lavezzo, *Angels on the Edge,* ch. 4, esp. pp. 95–6, 103.

Earth and Stone

York licensed Furness to exchange for nearer and more convenient possessions those which the abbey held in Ireland, in the Isle of Man, and elsewhere, 'so distant and so barren on account of floods of the sea that they yield little or no income'.[110] In a similar vein, in 1484 a papal decree granted a petition by Abbot Laurence of Furness, who had requested power to confer minor orders on monks and canons, to conduct blessing of sacred ornaments and to receive women and widows into the order. The abbot had set out his petition on the basis that the abbey was situated:

on the island of Fourneys, about eighty miles from the city of York, and that the archbishop had never been seen in the memory of man on that island or on those of Cartemell [to the east, also in Lancashire] or Copeland [to the west, in Cumberland] ... to which no one could approach except at low tide, and then not without danger of death, on account of two dangerous passes and of certain marshes which had caused the deaths of many.[111]

A critical appraisal of such statements would treat them less as statements of fact (albeit no doubt accurate descriptions of certain aspects of reality) than as statements of perception. Isolation and the perils of the sea are themes strongly at work in both these documents. The forbearance of the former at least was an important theme of Cistercian monasticism more generally. The motif of remoteness could be found in these low western peninsulas around Morecambe Bay, as much as it could be in the 'great waste' of the border hills in the east marches. If the reputation of Furness Fells as a terrain for medieval fugitives survived for Wordsworth to note it in the nineteenth century,[112] the Cheviots also carried a reputation as a place in which wanted men might disappear, as reflected in one fourteenth-century chronicle account. Following an exchange of large-scale border raids in 1383, the duke of Lancaster as warden sought certain English '*armigeri de partibus borealibus*' to be surrendered to the Scots. These unnamed northern squires declined to heed the warden's wishes, formed an armed band and went into hiding in the Cheviot Hills ('*coadunata multitudine armatorum inter montes de Chiveot latuerunt*').[113] Even if historians should hesitate to take such accounts of outlaws seeking refuge at face value, what is clear in this vignette is a general sense of the

---

[110] *Cal. Papal Reg.*, vii, 127. On the abbey's wealth, see Bennett, *Community, Class and Careerism*, 78.
[111] *Cal. Papal Reg.*, xv, 23.
[112] W. Wordsworth, *A Description of the Scenery of the Lakes in the North of England* (London, 1823), 40. W.G. Collingwood, *The Book of Coniston* (Kendal, 1897), 33–4, relates an episode from the reign of Edward III.
[113] *Westminster Chronicle*, 42–3. Cf. King, 'Best of Enemies', 129; Macdonald, *Border Bloodshed*, 72.

Part I

border terrain as a hilly vastness, a sign of the 'frontier wasteland' view noted above.

The upland parts of the English north, and the marches in particular, have resonated in prevailing understandings of its landscape. In the early twentieth century, there emerged a treatment of British topography which understood the island to be divided into two zones: a 'highland' north and west and a 'lowland' south and east. This paradigm was set by Sir Halford Mackinder and Sir Cyril Fox.[114] In the post-war decades, medievalists and early modernists readily applied this influential view to England alone.[115] The Pennines, Cheviots and Lakeland fells came to be seen as the dominating features of England north of the Humber and Mersey, and this is a view which continues in some recent scholarship. Historical discussions of the northern marches are frequently shaped by appraisals of the far north as predominantly upland, pastoral, with dispersed settlement patterns over terrain characterised as 'bleak, wild and inhospitable'.[116] Concerning the sixteenth century, a peculiar cul de sac disagreement has emerged, linked to questions of topography, about whether the English east marches were more settled and peaceable than the west marches. Both sides of the argument neglect to see beyond to a wider view of the framework in which it is set.[117] The pattern was fixed in work of the 1960s and 1970s, which acknowledged contrasts between upland and low-lying areas in the late medieval and early modern marches, but nevertheless viewed the area predominantly in terms of an economy focused on pastoral husbandry, particularly given to poverty and overpopulation in the hills.[118] Here, so it is argued, were to be found 'archaic communities' ensconced in Redesdale, Tynedale and Coquetdale or in the 'remoter and wilder parts of Durham'. Here the kinship group 'centred on the farmstead hearth' provided the strongest social tie.[119] Here, so it has been argued, the 'Surname' groups emerged 'as the basis of social organisation' when the

---

[114] H.J. Mackinder, *Britain and the British Seas* (London, 1902), 46–62; followed by C. Fox, *The Personality of Britain* (Cardiff, 1932). On this, see MacCannell, 'Dark Corners of the Land'.

[115] C. Brooke, *From Alfred to Henry III: 871–1272* (London, 1961), 14–15; Thirsk, (ed.), *Agrarian History*, 2–5, 8, 15. See also Armstrong, 'Centre, Periphery, Locality, Province'; Roberts and Wrathmell, *Region and Place*, 33.

[116] Ellis, *Defending English Ground*, 17 (quote). See also Dixon, 'Border Towers'; Summerson, 'Peacekeepers and Lawbreakers', 60; Bernard, *Power of the Early Tudor Nobility*, 109, and, more generally, T.C. Smout, *Nature Contested: Environmental History in Scotland and Northern England since 1600* (Edinburgh, 2000), 8, 116. More balanced comment is found in Goodman, 'Religion and Warfare', 246.

[117] For this argument, see Meikle, *A British Frontier*; Ellis, *Defending English Ground*.

[118] Tuck, 'Richard II', 28. See also Tuck, 'War and Society', 36.

[119] James, *Change and Continuity*, 6 ('archaic communities'); James, *Family, Lineage and Civil Society*, 4–7 ('remoter . . . hearth').

Earth and Stone

pressures of fourteenth-century warfare led to the failure of lordship and the 'collapse of law and order'.[120]

In turn, such appraisals emerged in the wake of Braudel's monumental geohistorical study, *The Mediterranean*, which was published in French in 1949 and in English translation in 1972–3. It seems that in these decades an existing understanding of 'highland' and 'lowland' England (and Britain) was blended with ideas imported from Braudel's *longue durée* approach which concentrated its attention (at the level of *histoire événementielle*) on the sixteenth century. In Braudel's first chapter he addressed the topographical, social and cultural characteristics of mountains, plateaux and plains. His most dramatic comments were those about 'mountain freedom' and the resistance of 'the highland world' to the penetration of lowland, urban civilisation and 'the establishment of the state'. In the Mediterranean highlands, the 'social archaisms' of vendetta and primitive magical beliefs thrived, and if the terrain offered poverty and demanded self-sufficiency, it was also 'a refuge, a land of the free'. For example, the Balkan mountain ranges formed 'a combat region, a frontier zone facing the Turks'.[121] For Braudel, the history of mountains was to

remain almost always on the fringe of the great waves of civilisation ... which may spread over great distances in the horizontal plane but are powerless to move vertically when faced with an obstacle of a few hundred metres. To these hilltop worlds, out of touch with the towns, even Rome itself, in all its years of power, can have meant very little.[122]

These claims have informed the wider framework of thought which late twentieth-century scholars applied to the Anglo-Scottish borderlands generally.[123] This is especially so with regard to the sixteenth century, that which is best captured in the border ballads of reivers and the riding 'Surnames'.[124] There are two concerns to raise about this. The first relates to the basis of Braudel's analysis in itself, for it is built primarily upon literary images created by urban elites and is unsubstantiated by archival sources; however, a critique in this regard need not detain us.[125] The

---

[120] Tuck, 'Northumbrian Society', 27–8 (citing work including that of Marc Bloch).

[121] F. Braudel, *The Mediterranean and the Mediterranean World in the Age of Philip II,* trans. Siân Reynolds, 2 vols (London, 1972–3), i, 37–9, 57 ('a combat ... Turks').

[122] Braudel, *The Mediterranean,* i, p. 34.

[123] A direct application of Braudel to the marches is found in Hay, 'England, Scotland and Europe'. For Scotland, see T.I. Rae, *The Administration of the Scottish Frontier, 1513–1603* (Edinburgh, 1966), 1–4, concentrating on 'the difficult country of plateaux and dales' (2).

[124] On ballads, see Reed, 'The Ballad and the Source'.

[125] See the evaluation in S.K. Cohn, 'Highlands and Lowlands in Late Medieval Tuscany', in Broun and MacGregor (eds), *Mìorun Mòr nan Gall,* 110–27, at 110–12.

Part I

second relates to a misapplication of Braudel's analysis of Mediterranean mountains to the hills of England's far north. The topographical elevation of Braudel's mountain region was above 500 metres, even exceeding 900 metres. By contrast, he is keen to claim that 'the half-mountainous region of plateaux, hills, and foothills' in no way resembled 'the real mountains', that 'hillside civilisation' he placed on land of 200–400 metres elevation.[126] In terms of the highest peaks in the far north, there are the Cheviot (816 m), Cross Fell in the Pennines (890 m) and four peaks in Lakes exceeding 900 metres, including Scafell Pike (978 m). But the vast majority of land in the three northern counties sits below 400 metres elevation, and a leading environmental history of the region identifies the 300-metre contour as the effective upland boundary.[127] It is true that Braudel's attention was on the warmer Mediterranean basin, not a North Atlantic archipelago, and his hillside zone emphasised settled agriculture supporting vineyards and olive groves to an extent exceeding what is possible in a British climate where rough grazing surely takes over at lower altitude in the Pennines than it does in the Apennine range (where four peaks surpass 2,100 m). All the same, the point to be made here is twofold. First, care should be taken in historical geographical investigations not to assume topography's overarching, even deterministic, importance in shaping human societies and cultures. Second, if Braudel's influential ideas must loom in the background of historical comment on England's northern marches – as they loom behind so much work on pre-modern landscapes[128] – caution is called for in how far his 'mountain' habitat, and the features to which he attributed it, are transposed. It is Braudel's zone of plateaux, hills and foothills which is, at least as far as it involved mixed agriculture, an environment more comparable to the upland areas of middle Britain.

In our region the mixed agriculture undertaken on fertile lowland soil, and its relationship with nearby hill farming, must be kept in perspective. Too far has the northern upland 'waste' (often classified as forest for game and rough grazing) been exaggerated by modern historians, much as it often was by late medieval northerners. As a result, significant areas of productive fertile plain and valley lowland tend to be minimised, or ignored, in accounts of the northern marches. One writer has astutely observed that there is all too often a focus on what the region lacks rather

---

[126] Braudel, *The Mediterranean*, i, 42 (mountain elevation), 53 (quote), 55 (hillside civilisation elevation), 53–60.

[127] Winchester, *Harvest of the Hills*, 6 (see also Roberts and Wrathmell, *Region and Place*, 37; Winchester, *Landscape and Society*, 8). Pollard, *North-Eastern England*, 28–9 (map showing land over approximately 150 m).

[128] For comment, see Cohen and Madeline (eds), *Space in the Medieval West*, 2–4.

Earth and Stone

than on its diverse forms of productivity.[129] The fells themselves provided a rich source of peat fuel and thatching materials; a number of areas supported mining of coal, lead and other minerals; and woodlands yielded their own resources too. The *Agrarian History of England and Wales* identifies two main farming regions in our area, the first being open pasture for cattle and sheep, with some dairying (in higher land), and the second being mixed farming of corn and stock in various combinations (in lowland areas). The latter represented an agricultural landscape by no means confined to the far north – indeed, comparable mixed farming was also to be found, for example, in Felden Warwickshire.[130] The northern lowlands expected the same mean temperature as the Midlands and East Anglia, and average rainfall on the Northumberland plain matched that of Norfolk.[131] All this is to point out that the coastal plains and well-drained valley floors offered open arable land. In Cumberland and Westmorland, plough land and open fields were to be found in the margins of the fells, and medieval settlements like Buttermere and High and Low Lorton (both in Cumberland) are examples of nucleated villages situated in valley floors. In these areas (as in the lowlands east of the Pennines) the husbandland or 'bovate' was the main form of customary peasant holding.[132] In earlier centuries large blocks of Lakeland and Pennine moorland had been controlled directly by feudal superiors as baronial forest. Between the upper moors and the valley floors was often a zone of woodland. By the end of the thirteenth century, a significant portion of these woodlands, and the slopes of the fells above them, came to be divided up between the adjacent townships in a process of upwards expansion of settlement into formerly open moorland. This occurred both through the leasing and subdivision of upland holdings and through the conversion of existing summer pastures to permanent settlements.[133] Whillimoor in Copeland is an example of a

---

[129] Winchester, *Harvest of the Hills*, 3. See also Pollard, *North-Eastern England*, 13–14, 43, 45–50; Dobson, *Durham Priory*, 250–96.

[130] Thirsk (ed.), *Agrarian History*, 4 (re-presented in Roberts and Wrathmell, *Region and Place*, 60), 8, 15. For the 'northern borders' before 1500 in the same series, see J.A. Tuck, 'The Northern Borders', in E. Miller (ed.), *The Agrarian History of England and Wales, III: 1348–1500* (Cambridge, 1991), 34–41, 175–81, 587–95.

[131] Roberts and Wrathmell, *Region and Place*, 38; E. Miller, 'Farming in Northern England during the Twelfth and Thirteenth Centuries', *Northern History*, 11 (1976 for 1975), 1–16, at 2.

[132] Winchester, *Landscape and Society*, 20, 32, 64–72, 74, 140–7; Winchester, *Harvest of the Hills*, 61–6; R.A. 'Developments in Land Tenure on the Prior of Durham's Estate in the Later Middle Ages', *Northern History*, 13 (1977), 27–43.

[133] A.J.L. Winchester, 'Hill Farming Landscapes of Medieval Northern England', in D. Hooke (ed.), *Landscape: The Richest Historical Record* (Amesbury, 2000), 75–84; J. McDonnell, 'Upland Pennine Hamlets', *Northern History*, 26 (1990), 20–39. These articles examine how the leasing of upland demesne stock farms could lead to clusters of tenants sharing a common surname (e.g., the

Part I

waste that came to be divided among its neighbouring townships by the fourteenth century, with its former unity remembered in a boundary described in 1447.[134] Following the general decline in population experienced in the fourteenth century due to the adversities of famine, livestock disease and pestilence, a renewed period of expansion into moorland occurred in the century following 1450.[135]

The farming year west of the Pennines was shaped by the 'open' and 'closed' seasons of infield–outfield cultivation, allowing livestock to graze and manure within the head–dyke boundary during the winter (open), and expelling them to moorland pasture in summer (closed). East of the Pennines, systems of field rotation were more common than such infield–outfield farming. Across the entire region there was natural integration between lowland and upland resources. In this way, arrangements were commonly made for the 'agistment' of lowland livestock on upland wastes during the summer grazing season (May to August).[136] It seems that a considerable amount of such 'seasonal intercommoning', or transhumance, was conducted informally across manorial boundaries. In northern and eastern Cumberland, the use of shieling huts located several miles away from manorial farms was common throughout our period. By contrast, in the Lakeland fells migrations to summer shielings, which tended to be located closer to villages there, declined from about 1350 onwards.[137] By contrast, in the north Pennines and Border hills summer grazing practices continued into the fifteenth and sixteenth centuries, in shieling grounds notably in the Pennines (as at Allendale in Hexhamshire) and North Tynedale, Redesdale and Kidland. These areas were not permanently settled until the mid-sixteenth century or later.[138]

What counts in this discussion of topography and farming practices in the historical environment are the patterns of human habitation: whether people were thick or thin on the ground. Roberts and Wrathmell's study of historical landscapes across England has identified three broad national or 'settlement provinces' – approximations which express particular areas of landscape and patterns of rural settlement (see Map 6). These are an

---

Aldersons of Keld and Angram in Swaledale, Yorks.). See also W.P. Hedley, 'The Medieval Forests of Northumberland', *Archaeologia Aeliana*, 4th ser., 28 (1950), 96–104.

[134] Winchester, *Landscape and Society*, 85–7.

[135] Winchester, *Landscape and Society*, 44, 51–5, 64, 101; Winchester, 'Hill Farming', 80.

[136] Winchester, *Landscape and Society*, 135; Winchester, *Harvest of the Hills*, 54–5, 66, 94, 96.

[137] Winchester, *Landscape and Society*, 91–6. The reasons cited are the expansion of permanent settlement in the moorlands and a shift from cattle to sheep stock.

[138] Winchester, 'Hill Farming', 79–81 (attributing the relative 'delay' to border turbulence); Winchester, *Harvest of the Hills*, 86 (for the 'hopes' or side valleys of Redesdale in the seventeenth century), 93–4; J. McDonnell, 'The Role of Transhumance in Northern England', *Northern History*, 24 (1988), 1–17, at 14.

Earth and Stone

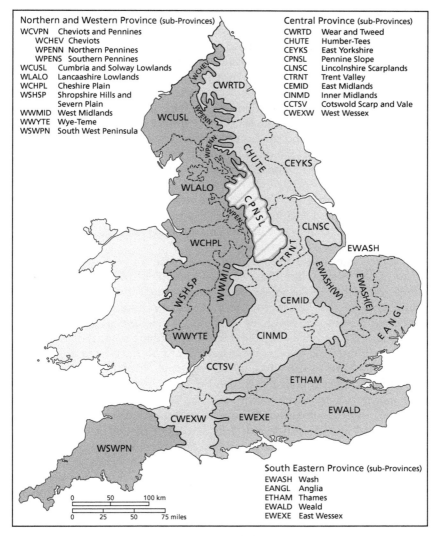

Map 6 Rural 'Settlement Provinces' (after Roberts and Wrathmell)

'inner' province (called by the authors the 'Central Province') running approximately from Somerset in a band north-eastward to encompass Northumberland's eastern plain as far as the mouth of the Tweed. This inner province is characterised by champion, open fields and a preponderance of compact and nucleated villages. It is flanked by two 'outer'

Part I

provinces – one called the 'South Eastern Province' reaching approximately from Bournemouth on the southern coast around to the Wash, and the other called the 'Northern and Western Province'. The latter includes the south-western peninsula of Devon and Cornwall, and runs from the mouth of the Wye northwards to Cumberland and the Cheviots. These outer provinces are characterised by woodland and a more dispersed pattern of settlement.[139] Thus in our area of interest in the far north there are two provinces to consider – the 'inner' to the east of the Pennine ridge and the 'outer' to the west. The boundary selected by the authors is the 300-metre contour on the eastern slopes of the Pennines and Cheviots, so allocating the 'deeply incised main dales' to the outer province of the west.[140] Other studies have reinforced the point that the distribution of nucleated medieval villages in England is largely concentrated within the inner province identified by Roberts and Wrathmell (and so does not include areas elsewhere, such as Hampshire, Surrey, Kent, Essex and East Anglia).[141]

Thus in eastern Northumberland were to be found a preponderance of nucleated villages like Ogle or East Matfen. Even closer to the hills (albeit still below 300 m in elevation) smaller nucleations occurred. Such is the case of the 'ten towns of Coquetdale', eight of which were contained within the parish of Alwinton, itself one of the townships concentrated on a bifocal village. However, the inhabitants of Alwinton and its neighbouring villages were more likely to have been engaged in cereal agriculture in surrounding field systems, primarily as a means of supporting stockraising in the Kidland pastures just over their shoulders, than in the intensive cultivation of corn.[142] Northumberland and the territory east of the Pennines had much greater agricultural potential than Cumberland and Westmorland. Still, it contained 'diverse terrains and diverse field systems'.[143] West of the Pennines diversity was also an important characteristic, where the manorialised lowlands of the Eden valley contrasted with the dispersed settlement which predominated in the southern barony of Kendale. Examples of dispersed settlements in

---

[139] Roberts and Wrathmell, *Region and Place*, 6–12 (and figure 1.4 at p. 10), also maps at 32 (English physical regions and terrains), 64 (landscape types) and 178 (a convenient overlay of county boundaries).

[140] Roberts and Wrathmell, *Region and Place,* 37, noting that the 300-metre contour is often followed by the head dyke.

[141] Palliser, *Towns and Local Communities,* c. II, 5–7 (and see map of the distribution of nucleated villages at 6). On nucleation, see Roberts and Wrathmell, *Region and Place,* 5, 11, 65–8, 173–4.

[142] Northumberland National Park Authority, 'Alwinton, Northumberland: An Archaeological and Historical Study of a Border Township', *Northumberland National Park Historic Village Atlas* (2004), 27–35, www.dartmoor.gov.uk ; accessed 1 October 2015.

[143] Roberts and Wrathmell, *Region and Place,* 131–3.

Earth and Stone

Cumberland, like Setmurthy and Kinniside (both in Copeland), have been shown to have existed as a scatter of farms without a nucleated focus.[144] The major anomaly in Cumberland and Westmorland was the rich Eden valley, which was in effect an outlier of the inner province. In it were to be found a string of planned nucleated villages, conducting continuous cultivation of fields in two- and three-course rotations.[145] Diversity should also be foremost in mind when reflecting on Kapelle's well-known proposition of the 'oat bread line' (projected from the Wansbeck in Northumberland to the Pennine hills of the West Riding) and its attendant claims about the limits of cereal cultivation in the far north. Kapelle argues that to the north-west of this line the crops which predominated were oats and barley and, to its south-east, wheat and rye.[146] Aeneas Sylvius Piccolomini's account of the wonder of 'barbarous' Northumbrian peasants when he offered them wine and white bread as he passed through in 1435 seems relevant, if bread made from wheaten flour was truly such a novelty to them. If this is an accurate account (rather than an oblique comment on the curatorial efforts of the local priest who welcomed him to supper), these peasants were unlike their peers who, on more than fifty occasions, were involved in cases heard before the justices of gaol delivery on both sides of the Pennines which involved the theft of quantities of wheat, or wheat flour, evidently of local origin.[147]

This examination of the interpretation and significance of fortifications and landscapes draws to a close with a plea. It is a plea for a more nuanced interpretation of what late medieval borderers said about life at the frontier, and in this regard a plea to keep an eye ready for the conventions of rhetoric and the utility of exaggeration. It is also a plea for caution and perspective on familiar claims for the militarisation of border society, so far anyway as this is evidenced by the built heritage of the marches in the later middle ages, and the fifteenth century in particular.[148] It is also difficult to conceive that the inhabitants of the fifteenth-century marches did not

---

[144] Winchester, *Landscape and Society*, 20, 32, 69, 74, for diversity. For Setmurthy and Kinniside, see ibid., 72, 149, 158–9.

[145] Roberts and Wrathmell, *Region and Place*, 128–9, and 3 for a critique of H.L. Gray, *English Field Systems* (Cambridge, MA, 1915).

[146] W.E. Kapelle, *The Norman Conquest of the North: The Region and Its Transformation, 1000–1135* (Chapel Hill, 1979), 213–30. On oats, see also Miller, 'Farming in Northern England', 9–10, part of a generally pessimistic appraisal of northern agriculture.

[147] *Enea Silvio Piccolomini, Papa Pio II, I Commentarii*, ed. and trans. L. Totaro, 2 vols (Milan, 1984), i, 26. See further discussion of this account in Chapter 8.

[148] On militarisation: Storey, 'The North of England', 130; Goodman, 'Introduction', in Tuck and Goodman (eds), *War and Border Societies*, 9; Harriss, *Shaping the Nation*, 528; King, 'Fortresses and Fashion Statements', 386, 396.

103

Part I

appreciate the complex diversity of landscapes in which they lived and worked. It is equally difficult to imagine that they did not predominantly orientate their social interactions towards the river valleys and coasts; these were the natural routes of communication along which they lived. Thus it is a plea for an appreciation of such geographical diversity and for care and caution when generalised social and political characteristics are taken to be determined by geography.

This vantage point offers a useful opportunity for a brief topographical comparison of the border counties with other parts of England, and existing local studies serve as a helpful guide. In terms of landscape, agriculture and settlement, the shires of the march had most in common with other northern territories. In Cheshire and Lancashire, part of what we have already identified as *Chester-Lancaster-Furness*,[149] the land rises eastwards into the ridge of the Pennine Hills, while on both sides of the Mersey better arable farming areas are situated in the lower lying coastal plains.[150] In the bishopric of Durham, part of what we have already identified as *Newcastle-Durham*,[151] the southern and eastern parts of the bishopric possessed nucleated settlements, and manors with substantial arable lowland and meadow. It was this area which was the more densely populated. By contrast, as one moved further west into the Pennine districts, dispersed farmsteads became the norm with an increasing focus on pastoralism.[152] In Yorkshire, we find a similar story, but more a patchwork of landscapes and modes of agriculture, from rich arable manors in the Vale of York and other fertile lowlands to the uplands of the Pennines and the North York Moors which were given to sheep and cattle husbandry.[153] However, for a county sitting at more substantial distance from the northern marches, perhaps the best comparator is Derbyshire. Wright's study of local society in that county found the chief geographical division was between the north-west, encompassing the High Peak at the southern end of the Pennine Hills with dispersed settlements and animal husbandry, and the more populous south-east, containing nucleated villages and arable farmland.[154] This main division within Derbyshire approximately matches the boundary between the

---

[149] See Map 1 and above, p. 42. See also Armstrong, 'Centre, Periphery, Locality, Province', 267–70.

[150] Bennett, *Community, Class and Careerism*, 8–9. See also N.J. Higham, *A Frontier Landscape: The North West in the Middle Ages* (Macclesfield, 2004).

[151] See Map 1 and above, p. 42.

[152] Liddy, *Bishopric of Durham*, 30–3, 41–7, 53; Dobson, *Durham Priory*, 274–7, 279. See also B. Dodds, *Peasants and Production in the Medieval North-East: The Evidence from Tithes, 1270–1536* (Woodbridge, 2007), 71–100, 101–21.

[153] Pollard, *North-Eastern England*, 30–8, 58–63, quote from 32.

[154] Wright, *Derbyshire Gentry*, 12–14, 18–20. Wright notes further local subdivisions.

104

Earth and Stone

'Northern and Western' and the 'Central' rural settlement provinces proposed by Roberts and Wrathmell as it runs through the Midlands (see Map 6).[155] Thus the arable and nucleated parts of Derbyshire match what we have observed of farming and settlement in lowland Northumberland. Just a little further to the south, in Warwickshire, it is worth noting that Roberts and Wrathmell's imaginary line divided the 'two distinct segments' of the Feldon from the Arden in the county, the latter area supporting not an insignificant amount of livestock rearing among dispersed settlements. That Feldon–Arden boundary, as Carpenter observes in her own local study, marked a geographical-economic divide and a persistent separation of the orientations and affairs of the local gentry.[156] If we follow further south the line between the 'northern and western' and the 'central' rural settlement provinces, the boundary runs with the Severn to the sea, reappearing in the western parts of Somerset and Dorset. In this framework, Cornwall and Devonshire sit entirely within the same settlement province that encompassed the western part of the northern marches. Cornwall and Devonshire, albeit without contour levels to match the Lakeland or Pennine fells, featured mixed agricultural regimes and a predominance of dispersed settlements.[157] What is most important to note in this short and select overview is simply that variety across local landscapes was typical of many English localities and, thus, that the diversity to be found in the northern marches was no different in this regard.

CONCLUSION AT PART I

So far we have established the main features of the historiography of late medieval England and its far north, and the topics of conflict and governance. It has been proposed that the ideas of centre and periphery are not helpful in understanding the northern marches. In this first part we have also examined the ideas and terminology of the frontier, towers and castles; the nature of the landscape and agricultural practices; and

---

[155] Roberts and Wrathmell, *Region and Place*, figures at pp. 10, 178. Phythian-Adams's framework of 'cultural provinces' treats this locality as another transitional area, situated within 'Trent' but shading towards 'Yorkshire Ouse' (Phythian-Adams, *Societies, Cultures and Kinship*, figure at p. xviii).

[156] Carpenter, *Locality and Polity*, 19, 19–30, 296, 609. See also A. Watkins, 'Landowners and Their Estates in the Forest of Arden in the Fifteenth Century', *Agricultural History Review*, 45 (1997), 18–33. Phythian-Adams treats the Arden as one of many 'overlap zones' across the English landscape, this one set within the cultural province of 'Severn/Avon' but orientated towards 'Trent' (Phythian-Adams, *Societies, Cultures and Kinship*, figure at p. xviii).

[157] J. Hatcher, *Rural Economy and Society in the Duchy of Cornwall, 1300–1500* (Cambridge, 1970), 8–36.

Part I

patterns of human habitation. The goal in all of this has been to explore these subject areas with a view to identifying their nuance and complexity and, in some cases, to connect together more niche areas of scholarship and draw them into a wider discussion of the region. To that end, the thrust of argumentation so far has been to encourage due recognition of the different functions of the frontier and the ways in which it was understood (being the only land frontier in the British–Irish Isles between two independent kingdoms) and of the diversity of landscape and economy in the border counties. Of course, the march was shaped by more than border defence and raiding, and for all its uplands it was also more than a pastoral region devoted to livestock rearing. As we have seen, and as we have been reminded by other studies touching the region, it supported mixed agriculture and contained significant areas of nucleated settlement. If I have stated my case rather strongly in places, the reason is to clear away the brush for the analysis to follow, which seeks to build an understanding of the far north, and what it tells us about the wider English polity, through the prism of conflict. What follows examines lordship, kinship, law, violence and peacemaking. In so doing, it treats the effects of war when it happened, an upland landscape where it existed, and distance from Westminster where relevant, with due regard and proportionality, but not as the defining features of the region.

PART II

4

THE NOBILITY, GENTRY
AND RELIGIOUS HOUSES

Before proceeding any further with our analysis, this short chapter offers an overview of the landowners of the northern marches. By 1399, the greatest border lords were relative newcomers. Fourteenth-century warfare had eliminated the cross-border landownership which been prevalent in the thirteenth century and had led to an increasing level of seigneurial absenteeism. The Percy earls of Northumberland (created 1377, and who suffered forfeitures in 1405–16 and 1461–70) were the only magnates frequently resident in the far north-east. However, as great magnates, their other responsibilities meant they were seldom in the marches for long. The family had gained extensive lands in Northumberland during the fourteenth century (including the baronies of Alnwick, Warkworth, Beanley, Langley and Prudhoe, and the manors of Rothbury, Corbridge, Newburn, Thirston, Newham, Ellingham and Newstead). Their territories included the 'Talbot Lands' within northern Tynedale, which alone extended to nearly 6,000 acres.[1] In Cumberland, they had also acquired Egremont and Cockermouth.[2] The sons of the second earl of Northumberland maintained a family presence in the marches: Thomas (Lord Egremont from 1449) was active on the family's Cumberland estates in the 1450s; Henry (Lord Poynings from 1446 and third earl from 1455) was warden of the east march and keeper of Berwick from 1440; Sir Ralph (d. 1464), was active in the 1450s and early 1460s as deputy and later constable of Dunstanburgh Castle.[3]

---

[1] The 'Talbot Lands' were members of the barony of Wark in Tynedale and included portions of Tarset and Kielder manors (*CPR 1461–7*, 340–1; *NCH*, XV, 245–8, 266–8).

[2] This was the Lucy inheritance. The 'Fitzwalter lands' within the barony of Egremont (*CCR 1402–5*, 128; *CPR 1405–8*, 47) became part of the crown revenues allocated to the west march warden (Summerson, *Medieval Carlisle*, II, 406). Walter, Lord Fitzwalter, was designated lord of Egremont c. 1401–2 (C 1/3/39; C 1/69/177).

[3] 'Percy, Sir Ralph (1425–1464)', *Oxford DNB*, XLIII, 735–6, by P. W. Hammond.

109

Part II

The Nevilles of Raby in Durham had been advanced as a counter-balance to Percy power in the marches under Richard II. In 1397 Ralph Neville was created earl of Westmorland and given lordships in Cumberland (Penrith and Sowerby), and a further grant two years later included the Richmond fee of the barony of Kendale in Westmorland. The first earl arranged for his children by his second wife to inherit the bulk of his estates. Consequently, following his death in 1425, the senior branch of the Nevilles was left with a reduced patrimony (consisting of Brancepath in Durham and in Northumberland the baronies of Bywell and Styford and other lands within the liberty of Bedlingtonshire). The junior branch of the family inherited the earl's estates at Middleham in Yorkshire, and Penrith in Cumberland. The inheritance was disputed but finally resolved in 1443 in favour of the junior house, whose scions also married into other inheritances and became the 'great' Nevilles of the fifteenth century, led by Richard Neville, earl of Salisbury (1400–60) and his numerous sons, including Richard, earl of Warwick (1428–71), and John, marquess of Montague (c. 1431–71). Although these men frequently served as wardens, they were not normally resident in the marches, and their local influence was derived primarily through office-holding.[4] Another branch of the junior Nevilles were the Lords Latimer, who by marriage obtained a few manors in Cumberland and Westmorland. After 1450 during the insanity of Lord George (d. 1469), these properties came into the custody of his brother the earl of Salisbury.[5] Following the elimination of the 'great' Nevilles in 1471, the Middleham inheritance became the northern territorial base of the king's brother Richard, duke of Gloucester.

For much of our period of interest Henry, Lord Bourchier (b. 1408, created Viscount Bourchier in 1445–6 and earl of Essex in 1461, d. 1483) was the absentee lord of Tynedale. Early in the century, the liberty had been inherited by Edward, duke of York, who arranged in 1412 to sell it to the Northumberland knight, Thomas Grey of Heton. As part of the deal, Grey's son (another Thomas) was to marry York's niece Isabel, daughter of Richard, earl of Cambridge. In 1415 Grey and Cambridge were executed for their part in the Southampton Plot, and the duke of York was killed at Agincourt. Isabel, now lady of Tynedale, was later widowed, and she took Bourchier as her second husband in 1426. Henry

---

[4] Salisbury's brother, William, Lord Fauconberg (d. 1463), served as warden of Roxburgh Castle in the 1440s and 1450s (*CDS*, IV, 237–8, 253, 260).

[5] The Latimer manors were Bolton in Allerdale (Cbl.), Warcop and Morland (Wml.), and Heversham (Kendale barony, Wml.).

The Nobility, Gentry and Religious Houses

and Isabel jointly held the liberty until their deaths in 1483 and 1484.[6] After this, Tynedale reverted to the crown through Richard III's disregard for an earlier grant by Edward IV.[7] Wark in north Tynedale was the *caput* of the liberty (and of the barony of Wark within the liberty), but there is also evidence for courts being held at other locations.[8]

The English crown also held some, but not a great amount, of land in the marches. Within Cumberland, this included the barony of Liddel, the forest of Inglewood and part of the barony of Copeland.[9] Within Northumberland, the crown had the duchy of Lancaster estates centred on Dunstanburgh and Bamburgh castles, and of course Tynedale from 1483. During the first Percy forfeiture, Henry IV granted their lands to his son, Prince John of Lancaster, the east march warden.[10] When Prince John was created duke of Bedford and earl of Kendale in 1414, he obtained the reversion of the honour of Richmond after the death of the first earl of Westmorland. In 1425, this brought Bedford the Richmond fee of the barony of Kendale, which reverted to the crown at his death in 1435, although his widow, Duchess Jaquetta, was to live with her dower until 1472.[11]

Among the lesser nobility, the Dacres stand out as the only family of this rank resident in the far north-west. Their lands included the baronies of Dacre, Gilsland and Burgh-by-Sands in Cumberland, and these were retained in 1458 by virtue of an entail, despite losses elsewhere. As Lancastrian partisans, they suffered attainder between 1461 and 1473, during which time the heirs general gained possession of the patrimony. The family was of relatively humble means, being assessed at a landed income of only £320 in 1436.[12] Further south in Cumberland was the

---

[6] CPR 1408–13, 383, 399; CPR 1413–16, 411; CCR 1435–41, 6; GEC, V, 137–8; NCH, XI, 41–2; NCH, XV, 285; L.S. Woodger [now Clark], 'Henry Bourgchier, Earl of Essex, and His Family, 1408–83', DPhil thesis University of Oxford (1974), 17, 183–5, 198, 209. For Tynedale before 1400, see Holford and Stringer, Border Liberties, 291–358.

[7] CPR 1476–85, 495.

[8] In April 1405 Edward, duke of York, held a court at Newburgh, transacting a sale of land in the presence some Nbl. JPs (CAC, Carlisle: D/Mus/2/ box 38 no. A56).

[9] T.H.B. Graham, 'The Barony of Liddel and Its Occupants', TCWAAS, n.s., 11 (1911), 55–83, at 55; F.H.M. Parker, 'Inglewood Forest', TCWAAS, n.s., 5 (1905), 35–61; 11 (1911), 1–37.

[10] Cockermouth and Egremont were granted to Ralph, earl of Westmorland (CPR 1405–8, 40, 50). The barony of Langley was granted to Sir Robert Umfraville (CPR 1429–36, 532).

[11] CPR 1429–36, 297–8; CPR 1436–41, 18, 51, 63, 89, 247, 255, 284, 392; CCR 1435–41, 146; CPR 1441–6, 453; CPR 1446–52, 263, 335; CPR 1452–61, 335; Nicolson and Burn, History and Antiquities, i, 34–63.

[12] GEC, IV, 1–18, 18–26; GEC, VI; 197, 201–2; GEC, XIV, 231; Ellis, 'A Border Baron', 258; Dunning, 'Thomas, Lord Dacre', 95–9. See H.L. Gray, 'Incomes from Land in England in 1436', EHR, 49 (1934), 607–39, at 614–18, 621, 629; T.B. Pugh and C.D. Ross, 'The English Baronage and the Income Tax of 1436', BIHR 26 (1953), 1–28. The nobility holding substantial lands in the border shires were Richard Neville, earl of Salisbury (assessed at £1238); Henry Percy, earl of

Part II

barony of Greystoke and the lords of that name. The Lords Greystoke also owned the barony of Morpeth in Northumberland, and lands in Westmorland, Durham and Yorkshire. In the early 1420s John, Lord Greystoke, served as warden of Roxburgh Castle, but the family's principal residence was in Yorkshire. They were assessed at £650 in 1436. On the death of Ralph, Lord Greystoke, in 1487, much of these lands passed to the Dacres, by marriage of Thomas, Lord Dacre, to Elizabeth, Lord Greystoke's grand-daughter and heir-general. The Dacres gained the rest of the Greystoke inheritance in 1508.[13] Apart from the Lords Harrington, who were primarily based in Furness (Lancashire) and who became extinct in 1458,[14] the other baronial house in the far north-west was that of the Cliffords, barons of Westmorland, who also normally resided on their Yorkshire estates. Lord Clifford had been assessed at an income of £250 in 1436. The family owned all of the barony of Westmorland, containing the castles of Appleby, Brough and Brougham. They suffered attainder in 1461 (their lands passing to Warwick and then to the Parrs) but were restored in 1485.[15] The Cliffords (like the Percys and the Middleham affinity which passed from the Nevilles to Gloucester)[16] illustrate the point that, despite the century's upheavals, stability prevailed in the regional distribution of landed power if we take the period as a whole.

Turning to sub-baronial landowners, certain records (of the oaths of 1434 and the income tax of 1436), although not exhaustive guides, help to identify the gentry of the marches. For those listed as oath-takers in 1434, we have evidence for Cumberland and Northumberland only, and a quick count shows that, while seventy-six men were named for the former county, only forty-four were named for the latter. This indicates that, in Cumberland, gentle status was spread amongst a larger group of local families.[17] The tax assessments of 1436 reveal a similar pattern and tell us about all three counties. While only thirty-nine tax-payers were

---

Northumberland (£1210); Joan Neville, countess of Westmorland (£667); John, Lord Greystoke (£650); William Neville, Lord Fauconberg (£325); Thomas, Lord Dacre (£320); Thomas, Lord Clifford (£250); and George Neville, Lord Latimer (£175).

[13] *CDS*, IV, 182; *CIPM*, Series 2, i, nos 231, 243, 245, 304, 307, 432, pp. 102, 107–9, 133, 182–3; *Select Cases,* ed. Bayne and Dunham, 20–2; *GEC*, IV, 18–26.

[14] 'Harrington family (per. c. 1300–1512)', *Oxford DNB*, XXV, 383–5, by R. Horrox.

[15] F.W. Ragg, 'The Feoffees of the Cliffords from 1283–1482', *TCWAAS*, n.s., 8 (1908), 253–330; G.W.S. Barrow, 'The Pattern of Lordship and Feudal Settlement in Cumbria', *Journal of Medieval History*, 1 (1975), 117–38, at 121–4; *PROME*, November 1461, items 20, 27, 28; November 1485, item 6 [11].

[16] Horrox, *Richard III*, ch. 1.

[17] *CPR 1429–36*, 383, 396. For Cbl., the two gentry commissioners, Laton and Legh, have been added in to arrive at this total. The same has been done for Nbl. (Lilburn and Cartington).

The Nobility, Gentry and Religious Houses

assessed in Northumberland, there were fifty-seven in Cumberland and fifty-three in Westmorland. Like the oaths, the tax assessments suggest that Northumberland's landed wealth was concentrated in relatively fewer hands and that, in the north-west, landholding was more diffuse. At the top end of reported incomes, there were four knights assessed at more than one hundred pounds. In Cumberland, these were Sir John Skelton (£118 6s. 8d), Sir Richard Huddleston (£100) and, in Northumberland, Sir William Eure (£100) and Sir Robert Umfraville (£400). Umfraville's outstanding wealth placed him even higher up the scale than Lords Fauconberg, Dacre, Clifford and Latimer, all of whom held substantial lands in these counties.[18] Yet such rough guides to the landed elite do not reveal the numbers of even more obscure gentry in the area, of the sort who appear in local legal records from these counties.[19]

A few gentry families had significant lordships in the marches. The Parrs of Kendal held one-fifth of Kendale barony and were the only resident chief tenants of the barony.[20] They would benefit as royal stewards and servants in Westmorland under Edward IV during the forfeiture of the Cliffords.[21] The lordship of Millom in south-western Cumberland was owned by the Huddlestons, another family of prominent gentry who were also normally resident in the march. Closer to the border itself, in Northumberland, were the lands of the Umfravilles and their heirs, the Tailboys. The wealthy Sir Robert Umfraville's lands in Northumberland were centred on the liberty of Redesdale, with castles at Harbottle and Otterburn.[22] He also owned the 'ten towns of Coquetdale', being Alwinton, Biddlestone, Clennell, Netherton,

---

[18] E 179/195/32 (Wml.); E 179/90/26 (Cbl.); E 179/359/29 m. 6d (Nbl.); E 179/359/29 m. 7 (barons). Peers were assessed separately from the gentry: Gray, 'Incomes', 614–18, 621, 629.

[19] For example, the following 'gentlemen' (among others) did not appear as oath-takers or tax payers in Nbl.: Alan Killingworth of Killingworth, Robert Langewayth of Newburn, and William Yonge of Throckley, 1435 (JUST 3/54/16 m. 4); Thomas Home of Alnham, William Jakson of Fenwick, and John Haysande of Throklaw, 1438 (JUST 3/54/19 m. 10). John Clenell (elsewhere 'esquire'), 1438 (JUST 3/54/19 m. 20), 1441 (JUST 3/54/24 mm. 5,6), and 1443 (JUST 3/54/26 m. 10).

[20] The three-fifths Richmond fee of Kendale has been traced above. The final fifth, the Lumley fee, was held by the barons Lumley (prominent in Durham and Yorks.). George, son of Thomas, second Lord Lumley, was active in Nbl. (*CPR 1461–7*, 66, 233, 569; *CPR 1476–85*, 568; *CPR 1485–94*, 39; *REM*, I, 357; *LOS*, 98).

[21] *CPR 1461–7*, 86; S.E. James, 'Henry VII and *Prerogativa Regis*: The Case of Mabel Dacre', *TCWAAS*, n.s., 99 (1999), 177–84; S.E. James, 'Sir Thomas Parr (1407–1461)', *TCWAAS*, 81 (1981), 15–25; S.E. James, 'Sir William Parr of Kendal: Part I, 1434–1471', *TCWAAS*, 93 (1993), 99–114; S.E. James, 'Sir William Parr of Kendal: Part II, 1471–1483', *TCWAAS*, 94 (1994), 106–20; 'Sir John Parr of Kendal, 1437–1477', *TCWAAS*, 96 (1996), 71–86.

[22] Early in the century a Peter de Stokhalgh was employed as keeper of the 'fortlet' at Otterburn (*CIM, VII (1399–1422)*, no. 233, p. 118; *CPR 1401–5*, 372; *CDS*, IV, no. 652, p. 137). For Redesdale before 1400, see Holford and Stringer, *Border Liberties*, 359–411.

113

Part II

Burradon, Sharperton, Farnham, Fawdon, Ingram (with its 'members' of Reaveley and Hartside) and Shirmunden.[23] Upon Umfraville's death in 1437, his estates passed under entail to Walter Tailboys, esquire of Goltho, Lincolnshire.[24] Unlike the Umfravilles, the Tailboys were absentees, although the quarrelsome William, Walter's son and heir, proved a committed Lancastrian adherent and was captured and executed after the battle of Hexham in 1464.[25] During the attainder of the Tailboys (1461–72),[26] Redesdale was granted to the Ogles of Ogle in Northumberland. The Ogles, a prominent knightly family, benefitted from their adherence to the Nevilles and Edward IV, and Sir Robert Ogle was summoned as Lord Ogle to Edward IV's first parliament in 1461. He also received grants of some other Lancastrian forfeitures in Northumberland and the stewardship of more lands, notably those formerly of the Percys. Robert, first Lord Ogle, who died in 1469, was succeeded by his second son, Owen, who was not very active.[27] The Ogles at least were resident in the county, and Redesdale reverted back to absentee ownership once it was returned to the Tailboys in 1472.[28] While most, but by no means all, of the greater landowners were absent from their lands in the marches, the resident gentry, of which many of these families are examples, assumed much local responsibility and authority, for example, serving as wardens of Roxburgh Castle before its loss in 1460.[29]

---

[23] C 139/83, no. 57; *NCH*, XV, 299.

[24] By a deed of 1437 Walter Tailboys confirmed William Clenell ['Glenhill'], esq., as constable of Harbottle, granted by Sir Robert Umfraville (Bodleian: Dodsworth MS, 49, fol. 82r). In 1438 Tailboys appointed Roger Widdrington, esq., constable of Harbottle and lieutenant of Redesdale (ibid., fol. 88v; MS 68, fol. 122r. See *Northumberland and Durham Deeds*, nos 7–8., pp. 221–2.

[25] C 140/15/49 m. 1 (Redesdale); *PROME*, November 1449, item 56; 'Tailboys, Sir William (c. 1416–1464)', *Oxford DNB*, LIII, 647–8, by R. Virgoe. In 1452 John Heron of Ford was lieutenant of Redesdale (*PPC*, VI, 125–6, 127).

[26] William's heir Robert Tailboys (d. 1495) was restored in 1472 (*PROME*, October 1472, item 17; Bodleian: Dodsworth MS, 49, fol. 81; *Northumberland and Durham Deeds*, no. 10, p. 222; Hodgson, *Northumberland*, II, i, 62–3; *CIPM*, Series 2, i, no. 971, pp. 414–15.

[27] *CPR 1461–7*, 29, 113–14, 466; Hedley, *Northumberland*, ii, 146–8; Pollard, *North-Eastern England*, 270, 285, 288, 298.

[28] On 15 December 1483 Sir Robert Tailboys appointed Richard Musgrave, esq., as his lieutenant of Redesdale (Bodleian: Dodsworth MS, 49, fol. 81v; *Northumberland and Durham Deeds*, no. 11, p. 222; *NCH*, XV, 475). In 1490 John Heron of Harbottle, esq., was bailiff of Redesdale (*CDS*, IV, 317).

[29] Wardens of Roxburgh: Sir Robert Umfraville, 1412–15 (*CDS*, IV, 163); John Burrell, esq., 1415 (*CDS*, IV, 173); Sir John Bertram and Sir John Heton, 1416–18 (*CDS*, IV, 175, 177); Robert Harbottle, 1419 (*CDS*, IV, 179–80); Sir John Bertram, 1420 (*CDS*, IV, 181–4); Sir Robert Ogle 1425–35, 1438 (*CDS*, IV, 202, 222); Sir Ralph Grey 1435–41 (*CDS*, IV, 224, 233); Sir Ralph Grey and William Neville, lord Fauconberg in the 1450s (*CDS*, IV, 260).

The Nobility, Gentry and Religious Houses

Religious houses were also important landowners in the marches.[30] As will be noted below, the palatine capacity of the bishop of Durham was of significance not only south of the Tyne but throughout the wider north, including the bishop's franchise territories in Northumberland.[31] Separate from the bishop and his administration, Durham Priory was the greatest of the marcher religious houses, with dependent cells at Holy Island, Farne Island, Warkworth and, across the border, at Coldingham.[32] Another important Benedictine house in Northumberland was Tynemouth Priory (protected by a castle), and Tynemouth itself had a cell at Coquet Island. Further west was the Augustinian priory at Hexham, within the liberty of Hexhamshire.[33] Five other Augustinian houses were to be found in the county, including the nunnery of Holystone in Redesdale.[34] The Cistercians had an abbey at Newminster near Morpeth, and houses of other orders were located elsewhere in Northumberland.[35] In Westmorland, the only significant house was the Premonstratensian abbey of Shap.[36] In Cumberland, St Bees Priory on the coast and Wetheral Priory east of Carlisle were both Benedictine dependencies of St Mary's Abbey, York.[37] Within Inglewood Forest were the Benedictine nuns of Armathwaite Priory.[38] The Cistercians of Melrose had a dependent abbey at Holm Cultram in north-western Cumberland, and, south of St Bees, there was also the independent Cistercian abbey of Calder. The cathedral priory of Carlisle was an Augustinian house, and others of the order were located at Lanercost Priory in Gilsland. In 1409 the canons of Lanercost were granted a financial exemption on account of burnings inflicted by the Scots.[39] Four years earlier, in July 1405, Henry IV made a similar allowance to Hexham Priory, impoverished by Scottish 'burning and destruction'.

---

[30] See Cardew, 'Anglo-Scottish', 35–56; Goodman 'Religion and Warfare', 245–6.

[31] See below, p. 178, and above, p. 13.

[32] Dobson, *Durham Priory*, ch. 9; Dobson, 'Last English Monks'.

[33] Holford and Stringer, *Border Liberties*, 173–203 (Hexhamshire); 203–27 (Tynemouthshire).

[34] Bamburgh, Brinkburn, Ovingham (a cell of Hexham) and Carham (a cell of Kirkham Priory, Yorks.).

[35] Newcastle (Trinitarian house of canons), Newcastle Priory (Benedictine nuns), Alnwick Abbey (Premonstratensian), Blanchland Abbey (Premonstratensian), Lambley Priory (Benedictine nuns) south of Haltwhistle, Newcastle Friary (Dominican), Newcastle Friary (Franciscan), Newcastle Friary (Carmelite), Newcastle Friary (Augustinian), Bamburgh Friary (Dominican), Berwick Friary (Franciscan), Berwick Friary (Augustinian), Hulne Friary (Carmelite).

[36] Also in Wml. was the Cistercian grange of Bleatarn, dependent on Byland Abbey. Appleby had a Carmelite friary.

[37] R. Midmer, *English Medieval Monasteries 1066–1540: A Summary* (London, 1979), 325.

[38] *CPR 1467–77*, 392. There were also Benedictine nuns at Seton Priory, near Workington.

[39] *Priory of Hexham*, ed. Raine, i, p. xcv, no. lxxiv. There were also friaries in Carlisle (Dominican and Franciscan), and Augustinians at Penrith.

Part II

Only days later Henry IV granted protection across the border to Melrose Abbey, in exchange for victuals to be purveyed at a fair price to the English garrison at Roxburgh.[40] In 1438 an English protection was issued for Coldingham Priory, in light of the 'constant depredations of the king's forces when invading Scotland and the Scots when making reprisals [so that] they have neither meat nor drink'.[41] Although they surely suffered in the path of international conflict, border religious houses also showed skilful deployment of frontier rhetoric.[42]

It should also be observed that abbeys and priories were focal points for the most prominent cross-border links within landed society, and this was particularly true of the monks of Durham and their cell of Coldingham in Berwickshire. The continued presence of this English priory in Scotland, despite more than a century of warfare, was testament to the long-standing spiritual weight of Durham's patron, St. Cuthbert, from the Tees to the Forth. Until the 1440s, the prior of Durham relied upon direct ties with Scottish magnates and lairds for Coldingham's administration. The office of bailie of Coldingham became the subject of a violent quarrel in the 1440s, and Durham's direct role in local political affairs across the border evaporated by the middle of the decade.[43] It is in the context of this dispute that we also find the only evidence for cross-border links among lay lords, which occurs in the tantalising remark of the Scottish laird David Hume of Wedderburn, in 1443, that it had been at the request of 'an noble & mighty my lorde of Northwmbre' (Henry Percy, second earl of Northumberland), that the prior of Durham had earlier granted him an exchange of lands.[44] Other religious cross-border links within landed society are revealed in the prior of Hexham's letters from 1456 in favour of George, earl of Angus, granting that the earl would be remembered in their prayers, and upon his death, as a mark of special favour, the canons would perform for him the same intercessory service as would be done for a brother of their order. This gesture is perhaps best seen as a strategic olive branch offered across the border to the recent successor to Black Douglas power in the marches, following the defeat of the latter family in a Scottish civil conflict.[45] Other such ties were maintained by Melrose Abbey, which owned tenements in English-held Berwick, which it was renting in 1442. Thirty years later, the abbot of

---

[40] '*par larsure et destruccion des Escotz*' (PSO 1/4/167). See also *CSL*, no. 410, p. 96; *CPR 1405–8*, 51; *CDS*, IV, 143; *Liber Sancte Marie de Melros*, ed. C. Innes, Bannatyne Club, 2 vols (1837), ii, no. 498, p. 473. In 1472 Melrose received a general protection from the Scottish king, James III (ibid., no. 573, pp. 591–2).

[41] *CDS*, IV, 227.   [42] See above, pp. 94–5.   [43] Armstrong, 'The "Fyre of Ire Kyndild"'.

[44] *Coldingham*, no. 160, p. 147; Brown, *Black Douglases*, 320.   [45] *Douglas Book*, III, no. 86, p. 82.

116

The Nobility, Gentry and Religious Houses

Melrose visited his dependent abbey of Holm Cultram in Cumberland, in order to supervise the election of the new abbot there.[46]

A few points from this brief survey should be reiterated by way of conclusion. The first is an extension of the point just made, about religious houses in the northern marches. Whereas the era of Anglo-Scottish cross-border landholding among the secular nobility had long come to its end, well into the fifteenth century it was the abbeys and priories of the region which retained and exercised the most significant cross-border ties of affiliation and landownership, although, as we have seen, these too dwindled out in the 1460s coinciding with the end of English control in Tweeddale and Teviotdale.[47] Second, absentee lordship was widespread, even if a number of absentees resided at no great distance in Yorkshire or the bishopric of Durham. The only magnates who were regularly resident in the marches were the Percy earls with their estates in Northumberland and Cumberland. Similarly, the Dacres were the only baronial family also normally resident and active in the marches, and thus Dacre and Percy connections with lesser men in the region as we find them in what follows are to be noted with this significance in mind. Just as in other English counties, throughout the marches there were variations in patterns of landownership, and for the lower rungs of political society some rough comparisons can be drawn with neighbouring shires. Whereas the records of oath-takers and taxpayers suggest that Westmorland and Cumberland had a relatively diffuse gentry society, and Northumberland a more concentrated one, it seems the opposite of this east–west pattern is to be found just to the south of the marches. In the bishopric of Durham, some seventy-four men took the oath of 1434, almost exactly the same number as for Cumberland.[48] And in Lancashire, indications of a county-wide gentry assembly of thirty-eight men in 1414 suggest a number almost exactly the same as for taxpayers for Northumberland in 1436.[49] The east–west and north–south differences here across these counties (and thus the proposed 'country-provinces' identified in Map 1) should not be overstated. In all, by the standards of the rest of the kingdom, these northern counties seem to have had relatively small populations of knights, esquires and more

---

[46] *Liber de Melros*, II, nos 550, 577, pp. 551–2, 596–9; *The Register and Records of Holm Cultram*, ed. F. Grainger and W.C. Collingwood, CWAAS, Record ser., 7 (1929), 149–50; Fawcett and Oram, *Melrose Abbey*, 248–9.

[47] See above, p. 59.

[48] *The Register of Thomas Langley, Bishop of Durham 1406–37*, ed. R.L. Storey, 6 vols, (Durham, 1949–67), iv, 142–3. Liddy, *Bishopric of Durham*, 68 (table 3), 70.

[49] Bennett, *Community, Class and Careerism*, 8, 50–1, 56 and 22–3, noting assemblies of sixty-three Cheshire gentry in 1412, and thirty-eight Lancashire gentry in 1414.

Part II

minor landowners. Derbyshire, noted above as a county meriting comparison in topographical terms, contained significantly more families of the same social range: 330 oath-takers in 1434 and 106 men assessed for tax in 1436, and Wright has tabulated some 167 families active c. 1430–50 in her directory of Derbyshire political society.[50] In this snapshot, Westmorland had (after Huntingdonshire) the lowest amount of taxable wealth in England, and Cumberland and Northumberland were not far behind.[51]

---

[50] See above, p. 104. Wright, *Derbyshire Gentry,* 4, 6, 9, 11, 196–202 (appendix 1), and 203–4 (appendix 2).

[51] Payling, *Political Society,* 17 (table 1.6).

5

LORDSHIP, KINSHIP AND THE SURNAMES

Wherby after the lawes and custumes of the borders of the saide reymes they haue doon and committed felonye and treason . . . all the surnames of the saide Charletons Redes hedleyes Robsons milbournes Wilkynsons Cressopes doddis hogges hunters Oblissons and ffenwykkes inhabitauntes of the saide Tynedale and Ryddysdale bere fauour socour and maynteigne the said murderers.[1]

—Patent Roll 582

The concern of this chapter is some fundamental elements of the structure of local society in the marches. At the outset we highlighted the theoretical importance of kinship and lordship in conflict management, and now we return to these themes with the goal to address directly the vague generalisations that have been made concerning 'the clannish loyalties of border society', and which build on certain (and enduring) assumptions about the strength of kinship in the region and its correlation with weak governmental structures.[2] By evaluating the importance of social relationships of lordship and kinship, the aim is to build the ground upon which to assess local conflict in the marches. More broadly, it is to explore how kinship was conceived and expressed at different social levels, beginning with landed society and then extending the analysis to encompass common inhabitants of the border shires. This discussion relies heavily for its source materials on court records, which will be introduced in the course of discussion below and more fully in a subsequent chapter.[3]

---

[1] C 66/582 m. 6d, a royal instruction for the sheriff of Northumberland to make a proclamation in 1498.

[2] See above, pp. 8 and 22–36. For example, Dunlop, 'Redresses', 348 (quote). See also Ellis, *Defending English Ground*, 40–1; Reid, *King's Council in the North*, 6; Bean, *Estates of the Percy Family*, 2–4.

[3] See below, pp. 130, 201 and 230.

Part II

LORDS AND MEN

As we have already noted, explicit contracts between lords and men in England are well known in the form of indentures of retainer. Discussions of political behaviour have often fixated on the phenomenon of 'bastard feudalism' expressed through these indentures and other less formal links.[4] By their written bonds, men pledged personal service (usually for life) in peace and war to their lord, often in exchange for a money fee. It is now well established that, far from being the means by which an ideal feudal world of military landholding was corrupted, these indentures were just one tool among many by which the vital relationship between nobles and gentry was tangibly expressed. By the fifteenth century, legislative change had long meant that English lords were no longer able to use land to make new subinfeudiations in their property.[5] While tenurial ties are seen as relatively meaningless by this time, other tangible expressions of lord–man bonds included grants of annuities or livery robes and badges, and appointment to offices of estate and household administration.[6]

The purpose of such links was to symbolise the obligation of lords to provide 'good lordship' to their followers, and some indentures stated this explicitly.[7] But good lordship viewed by one party could be unfair influence when viewed by another. Parliament sustained decades of debate over the disruptions caused by fee'd men in the fourteenth century. Retaining and the distribution of liveries was curtailed, with legislation and proclamations on the issue first appearing in 1390 and 1399, and later in 1406, 1413 and 1429.[8] At the beginning of his reign in 1461 Edward IV repeated these, but specifically made exception for the wardens of the march.[9] Two prominent wardens of this period, Richard

---

[4] See above, pp. 9–10; McFarlane, 'Bastard Feudalism', in *England in the Fifteenth Century*, 23.

[5] From the thirteenth century onwards, 'feudal' lord–man ties are considered to have only a minor residual importance, and land conveyancing is viewed almost entirely in terms of economic exchange: Jones and Walker, 'Private Indentures', 12–13. For the view that tenurial lordship (sometimes called 'mesne feudalism') retained an importance in the English far north, see Pollard, *North-Eastern England*, 96–9; Bean, *Estates of the Percy Family*; James, 'The First Earl of Cumberland', 48–9; and the contrary view by R.W. Hoyle, 'The First Earl of Cumberland: A Reputation Reassessed', *Northern History*, 22 (1986), 63–94, at 65–6, 72.

[6] Carpenter, *Locality and Polity*, esp. chs 1 and 9, and 263–77, 288; Walker, *Lancastrian Affinity*; Jones and Walker, 'Private Indentures', 12–13, 25.

[7] Notably those of William, Lord Hastings. See W.H. Dunham, *Lord Hastings' Indentured Retainers 1461–1483* (New Haven, 1955), 10, 125; Jones and Walker, 'Private Indentures', 25.

[8] G. McKelvie, 'The Livery Act of 1429', in L. Clark (ed.), *The Fifteenth Century XIV* (Woodbridge, 2015), 55–65.

[9] Exception was also made for others acting by the king's special commandment, when raising soldiers for the defence of the realm and the suppression of enemies. *PROME*, October 1399, item 84; March 1406, item 137; September 1429, item 35; November 1461, item 39; Jones and Walker, 'Private Indentures', 31–3.

Lordship, Kinship and the Surnames

Neville, earl of Salisbury (d. 1460), and Henry Percy, second earl of Northumberland (d. 1455), have been estimated to have spent, respectively, 25 and 33 per cent of their incomes on retaining, rather higher than the national average of 10 per cent.[10] However, in 1468, the statute of livery radically curtailed the practice of retaining, over which the king appears to have sought to exert control through licensing. Some of those close to the king, like Richard, duke of Gloucester, and William, Lord Hastings, continued to retain, but, after this point, the practice was to dwindle rapidly.[11] Of course, the relationships themselves continued and underwent further regulation by Henry VII.[12]

In the marches it seems that indentures of retainer (normally including a fee payment), or adaptations of these indentures, endured as an important form of new lord–man bonds at least through the 1470s, despite the fading of the practice further south.[13] In 1484–5, at least twenty-five gentry retainers were receiving fees from the earl of Northumberland's Cockermouth estates.[14] It is undeniable that the scope for military service to be included in these bonds remained a relevant consideration.[15] The point is illustrated by the career of the esquire Christopher Curwen of Workington, a Percy tenant. Within months of the fourth earl's restoration in 1470, Curwen was retained by Percy in a gathering of the affinity at Cockermouth Castle, the seat of the Honour of Cockermouth, and the esquire promised to serve his lord in peace and war for a fee. Eleven

---

[10] Griffiths, *Henry VI*, 134; Bean, *Estates of the Percy Family*, 93–4, 96–7, 106–7; Pollard, 'Northern Retainers of Richard Nevill, Earl of Salisbury', 52–69, esp. 65; Pollard, *North-Eastern England*, 260; Carpenter, *Wars of the Roses*, 56. Salisbury's retaining fees were not drawn from his salary as warden but from the honour of Penrith: Booth, 'Landed Society', 40, 43–4, 46 (and see also discussion of Percy fees at 36–7). Summerson has suggested that Salisbury's warden salary was used for retaining: *Medieval Carlisle*, II, 407.

[11] Dunham, *Lord Hastings' Indentured Retainers*, 53; Jones and Walker, 'Private Indentures', 31–3; Ross, *Edward IV*, 412–13; Hicks, 'The 1468 Statute of Livery', 15–28.

[12] D.A. Luckett, 'Crown Office and Licensed Retinues in the Reign of Henry VII', in R.E. Archer and S. Walker (eds), *Rulers and Ruled in Late Medieval England* (London, 1995), 223–38; Gunn, *Early Tudor Government*, 38–40.

[13] See Jones and Walker, 'Private Indentures', nos 99, 100, 102, 103, 105, 120, 121, 127, 128, 132, 140, 143, 144, 145. See esp. no. 148 (Lord Greystoke and John Fleming of Rydal, 1467), nos 149 and 150 (Sandford of Askham, 1468, 1469), no. 151 (Henry, earl of Northumberland and Christopher Curwen, 1470), no. 152 (Gloucester and William Burgh, 1471), no. 153 (Gloucester and Henry Denton, 1473), no. 154 (Gloucester and Henry, earl of Northumberland, 1474), no. 155 (Gloucester and Scrope of Masham, 1476). See also DL 29/648/10485 fol. 12 (mm. 12–14): Thomas Tunstall, esquire, retained by Gloucester in November 1471; Robert Clifford, esquire, retained by Gloucester in October 1471; John Redmane, esquire, retained by Gloucester in March 1473. See also Geoffrey Wharton, esquire, a royal serjeant-at-arms from April 1483, receiving by letters patent in 1484 an annuity of £10 (*CPR 1476–85*, 367, 444).

[14] CAC, Whitehaven: D/Lec 29/8.

[15] See Jones and Walker, 'Private Indentures', 22, on the decline of military service in the later fifteenth century.

Part II

years later, Curwen was knighted by Percy at Cessford ['Sefford'] in Scotland, and, no doubt, in 1482 he followed his lord to besiege Edinburgh.[16] The need to be able to call upon armed protection south of the marches was also important. The same earl's retainers whom he summoned to attend him in arms while supervising the tax collection at Cocklodge in Yorkshire in 1489 ultimately failed to preserve their lord.[17] The fifth earl's retinue found themselves drawn into a well-documented affray at Fulford in Yorkshire in 1504.[18]

The text of some indentures of retainer offers particular insight into features of the structure of landed society. Some stand out for a specific clause whereby the retained man's service to his new lord was granted with reservation to his own 'kyn or alye'.[19] It seems significant that all but one of the six surviving English indentures of retainer which include such a clause concern the north in the fifteenth century, and three of these were made by Richard Neville, earl of Salisbury.[20] In 1456 he contracted the allegiance of Richard Musgrave the younger, esquire, excepting the latter's brother-in-law, John, ninth Lord Clifford, and Clifford's own grandfather Thomas, sixth Lord Dacre.[21] A decade earlier Salisbury had indented with the Yorkshire knight James Strangeways, excepting two relatives of the earl, and the knight's 'kynne and alies ... at and within the thride degree of mariage'.[22] Two other examples excepted brothers,

---

[16] CAC, Carlisle: D/Lons/WO 8 (16 December 1470); W.C. Metcalfe, *A Book of Knights Banneret, Knights of the Bath, and Knights Bachelor* (London, 1885), 6–7. It is not known whether Curwen accompanied Percy on the French campaign of 1475 (for which Ross, *Edward IV*, 206–14). On 14 December 1470, the earl also received his tenant, John Pennington, esquire, at Cockermouth and made him bailiff of Copeland (CAC, Whitehaven: D/Pen/Family Docs Bundle A/ no. 3). The tradition of Percy service by the Curwens was strong. See Thomas Curwen, esquire (1447 lease of lands; CAC, Carlisle: D/Lons/WY 4; Ragg, 'De Culwen', 422); Christopher Curwen (1424, homage and fealty for lands within the honour: Alnwick Castle: Northumberland MSS, box 761, no. 19; printed in C.H. Hartshorne, *Feudal and Military Antiquities of Northumberland and the Scottish Borders* (London, 1858), appendix XV, no. 18).

[17] *Plumpton Letters*, no. 74, p. 84 (the earl of Northumberland to Sir Robert Plumpton, 24 April 1489). See p. 223, and M.E. James, 'The murder at Cocklodge, 28 April 1489', *Durham University Journal*, 57 (1965), 80–7.

[18] R.W. Hoyle, 'The Earl, the Archbishop and the Council: The Affray at Fulford, May 1504', in R. Archer and S. Walker (eds), *Rulers and Ruled in Late Medieval England* (London, 1995), 239–56.

[19] A point noted in Jones and Walker, 'Private Indentures', 21. Quotation from John Wensley to William, Lord FitzHugh, Yorkshire, 1433 (ibid., no. 119, p. 149).

[20] The exception is from 1297, Hardreshull-Stafford, '*mon frere, ke je forpreng sus touz autres*' (Jones and Walker, 'Private Indentures', no. 8, p. 41).

[21] Lord Dacre was an associate of Musgrave's grandfather (still living in 1456), and his daughter Joan Dacre had married Thomas, eighth Lord Clifford (ibid., no. 132; CAC, Carlisle: D/Mus/2/3 box 25, no. 123 (original); CAC, Kendal: WD/Hoth/BR, vol. 2, 375–7 (Clifford–Dacre marriage); CCR 1435–41, 263).

[22] The Neville relations were Katherine Neville, duchess of Norfolk, and Robert Neville, bishop of Durham (Jones and Walker, 'Private Indentures', no. 126, p. 156).

Lordship, Kinship and the Surnames

fathers, children and affinal kinsmen.[23] The privileging of certain kin relationships for exemption suggests that, at least in the eyes of these indenting parties, kinship trumped lordship in importance, and this merited explicit statement. What seems clear in these examples is that the creation of new ties of lordship was not aimed at establishing bonds capable of intervening between kinsmen (or 'alye', in the sense of relatives or relations). Here, kinship ties appear to be held apart as a distinctive set of relations from those between lords and the men they retained.

In the marches on the English side of the border we also find the use of the word 'manrent', which is of course best known from its Scottish context. Yet this is not surprising given the northern English origins of the word 'manraed'. Over the centuries it went through a variety of meanings in Middle English and Middle Scots, and continued to be used in England throughout the later middle ages and the sixteenth century.[24] By the late fifteenth century, in an English context the word implied the leadership of fighting men, and this is illustrated in a Cumberland arbitration award of 1497, which was concerned in part with the 'man-ryddyn of certen men' living in lands which were in debate between the parties.[25] It also appears in a Westmorland bond from 1471, between the esquire Thomas Sandford of Askham and his son William, on the one part, and, on the other, William Yate of Leadgate in Cumberland, who was almost certainly a prominent yeoman.[26] The terms of this agreement were for the Sandfords to have rule and governance and the 'manrydyn' of the place of Leadgate during their lives, for Yate to let the land and for the Sandfords to 'trewly manttene and forteffy' Leadgate as they did their own lands.[27] This was in a sense a 'bastard' indenture of retainer – a

---

[23] The first is Robert Eure, esquire to Joan, Countess of Westmorland and Richard, earl of Salisbury, Durham, 1435, 'his brother and with his children' (Jones and Walker, 'Private Indentures', no. 121, p. 151). The second is John Clibburn of Bampton, gentleman to Thomas Sandford of Askham, esq., Wml., 1469, 'except ye kynge and Rowland Clybburn hys awn fader wt all hys awn Breder and Sir Thos Curwen hys fadyr in law wt all hys chylldyr' (Jones and Walker, 'Private Indentures', no. 150, p. 174; CAC, Carlisle: D/Lons/L/Medieval Deeds/BM 119).

[24] J. Wormald, *Lords and Men in Scotland: Bonds of Manrent 1442–1603* (Edinburgh, 1985), 15–18, 419nn 7–8. For *manraed* in sixteenth-century Cumberland, see Ellis, 'A Crisis of the Aristocracy?', 331.

[25] Pennington *v.* Irton, 1497 (CAC, Whitehaven: D/Pen/bundle 23/no. 2).

[26] Sandford himself had been a Warwick retainer (CAC, Carlisle: D/Lons/L5/1/3/64, formerly AS 59).

[27] William of Yate was the son of John of Yate, heir to the place of the 'Led Yate' (presumably Leadgate in Inglewood Forest). Yate (presumably the heir to a heritable lease) was to let to farm and lawfully distrain for the farm of the 'tennantte' of the place of the Led Yate (CAC, Carlisle: D/Lons/L5/1/3/72, formerly D/Lons/MD/AS 66). See also Jones and Walker, 'Private Indentures', 32, 174n 372; Ragg, 'De Cundal, Bampton Cundal and Butterwick', 317. For the Sandford estates, see *HOP*, IV, 298–9, 299–300.

123

Part II

monetary bond used by Sandford to evade the legal restrictions of the 1468 statute of livery and still achieve a similar effect as if he had retained directly. Still it was not typical of such contracts in that it explicitly incorporated expectations of the lord's faithful protection by force, in exchange for the leadership of the local men in violence. Such relationships between gentry and their peasant tenants were normally just implicit elsewhere in England and mostly have to be inferred.[28] However, Sandford's bond is also unexpected in that it formalises his influence over a family of yeomen who were not already linked to him by tenure. In this regard, it does not resemble what would be expected further south in England. We shall return to some similar arrangements made by Sandford in due course.

KINSHIP AND LANDED SOCIETY

Studies of kinship in English landed society have tended to find a 'range of sentiment' directed to the wider kin[29] and that the strength of family alliances (as established by marriage) lay only 'in a continued interdependence of interest'.[30] No great prominence has been ascribed to the wider bonds of kinship in landed society. Yet in the parliament of 1399, no less a figure than Henry of Lancaster claimed that, through God's grace and 'with helpe of my kyn and of my frendes', he had rightfully been able to recover the crown.[31] Sir John Fortescue's famous late fifteenth-century treatise on the governance of England was critical of the nobility's counsel to the king on grounds that lords were preoccupied with 'maters off thair kynne, servauntes, and tenantes'.[32] Border magnates were certainly among those who expressed an awareness of kinship bonds. Writing to Henry IV to ask for assistance in 1400, George

---

[28] M.C. Carpenter (ed.), *The Armburgh Papers: The Brokholes Inheritance in Warwickshire, Hertfordshire and Essex c. 1417–c. 1453* (Woodbridge, 1998), 48–9; *Stonor Letters*, introduction, 19–20; Carpenter, *Wars of the Roses*, 35.

[29] E. Acheson, *A Gentry Community: Leicestershire in the Fifteenth Century, c. 1422–c. 1485* (Cambridge, 1992), 150.

[30] Wright, *Derbyshire Gentry*, 58 (quotation). See also McFarlane, 'Service, Maintenance, and Politics', in *Nobility*, 102–21; Houlbrooke, *The English Family*, 45; Carpenter, *Locality and Polity*, 260–2, 620–1; Hicks, 'Cement or Solvent?', 31–46; J.R. Lander, 'Family, "Friends," and Politics in Fifteenth-Century England', in Griffiths and Sherborne, *Kings and Nobles*, 35–7; and more generally R. Eales and S. Tyas (eds), *Family and Dynasty in Late Medieval England* (Donington, 2003).

[31] *PROME*, October 1399 (Roll), item 53. Similarly, the chronicler John Hardyng wrote of the 'great vexacion' of the 'kynne and progenye' of Richard II's queen, Isabel, sent back to France by Henry IV (*Chron. Hardyng*, 408).

[32] A few lines later this is reiterated as 'thair cosyns, ther servantes, tenantes, or such other as thai owed ffauor vnto': J. Fortescue, *The Governance of England*, ed. C. Plummer (Oxford, 1885), 145.

Lordship, Kinship and the Surnames

Dunbar, the Scottish earl of March, invoked the tie of kinship between himself and the English king on grounds that the two men were third cousins, sharing a great-great grandfather. Thus, Earl George told the king, they were kin in the fourth degree which, he qualified, 'in alde tyme was callit neir'.[33] Extended kinship was also raised by the second earl of Northumberland, in an undated letter to the prior of Durham. The earl asked the prelate to find a benefice for Henry Strother, 'our sybman', the son of the earl's 'right welbeloued squier and cousin' William Strother of Northumberland. This was a gesture of patronage in favour of a relation residing quite a step down the social scale. Such examples demonstrate the currency of kinship as a concept that was invoked at the highest levels of political society.[34] It was apparent in an urban context, too. At Berwick-upon-Tweed in 1505, the guild of the town laid down numerous local ordinances. These included the rights of the 'kinsemenne' of a freeman dying in debt, specifically, 'the most next of his kynrede' to claim any residue of proceeds from the sale of his property.[35]

In an influential study James argued that the pastoral upland regions of the north remained more kin-dependent than lowland parts of the north well into the early modern period.[36] Yet as has just been noted, the greater importance of nuclear family bonds over those to more distant kin has been emphasised for the kingdom generally, and the fifteenth-century evidence suggests that in some ways landowners across the far north were no different. In general, English gentry have been found to have placed the greatest weight on their 'vertical' kinship ties of lineage, an expression of the importance of the inheritance and possession of land. Of the Midlands gentry it has been observed that while the concept of an all-embracing extended family is unfitting, 'horizontal' kinship ties could still serve as a reservoir of supporters, where close kin acted as regular associates and more distant relatives might be called upon in a crisis.[37]

---

[33] BL: MS Cotton Vespasian, F VII, fol. 22, printed in *Royal and Historical Letters during the Reign of Henry the Fourth*, ed. F.C. Hingeston, 2 vols (London, 1860–4), I, no. 24, p. 449.

[34] DUL, DCM: Loc. XXV, no. 164 (undated). On kinship and the nobility, see Hicks, 'Cement or Solvent?', 31–46; McFarlane, 'Service, Maintenance, and Politics', in *Nobility*, 102–21; Rock, 'Shadow Royals?', in Eales and Tyas, *Family and Dynasty*, 193–210.

[35] *HMC, Report on Manuscripts in Various Collections*, i (1901), 11. See also at 9 mention of restricted actions in favour of 'hys frendes nor kensemane'.

[36] James, *Family, Lineage and Civil Society*, 19–40, 177–98. For a critique, see Gunn, *Early Tudor Government*, 6–7. Yorks. gentlemen financed the military service of their brothers and sons under Henry V (Goodman, 'Responses to Requests', 248).

[37] Carpenter, *Locality and Polity*, 260–2, 311, 620; Wright, *Derbyshire Gentry*, 51–9, 143, 147. For a clear statement on kinship by a Bucks. gentleman, see *Stonor Letters*, no. 130, p. 224. See also K. Mertes, *The English Noble Household, 1250–1600* (Oxford, 1988).

Part II

But it is in arrangements for the settlement of land that some of the clearest indications of conceptions of kinship emerge. Settlement in tail male aimed to keep lands intact and to perpetuate the family name, thus seeking to avoid the potential disaster of lands being divided amongst co-heiresses, and subsumed by their husbands' families. Male entail was unusual prior to the end of the fifteenth century, and, among the gentry, the choice to entail lands in this way was by no means universal. When a family had sufficient wealth, younger sons could be endowed with lands, thus establishing cadet branches sometimes residing at great distance from the primary estate.[38] One family from the marches illustrates the endowment of younger sons along the lines of what would be expected elsewhere in England. In 1410 the Northumberland knight Robert Ogle died, and his lands were divided between two of his sons: Robert inherited the family seat and manor at Ogle, and John took the surname of Bertram when he received the inheritance of the castle and manor of Bothal, brought into the family by John's grandmother, Helen Bertram, sole heiress of Bothal.[39] Evidently, the intention here was to resuscitate another family whose male line had expired, by allowing a younger son to inherit through the female line. In this regard, at least, the arrangement (focused on directing the inheritance of the next generation) was not at all exceptional. Other families, too, can be shown to have made provision for their living sons. The sixth Lord Dacre, for instance, a Cumberland baron of relatively humble means, sought to entail lands to his younger sons so that they might hold for life, and so that the lands reverted to Lord Dacre's heirs male upon their deaths.[40]

The northern marches do, however, produce some less usual examples which suggest that horizontal kinship ties in the border counties held greater importance for landowners than they did further south. For instance, some gentry of Northumberland took care to endow their kin of the same generation. In 1487, Sir Ralph Harbottle granted and leased some of his lands in Northumberland and in the bishopric of Durham to his brother Anthony and his wife, for their lives and the life of their heir. Similarly, in 1472, John Fenwick, the son of a Northumberland esquire, granted the manor of Gunnerton jointly to his brothers William and

---

[38] Carpenter, *Locality and Polity*, 246–54; C. Given-Wilson, *The English Nobility in the Late Middle Ages* (London, 1987), 139–42, 163–6; Wright, *Derbyshire Gentry*, 35–8, 42–4; Payling, *Political Society*, 68–73.

[39] *CPR 1405–8*, 144; *CPR 1408–13*, 116; Hodgson, *Northumberland*, II, i, 382–3, iii, 126–8.

[40] For various Dacre settlements, see Castle Howard: A.1/169, cited in Booth, 'Landed Society', 66; *CPR 1408–13*, 355; *CCR 1435–41*, 340, 342–3; *CCR 1454–61*, 327–9.

Lordship, Kinship and the Surnames

Robert for the term of their lives.[41] Furthermore, it was not just that endowment went well beyond the direct lineage, for there seems to have been a reverence for the family name as well. There are indications that landholders in the far north were concerned to restrict the inheritance of their patrimony to male heirs earlier in the century than was common further south, thus ensuring the joint survival of the family name and lands. Before 1426, Patrick Southayk of Skelton, a minor Cumberland gentleman, entailed his lands to his son William and the heirs male of William's body, and with final remainder to the son's heirs general.[42] Most extraordinary is an entail relating to the Ogle–Bertram inheritance just mentioned. In 1406 Sir Robert Ogle Sr entailed part of his mother's Bothal inheritance (excluding the castle and manor of Bothal itself) to his elder son, Robert. The entail went to Robert the son's heirs male, with remainder to his younger son John, and John the son's heirs male, and then to Sir Robert's own heirs male, and then to his right heirs, so that 'each of the said male heirs bear the name and arms of Ogle and Bertram quartered'.[43] A settlement in tail male of the Swinburne lands in Northumberland in 1378 applied a similarly explicit 'name and arms' restriction.[44]

Provision for siblings and restrictions on inheritance had an important impact on a family's cadet branches. Before 1434 Sir John Lancaster and his wife Dame Katherine set out an entail that would serve to carry their manors of Rydal and Loughrigg in Westmorland to the male heirs of various Lancaster cadets in turn.[45] This highly specific entail, going so far into the collateral male kin, demonstrates an exceptional degree of concern to enumerate and recognise the wider agnatic kinship pool.[46] Even so, the Lancasters were not the only family with a large number of

---

[41] NA, Woodhorn: ZSW 2/65, 66 (Harbottle); ZSW 2/63 (John Fenwick, son of John Fenwick of Wallington, esquire); cf. Meikle, *British Frontier*, 24–5, 174–5. The younger brothers of Midlands gentry might only expect to receive bequests of goods; see Carpenter, *Locality and Polity*, 211–15; M.C. Carpenter, 'The Fifteenth-Century English Gentry and Their Estates', in M.C.E. Jones (ed.), *Gentry and Lesser Nobility in Late Medieval Europe* (Gloucester, 1986), 51.

[42] *CPR 1422–9*, 343 (Southayk). For a comparably specific male entail by esquire Thomas Beetham of Beetham (Wml.), before 1472, see *CCR 1476–85*, no. 707, pp. 205–6.

[43] *CPR 1405–8*, 144; *CPR 1408–13*, 116.

[44] NA, Woodhorn: ZSW 1/78. For recent comment, see B. Wells-Furby, 'The Origin of the "Name and Arms" Clause and the Development of the Lineage Culture in Fourteenth-Century England', *Nottingham Medieval Studies*, 59 (2015), 77–111, at 92–3.

[45] Failing John and Katherine's heirs male, the inheritors were to be, first, Sir John's brother Robert, for life; second, John, the son of William Lancaster of Yanwath; third, Christopher, William's other son; fourth, William, the son of Robert; and fifth, William Lancaster of Hartsop. Each remainderman's heirs male had to be exhausted for the next to inherit (*CPR 1429–36*, 455). Other Lancaster cadets in Wml. included Roger Lancaster of Sockbridge. John Lancaster of Howgill appears to be the son of Sir John and his second wife, Dame Katherine (*CPR 1436–41*, 273; *CPR 1436–41*, 576).

[46] Carpenter, *Locality and Polity*, 211–15, finds different expectations in the Midlands.

Part II

cadet branches. The Blenkinsops, the Musgraves and the Middletons can all be identified with branches on both sides of the Pennines, but what is most outstanding is the apparent geographical concentration of some groups of cadets.[47] In northern Northumberland the Maners family had a senior branch of esquires at Etal, and gentlemen cadets at Cheswick, Berrington and, further south, at Framlington.[48] The Strothers, Greys and Herons all had comparable clusters of landed relatives in this area,[49] and numerous cadets can also be found among west march families.[50]

The evidence also reveals more distant kin acting together. As we shall see below, John Middleton and his mother lost the castle of Bewcastle to a Scottish force in 1401. Subsequently, as their royal pardon noted, they were able to recover it 'by the aid of God and their cousins and friends'.[51] Court records also reveal conceptions of kinship among the gentry.[52] One example of an English border gentry kin group operating together in local politics and local violence whose activities are worth looking at more closely are the Fenwicks.[53] With close ties to the Percys, Sir Alan Fenwick appears to have married no less a bride than Margaret, the sister of Henry 'Hotspur' Percy.[54] Their son and heir was Henry

---

[47] E 179/195/32 (1436 tax for Wml.); E 179/359/29 (1436 tax for Nbl.); *CPR 1429–36*, 370–413; Hodgson, *Northumberland*, III, i, 26–9.

[48] Robert Maners of Berrington and Edward Maners of Framlington: KB 27/672 rots 60, 60d, 60(a), 70; JUST 3/54/24 mm. 1–3; W.P. Hedley, *Northumberland Families*, 2 vols (Newcastle, 1968–70), II, 246–8; Hodgson, *Northumberland*, III, i, 26–9.

[49] Strother cadets were at Moneylaws, Newton and Lanton in Glendale, Bolton and Wallington (*CPR 1422–9*, 331, 361; *CPR 1436–41*, 258–9, 350; *CCR 1435–41*, 300–2; KB 27/672 rots 60, 60d, 60(a), 70; Hodgson, *Northumberland*, III, i, 26–9; *CCR 1419–22*, 152). The Greys of Heton and Wark had relations at Horton. The Herons of Ford had cadets at Coupland, Eshott, Cornhill, Chipchase, Bockenfield, Netherton and Meldon (E 179/359/29 (1436 tax for Nbl.); *CPR 1429–36*, 370–413; Hedley, *Northumberland*, II, 43–7; JUST 3/54/31 m. 6; JUST 3/54/32 m. 7; JUST 3/54/35 m. 3; JUST 3/54/36 m. 7).

[50] The Lowthers had cadets at Askham (Wml.) and at Rose Castle, Allerby ['Alwardby'] and Crookdale ['Crokedayle'] in Cbl., in addition to their senior line with lands in both counties. The Warcops of Wml. had branches along the Eden valley at Warcop, Sandford and Lammerside, and another cadet in Cbl. See E 179/195/32 (1436 tax for Wml.); E 179/90/26 (1436 tax for Cbl.); *CPR 1429–36*, 370–413; *CPR 1429–36*, 455.

[51] *CDS*, IV, no. 585, p. 121. See below, p. 245.

[52] See below, p. 294, for the Moresbys as an example of a gentry family with common members among its number.

[53] See the family description in Dendy, 'Heton–Fenwick–Denton', including 177–8 (pedigree). For the Fenwicks before 1400, see Holford and Stringer, *Border Liberties*, 339–41, 345, 351–2.

[54] Margaret Percy was the wife of Sir Alan. His father, Sir John Fenwick (dead by 1402), held Fenwick, East Matfen, Cambo, Hartington and Walker (Nbl.). His mother, Elizabeth Heton, brought lands including Lowick, Coldmartin and Ingram. Sir Alan, who was dead by 1406, had a brother, another John, who also outlived him, was knighted by Henry V in France and was active on the border (*CPR 1396–9*, 584; Bodleian: Dodsworth MS, 45, fol. 39v (10); *Northumberland and Durham Deeds*, ed. Oliver, p. 56, no. 36; *CPR 1408–13*, 383, 399; *CCR 1435–41*, 6; Neville, *Violence, Custom and Law*, 129–30, 148nn 32, 34; *CDS*, IV, no. 21, pp. 404–6; *Calendarium Inquisitionum Post Mortem*, ed. Caley and Bayley, iv, 81, no. 39).

128

Lordship, Kinship and the Surnames

Fenwick,[55] who entered Percy service in the 1430s and was involved in march administration, remaining active until his death in 1458.[56] Henry and his wife Joan (daughter of Sir William Legh of Isel) failed to produce a son. They had six daughters, all of whom married into the Cumberland gentry. However, an evident male entail took his lands to his cousin, John, esquire, the husband of Mary Strother, the heiress of Wallington in Northumberland. John Fenwick of Wallington was involved in a violent dispute in 1455[57] and seems to have had two younger brothers, Roger and Thomas, who were minor Northumberland gentlemen active between the 1420s and 1450s.[58] The Fenwicks faced misfortune under the Yorkist regime, losing part of their lands to their relations by marriage in Cumberland.[59] From the 1460s the family appears to have fallen into decline, holding land but showing no sign of their former authority. By the mid-1470s, the Fenwicks appear with blood on their hands and with renewed Percy links. Five Fenwick gentlemen were appealed in Michaelmas Term 1474 for the (undated) death of one Henry Carr. These men were Thomas and George, both lately of Littleharle (beside Wallington); Robert, lately of 'Rowley'; and Roger and Ralph, both lately of Chipchase. One of the accessories to the killing was John Widdrington, esquire lately of Chipchase.[60] Widdrington was a close associate of the fourth Percy earl, and John Fenwick was married to Widdrington's sister Elizabeth.[61] The Fenwicks were not to regain

---

[55] CCR 1422–9, 286; CCR 1422–9, 437; LOS, 98; REM, I, 38.

[56] E 179/90/26 (1436 tax for Cbl., which states he had income of £60 from that county as well as Nbl.); CPR 1429–36, 370–413; CPR 1436–41, 49, 88. Henry was linked to Lord Egremont, and supported him in Yorks. in 1453 (CAC, Kendal: WD/Ry/Box 92/Nos 93, 94; Griffiths, 'Local Rivalries', 596, 601n 3, 604; PPC, VI, 154; KB 9/149/1/6 m. 8; KB 9/149/1/11 m. 16; LOS, 27. See also KB 27/786 rot. 41; KB 27/790 rot. 125d.

[57] Following shortly after the death of the second earl at St Albans, local esquires with Percy connections arbitrated on 2 September 1455 between Fenwick and Walter Boynton, esq. (NA, Woodhorn: ZSW 2/60).

[58] John, Roger and Thomas Fenwick were jurors at various gaol delivery sessions between 1429 and 1452 (JUST 3/54/7 m. 18; 8 m. 11; 10 m. 10; 12 m. 25; 12 m. 26; 13 mm. 13–15; 14 m. 12; 16 mm. 16–17; 19 m. 20; 24 m. 2; 26 m. 10; 29 m. 8; 34 m. 9; 35 m. 3; 36 m. 7). In 1421, Roger Fenwick and John Strother were victims of sheep theft at Capheaton (JUST 3/208 rot. 23). Roger and Thomas Fenwick were active litigants in 1450 (KB 27/758 rot. 61).

[59] Bodleian: Dodsworth MS, 45 fol. 43v (62); Northumberland and Durham Deeds, ed. Oliver, p. 60, no. 55.

[60] KB 27/853 rot. 1d ('Lytill Harle'): the appeal was made by Robert, the victim's brother. The accessories included the gentleman Gerard Redde. Chipchase is near Gunnerton. See the Gunnerton grant above, at p. 126–7.

[61] Widdrington gained Chipchase by marriage (Hedley, Northumberland, II, 45, 147, 154; Hodgson, Northumberland, II, iii, 234–5). He served as sheriff of Nbl. in the early 1470s and as a Percy official. He was a knight before March 1472, although he (or a son?) appears as esquire of Chipchase in 1477, and he is mentioned in the Gloucester–Percy indenture of 1474 (for which see p. 218). CCR 1461–8, 55; CPR 1461–7, 349; CPR 1467–77, 350, 407, 463, 467, 490, 624; CCR 1476–85,

Part II

official influence before the reign of Henry VII.[62] During their period of eclipse under Yorkist ascendancy they appear to have drawn upon a concentration of cadet gentlemen for support in the course of violent action.

On the basis of the evidence reviewed here the northern marches were, indeed, more kin-conscious than parts of the realm further south. In general, disputes among the English gentry are better known for involving supporters drawn from ties of lordship and from local networks of friends than from more distant kinsmen, who were only occasionally called upon.[63] Different patterns in the far north are evident in exceptions for allegiance to kinsmen written into indentures of retainer, in the provision for distant relations in the settlement of property and in the reliance upon cadet branches within the wider cousinage in episodes of local disputing. This description seems to have been especially apt for landed families in Westmorland and in northern Northumberland. These areas of concentration will be significant when we come to a wider evaluation below, and,[64] in the chapters yet to come, we shall look more closely at the importance of such relationships in processes of violent disputing and the making of peace.[65]

NAMING CUSTOMS AND PRACTICES

The sources harnessed for this study present an opportunity to extend this discussion of aspects of kinship down, across the social boundary that separated gentry landowners from the higher peasantry who were their tenants. It is possible to examine phenomena associated with naming customs and practices in the far north, with particular regard to their implications for ideas of kinship among the yeomanry of the region. The data gathered from the gaol delivery rolls for the three marcher counties between 1401 and 1459 includes a corpus of some 6,509 names appearing in the rolls. Elsewhere I have published on the concepts of kinship which may be deduced through an investigation of these names.[66] That exercise drew guidance from onomastics (the study of proper names) and in

---

no. 129, p. 38; Alnwick Castle: Northumberland MSS (Syon House), C. VI, 2a (BL: microfilm reel 373); Hodgson, *Percy Bailiff's Rolls*, 18; Hicks, 'Dynastic Change', 83, 107.

[62] Roger Fenwick was sheriff of Nbl. in 1492–3 (*LOS*, 98).

[63] For example, see Carpenter, *Locality and Polity*, 246, 260–2, 620–5; Harriss, 'Political Society', 51; Payling, *Political Society*, 202–5; Bennett, *Community, Class and Careerism*, 220–3.

[64] See below, p. 160–3.   [65] See below, p. 292–4.

[66] See below, pp. 201 and 230; J.W. Armstrong, 'Concepts of Kinship in Lancastrian Westmorland', in B. Thompson and J. Watts (eds), *Political Society in Later Medieval England: A Festschrift for Christine Carpenter* (Woodbridge, 2015), 146–65.

Lordship, Kinship and the Surnames

particular from anthroponymy (the study of personal names) and associated customs and practices.[67] Aspects of the process by which hereditary surnames in the modern sense appeared and stabilised throughout late medieval England (a process paralleled in much of France) may be summarised briefly.[68] Such considerations are directly relevant to concepts of kinship, notably at the social boundaries of an aristocratic culture which, for some time,[69] had prized the dynastic name as one distinctive marker of noblesse and patrilineage traceable to a particular place of origin.[70] The use of hereditary surnames by the ordinary inhabitants of the realm became widely established in southern England during the fourteenth century, but this took longer in the north.[71] The process involved 'by-names', a term for designations used in addition to single personal names. Unlike a personal name given at baptism, by-names might only be temporary tools of identification, changed at convenience. The later middle ages were a transitional period, in which older by-names coexisted with newer hereditary surnames as types of *cognomina* (second names). Consequently, it is not always possible to distinguish one from the other.[72] By-names typically derived from occupations, topographical features, toponyms, the body and personal characteristics, animal names and interpersonal relationships denoting kinship (and so taking a suffix such as *-cousin*, *-son* or *-daughter*), among numerous other potential sources and combinations.[73] Employment was one such source, whereby the suffix *-man/woman* or *-servant* could indicate the relationship, as in the case of Gibbe Roderfordman, the servant of Gilbert Rutherford.[74] Less commonly, by-names could describe intimate events,

---

[67] G.T. Beech, M. Bourin, P. Chareille (eds), *Personal Names Studies of Medieval Europe: Social Identity and Familial Structures* (Kalamazoo, MI, 2002); D.W. Sabean, S. Teuscher and J. Mathieu (eds), *Kinship in Europe: Approaches to Long-Term Development (1300–1900)* (New York, 2007).

[68] P. Beck, 'Personal Naming among the Rural Populations in France at the End of the Middle Ages', in Beech, Bourin and Chareille (eds), *Personal Names Studies*, 143–56, at 144–5, 153.

[69] Work reassessing the accepted timeline of a 'patrilineal turn' in European kinship (formerly concentrated in the eleventh century, more recently placed c. 1400–c. 1700) is surveyed in D. W. Sabean and S. Teuscher, 'Kinship in Europe', in Sabean, Teuscher and Mathieu (eds), *Kinship in Europe*, ch. 1, at 4–6 and 10.

[70] D. Crouch, *The Birth of Nobility: Constructing Aristocracy in England and France, 900–1300* (London, 2005), chs 4 and 5. See the further works cited in Armstrong, 'Concepts of Kinship', 153.

[71] P.H. Reaney, *The Origin of English Surnames* (London, 1967; repr., 1991), introduction. On the English north, see P.H. Reaney, *A Dictionary of English Surnames* (3rd edn, London, 1991), l–liii; D. Postles, *The North through Its Names: A Phenomenology of Medieval and Early-Modern Northern England* (Oxford, 2007).

[72] R. McKinley, *The Surnames of Lancashire* (London, 1981), 3.

[73] Postles, *The North through Its Names*, esp. 7–9, 72, 163; Reaney, *Dictionary of English Surnames*, xix, l–liii; McKinley, *Lancashire*, 3, 322–36; G. Redmonds, *Yorkshire, West Riding* (Chichester, 1973), 9–69.

[74] KB 9/1056 m. 23: '*Gilbertus seruiens Gilberti Roderford alias dictus litill Gibbe Roderfordman de Werk*'.

Part II

perhaps best illustrated by John Twysontheday, an English harper who received a pardon in 1411.[75] All of these different types of by-names could become 'frozen' into hereditary usage as a modern surname, but by-names in the late medieval north retained a flavour that was 'transient and ephemeral'.[76] The appellation 'Agnes Huchunsondoghter', captures this complexity.[77] Patronymic naming patterns varied significantly throughout late medieval England. Postles's study of this period argues that the most significant onomastic feature of the six northernmost counties was the proliferation and intensity of patronymic and matronymic forms of by-name and surname with the suffix '-son', which are sometimes known as filial names.[78] In work along the same lines another scholar found more '-son' names in Lancashire than in Yorkshire, with the highest numbers in Lonsdale hundred in northern Lancashire, adjacent to Westmorland.[79] It is worth highlighting that these '-son' names (appearing in manor court rolls or lay subsidy records) are not Latinate but vernacular forms incorporated into Latin text. The usual result – one variation familiar to documentary researchers – is a hybrid form (e.g., 'Johannes Nicolson') in which the forename is rendered in Latin, and the second name rendered in the vernacular.[80] All this complexity gives significant grounds for caution in the interpretation of names, not least when using them as a basis for study of kinship.[81] However, it offers potential avenues through which to explore patronymic naming patterns and the conceptions of kinship that they might imply or express.

The corpus of names from the gaol delivery rolls reveals that, across the collection, *cognomina* ending in '-son' appeared at a remarkable rate of just under one in four (1,593 names from a total of 6,509). Westmorland closely matched this overall average, while Cumberland had a slightly higher rate, and Northumberland a slightly lower one.[82] Of course, it is

---

[75] *CPR 1408–13*, 252.   [76] Reaney, *Dictionary of English Surnames,* l, writing specifically of Yorks.

[77] *CIPM XXII 1422–7,* no. 306, p. 284 (a tenant at Brough Sowerby in Wml., 1421).

[78] Postles, *The North through Its Names,* ch. 2, esp. 34, 222; D. Postles, *The Surnames of Leicestershire and Rutland* (Oxford, 1998), 19; Reaney, *Origin of English Surnames,* 87; Redmonds, *Yorkshire, West Riding,* 29–31, 36.

[79] McKinley, *Lancashire,* 331–2; Reaney, *Dictionary,* xxi, l–lii.

[80] Compare the purely Latinate form '*Robertus filius Symonis filii Rogeri*' (*sic*) in northern Cheshire in 1360, as well as the appearances of a single person variously as '*Wadkyn del Haghe*', '*Waltero filio Radulfi*', and '*Watkyn Rowessone*': *Extent of the Lordship of Longdendale 1360,* ed. J. Harrop. P. Booth, and S. Harrop (Record Society of Lancashire and Cheshire, 2005), 2–3, 95.

[81] J. M. Bennett, 'Spouses, Siblings and Surnames: Reconstructing Families from Medieval Village Court Rolls', *Journal of British Studies,* 23 (1983), 26–46, esp. 36–40.

[82] The overall rate by person was 24.47 per cent (1,593 out of 6,509). The rates by county were: Wml., 25.26 per cent (261 out of 1,033); Cbl., 28.50 per cent (632 out of 2,217); and Nbl., 21.47 per cent (700 out of 3,259).

Lordship, Kinship and the Surnames

impossible to determine to what extent these '*–son*' names were being used either as patronymic by-names or as stable, hereditary surnames. However, it is possible to identify particular cases appearing in the rolls with circumstantial evidence of genuine patronymic usage. For instance, of just six such suggestive occurrences from Northumberland, one featured William Andreson of Tynedale, alias William Stokhalgh, the son of Andrew Stokhalgh.[83] Here we find what appears to be a patronymic by-name and a hereditary surname used interchangeably. Other Northumberland cases included Little ['*Parvus*'] William Robson, son of Robert Joly, and John Johnson, the son of John Thomson, which are doubtless clear examples of patronymic usage.[84] But these are uncommon in the east, where a much more typical example of a hereditary *cognomen* is that of John Atkynson, son of William Atkynson, a serf from the liberty of Norham manumitted in 1434 so he could become a priest.[85] Occurrences offering internal guidance on genuine patronymic usage appear more frequently west of the Pennines.[86] In Cumberland we find similar examples of usage, like Thomas Johnson, son of John Thomlynson.[87] That county also produced further occurrences of names used interchangeably, like William Marsshall alias William Adamson, and some examples of two-part compound names such as John Thomson Hartlawe, the latter suggestive of a patronymic element.[88] Of the three counties considered, Westmorland presents by far the highest rate of cases with such internal evidence for genuine patronymic usage. It also provides examples of two-part compound names, such as those used by the tailor William Robynson Hynne and the yeomen Richard Jakson Lambee and John Richardson Wynter.[89] Such compound names, it is

---

[83] JUST 3/199 rot. 17.   [84] JUST 3/191 rot. 52 (Johnson); JUST 3/208 rot. 24 (Robson).

[85] *Register of Thomas Langley*, ed. Storey, iv, 126.

[86] The rates for such cases by county were: Wml., 11.42 per cent (36 out of 315); Cbl., 24 per cent (29 out of 894); Nbl., 0.44 per cent (6 out of 1,357). As these numbers are by case, not person, they include examples where one individual person might appear in two or more different cases.

[87] JUST 3/191 rot. 59d (Johnson). Another is the miller William Henryson, son of Henry Milner (JUST 3/199 rot. 26d), and also John Wilson, son of William Symson, accused with William Symson his brother (JUST 3/184 rot. 16d), which suggests some fluidity of usage, sibling to sibling.

[88] JUST 3/208 rot. 39d (Marsshall); JUST 3/191 rot. 57 (Hartlawe). See also John Wilson Shephird, yeoman (JUST 3/208 rot. 44d) and John Wylson Shepherd and John Wylson Bernard, tenants at Blindcrake in Cbl. in 1439: *CIPM XXV 1437–42*, no. 250, p. 180. For compounds of this type, see McKinley, *Lancashire*, pp 325–36.

[89] JUST 3/211 rot. 47d (Hynne); JUST 3/208 rot. 47 (Lambee, Wynter). Men from just across the county boundary in Lancs. appearing in Wml. cases also used compounds: Robert Thomson ffleccher, Thomas Robynson ffleccher, both yeomen from Yealand Conyers, and William Thomson Milner, yeoman, and Richard Thomson Milner, miller, from Priest Hutton (JUST 3/211 rots 49–49d).

Part II

reasonable to conjecture, described a family relationship by adding a patronym to a hereditary surname, in order to assist identification.[90]

My examination of concepts of kinship found that Westmorland was also the county which produced the highest rate of compound names with 'double patronyms', that is to say, names written in the form 'William Atkynson Dykson'. The corpus of gaol delivery material produces such occurrences only in Westmorland and Cumberland – none in Northumberland.[91] Upon closer scrutiny the intended meaning of such double patronyms is difficult to discern. They do not appear simply to involve a patronym added like a nickname (what came to be known as a to-name in the borderlands) in the examples just given, which is the solution proposed by one writer.[92] The interpretation of these names concerns the direction in which the double patronyms should be read. Drawing especially on the information given in the name Idonia Johndoghter Amyson and on the names of apparently related yeomen listed together in some cases, my argument is that the intended direction of reading in such compounds is *forwards* with the text. In this way the name itself becomes a pedigree: Idonia is John's daughter, and John is Amey's son.[93] Furthermore, I argue that these name forms are suggestive of fundamental incongruities in concepts of kinship and family that have been established for England as a whole, over and above more superficial regional variations detected in other studies.[94] What such multiple patronymic elements in the form of names like Thomas Johnson Atkynson suggest is the existence and social recognition of agnatic descent groups of patrilineal cousins among the upper peasantry, which were reckoned through such naming practices.[95] Such a descent group would count its parentage back two generations, to a common grandparent.

All this matters for a few reasons. Such a shallow, horizontal kin group would encompass one's first cousins by that grandparent, rather than any more widely extended network of relations. Patronyms derived from masculine forenames are represented in the preponderance of cases identified, which suggests that the descent group recognised in this formulation shared a common paternal grandfather, and so consisted of

---

[90] See Armstrong, 'Concepts of Kinship', 155, for several Ruds of Sandford, Wml., who used added patronyms.

[91] The rates for such persons by county were: Wml., 4.55 per cent (47 out of 1,033); Cbl., 0.81 per cent (18 out of 2,217); Nbl., nil.

[92] Summerson, 'Crime and Society', 119.

[93] CAC, Whitehaven: D/Pen/Bundle 29/15, from Seaton in Cbl.; Armstrong, 'Concepts of Kinship', 157.

[94] Armstrong, 'Concepts of Kinship', 148.

[95] He appears with the double patronym in the roll, JUST 3/208 rot. 50, and without a double patronym in the corresponding jury list, JUST 3/70/10 mm. 2–3.

Lordship, Kinship and the Surnames

the patrilineal first cousins. Furthermore, from the examples detected, this phenomenon was concentrated among the yeomanry, the social level from which were drawn gaol delivery jurors and mainpernors, as well as minor officials of landed estates and participants in local transactions.[96] The evidence suggests that west of the Pennines, and especially in Westmorland, double patronyms were one hallmark of independence among the peasant elite. Although by no means used by all, it was a practice prevalent enough to serve simultaneously to indicate ungentle status and to confirm a role in the lowest rung of political society. By the same token, what indications survive are that those who would assert tenuous gentle status chose to drop the double patronym and adopt a fixed family name. There are implications in these findings for our understanding of the social structure of late medieval England. It would appear that multiple concepts of kinship operated at the threshold of gentility in this area. The members of political society who used or recognised double patronyms as name forms thus navigated between local conceptions of kinship (which emphasised the cousinage who shared a grandfather) and national ones (which prised the paternal lineage). For our understanding of kinship in the far north there are implications too. This indicates some diversity and perhaps unexpected complexity. It is no novelty to observe the importance of kinship in the region generally, but the phenomenon of double patronyms indicates that kinship across the march counties was reckoned in different ways – in this case of relatively shallow, horizontal kin groups of first cousins. This was quite different from (more familiar) patterns among the peasantry and among the established gentry, and indeed different from the Surnames which will be considered presently.[97] Furthermore the geographical concentration of evidence for this phenomenon suggests it flourished especially in *Chester–Lancaster–Furness*, which was orientated away from the Scottish border itself.[98] Whereas my study was also able to point to comparable practices much further afield (in mid- and western Cornwall), additional occurrences can now be observed. These arise in deeds dating between 1370 and 1450 in the south-west of Cheshire (at Edge and Malpas) and thus further reinforce the impression of a

---

[96] For instance, see *The Duke of Norfolk's Deeds at Arundel Castle*, ed. H. Warne, 2 vols (Chichester, 2006–10), i, 159 (CW 301), for 'John Wilson Addeson of Overton' among witnesses to a Dacre transaction in Wml. in 1449.

[97] Armstrong, 'Concepts of Kinship', 152, 157–8, 161–3, 165.

[98] See Map 1 and above, p. 42. Similar examples from Cbl., Lancs., Yorks. and Durham can be found: Postles, *The North through Its Names*, 48, 61–2; Reaney, *Dictionary*, xxi, l–lii; Reaney, *Origin*, 88; Redmonds, *Yorkshire, West Riding*, 33; McKinley, *Lancashire*, 325–36; Summerson, 'Crime and Society', 119.

Part II

concentration in the *Chester–Lancaster–Furness* area.[99] For example, one David Jonesson Wylmesson was the recipient in 1424 of a grant of which he had previously given to trustees. Here it is worth noting that several of the bearers of such names in Cheshire were not merely tenants but the holders of lands in fee.[100] Further work on this phenomenon is required, but for present purposes it serves helpfully to complicate our picture of how kinship was reckoned at the boundary between gentility and commonalty in the marches. In this regard, part of the far north displayed a strong expression of the strength of kinship ties among patrilineal first cousins among the upper yeomanry, but it did so in a way which is not yet well understood and whose parallels in other, especially western, areas may yet reveal stronger similarities than differences with other parts of the kingdom.[101]

THE SURNAMES

The patronymic naming patterns we have observed demonstrate the importance of kinship in local society, but they also suggest that the concept of a wider kin group sharing a surname was irrelevant for many. Still, some of the evidence just reviewed clearly shows the use of apparently stable surnames among the peasantry of the marches, sometimes alongside patronymic by-names. All the same it should be noted that the importance of the wider kin is downplayed as much amongst the peasantry as amongst landed society in discussions of English kinship.[102] By contrast the Anglo-Scottish marches are well known for a particular type of kinship grouping, the notorious riding Surnames, so prominent in sixteenth-century evidence.[103] For the Surnames the use of a hereditary *cognomen* or second name was an important sign of membership in a wider agnatic kin group. Their presence in the Northumbrian liberties of Tynedale and Redesdale has been emphasised, but so has the existence of

---

[99] Cheshire Archives and Local Studies: DCH (Cholmondeley of Cholmondeley)/C/25, 26, 28, 38 and 339; also DCH/B/21 and 22; accessed through TNA online catalogue, *Discovery*, http://discovery.nationalarchives.gov.uk; accessed 9 September 2014. I am grateful to Matt Tompkins for alerting me to the Cholmondeley references. There are also occurrences from Wales that have been noted: O. Padel, 'Names in -*kin* in Medieval Wales', in D. Hooke and D. Postles (eds), *Names, Time and Place: Essays in Memory of Richard McKinley* (Amersham, 2003), 117–26.

[100] Cheshire Archives and Local Studies: DCH/C/38 (accessed via TNA online catalogue as above).

[101] Armstrong, 'Concepts of Kinship', 159.

[102] Studies of the peasantry focused further south have generally downplayed the wider kin group. For example: R.J. Faith, 'Peasant Families and Inheritance Customs in Medieval England', *Agricultural History Review* 14 (1966), 77–95; Smith (ed.), *Land, Kinship and Life-Cycle*; Fleming, *Family and Household in Medieval England*, 76–9.

[103] See above, pp. 22–5.

136

Lordship, Kinship and the Surnames

similar groups like the Nixons in northern Cumberland.[104] This turns our attention northwards, geographically to *Carlisle-Solway*, and *Newcastle-Durham*, towards the border with Scotland.[105] Indeed, the riding Surnames are best understood as a cross-border phenomenon. They are clearly evident in Scottish records from the sixteenth century, and more generally they fit well into wider patterns of kinship familiar in lowland Scotland.[106]

The earliest known use of the term 'Surnames' with reference to the border kin groups on either side of the marches occurs in 1498. In that year, Henry VII commanded the sheriff of Northumberland to proclaim certain truce-breakers as outlaws, and charged the 'surnames of Charletons, Redes, Hedleys, Robsons, Milbournes, Wilkynsons, Cressopes, Dodds, Hogges, Hunters, Oblissons and Fenwykkes, dwelling in Tyndale and Redesdale' to deliver the outlaws they were sheltering to the authorities.[107] The Surnames have often been equated with 'clans', but the latter is a not a word (translated from the Gaelic *clann*) which appears in fifteenth-century records relating to the marches, in England or Scotland. Indeed, although 'freindis and surname' are terms which appear in a bond made in Edinburgh in 1455, the word 'Surname' used in the border sense has not been found in Scotland earlier than 1516.[108] John Hardyng's usage in his *Chronicle* might be expected to offer some insight into this terminology in the borderlands in our period. Interestingly, Hardyng deploys the term 'surname' but he uses it by reference to the epithets for figures from Monmouth's *Historia* (such as Brutus Greneshilde) or to the dynastic name (Montagu) of his contemporary nobleman Thomas, fourth earl of Salisbury. As for himself, he recorded that his 'booke' he called 'after my name Hardyng', which is suggestive that in his conception 'surname' might well be a term to be reserved especially for the appellations of magnates and kings (in a sense similar to the terminology of the 'noble howses and blodes of Lancastre and York'

---

[104] James, *Change and Continuity*, 6–9; James, *A Tudor Magnate and the Tudor State*, 10–11, 30; Ellis, *Tudor Frontiers*, 60–76; Etty, 'A Tudor Solution'; Etty, 'Neighbours from Hell'.

[105] See Map 1 and above, p. 42.

[106] Rae, *Administration of the Scottish Frontier*, 6–7; Groundwater, *Scottish Middle March*, 52–62.

[107] C 66/582/ m. 6d, also calendared in: *CPR 1494–1509*, 160; *CDS*, iv, pp. 331–2, no. 1649. The king's order evidently followed upon a recent border diet (NRS: AD 1/83).

[108] Limited work on English border Surnames before the sixteenth century includes Tuck, 'Richard II', 27–30; Ellis, *Tudor Frontiers*, 60–76; R. Robson, *The English Highland Clans: Tudor Responses to a Mediaeval Problem* (Edinburgh, 1989); E. Charlton, *The Memorials of North Tynedale and Its Four Surnames* (Newcastle, 1870). Holford and Stringer, *Border Liberties*, 328, did not find 'any allusion to such solidarities' before 1400. For 'Surname' used in 1516 in Scotland, see the documents cited in Armstrong, *Liddesdale*, I, 206–8. For 1455, see *Charters and Other Documents Relating to the City of Edinburgh. A.D. 1143–1540*, ed. J.D. Marwick (Edinburgh, 1871), 79.

137

Part II

as recalled in a decree of excommunication in 1487).[109] Thus in the early fifteenth century the term had not yet obtained the sense it carried when, in an English judicial bond of 1506, 'surname' appears as a synonym for 'clan'.[110] The first clear reference to the riding Surnames in 1498 also directly links them with Tynedale and Redesdale, areas which (as we shall see in Chapters 7 and 8) produced troublemakers in the fifteenth century. Long before this date there are a number of complaints and orders issued that, like one from 1447, cite the 'evildoers, robbers and highwaymen dwelling in the lordships of Tynedale and Redesdale, who mutilate, rob and slay the people thereof'.[111] However, in none of these examples are specific trouble-making kin groups identified. The origins of these groups have been a matter of conjecture.[112] Work on the surviving records of the gaol delivery sessions for the English marcher counties has detected isolated occurrences of apparent antecedents of these sixteenth-century Surname groups, notably, certain men of the name of Elwald in Cumberland.[113] Much stronger fifteenth-century evidence can be found for the activities of those going by the Surnames listed in 1498, suggesting that these kin groups were already well established by the reign of Henry VII even if the terminology of the riding 'Surnames' had not yet taken hold. Historians have tended to regard the social status of the Surnames as common rather than landed, although members of certain Surnames such as the Grahams in northern Cumberland were clearly landowners in their own right.[114] Thus there is an unresolved question of who led these apparent Surnames. Some were entirely made up of gentry, most were purely common, but, in some cases, there were mixtures of the two, encompassing members across a wide spectrum of social status. In such cases, it would be natural for the

---

[109] *Chron. Hardyng,* 50, 65, 95, 106, 117, 247, 273, 387, 422 ('my name Hardyng'). *Register of Thomas Rotherham, Archbishop of York 1480–1500,* ed. E.E. Barker (Torquay, 1976), 221.

[110] *Cata. Deeds,* iii, 497 (D 790). For the 'clannis and surnaimis of Armstrang and Tailzour' (in 1517), see *Registrum Secreti Sigilli Regum Scotorum,* ed. M. Livingstone et al., 8 vols (Edinburgh, 1908–82), i, p. 454, no. 2904.

[111] *CPR 1446–52,* 137. In 1446, John Heron, esq., complained of cattle raids by the 'thieves of Redesdale' (*Dunelmensis, Historiae, Scriptores Tres,* ed. J. Raine (1839), appendix, 309). In 1450, the prior complained to Sir Robert Ogle about thefts by men under Ogle's rule in Redesdale (DUL, DCM: Reg. Parv. III, fol. 42v; *Priory of Hexham,* ed. Raine, i, appendix, p. cvi, note a). Further disturbances in these liberties and in Hexhamshire are noted in 1467 (ibid., ii, pp. 153–4, no. lvi) and 1474 (ibid., i, appendix, pp. cv–cvi, no. lxxxiii; *Coldingham,* 191; DCM: Reg. Parv. III, fols 117r, 159v–160r).

[112] *CPR 1494–1509,* 160 (1498). See Tuck, 'Richard II', 29–30; Tuck, 'War and Society', 51–2; Ellis, *Tudor Frontiers,* 61–2; Houlbrooke, *The English Family,* 50–1; Postles, *The North through Its Names,* 11.

[113] Summerson, 'Crime and Society', 118–19. See also Neville, 'Local Sentiment'.

[114] For instance, Etty, 'Neighbours from Hell?'. On the Grahams, see Spence, 'Pacification'.

Lordship, Kinship and the Surnames

group to seek leadership from its landed relatives. However, for wholly common kin groups, leadership would most likely have to be found elsewhere. All these questions will shape the following investigation of fifteenth-century evidence for several of the Surnames that would go on to become notorious in the Tudor period. Two groups are to be examined: the first consisting of some of those Surnames listed in 1498, the second of certain English Surnames with notable Scottish dimensions.

THE SURNAMES OF 1498

Among the first group, the first and the last of the Surnames identified in 1498 both stand out as the *cognomina* of prominent gentry. We have already seen that the Fenwicks were close Percy adherents tied to the Lancastrian regime and that their standing fell drastically with the advancement of the Nevilles under Edward IV. They are found committing violent offences in a group of gentlemen who were apparently related in and near Tynedale in the 1470s, still maintaining links to the Percys.[115] Like the Fenwicks, the Charltons were prominent and long-established gentry in the liberty, active in North Tynedale since the thirteenth century.[116] One William Charlton was involved with the earl of Northumberland in the administration of a judicial duel in Tynedale in 1398–9. Then, in 1408, the esquire Walter Charlton was found in the court of common pleas. About the 1420s a draper named William Charlton was to join the Berwick garrison under the second earl of Northumberland.[117] After this point in time, references to the name dwindle, but those which do occur point to minor gentlemen or very prominent yeomen. These include John Charlton, bailiff of the lordship of Redesdale in 1440; Richard Chearleton, a joint lease-holder of Fourstones in the Percy barony of Langley in the mid-1470s; and John Carlton, serving the Percys as bailiff of Alnwick barony in 1482. In the next decade, the brothers Alexander and George Charlton were accused

---

[115] See above, p. 128.

[116] For the Charltons before 1400, see Holford and Stringer, *Border Liberties*, 254, 268–9, 272, 283, 336n, 347. Throughout the fifteenth century, a family of minor gentlemen known as Carleton resided at Penrith: NA, Woodhorn: ZHW 1/50–96. Carleton was the name of lands near the town and in a number of other places in the county. The similarity of this name with Charlton presents an obvious danger of confusion.

[117] *CPR 1396–9*, 507; *CPR 1399–1401*, 119; *CPR 1408–13*, 8; *CDS*, V, 557. In 1395, one 'Magete' Charlton was a victim of theft in Northumberland (JUST 3/191 rot. 45), see below, pp. 184 and 306. Sir Edward Charlton, who joined Henry IV's invasion of Scotland in 1400, was probably the future fifth Lord Powys (*CPR 1399–1401*, 353).

Part II

of troublemaking in the west march.[118] In the command of 1498 several men of the name Charleton were identified specifically: William (otherwise called Willy), Hob, Sandy, George, Thomas, Percival, William (the son of William), Robert and one 'Cok Fenwyk the maugh of Willy Charleton', the latter indicative of a link by marriage between these families.[119]

Rather more can be said about the Redes. The most prominent figure bearing this *cognomen* in our period was Robert Rede, briefly bishop of Carlisle in 1396–7, although he was not apparently a native of the marches himself. This is a point which highlights some of the difficulties of this approach of identifying probable antecedents of the Surnames.[120] Among the 400 archers serving Prince John of Lancaster at Berwick in 1403 were two men with the name Rede.[121] Although there is no certainty that any of them were related, seventeen Redes appear in the gaol delivery rolls, and, of these, twelve were accused felons. Only one was from Cumberland, a John Rede of Dockray west of Carlisle, accused of depredations in 1408.[122] Different pockets of non-gentle Redes are to be found in Northumberland, especially in the north near Bamburgh and around Coquetdale and Redesdale. These Northumbrian Redes included Robert and Richard, a Thomas of Learchild (beside Alnwick), and three men from upper Coquetdale: Andrew and Alexander, both of Prendwick, and William of Flotterton, just outside of Redesdale.[123] Further south, four people of this name appeared in Newcastle, and one near Ponteland.[124] While all these different pockets of Redes appear to be non-gentle, some landowners of this name (albeit very minor figures), do appear throughout the century. For instance, one gentleman of 'Rowlay', Robert Rede, appeared as a mainpernor in Northumberland in 1418–19.[125] He may have been the same person who, among

[118] See JUST 3/54/22 m. 1d; Alnwick Castle, Northumberland MSS (Syon House), C. VIII, 1i (consulted via BL microfilm reel 358); Hodgson, *Percy Bailiff's Rolls*, 88; CDS, IV, 324.

[119] C 66/582/ m. 6d. See *OED*, s.v. 'maugh': a close male relative.

[120] 'Rede , Robert (d. 1415)', *Oxford DNB*, XLVI, 252–3, by R.G. Davies.

[121] E 101/43/26; CDS, IV, 140.   [122] JUST 3/191 rot. 59d ('Dokwra').

[123] JUST 3/199 rot. 22; JUST 3/211 rot. 27d; JUST 3/208 rots 25 ('Flotwaton'), 31, 34 (Prendwick); JUST 3/213 rot. 15d ('Leuerchild'). Richard Rede, yeoman of Etal, was accused in the *Causa de Heron*: JUST 3/54/24 mm. 2,3; KB 27/672, rot. 60. Near Bamburgh, see JUST 3/191 rots 47 (Newham), 51, 51d, 52 (Belford); JUST 3/199 rot. 23d; JUST 3/208 rots 35d, 37. The jury on an inquest by Bamburgh (1444) included Robert Rede: KB 9/245 mm. 98, 99.

[124] JUST 3/199 rots 18d ('Edderslawe'), 19 ('Hedirslawe'), Heatherslaw near Ponteland; JUST 3/211 rot. 36 (Newcastle). Husband and wife William and Alice Rede were jurors at Newcastle, and so was Thomas Rede: JUST 3/54/4 m. 4; JUST 3/54/24 mm. 5, 6; JUST 3/54/13 m. 15; JUST 3/54/15 m. 7. In 1438 and 1445, Alan and William Rede were involved in Newcastle commercial disputes: KB 27/710 rot. 51; KB 27/738 rots 29,29d.

[125] Perhaps this was the Rowley Burn or Rowley Head, in Hexhamshire: JUST 3/54/3 m. 5.

Lordship, Kinship and the Surnames

others, was pardoned in 1405 at Warkworth in connection with the Percy rebellion that same year.[126] Later, in 1474, Gerard 'Redde', gentleman lately of Kirkharle, was accused as an accessory to the killing of Henry Carr.[127] Another man with enough local standing to hold office in border administration was John Rede, bailiff to the east march warden in the early 1480s.[128] Whether these gentle Redes were related is unclear; more can be said about the most visible Rede in the 1430s and 1440s, Thomas, gentleman of Otterburn in Redesdale. He was an oath-taker for Northumberland in 1434 and a juror for the inquisition post mortem at Newcastle for the lands of Sir Robert Umfraville in 1437.[129] Also in 1434 this Thomas was accused of bringing a raiding party of twenty men from Redesdale '*armees et araies en maner de guerre*' to plunder £50 worth of animals at Houghton (near Prudhoe) from the coroner Nicholas Turpyn. Thomas was indicted with John Rede, another gentleman of Otterburn, and Alexander Rede, gentleman of 'Kirklaw', who were, in all probability, his relations.[130] The origins of this particular dispute were in claims to Turpyn's Northumbrian inheritance and more specifically the lease of twenty acres of land at Houghton.[131] These Redes were pursued in king's bench for nearly fifteen years until the crown finally dropped its suit against them (though not against their accomplices) in 1449. By this time they had obtained pardons.[132] Nicholas Turpyn's dealings with these men had been warmer in 1429 and 1431 when Thomas Rede and Robert Rede had stood as his own mainpernors.[133] Perhaps these mid-century Redes were descended from Thomas Rede 'of Redesdale' (or 'of Otterburn'), who was active as a tax commissioner in Northumberland in the late 1390s and who appeared in a bond

---

[126] *CPR 1405–8*, 76 (those pardoned included a Hunter of Guizance, Nbl., a Hall, and a Wilkinson).

[127] KB 27/853 rot. 1d. See below, pp. 219 and 305.

[128] Alnwick Castle, Northumberland MSS, (Syon House), C. VI, 2c, 4d (consulted via BL microfilm reel 373).

[129] *CPR 1429–36*, 396. The jury included Thomas Rede, John Reyde and Robert Fenwyk: *CIPM XXIV 1432–7*, no. 698, pp. 483–4.

[130] See below, pp. 213, 246–7, 250–1, 280. As coroner, Turpyn himself indicted these men (KB 9/940 mm. 23,24; KB 27/698 rots 24d, 72d; KB 27/754 *rex* rot. 5). He also petitioned for remedy (C 1/12/221), claiming that Rede's party had come to Houghton ('*iuxta* Heddan') '*en affray de tout le people dicell pais*', and took the animals to Otterburn. On the Redes of Otterburn in the earlier fourteenth century, see Holford and Stringer, *Border Liberties*, 392, 411.

[131] Thomas Rede claimed that the lands had been leased to him by William Buticom ('Botycombe'), esq., and that he also had permission to move the animals. Nicholas Turpyn claimed that he in fact held the lease of the lands: KB 27/702 *rex* rot. 56. 'William Butecom' sat on an inquest at Newcastle in 1412 (*CDS*, IV, 165) and he held the tower of Troughend, near Otterburn in Redesdale, in 1415–16: Hodgson, *Northumberland*, III, i, 26–9.

[132] KB 27/706 *rex* rot. 23d; KB 27/710 *rex* rot. 10d; KB 27/714 *rex* rot. 27d; KB 27/718 rot. 100; KB 27/722 *rex* rot. 17d; KB 27/746 *rex* rot. 13; KB 27/754 *rex* rot. 5.

[133] KB 27/674 *rex* rot. 8d; KB 27/682 *rex* rot. 17d.

141

Part II

in 1400.[134] In the command of 1498 Hob Rede and one Thomas the son of Willy Rede were identified as malefactors, although their precise residences are not specified. All this suggests that the Redes' trajectory of local significance followed an arc similar to that of the Fenwicks and Charltons, whereby they enjoyed much less prominence during the decades of Yorkist ascendancy.[135]

Hedley is the next Surname listed in the command of 1498, and five yeomen of this *cognomen* from Redesdale were, in fact, among the accomplices of the Redes in the Houghton case just mentioned. That crown suit against these Hedleys and others continued until the regime change of 1461.[136] One Robert Hedley was among a group of Umfraville retainers connected to Redesdale in 1385.[137] Behaviour more typical of the later Surnames can be detected in 1408, when one Robert Hedle was accused of leading Scots to raid cattle in Hexhamshire.[138] In the 1470s yeomen Hedleys are found as jurors in Tynedale and also as troublemakers entering Northumberland from the bishopric of Durham.[139] We can also clearly find related Hedleys committing offences together. In 1422, William Hedley and his son Thomas were tried and acquitted of stealing cattle 'belonging to the king', at their residence of Kirkwhelpington (just in Northumberland proper beyond the southeastern boundaries of Tynedale and Redesdale).[140] Perhaps this was the same William who himself was the victim of animal theft at Kirkwhelpington in 1428, or the same Thomas Hedley, yeoman, who lifted sheep from Robert Ussher there in 1432.[141] In the king's command of 1498 several individual Hedleys lead the list of offenders, including 'William

---

[134] Thomas Rede named as a royal taxer in Northumberland in 1395 (listed as 'of Otyrburn') and in 1398 (*CFR 1391–9*, 139, 265) was presumably the same Thomas Rede 'de Redysdall' who entered a bond at Haughton in Tynedale in May 1400: NA, Woodhorn: ZSW 1/110; Hodgson, *Northumberland*, II, ii, 136.

[135] C 66/582/ m. 6d.

[136] The five Hedley yeomen of Redesdale named in the indictment were John, Robert and Roland Hedle of Saynt Mareshele, John and 'Wally'/Walter Hedle of Woodburn; they were joined by John Hall of Ralees: KB 9/940 mm. 23, 24; KB 27/706 *rex* rot. 23d; KB 27/710 *rex* rot. 10d; KB 27/714 *rex* rot. 27d; KB 27/710 *rex* rot. 17d; KB 27/746 *rex* rot. 13; KB 27/758 *rex* rot. 10d; KB 27/778 *rex* rot. 18; KB 27/790 *rex* rot. 32d; KB 27/798 *rex* rot. 19d.

[137] Holford and Stringer, *Border Liberties*, 407.

[138] JUST 3/54/4 m. 1 (cited in Neville, 'Law of Treason', 14, but given in error as 'Hodle').

[139] KB 27/845 rot. 118 (1472, Roland and William Hedle from Rookhope ['Rucoppe'] in Durham); KB 9/343 mm. 70–1 (1476, Andrew and William Hedlee, jurors at Sewing Shields ['Suwynsheles'] in Tynedale). In 1455 Robert Hedle, 'turnour' of Ebchester near Prudhoe, was accused of trespasses in the bishopric (DURH 13/227 m. 18). John Hedley, yeoman, had a tenement in Gateshead in 1451 (*Cata. Deeds*, iii, 272).

[140] JUST 3/199 rot. 21d ('*tres vaccas precij xx s. de bonis et catallis domini regis apud Whelpyngton*'; '*ij stirkes precijj v s de bonis et catallis domini regis apud Whelpyngton*').

[141] JUST 3/208 rots 25d, 31d.

Lordship, Kinship and the Surnames

Hedle otherwise called Weykspere[,] Hogge of Hedle broder to the same William[,] Hob Rede [and] Crysty Mylbourne the son of Cryspy of Hedle'. The naming of the latter two men as father and son may well suggest a marriage link between the Hedleys and another family, the Milburns. It might also be suggestive of illegitimacy or of a slippery usage whereby the son adopted a different *cognomen* from that of his father.[142] However, unlike the Hedleys, men called Milburn are almost totally absent from the records consulted in this study.[143] Only one Hedley appeared in Cumberland. He was a yeoman from Gilsland who stole eight horses in 1432 and was received following his offence by the parson of Croglin.[144]

The Wilkinsons, another name on the list of 1498, are also visible in the fifteenth century. One Robert Wilkynson of Redesdale was among the soldiers defending Roxburgh in 1400. Two men of this name, William and John, were identified among truce-breakers to be arrested in 1415.[145] Wilkinsons are in evidence in Westmorland in the first decade of the century and again in the 1470s.[146] In the gaol delivery rolls, there are forty-two instances of Wilkinsons, mostly in Northumberland. A notable case from October 1420 shows several men of this name working together in animal theft. Two husbandmen, Robert and John Wilkynson, one from near to Rothbury in Coquetdale, stole eight pigs from a father and son. They were received by Thomas Wilkynson and another husbandman, at nearby Todburn.[147] The same Robert also appears to have been accused of stealing a cow in 1425, and he himself may also have been the victim of animal theft in 1421.[148] Other Wilkinsons were scattered about the county, some in Percy service.[149] The brothers Richard and Hugh Wilkynson were among troublemakers

---

[142] C 66/582/ m. 6d.

[143] The only occurrences found are for William Milburn (JUST 3/191 rot. 50), the victim of animal theft at Buteland in Tynedale in 1405; and for John Milneburn of 'Redeswod' in Tynedale, accused of theft at nearby Birtley in 1430 and released on an insufficient indictment in 1433 (JUST 3/208 rot. 30).

[144] JUST 3/208 rot. 44d. See also Peter Hedley below at p. 159.

[145] E 101/42/40; *CDS*, IV, 118 (Robert); *CPR 1413–16*, 343 (William and John).

[146] John, a juror at Appleby (Wml.) in 1408: KB 9/195/2 mm. 18, 19. See below, p. 156 (Sandford-Nobles), p. 296 (Sandford-Wilkinsons), p. 331 (Sandford-Walkers).

[147] Robert was from Garrett Lee ['Gerard Lee'] and John was from 'Greneheley' [Greenlee in Tynedale?]. By the time the principals and receivers were acquitted in 1423, John was dead: JUST 3/199 rots 20, 20d. The other receiver was William Gibson from 'Haysand', and the pig theft occurred at 'Whithale'.

[148] JUST 3/199 rots 18d (1425, theft from Alicia Elyngton), 20d (1425, victim of William Clerk and Robert Watson, yeomen, who were received at 'Newmoorehouse' by Henry Watson, father of the thief, from Roddam).

[149] Thomas was a collier from Heddon-on-the-wall in 1422 (JUST 3/199 rot. 19d). He may be the same man accused of theft in 1446 (JUST 3/211 rot. 33d); E 179/158/41 m. 2 (Robert Wilkenson constable of Warden vill, 1440), 41 m. 6 (Thomas Wilkynson constable of Fawdon vill, 1440). In

143

Part II

in the west march in 1494, and in the list of Surnames of 1498 George and Cuthbert Wilkynson are named offenders.[150] Probably an important reason for the relatively greater numbers of people to be found with this name is that it takes a common patronymic form, ending in -son, which as we have seen was familiar practice in the marches. This makes it difficult to know if any particular Wilkinson used this *cognomen* as a genuine patronymic or indeed as a hereditary second name signifying potential membership in a precursor Surname group.

The final example taken from the list of 1498 is Obilson (spelled 'Oblisson' in 1498 and now usually 'Olbison', apparently originating from a patronymic). Bearers of this name are not numerous, but those who can be located are noticeably concentrated in upper Coquetdale and implicated in illicit activities. For example, William Obylson, yeoman of 'Cleughtfeld' in Northumberland, a 'known and notorious thief', was tried and acquitted of conducting John Hunter, a Scot, back into Scotland after Hunter had burgled a house at Linshiels in upper Coquetdale, within the lordship of Redesdale, in November 1428.[151] Alwinton in upper Coquetdale was the residence of three other offending Obylson yeomen: William, Stephen and Thomas, who were tried and acquitted at different sessions for livestock thefts in the area between 1428 and 1432. Similarly, another Stephen Obylson, yeoman of 'Derhall' in Redesdale, was acquitted at the 1454 session for an alleged theft done at Burradon, also in the upper Coquet, in 1441.[152] Once again, there is no certainty that these men were interrelated, but their concentration in one area makes speculation along these lines tempting. A similar enumeration could be performed for other Surnames appearing in the royal command of 1498 – the Robsons, Cressopes (or Kershopes), Hoggs and Hunters – but this would only reinforce the impression made already, that men bearing these names in the fifteenth century are to be found in the marches, many behaving in much the same way as would their better-documented namesakes of the sixteenth century.[153]

1444, John Wylkynson appeared at the view of the body of the slain esquire Alexander Lermoth at Bamburgh (KB 9/245 mm. 98, 99). Between 1472 and 1482, William and Thomas Wylkynson served the Percys as reeves of Swinhoe and South Charlton in Alnwick barony: Alnwick Castle: Syon House MSS, C. VIII, 1i; C. VIII, 1g; C. VI, 2b m34 (consulted via BL microfilm reels 358, 373).

[150] *CDS*, IV, 324; C 66/582/ m. 6d.

[151] JUST 3/208 rot. 25d (Obylson): 'Lynscheles in Ridesdale'. Obylson was also accused of stealing cattle.

[152] JUST 3/208 rots 27 (William, 1428), 34 (Stephen, 1432); JUST 3/211 rots 31d (Thomas, 1432); JUST 3/213 rot. 14 (Stephen, 1441).

[153] See further detail given in Armstrong, 'Local Conflict', ch. 6. Also for Hogg and Hunter in the late fourteenth century, see Holford and Stringer, *Border Liberties*, 333–4.

Lordship, Kinship and the Surnames

ENGLISH SURNAMES WITH SCOTTISH DIMENSIONS

Turning now to the second group of Surnames, notorious under the Tudors but not listed in 1498, fifteenth-century evidence can be traced for the Halls, Bells, Elwalds, Armstrongs and Grahams, and some of their activities. To varying degrees, all of these *cognomina* can be shown to have had a notable Scottish dimension, with counterparts over the border. The first of these names, Hall, was quite common, making forty-eight appearances in the gaol delivery rolls. There was evidently a family of prominent merchants in Newcastle, producing a sheriff of the town.[154] Other Halls can be found elsewhere in Northumberland,[155] and between the 1420s and 1440s, Halls appear as offenders in Redesdale and upper Coquetdale.[156] Certain yeomen of this name from the bishopric of Durham were accused of trespasses committed in Northumberland in 1472.[157] Beyond the Pennines, in Cumberland, where one William Hall was a long-serving forester of the upper ward of Inglewood, several Halls from Gilsland caused trouble between 1418 and 1429.[158] Although landed Halls living north of the border in our period are not identifiable, one Nichol Hall served as Robert, duke of Albany's man of business in England in 1401.[159] An instructive indication of ideas of kinship and social status, albeit from north of the border, arises in connection with one Peter Hall 'in Newbiggin' ('in' was a Scottish territorial designation indicating this man's social status was that of tenant, not landowner).[160] In 1493 the Scottish justice ayre at Roxburgh recorded the pardon

---

[154] Richard de Hall was sheriff of Newcastle in 1431 (*CPR 1429–36*, 118; *CPR 1441–6*, 23). See below, pp. 159, 184, and 306 for Robert de Hall c. 1398.

[155] John Hall, chaplain, acted as a trustee for various gentry in Nbl.: for Robert de Clifford, 1415 (*CPR 1413–16*, 379); for Sir Thomas Grey of Horton, 1430 (*CPR 1429–36*, 56); for Sir John Bertram 1436 (*CPR 1429–36*, 595; *CPR 1447–54*, 209). Three Halls were among archers at Berwick in 1403 (E 101/43/26; *CDS*, IV, 140). See William de Halle, 1405 (*CPR 1405–8*, 127).

[156] 1430 Robert, of Raylees ['Raleye'] in Redesdale, by then dead, had allegedly stolen five cows at Alnham in 1429 (KB 9/940 mm. 23, 24). John, from the same place, was among the accomplices of the Redes in the Houghton case mentioned earlier. In 1420, Thomas de Hall of 'Fylton More', labourer and servant of Nicholas Turpyn, was accused of theft (KB 9/213 m. 59; KB 9/216/2 m. 5; KB 27/646 *rex* rots 25, 25d, 25(a); KB 27/694 *rex* rot. 18d. See also JUST 3/208 rot. 25 (1429); JUST 3/211 rot. 32 (1444); KB 27/738 *rex* rot. 53d (1445); and the killing of Henry Hall of Ilderton, at Lorbottle in Coquetdale in 1447 (*CPR 1446–52*, 136).

[157] KB 27/845 rot. 188 (John, Geoffrey Sr and Jr, Roland, and William Hall, from 'Bemysheparke', 'Sagerstaynhugh' and 'Holmesyde').

[158] William served as forester from 1408 to 1442 (*CPR 1436–41*, 150, 197; *CPR 1441–6*, 73). See JUST 3/199 rot. 30 (Henry, 1418); JUST 3/199 rot. 26 (Richard of Kingsbridge in Gilsland, 1423); JUST 3/199 rot. 26d (Thomas of Farlame in Gilsland, 1423); JUST 3/208 rot. 39 (Thomas of Farlame in Gilsland, 1429, twice).

[159] *CDS*, IV, 119.

[160] M.H.B. Sanderson, *Scottish Rural Society in the Sixteenth Century* (Edinburgh, 1982), 44, 177, 182.

145

Part II

granted to Peter. The offence of which he had been accused was the killing of an unidentified person in Jedforest described only as *unius heris* of his own *cognomen*.[161] The language of the record is Latin, so the use of *cognomen* here rather than 'name' or 'surname' is not unexpected, but *heris* appears to be a (Latinised) Scots vernacular intrusion. The word denotes a lord or chief, in the sense of Dutch *heer* or German *herr*.[162] This source suggests that by the end of the century non-landed Halls on the Scottish side of the border were presumed to recognise a leadership structure within the Hall kindred itself, even if these senior representatives of the family were not sufficiently prominent at the time to be identifiable in the surviving evidence. In Scotland the vernacular terminology of the fifteenth century – to cite examples from 1455, 1485 and 1491 – more typically referred to the *hedismen* of the borders, a term which encompassed all the local leading men, including heads of kin.[163] In this sense *hedismen* was a term synonymous with *heris*. There is evidence from the sixteenth century at least to suggest that 'headsmen' was a term adopted across the border in England.[164] What cannot be determined for the fifteenth century is whether a shared kinship, let alone shared seniority or leadership, was acknowledged between English and Scottish Halls. But it would be difficult to expect that south of the border, the idea of there being certain leading *heris* among the Halls was wholly an alien concept.

Bells also appear frequently in English legal records.[165] The only landed English Bell was William, who served as MP for Carlisle in 1416, although his background is otherwise obscure.[166] Several accused Bells are to be found in Cumberland and Westmorland, including Alexander Bell of Gilsland, accused of trespass in 1412, and Thomas Bell alias Thomas Scot, a labourer hanged for assault and theft at Dacre in 1442.[167] One Robert Bell, yeoman of Paterdale, was impleaded by Sir

---

[161] See Map 4. NRS: JC 1/1, fol. 16r: '*pro interfeccione unius heris in Jedforest ex proprio cognomine*'.

[162] *DSL*, s.v. 'here'.

[163] In 1455, an act of parliament ordered that the 'saide statutis be deliueryt to ye hedis men' of the borders (*RPS*, 1455/10/13). See also comparable terms in 1485 (*ADC*, I, 95*), and 1491 (*TA*, I, 182).

[164] For example, see Bowes and Ellerker's survey of 1541 which describes the houses of 'headsmen' in North Tynedale, printed in Bates, *Border Holds*, 49.

[165] The gaol delivery rolls contain fifty-one occurrences of Bells, thirty-five of whom were accused offenders. The vast majority (thirty-nine) came from Nbl., thirteen from Cbl., and only two from Wml.

[166] *REM*, I, 287; *HOP*, II, 179. Of course, Richard Bell, whose origins are also unclear, was prior of Durham (1464–78) and later bishop of Carlisle (1478–95): Dobson, 'Richard Bell', 182–221. In 1396–7 the chaplain John Bell was feoffee for Sir William Threlkeld in Cbl.: *Cal. Deeds*, vol. 152, 41.

[167] KB 27/606 rot. 72d (1412 case); JUST 3/211 rot. 41; JUST 3/11/14 m. 4 (1442 case).

Lordship, Kinship and the Surnames

John Greystoke in 1429. This Robert had been sheltered by the late sheriff Thomas Delamore, esquire. His possible relations Thomas and Alexander Bell were mainpernors in the case.[168] In other instances, yeomen Bells were appealed for involvement in Westmorland killings in 1445, 1447 and 1448.[169] In Northumberland, there appears to have been a concentration of Bells living in Tynedale ward, just outside the south-eastern boundary of the liberty. Two John Bells from Colwell (the senior a husbandman, the junior a herd) were accused as accomplices of Nicholas Turpyn in 1420. Thirty years later, William Bell of Kirkharle was impleaded for trespass.[170] Another Bell was a juror at Corbridge in 1451.[171] The Bells can also be found further north, including five archers at Berwick in 1403, and one serving the Percys as reeve of Alnwick Castle in the 1470s.[172] As for Scottish Bells, we have seen already that some crossed the border into England and were involved in a Northumberland kidnapping in 1420.[173] Given his alias of Scot, it is plausible that the Thomas Bell hanged in 1442 just noted above was also of Scottish origin, although he may have been normally resident in England. North of the border, the Bells comprised a large kindred focused in the west march.[174] One William Bell received a grant of Kirkconnel in Annandale from the fourth earl of Douglas between 1409 and 1414.[175] He was perhaps a relative John Bell, a Scottish prisoner held in England in

---

[168] KB 27/674 rot. 122; KB 27/682 rot. 37d; KB 27/686 rot. 43d: Alexander was mainpernor for Delamore, and Thomas was mainpernor for Robert. See also KB 9/252/1 mm. 75, 76 (William Bell of Windermere, abetted theft in 1442); KB 27/782 rots 1d, 35 (John Bell of Netherhertsop, impleaded by Thomas Baty in 1456).

[169] KB 27/742 rots 6, 26d (William of Crook in Kendal and William of Windermere, 1445–6); KB 27/746 rot. 2 (William, Roland and Robert of Applethwaite, 1447); KB 9/385 mm. 23, 24 (John Bell of Staveley, 1488). Edward Bell of Paterdale was accused in 1491 of trespass with Richard Threlkeld, gentleman: KB 27/921 rots 5d, 72.

[170] KB 9/213 mm. 58, 59; KB 9/216/2 mm. 4, 5 (John Bell Sr, husbandman and John Bell Jr, herd); KB 27/758 rot. 61 (William Bell of Kirkharle). For Bells in Newcastle, see KB 27/738 rots 29, 29d; KB 27/650 rot. 49. See also C 1/47/145 (Thomas Bell). The lay subsidy of 1336 had taxed certain Bells living in Redesdale also with lands outside the liberty: Holford and Stringer, *Border Liberties*, 382n 92.

[171] KB 9/265 m. 161, for Patrick Bell, juror at Corbridge, 1451. The other jurors were Roger, John, William and Roland Vssher; Roland Elryngton; William Shafthowe; Thomas Armstrang; George Story; John Redle; William Restowe; and Robert Chetson.

[172] Archers: E 101/43/26; *CDS*, IV, 140. Lionel Bell, merchant of North Shiels, victualed Berwick in 1487: *CPR 1485–94*, 139; *CDS*, IV, 312; Richard Bell, juror in 1445 at 'Emyldon': KB 9/252/1 mm. 9, 10, 11; Matthew Bell was the reeve of Alnwick Castle: Alnwick Castle: Syon House MSS, C. VI, 2a (consulted via BL microfilm reel 373); Hodgson, *Percy Bailiff's Rolls*, 1, 87. See also Alan Bell killed in 1444: *CPR 1441–6*, 228.

[173] JUST 3/199 rot. 17. See p. 257n 93.

[174] For a fuller account of the Scottish Bells, Elwalds, Armstrongs, Grahams and others, see Armstrong, 'Local Conflict', 247–55.

[175] *RMS*, II, no. 85, p. 16 ('Kirkconveth').

147

Part II

1422, and of the esquire Adam Bell, who followed the earl of March into English allegiance before 1409[176] and whose name is evocative of an early fifteenth-century ballad.[177] William of Kirkconnel appears to have been the most prominent Bell at the time, and he and his sons may be the five Bells who witnessed an instrument in Annandale in 1432.[178] Others appear with landed interests in the same lordship in 1450.[179] Several Bells emerge in Scottish financial records for justice ayres in the west march in the later 1450s and 1460s, and many of these men are given territorial designations suggesting that they held land, if only in small parcels.[180] For instance, in the Annandale ayre held in 1464–5, it was recorded that several landed Bells had paid fines at the ayre; others were listed without a territorial designation.[181] Still more Bells are to be found in the marches as clerics, and one nun of Eccles convent near Coldstream was a Bell who entered English allegiance in 1409.[182] Although there is no explicit recognition of a common kinship, the Scottish Bells typify a kindred in that realm with a large number of minor landholders and non-landed members. They were concentrated in the west march but were not confined there.[183] Some can be seen to have crossed the border for various reasons, including nefarious deeds. Although their English

---

[176] The prisoner John Bell was held by Geoffrey Lowther: *CDS*, IV, 184. Adam received a pardon for abetting the men of the exiled George Dunbar, earl of March, in an affray in Lincolnshire in 1407. He was then called Dunbar's esquire. Later he received an annuity as the English king's liege esquire. See *Select Cases in the Court of King's Bench under Richard II, Henry IV and Henry V*, ed. G.O. Sayles (1971), no. 43, pp. 187–9; *CPR 1405–8*, 332; *CPR 1408–13*, 115; *CDS*, IV, 150, 158.

[177] On the ballad, see S. Knight and T.H. Ohlgren, 'Adam Bell, Clim of the Clough, and William Cloudesley: Introduction', in Knight and Ohlgren (eds), *Robin Hood and Other Outlaw Tales* (Kalamazoo, MI, 1997); Summerson, *Medieval Carlisle*, ii, 432–3.

[178] *Calendar of the Laing Charters, 854–1837*, ed. J. Anderson (Edinburgh, 1899), no. 109, p. 28.

[179] *RMS*, II, no. 297, p. 67; *HMC, 15th Report*, appendix, part VIII, no. 129, p. 64.

[180] Minor landed Bells were fined in the 1458 and 1459 ayres at Dumfries, including Richard of 'Sedehill', David of 'Maynezhill', William of Albie ['Aldby'], John of Blackethouse ['Blakwod-house'], Richard of Allerbeck ['Ellyrbek'], Thomas of 'Bagthropill', Thomas of 'Kowholm', David of Middlebie ['Middilby'], William of Wauchopdale and William of 'the Crag'. John Bell and John Bell Jr were also mentioned without a designation (*ER*, VI, 552–6, 557–8).

[181] John of Blackethouse, Walter of Middlebie and Richard of Allerbeck, mentioned in the preceding note, made composition. Named here for the first time were also Thomas of 'Culness' and William of Dryfe ['Driff']. Others who composed were David Bell Wagfute, John Bell Prestmache, William Bell Watsone, David Bell and William Bell. Richard Bell, who had nothing to distrain, was fined £20 (*ER*, VII, 310–12).

[182] John Bell, notary, drew up an instrument at Dumfries in 1469 (*RMS*, II, no. 976, p. 202), and William Bell was rector of Upsettlington in Berwickshire c. 1467–88 (*RMS*, II, nos 924, 941, 1773, pp. 193, 196, 375). For Emma Bell, nun of Eccles, see *CDS*, IV, 159.

[183] In 1451 Thomas Bell travelled abroad in the entourage of the earl of Douglas (*CDS*, IV, 250). In 1495, see also David, Patrick, Nicholas, William and George Bell, and Thomas Bell of 'Kyrk-connel', David Bell of Pennersaughs ['Pennersax'] and John Bell of 'Thoftgatis' in Annandale (NRS: AD 1/81).

Lordship, Kinship and the Surnames

counterparts were numerous, the most prominent Bells in the marches appear to have lived north of the border.

Elwald (a variant of Elliot) is a second additional Surname. The Elwalds present some of the most indicative evidence for a kin group of mixed status engaged in illicit activity in the English marches, chiefly in northern Cumberland.[184] The most prominent man of this name early in the century appears to have been William Elwald, gentleman of Gilsland, tried for animal thefts in 1426 and 1429. This William would have been a tenant of Thomas, Lord Dacre, who held the barony of Gilsland. After a relatively meagre theft in 1389 of two oxen and cows south of Carlisle, Little ['*Parvus*'] Richard Elwald harboured the thieves Thomas Elwald and one-eyed ['*monoculus*'] William Elwald, who were his probable kinsmen.[185] Another instance of Elwalds supporting others of the same name comes from a case tried in 1434, in which William and Robert Elwald, yeomen of Walton, were accused of receiving Thomas Elwald and another cattle thief eleven years earlier. They were acquitted since the principals were now dead. These accused men had been released on mainprise in 1429 to the yeomen William Elwald of Triermain and Alexander Elwald of Askerton.[186] Other English Elwalds from Gilsland were alleged to have stolen animals in 1406, 1434 and 1446.[187] Only two men of this name can be found in the other border counties.[188] In 1461 three other yeomen Elwalds from Cumberland were impleaded for trespass: Robert, of 'Crosbygyll', and Gilbert and Andrew, both of 'Nulandes' – possibly referring to Newlands across the Scottish border in Liddesdale.[189] The English gaol delivery sessions highlight several Scottish Elwalds such as Robert who, with other Scotsmen, allegedly met Englishman William Smart in order to steal thirty animals from William Wilkinson in 1417.[190] One

---

[184] For sixty-six different spellings of Elliot, see Armstrong, *Liddesdale*, I, 178n 67. The placename 'Elwaldsyd' occurs in Nbl. (Bodleian: Dodsworth MS, 32 fol. 124v (34); *Northumberland and Durham Deeds,* ed. Oliver, 156, no. 47).

[185] JUST 3/208 rot. 44 (William Elwald, gentleman of Gilsland). Dacre's feodary of Gilsland barony in 1423 does not mention this William (DUL: HNP C/201/1). JUST 3/191 rot. 55d (Elwalds, 1389, theft from Beatrice Batycombe).

[186] The theft was of four cows at Corby (JUST 3/208 rot. 42d; JUST 3/11/4 m. 6).

[187] JUST 3/191 rot. 58d (John Elwald, 1406); JUST 3/208 rot. 44 (Hugh Elwald of Cumwhitton, yeoman, 1434); JUST 3/211 rot. 43 (Richard Elwald of Lanercost, 1446).

[188] Henry Ellewald was an archer at Berwick in 1403 (E 101/43/26; *CDS*, IV, 140). Robert Elwald, yeoman from Maulds Meaburn in Westmorland, was appealed as an accessory to the death of Robert Crackenthorpe in 1439 (KB 27/714 rot. 36).

[189] See Maps 3 and 4. KB 27/802 rots 58, 58d.

[190] Smart, called a traitor, was the principal offender of this theft done in November at Aydon ['Ayden'] in Northumberland. He was acquitted of this and of another cattle theft: JUST 3/199 rot. 18.

149

Part II

Henry Elwald received goods stolen by Englishmen in 1419.[191] Similarly, Humphrey Elwald received goods stolen at Filton in 1429, and, in 1441, Henry and John Elwald received goods stolen at Blenkinsop in Tynedale.[192] Among those aliens in England enumerated in 1440 was Mariota Elwald, a Scottish servant dwelling in a household south of Carlisle.[193] North of the border, the Elwalds were concentrated in Roxburghshire (Teviotdale) and Dumfriesshire. They appear there in the former in the mid-1420s.[194] A decade later John Elwald witnessed a deed in Jedworth Forest and, in the 1450s, another is found in Jedburgh and three appear in Ewesdale. At the Dumfries justice ayre of 1458, two John Elwalds were fined, one whose territorial designation indicates that he was an Eskdale landowner.[195] By this time (and possibly much earlier), the senior Elwalds were established in the lands of Redheugh in Liddesdale.[196] In the 1470s and 1480s Robert Elwald of Redheugh received further grants in that lordship from Archibald, earl of Angus.[197] By 1488 Elwald cadets were evident elsewhere in Liddesdale.[198] In 1491 the main line can be seen to have been even more closely connected with Angus, for in an illicit agreement between the Scottish earl and Henry VII the king promised to release 'Robert Elwolde, son to Robert Elwold of the Hermitage, yonger, which late deceassid'.[199] A retour of 1498 for Robert Elwald as heir to his grandfather marks at least three generations of the senior line dwelling in

---

[191] William and Thomas Berehalgh of Thorngrafton in Tynedale had stolen the goods from Oderd Ridley: JUST 3/199 rot. 17. Odard Ridley was the Percy's captain of Langley castle in 1403: *PPC*, I, 211–13. He was also a victim in 1416 and 1419 (JUST 3/199 rot. 17), 1420 (JUST 3/208 rot. 39d) and 1427 (JUST 3/208 rot. 24d).

[192] JUST 3/208 rot. 26 (1429, theft by John Gray); JUST 3/211 rot. 32d (1441, theft by John Pykeryng).

[193] E 179/90/27 m. 2d: her employer was Thomas Pinkeny ['Pynkene'] of Blackhall.

[194] Dowager Lady D.F.A. Eliott of Stobs and A.F.A.B. Eliott, *The Elliots: The Story of a Border Clan* (Chatham, 1974; repr., Chippenham, 1986); Armstrong, *Liddesdale*, I, 178–80, esp. 179nn.

[195] *HMC Milne-Home*, nos 5–6, p. 20 (1436); *HMC, 14th Report*, appendix, part III, 9 (1453); *Douglas Book*, III, nos 88–9, pp. 84–5, (1457); *ER*, VI, 557–8 (fines, including that of John Elwald 'of Dauduran'). Armstrong, *Liddesdale*, I, 159, gives the place name 'Dalduriane' and 'Daldoran' in Eskdale.

[196] For Redheugh, see the extent made in 1376: *Morton Register. Registrum Honoris de Morton*, ed. T. Thomson, A. Macdonald and C. Innes, 2 vols (1853), I, appendix, no. 17; Eliott, *The Elliots*, 11, and 11n.

[197] Various grants dated 1476(?), 1480, 1484: Eliott, *The Elliots*, 11; Elliot, *The Border Elliots*, appendix, pedigree of 1704.

[198] John Elwald of Thorleshop in Liddesdale and his brother Patrick (1488): *Scotts of Buccleuch*, II, no. 94, pp. 91–2, 92n.

[199] Armstrong, *Liddesdale*, I, appendix, no. ix, p. xiv. Robert Elwald appears elsewhere in the marches in 1490 (*The Lag Charters, 1400–1720*, ed. A.L. Murray and P.J. Hamilton-Grierson (1958), no. 37, pp. 15–16) and 1492 (NRS: GD 6/593, 594).

150

Lordship, Kinship and the Surnames

Roxburghshire.[200] The Elwalds are outstanding as minor Scottish landowners with links to greater magnates, and they were active on both sides of the border, throughout the whole of the century.

Turning to consider the Armstrongs, only five emerge in the gaol delivery records, and just one man of this *cognomen* has been found west of the Pennines in our period, being one Andrew Armestraunge of Walby near Carlisle, in 1399.[201] Most English Armstrongs are found as Percy tenants along the South Tyne in Northumberland. The yeoman Thomas Armstrang from Beaufront Tower, near Corbridge, was acquitted of breaking into Ponteland mill in 1422 to steal wheat. He may be the same Thomas who was on the jury for the coroner's inquest held at Corbridge in 1451, when a man was indicted for stealing seventy-two sheep.[202] Another Armstrong yeoman, John, of Woodshield ['Wodshell'], nearby in Langley barony, was tried and acquitted for thefts at Chollerton in 1438. He may have been a relative of Gilbert and Richard Armestrange, who were tenants at Woodshield in the mid-1470s.[203] Other Armstrongs appear elsewhere in the county, including a cleric of Hexham.[204] William Armstrong, yeoman from Belsay ['Belsowe'], was acquitted of stealing two cows from John Brandlyng in November 1434 at Trewhitt ['Trewyk'] in upper Coquetdale. He may be the same William Armistrang from Belsay who, in August 1433, lost a cow to theft.[205] No English Armstrongs claimed gentle status at this time. By contrast, it was in Scotland that Armstrongs held land, with the senior line established in Liddesdale from at least 1376. The head of that family, Alexander Armstrong of Mangerton, agreed an indenture with the lord of Liddesdale in 1389. In the truce of 1398, Alexander, Geoffrey and Davy Armstrong appeared as surety for the third earl of Douglas as march warden.[206] Still,

---

[200] On retours, the findings of inquests into succession to heritable property, see P. Gouldesbrough, *Formulary of Old Scots Legal Documents* (Edinburgh, 1985), 74–80. Robert Elwald the grandfather died about 3 May 1497 (Armstrong, *Liddesdale*, I, 144n 1; appendix, pp. xvi–xvii, no. xi; *HMC, 7th Report*, appendix, part II, p. 729, no. 22; Eliott, *The Elliots*, 12).

[201] *CPR 1399–1401*, 166 (pardoned in October 1399, for not answering a £6 debt). The earliest recorded Armstrongs, from the thirteenth century, are from Cbl. (SC 1/27/18; CAC, Carlisle: D/Mus/2/2 box 20, nos 27, 49, 52; Armstrong, *Liddesdale*, I, 175–6).

[202] JUST 3/208 rot. 23d (1422). For the inquest at Corbridge, see KB 9/265 m. 161.

[203] JUST 3/211 rot. 27 (1438); Hodgson, *Percy Bailiff's Rolls*, 89. John Armestrange was paid in 1472 for building a stone wall in Westpark for the earl of Northumberland: ibid., 19.

[204] Andrew Armstrong obtained permission for ordination in 1486: *Register of Thomas Rotherham*, ed. Barker, 210.

[205] JUST 3/208 rot. 35 (1434); JUST 3/208 rot. 31 (1433); In 1440 Nicholas Armstrang was another victim of theft, at Morpeth, having three pelts of cow leather stolen (JUST 3/211 rot. 31). One Richard Armestrong witnessed a lease in Morpeth in 1417 (NA, Woodhorn: ZSW 2/48).

[206] *Morton Reg.*, I, appendix, no. 17; see Armstrong, *Liddesdale*, I, 135, and appendix, no. i, pp. iii–vii; NRS: GD 150/78 (1389 indenture); *Foedera*, III, iv, 152 (1398 truce); *Douglas Book*, II, 21–3.

151

Part II

we hear nothing more of the Armstrongs in Scotland until 1456, when David Armstrong of Sourby and Archibald Armstrong witnessed an instrument at Branxholm. Later that year, Archibald and Alexander Armstrong were concerned in a deed over lands in Ewesdale granted to George, the fourth earl of Angus. In the Selkirk justice ayre of 1466, David and Archibald Armstrong of Liddesdale had fines laid against them for failing as the pledges for the appearance of an offender.[207] Then, the Armstrongs disappear from record once again for nearly two decades, only to re-emerge in 1482 when Thomas Armstrong resigned Mangerton to Archibald, the fifth earl of Angus. The lands came for a time to David Scott of Buccleuch.[208] It would seem that Angus and Scott pressured Armstrong to give up his lands, and a plausible explanation could be that Armstrong had incurred the wrath of Angus (a march warden) by tacitly supporting the English invasion of July 1482, apparently joining some of their Elwald neighbours in this treason.[209] The Armstrongs were clearly troublemakers in Liddesdale in the 1490s, and by early in the next century they appear to have returned to Mangerton.[210] As very minor landholders north of the border, they appear to have fallen foul of the growing power of the Scotts of Buccleuch, who were sponsored by the Red Douglases, from the 1460s onwards.[211]

Finally, the Grahams. These illustrate well how kinship ties could be constructed, reckoned and just as easily confused or forgotten. 'Long Will Graham' is the reputed Scottish exile and early sixteenth-century founder of the various branches of the Graham kindred along the Esk in northern Cumberland.[212] The putative primacy of Long Will arises from the tabular pedigree prepared by a march official for William Cecil, Lord Burghley, in 1596.[213] The Graham pedigree has influenced modern

---

[207] *Scotts of Buccleuch*, II, no. 59, pp. 55–6; *Douglas Book*, III, nos 88–9, pp. 84–5; *ER*, VIII, 4–5 (Selkirk justice ayre).

[208] *Scotts of Buccleuch*, II, nos 79, 81, pp. 77–80; NRS: GD 224/890/20/1; Armstrong, *Liddesdale*, I, 142n. 1.

[209] In August 1481 Edward IV empowered the duke of Gloucester and the exiled earl of Douglas to promise rewards to Scots who would collaborate with them (*CDS*, IV, no. 1470 p. 299). In March 1482 James III offered pardon to all borderers who had committed treason, excepting a few named men (*RPS*, 1482/3/44, A1482/3/2). James, Laurence, Simon and John Elwald were captured as rebels c. 1482: *ER*, IX, pp. xxxix, 295–6, 347, 454, 551.

[210] In 1493 Archibald Armstrong was outlawed for the slaughter of the laird of Eildmer (NRS: JC 1/1, fol. 9v). For various Armstrongs in Liddesdale, see NRS: JC 1/1, fols 25v–27r.

[211] On the Red Douglases, the crown, the Scotts and other local families, see Boardman, 'Politics and the Feud', 111–32; Brown, *Black Douglases*, 315–19, 330–1.

[212] The most senior being the Grahams of Netherby: Reid, 'The Border Grahams', 85–107 (esp. 86, 91); Spence, 'The Graham Clans', 79–81; Spence, 'Pacification', 60–2.

[213] 'A breefe relacion of the begininge and discent of the Grames now inhabiting the Debateable grounde neare the River of Eske in England', in *Calendar of Border Papers,* ed. J. Bain, 2 vols (Edinburgh, 1894–6), ii, 826–7.

Lordship, Kinship and the Surnames

writers as much as it captured the horizons of local memory in the sixteenth century. It relates that 'William Grame, alias Longe Will, bannished out of Scotland about 80 yeares since, came into England and brought with him eight sonnes, whome he planted neare the said river of Eske', and sets out the descendants of each son. This account would thus place the establishment of the Grahams on the Esk about 1516. But, while useful to describe the horizontal relations between various branches in the 1590s, and significant in noting the cross-border dimension of this family, the pedigree provides a misleading, or at least incomplete, account of the past. It is very clear from the earlier evidence that 'Grames' lived in the area well before Long Will's arrival. For instance, in 1418, Thomas Grame had six cows stolen at Alstonby, on the River Lyne, halfway between Carlisle and the border. The acquitted thief was called a 'marcheman', from nearby Arthuret. This Thomas Grame may be the same man, described as a gentleman of Linstock, who stood pledge for a fine in 1430 and, as mainpernor for a yeoman from Ainstable in 1437, at the gaol delivery sessions in those years. The following year he was outlawed for failing in these obligations.[214] He may well have been closely related to John Grame, gentleman, dwelling on the water of Esk near Carlisle in 1415, appealed by a Buckinghamshire coin-clipper in 1436.[215] That the compiler of the pedigree of 1596 ignored Grahams living on the Esk predating Long Will suggests that the origins of the Surnames, even in their Elizabethan heyday, were not well understood and subject to fuzzy recollection or creative misremembering. Burghley's annotations suggest he was aware of but confounded by a more complicated picture of the Graham kindred.[216] Still other Grahams are to be found in the northern marches in our period. Elsewhere in Cumberland, Margaret Grame was the victim of rape and abduction in 1439 at Hutton-in-the-Forest. Around mid-century three Grames, doubtless Scots, appeared in the alien subsidies as resident in Cumberland, and one in Northumberland.[217] Only a few other Grames are to be found in Northumberland. Of these, the yeoman William, of 'Neuburgh' in Tynedale, was a suspected felon in 1458 and,

---

[214] JUST 3/199 rot. 30d (1418, the 'marcheman' was James Ra); JUST 3/11/4 m. 5 (1430); JUST 3/208 rot. 46 (1437, 'Aynstaplith').

[215] CDS, iv, 224. See also J. Bain, 'The Grahams or Graemes of the Debateable Land', *Archaeological Journal*, 43 (1886), 116–23, at 120.

[216] The annotations on the pedigree, however, observe that 'there are also another sort of Grames which inhabit upon the rivers Levyn [Lyne] and Sarke, which are not of this race' but which had over time intermarried with the Grahams of Esk (*Calendar of Border Papers,* ed. Bain, ii, 827).

[217] In Cbl.: E 179/90/34 m. 1 (Henry, 1455); E 179/90/36 m. 3 (John, 1450); E 179/90/39 m. 1 (William, servant of Clement Skelton, 1464); and in Nbl.: E 179/158/41 m. 6 (David, 1440, at North Dissington).

Part II

in 1482, Robert Grame was a Percy officer.[218] Indeed, Bain long ago observed that in the thirteenth century two knightly families of this name had held land in Northumberland, at Simonburn in Tynedale and at Wooler.[219] Grahams thus inhabited England's northern marches long before 1500, and in the fifteenth century the bearers of this *cognomen* straddled the social boundary between yeoman and gentleman.

More notable landowners among the Grahams were to be found dwelling in the marches north of the border, concentrated in Dumfriesshire.[220] Landed Grahams appear in Annandale and Ewesdale, and with links to the earls of Douglas in the 1430s and 1450s.[221] Some time in the reign of James III three Grames who identified themselves as 'marche men' claimed to have held the lands of Hutton in Annandale for a century and more.[222] The most prominent Graham house in the marches at this time was seated at Mosskesso in Dumfriesshire, and indeed it has been suggested that 'Long Will Graham' was in fact William Graham of Mosskesso, a Scottish laird driven out of his lands by debt about 1516.[223] A charter of 1465 shows three generations of the family then alive and in possession of Dryfe Tower in Annandale. The Mosskesso branch, and the Grahams of Gillesbie, were tied closely to the earls of Morton, their immediate feudal superiors.[224] In ayres held at Dumfries in the late 1450s and mid-1460s, several apparently landless Grahams came before the court.[225] English gaol delivery records reveal that two Scottish Grahams, Thomas and William, entered Northumberland to kidnap an

---

[218] JUST 3/213 rot. 15 (1458). Robert was reeve of Rugley in Alnwick barony (Alnwick Castle: Syon House MSS, C. VIII, 1i (consulted via BL microfilm reel 358)). In 1422 Thomas Grame was the victim of theft at 'Newtongrange' (JUST 3/199 rot. 21d).

[219] Bain, 'The Grahams', 121–2; Reid, 'The Border Grahams', 85. See also Holford and Stringer, *Border Liberties*, 245–8, 251, 268.

[220] Reid, 'The Border Grahams', 87–9; Holford and Stringer, *Border Liberties*, 290, 297, note the Grahams in Tynedale who came into English allegiance under Edward I reverted to Scottish adherence in the reign of Edward II.

[221] For instance, Thomas Grame, lord of Roucan near Dumfries, witnessed a retour in 1432 (*Calendar of the Laing Charters*, no. 109, p. 28). This may be the same man who joined the earl of Douglas abroad in 1451 (*CDS*, iv, 250). For Ewesdale: *Douglas Book*, III, no. 89, p. 85.

[222] *HMC, Report on Manuscripts in Various Collections*, v (1909), 77: Wylzame the Grame, Richarde the Grame and Henry the Grame.

[223] See Reid, 'The Border Grahams', 89.

[224] NRS: GD 150/135; 150/103; 150/121. See Reid, 'Gillesbie Tower', 377. Morton granted various lands in Hutton to Graham of Gillesbie and Graham of Mosskesso in the 1470s (NRS: GD 150/148; 150/238).

[225] Richard, Walter his son, Gavin, and Richard Graham Jr secured remission of fines in 1458–9 (*ER*, VI, 552–6). Geoffrey Graham, fined £10 1459–60 (ibid., VI, 618–19). Galwin, George, James and William Graham componed with the lords of council in 1464–5 (ibid., VII, 310–12).

Lordship, Kinship and the Surnames

Englishman in 1410.[226] Thus in Scotland the Grahams, like the Bells, were a family of mixed status, consisting of several landed lineages with links to greater magnates, and there is evidence of Grahams in cross-border activity. As with the other families examined here, no clear indication of collaboration between English and Scottish Grahams has been found. Still the Scottish Grahams offer a useful illustration of how the wide collateral kin could be reckoned among a landowner's relations, in a way that is at least suggestive of the potential for extended ties of kinship to be recognised among relations across the border. The entail (or tailzie in Scotland) of patrimony restricting inheritance in the male line might also serve as a written articulation of the wider family pedigree, or at least of the senior membership of a kin group sharing a *cognomen*. Reminiscent of the complex English entail by the Lancasters of Rydal observed earlier,[227] but going much further, was the settlement arranged in 1465 by William le Graham of Mosskesso concerning his lands of the same name and the tower of Dryfe, just noted. This tailzie started with the grandson and eventual heir apparent of the current incumbent, and then worked down the line of seniority among the grandson's uncles.[228] Going so far into the male kin, these arrangements were far more specific, and concerned to avoid dismemberment through female inheritance, than was common in England at this time. Much as with the *here* of the Halls noted earlier, it is difficult to expect that such a reckoning would be entirely alien to Grahams living in the English marches, and, as we have seen, there may have been more importance given to the wider male kin in settlements and family dynamics in the border counties than further south in England.

MODELS AND INDICATIONS OF LEADERSHIP
AMONG THE SURNAMES

Even if such collections of people sharing a name and, in some cases, an area of residence do not put past all doubt the presence of coherent 'Surname' groups in this period, they serve as very strong indications that such a phenomenon was a reality long before 1498. Significantly, even

---

[226] Thomas and William Grame; their residence is not given (JUST 3/191 rot. 51d).

[227] See above, p. 127.

[228] NRS: GD 150/135. The grandson and recipient, Patrick le Grahame, ratified the charter made to him by the earl of Morton, by which Patrick and the heirs male of his body received the lands. Failing this, the lands were to pass successively to his uncles John, Patrick, James, Thomas, John and Geoffrey and, failing them, to William the grandfather and William, Patrick's own father, the eldest son and heir apparent of William the grandfather. Liferent was reserved to both Williams and a terce to their wives.

Part II

though kin groups in England, as we have seen, tended not to cross the social divide between gentle and common, it seems that several precursor Surnames did have landed members. Those with gentry among them – the Fenwicks, Charltons, Redes, Cressopes, Elwalds and Grahams – might be able to look to their own senior kinsmen for leadership. There is also evidence to show members of these groups linked with other landowners outside the kindred, and these ties would be especially significant for those 'Surnames' without landed kinsmen.

Examples of leadership of local families provided by middling gentry outside the kin group can be found in Westmorland. The bond of 1471 between the Sandfords of Askham and the Yates of Leadgate, already discussed, reveals an English esquire and his heir clearly establishing their 'rule' over a sub-gentry lineage.[229] Thomas Sandford did not stop with the Yates, for his associations with the local yeomanry are well documented, and his links with several Wilkinsons (a 'Surname' identified above) and other families will be discussed in another context below.[230] In January 1477, Sandford made a similar arrangement, allying himself with several members of the Noble family (also to become a notable 'Surname' in the next century). This took the form of a monetary bond from William Nobill Sr, William Nobill Jr and John, son of William Jr, yeomen from Butterwick, who obliged themselves in £40 to abide Sandford's 'reull and gouernance'.[231] What was happening here was a local kindred of yeoman status, the Nobles, entered into what amounted to a contract of lordship with Sandford, a local esquire who, to judge by the testamentary sentiment of one of his ancestors, carried an awareness of his own horizontal cousinage. This was the integration of minor kin groups into greater networks of power.[232]

---

[229] See above, p. 123.

[230] See below, p. 296 (Sandford-Wilkinsons) and p. 331 (Sandford-Walkers). Many of the yeoman families who associated with Sandford formed a long-standing local network and are traceable together in a case beginning in 1438 (KB 9/229/4 mm. 25, 26; KB 27/710 *rex* rot. 17d).

[231] CAC, Carlisle: D/Lons/L5/1/3/81, formerly D/Lons/MD/AS 72. Noted in Jones and Walker, 'Private Indentures', 32, and 174n. 372. Others concerned in the bond were the gentleman, William 'Soucaf [Southayk?] of Eamont Bridge[?] in Cbl., and the Wml. yeomen William Loghorn of 'Helton Helham' and John Nobill of 'Burkby'. The men of Butterwick may have been Sandford's tenants, but the extent of Sandford's holdings there is unclear. John Nobyll, yeoman of 'Bampton Condale' (near Butterwick), a Sandford tenant, was indicted for offences in 1452 (KB 27/766 *rex* rot. 25d). For two Nobles in Nbl. in 1407 and 1419, see JUST 3/191 rot. 52; JUST 3/199 rot. 23d.

[232] The sense of a wider cousinage is evident in Thomas Sandford of Sandford's will of 1380, in which he left half of his wool '*ad distribuendum inter mediocres de parentalia mea et alios maxime indiguentes*'. Printed in *Testamenta Karleolensia*, ed. R.S. Ferguson, CWAAS, extra ser., 9 (1893), no. 143. See also *HOP*, IV, 298–9, 299–300.

156

Lordship, Kinship and the Surnames

In Northumberland the Swinburnes were an old knightly family with lands close to the border,[233] which also established links, though not necessarily amicable ones, with a precursor Surname group.[234] They had lands within Redesdale, and an important connection between the Swinburnes and the Redes is found in a bond of May 1400. In this document Thomas Rede of Redesdale, who was perhaps the same as Thomas, gentleman of Otterburn and most senior member of the family already noted, bound himself to pay £20 to Sir William Swinburne, 'without fraud or guile'. This was to fund the *redempcione* of William Moscrop of Teviotdale ['Teuedall'], evidently Swinburne's man who had been captured by the Scots. It is not clear that Rede was acting freely in this and he may have been under pressure to sign the bond.[235] In 1447, Sir William Swinburne received a royal pardon, the need for which may have been connected with the activities of Alan Swinburne of Newbrough ['Newburgh'], gentleman, and John Swinburne of 'Hawden', yeoman, both tried in 1446 for separate offences.[236] The latter's status suggests that the Swinburnes, like the Redes, were also a mixed status kin group, although not themselves later to be counted among the riding Surnames. They continued to be implicated in local turbulence in the 1470s.[237]

Among English barons and earls in the marches we have noted the Dacre and Percy families as normally resident, and they can also be linked to men of the 'Surnames'. In the English west march, the Dacres had connections with groups of mixed and entirely sub-gentry status. For

---

[233] William Swinburne held Capheaton and Robert Swinburne held Harnham Hall in 1415–16 (Hodgson, *Northumberland*, III, i, 26–9). In 1437 Sir William Swinburne mortgaged lands in Tynedale to Lord Dacre (NA, Woodhorn: ZSW 1/151; also recited in Bodleian: Dodsworth MS, 45 fol. 52v (64); *Northumberland and Durham Deeds*, ed. Oliver, p. 213, no. 94). In 1416 William Swinburne was keeper of the castle of Marck in France (E 101/69/8/528).

[234] In 1443 three generations of Swinburnes (Sir William Sr, Sir William Jr, and John the grandson) made arrangements to settle their patrimony in tail male. That year Sir William Jr married Elizabeth, daughter of John Collingwood of Etal (NA, Woodhorn: ZSW 5/66, 67; ZSW 1/153, 154). See also Hedley, *Northumberland*, I, 102–3; Hodgson, *Northumberland*, II, i, 212; *HOP*, IV, 544–5; ibid., 545–7; ibid., 547–50; ibid., 550–1; ibid., 552–4.

[235] NA, Woodhorn: ZSW 1/110. See above p. 142n 134; Hodgson, *Northumberland*, II, ii, 136. Rede was to pay two instalments of £10 '*sine fraude et dolo*' at Haughton in Tynedale on 1 August and 11 November.

[236] The pardon was granted in recognition of good service in the east march, for offences done before 4 March 1447 (*CPR 1446–52*, 31–2). Alan stole a horse from Alan Robson at Settlingstones in 1445. John stole three ewes from Agnes Broun at Fourstones in 1443 (JUST 3/211 rot. 33). In 1446 Sir William Swinburne granted Ottercops in Redesdale to Robert Mitford (NA, Woodhorn: ZSW 1/157; Bodleian: Dodsworth MS, 45, fol. 50v (38); *Northumberland and Durham Deeds*, ed. Oliver, p. 214, no. 97).

[237] Gilbert Swinburne, gentleman lately of Nafferton, was implicated in a homicide in 1476 (KB 9/343 mm. 70, 71).

Part II

instance, in September 1416, Thomas, sixth Lord Dacre, had taken a retinue of soldiers from Cumberland to France that included Alexander Belle and William Robson.[238] Further south in England, tenantry regularly turned out in support of their lord, and we can see presumed members of Surname groups doing this in the marches.[239] The Dacres seem to have relied on the Elwalds and Bells in this way. William Elwald, the gentleman of Gilsland noted above, was tried in August 1435 for stealing twenty-six oxen and cows at Plumpton in 1429, and twelve cattle from the earl of Salisbury at the same place three years earlier.[240] Dacre, who was Elwald's landlord, had been at odds with Salisbury in 1429, and so he may well have condoned or instigated Elwald's raids. Nevertheless, Dacre's eldest son was retained by Salisbury in April 1435, an arrangement possibly made under some duress.[241] It may be that Elwald's appearance in court (where he was acquitted) was engineered by the earl as a pressure tactic to secure the Dacres' allegiance. Further links between the Lancastrian eighth Lord Dacre and a number of yeomen Elwalds and Bells are to be found in 1464, when Dacre was pursued in court for the deaths of two men.[242] His associates included Gilbert and Robert Ellewald, and five Belles, all described as lately of Naworth, evidently an indication of association with Dacre more than of permanent residence.[243] This later example suggests that the Elwalds and Bells were acting as local kin groups in Dacre service.

[238] *CCR 1413–19*, 321. Dacre's soldiers included John Twedale and John Whelpdale. Dacre had not accompanied the king on the 1415 Agincourt campaign (Curry, *Agincourt*, 67).

[239] On tenant armies, see Carpenter, *Locality and Polity*, 283, 335, 377, 379.

[240] JUST 3/208 rot. 44. The victim at Plumpton in 1429 was Roger Garth, probably the same man who was bailiff of the forestership in Penrith ward in Inglewood Forest, and from a local gentry family connected to the Dacres in 1411, and Cliffords in 1422. Salisbury was keeper of the king's forests north of Trent (thus including Inglewood), and he held the honour of Penrith, adjacent to Plumpton (*CPR 1399–1401*, 34; *CPR 1408–13*, 355; *CPR 1413–16*, 42; *CCR 1422–9*, 5; *CPR 1422–9*, 68, 411; *CPR 1436–41*, 196).

[241] For Dacre's indenture, see Jones and Walker, 'Private Indentures', no. 120, p. 150; Summerson, *Medieval Carlisle*, ii, 407, 410; R.W. Dunning, 'Thomas, Lord Dacre and the West March towards Scotland, 1435', *BIHR* 41 (1968), 95–9; Griffiths, *Henry VI*, 161.

[242] Dacre and Sir Henry Bellingham, Robert Bellingham, esq., and Alexander Bellingham, gentleman, were pursued along with fifty-two accomplices. All the principals were described as lately of Naworth ['Naward'], in Cbl., Dacre's seat. In the Richard Weddale killing, the gentlemen (both lately of Naworth) Richard Kirkby and John Ratcliffe were additional principals. In Thomas Nevynson's killing, the additional principals (all lately of Naworth) were the chaplain John Ellergyll and yeomen John Wardrop and John Hunt (KB 27/814 rots 47, 47d).

[243] The Belles were William, John, Andrew, Thomas and Alan. John Whelpdale was also named, perhaps the same yeoman who had served with Lord Dacre in 1416. The accessories to both cases included Robert Waleys, gentleman; Alexander Wharton ['Querton'], yeoman; and John Caldbeke, chaplain. The Nevynson case also named as accessories Kirkby and Ratcliffe (KB 27/814 rots 47, 47d).

Lordship, Kinship and the Surnames

We have seen the close connection between the Percys and the gentle Fenwicks,[244] and many representatives of the Surnames surveyed here have been found living on Percy estates, which is not entirely surprising given the extent of their lands. But the Dodds provide a good example of links between the earls of Northumberland and non-landed men of this *cognomen* dwelling near to the frontier. In early 1397, the first Percy earl procured a pardon for Robert Dodd, son of William Dodd, and for John Dodd of Tarset in north Tynedale, for offences committed before January 1396. Tarset was a Percy manor. The earl sought and received a similar pardon for Henry Dodd, the son of William Dodd of Thorney-burn in north Tynedale, as well as one for Peter Hedley and his son Robert Hedley, of Redesdale (not a lordship in the earl's possession), who were pardoned of all felonies committed before Christmas 1396. It may be that these borderers required pardons for handling the Percys' dirty work in the border liberties or that they had submitted to a compromise imposed by the earl, in exchange for a reprieve.[245] In subsequent decades other Dodds were to be involved in local turbulence. A rare conviction at gaol delivery occurred in the case of the notorious yeoman thief Walter Dod of Blakelaw in Tynedale, who had committed livestock thefts near Morpeth in 1424.[246] At Corbridge the following spring, one William Dodd met his death in connection with the actions of two yeomen, John and David Baxter, who had been lying in wait at night with others, intent on killing someone else.[247] There were no clear Percy links among these men, but in the 1470s certain other Dodds are to be found in Percy service in Northumberland.[248] These Percy connections indicate that small groups of related peasants, sometimes their tenants, from families later to be held to be Surnames were employed in their service in the marches. All this evidence so far suggests that

---

[244] See above, p. 128.

[245] *CPR 1396–9*, 62, 72. Those pardoned by the king at Warkworth in 1405 for participating in the Percy rebellion include Henry Fenwick, chaplain, and others including Robert Rede, Robert de Hall, Robert Wilkynson and William Hunter of Guyzance. Lands worth £40 forfeit by a Roger Hall were granted in 1406 (*CPR 1405–8*, 76, 116).

[246] See below, p. 177.

[247] JUST 3/199 rot. 19d (Walter Dod of 'Blaklawe'); JUST 3/199 rot. 18 (William Dodd; the Baxters' intended victim was Lionel de Chester; the coroner was Nicholas Turpyn). In 1430 William Dode, Thomas and Robert Baxter, Robert Dixon and Stephen Hunter were named as burgesses of Hexham: Warne (ed.), *The Duke of Norfolk's Deeds at Arundel Castle*, i, 124 (CW 255).

[248] Alnwick Castle: Syon House MSS, C. VIII, 6 (consulted via BL microfilm reel 358): in 1474, Walter Dod was reeve of Prudhoe; at the same time Richard Dodd was lately a cottager in Langley barony (Hodgson, *Percy Bailiffs' Rolls*, 89). In 1494, Robert Doddys and his son Arche stood under accusation in the west march (*CDS*, IV, 324).

Part II

certain kin groups existed in parts of the English marches, many with a mixed-status composition and links to landed society.

We can now draw some wider conclusions about relations of lordship, and of kinship, in particular expressions of kin solidarity through certain naming practices in the English far north. This is a discussion of social bonds which has necessarily moved back and forth across the status boundary of commonalty and gentility. By the end of our period new indentures of retainer had ceased to be made. Yet well into the 1470s indentures continued to be sealed in the marches in greater number than further south, and this seems to be a result of wardens cultivating their retinues. Retainers in the north could sometimes make explicit exceptions for allegiance to kinsmen, an expression of the relative strength of kinship ties. All these formal links within landed society were important for political alignments and for the recruitment of support in episodes of conflict.[249] In what is yet to come we shall look more closely at the importance of such relationships in processes of violent disputing and the making of peace. Landowners in the marches, it is fair to conclude, seem to have been more kin-conscious than would be expected in parts of the realm further south. This seems to have been especially true of landed families in Westmorland and in northern Northumberland.

There appear to be two typologies of particularly strong kinship solidarities in evidence: the use of double patronyms and the use of certain *cognomina* by those whose activities and associations are highly suggestive of being antecedents of the riding Surnames. Both of these forms were concentrated in different parts of the marches, and in both cases they were part of a more diverse field of personal naming practices. In the former, Westmorland stands out. That county shows by far the highest rate of double patronyms and genuine patronymic usage more widely. This suggests its inhabitants had a strong sense of their kinship ties, especially encompassing first cousins in the male line. All this indicates a complex picture of conceptions of kinship, for, although the extended kin group was important, some English marchers like other inhabitants of the wider English north did not make use of a stable and hereditary *cognomen*. As for the Surnames, their precursors appear to be present long before 1498. The sources reveal people with the right names in the right areas, taking part in the right sort of illicit activities. These groups are most evident in the lands closest to the frontier, in northern Cumberland, Tynedale and Redesdale. They can sometimes be found

---

[249] See below, p. 218.

Lordship, Kinship and the Surnames

involved in the type of cross-border misdeeds that will be expounded fully in Chapter 8.

There is little evidence that this was so because of the military pressure of an armed frontier. Rather, the Surnames seem to be one expression in the region of a prevailing culture which observed strong kin-based solidarities. Yet if the evidence suggests this phenomenon did exist in the fifteenth century, the terminology which came to describe it was not in place until the 1490s. The history of the term is of course not the same as the history of the phenomenon. Hardyng's writing shows the term 'surname' was not used in the same way in the early fifteenth century (when it was reserved especially for the appellations of great magnates and kings). This was a time when naming practices were still fluid, and not all in the north used a stable hereditary second name.[250] The terminological jump came in the 1490s when 'surname' expanded its meaning beyond the sense in which Hardyng had used it, to refer not merely to a form of name but to a group of people sharing a *cognomen*. The sense of a group becomes explicit in other sources from the 1490s. We have seen that some of these Surnames had reference points across the border, and it is in the Scottish ayre records of that decade that collective references such as 'le Diksons', 'le Turnbulis', or 'le Elwaldis Armstrangis & Forstaris' appear in connection with particular offenders and their accused associates.[251] In the first case of 'le Diksons', this group (the kinsmen of the offender Andrew Dikson, tenant in Buccleuch) was described as 'traitors of Levyn'. We have seen in an earlier chapter that there is reason to identify these groups as Englishmen, resident between the Esk and the Lyne in Cumberland. This reference from 1495, there-fore, might be the clearest indication of cross-border cooperation by kinsmen sharing a *cognomen* in the period.[252]

Some of the supposed Surname families (like the Fenwicks, Charltons and Redes) had deep roots in the marches, reaching back into the thirteenth century and progressing into associations with the Percys in the late fourteenth century and the early fifteenth century. They entered a period of obscurity in the 1460s and 1470s, to emerge again into view in

---

[250] Postles, *The North through Its Names*, 7–11.

[251] NRS: JC 1/1, fols 21v, 24r, 32r. See also at fol. 21v: '*Willot Elwald et Rollandj Elwald et quinque fratrem de Armstrangis proditorum de Levyn*'.

[252] NRS: JC 1/1, fol. 32r: The inbringing of '*Diksons consanguineorum suorum proditorum de Levyn*'. For the rebels of Levyn, see above, pp. 61–3. See also ibid., fol. 30r: William Dicsone in Laidhop accused of treasonably aiding '*Johannis Dicsone et Alexandri Dicsone proditorum de Levyn*'. For other Dixons, see Henry Aldstanmor, alias Dikson, who received a protection for service at Roxburgh Castle in 1438: *CDS*, v, 562. Also for William Dixon of Kirkhaugh in South Tynedale, active in Nicholforest in the late fourteenth century, see Holford and Stringer, *Border Liberties*, 335n 171.

Part II

the 1490s as identifiable Surnames, certainly by 1498. As we have seen, some of these lineage groups had clear Scottish dimensions. What evidence does survive is very suggestive that Anglo-Scottish cooperation among namesakes (as just noted with the Dixons) occurred but went largely unrecorded. The Elwalds, Bells, Armstrongs and Grahams in England may indeed have interacted with the landowners of these families in Scotland, and the evidence of the alien subsidies certainly reveals plentiful cross-border migration.[253] There is no equivalent source with which to identify English aliens resident in Scotland, but there is every reason to assume such traffic was two-directional. All the same, the weight of evidence suggests that we might not expect the reverse scenario, of a landowning family in England interacting with non-landed Scots of the same *cognomen*, to have been quite so probable. Even so, the social structure of a mixed status kin group, with a wide sense of shared kinship among distant relations of a form that was familiar in lowland Scottish society, seems to be evident as well in parts of the English far north. Some Surnames – the Redes and the much lesser Cressopes, Elwalds and Grahams – appear to have had members of mixed social status. And we shall see in what is yet to follow still further evidence for the mixing of status among and below the gentry within apparent kin groups.[254] As in Scotland, within England the Surnames can be found in geographical clusters, most probably of satellite cadet branches focused around a senior household. This clustering appears to be a pattern followed even by some non-landed English kindreds, like the Obilsons in upper Coquetdale, the Halls in Gilsland and the Dodds in Tarset. While many of the Surnames appear to be landless, they were hardly cut off from resident landowners: the Dodds were linked to the Percys, the Hedleys to the Redes and to the Percys, and the Halls, Bells and Robsons to the Dacres. Similarly, those of mixed status also established links with landowners of higher social rank, like the Redes to the Swinburnes and the Elwalds to the Dacres. Such ties could be formalised through written contracts, and this returns to the theme of lord–man relations. In Westmorland, far from the border itself, the esquire Thomas Sandford of Askham received several contracts of service from local yeomen and their relations (in the form of monetary bonds to evade the 1468 statute of livery). Sandford's bonds were written expressions of the sort of relationships between gentry and their lesser adherents, of which we

---

[253] See the E 179 records cited above in nn 193, 217.
[254] See below, p. 294, and also comment on large groups of yeomen acting in lethal violence (p. 303).

Lordship, Kinship and the Surnames

shall see more in due course.[255] Sandford is remarkable for using these written bonds to place himself and his heir not just in charge of those who were his own tenants but also in the lead of local non-gentle kin groups who, like the Yates of Leadgate, were not.[256]

All things considered, the evidence for the Surnames before the 1490s is modest, and much is probably hidden behind the cloak of Percy and Neville regional dominance in the period. These magnates had local dealings which were not recorded by the royal government. Yet it does not seem that the Surnames originated as a product of Tudor interference in the marches.[257] Indications of their existence can be found from the very beginning of our period. We have not seen evidence that they formed in reaction to Anglo-Scottish warfare. Rather, the impression given by the sources is of a late medieval expression of an older and deeper set of ideas about kinship in a society straddling what became England and Scotland, whereby conceptions of an extended kin group came to focus on a shared hereditary second name in parts close to the border. Over time, kinship terminology adapted to describe this phenomenon as the riding Surnames. By contrast, the different phenomenon of double patronyms concentrated in Westmorland never acquired its own specific terminology, and the evidence suggests that its origins are to be found not in any older cross-border cultural heritage but in patterns that were indigenous to western parts of the English kingdom (with comparators to be found in Cheshire and Cornwall). As we shall see in what follows, an appreciation of such nuances in ideas of kinship is an important basis for understanding how conflict worked in the region, especially within a framework of accustomed practices related to feud. In the borderlands, kinship also influenced conceptions of friendship and lordship. Friends and enemies relied especially upon these relationships as they sought justice during the course of local conflicts. It is to the administration of justice that we now turn.

CONCLUSION AT PART II

Whereas the first part of the book set out the ways in which the far north's reputation for being exceptional and distinct should be treated with caution and perspective, this part has examined ways in which the border counties do reveal some differences with other parts of England. Through a focus on landownership, lordship and kinship, the most

---

[255] See below, pp. 250–1, 265.   [256] See above, pp. 123 and 156, and below, p. 296.
[257] By contrast, see Tuck, 'War and Society', 50–2; Lomas, *North-East England*, 64–5; Etty, 'A Tudor Solution', 209–12, 224–6.

Part II

significant points to recall at this stage are about the strength of kin-consciousness in the region. Awareness of kin and expressions of kinship solidarities here in some ways show similarities with Scotland. What is more, in some cases, this point reaches beyond mere similarity to suggest actual Scottish dimensions, as in the example of the Surnames which have been discussed. This chapter has attempted a more comprehensive and nuanced investigation of the precursors of the Surnames than has been done before, and I have argued that the phenomenon is to be found across the fifteenth century. But it would be injudicious to see this point as anything other than a cautious one, not least when recalling that the strong sense of kinship in the region was neither simply a matter of the Surnames nor of proximity to the border. The usage of double patronyms among the highest rungs of the peasantry concentrated west of the Pennines and especially in Westmorland is a firm reminder of complexities around ideas of kinship. Above all, it is a reminder of the need to think in terms of kin-consciousness as a phenomenon of a diverse and varied England, not simply a cross-border import.

PART III

6

THE ADMINISTRATION OF JUSTICE

In Part III we direct our attention to the topic of conflict from a number of interrelated angles. In doing so, this part of the book proceeds as follows, beginning with examination of the administration of justice (this chapter), patterns of local conflict especially as documented in various court records (Chapter 7) and aspects of conflict specifically identifiable in a cross-border context (Chapter 8). Then, we shall explore more qualitative features of discord (Chapter 9) and concord (Chapter 10) in local disputes in the marches.

This chapter examines justice and its administration in the borderlands. It addresses how march inhabitants obtained remedy of injury through the systems of royal justice and border justice which served as the two primary legal systems regulating local conflict in the area. To that extent, it is concerned with the apparatus of royal justice offered chiefly by the English common law and of border justice offered by Anglo-Scottish march law, and with an overview of the main features of each. It assesses the official mechanisms which the English government, its officers and individual parties had at their disposal in the management of local conflict. It was noted earlier that such mechanisms are but one tool available to disputants in pursuing their objectives.[1] However, the complexity of these systems meant that law itself was more of a toolbox than a single tool, leading to a further array of options and possible outcomes. March law and its administration, concerned with border-related offences, was less complex than common law; however, both relied on the active participation of members of local society. Neither were 'external' impositions but systems actively shaped by local usage. Understanding that interaction is a vital part of the agenda of this book.

---

[1] See above, p. 26.

Part III

JUSTICE IN ENGLAND AND EUROPE

When King Oswald was about to give battle to the heathen, he set up the sign of the holy cross ... This done he summoned his army with a loud shout, crying 'Let us all kneel together, and ask [God] of his mercy to protect us from the arrogant savagery of our enemies, since he knows that we fight in a just cause to save our nation.' The whole army did as he ordered and, advancing against the enemy at the first light of dawn, won the victory that their faith deserved. At this spot where the king prayed, innumerable miracles of healing are known to have been performed ... This place is called in English Hefenfelth, meaning 'the heavenly field'.[2]

—Bede, *Ecclesiastical History*

In the later middle ages the site of St Oswald's seventh-century exhortation before combat with Cadwallon was marked with a chapel (St Oswald in Lee, or Heavenfield), about four miles north of Hexham. By the fifteenth century the monks of Durham and of numerous other monasteries cared for several of his relics, and the cult of this Northumbrian king had become continental in scope, with particular traction in the German-speaking lands.[3] The account given by Bede, who remained the premier authority on the life of this king and martyr, recorded Oswald's victory primarily as a story about the kingly and heavenly nature of justice. But it was also a story of the justice of vengeance, for Oswald had fought to triumph over his brother's killer and to recover the kingdom taken from his father. These elements resonated with wider late medieval thinking about justice which was concerned with the vindication of rights and redress of grievances according to law.[4] The cult of the saint, which venerated in addition to the king's severed head his blessed and uncorrupted right arm, and his ability to heal the broken arms of the faithful (and diverse other curative powers), spoke to another, dual, sense of justice which achieved redress of injury inflicted by enemies, and remedy from physical injury as well. This duality mirrored late medieval ideas of rectificatory justice (a balanced exchange between parties), on the one hand, and distributive justice (a proportional distribution of

---

[2] Bede, *Ecclesiastical History of the English People,* ed. L. Sherley-Price (rev. edn, London, 1990), 144. For comment, see C. Stancliffe, 'Oswald, "Most Holy and Most Victorious King of the Northumbrians"', in C. Stancliffe and E. Cambridge (eds), *Oswald: Northumbrian King to European Saint* (Stamford, 1995), 44–5.

[3] D. Rollason, 'St Oswald in Post-Conquest England', in Stancliffe and Cambridge (eds), *Oswald,* 168; A. Binns, 'Pre-Reformation Dedications to St Oswald in England and Scotland: A Gazetteer', in Stancliffe and Cambridge (eds), *Oswald,* 255.

[4] Stancliffe, 'Oswald', 33. On justice, see Black, *Political Thought in Europe,* 35. However, for thirteenth-century canonists' views on unlimited vengeance as an insufficient cause of just war, see F.H. Russell, *The Just War in the Middle Ages* (Cambridge, 1975), 131–3.

The Administration of Justice

reward according to virtue and service), on the other.[5] Justice was a broad idea which drew together questions of law, economy and faith; through each lens it points to the foundations of social interaction.

In England, the monarch's duty was to guarantee his law and see justice dispensed according to it. In order to achieve this, the king required the consent and cooperation of landowners, because they implemented his authority and governed his subjects.[6] The landowners of the realm were the law's primary administrators, and also its most important 'consumers'. It was they who, with a reliance on specialist common lawyers, shaped the growth and use of the law in pursuit and defence of their rights, especially in property. All the same, resort to law was but one possible step in the course of disputing. England's localities were first and foremost self-policing, and while social pressure from one's peers and superiors could steer a disputant towards a particular set of choices, self-help, involving the use of force, remained not just an outside option but at times a necessity. Violent disputing and extra-judicial peacemaking were once understood simply to demonstrate the failure of government to preserve public order in the later middle ages. No longer is this the case. Studies of conflict among English local elites now see such phenomena as part of an 'acceptable amalgam' of private power and public authority. Landowners had the right and means to use violence, but, while it was intended that force should be used to maintain public authority, if violence was misused, the access and means to use it, and the undermining of authority from such abuse, were highly destabilising.[7] In this regard the gentry and nobility shared a consensus in the form of 'a tacit agreement as to the ground rules of disputes', and the acceptable boundaries for the use of force. This meant that land-owners shared an aversion to the use of violence, and especially interper-sonal violence which risked undermining public authority, as anything other than a last resort.[8] In addition to this, 'private' processes of dispute resolution, typically arbitrations done either under the auspices of a great lord or through the cooperative networks of local gentry, have come to

---

[5] J. Kaye, *Economy and Nature in the Fourteenth Century: Money, Market Exchange, and the Emergence of Scientific Thought* (Cambridge, 1998), 41, 106 (on the scales of justice and exchange); see also D. Wood, *Medieval Economic Thought* (Cambridge, 2002), 13–14, 133–4, noting Aristotle's emphasis on justice, or virtue, as the application of moderation to human behaviour.

[6] The discussion here develops more fully the theme introduced above, p. 40.

[7] Baker, *Introduction to English Legal History*, 178–85; Carpenter, *Wars of the Roses*, 60 (quotation); Harriss, 'Political Society', 48–9; Maddern, *Violence and Social Order*, 16, 18–20, 228–34; Powell, *Kingship, Law, and Society*, chs 1, 4, 10; Wright, *Derbyshire Gentry*, 119, 122.

[8] See above, p. 4. Maddern, *Violence and Social Order*, 34 (quotation); Carpenter, 'Law, Justice and Landowners', 235; Carpenter, *Locality and Polity*, 358–9, 397, 433, 561, 572, 581, 610, 612, 620–2; Harriss, 'Political Society', 51.

Part III

be considered as adjuncts to, not aberrations from, the system of royal justice, and most arbitrations can be shown to have happened in conjunction with the use of the legal system.[9]

Elsewhere in Europe other patterns emerged in relation to the ways that the powerful approached justice and the redress of injury. Three brief illustrations may be drawn. First, as we have seen,[10] in the German-speaking lands the practice of 'feud' among late medieval and early modern noblemen and princes is a well-attested phenomenon. What this entailed was a range of violent actions (small-scale raiding, burning, looting, cattle rustling, kidnapping) which were 'regulated by accepted rules of conduct and by a more or less fixed repertoire of sanctioned methods'.[11] This included requirements that attacks on opponents be preceded by formal announcement. Thus documents known as 'cartels of defiance' came to be accepted as formal declarations of legitimate hostilities. 'Feud was neither a generally undisputed legal institution, nor a legally prohibited practice.'[12] It involved not only noblemen but also prelates and princes, and towns as corporate bodies; even peasants might become engaged as principal parties in feuding, which was an important means for the 'activation of the law' in the jurisdictionally fragmented territory of the Holy Roman Empire. The practice served as a framework through which to assert and defend rights.[13] If this might seem distant from English experience, recent work notes the strong two-way flow of contacts and exchange between England the Empire in the later middle ages. This was, for instance, the world which wealthy crusaders encountered when participating in the *Reyse* in Prussia and its eastern borderlands, especially in the later decades of the fourteenth and the first decade of the fifteenth century.[14]

Second, France has furnished an enriching discussion of violence and feud which offers another point of comparison.[15] Recent work on late medieval southern France has examined the phenomenon of 'seigneurial warfare' among noblemen and found that 'warfare remained a vigorous local tradition' in the period at least up to 1380, involving sieges, raiding, burning, kidnapping and similar violence. One way in which French

---

[9] See above, p. 39, and below, pp. 309–15.   [10] See above, pp. 22–36.

[11] Zmora, *The Feud,* 25, 44 (quote), 53.

[12] Zmora, *The Feud,* 34, 41 (quote), 61; O. Volckart, 'The Economics of Feuding in Late Medieval Germany', *Explorations in Economic History,* 41 (2004), 287–91.

[13] Reinle, 'Peasants' Feuds in Late Medieval Bavaria'; Zmora, *State and Nobility,* 127–8; Zmora, *The Feud,* 9, 14–16, 125 (quote).

[14] L. Scales, 'The Empire in Translation: English Perspectives on Imperium and Emperors, 1220–1440', in Crooks, Green and Ormrod (eds), *The Plantagenet Empire,* 58–63; Harriss, *Shaping the Nation,* 131; C. Tyerman, *England and the Crusades 1095–1588* (Chicago, 1988), 266–76.

[15] On the early modern period, see Carroll, *Blood and Violence.*

170

The Administration of Justice

royal officials sought to insert the power of the crown into conflicts arising between local parties was through the extension of royal letters of safeguard which promised protection and marked it out with public proclamation, including display of fleur-de-lis pennants.[16] A similar view of the extension of royal power in France has been taken in the study of royal grace. Mercy, in the form of royal pardons, was a means by which the crown and its agents could project the supremacy of royal jurisdiction.[17] Other work has studied the courts of Marseille, and there has identified 'hatreds' (typically recorded as *inimicitia, odium* or *rancor*) motivating vengeance among townspeople who sought to have their enmities notarised in open court.[18] For now it is worth noting that the English in France were not ignorant of such practices. For example, there was reference to '*maxima inimicica*' in an English grant in favour of the lord of Garro in Gascony in 1378.[19] It is also worth noting the range of options considered by one party in a suit between Englishmen in northern France in 1426. There the relevant court recorded that one litigant '*en fu mal content et pensa comment il s'en vengeroit, et mist x ou xij homes armes ... pour le grever*'.[20]

Third, a final comparative gesture may briefly be drawn with Scotland. Scottish feuding has been understood to be both a legal phenomenon and one which underwent a transformation and challenge in the sixteenth century through both the growth of 'public' justice and legal culture and the rhetoric of the reformed church after 1560.[21] For the fifteenth century, the emphasis has been on the degree to which feuding among landowners served to link local and national politics and shape crown–nobility relations. The study of justice and feud has also relied heavily on the surviving evidence in the form of arbitration awards between parties and bonds between noblemen, which often served to

---

[16] Firnhaber-Baker, 'Seigneurial War and Royal Power', 41, 44, 46–7, 71–2, 75.

[17] Gauvard, '*De grace especial*', i, ch. 2, 20; Gauvard, 'La justice pénale du roi'.

[18] See below, pp. 279–80; Smail, 'Hatred as a Social Institution', 90, 108; Smail, *Consumption of Justice*, ch. 2.

[19] The Gascon Rolls Project 1317–1468, ed. A. Curry, P. Morgan and P. Spence et al., C 61/91 m. 7, entry 64, www.gasconrolls.org/en/edition/images/C61_91/m7.html; accessed 1 April 2016.

[20] *English Suits before the Parlement of Paris, 1420–1436*, ed. C.T. Allmand and C.A.J. Armstrong (Cambridge, 1982), 117.

[21] J.M. Wormald, 'Bloodfeud, Kindred and Government in Early Modern Scotland', *Past & Present*, 87 (1980), 54–97; Brown, *Bloodfeud in Scotland*; A.M. Godfrey, *Civil Justice in Renaissance Scotland: The Origins of a Central Court* (Leiden, 2009), esp. 401–9, 448–9; A.M. Godfrey, 'Rethinking the Justice of the Feud in Sixteenth-Century Scotland', in S. Boardman and J. Goodare (eds), *Kings, Lord and Men in Scotland and Britain, 1300–1625: Essays in Honour of Jenny Wormald* (Edinburgh, 2014), 136–54.

Part III

recruit supporters in the course of disputes.[22] An examination of the earliest surviving records of the Scottish justice ayre, an itinerant court which circuited the realm (and in this case the border sheriffdoms in the 1490s), underscores the importance of mercy and pardon in Scotland and points to a more than passing resemblance to French practices. It also shows the extent to which these were interlinked with the payment of compensation ('assythement') in redress of wrong. In Scotland royal (or 'public') pardon frequently *preceded* the payment of compensation to the offended party, and written receipts for the latter in effect served as a parallel 'private' pardon.[23] Royal justice in Scotland was more compensatory than retributive in its emphasis.

The numerous differences between these parts of western Europe beyond England are readily apparent. Yet there are some connective tissues to be found running between them. In all three areas, 'feud' or something like it was shaped by legal frameworks, in which written documents (for declaring hostilities, obtaining and asserting protection, or making peace) were important. This focus on written authority concentrated attention on the use of particular words and formulae in the progression of different stages of dispute, including in the ways in which peace was sought and made and the ways in which law courts were involved. The patterns of behaviour here were mostly enacted by landowners (lay and spiritual), but peasants and towns could also become involved as parties. Redress in the form of legally defined compensation for injury was an important theme, and, in the assertion of rights and claims through acts of violence, there seems always to have been in play a collection of tacit rules about acceptable and unacceptable behaviour. This in particular resembles the arguments noted above about English landed society. The preliminary point to be made here is that the pursuit of justice in England may have looked rather more like it did in Germany, France and Scotland than has been appreciated to date.[24]

ROYAL JUSTICE AND ENGLISH COMMON LAW

We now turn to examine the first of two systems of law and justice in England's far north selected for consideration here, that is to say, the

---

[22] S.I. Boardman, 'Politics and the Feud in Late Medieval Scotland', PhD thesis, University of St Andrews (1989). See also Armstrong, 'The "Fyre of Ire Kyndild"', 51–84; A. Grant, 'Murder Will Out: Kingship, Kinship and Killing in Medieval Scotland', in S. Boardman and J. Goodare (eds), *Kings, Lord and Men in Scotland and Britain, 1300–1625: Essays in Honour of Jenny Wormald* (Edinburgh, 2014), 193–226.

[23] Armstrong, 'The Justice Ayre', 30–2.

[24] The topic of feud will be expounded below in Chapters 9 and 10.

The Administration of Justice

royal justice offered by the king of England in his capacity as guarantor of the common law of the realm. For the administration of its shires, the English crown relied on the local gentry to serve as various royal officers. The post of sheriff, normally held for a year at a time, was the most important of these (other posts included that of coroner and escheator). The sheriff's duties facilitated the operation of the king's judicial system, notably, executing and returning writs, summoning juries and maintaining county gaols.[25] Cumberland and Northumberland had an annual turnover of sheriffs, the western county sharing the office among twenty-six families of the upper gentry between 1399 and 1488, the eastern one among thirty-five in the same period. Considering the comparatively large number of landed families observable in Cumberland, that county shows greater exclusivity of participation in this office than its neighbour to the east. The custom that every third year, and every fourth year (thus twice in seven years) the sheriff of Northumberland raised a financial levy known as 'hede penes' on the commons of the county was brought to an end by petition to parliament in 1445.[26] The shrievalty of Westmorland was, by contrast, held in heredity by the Cliffords, who normally exercised the office through undersheriffs found among their county tenants serving for a few years at a time. This was shared among an even more exclusive group of fifteen families.[27] In 1462, following the Clifford attainder, the shrievalty was granted to John Parr, esquire. Three years later the office came to Richard, earl of Warwick. After Warwick's death and confiscation following the Readeption of 1470–1, Parr again obtained the shrievalty, holding it till his death in 1475. In that same year, his brother, Sir William, received the office for life, and he held it until his death in 1483. In November 1485, Henry VII restored Henry, tenth Lord Clifford, to his inheritance, including the shrievalty.[28] In Cumberland and Northumberland the pattern of annual tenures of

---

[25] On the local officers, see Carpenter, *Locality and Polity,* ch. 8. See also R. Gorski, *The Fourteenth-Century Sheriff* (Woodbridge, 2003); Carpenter, 'General Introduction', in *CIPM XXII* 1422–7.

[26] *PROME,* February 1445, item 34; April 1425, item 40. The 'poure communes' of the county asked for the practice to cease as of the feast of St John the Baptist in 1446, suggesting that the seven-year cycle fell in 1446, 1439, 1432, 1425, 1418, 1411, 1404, 1397 and so on.

[27] See Chapter 4. Wml.'s count includes three branches of the Lancasters, and Nbl.'s count includes at least three branches of the Herons. These numbers are for sheriffs, and undersheriffs serving hereditary sheriffs, taken from *LOS,* 27, 91, 98, 150–1. All hereditary sheriffs are included.

[28] In 1397 the Cliffords were briefly deprived of the office, when Richard II granted it to Ralph, earl of Westmorland, but the grant was soon reversed. In 1467 Warwick's undersheriff was Ralph Blenkinsopp, and, in 1485, Lord Clifford's brother exercised the office. Sir Richard Ratcliffe was sheriff from November 1483, and Roger Bellingham was briefly in office after Bosworth (*GEC,* III, 290; *CPR 1396–9,* 267, 361–2; *CPR 1461–7,* 187, 280, 435; Tuck, 'Emergence of a Northern Nobility', 14; Cardew, 'Anglo-Scottish', 378–9, 445–6; Booth, 'Landed Society', 14, 152–3, 219, 221).

173

Part III

the shrievalty changed in the reign of Edward IV. From 1466 till his death in 1471, John Neville of Montague, earl of Northumberland, held a life grant of the office in that county. Then, in 1474, the king granted it for life to Henry Percy, fourth earl of Northumberland. The following year, Richard, duke of Gloucester, received a similar grant concerning Cumberland. Gloucester exercised the Cumberland office by undersheriff until he became king in 1483, when he appointed a local esquire as his replacement. After 1485, the office returned to its normal pattern of annual appointment. Similarly, Percy exercised the Northumberland office by undersheriff and held it until 1488, when the king diminished the earl's life-tenure to a grant during pleasure. After the earl's death in 1489, the shrievalty returned to a system of annual tenure.[29]

The work of the sheriffs and other local officers supported the operation of the common law. The two premier courts of the king's common law sat at Westminster. While the first of these, the common pleas, was concerned with private litigation, the second, the king's bench, did the same and also dealt with cases concerning royal interests and crown prosecutions. A well-developed legal profession provided necessary and costly services to litigants, and there was plenty of opportunity for delay.[30] Apart from the common law courts, English subjects could make direct appeals for equity, by petition to chancery, the royal council or parliament.[31] A chancery petition from Cumberland, datable to the late 1390s, illustrates this type of resort and the importance of the sheriff as the official link between Westminster and the localities in the system. Here the petitioners complained that they could not proceed at common law against a violent opponent because he was married to the sheriff's cousin, who was also the sister of the undersheriff.[32] Both the chancery and the council could implement mainprises and recognizances for parties to keep the peace. Such was the case in 1402 when certain men guaranteed that a Cumberland esquire, Richard Orfevre, would not harm William Egremont, the parson of Workington. Egremont had petitioned

---

[29] *CPR 1467–77*, 467, 485, 525, 531–2; *CFR 1485–1509*, nos 40, 81; *LOS*, 27, 98; Cardew, 'Anglo-Scottish', 378–84, 443–6; Booth, 'Landed Society', 125–7, 168, 178.

[30] An essential overview is offered in Maddern, *Violence and Social Order*, 27–74. See also M. Hastings, *The Court of Common Pleas in Fifteenth Century England* (Ithaca, 1947); M. Blatcher, *The Court of King's Bench, 1450–1550* (London, 1978), 1–7; Baker, *Introduction to English Legal History*, 17, 64–71, 76–7; Musson and Ormrod, *Evolution of English Justice*, 8–9, 12–13, 16–19.

[31] J.B. Post, 'Equitable Resorts before 1450', in E.W. Ives and A.H. Manchester (eds), *Law, Litigants and the Legal Profession* (London, 1983), 68–79; J.A. Guy, 'The Development of Equitable Jurisdictions, 1450–1550', in ibid., 80–6; Musson and Ormrod, *Evolution of English Justice*, 20–8.

[32] C 1/7/313: '*qas espuse la cosyne le viscont du dit conte qest la soere de son souzviscount*'.

The Administration of Justice

chancery about the violent attacks of his adversaries.[33] Decades later, Richard III established a new conciliar tribunal, creating the 'council in the north' in 1484, a body subordinate to the royal council with wide judicial authority over trespass and felony. Special ordinances gave it jurisdiction over riots and forcible entries, 'debates' and misbehaviours against the peace. An element of compromise in decisions was stressed: 'thassent of the parties' was to be necessary for determinations in matters of land.[34]

Second only to the sheriff in local importance were the justices of the peace (JPs). They conducted a large amount of judicial business in their own 'quarter sessions of the peace' and in support of itinerant justices who presided over other local courts, such as the assize and gaol delivery sessions, which in the north were typically held once a year.[35] Commissions of oyer and terminer and other special commissions of inquiry supplemented this system and were often initiated by the petition of an injured party.[36] Throughout England by the late fourteenth century, accused felons were regularly indicted at the peace sessions, normally on the basis of bills of indictment brought before the court.[37] Many prosecutions in the border counties originated in this way. As in other parts of the kingdom, despite fluctuation in the numbers of commissioned JPs during the century,[38] indictments were often found before only two or three named JPs actually sitting, frequently in a dual role as

---

[33] *CCR 1402–5*, 128; C 1/3/39; C 1/69/177. On recognizances and arbitration, see Powell, 'Settlement of Disputes', 33, 36–8.

[34] *British Library Harleian Manuscript 433*, ed. R. Horrox and P. Hammond, 4 vols (Gloucester, 1979–83), III, 107–8, 114–15; R.R. Reid, *The King's Council in the North* (London, 1921), 59–70, 83, 108; F.W. Brooks, *The Council of the North* (rev. edn, London, 1966), 11–12. Reid and Brooks suggest that the council's jurisdiction applied only within Yorks., but this is by no means clear.

[35] On the JPs' powers, see Powell, *Kingship, Law, and Society*, 12–20, 56–9; J.R. Lander, *English Justices of the Peace 1461–1509* (Gloucester, 1989), ch. 1; D.J. Clayton, 'Peace Bonds and the Maintenance of Law and Order in Late Medieval England: The Example of Cheshire', *BIHR*, 58 (1985), 133–4, 145–6; S. Walker, *Political Culture in Later Medieval England*, ed. M.J. Braddick (Manchester, 2006), ch. 4, 81–2.

[36] Cockburn, 'The Northern Assize Circuit'; Musson and Ormrod, *Evolution of English Justice*, 9–10, 42–53; R.C.E. Hayes, '"Ancient Indictments" for the North of England, 1461–1509', in Pollard (ed.), *Age of Richard III*, 20–1; Maddern, *Violence and Social Order*, 44–6; N.J. Coates, 'The Law Enforcement Policy of Edward IV', PhD thesis, University of Cambridge (2005), 43–4.

[37] Baker, *Introduction to English Legal History*, 576; Powell, *Kingship, Law, and Society*, 65–74; Coates, 'Law Enforcement Policy', 25–7, 40; Bellamy, *Criminal Trial*, 20–7.

[38] Roughly, average numbers of JPs named on the commissions for each border county rose from about ten in 1400–30, to about fifteen in 1430–60, and settled back to about thirteen in 1460–90. Larger commissions (reaching twenty for Cbl. in 1473: *CPR 1467–77*, 610) tended to be issued when different political interests were being accommodated (see the comments of Booth, 'Landed Society', 57, 183). Compare with Carpenter, *Locality and Polity*, 267–9; Walker, *Political Culture*, 90, 99–104; Wright, *Derbyshire Gentry*, 94.

175

Part III

justices of oyer and terminer.[39] There are numerous examples from the gaol delivery and king's bench records of indictments found before the JPs in the Lancastrian period. However, king's bench records between 1461 and 1494 reveal indictments from only *six* peace sessions in our counties.[40] Starting in the reign of Edward IV, prosecutions originating here with the JPs only very rarely made it into king's bench. A logical explanation for this is that most of these cases were in fact dealt with at gaol delivery, but records do not survive from this period by which the explanation could be tested.[41]

The counties of the English far north consisted of wards rather than hundreds, and the wards do not appear to have had courts. The sheriff's tourn, an element of the frankpledge system based on the hundred courts further south in England,[42] was introduced in our counties only in the thirteenth century, and its imposition on Northumberland, at least, was soon remitted.[43] Our period reveals eight explicit references to presentments made on the sheriff's tourn in Westmorland, and two in Cumberland, and there are many more instances from both of these counties to presentments made 'before the sheriff', implying the same thing.[44] As hereditary sheriffs, the Cliffords had complete control of this system in Westmorland (excepting the barony of Kendale), and, at their castle of Appleby, their undersheriff held the county court, maintained the county gaol (called the 'king's prison') and entertained the justices who came there to hold the sessions of the peace, assize and gaol delivery.[45] By

[39] For citation of individual oyer and terminer commissions across the century, see Armstrong, 'Local Conflict', 69.

[40] There is a dearth of peace session rolls surviving from the fifteenth century. The KB 9 indictments provide an indirect source of information on the sessions. They reveal a continually healthy number of indictments taken at the peace sessions before 1461. After 1461, the six sessions are 1474, Cbl. (KB 9/339 mm. 13, 14; see also KB 27/857 *rex* rots 7, 7d); 1475, Carlisle City (KB 9/343 m. 34); 1475, Nbl. (KB 9/343 m. 56); 1479, Cbl. (KB 9/361 mm. 11,12); 1489, Cbl. (KB 9/389 mm. 15,16); and 1493, Wml. (KB 9/396 m. 4).

[41] Carpenter, *Locality and Polity*, ch. 13, detects a similar trend in Warks., but finds some cases in common pleas.

[42] W.A. Morris, *The Frankpledge System* (New York, 1910), 42–68; D.A. Crowley, 'The Later History of Frankpledge', *BIHR*, 48 (1975), 1–2.

[43] *North Durham*, ed. Raine, 3; Nicolson and Burn, *History and Antiquities*, i, 107; Morris, *Frankpledge System*, 44, 47–9, 51; J.E.A. Jolliffe, 'Northumbrian Institutions', *EHR*, 41 (1926), 2–5, 15, 26–35, 37; C.M. Fraser, 'The Northumberland Eyre of 1293', *Northern History*, 36 (2000), 18, 22, 30.

[44] Wml.: 1408 (JUST 3/191 rot. 67d); 1423 (×2) (JUST 3/199 rot. 32d); 1425 (JUST 3/199 rot. 31); 1437 (JUST 3/208 rot. 50d); 1440 (JUST 3/211 rot. 47); 1451 (JUST 3/211 rot. 51); 1453 (JUST 3/211 rot. 51d). Cbl.: 1430 (JUST 3/208 rot. 40); 1410 (KB 9/164/2 mm. 1–2). By this time, the verb '*indictare*' referred to both presentment and indictment. I am grateful to discussion with Christine Carpenter on this point.

[45] Booth, 'Landed Society', 14. A reference to frankpledge within the liberty of Kendale barony in 1505 is discussed in Hayes, 'Ancient Indictments', 29. For '*prisone dicti domini regis de Appulby*', see KB 27/714 rot. 36 (1439); KB 27/818 rot. 41d (1465).

The Administration of Justice

contrast there is no evidence for the sheriff's tourn in the county of Northumberland; however, the exterior jurisdictions of Newcastle (administered as a 'county borough' from 1400, with its own customs and liberties) and the liberty of Redesdale show otherwise.[46] In Northumberland itself the local 'peace' system relied on presentments made to the coroners. The peculiarly extended judicial role of these officials in this county is illustrated by the fact that it was not the sheriff but the coroners who prepared the calendar of offences for trial at the gaol delivery sessions.[47]

The private appeal of felony was another way to initiate prosecution.[48] An appeal could be launched by the victim, his relatives or a felon seeking reprieve in exchange for assistance in crown prosecution.[49] A number of such examples from the area of this study can be found in king's bench,[50] and the border gaol delivery sessions also reveal at least thirteen private appeals prosecuted locally between 1399 and 1459.[51] The high conviction rate on these appeals at gaol delivery (eight of thirteen) suggests that they were treated very seriously by otherwise lenient local juries, for the conviction rate at gaol delivery in the far north was a very low 5–7 per cent, lower than was typical in counties further south. By contrast with this usual rate of conviction in the border counties, when 'known and notorious' felons earned local opprobrium, their chances

---

[46] Newcastle-upon-Tyne has evidence for a tourn in 1489 (KB 9/382 mm. 6–7). In 1437 and 1444 inquisition post mortem juries attested to 'two annual views of frankpledge held after Easter and Michaelmas' in the liberty of Redesdale: *CIPM XXIV 1432–7*, no. 698, pp. 483–4; *CIPM XXVI 1442–7*, no. 217, pp. 125–6.

[47] For example, see JUST 3/54/3 mm. 1–4. M.E.H.J. Gollancz, 'The System of Gaol Delivery Rolls of the Fifteenth Century', MA thesis, University of London (1936), 25. See also R.F. Hunnisett, *The Medieval Coroner* (Cambridge, 1961), 5, 7, 95; Fraser, 'Northumberland Eyre', 19, 22, 30.

[48] Prosecution also began more rarely by trial upon 'record', or the laying of information: A. Harding, *A Social History of English Law* (Harmondsworth, 1966; repr. Gloucester, MA, 1973), 76–8; Neville, 'Gaol Delivery', 49.

[49] Powell, *Kingship, Law, and Society*, 71; Musson and Ormrod, *Evolution of English Justice*, 169–72; Bellamy, *Criminal Trial*, 37; Baker, *Introduction to English Legal History*, 574–6.

[50] For example, see Cbl., 1399, appeal, for mayhem (KB 27/554 rot. 19d); Nbl., 1429, appeal, for homicide (KB 27/672 rot. 60); Wml., 1439, appeal, for homicide (KB 27/714 rot. 36); Nbl., 1476, appeal, for homicide (KB 27/861 *rex* rot. 15).

[51] Wml., 1401, theft *vi et armis*, two different appeals against the same man (JUST 3/191 rot. 63); Wml., 1407, rape (JUST 3/191 rot. 66); Wml., 1411, rape, appealed before the county court of Wml. (JUST 3/191 rot. 69, also prosecuted by the crown); Cbl., 1422, theft (JUST 3/199 rot. 29d; also (rot. 30) indicted before the JPs); Nbl., 1423, depredation (JUST 3/199 rot. 21); Wml., 1438, depredation (JUST 3/208 rot. 51); Nbl., 1438, theft (JUST 3/208 rot. 36); Nbl., 1438, theft (JUST 3/208 rot. 36; also presented before the coroner); Nbl., 1438, theft (JUST 3/208 rot. 36; also presented before the coroner); Cbl., 1440, theft (JUST 3/211 rot. 39); Nbl., 1441, homicide (JUST 3/211 rot. 28d); Nbl., 1442, theft (JUST 3/211 rot. 30; also presented before the coroner); Cbl., 1442, assault and depredation (JUST 3/211 rot. 41).

Part III

were not good.[52] This was well understood by the yeoman John Maughan of Brokenheugh in Northumberland, indicted for theft and locally notorious. At dawn on the day he faced trial in 1434, he bit off his own tongue. Though the jurors (who related this tale) found him guilty, he was unable to answer the court, and he was remanded to prison.[53] By this desperate tactic Maughan may have hoped to buy time to secure a royal pardon.[54] Now silenced, he was able to convince no one of his worth, and he died in prison two years later. Maughan's case is also telling of the extent to which English common law relied on strict adherence to fixed procedures; in this instance an accused man created for himself a technical advantage. English legal culture placed high authority in the written record and its accuracy. The precise language used in a writ or indictment was vital, and the smallest errors or omissions from a set formula could make a document inadmissible and see a case thrown out of court.[55] All this ensured a measure of predictability, even fairness, before the law, but it also exposed the system's rigidity and left it open to manipulation.

The jurisdiction of royal officials and justices did not normally extend into privately held liberties, where the lord in question employed his own officers. The most complete franchises in our area ('royal liberties' or regalities) were those held by the bishop of Durham (Norhamshire and Islandshire), the archbishop of York (Hexhamshire) and the lord of Tynedale.[56] For example, Lord Bourchier employed the prior of Hexham as his chancellor within Tynedale in 1434.[57] In Norhamshire and Islandshire, the bishop of Durham had the full range of local royal officials paralleled in miniature. These posts were staffed by local gentry, usually for periods of several years. Multiple office-holding by one person was common.[58] The unruly reputation of some of the English

---

[52] A higher overall conviction rate at 30 per cent was typical of southern counties. As Neville points out, this is consistent with the general observation that conviction rates decreased as distance from London increased (Neville, 'Gaol Delivery', 57, 59; H.R.T. Summerson, 'Crime and Society in Medieval Cumberland', *TCWAAS*, n.s., 82 (1982), 111–24, at 111, 117; Powell, *Kingship, Law, and Society*, 82; Storey, *Thomas Langley*, 140; Hanawalt, *Crime and Conflict*, 56, 58–9).

[53] JUST 3/208 rot. 31d; JUST 3/54/14 m. 6. See also JUST 3/199 rot. 19 (1422).

[54] On the use of pardons in England, see Powell, *Kingship, Law, and Society*, 229–40; Musson and Ormrod, *Evolution of English Justice*, 82; T.A. Green, 'Societal Concepts of Criminal Liability for Homicide in Medieval England', *Speculum*, 47 (1972), 669–94.

[55] Carpenter, *Locality and Polity*, 705; Baker, *Introduction to English Legal History*, 103.

[56] On the different types of liberties in the region, see Holford and Stringer, *Border Liberties*, 2–3, 9, 173, 368.

[57] The chancellor issued a pardon to one Alan Marschale of Haughton, 27 November 1434 (NA: ZSW 2/55).

[58] From 1404 to 1476 the Ogles dominated these offices. Thereafter it was held by various gentry (and jointly by the earl of Northumberland in 1481–2). See *North Durham*, ed. Raine, 7–12; *LOS*,

178

The Administration of Justice

border liberties has already been cited, and an abundance of franchises meant that felons could readily criss-cross jurisdictions to escape a pursuing officer. Poor cooperation between officials was often bewailed.[59] In 1414 the commons of Northumberland petitioned parliament that the autonomy of Tynedale, Redesdale and Hexhamshire was exacerbating local turbulence. In response, a statute permitted common law to operate within Tynedale and Hexhamshire.[60] This marked an intrusion into these two 'royal liberties', but it left unmolested the more ambiguous return-of-writs franchise held by the lord of Redesdale. A similar franchise was held by Tynemouth Priory over its manors scattered around county, but fragmented Tynemouthshire was not singled out as a source of misconduct.[61] The focus of anxiety was over concentrated blocks of territory with exemptions from the jurisdiction of the king's officers. Yet again, in 1421 the 'poor commons' of all three march counties complained to parliament on the same theme. They asked for an ordinance for the lords of the liberties to appoint sufficient justices, and to hold their sessions and gaol deliveries at least twice a year. In response, the government extended the statute of 1414 to cover Redesdale as well.[62] Thus royal government responded to the turbulent reputation of the northern liberties, albeit clumsily. Nor was this to be the end of the story. In 1422 William and Mary Stapleton found it suited their claim to the Alston Moor mine on the South Tyne to assert the age-old and continuing status of Tynedale as a *'dominium regale'* contiguous with the county of Cumberland.[63] In 1437 and again in 1444 the inquisitions post mortem for lords of Redesdale attested to the right of tenants to hold rent-free in time of war 'except their aid to their lord in keeping the valley of Redesdale ... from wolves and robbers', and to the wide range of

---

91; C.H. Hunter Blair, 'The Sheriffs of Northumberland, Part III, the Sheriffs of Norham', *Archaeologia Aeliana*, 4th ser., 21 (1943), 72–89.

[59] See above, p. 13. On flight, see Summerson, 'Crime and Society', 113; Neville, *Violence, Custom and Law*, 115, 192.

[60] *'plusours gentz des Fraunchises de Tyndale Riddesdale et Exhamshire adjoignantz a les marches d'Escoce'* were daily afflicting the commons with *'plusours murders tresons homicides et robberies et autres maffaitz'*. And the *'gentz'* were harbouring Scots, with whom they stole goods and conducted kidnappings. The petitioners complained that the sheriff was unable, *'saunz tres graunde force et poair des gentz de mesme le Comtee' . . . 'et pur doute de morte'* to execute the law in these franchises, and did not dare to do so (*PROME*, April 1414, item 20; *SR*, II, 177–8). See Holford and Stringer, *Border Liberties*, 202, 327, 368, 409.

[61] Holford and Stringer, *Border Liberties*, 203–27.

[62] *'ne nul commune droit ou justice illoeqes est fait par minustres du roi ne par autre juge suffisant'* (SC 8/130/6459; *PROME*, May 1421, item 22; *SR*, II, 206–7, 177–8). On these petitions, see Storey, *Thomas Langley*, 140, 153; Powell, *Kingship, Law, and Society*, 265; Neville, *Violence, Custom and Law*, 110–11, 115.

[63] C 44/27/17, and KB 27/652 *rex* rots 10–10d. See Holford and Stringer, *Border Liberties*, 347–8.

Part III

governmental and judicial rights in the liberty allowed since the reigns of Edward I and Edward III by title of prescription, including exemption from interference by sheriffs or other royal officers except in default of the lord's bailiffs.[64] Thus the local advantages of these liberties could also be asserted. Still further tweaking continued in 1466, when the archbishop of York was given full power to receive into the king's protection any persons indicted of treason within Hexhamshire and Tynedale. Following the reversion to the crown of the latter in 1483, Henry VII abolished the liberty in 1495 and included Tynedale as parcel of the county of Northumberland.[65] Nevertheless, both Tynedale and Redesdale would remain troublesome into the next century.[66] All these interventions should be understood in terms of a mixture of genuine local frustrations over the jurisdictional complexities posed by franchises, the tendency to frame those frustrations in terms of the frontier rhetoric already discussed (or to disregard them when there were advantages in so doing) and, as we shall see, evidence that certain franchises did in fact house the troublemakers of which petitioners complained.[67]

Although there were some differences among the English border counties, the manner in which the system of royal justice operated was essentially the same across the far north. Throughout the English realm, this system did not rest solely on the expectation of a strong king imposing 'law and order' on the localities, as an older school of thought once accepted.[68] On the contrary, historians now appreciate the role of the gentry and the nobility in managing conflict among their social equals and inferiors. The local power of magnates and their affinities was not necessarily a force for disruption, but potentially a mechanism for good rule. In order to rule effectively, a successful king, like Henry V or Edward IV, was able to harness the private power of the magnates and gentry and forge this together with the public authority of the crown.[69] This chapter began with comment on the late medieval view of an early medieval ruler, King Oswald. For his late medieval successors much, of course, had changed.

---

[64] *CIPM XXVI 1442–7*, no. 217, pp. 125–6 (quotation); *CIPM XXIV 1432–7*, no. 698, pp. 483–4.

[65] *CPR 1461–67*, 525; *CPR 1476–85*, 495; *NCH*, XV, 158, citing *SR*, II, 575 (c. 9). See also Pollard, *North-Eastern England*, 100.

[66] C66/582, part 1, m 6d, calendared in *CPR 1494–1509*, 160 (identifying the 'surnames' there in 1498). See also Bishop Fox's monition of the same year against the '*latrones, fures, raptores, depredatores famosos et manifestos*' of Tynedale and Redesdale (*Depositions and Other Ecclesiastical Proceedings from the Courts of Durham*, ed. J. Raine (1845), 37–41; *Fox's Register*, 121). For comment, see Tuck, 'War and Society', 51–2. The crown purchased Redesdale in 1546 (Meikle, *British Frontier*, 88).

[67] See above, pp. 90–3, and below, pp. 236–8.   [68] See the topic introduced above, pp. 39–40.

[69] For example: Carpenter, 'Law, Justice and Landowners', 205; Powell, *Kingship, Law, and Society*, ch. 1; Maddern, *Violence and Social Order*, ch. 7; Castor, *Duchy of Lancaster*, 227–34.

The Administration of Justice

The law had grown more complex, and legal and other governmental institutions had become comparatively elaborate. Late medieval kings had responsibility to direct landowners to cooperate to ensure the continuous functioning of the organs of government. All the same, in doing so, kings might still rule by the sheer force of personality, demanding the resolution of conflict beyond this system altogether. John Hardyng gave an apt illustration of this aspect of successful kingship when encouraging Edward IV to follow the example set by Henry V. The chronicler related a story in which two knights informed the king:

> That none might them accorde or treate to peace,
> Ne iustyce none of fyghting might them cease.
> The lordes then greatly counsayled the kyng
> To make them fynde suretye to kepe the peace,
> The kyng answered anon without tarying,
> I shalbe youre borowe now or I cease,
> For of this thyng I may not longe you prease;
> But what case fall that slaine is one of you,
> That other shall dye to God I make a vowe.
> They heryng this, anon they were accorde
> By frendes that treated yt time betwene them two,
> And after that they were no more at discorde.[70]

This tale alludes to the process of peacemaking and compromise, by arbitration or other means, to which we have already referred, and upon which we shall expand in Chapter 10.

BORDER JUSTICE AND MARCH LAW

The second apparatus in England's far north which related primarily to the regulation of local conflict was that of border justice underpinned by the Anglo-Scottish law of the march.[71] In the borderlands a unique body of international law applied. The first recorded meeting of local representatives to address a boundary dispute between the realms was in 1245, and, four years later, a meeting was held to set down the first surviving written 'recognisance' of the laws of the march, which had existed as unwritten custom (of uncertain antiquity) until this time.[72] March law

---

[70] *Chron. Hardyng*, 383. (Carpenter, *Locality and Polity*, 514, 534–45, shows that Edward IV came to intervene in precisely this way in certain disputes, especially later in his second reign.)

[71] The law of the march has been introduced above, pp. 16, 57 and 67.

[72] *Leges Marchiarum*, ed. W. Nicolson (London, 1705); *The Acts of the Parliaments of Scotland*, ed. T. Thomson and C. Innes, 12 vols (Edinburgh, 1814–75), i, 413–16; *CDS*, I, nos 827, 832, 1676, 1699; *Anglo-Scottish Relations*, ed. Stones, 27, 38–53, 54–7; Neilson, 'March Laws'; Barrow, 'The Anglo-Scottish Border: Growth and Structure', 197–212; Summerson, 'Early Development',

Part III

continued to evolve in both customary and written form over the next three centuries, periodically recodified by indentures sealed between England and Scotland. After war erupted in 1296, most of these indentures took the form of truces which also set out mutually agreed rule changes. March law was administered through various courts, held both within each realm and on the border. The latter were known variously as days of march or days of truce, in which panels of men known as 'conservators of the truce' heard and determined offences.[73] In what follows we shall examine march law in its domestic and international contexts.

The extent of the administrative framework of the march has already been noted; each subdivision of the English frontier was under the jurisdiction of its own crown-appointed warden. The law of the march took on a domestic jurisdiction in both adjoining kingdoms. In England wardenial jurisdiction covered private franchises and, as such, made them the sole royal officials with such latitude in the marches.[74] English warden courts were subject to conciliar and parliamentary oversight. In 1423 a decision of the warden court of the east march concerning a Scottish prisoner was appealed by petition to the royal council, and an investigatory commission was appointed. That body included three men learned in canon and civil law.[75] In 1434 the same warden court found an accused esquire guilty of truce breaking and bound him over to the bishop of Durham for his offence.[76] Two years later, the council empowered Sir Robert Umfraville to hear pleas in the court of the east march until a new warden was appointed.[77] From the 1440s there survive various examples of English wardens taking the faith of Scots swearing their allegiance to the English king, presumably done in the warden court.[78]

A prominent concern of domestic march law was the offence of treason. The subject has been explored by Neville, who has shown that accused traitors were often tried before the local common law courts, under the treasonable offences of adhering to or aiding the king's

---

29–42; Dunlop, 'Redresses and Reparacons', 344n 24; Neville, 'Scottish Influences', 161–85; Neville, *Violence, Custom and Law*, 2–11.

[73] Summerson, 'Early Development', 37–41; Neville, *Violence, Custom and Law*, 22, 32, 37–8, 52, 58, 69, 78, 109, 126–9, 133, 154, 163, 174, 192–3.

[74] For the extent of the English march, and its division into the east, west and middle marches, see above, p. 58.

[75] *CPR 1422–9*, 78.

[76] DURH 3/37 m. 8d, abstracted in *Thirty-Third Annual Report of the Deputy Keeper of the Public Records* (1872), app. no. 2, p. 164.

[77] *CDS*, V, 294, citing E 28/58; *Rot. Scot.*, II, 296.

[78] Alnwick Castle: Northumberland MSS, Box 761, no. 21; CAC, Carlisle: D/Lons/C 58.

The Administration of Justice

enemies and of levying war against the king, set out by statute in 1352. The warden courts also heard and determined such cases (high treason), as well as those of truce-breaking (march treason), but in our period only patchy evidence for this is to be found.[79] For example, the west march warden was remunerated in 1401 'for the arrest of six traitors of the marches of Scotland put to death because of their treason'.[80] The following year, the east march warden executed a Scottish knight, captured at the battle of Humbleton Hill, for treason on the grounds that he had been born in Teviotdale when that territory was under English allegiance; thus, he was convicted for his subsequent adherence to the Scottish king.[81] A major change to English treason law came in 1414, under the statute of truces, whereby the definition of high treason ('*haut traisone*') was expanded to include truce-breaking. The effect of this legislation was to remove the wardens' jurisdiction over cases involving truce-breaking (march treason) and place it in the common law courts.[82] This move exemplifies the lack of confidence in the system of march law exhibited by Henry V. The king sought to address truce-breaking with at least one special commission to the east march warden's officers, but the whole state of affairs proved ineffective.[83] As a result of the statute of truces, international march days (for the redress of breaches of the truce) ceased to be held with the Scots. Despite the statute, these were resumed in August 1425, when the English government issued commissions to this effect.[84] After years of complaints from the borders, the act was suspended in 1442 and superseded in 1450.[85] After this time, the English wardens' jurisdiction over march treason resumed, as was made clear by legislation in 1453.[86]

---

[79] *SR*, I, 320; Neville, 'Law of Treason', 7–8.

[80] '*et pur la prise de sys traitours [des] marches descoce mys a mort a cause de leur treison trente liures*': E 404/16/695; Summerson, 'Early Development', 38; Neville, *Violence, Custom and Law*, 85.

[81] The knight was Sir William Stewart of the Forest (Jedworth Forest): *Scotichronicon*, viii, 46–9.

[82] *PROME*, April 1414, item 23; *SR*, II, 178–81 (c. vi). The English wardens' commissions ceased to include the power to punish truce-breakers, as they had in 1399, 1404 and 1412. From the time of the truce of 1449 the English wardens' power was restored: *Rot. Scot.*, II, 146, 166, 171, 200–1, 372. See Neville, 'Law of Treason', 15, 19; Neville, *Violence, Custom and Law*, 107, 111–12, 121n 98, 125.

[83] *CPR 1413–16*, 343. This was a commission to arrest specific offenders (dated 6 May 1415), not an oyer and terminer commission, as per Neville, *Violence, Custom and Law*, 113.

[84] *Foedera*, IV, iv, 117; *PPC*, III, 171–4; *Rot. Scot.*, II, 253.

[85] SC 8/130/6459; *PROME*, November 1415, item 10; ibid., October 1416, item 31; ibid., May 1421, item 22; ibid., November 1450, item 20; *SR*, II, 358–9. Neville, 'Law of Treason', 14–15, 19–21. On march treason, see also Reid, 'Office of Warden', 484nn 29, 30.

[86] 'for to answere to enditementz taken in the courtes called the wardeyn courtes of the seid marches, for attemptates supposid to be doon ayenst the vertue of the treuxe within the said shires': *PROME*, March 1453, item 66.

Part III

Evidence from either side of the border also exists for cases of treason in the marches which were prosecuted by judicial duel. In England during the 1390s, one Robert del Hall appealed a Robert Dodd ['Dode'] of treason before the earl of Northumberland, then warden of the east march, and pursued the appeal to a duel in which he was killed by Dodd and his goods were forfeited to the king.[87] It is not clearly stated that the duel took place in the context of the domestic warden court, but the warden's presence suggests this may well have been so. The parties were probably all of yeoman status, suggesting that, rather than being duels of chivalry, these were non-chivalric duels of law. Wager of battle, known as 'handwarsil', had featured in march law (and in the common law of England and of Scotland) during the thirteenth century, but, by 1400, as a method of proof in civil litigation, trial by battle had been outdated for more than a century.[88] However, an extraordinary case from 1423 over a manor in Cumberland between Sir Peter Tilliol and Henry, earl of Northumberland, was pursued to a battle by champions but not actually fought.[89] Where duels of law did persist in England, it was only in battles fought by approvers, and the last record of an approver's duel dates from mid-century.[90] It would seem that for cases of treason, combat remained justiciable in English domestic march law early in the fifteenth century, and such treason duels before the wardens could be transmuted to duels of chivalry: between 1399 and 1401, Sir Gerard Heron received payment for the making of (jousting) lists for five battles touching treason which the east march warden had ordered to be held on 15 May 1396 at Berwick.[91] Scholars have observed the overlap, made obvious here, between march law and the chivalric law of arms, which includes the laws of war: in 1386 the earl of Northumberland as warden was

---

[87] The Hall–Dodd duel would probably have occurred between June 1391 and June 1396, when the earl was warden of the east march: *CPR 1399–1401*, 119; *Foedera*, III, iv, 167. See pp. 159 and 306.

[88] Neilson, *Trial by Combat* (Glasgow, 1890), chs 15, 36, 37, 64, 88; Neilson, 'March Laws', 17, 20, 22–3, 67; M.J. Russell, 'I Trial by Battle and the Writ of Right', *JLH*, 1 (1980), 111–34; M.J. Russell, 'II Trial by Battle and the Appeals of Felony', *JLH*, 1 (1980), 144; J.B. Post, 'The Evidential Value of Approvers' Appeals: The Case of William Rose, 1389', *Law and History Review*, 3 (1985), 91–100.

[89] The earl impleaded Tilliol on a writ of right concerning the manor of Torpenhow (Cbl.). In the end Percy's champion defaulted, almost certainly by prearrangement: C.H. Williams (ed.), *Year Books of Henry VI: 1 Henry VI* (1933), 95–100; Neilson, *Trial by Combat*, 31–74, 149–60. In 1410 Sir Henry Percy of Atholl (the second earl's first cousin) gave a 200-mark recognisance to Tilliol, indicating real tension: *CCR 1409–13*, 55.

[90] F.C. Hamil, 'The King's Approvers: A Chapter in the History of English Criminal Law', *Speculum* 11 (1936), 238–58, at 256–7; A.J. Musson, 'Turning King's Evidence: The Prosecution of Crime in Late Medieval England', *Oxford Journal of Legal Studies*, 19 (1999), 467–79; Powell, *Kingship, Law and Society*, 71–3.

[91] E 28/26, printed in *CDS*, V, 282.

The Administration of Justice

empowered to punish those who released Scottish prisoners without permission 'according to the courts of arms and the customs of the marches' (*secundam foros armorum et consuetudines marchiarum*).[92] Just as the English warden courts shared their jurisdiction over treason with the royal courts, so too they shared jurisdiction with the military court of chivalry. This latter tribunal sat at Berwick in May 1408 where it condemned a knight to death for treason done in league with the rebellious earl of Northumberland, and it was again active in the north during the strife of the 1460s.[93] As we shall see below, judicial duels also featured in cross-border disputes around the turn of the century, and they suggest one way in which accustomed practices in the far north, particularly those related to the law of arms, interpenetrated with domestic march law and common law.

March law in its international guise was exercised in the border tribunals known as days of march or days of truce. These assemblies were the equivalent of lovedays in the Irish and Welsh marches and '*jours en marche*' in the frontier around English-held Gascony. They were convened intermittently at customary locations near the frontier, such as Reddenburn in the east march.[94] Financial records from both sides of the border document these meetings throughout the century, frequently in the form of reimbursements for the expenses incurred by officials (*pur les jours des marches et Reparacons des attemptates countre les dites trieues*).[95] At march days, the wardens and their officers, and the panels of conservators from both realms, met to hear and determine bills of complaint submitted by individual borderers. The accused, if found and brought before the court, were subjected to the testimony of mixed juries (a practice revived in 1429 after a period of lapse), consisting of even numbers of

---

[92] *Rot. Scot.*, II, 79; Summerson, 'Early Development', 38–40; Neville, *Violence, Custom and Law*, 84–5.

[93] M.H. Keen, 'The Jurisdiction and Origins of the Constable's Court', in J. Gillingham and J.C. Holt (eds), *War and Government in the Middle Ages* (Cambridge, 1984), 159–69; M.H. Keen, 'Treason Trials under the Law of Arms', *TRHS*, 5th ser., 12 (1962), 85–103, at 85, 90, 100; Keen, *Chivalry*, 175–6; Ross, *Edward IV*, 16; Bellamy, *Law of Treason*, 145–76. In 1395 a duel was to be fought before the constable of England by a Scot against the man whom he had appealed of treason: *Foedera*, III, iv, 110; *Rot. Scot.*, II, 129; *Cal. Deeds*, vol. 158, p. 164; Neilson, 'March Laws', 67n 3.

[94] See above at p. 67. See also Davies, *Lordship and Society*, 219–20; R. Frame, *English Lordship in Ireland, 1318–1361* (Oxford, 1982), 38–9.

[95] The wording of the warrant for payment to Sir Robert Umfraville which also specifies a day of march to be held at Reddenburn, 1426 (E 404/42/297); see also references to Haddenstank, 1431 and 1451 (E 404/47/326; E 28/81/46). For Scottish records, see, for example, *ER*, III, 635–6, *ER*, IV, 163, 224, 253 (the latter noting the expenses of the abbot of Kelso for '*diei marchiarum pro treugis*', in 1416, and those of the earl of Douglas). See also *TA*, I, 45 (1473), 48 (1474), 96 (1488), 173 (1490), 172, 178, 183 (1491).

185

Part III

Scottishmen and Englishmen.[96] After 1484, when the wardens ceased to be conservators as well, they acted as the presidents of these tribunals.[97] The books, rolls and documents of the courts were kept personally by the wardens. From the 1340s, notaries and clerks trained in civil law became increasingly involved in proceedings, and the attendance of clerks at days of march was required after 1429.[98] Record-keeping and the involvement of lawyers suggests a well-developed legal system, so much that, in 1492, the Scottish conciliar session relied upon the 'rolment' of the warden's court for proof concerning a case of delayed payment of redress and redemption of a pledge entered in England at a day of march.[99] The wardens might exert pressure on their countrymen to ensure attendance at the border courts, as is illustrated by two letters from the earl of Northumberland datable to the 1390s. The earl wrote to two unnamed men concerning their plans not to attend a '*iour de marche*' to be held at Kershope Bridge in the west march. Their attendance was commanded 'to do and take as reason will for what will be determined there upon you and your men', and they were threatened with distraint of body and goods. The use of '*reson*' in the earl's phrasing suggests not a vague sense of equity but, rather, a synonym for 'law' familiar from Scottish plaints of 'wrang and unreson' or 'wrang and unlaw' – in this case that law being the law of the march.[100]

Of greater weight than days of march, but not so great as a full embassy, were the international border 'diets'.[101] On these occasions, which were sometimes called 'great' days of march, crown-appointed

[96] For the submission of pre-trial bills, see *CCR 1429–35*, 292–3; *PPC*, IV, 350–2. The procedure for march days is outlined in NRS: SP 6/20 (29 September 1458), and similar provisions appear in the indentures of 1429 and 1449: *Foedera*, IV, iv, 148–9; ibid., V, ii, 15–19, 25; *Rot. Scot.*, II, 337–41, discussed in Neville, *Violence, Custom and Law*, 131, 133, 139–40, 144; Cardew, 'Anglo-Scottish', 291–300. On the development of mixed juries, see Neville, *Violence, Custom and Law*, 41, 132–3, 144; Summerson, 'Early Development', 37.

[97] Neville, *Violence, Custom and Law*, 174; Reid, 'Office of Warden', 483.

[98] In 1434 the earl of Salisbury, as joint warden of the west and each marches, requested that the relevant court books be transferred to his custody: *PPC*, IV, 268–77; Neville, *Violence, Custom and Law*, 137, and on march lawyers see 33, 59, 131, 155; Neville, 'Keeping the Peace', 10–11. The earliest surviving records of presentments made to a warden court date from about 1500 and relate to the English east march: Summerson, 'Early Development', 38.

[99] *ADC*, I, 208.

[100] NA: ZSW 1/101: '*pur faire et prendre come reson voet qar de ce que serra determine illoeqs sur vous et voz gentz*'. See also ZSW 1/102. A date of c. 1381 has also been suggested for these two letters: Neville, 'Keeping the Peace', 9n 5. On plaints of 'wrang and unreson', see A. Harding, 'Rights, Wrongs and Remedies in Late Medieval English and Scots Law', in *Miscellany IV*, Stair Society (Edinburgh, 2002), 2; H.L. MacQueen, 'Some Notes on Wrang and Unlaw', *Miscellany V*, Stair Society (Edinburgh, 2005), 15, 17, 23.

[101] For Scottish evidence of '*dieta marchiarum*', see *ER*, III, 646 (1405); *ER*, IV, 115 (1410); *TA*, I, 48 (1474). More important ambassadorial meetings are recorded in *ER*, IV, 466 (James I's meeting at Coldingham with Cardinal Beaufort, 1429); *ER*, V, 52 (ambassadors to England, 1438).

The Administration of Justice

commissioners (usually including the wardens) would meet to discuss major border incidents (called '*attemptats*' against the truce) or to negotiate a prorogation of the armistice.[102] They could also handle more minor matters, as was planned for a diet in 1471 at Alnwick, before which it was proclaimed that all complainants should appear before the commissioners on the assigned day 'according to the old use and custom wont at such meetings to be observed'.[103] A similar meeting at Reddenburn in 1458 handled major issues like reparation for an English raid by sea on Kirkcudbright and the harbouring of the exiled earl of Douglas and his associates in England, but the commissioners off-loaded unfinished minor business to the wardens at the upcoming days of march.[104] If the mutual political will existed for international cooperation, these diets could be productive problem-solving assemblies.[105] Equally, a narrative of a diet held over four days in October 1401 shows that they could serve as occasions for diplomatic posturing.[106] Less formal diplomacy might also be conducted by border gentry. For example, the Northumberland knight Robert Maners, called the 'Larde of Etoll, Inglisman', met with James III and had servants who conveyed letters to the Scottish king. Similar cross-border exchanges may be detected in Scottish records.[107]

The primary concern of march law was the regulation of behaviour between English and Scottish inhabitants of the borders. It provided a framework for the redress of wrong, particularly violent wrong resulting from truce-breaking, such as when marchers crossed the border to steal goods or livestock, to kidnap victims to be held for ransom, or to kill.[108] Thus, march law was one normative system for the management of conflict in the region, albeit one of a strongly international nature. In part, it reflected the norms of English royal justice, for the chief administrators of the marches were wardens acting under royal authority, and, as we have seen, the domestic warden courts were subject to oversight by the council and parliament. The indentures by which late medieval

---

[102] For example, a meeting at Reddenburn in 1426 was to make '*reparation sur les attemptas faitz et perpetreez par les subgiz de l'une et l'autre coustee seloncque la teneur des dits trieuves*': PPC, III, 205–6. '*Attemptats*' and its cognate renderings was a term common to documents in English, French and Latin.

[103] CCR 1468–71, no. 772, p. 208. See also TA, I, 43–5, 67.   [104] NRS: SP 6/20.

[105] Dunlop, 'Redresses and Reparacons', 344.

[106] Anglo-Scottish Relations, ed. Stones, 173–82; CDS, V, 279. See above, p. 68.

[107] Maners of Etal received £44 for his expenses in 1474 (TA, I, 70). For the period 1455–6, the expenses of the visits of other Northumbrian gentlemen, Thomas Ogle ['Ogill'] and William Maners, and, in 1459, of William Bertram, to the household of the accountant of the wool customs in Edinburgh are recorded (ER, VI, 121, 499).

[108] On violence, see below, pp. 199–201, 232–6, 270–3 and 297–307. For the most recent summary of march law, see Neville, Violence, Custom and Law, 184–95.

Part III

international march law was modified and codified were framed as contracts between the kings of England and Scotland, negotiated under royal commission and personally ratified by them. Nevertheless, the law itself originated in local usage and was negotiated locally; it was not the law of one realm or one king. It allowed significant room for the accommodation of local accustomed practices of conflict management, many of which became codified within its remit.[109] This is most thoroughly demonstrated by march law's emphasis not on punishment but on compensation and redress, through the restitution of plundered goods. In this regard, the exchange of pledges (or 'borrowis') as surety for the performance of various obligations, especially the payment of court-ordered reparations, was an important and long-standing mechanism of march law.[110] It put an element of trust into cross-border dispute resolution and the arrangement of compensation, as well as placing clear personal liability on disputants, a pressure which many must have sought to evade. Cases may be identified in Scottish court records where disputes arose over the capture and escape of men to be handed over into England as pledges 'to mak redress ... according to the lawis of the merchis'.[111] A further indication that trust, and reputation for trustworthiness, were crucial in this context is demonstrated by the practice (which did not become codified and which is not attested until the sixteenth century) of 'baughling'. This was a public denouncement – and provocation – of one who broke his word, performed by displaying a glove on a spear point to symbolise the 'false hand' of the accused. Although this has been identified with the late medieval procedure of 'dishonour', the latter tended to focus on actions of the reversal or defacement of heraldic arms to accompany accusations of treason or breach of promise (such as for non-payment of ransoms).[112] Despite certain similarities with this procedure, which was by no means confined to English chivalry, the context in which 'baughling' appears in the

---

[109] See above, p. 36. The idea of 'accustomed practices' advanced in the present study (as in Armstrong, 'Local Conflict') resembles the concept of 'behaviour-custom' as discussed in E. Kadens, 'Custom's Two Bodies', in K.L. Jansen, G. Geltner and A.E. Lester (eds), *Center and Periphery: Studies on Power in the Medieval World in Honor of William Chester Jordan* (Leiden, 2013), 239–48.

[110] See below, pp. 328–31; Summerson, 'Early Development', 33–5; Neville, 'Scottish Influences', 167, 177–9.

[111] *ADC*, I, 48–9 (1480). A case from 1493 concerns redress in exchange for a pledge held in England: *ADA*, 173.

[112] Neilson, 'March Laws', 64–6. Summerson, 'Early Development', 38, connects baughling with dishonour, as discussed in Keen, *Laws of War*, 173. For a better-known example of defacement of arms and accusations of treason, see H.R. Castor, '"Walter Blount is gone to serve Traytours": The Sack of Elvaston and the Politics of the North Midlands in 1454', *Midland History*, 19 (1994), 31.

The Administration of Justice

Anglo-Scottish borderlands is rather more suggestive of an overt challenge by the armigerous, somewhat like the throwing down of gauntlets to offer wager of battle[113] and somewhat like the German cartel of defiance, which initiated a state of 'feud'.[114] Fifteenth-century English comparators, in broad terms, should perhaps include the written declarations of hostilities before 'private' battles such as those at Clyst (1455) and Nibley Green (1470).[115]

Direct mechanisms of redress existed under border law, such as what came to be known as the 'trod', an old custom of the march which was a sanction for the recovery by force of stolen goods from across the border.[116] It was given clear expression in the truce indenture of 1386, which made provision for 'men folwand thar gudes with hond or without horn or with bathe without spere or bowe, and whasa makes lettyng to silk followyng sal mak asseth for the gudes'.[117] The need for such articulation may have become elevated following a conspicuous incident of 1379 where goods were forcefully recovered.[118] This ritual of pursuit was reiterated in the truce indenture of 1398, with the addition that a person impeding the trod was liable to loss of life and limb.[119] In practice, those following the trod ran the risk of being accused of raiding and breaking the truce, and an important consequence of the English statute of truces of 1414 was that it restricted the ability of English borderers to take reprisals on the Scots, for all truce-breaking was thenceforward to be construed as high treason.[120] This situation may have influenced the further elaboration of the trod in 1424, when the

---

[113] As did the lords appellant in parliament in 1388: '*les seignurs appelantz devant le roy en plein parlement on ewages les gauns et toutz les seignurs piers du roiaume et plusours chivalers et esquiers illoeqes gageront ensi lour gauntes et getteront devant le roy a number de ccc. gauntz v. qe le dit [Nicholas Brembre] est faux traitour*': *Westminster Chronicle*, 282.

[114] Zmora, *The Feud*, 5–6, 65–6. Lesley's 'Historie' of 1578 described (but did not name) baughling in a discussion of '*capitale odium*' and asserted its purpose was to shame the target and prompt his companions to demand his '*honesta morte*': J. Leslie, *De origine, moribus & rebus gestis Scotorum libri decem* (Rome, 1675), 59–60.

[115] Blow, 'Nibley Green', 106; M. Cherry, 'The Struggle for Power in Mid-Fifteenth Century Devonshire', in R.A. Griffiths (ed.), *Patronage, the Crown and the Provinces in Later Medieval England* (Gloucester, 1981), 123–44, at 123, 136.

[116] Neilson, 'March Laws', 24; Summerson, 'Early Development', 35–6. See the chancery case of Henry Scot in 1279: *CIM, 1219–1307*, no. 1208; *CDS*, II, no. 183, pp. 58–60.

[117] 'Men following their goods with hound or without horn or with both without spear or bow, and he who delays this following shall pay compensation for the goods.' Within the same six days, the offended party had the option to complain to the opposite warden or his deputy to see that justice was done: *Foedera*, III, iii, 205.

[118] This was William Heron's forceful poinding (distraint) from Scots in 1379 for what he claimed to be stolen goods: *PROME*, April 1379, appendix, item 24; printed in *RP*, III, 255–6, which lists it with petitions for 1387–8.

[119] *Foedera*, III, iv, 151.

[120] See p. 183. Neville, 'Law of Treason', 14–16; Neville, *Violence, Custom and Law*, 111.

Part III

truce agreement allowed that fugitives could be pursued across the border for a period of six days, during which time the pursuers were not required to hold letters of safe conduct.[121] The 1429 truce indenture referred to the right of any man to make 'lauchful sluthe as the trewis wil' of his stolen goods.[122] Evidence for the operation of the trod can be found about this time. In one example, William Douglas of Drumlanrig complained that two knights from the English west march had led a raid to burn his Eskdale lands against the truce in April 1424. He alleged that the attackers, retreating with thousands of livestock and £20 of other booty, had set up a *'subtill embuschement fait au gentz que voloyent avoir rescowe lour ditz biens solonc vertue de triwes'*. This appears to have been an ambush specifically designed to trap any who sought to follow the trod and rescue their stolen property.[123] A second example comes from Northumberland in 1433, when one William Brandlyng of Kilham (in the far north of the county) was accused of having treasonably fore-warned Nicholas Rutherford, a Scot, of another Englishman's plans to ride into Scotland to recover his stolen goods.[124] In 1451 trod procedure was expanded further, requiring the pursuers to announce their presence and their purpose to the first person they met upon entering the opposite realm. Finally, in 1484, the local inhabitants were no longer obliged just to permit the trod but to assist in it.[125] The authority of the truce gave formal legitimacy to the trod, concerned as it was with the forceful recovery of moveable property. This became a fact of practice which was recognised beyond the strict confines of march law. A bond of 1506 for the good behaviour of several Nixon yeomen in Cumberland was typical of contracts made on condition and enforceable at common law. This twenty-mark bond was from the Nixons to the bishop of Carlisle; Lord Dacre, the west march warden; and two others. It included provision that if any 'grownd' where the Nixons or any of their 'surname or clannes haith habitacon or rewll owd' should be intruded by 'any

---

[121] *Foedera*, IV, iv, 109–11 (1424); Armstrong, *History of Liddesdale*, 46; Neville, *Violence, Custom and Law*, 81–2, 115–17.

[122] *CDS*, IV, appendix 1, no. 21, p. 404.

[123] *PPC*, III, 353–4. The knights were Robert Tilliol and Thomas Lucy. In 1427 William Douglas was retoured as heir to his father, William Douglas of Drumlanrig, in the barony of Hawick: *The Scotts of Buccleuch,* ed. W. Fraser, 2 vols (Edinburgh, 1878), II, 26.

[124] The other man was Thomas Hayland. Brandlyng was acquitted at trial in 1435 (JUST 3/208m34d; see also JUST 3/54/16m11). See p. 249n 40.

[125] *Rot. Scot.*, II, 349–54, at 352 (1451); Neilson, 'March Laws', 68; *Foedera*, IV, iv, 170–1 (1430); V, ii, 36 (1451); V, iii, 150–3 (1484); Neville, 'Keeping the Peace', 22; Cardew, 'Anglo-Scottish', 262–4. See also the details of the trod articulated in the indenture of the border diet held on 29 September 1459 at Reddenburn: NRS: SP 6/20. R.B. Armstrong observes the clauses of the 1451 indenture appearing in 1457, 1464, 1493, 1528, 1533–34, 1543, 1549 and 1551, with the option of complaint to the warden omitted in 1493: Armstrong, *History of Liddesdale*, 46.

The Administration of Justice

Englisheman to folow his trod of his gude stolin', then they must 'make restitucon of the said godes or els uttren the sayd trod outt of ther grownde'. Elsewhere the document obliged them to see stolen goods restored to the rightful owners within six or eight days of a demand being made.[126] The trod was sanctioned retaliatory violence, comparable in many respects to the taking of 'distresses' under the march law of Ireland.[127] Its method came to be engrossed with additional rules about timing and open declaration of intent. During the period 1398–1459 truce indentures extended comparable provision to the recovery of immoveable property, too. Several such agreements included a clause allowing a party ejected by assault to recover a captured fortress by whatever means possible ('*per ... quoquo modo prout melius poterit*') and for them to punish the invaders. The truce conservators of the offending party's realm were obliged to assist in the recovery and restoration of the building to the injured party.[128] The case of Jedburgh Castle in 1394–5 may have made the articulation of such procedures pressing.[129] Why they should be omitted after 1459 is not clear. Nevertheless, in allowing for the licit and forceful recovery of property, as much it did through an emphasis on redress and compensation, march law accommodated and gave shape to a patterned repertoire of local practices.

Further illustration of redress and retaliation under march law concerns cross-border homicide. The usual remedy for slaughter on the marches in the thirteenth century was compensation, for the 1249 code spoke of a '*manbote*' to be paid to the appellant in such cases.[130] By 1398 the truce

---

[126] *Cata. Deeds*, iii, 497 (D 790). The obliged men were Arche Nykson, Davy Nykson, Clement Nikson and Quyntyn Nikson.

[127] For the Irish context, see Crooks, 'Factions, Feuds and Noble Power', 438 and the works surveyed there.

[128] *Foedera*, III, iv, 150 (truce of 1398); *Foedera*, IV, iv, 110 (truce of 1424); *Foedera*, IV, iv, 169–71 (truce of 1430); *Foedera*, V, i, 47–50 (truce of 1438); *Rot. Scot.*, II, 337–41 (truce of 1449); *Rot. Scot.*, II, 349–54 (truce of 1451); *Rot. Scot.*, II, 363–68 (truce of 1453); *Rot. Scot.*, II, 381 (truce of 1457), 395 (truce of 1459); the latter two cited in Cardew, 'Anglo-Scottish', 277, who notes that this clause was omitted after 1459. Expenses incurred in the lawful recovery of the fortress were to be extracted from the offenders. The injured party could leave the recovery of the fortress up to the officials of the other realm. See Armstrong, *History of Liddesdale*, 60–1.

[129] In 1394 a Scottish party led by Sir William Inglis had briefly captured Jedburgh Castle during truce. After recovering the castle, Sir Thomas Strother, the English keeper, challenged Inglis to a duel, presumably under march law, at which the wardens presided. It was held at Rulehaugh in Roxburghshire, and Strother was killed: *Scotichronicon*, viii, 6–11; 'Annales Ricardi Secundi et Henrici Quarti', in *Johannis de Trokelowe et Henrici de Blaneforde monachorum S Albani, necnon quorundam anonymorum, Chronica et Annales*, ed. H.T. Riley (1866), 166–7; Neville, *Violence, Custom and Law*, 79n 126; Goodman, 'Defence of Northumberland', 165.

[130] An important discussion of '*botes*' is found in Wormald, 'Bloodfeud, Kindred and Government', 62–3; Neville, 'Scottish Influences', 176; Neilson, 'March Laws', 21; Scott, 'March Laws Reconsidered', esp. 120.

Part III

specifically placed the application of justice in the hands of the victim's relations. It included a clause touching harm done in the opposite realm: if found guilty, the offender was to be delivered to the injured party 'to sla or raunsoun at thair lykyng'.[131] A different approach was implemented in 1429, when punishment came to supersede compensation in cases of border killings. That year it was laid down that the culprit was to be delivered to the warden of the injured party's realm, to be punished by the law of that country.[132] The emphasis in such a regulation was for march law to function as a means to enable the application of relevant domestic law, rather than to place a decision with the complaining party or to promote the payment of reparations. Yet the rules changed again in 1473, reverting back to terms familiar from earlier in the century. In that year it was specified that, should an Englishman slay a Scot within Scotland, or vice-versa, 'the Slaar or the Slaars shall be takyn be the Wardains Leutennants or Deputis, and Deliverit on to the Partye Complenyng, to be Justifiet or Raunsoned at the Will of the Partye Complenyng'.[133] For the slayer to be 'justified' was to be condemned to death; this amounts to licit revenge killing. It is not a practice familiar from north of the border. Within England, the privilege of victorious appellants or a victim's kin to carry out the death penalty was to be found in the laws of Cnut, and in some cases it endured into the thirteenth century, in Northumberland and elsewhere.[134] From fifteenth-century Kent there are custumal rules prescribing the execution by drowning of condemned thieves in Fordwich, where it was the obligation of the suitor to carry out the punishment.[135] If the principle was thus not peculiar to the marches, all the same such practices were offensive to some thinkers. For instance the author of the well-known spiritual dialogue *Dives and Pauper*, written early in the century, stressed that for execution to be just, the judge, pursuers and officers ought to act not 'for

---

[131] *Foedera*, III, iv, 151, 153: 'harm' was specified as 'takyng or Slaghtir of Men, or Takyng of Gudis, or Brynnyg of Housis, or Takyng of Castell or Forteresce'. See also Armstrong, *History of Liddesdale*, 60.

[132] *CDS*, IV, appendix 1, no. 21, p. 404 (printed indenture of 1429); Neville, *Violence, Custom and Law*, 130.

[133] *Foedera*, V, iii, 34. For comment, see Neville, *Violence, Custom and Law*, 157–8.

[134] See p. 299n 174. *DSL*, s.v. 'Justify, -fé, Justefy'. F. Pollock and F.W. Maitland, *History of English Law*, 2 vols (2nd edn, Cambridge, 1898), II, 160, 496; P.R. Hyams, 'Feud and the State in Late Anglo-Saxon England', *Journal of British Studies*, 40 (2001), 40; Hyams, *Rancor and Reconciliation*, 242–66. For similarities between march law and Anglo-Saxon law codes, see Summerson, 'Early Development', 31 (for Cnut); Reid, 'Office of Warden', 480–1 (for Athelstan and Edgar).

[135] *Borough Customs*, ed. M. Bateson (1904–6), i, pp. xxvii, 76 (and see 73 for an earlier reference from Preston). For comment, see R.F. Green, 'Violence in the Early Robin Hood Poems', in M.D. Meyerson, D. Thiery and O. Falk (eds), *A Great Effusion of Blood? Interpreting Medieval Violence* (Toronto, 2004), 268–86, at 275.

The Administration of Justice

lykyng of venchance ne of cruelte'.[136] Yet the focus of the march law of homicide, it seems, did not heed this view. It moved away from promotion of compensation, and, for much of our period of interest, it seems that the border courts accommodated a procedure which channeled the urge to vengeance into their activity, but equally allowed for the option of seeking 'ransom' as an alternative measure. This was not so much the payment of compensation for homicide as the delivery of a guilty man's fate into the hands of the victim's party, perhaps more an incendiary measure than a pacificatory one. As with the trod and the recovery of captured buildings, the treatment of cross-border homicide was shaped by the formal law so as to leave significant latitude to individual parties in determining the course of action to be taken.

Judicial duels, another type of legitimate violence, have already been considered under domestic march law. They also are to be found in international law, and this shows a further cooperation with accustomed practices, particularly those related to the law of arms. In some cross-border cases, wager of battle under march law appears to have been transmuted to the duel of chivalry. Indeed, from the early 1380s, Richard II encouraged judicial combat under royal licence for march-related disputes, and similar interest was taken by Robert III in the 1390s.[137] Thus, with such royal backing, duels in 1380, 1381 and 1395 took place at customary sites for march days, like Lilliot Cross and Rulehaugh, before the wardens.[138] Unlike some more famous duels of chivalry in Scotland and England at this time which were stopped (and an inclination to use judicial combat in this way may have informed Richard II's thinking in the Mowbray–Bolingbroke duel of 1398), we know that at least the border duel of 1395 was fought to the death.[139] Yet, between 1387 and 1414, there was also a flurry of Anglo-Scottish chivalric tournaments, or at least arrangements for them to be held, none of which was an

---

[136] *Dives and Pauper,* ed. P.H. Barnum, 2 vols in 3 (Oxford, 1976–2004), I, ii, 36–7. Deuteronomy 19:12 lays down provisions for execution by the victim's next of kin.

[137] Neilson, 'March Laws', 17, 20, 22–3, 67; Neville, 'Keeping the Peace', 14–15; Neville, 'Scottish Influences', 165; Neville, *Violence, Custom and Law,* 77, 190; Macdonald, *Border Bloodshed,* 182.

[138] Grant-Strother, at Lilliot Cross, before Henry, earl of Northumberland, 1380 (*Foedera,* III, iii, 108); Chattowe-Badby, at Lilliot Cross, before Henry 'Hotspur' Percy, Ralph Neville, John de Harleston and William Farendon, 1381 (*Foedera,* III, iii, 130–1; *CDS,* IV, no. 309, p. 68); Inglis-Strother, at Rulehaugh, before Archibald, earl of Douglas, and Henry, earl of Northumberland, 1395 (*Scotichronicon,* viii, 6–11; 'Annales Ricardi Secundi et Henrici Quarti', 166–7). See also Russell, 'II Trial by Battle', 144nn 133–43; Neville, *Violence, Custom and Law,* 71, 74, 77, 79, 82; Goodman, 'Defence of Northumberland', 165; Macdonald, *Border Bloodshed,* 125–6.

[139] J.G. Edwards, 'The Parliamentary Committee of 1398', *EHR,* 40 (1925), 321–33; W.D.H. Sellar, 'Courtesy, Battle and the Brieve of Right, 1368 – A Story Continued', *Miscellany II,* Stair Society (Edinburgh, 1984), 1–12.

Part III

explicitly judicial duel.[140] One such contest carried overseas to a furious affray on the streets of Königsberg in Prussia in 1391, where Thomas, Lord Clifford (and other Englishmen, Germans and men of Bohemia and Guelders), killed Sir William Douglas and two other Scots (who were backed by French supporters).[141] Neville suggests that these knightly encounters stemmed, nevertheless, from border offences, now settled 'under the guise of chivalric pursuits', and, similarly, Macdonald argues that they were truce-time venues for the continued pursuit of war-time grievances.[142] Both points are tenable, but for present purposes what matters is the accommodation of customs associated with the law of arms. The wardens were involved in some of these chivalric contests: in 1404 John, the son of Sir Thomas Grey of Heton and Wark, obtained a licence for a joust against two Scots, to be judged by the earl of Westmorland, warden of the west march.[143] A decade later, in December 1414, John, Lord Clifford, was permitted to perform feats of arms against William Douglas of Drumlanrig, and he asked the English king to order the west march warden to appoint a place at Carlisle for the event. The involvement of the warden in the process may indicate a border-related dispute.[144] In this case, again we find the administration of the march accommodating customary procedures (in the context of the duels of law mentioned above, cross-border duels of chivalry or ritualised violent encounters at chivalric tournaments) into its own normative system.[145]

---

[140] Thomas, sixth Lord Clifford, feats of arms, 1387 (*Foedera*, III, iv, 12; *Rot. Scot.*, II, 87); Tempest *v.* various Scots, feats of arms, 1387 (*Rot. Scot.*, II, 90); Sir William Dalzell, tournament at Smithfield, 1390 (*Scotichronicon*, viii, 15–18; *CDS*, IV, no. 411); Neville-Lindsay and Colville, Etton, Saveyn, Lowther, Croypole, Warde, feats of arms, 1391 (*CDS*, IV, no. 425, p. 94; *Rot. Scot.*, II, 111); John, earl of Huntingdon, at Berwick, feats of arms, 1392 (*CDS*, IV, no. 439, p. 96; *Rot. Scot.*, II, 117); Redmane-Haliburton, including Barde, Douglas of Strathbrock, 'joust in war', at Carlisle 1393 (*CDS*, IV, nos 452–3, pp. 97–8; *Rot. Scot.*, II, 119); 1398, Morley v. Douglas of Strathbrock (*Scotichronicon*, viii, 11–12; *ER*, III, 436); Alexander, earl of Mar, hastilude at Smithfield, 1405 (*Incerti*, 43; *English Chron.*, 43); Douglas of Drumlanrig and Murray, feats of arms, 1405 (*CDS*, IV, no. 711, p. 146). See also J.R.V. Barker, *The Tournament in England, 1100–1400* (Woodbridge, 1986), 35–6.

[141] Tyerman, *England and the Crusades*, 271–2; *Westminster Chronicle*, 474–7. Clifford had in the preceding year arranged a safe conduct for Douglas to travel to England (*Rot. Scot.*, II, 105–6).

[142] Neville, 'Keeping the Peace', 15 (quote); Neville, *Violence, Custom and Law*, 102–3; Macdonald, *Border Bloodshed*, 122–3, 125–6, 181–3.

[143] (29 June 1404) *Foedera*, IV, i, 68; *CDS*, IV, no. 659, p. 138; *CPR 1401–5*, 410. The bond for payment made on 10 April 1404 by Sir John Stewart of Scotland to Westmorland may be related to the event: *Cata. Deeds*, iii, 544 (D 1163). On 6 August 1404 Sir Thomas Grey of Heton was retained by Westmorland: 'Private Indentures for Life Service in Peace and War 1278–1476', ed. M. Jones and S. Walker, in *Camden Miscellany XXXII* (Camden Society, 5th ser., 3, (London, 1994), 100.

[144] (13 and 16 December 1414). It was to occur on a day assigned by Clifford and agreed between the parties: E 28/30, printed in *CDS*, V, 285; *Rot. Scot.*, II, 212; *Foedera*, IV, ii, 89, 100.

[145] See pp. 297–99. Further on tournament, see K. Stevenson, *Chivalry and Knighthood in Scotland, 1424–1513* (Woodbridge, 2006), 63–102; Maddern, *Violence and Social Order*, 12–13.

The Administration of Justice

Neville has noted the end of cross-border duelling and chivalric activity by the third decade of the century, which led her to suggest that armed gatherings were coming to be seen by the wardens as too dangerously at risk of degenerating into 'pitched battle'.[146] Yet the Percy wager of battle in 1423, noted above, can hardly be seen as a step in this direction.[147] The disappearance of resort to battle in the marches may be better explained as yet another consequence of the cumbersome English statute of truces, promulgated in the spring of 1414.[148] We have seen that this national legislation expanded the scope of high treason to include truce-breaking, and thus removed the English wardens' jurisdiction over offences of this type. Consequently, if English wardens lost their competence to handle domestic cases of march treason, and thus the duels of law by which cases of this sort might proceed, it could well follow that they also lost the power to supervise cross-border combats. In this way parliamentary legislation acted to restrict the ability of crown-appointed wardens to administer border justice. Certainly, petitions to parliament against the statute, in 1429 and 1433, complained that English wardens could no longer deal with truce-breaking 'in a similar way' to their Scottish counterparts.[149] North of the border, duels of law continued to be used in some treason cases into the sixteenth century.[150] The last recorded cross-border chivalric encounter of this period was between Clifford and Douglas of Drumlanrig in December 1414, and, for this, Clifford asked the king not only to grant his licence but specifically to order the warden to preside, which would have been a necessary delegation of power in light of the recent statute. Clifford's case may have been a special concession by Henry V, a king who disapproved of tournaments and feats of arms and preferred real war.[151] The coincidence of the statute of truces and the end of border combats also clarifies the seemingly anachronistic wager of battle by Percy (himself warden of the east march) before the court of common pleas at Westminster in 1423. Percy's case may be explained as an attempt to normalise this violent method of proof early in the new reign, lending credibility to its potential for continued use in the marches.

We may now take stock of this examination of justice in the borderlands. This chapter began with a reference to the cult of St Oswald and an episode from that king's life which emphasised divine vindication and

---

[146] Neville, *Violence, Custom and Law*, 134 (quote); Neville, 'Keeping the Peace', 15.
[147] See p. 184. [148] See p. 183.
[149] *PROME*, September 1429, item 43: '*en semblable fourme qe lez conservatours et gardeins en lez partiez d'Escoce*'; ibid., July 1433, item 58.
[150] Stevenson, *Chivalry and Knighthood*, 64–5.
[151] C. Taylor, 'Henry V, Flower of Chivalry', in Dodd (ed.), *Henry V: New Interpretations*, 219–20.

195

Part III

the expectation of heavenly judgment. That story also alluded to vengeance and retaliation as just means to achieve redress and the restoration of right. Its relevance to our discussion lies not in the early medieval career of Oswald but, rather, in his late medieval afterlife and veneration, and the reasonable expectation that the stories associated with this saint revered at Durham and in numerous churches bearing his dedication in the march counties convey an important spiritual backdrop of late medieval thought about justice. Neither royal justice nor border justice were constant; they entertained their own complexities, changes and evolutions across our period. One such evolutionary pattern readily identifiable in the foregoing discussion is that the relative fragmentation of the far north into several common law and franchisal jurisdictions came to be reduced over the fifteenth century, a trend that is particularly evident in the gradual watering-down of the autonomy of the Northumberland liberties. At the same time there was a flourishing of the law of the march and a continued vibrancy in its provisions, even if that vibrancy might be uneven, as was noted with the jurisdiction of the English wardens over treason and wager of battle falling under restriction from 1414 (finally restored by 1453). Whereas common law paid heed to the significance of particular words in documents like writs and the precise narrative of events set forth in indictments, a number of features of march law discussed above, by contrast, emphasise immediacy of action on the ground. The trod and its declaration, the duty of protection for those following the trod, and measures for the recapture of buildings all relied upon actions which were not to be taken at random but which, according to codified formulae, amounted to self-evident assertions of legitimacy and right. Such practices served as a means for the activation of jurisdictional frameworks or the invocation of march law and its sanctions. And this was not just the activation of abstract legal processes but, in certain instances, the initiation of a framework for the use of violent force. In this way march law accommodated local accustomed practices of conflict management.[152] Kings were not paramount in border justice, even if English wardens were subject to the decisions of their own parliament and council. It was the diplomacy of the continuously recodified truce which was the ultimate authority that was invoked. Breaches of the truce, not breaches of a king's peace, were the focus of this law. In rectifying such infractions, the focus of march law, as we have seen, was primarily on processes of redress and reparation rather than punishment. Even the rules to be applied in cases of homicide put the option of

---

[152] See above, p. 188.

The Administration of Justice

arranging compensation (by means of charging ransom) to the fore. All this seems exceptional in a wider English context and certainly also stands out in contrast to the provisions of royal justice and common law as they were applied in the far north. These differences require explanation, and one which considers the interaction of local usage with broader frameworks. To this end it is not satisfactory to assert that 'distance from the centre of government ... undoubtedly favoured the perpetuation of local custom against the levelling influence of the common law'.[153] Indeed, the similarities with certain features of Scottish justice, not least in the emphasis on compensation rather than retribution, have already been observed. What is more, the wider set of practices examined here seems rather less out of place when the Scottish, French and German contexts observed at the outset are taken into consideration. The concluding point to be made is that justice in the far north cannot be understood in straightforward terms; there were other legal frameworks in play beyond the two considered here (that of the church in particular). What can be said of this complexity is that while it may seem to have certain extraordinary features, not typical of what has been found in studies based upon common law records elsewhere in England, the repertoire of practices and assumptions that were built into the law of the march suggests a local society with an approach to justice that was broadly comparable to certain other parts of late medieval Europe at the same time.

CONCLUSION AT CHAPTER 6

This first chapter of the third part turns our attention to conflict in the northern marches with a view to different frameworks of justice and law. Here we see simultaneously the signs of an increasingly less fragmented system of royal justice through the common law (not least as it was applied to address the complexities posed by the border liberties) and a thriving framework of border justice through the law of the march. The latter adapted local customs of conflict management, what have been called here 'accustomed practices'. Especially in particular aspects of march law, the chapter suggests some broad points of comparison with approaches to justice in other European contexts and also some differences with other localities of England which have been studied through common law records. Unsurprisingly, the countries to which we have looked for comparison include Scotland, but we have also seen ways in

---

[153] Neville, 'Scottish Influences', 181.

Part III

which the French and German contexts are equally instructive. The point of this is to help enrich our view of the far north as in some ways distinctive from other parts of England but also to draw our attention away from the frontier itself as an explanation for such apparent distinctiveness. In other words, it is to prompt the wider question, to be developed in subsequent chapters and to which we return in the book's conclusions, of how far other English localities may have been, like the border counties, accepting of different frameworks of justice in the regulation of local conflict.

7

PATTERNS OF CONFLICT

Willelmus Jakson de Gamelsby in comitatus Cumbr' yoman captus pro eo quod ubi Henricus Whitwham de Gillesland in comitatus Cumbr' yoman in festo sancti martini anno regni regis Henrici sexti secundo apud Gameslby ij vaccas precij xx s' de bonis et catallis Willelmi Helton de Gamelsby furtive furatus fuit . Ibi predictus Willelmus Jakson felonice receptauit predictam Henricum apud Gamelsby ipsum fecisse feloniam predictam.[1]

—Gaol Delivery Roll 199

The goal of this chapter is to establish an overview of the patterns of conflict in the border counties. The purpose here is, as far as possible, to make a quantitative analysis of conflict derived from court evidence. The first section below presents the records which underpin the analysis that follows. The archives of the court of king's bench are useful for establishing a chronology of affairs at law. Private litigation among landowners features predominantly on the *coram rege* side this court, and on the *rex* side it heard most crown and private charges against gentry and nobility. It also heard quite a lot of crown charges of felony or trespass against perpetrators from the lower social orders, but even so such cases were frequently associated with disputes among landed antagonists. Thus, litigation in king's bench should be an important indicator of tensions in political society.[2] The itinerant gaol delivery court records focus, by contrast, much more on crown prosecutions of felonies perpetrated by culprits of yeoman status or lower; accordingly, they point towards more local social tensions and concerns of a much less politically significant flavour.[3] There are no surviving records of the warden courts

---

[1] JUST 3/199 rot. 27d.

[2] See above, p. 174. On king's bench litigation and political society: Carpenter, *Locality and Polity*, 393–4, 705–9; Maddern, *Violence and Social Order*, 38, 46.

[3] Neville, 'Gaol Delivery', 45–60; Maddern, *Violence and Social Order*, 49, and, on court records, violence and social tensions generally, 27–74, 111–34.

199

Part III

to examine by way of comparison. By tracing a chronology of conflict derived from legal records[4] and matching this with major events, especially political upheavals, the second section below examines the extent to which the border counties were affected by the wider national context, including what local effects were caused by greater disputes among magnates. King's bench records provide the main pool of evidence used in this section. Third, the chapter considers the effect of Anglo-Scottish war and truce on patterns of conflict and litigation in order to continue to address the question of whether the military aspect of the frontier had the effect of making the marches more prone to conflict, especially violent conflict, than elsewhere. This will be done with the king's bench data and the gaol delivery data separately, and here the gaol delivery evidence will be more fully discussed.[5] Fourth, the chapter will assess, where possible, the level and nature of violence. Finally, it will consider the role of the border liberties in local conflict. In these final two sections the evidence from both king's bench and gaol delivery will be employed. Further supplementary evidence will be used throughout this chapter where relevant.[6] Of course, where we are concerned with 'violence' it should be recalled that this is a broad heading under which can be grouped a number of aggressive actions involving the use of force, both against the person (including physical assault, rape, abduction, detention and killing) and against property (including plundering of goods and livestock and burning or destroying buildings, boundary-markers, crops or the like). Yet no objective measure of such behaviour exists; historians must rely upon the subjective accounts of those who bothered to record it; and it should be taken as read that legal records complicate analysis considerably. As will be noted below, cases begun with the general-purpose writs of trespass *vi et armis* are not treated on their own as encompassing genuine violence unless they feature more specific allegations.[7] It should also be observed that, although they have not been excluded from the comprehensive figures enumerated in this chapter, those cases with specifically cross-border

---

[4] On the problems associated with the use of legal records, see Post, 'Crime in Later Medieval England', 211–24; Powell, *Kingship, Law, and Society*, 91–7; Carpenter, *Locality and Polity*, 705–9. In response to Carpenter, see P. Tucker, 'Historians' Expectations of the Medieval Legal Records', in A. Musson (ed.), *Expectations of the Law in the Middle Ages* (Woodbridge, 2001), 191–202.

[5] See below, p. 230.

[6] Chancery petitions (class C 1), which pose difficulties with dating, are included among the supplementary evidence. Some sixty-seven chancery petitions relate to the border counties in our period of interest.

[7] On violence see above, p. 28. Litigants' choice of legal strategy affects the records substantially: see Maddern, *Violence and Social Order*, esp. 9–12. On trespass *vi et armis* see ibid., 22, 27, 31; Baker, *Introduction to English Legal History*, 72–5.

Patterns of Conflict

dimensions (which are more often to be found in gaol delivery than in king's bench records) will be a focus of Chapter 8.

COURT RECORDS AND FIGURES: THE EVIDENCE ASSEMBLED

The information gathered here requires a brief introduction. In this survey every case in the gaol delivery rolls between 1401 and 1459 has been recorded.[8] A major limitation of the gaol delivery rolls is their irregularity, a situation partly caused by Anglo-Scottish war. For all three counties before 1421, surviving enrolments are very limited.[9] Similar gaps are to be found for records for other parts of the realm, and this dearth is partly due to the suspension of the assizes in 1415, and the disruption of gaol deliveries for the rest of Henry V's reign. Records are complete between 1421 and 1435 for all three border counties, but it appears that in 1436 no sessions were held, presumably because of war with Scotland.[10] There are further discrepancies in the surviving records during the 1440s and 1450s.[11] For example, no gaol deliveries took place in Northumberland in 1445 or 1457, and there is no surviving enrolment of the session for 1443.[12]

The survey of the king's bench records for the three counties of Cumberland, Westmorland and Northumberland includes every indictment brought into the court from these counties for the period 1399–1494, and every case from the counties appearing in the court's plea rolls (KB 27s) for each Michaelmas term during the same period. It is important

[8] The corresponding gaol delivery files have been excluded from systematic inclusion. See also above, p. 130, and below, p. 230.

[9] For Henry IV, enrolments for the sessions in 1401, 1404, 1406, 1407, 1408 and 1411 alone survive, though Cbl. and Wml. have additional enrolments for 1409. Rolls for the border counties do not survive after 1459. (One case dated 1460 is an evident clerical misdating of a Nbl. case from the 1458 session: see JUST 3/213 rot. 15.) The rolls included here are JUST 3/191, 199, 208, 211 and 213. Unless otherwise indicated, sessions for Newcastle-upon-Tyne, enrolled separately from those for Nbl., have been grouped together with Nbl. cases.

[10] Maddern, *Violence and Social Order*, 21–3, 47–8; Powell, *Kingship, Law, and Society*, 248. For compurgation in 1419 for a clerk convicted of stealing a horse at Morpeth in Nbl. in 1413, see *Register of Thomas Langley*, ed. Storey, v, 125. This suggests the clerk was tried at gaol delivery in the period for which records are wanting.

[11] There is a gap in the Cbl. rolls for the years from 1449 to 1456 inclusive, in which no sessions were held. For the years 1449, 1454, 1455 and 1456, the clerk noted that no sessions were held 'because of the insurrection of the Scots'. The 1457 Cbl. session sat at Penrith (JUST 3/211 rots 44, 44d; JUST 3/213 rot. 16). A Cbl. session was held in 1459 at Carlisle (enrolled on JUST 3/213 rot. 16d). By contrast, Wml. missed sessions in only 1455 and 1456 (see JUST 3/213 rot. 17).

[12] On these records, see Neville, 'Gaol Delivery', 46–7. Neville notes (ibid., 46n 4) that the Nbl. file (JUST 3/54/39) dated 15 September 1457 corresponds to the session enrolled at (JUST 3/213 rot. 14d) dated 14 September 1456; this would seem to be a dating error, and thus in one of these two years no delivery occurred. A similar discrepancy occurs between the Wml. file (JUST 3/70/25) dated 11 September 1456 and the corresponding roll (JUST 3/213 rot. 17) dated 11 September 1457. Neville (ibid.) is mistaken that no Nbl. Gaol delivery was held in 1443; the file exists as JUST 3/54/26.

Part III

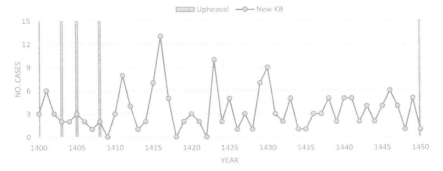

Figure 1   National upheaval and new KB (total), 1400–50

Figure 2   National upheaval and all KB (total), 1400–50

to note that while this analysis includes complete coverage of the king's bench indictment files (KB 9s), the data presented from the plea rolls sample only one term each year (albeit Michaelmas was the term with the largest plea roll). Where particularly relevant, the rolls for additional terms have been consulted, but the picture offered here is indicative rather than exhaustive.[13] Although the pleas in king's bench encompassed both private actions and crown prosecutions, in the figures where the data are displayed visually, all these cases have been treated together and are simply referred to as 'court activity'. It should be kept in mind that while not all king's bench cases involved allegations of violence, they were more likely to do so than cases in the court of common pleas.[14]

---

[13] I am grateful to Richard Hoyle and Rosemary Milligan-Hayes for allowing me access to transcripts of the northern KB 9 files from 1461 to 1509, which form the basis of Hayes, 'Ancient Indictments'.

[14] Carpenter, *Locality and Polity*, 707.

Patterns of Conflict

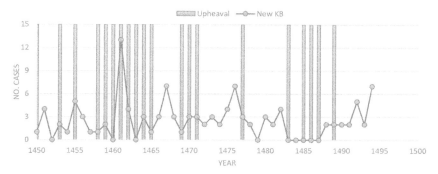

Figure 3   National upheaval and new KB (total), 1450–1500

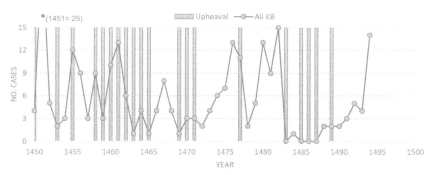

Figure 4   National upheaval and all KB (total), 1450–1500

Analysis is assisted by Figures 1–8 and 11–14, which summarise the numbers of cases appearing in the king's bench records for the three counties across the period 1400–94. Figures 1 and 2 cover the first part of this period, 1400–49, and Figures 3 and 4 cover the second part, 1450–94. Two charts are presented for each period in order to show clearly both the new cases appearing in the records (Figures 1 and 3) and all the cases appearing in the records (Figures 2 and 4). That is, the charts labelled 'new KB' show only those cases appearing for the first time, and the charts labelled 'all KB' show the total number of cases appearing by combining both new cases and those which recur that year.[15]

---

[15] For cases involving multiple allegations, each alleged offence has been counted separately. This produces a distortion in the total number of cases, but this is corrected by counting only one allegation between parties as a 'new' case (the one first appearing in court) and plotting new cases on their own.

Part III

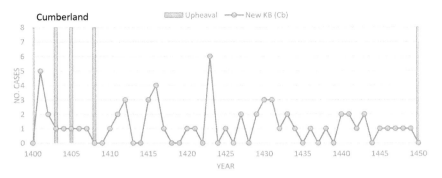

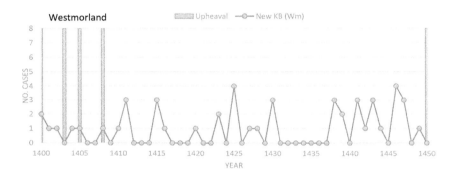

Figure 5 National upheaval and new KB (by county), 1400–50

Patterns of Conflict

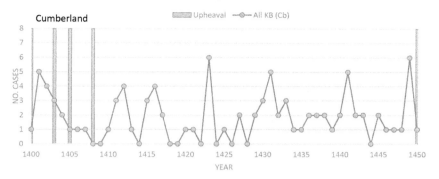

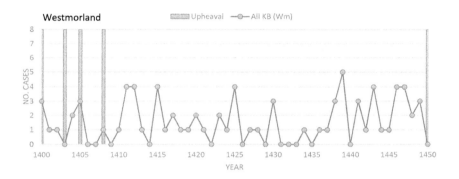

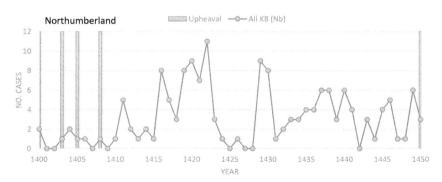

Figure 6 National upheaval and all KB (by county), 1400–50

Part III

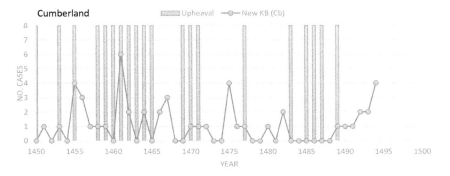

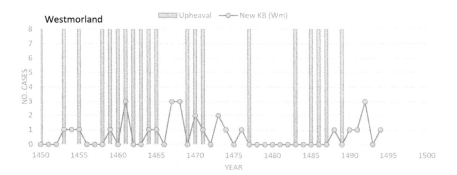

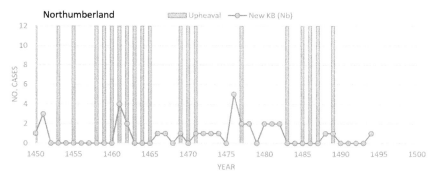

Figure 7 National upheaval and new KB (by county), 1450–1500

Patterns of Conflict

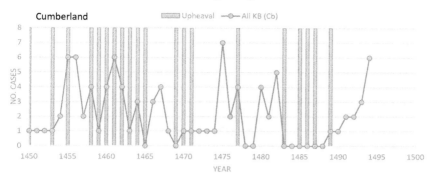

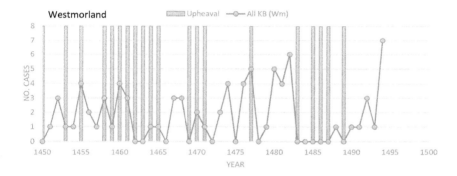

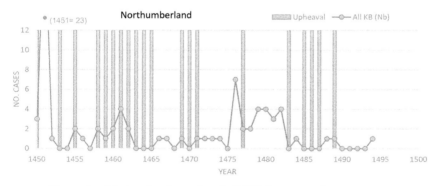

Figure 8   National upheaval and all KB (by county), 1450–1500

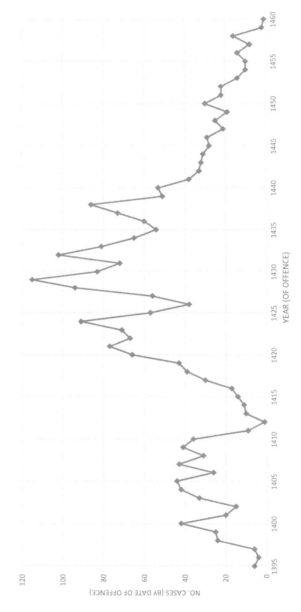

Figure 9   JUST 3 (gaol delivery) offences (total), 1395–1460

Patterns of Conflict

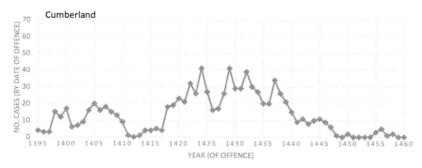

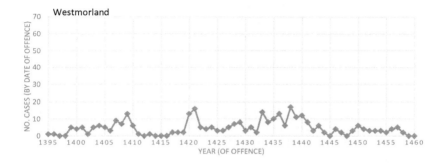

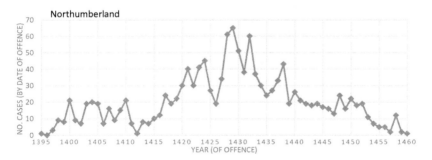

Figure 10 JUST 3 (gaol delivery) offences (by county), 1395–1460

This approach is different from that taken in the most comprehensive local study which achieved a complete sample of king's bench records. Carpenter's study carefully analysed cases and sorted them for display in a different type of chart which illustrated levels

Part III

of conflict.[16] For our purposes, neither the 'new KB' or 'all KB' charts purport to display levels of local conflict exhaustively, for the 'new KB' chart is too exclusive, and the 'all KB' chart is too blunt.[17] Since a survey of every term in every year has not been done, the two types of chart are presented for use together. The visual presentation of this large amount of data highlights a number of peaks and troughs in levels of activity over time. A peak in 'new KB' that is reflected in 'all KB' suggests new cases arising, and this can be read as an indication of increased local tension. However, a peak in 'all KB' that is not reflected in 'new KB' may suggest simply a continuation of judicial process or a new resumption of older cases, both to be treated with greater caution as a sign of local tension. Our interpretation throughout is heavily dependent on what can be gleaned from the surrounding context, including what is known about political events, evidence for disputing out of court, and related governmental actions. For instance, a rise in cases may result from prosecutions initiated by a commission of oyer and terminer.[18]

In the charts, the numbers of cases appearing each Michaelmas term have been plotted as a line running on top of vertical bars which have been inserted for certain years. These vertical bars represent a year in which significant political upheaval occurred in England, for instance, the final Percy rebellion (1408), the first battle of St Albans (1455) and the usurpation of Richard III (1483). (The effects of war with Scotland will be discussed separately below.) For the purposes of cross-county comparison, Figures 5–8 display exactly the same arrangement of information as the first four figures, except that here cases from Cumberland, Westmorland and Northumberland are displayed separately. The objective of plotting these first eight figures is simply to display the patterns of litigation in the court of king's bench, for the three counties collectively and individually, as against periods of particular national political upheaval. (Figures 9 and 10 present the gaol delivery evidence and will be discussed below.)

CONFLICT AND COURT ACTIVITY

A baseline assessment of court activity in the final years of the reign of Richard II reveals the effects of the advent of the Lancastrian regime in September 1399. The final gaol delivery roll of Richard's reign for the

[16] Carpenter, *Locality and Polity*, figs 9 and 13, 407 and 613, also appendix 4 for methodology.
[17] The 'new KB' chart excludes resumed cases and new indictments on old cases, which might be counted as new. The 'all KB' chart shows a total level of judicial process from these counties.
[18] See above, p. 175.

210

Patterns of Conflict

northern circuit covers the years 1397–1400. For Yorkshire it includes two sessions in 1397, three in 1398 and one (in the name of Henry IV) in 1400. For the normal circuit of the three border counties, it contains the sessions held in August 1398 alone, and this suggests that gaols were not delivered there in 1397, 1399 or 1400 (the year of Henry IV's Scottish campaign).[19] Richard II's arrest of leading magnates in the summer of 1397 may well have prompted the justices to progress no further than Yorkshire. The turbulence of 1399 appears to have kept the justices from their circuit into the marches, and so again in 1400 due to war; the assize rolls also confirm these absences.[20] As for king's bench there is greater continuity in the archives. The amount of business indicated by a count of the *rotuli* in Michaelmas term rolls from 1395 to 1398 shows that in the final years of Richard II a consistent level of court activity obtained.[21] It was only in Michaelmas 1399, at the very moment of the king's dethronement, that the volume of business dropped notably. Levels of activity familiar under Richard II resumed by the same term in 1400.[22] In fact, a count of the *rotuli* for all terms in 1399 and 1400 shows that the former pace of court business was reached again in Hilary 1400.[23] Such a pattern matches what is generally to be expected about use of the courts during uncertain periods of regime change, and similar occasions will be identified in the discussion below.[24]

The data in the present survey (Figures 1, 2, 5 and 6) clearly illustrate a declining number of cases from the three border counties in the reign of Henry IV. The Percy rebellions in 1403, 1405 and 1408 seem not to have affected this general trend. Neither did the general oyer and terminer commissions of 1403, 1405 and 1407 generate many cases for the court.[25] Others have argued that the removal of the Percys in 1405 destabilised the north,[26] but the evidence presented here cannot

---

[19] JUST 3/184 includes sessions for Nbl. (12 August 1398), Cbl. (15 August 1398) and Wml. (17 August 1398). See also A. Curry, A.R. Bell, A. King and D. Simpkin, 'New Regime, New Army? Henry IV's Scottish Expedition of 1400', *EHR*, 125 (2010), 1382–413.

[20] JUST 3/1509 records the 1398 assize sessions for all three counties on the dates given in the preceding note. JUST 1/1517 records their return in summer 1401.

[21] Richard II: 1395 (KB 27/538: 63 rots, 27 *rex* rots); 1396 (KB 27/542: 74 rots, 28 *rex* rots); 1397 (KB 27/546: 88 rots, 33 *rex* rots); 1398 (KB 27/550: 83 rots, 31 *rex* rots).

[22] Henry IV: 1399 (KB 27/554: 34 rots, 16 *rex* rots); 1400 (KB 27/558: 80 rots, 33 *rex* rots).

[23] Richard II: 1399, Hilary (KB 27/551: 60 rots, 20 *rex* rots); 1399, Easter (KB 27/552: 62 rots, 17 *rex* rots); 1399, Trinity (KB 27/553: 56 rots, 22 *rex* rots). Henry IV: 1400, Hilary (KB 27/555: 53 rots, 19 *rex* rots); 1400, Easter (KB 27/556: 56 rots, 15 *rex* rots); 1400, Trinity (KB 27/557: 54 rots, 22 *rex* rots).

[24] Carpenter, *Locality and Polity*, 393–6, 614, 709.

[25] 1403 (*CPR 1401–5*, 361); 1405 (*CPR 1405–8*, 59); 1407 (*CPR 1405–8*, 359).

[26] King, 'They have the Hertes of the People by North', 153–7. See also Neville, 'Keeping the Peace', 17–18.

Part III

confirm this, and there is not much to suggest a burst of extra-judicial disputing at this time.[27] Still, the most probable scenario is that a low level of court activity in part reflected political uncertainties. This trend of declining litigation dramatically turned around in 1411, and the notable rush to the courts at this time will be considered below with reference to war and truce.[28]

At the next peak, in 1415–17, a large number of new cases appear, most of which were pleas *coram rege*. These involved two killings in Westmorland and other allegations of violence in that county and in Cumberland.[29] This rise in judicial activity coincides with the king's French campaigns, on which he was joined by John, Lord Clifford, in 1415 and 1416, and by Thomas, Lord Dacre, in 1416. The absence of these barons seems to have contributed to local turbulence.[30] Also underway at this time, perhaps in part motivated by the sense of need for a magnate presence to address local unrest, were moves to restore the Percy heir. He returned from Scottish captivity in February 1416 and was restored to his grandfather's earldom before September,[31] when he accompanied the king to France for the first time.[32] It may be that litigants anticipated a need to assert and defend their rights which might come into question with a change of local leadership, but still only one of the relevant cases can be loosely connected to Percy interests. Thus, without examining the plea rolls from other terms in this period, the

---

[27] The KB 9 files of Henry IV are generally thin: Carpenter, *Locality and Polity*, 364. There is the notable exception of the Ogle dispute over Bothal Castle in 1410, and other hints of conflicts found in *CCR 1402–5*, 184; *CCR 1405–9*, 249, 272–3, 367, 487.

[28] See below, pp. 224–232.

[29] 1415 (KB 27/618 rots 22–88d, *rex* rot. 17d); 1416 (KB 27/622 rots 11d–96d); 1417 (KB 27/626 rots 14–78d, *rex* rot. 13d). Dacre himself is implicated in the violence of 1415, when he was still in England. This period also produced two chancery petitions concerning violent assaults in Wml. in 1415 (C 1/6/213; C 1/6/278), not included in the figures, for which see below, p. 300nn 180, 181.

[30] A. Curry, *Agincourt: A New History* (Stroud, 2005), 58, 62, 67–8. For Clifford's absence in 1416, see *CPR 1413–16*, 320; *CPR 1416–22*, 72, 77. He was at Southampton in August 1415, suggesting that he followed the king to Agincourt that year (*PROME*, November 1415, item 6). For Dacre in France in 1416, see *CCR 1413–19*, 317, 321, 322.

[31] Percy was appointed as captain of Berwick and warden of the east march in early 1417: E 101/73/3/44; *CDS*, IV, 174; ibid., V, 286; *CPR 1413–16*, 399; *PROME*, March 1416, item 12; *Rot. Scot.*, ii, 219–20; *PPC*, II, 208–9, 212–14; Bradley, 'Henry V's Scottish Policy', 181, 185.

[32] Curry has argued (*Agincourt*, 58) that the future second earl sent a retinue to France in 1415 (citing E 404/31/266; E 101/45/5 m. 5). However, this would have involved him recruiting across the border as a captive in Scotland. While not impossible, it seems more probable that it was his first cousin, Sir Henry Percy of Atholl, who indented with Henry V. The future earl indented with the king in 1416 (E 101/48/10/142). I am grateful to Anne Curry for a helpful exchange on this point and I note the revised edition of *Agincourt* (Stroud, 2015) omits the argument. For Percy of Atholl, see *CDS*, IV, 143, 147, 182; *CCR 1405–9*, 224–5; *CCR 1409–13*, 55; *CPR 1416–22*, 124; *CCR 1413–19*, 505–6; *CCR 1419–22*, 199, 226; Hodgson, *Northumberland*, ii, 53, 62.

Patterns of Conflict

proposed connection must remain partly speculative.[33] Overall it appears that both the French campaigns and the Percy restoration were factors that served to raise court activity.

The apparent jump in the total number of cases in Figure 2 between 1419 and 1422 is in fact produced by two particular groups of cases which generated a large number of allegations.[34] The first of these groupings concerns various thefts and other offences in Northumberland, notably against a group of victims that included two knights, allegedly perpetrated in the late 1410s by a gang of men from Redesdale.[35] The second grouping concerns the Turpyn–Whitley dispute in Northumberland.[36] There were further peaks of new litigation, in 1423, 1429–30 (to be addressed below) and in 1441, the latter mostly created by a number of existing cases being brought back into the court.[37] King's bench records capture some but not all of the serious turbulence that occurred in Westmorland during the 1430s. Details of those events are mostly forthcoming in petitions to chancery and parliament, which will be examined in a later chapter.[38]

Storey's claim that the border counties 'are almost entirely unrepresented' in king's bench records after 1440 can be safely discarded, for this survey shows continued activity in the court's plea rolls during that decade and after.[39] For example, the roll for Easter term 1446 includes Sir Thomas Parr of Kendal's petition against Robert and Thomas Bellingham and three others who had violently ambushed him in London as he travelled to parliament.[40] The year 1449 presents a peak that is best explained by the separate commissions of oyer and terminer issued for Cumberland and Northumberland in May 1449.[41] These

---

[33] Thomas Ampilforth, a chaplain of Cockermouth, was accused of trespass (KB 27/622 rots 66d, 73d).

[34] This distortion is corrected by reference to Figure 1 for the same period, which shows a smaller number of new cases, as opposed to proceedings on a particular case.

[35] KB 9/1056 m. 23. See below, p. 246.

[36] KB 9/213 mm. 58–9; KB 9/216/2 mm. 4–5; KB 27/646 *rex* rots 25, 25d, 25(a). See comment on the Turpyn-Whitley affair below, at pp. 246–7, 250–1 and 280.

[37] The oyer and terminer commission of 1438 for Nbl. (*CPR 1436–41*, 201) does not appear to have brought new cases into the court. For the 1441 cases, see KB 27/722 *rex* rots 14, 17d, 30d; KB 27/722 rots 67, 67d, 94; KB 9/235 mm. 79–80; KB 9/237 m. 66.

[38] Robert Crackenthorpe's widow Elizabeth appealed her husband's killers in 1439 (KB 27/711 rot. 36d; KB 27/713 rots 35, 35d; KB 27/714 rots 36, 82). The oyer and terminer commission issued in July 1441 for Wml. (*CPR 1436–41*, 576) related to these disputes. See below, pp. 301–3.

[39] Storey, *House of Lancaster*, 118. Storey's bibliography cites KB 9 and KB 27 records; it is, however, correct to state that the KB 9 files alone for the 1440s and 1450s do not reveal cases from the border counties.

[40] KB 27/740 rots 82–82d. See below, p. 301. This enrolment is missed by Storey, 'Disorders in Lancastrian Westmorland', 77–9; Storey, *House of Lancaster*, 120–1.

[41] *CPR 1446–52*, 269–70.

213

Part III

commissions resulted in renewed prosecution of old *rex*-side cases, and three of five new cases were also from the *rex* side. Many of these crown prosecutions would either disappear altogether after this year or not be resumed again for some time.[42] While turmoil engulfed the south of England in 1450, the north remained stable.[43] Southern events may have had some indirect effect on court activity in the far north. The apparent spike off the chart for all cases in 1451 (Figures 4 and 8) is, in one sense, another distortion, as all but four of the twenty-five cases appearing at this time relate to thefts done by two yeomen in Northumberland throughout the previous decade. However, they had been indicted before the JPs at Newcastle in April 1451, and, if this was a sign of a sterner judicial attitude, it may well have been in reaction to the unsettling events of the previous year.[44]

The impact of the national political struggles of the 1450s and 1460s is illustrated in Figures 3 and 4. The infamous Percy–Neville disputes of 1453–4 were concentrated in Yorkshire, where the major confrontations occurred and where indictments were taken.[45] There is some evidence for 'discensions, riotes and debates' in Cumberland in the early 1450s in the build-up to these outbursts, but this is not reflected in court activity.[46] During the volatile years between 1455 and 1461, the border counties generated a level of judicial activity that was no more than comparable to that of the previous decade. In 1455, following upon the first battle of St Albans and York's second protectorate, an effort to exert royal authority through the judicial system may explain the resumption of a number of older cases of felony on the *rex* side of the court. These came mostly from Cumberland and Westmorland and included the first appearance of indictments taken the previous year before justices at Appleby, and of those taken years earlier at Carlisle in 1448.[47] Three

---

[42] All of the ten cases making reappearances in 1449 were from this side of the court. KB 27/754 *rex* rots 5, 11, 11d, 13d, 16, 16d, 17d, 18d, 32; KB 27/754 rots 17, 57, 57d.

[43] The events of 1449–50 included Jack Cade's rebellion, the murder of two bishops, and the parliamentary impeachment, exile and killing of the duke of Suffolk (Carpenter, *Wars of the Roses*, 113–15).

[44] The yeomen were Robert Wan and John Jackson. Others were indicted at Newcastle-upon-Tyne, and, in this and the previous month, coroners brought further indictments from Corbridge and Morpeth (KB 9/265 mm. 158–62; KB 27/762 *rex* rots 3d–4).

[45] KB 9/148/1 m. 8; KB 9/149/1/4 mm. 25–7; KB 9/149/1/5 m. 3; KB 9/149/1/6 m. 8; KB 9/149/1/8 mm. 2,6; KB 9/149/1/9 m. 8; KB 9/149/1/11 m. 16; KB 27/778 rot. 3d; Griffiths, 'Local Rivalries'.

[46] *CCR 1447–54*, 470, 467–68; Griffiths, 'Local Rivalries', 592, 603, 619; Storey, *House of Lancaster*, 106–23, 126; Summerson, *Medieval Carlisle*, ii, 441, citing the assertions of two sheriffs of Cbl. in 1451–2 (Roland Vaux) and 1452–3 (Thomas Delamore), found at E 28/85/21–2, 26–7; E 28/87/20. See also Delamore's petition (SC 8/29/1446); *PROME*, March 1453, appendix, no. 28.

[47] KB 27/778 *rex* rots 3d, 4d, 16, 17d, 18, 20d; KB 27/778 rot. 87; KB 9/277 mm. 11–12; KB 9/276 m. 9.

Patterns of Conflict

years later, in Michaelmas 1458, at a time of Lancastrian ascendancy, almost all the cases appearing in court were reappearances on the *rex* side. Some of these can be identified as highly partisan uses of the royal judicial system by those in political favour. For example, the indictment file this year included the first mention of a decade-old case concerning the disputed inheritance of Scaleby Castle in northern Cumberland. The gentleman William Tilliol and his associates were pursued by Thomas and Margaret Crackenthorpe, who accused them of making a violent attack at Scaleby in 1449.[48] Tilliol was to face further accusations in 1459 and 1460.[49]

In contrast to the large numbers of old *rex*-side cases in the peaks of 1455 and 1458, the year 1461 produced mostly new cases, and these appeared on the *coram rege* side of the court. We have already noted the effects of crisis and uncertainty on the use of the courts, and a rapid rush to law might be expected following the establishment of Edward IV's regime such as has been observed, though not uniformly, elsewhere in the country.[50] However, in the far north, the peak in 1461 seems to reflect less a renewed confidence in government and the system of royal justice than a continued partisan use of the courts, now in favour of Yorkist proponents whose fortunes had been reversed. However, the new regime was far from secure in Northumberland, where Lancastrian resistance would continue until 1464.[51] It is unsurprising, then, that only three cases in 1461 came from that county, two lodged by the same plaintiff.[52] The rest of this year's cases arose west of the Pennines, and among them we

---

[48] William Tilliol (né Colville) 'of Scaleby' and his brother, Robert Colville of Carlisle, were indicted with others (KB 27/790 *rex* rots 22, 26d, 28, 29d, 32d; KB 9/288 mm. 1–5). The eventual co-heirs of Sir Peter Tilliol of Scaleby (d. 1434) were his two daughters. The first, Isabella (d. 1439), married John Colville and had two sons, William and Robert Colville (C 140/71/ no. 54, *i.p.m.* for William Colville, 1479). The second, Margaret (d. 1458), married James Moresby and later Thomas Crackenthorpe. Her son by Moresby was Christopher, who, at his death in 1461, held half of Scaleby. His own son, another Christopher (d. 1499), held all of Scaleby. See C 1/293/27; *LOE*, 26; *CPR 1436–41*, 346; *CFR 1437–45*, 51; *CFR 1452–61*, 214; *CFR 1461–71*, 3, 47, 50; *CCR 1461–8*, 5; *Calendarium Inquisitionum Post Mortem Sive Escaetarum*, ed. J. Caley and J. Bayley, 4 vols (London, 1806–28), iv, no. 30, p. 283 (Moresby, 1458); no. 35, p. 311 (Moresby, 1461); *CIPM, Henry VII*, II, no. 292, pp. 191–3 (Moresby, 1499); Booth, 'Landed Society', 68–70; Summerson, *Medieval Carlisle*, ii, 445; Denton, *Accompt*, 152–5; D.M. Yorath, 'Sir Christopher Moresby of Scaleby and Windermere, c. 1441–99', *Northern History*, 53 (2016), 173–88.

[49] KB 27/794 *rex* rot. 20; KB 27/798 rot. 103d; KB 27/798 *rex* rot. 35d.

[50] See above p. 211. Warks. shows a similar jump (Carpenter, *Locality and Polity*, 709), but Coates's work on Notts., Derbys., Herts. and Essex does not, until an apparent judicial campaign by Edward IV in 1462–3 (Coates, 'Law Enforcement Policy', 55, 158–60, 193–4).

[51] Carpenter, *Locality and Polity*, 511; Goodman, *Wars of the Roses*, 63–5.

[52] This was Thomas Colt, a Warwick adherent who was also active in Cbl. (J.C. Wedgwood, *Biographies of Members of the Commons House 1439–1509* (London, 1936), 208–9).

Part III

find William Tilliol initiating pleas against his erstwhile pursuers and others. Presumably, he had been inspired by the death of Thomas Crackenthorpe, apparently killed fighting for Henry VI at Towton.[53]

King's bench entertained relatively few cases from the border shires before 1467. Northumberland produced much less activity than its neighbouring counties to the west, and the obvious cause for this was the overwhelming civil strife which did not decline until the Lancastrian defeat at Hexham (1464) which was followed by the capture of Henry VI the following year. The eclipse of the Percys, Cliffords and Dacres during the 1460s did not provoke any exceptional conflicts beyond the bigger factional struggles, apart from two homicide appeals in 1464 against Sir Humphrey Dacre and a small disturbance in south-west Cumberland in February 1466.[54] The temporary abeyance of these noble dynasties did not, then, lead to the escalation of local disputes. Rather, the opposite seems to have happened. By 1465, John Neville of Montague, the new earl of Northumberland, was arbitrating in local quarrels, while some Westmorland gentry were also making peace among their peers.[55] It would seem that Montague's personal authority and the weight of the ascendant Neville family, combined with a general exhaustion with violent dissension, served as effective forces for peacemaking in the wide gap left by Percy, Clifford and Dacre. In the peak of 1467 there were six new pleas *coram rege* from Cumberland and Westmorland, a number of which were made by prominent gentry.[56] There is no clear explanation for so many new cases appearing in 1467.[57] However, this jump may well

---

[53] KB 27/802 rots 32, 37d, 58, 58d, 59d. Sir William Legh of Isel and Sir John Pennington, both attainted Lancastrians, were among Tilliol's opponents. Tilliol's brother Colville, and their cousin Christopher Moresby (whose son obtained Scaleby), were Neville supporters (*CFR 1452–61*, 286). See Booth, 'Landed Society', 58, 70–5, 105; C. Moor, 'Crackenthorpe of Newbiggin', *TCWAAS*, n.s., 33 (1933), 43–97.

[54] KB 27/814 rots 47, 47d; *CPR 1461–67*, 492. Among the troublemakers were members of the Pennington family, linked to Percys (Booth, 'Landed Society', 88).

[55] *CCR 1461–68*, 330; Bodleian: Dodsworth MS, 45, fol. 43v (62); *Northumberland and Durham Deeds from the Dodsworth MSS, in Bodley's Library, Oxford*, ed. A.M. Oliver (1929), no. 55, p. 60; F.W. Dendy, 'The Heton–Fenwick–Denton Line of Descent', *Archaeologia Aeliana*, 3rd ser., 14 (1917), 173–90, at 177–8, 187; CAC, Carlisle: D/Lons/L5/1/3/66, 67, formerly AS 61, 62.

[56] The knights Lancelot Threlkeld and William Martindale, and Robert Colville, esq., proceeded against local yeomen, husbandmen and tradesmen. In Wml. Sir Richard Redmane impleaded the minor gentleman Alexander Manzergh and his associates for trespass (KB 27/826 *rex* rot. 18d; KB 27/826 rots 9, 16d, 15, 62d, 67, 72d). The indictments this year included one (KB 9/316 mm. 37–8) for the killing of a Nbl. yeoman in 1461. The Hilary Term file from Yorks. contains the indictment (KB 9/315 mm. 55, 56) of various Lancastrian gentry, including men from Nbl., Cbl., Wml., and Furness.

[57] A similar peak has been detected in Essex and Herts. at this time and into the following year, which Coates ('Law Enforcement Policy', 181–4) has suggested signifies increasing instability. Likewise, Warks. in 1467 reveals elevated local tensions: Carpenter, *Locality and Polity*, 506–8, 613.

Patterns of Conflict

indicate that local tensions had cooled to the point where the common law could be used in conjunction with peacemaking out of court. In 1468–9, more bonds for arbitration are recorded.[58] A further sign of subsiding tensions at this time is the pardon of Sir Humphrey Dacre in 1468, the first step in his gradual restoration to royal favour in the west march, which culminated in his recognition as the Dacre heir male in 1473.[59]

Levels of king's bench activity remained low throughout the risings of 1469 and the whole period of the Readeption of Henry VI. Further political uncertainty, at least until 1471, may be the simple explanation for this, and this pattern has been observed elsewhere.[60] The northern risings of 1469 and 1470 were concentrated south of the marches, in Yorkshire, Lancashire and Lincolnshire.[61] The situation was stable enough in Cumberland and Westmorland for attempts to be made to resolve multiple local disputes between 1469 and 1471. For example, in January 1470, nine months before the Readeption, a violent dispute between the Briscos of Crofton and the Dentons of Cardew was put to arbitration.[62]

Judicial activity did not jump again until the mid-1470s. This occurred during a period of tension between the fourth earl of Northumberland (restored in 1469–70) and the duke of Gloucester, as these two noblemen sought to carve out their northern followings.[63] By 28 July 1474, they

---

[58] *CCR 1468–76*, nos 136, 278, 900, pp. 36, 71, 244; Rawson and Wyber *v*. Lancaster, 1468 (CAC, Kendal: WD/Hoth/Box 35/unnumbered doc. dated 10 March 1468); Gybson *v*. Bakstar, 1469 (CAC, Carlisle: D/Lons/L5/1/3/70, formerly AS 64).

[59] *GEC*, IV, 1–18; *PROME*, Oct. 1472, items 45–7; Pollard, *North-Eastern England*, 307.

[60] For instance, it has been found in Notts., Derbys., Herts. and Essex (Coates, 'Law Enforcement Policy', 223–4) and Warks. (Carpenter, *Locality and Polity*, 613). In addition to the general commission of oyer and terminer, a separate commission was issued in May 1469 for Yorks., Cbl. and Wml. (*CPR 1467–77*, 170).

[61] The only evident political unrest in the border shires is a failed rising attempt by Humphrey Neville of Brancepath and his brother in August 1469. The brothers had been in hiding since 1464 (Goodman, *Wars of the Roses*, 69–74; Ross, *Edward IV*, 127–37, esp. 134–5). On the Readeption, see Booth, 'Landed Society', 99–113. Pollard, *North-Eastern England*, 172, cites the cases relating to the Nbl. liberties from the Durham gaol deliveries of 1471–3 as signs of locals taking advantage of political uncertainty.

[62] Sir John Huddleston and the prior of St Mary's Carlisle gave the award on 27 January (CRO D/Lons/D 65). Huddleston was the earl of Warwick's agent in Cbl., with responsibility for the honour of Cockermouth and carrying out a policy of pacification and reconciliation towards former Percy adherents: Booth, 'Landed Society', 87–8, 92–7. See also Lancaster *v*. Sandford, 1471 (CAC, Carlisle: D/Lons L5/1/3/73, formerly AS 67). Thomas Sandford directed arbitrations among Wml. yeomen, in 1469 (CAC, Carlisle: D/Lons L5/1/3/70, formerly AS 64) and in 1470 (CAC, Carlisle: D/Lons L5/1/3/71, formerly AS 65).

[63] Both magnates were called before the council in May 1473: Ross, *Edward IV*, 199; Horrox, *Richard III*, ch. 1. For Percy's restoration, see E 39/99/91; *Rot. Scot.*, ii, 422–3; *CPR 1467–76*, 206; *CCR 1468–76*, no. 403, p. 100.

217

Part III

had reached an accommodation by which Gloucester retained Percy and each undertook not to meddle with the other's men.[64] In August, they served jointly as umpires in a Cumberland dispute,[65] and, as a further division of authority, the king granted Percy the Northumberland shrievalty for life in that same month. The following year, he gave comparable grants to Gloucester for Cumberland and to Sir William Parr for Westmorland.[66] In 1475 all three men – the duke, the earl and the knight – campaigned in France with the king. Although Percy and Gloucester are widely understood to have cooperated to a certain degree for the rest of the reign, we shall see that things were not so restrained.[67] Turning now to the statistics, Figures 7 and 8 demonstrate that Cumberland's peak of cases came before that in the other counties, in 1475. In this year, we find a resumption of the Brisco–Denton affair. King's bench heard indictments against the Briscos, concerning threats, depredations and thefts dating from 1471, 1472 and 1474. Robert Brisco, esquire, and his gentle kinsmen and their followers had allegedly victimised John Denton, esquire, and Sir William Legh of Isel (a Percy tenant and sheriff of Cumberland in 1473–4) and their non-gentle associates.[68]

The Brisco–Denton affair illustrates the effect on local conflict of both the presence of great magnates and their absence on a royal military campaign. Following the arrival of Gloucester in the north, John Denton's son Herry had become the duke's retainer in October 1473, an evident intrusion into Percy allegiances.[69] The next year, in June 1474, and only a month before Gloucester's agreement with the earl of Northumberland, a jury including Henry Denton and various Percy

---

[64] The duke was not to retain any of Percy's men except John Widdrington: Alnwick Castle: Syon House MSS, Y. II, 28 (consulted via BL microfilm reel 358); calendared in *HMC, 6th Report*, appendix, part I, 223–4; Jones and Walker, 'Private Indentures', no. 154, pp. 177–8. See also Bean, *Estates of the Percy Family*, 128–35.

[65] Huddleston v. Pennington, 1474 (Bodleian: Dodsworth MS, 41, fol. 113d [36]); *CCR 1468–76*, no. 1317, p. 365; CAC, Carlisle: D/Hud/5/1. Percy appointed John Pennington esquire as his bailiff of Copeland in December 1470 (CAC, Whitehaven: D/Pen/Family Docs Bundle A/no. 3).

[66] *CPR 1467–77*, 467, 485, 531–32, Booth, 'Landed Society', 125–7, 168, 178.

[67] See below, p. 305; *CPR 1476–85*, 145; Horrox, *Richard III*, 69–70; Ross, *Edward IV*, 206–14; Hayes, 'Ancient Indictments', 37–44; Booth, 'Landed Society', 129–30, 165; C.L. Scofield, *The Life and Reign of Edward the Fourth*, 2 vols (London, 1923), II, 167. Early in 1475 the northern part of the Warwick inheritance strengthened Gloucester's hand in northern Yorks. but limited his role in Cbl. (M. Hicks, 'Descent, Partition and Extinction: The "Warwick Inheritance" [1471–75]', *BIHR*, 52 (1979), 116–28; *PROME*, October 1472, items 16–17, 20–4; *CPR 1467–77*, 483).

[68] KB 9/339 mm. 13, 14; KB 27/857 *rex* rots 7–7d; *LOS*, 27.

[69] CAC, Carlisle: D/Lons/D 65; printed in Jones and Walker, 'Private Indentures', no. 153, p. 177.

Patterns of Conflict

associates indicted the Brisco party before the Cumberland JPs.[70] Evidently, both Gloucester and Percy were trying to exert influence on the same side of this dispute. The Briscos petitioned chancery with allegations against the sheriff, Sir William Legh of Isel, and a gentleman called William Dykes.[71] It was not until Trinity term 1475, immediately before Gloucester, Percy and Parr were to depart with the king for France, that the previous year's indictments appeared in king's bench. Pending the uncertain journey, Gloucester's man Denton evidently sought to put pressure on his opponents by taking them to court. Shortly after the return of the military expedition in September 1475, the cases were despatched inconclusively, to all purposes suggesting an out-of-court compromise.[72]

The peak of court activity from Northumberland in 1476 needs some explanation. This year produced the highest peak for new cases from Northumberland since mid-century. These cases included depredations perpetrated by a large group of Newcastle men in July 1475 and thefts carried out by a family of yeomen – John, Thomas, Adam and Herbert Tweddall – over the preceding three years. All but one of these indictments were taken before the JPs at Newcastle, immediately following the return from France of the king, Percy and Gloucester in the autumn of 1475. Those who sat in these sessions were Percy men. This was no royal judicial drive[73] but, rather, a legal assault by the Percy affinity on local adversaries.[74] The origin of these tensions is obscure, but matters had already become lethal sometime before the autumn of 1474, by which time one man had been killed by Percy associates (including John Widdrington). That incident was perhaps the catalyst for the Percy–Gloucester indenture of July 1474, which mentioned Widdrington specifically.[75]

---

[70] The Percy-linked jurors included John Legh Sr; William Dykes, gentleman; and Alexander Dykes (for the Dykes in the Cockermouth affinity, see CAC, Whitehaven: D/Lec 29/2; 29/3). The Cbl. peace commission had been issued on 20 June 1473 and named twenty men, including both Gloucester and Percy. The only two JPs sitting at Carlisle, Roland Thornburgh and William Beaulieu, were very minor figures. *CPR 1467–77*, 610; KB 9/339 mm. 13, 14; KB27/857 *rex* rots 7–7d.

[71] The petitioners were Robert Brisco esq. and his brother Edward, gentleman, who complained of repeated false pleas and fines in the shire court and of harassment, plunder and kidnapping by Dykes and his men, keeping them from the shire day (C 1/48/13). Their supplication to the bishop of Durham as chancellor may be dated to 1474 as Bishop Laurence Booth was chancellor in 1473–4 ('Booth [Bothe], Laurence (c. 1420–1480)', *Oxford DNB*, VI, 626–8, by R. O'Day).

[72] For an affair timed similarly in Essex (1475), see Coates, 'Law Enforcement Policy', 270–1.

[73] There was a special oyer and terminer commission issued in 1476, but this was specifically for counterfeiting in Cbl. and Wml. (*CPR 1467–77*, 606). Coates, 'Law Enforcement Policy', 271–2, 275, 295, detects a post-campaign judicial drive further south.

[74] KB 9/343 mm. 34, 56. The JPs sitting on 4 September and 25 October 1475 (m 56) were Percy's undersheriff, John Lilburn esq., and John Cartington. Both were associated with Percy's man John Widdrington (*CPR 1467–77*, 407; *LOS*, 98). The mayor and aldermen of Newcastle-upon-Tyne sat as JPs for the town on 23 November 1475 (KB 9/343 m. 34).

[75] The slain man was Henry Carr. See below, p. 305.

219

Part III

This manoeuvre against the Tweddalls in 1475 provoked a dramatic escalation of tensions the following summer. The cases of 1476 include the indictment for the killing of Richard Tweddall – Adam's brother – in Tynedale in June of that year. Those accused in this case included eleven Northumberland gentry, six yeomen and others unknown, numbering two hundred, including some Scots. Their leader was the earl's relative, Sir Henry Percy of Bamburgh.[76] At this stage the king himself seems to have become personally involved, directing the court to release Tweddall's killers and pressuring Tweddall's brother to drop his private suit against them.[77] In general Edward IV seems to have paid close personal attention to cases involving his Duchy of Lancaster lands and tenants, among which Percy the knight of Bamburgh was to be counted.[78]

The situation at this time in Westmorland may also be partly explained by tensions among magnates. Sir William Parr was the dominant force in that county after 1471. The king had given him extensive influence there, including a grant of the Clifford barony of Westmorland and the shrievalty.[79] Edward IV relied upon this knight as his premier agent in the far north-west. Although Parr was a potential rival to Gloucester, the two men shared in their opposition to Percy.[80] It is indicative that some of the Westmorland cases pursued in the mid-1470s, all but two being old ones, were against the Bellinghams of Burneside, who were rivals to Parr connected to the Percys. Another case involved the killing of a yeoman by Thomas Pennington of Egremont, a gentleman with obvious

---

[76] The view of Tweddall's body by the king's coroner within the earl of Essex's liberty of Tynedale is found at KB 9/343 mm. 70, 71. Among Tweddall's other accused killers were the esquires Giles Thornton of Witton-by-the-Water, Robert Harbottle of Prudhoe, Henry Swinhowe of Rock and Scremerston, William Lisle of Felton, and Robert Howpnum of Elford; and the gentlemen Gilbert Swinburne of Nafferton, Cuthbert Ogle of Ogle, Christopher Errington of Denton, Thomas Cramlington of Newsham, and Edward Carr of Lucker. The appeal by Tweddall's brother Adam (KB 27/861 *rex* rot. 15) named only Percy, Cramlington and Thornton as principals.

[77] Lilburn, Percy's undersheriff, was fined for failure to return a writ of attachment issued upon Adam Tweddall's appeal for the death of his brother (KB 27/861 rot. 118). Percy, Thornton and Cramlington were released from the court in Michaelmas 1476 when Adam failed to prosecute his appeal. At the same time, the crown attorney presented a signet letter mandating the discharge of the king's suit against the three men (KB 27/861 *rex* rot. 15).

[78] Percy of Bamburgh became a Duchy official as porter of Bamburgh Castle in 1483 (*CPR 1476–85*, 346). He was presumably a close relative of the earl, employed by him as lieutenant-warden of the east marches in the early 1480s (Alnwick Castle: Syon House MSS, C VI, 2c and 4d [BL microfilm reel 373]; Cardew, 'Anglo-Scottish', 371; *CDS*, IV, 306; *CPR 1485–94*, 39, 495). On Edward's use of the small seals to manipulate the courts, see Coates, 'Law Enforcement Policy', 77–97, 86–8. See also Carpenter, *Locality and Polity*, 518, 535–47; T.M. Westervelt, 'William Lord Hastings and the Governance of Edward IV, with Special Reference to the Second Reign (1471–83)', PhD thesis, University of Cambridge (2001), 56–62, 67, 72, 74, 126.

[79] *CPR 1461–77*, 187, 280 (John Parr); *CPR 1467–77*, 531–2 (William Parr).

[80] *CPR 1467–77*, 264, 423, 467, 485; *CFR 1471–85*, 116.

Patterns of Conflict

Percy links.[81] These cases from Westmorland could reflect Parr's own antipathy to the Percy interest.

The elimination of Gloucester's brother Clarence in 1477–8 gave him a much freer hand to conduct his affairs in the north,[82] and perhaps greater leverage to direct dispute resolutions.[83] This may well help to explain why litigation in the north seems to subside after 1477. Levels of judicial activity do not rise again until 1480–2, and Figures 7 and 8 demonstrate that this new peak concerned mostly old *rex*-side cases from Cumberland and Westmorland but also some new violence in Northumberland.[84] What is remarkable about a number of these cases is their antiquity. Many dated back decades and had long since been abandoned. Among them were one from 1429,[85] two from 1438,[86] three from the 1440s,[87] one from 1455[88] and one from 1466.[89] The reappearance of such old cases reflects the undoubted security of the Yorkist regime and may have been intended as a public statement to that effect at the high point of Edward IV's authority. The pursuit of long-standing offenders would also have been a means by which Gloucester could exert his personal clout in the marches. Booth has suggested that there was increased cooperation between Gloucester and Parr at this time, and, among the cases being pursued, there continued the pleas against the Bellinghams, a further suggestion that Gloucester had Parr's interests at heart.[90] While these old cases were numerous, Westmorland produced almost no new cases in the decade following 1477. Although Hayes found no king's bench indictments from Westmorland for the entire Yorkist period, the plea rolls show continuing

---

[81] 1474 (KB 27/ 853 *rex* rots 21d, 22, 38d); 1476 (KB 27/861 rot. 14d; KB 27/861 *rex* rots 22, 25d, 26); 1477 (KB 27/865 *rex* rots 20d, 21, 22, 22d, 23).

[82] Booth, 'Landed Society', 128–31; Carpenter, *Locality and Polity*, 521, 533.

[83] See below, p. 314.

[84] The Easter and Trinity term rolls for 1480 record the killing of Nicholas Reymes by several Ogles from North Middleton in the parish of Hertburn, Nbl. (KB 27/874 rot. 13; KB 27/875 rot. 8).

[85] 1429 (KB 9/224 mm. 66–7); 1449 (KB 27/754 *rex* rot. 11); 1480 (KB 27/876 *rex* rot. 49).

[86] 1438 (KB 9/229/4 mm. 25–6); 1480 (KB 27/876 *rex* rot. 49d); 1481 (KB 27/880 *rex* rot. 31d, 36); 1482 (KB 27/884 *rex* rot. 41d); 1438 (KB 27/710 *rex* rot. 64); 1439 (KB 9/230B mm. 90, 91); 1480 (KB 27/876 *rex* rot. 46d); 1482 (KB 27/884 *rex* rot. 41d).

[87] 1446 (KB 27/742 *rex* rots 26–26d); 1480 (KB 27/876 *rex* rot. 48d); 1482 (KB 27/884 *rex* rot. 42); 1446 (KB 9/252/1 mm. 75–6); 1480 (KB 27/876 *rex* rot. 46d); 1482 (KB 27/884 *rex* rot. 43); 1449 (KB 27/754 *rex* rot. 18d); 1480 (KB 27/876 *rex* rot. 49d); 1482 (KB 27/884 *rex* rot. 42d).

[88] 1455 (KB 9/277 mm. 11, 12); 1480 (KB 27/876 *rex* rot. 48d); 1481 (KB 27/880 *rex* rot. 36); 1482 (KB 27/884 *rex* rot. 42d).

[89] 1466 (KB 27/822 *rex* rot. 23d); 1480 (KB 27/876 *rex* rot. 49d); 1481 (KB 27/880 *rex* rot. 36); 1482 (KB 27/884 *rex* rot. 42d).

[90] Booth, 'Landed Society', 179, 181–2. Parr was controller of the royal household from 1471 to 1475, a member of the royal council from July 1471 and a member of Gloucester's council ('Parr, Sir William (1434–1483)', *Oxford DNB*, XLII, 854–5, by R. Horrox). See KB 27/853 *rex* rot. 22; KB 27/865 *rex* rots 25d, 26; KB 27/865 *rex* rot. 21; KB 27/876 *rex* rots 46d, 48d; KB 27/884 *rex* rots 42, 43. Many of these cases were held up by uncooperative sheriffs who failed to serve writs.

221

Part III

judicial process on old *rex*-side cases. Still, from Michaelmas term 1477 until Edward IV's demise, only two new cases came into king's bench from this small county, suggesting that Parr was handling local disputes personally or passing them up to the royal council before his own death in 1483.[91] There is certainly extra-judicial evidence to show that both lethal violence and local peacemaking continued in the county at this time.[92]

The usurpation of Gloucester as Richard III in 1483 coincided with a total flatline for new cases in the border counties (excluding Newcastle), which lasted until 1487. Westmorland had been at near zero since 1477, and now the cases coming from Northumberland and Cumberland dropped to nil as well.[93] The Michaelmas plea rolls for king's bench as a whole for 1483 and 1485 are small, reflecting the widespread uncertainty caused by the regime changes in these years. However, the rolls for 1484, 1486, 1487 and 1488 are much larger, indicating that, for court activity at least, the far north was now operating very differently from other parts of the realm.[94] By contrast, it seems that the same unease, much of it expressed through rebellion in the north in 1486 and 1487,[95] helped to discourage conflict from the border counties coming into king's bench.

Yet political turmoil is not an entirely satisfactory explanation for this lack of activity; even when outright civil war was waged in the early

[91] Hayes, 'Ancient Indictments', 25–6. The present survey of Michaelmas terms found just one new *rex*-side case from Wml. in the Yorkist period, in 1474 (KB 27/853 *rex* rot. 38d) but several new cases on the plea side before 1476. A supplemental review of plea rolls in all terms from 1476 to 1483 identified only the following new cases from the county: 1477 (Trinity: KB 27/864 rot. 68), 1482 (Hilary: KB 27/881 rot. 11d), (Easter: KB 27/882 rot. 10d).

[92] See below, p. 311. At least six killings between 1475 and 1479 are evident in Kirkby Lonsdale in southern Wml. and in nearby Sedbergh and Dent in the West Riding of Yorks. (DUL, DCM: Reg. IV, fols 184v–185r, 187r–v, 188v, 238r, printed in *Sanctuarium Dunelmense et Sanctuarium Beverlacense*, ed. J. Raine (1837), pp. 4–13, nos vii, ix, xii, xiii, xvi, xviii, xxx).

[93] A supplemental survey of plea rolls in all terms from 1483 to 1488 shows that Hilary 1483 (the last term of Edward IV's reign) contained cases from Cbl. and Nbl. (KB 27/885 rots 12d, 44, 61, 61d). Only three cases, all from Newcastle-upon-Tyne, appeared in 1484 (new: Trinity, KB 27/892 rot. 7; old: Michaelmas, KB 27/893/2 rot. 56d) and 1485 (new: Hilary, KB 27/894/1 rot. 56d). A memorandum of a quitclaim by a gentleman of Nbl. to a gentleman of London was recorded in 1485 (Trinity, KB 27/895 rot. 30d). It was in Hilary, Easter and Trinity 1488 that new cases appeared again from the border counties.

[94] 1483 (KB 27/889: 32 rots, 32 *rex* rots); 1484 (KB 27/893: 111 rots, 37 *rex* rots); 1485 (KB 27/897: 31 rots, 8 *rex* rots); 1486 (KB 27/901: 98 rots, 31 *rex* rots); 1487 (KB 27/905: 80 rots, 29 *rex* rots), 1488 (KB 27/905: 120 rots, 41 *rex* rots). For example, Carpenter found a high rate of activity from Warks. in king's bench in these same years which, she suggests, was a sign of political instability lasting into the early years of the Tudor regime. More generally, Carpenter highlights the frailty of Henry VII's rule before 1495 (*Locality and Polity*, 564–83, 595, 613; Carpenter, *Wars of the Roses*, 219–23, 235). For the king's regional expansion of power, see Pollard, *North-Eastern England*, 367–96, 404.

[95] In the spring of 1486 Viscount Lovell's rising began in Yorks. and fled into Furness, and, in June 1487, the earl of Lincoln's invaded at Furness and marched into Yorks. and Notts.: Pollard, *North-Eastern England*, 371–2, 375–8.

Patterns of Conflict

1460s, at least some litigants still made regular use of king's bench. In all probability, what was happening in the middle and later 1480s was that disputants were taking their plaints to other venues. Obvious alternatives included the royal council and the domestic warden courts, which have left little record from this time. Neither was new, although it is known that Henry VII generally used the council in a more interventionist way than did his predecessors.[96] On the other hand, what was new at this time was the council 'in the North Parties', created by Richard III in 1484 with the intention of reforming the administration of the region he had known so well as duke. The council in the north may have been the venue to which litigants now turned.[97] Thus, from the mid-1480s, the crown took a new approach to the management of conflict in the borders and the north as a whole, creating a more accessible forum for adjudication with wide powers and a close link to the king, potentially allowing more direct royal intervention in the region. A prompt local engagement with this new policy may be signalled by the lack of activity at Westminster. Records from the northern council at this time are very thin, and so we cannot confirm this supposition.[98] Still, if it is accurate, it may indicate that landowners as much as the crown were looking for a new artery of royal justice in the region.

Northern judicial activity in king's bench did creep back in the later 1480s. Even then it was really in Cumberland and Westmorland that court business picked up. Northumberland, on the other hand, generated only three cases after 1487, all of them new. The fourth Percy earl, restored on probation by Henry VII following Bosworth, served as president of the northern council at this time. This may explain the relative lack of cases from Northumberland, and all the more if his personal influence had become important to the council's operation, especially east of the Pennines.[99] But the assumption that the earl of Northumberland had matters firmly under control in the later 1480s seems mistaken.[100] The fourth earl's violent death in 1489 at the hands of tax rebels (while the earl's retainers declined to protect their lord) removed one of Henry's key supporters in the north and left an

---

[96] Gunn, *Early Tudor Government*, 62–7.

[97] See above, p. 175. Richard III appointed the earl of Lincoln as president of the council, but, under Henry VII, Northumberland soon assumed the role: *British Library Harleian Manuscript 433*, ed. Horrox and Hammond, III, 107–8, 114–15; 'Pole, John de la, earl of Lincoln (c. 1460–1487)', *Oxford DNB*, XLIV, 705–6, by R. Horrox.

[98] Reid, *King's Council in the North*, 67–8: the only evidence for council business at this time comes from three cases, all from Yorks., in 1484.

[99] Reid, *King's Council in the North*, 74–5, suggests that the earl's comital council was used to the exclusion of the northern council in the late 1480s.

[100] Pollard, *North-Eastern England*, 375: Pollard's assumption concerns Northumberland specifically.

Part III

eleven-year-old heir.[101] Within a month of Percy's killing, the king restored Thomas Howard as earl of Surrey, a former Ricardian stalwart without any northern connections, and gave him leadership of the council as lieutenant of the north.[102] The records of the royal council also show that, in late 1488 and early 1489, lethal riots were provoked in the west march by an inheritance dispute over Greystoke barony.[103] It is telling of the limited role of king's bench in the border counties in the later 1480s that this case appears not to have come before the court at all, and it may have been passed up from the northern council. All the same, no fewer than three separate homicides in the region were recorded in king's bench at this time.[104] All of this, not least the slaying of Northumberland and the installation of an outsider like Surrey as the king's agent, suggests that things were going rather badly awry in the later 1480s and that a straightforward diversion of quarrels to the council in the north is not a complete explanation in itself. It was not until 1494 that court activity from the borders resumed anything like the levels of Edward IV's second reign. In this year, even some of the older cases which had been resumed in the early 1480s once again reappeared in the court.[105] In more general terms, the cases from the border shires in king's bench during the fifteenth century do not, on the whole, reflect the wider trends of levels of business in the common law courts that have been detected in other studies.[106]

CONFLICT, WAR AND TRUCE

This chapter now examines the impact of Anglo-Scottish war and truce on patterns of conflict and litigation. We shall first continue our analysis using

---

[101] See above, p. 122; Hicks, 'Dynastic Change', 78–107.

[102] Pollard, North-Eastern England, 386; Reid, King's Council in the North, 77.

[103] CDS, IV, 182; CPR 1485–94, 285–6. Dacre's recommission as lieutenant of the west march was dated 12 July 1488 (CDS, IV, 314).

[104] KB 27/906 rot. 4 (Hilary 1488: Newcastle-upon-Tyne, killing of Arthur Horsley by five men surnamed Thorpe); KB 27/907 rot. 7 (Easter 1488: Wml., killing of William Conyers); KB 27/908 rot. 10 (Trinity 1488: mandate to the sheriff of Cbl. concerning the killing of Thomas Colvell).

[105] KB 27/933 rex rots 14, 15, 22. Hayes ('Ancient Indictments', 23–29) notes the dramatic rise in northern indictments coming into king's bench under Henry VII and suggests this may partly result from 1487 legislation on coroners. Parliament that year also established the notorious tribunal against riots: PROME, November 1487, items 17, 21; Hunnisett, Medieval Coroner, 115–16, 221–2; E.W. Ives, The Common Lawyers of Pre-Reformation England (Cambridge, 1983), 261–2. At this same time compare the situation in the north midlands, 'badly out of hand': Carpenter, Locality and Polity, 568.

[106] That is, that the profits from sealing fees show declining business after 1440: Blatcher, Court of King's Bench, appendix, 167–71.

Patterns of Conflict

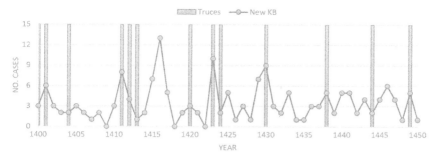

Figure 11 Truces and new KB (total), 1400–50

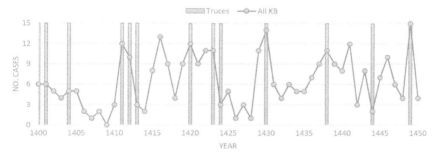

Figure 12 Truces and all KB (total), 1400–50

the king's bench data. The relationship between activity in the Westminster courts arising in the marches and Anglo-Scottish war remains almost entirely unexplored.[107] It is clear that warfare could disrupt the normal processes of the royal judicial system, for military conflict inhibited the regular travel of the itinerant justices to the border counties. Not only were the itinerant courts disrupted, but war could also suspend the business of the Westminster courts.[108] However, disruptions at Westminster did not happen often, and so the patterns of activity from the border counties in king's bench across the century offer a fairly consistent tool of assessment for the relationship between war, truce and judicial activity.

If we return to Figures 1 and 2, and consider years of Anglo-Scottish warfare, highlighting 1415, 1417–20, 1433–6 and 1448, the

---

[107] Almost every war in this period, especially Anglo-French war, generated surges of legal activity (Musson and Ormrod, *Evolution of English Justice*, 78–9, 80–2; Maddern, *Violence and Social Order*, 17–18).
[108] For example, see *CCR 1476–85*, no. 764, p. 227.

Part III

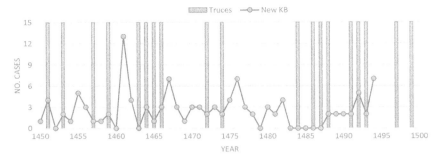

Figure 13   Truces and new KB (total), 1450–1500

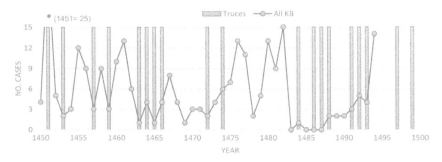

Figure 14   Truces and all KB (total), 1450–1500

impression given is that court activity could tend to decrease during wartime. However, after mid-century, this pattern seems to change. Looking at 1455, 1460–1 and 1480–2, which were years of major military activity against Scotland, we find that these were some of the busiest years for northern cases in king's bench. Thus, while Anglo-Scottish war seems to have lowered court activity earlier in the century, by the second half of our period, the same activity in court appears to be unhindered by war.[109]

Shifting our attention to truce, Figures 11–14 illustrate the same king's bench graphs from Figures 1–4, but they plot numbers of cases against years in which Anglo-Scottish truces were signed. It is revealing that many of the peaks of new cases appearing in Figure 11 (i.e., for the years 1401, 1411, 1420, 1423, 1430, 1438, and 1449) occur exactly in the years

---

[109] A point expanded upon below, p. 239.

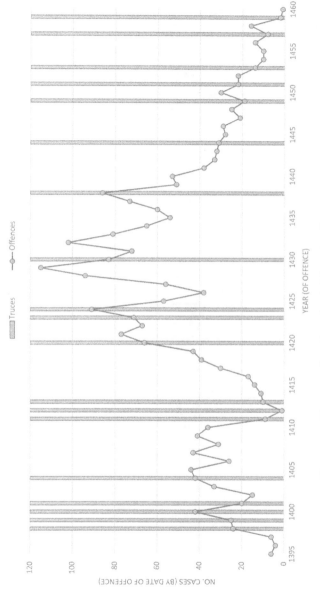

Figure 15 Truces and JUST 3 (gaol delivery) offences (total), 1395–1460

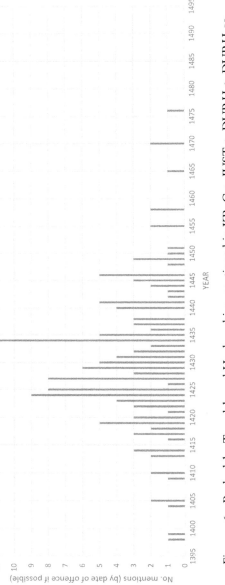

Figure 16 Redesdale, Tynedale and Hexhamshire mentioned in KB, C 1, JUST 3, DURH 3, DURH 19 (offence date used where possible) (total), 1395–1495

Patterns of Conflict

that truces were signed. Figure 12, showing all cases, also makes this point effectively, if less dramatically, in the years 1411, 1420, 1430, 1438 and 1449. There are some exceptions. It will be recalled that the truceless peak of 1416 seems to have resulted from a combination of the French campaigns and the Percy restoration that year.[110] A return to the courts could also happen when major international agreements and truce extensions were secured, even if they did not immediately terminate war, as in 1423–4 and 1429–30.[111] The truce extension of 1444 is the clearest exception, but, in the early 1440s, the threat posed from Scotland was low and the effect of the truce may therefore have been slight.[112] What all this might suggest is that English disputants held off pursuing legal quarrels with their countrymen during the prosecution of war with Scotland, preferring instead to cooperate (or at least not aggravate) each other when the need for collective defence was greatest. However, once a truce was signed (or negotiations were underway and signing was imminent) and the threat of open war had subsided, then disputants brought their claims against each other.

The timing of a dispute within the Percy affinity from 1438 helps to illustrate the point. On the last day of November that year, two Cumberland JPs[113] sitting at Isel took an indictment against the gentleman and Percy retainer Alexander Highmoore of Armathwaite,[114] and a number of yeomen including Thomas and William Fisher of Setmurthy ['Sacmorthowe'], for having destroyed the fish weirs (*'gurgitis'*) of Sir William Legh of Isel along the River Derwent and for disturbing Legh's other possessions in nearby Bassenthwaite and Blindcrake.[115] These intrusions came in June, only three months after the Scottish truce had been signed, and they appeared in court as soon as Michaelmas term of the same year.[116] From the same term, four further new cases appeared, as did

---

[110] See above, p. 213.

[111] Two indentures concerning march law were agreed upon in 1429 (*Foedera*, IV, iv, 148–49; E 39/92/39: *CDS*, IV, p. 211 no. 1030, printed in appendix 21 at pp. 404–6), and a truce extension was agreed in the following year (*Foedera*, IV, iv, 169–71; *Rot. Scot.*, ii, 268–69; *CCR 1429–35*, 118).

[112] For the extension of 1444, see *Foedera*, V, i, 132; *Rot. Scot.*, ii, 323; *CCR 1441–7*, 221.

[113] The JPs were Robert Warcop and Hugh Lowther. The Lowthers, Percy tenants at Wythop, on Bassenthwaite, in Derwent Fells, were married to the Leghs (CAC, Whitehaven: D/Lec box 29/3).

[114] Highmoore was also receiver of Cockermouth in 1441–2 (CAC, Whitehaven: D/Lec box 29/1; 29/2).

[115] Legh's lands were also in the Percy honour of Cockermouth, but north of the Derwent in the barony of Allerdale. He was dead by November 1439, leaving his widow Isabel, daughter of Sir Robert Lowther (*CCR 1435–41*, 295–6).

[116] The offences were framed as forcible entry and disseisin (KB 27/710 rot. 64; KB 9/230B mm. 90–4). For the truce of 1438, see *Rot. Scot.*, ii, 306–10; *Foedera*, V, i, 47–50.

229

Part III

several *rex*-side recurrences.[117] Other illustrations come from 1420 when, after a period of warfare, the Turpyn–Whitley dispute came to court, as did the indictments against the Redesdale offenders (noted earlier). Likewise, the large number of *rex*-side prosecutions recurring in 1449 may all be the result of judicial assertiveness following the cessation of major Anglo-Scottish conflict. We have seen that a commission of oyer and terminer for Cumberland and Westmorland coincides with this peak in 1449, but this is one of only two such commissions issued in a truce year. It should also be noted that the timing of commissions of the peace does not show a relationship with war or truce, at any time.[118]

This examination of Anglo-Scottish war and local conflict now broadens in scope to take into account evidence from the surviving fifteenth-century gaol delivery records.[119] Before resuming our analysis, it is important to set out that Figures 9, 10 and 15, which present the gaol delivery evidence, display the information in a different manner from the king's bench data, for the gaol delivery figures show the dates of alleged offences, rather than the dates on which cases appeared in court. The reason for this different approach is that nearly every gaol delivery case includes an offence date, a detail which is not regularly included in case entries in the king's bench plea rolls. We are on firmer ground in using offence dates in an attempt to gauge levels of local conflict, because these indicate the timing of a felony, rather than the timing of a defendant's capture and appearance before the justices. Problems still lurk, and it should be noted that because many gaol delivery trials dealt with offences committed a few years in the past,[120] and because of the uneven survival of the rolls, we have a poor record of any offences from the early 1410s, reflected in a trough in the relevant figures. A similar problem arises for the 1440s and 1450s, when case numbers trail off as the sessions advance towards their final surviving enrolment.

It could be argued that offences in the gaol delivery records tell us not about local conflict and tension but only about minor 'crime' among the lowest levels of society.[121] However, the cases appearing in the border gaol delivery rolls primarily record the misdeeds of local yeomen, accounting for somewhere in the range of half to three-quarters of

---

[117] KB 27/710 rots 17d, 64, 51; KB 27/710 *rex* rots 8d, 10d.

[118] See above, p. 214. Apart from the commission of oyer and terminer for Cbl. and Wml. in 1449 (*CPR 1446–52*, 269–70), the commission for Nbl. in 1438 can be counted in the same way (*CPR 1436–41*, 201).

[119] See above, p. 201.

[120] Maddern, *Violence and Social Order*, 37, presents figures for the 'lag' period between offence and trial.

[121] As per Summerson, 'Crime and Society', 111–24; Neville, 'Keeping the Peace', 6.

230

Patterns of Conflict

defendants.[122] Yeomen were the elite of the peasantry and could be quite wealthy and prominent in local terms. In those areas dominated by a pastoral economy in the far north, non-landed wealth was often invested in large and mobile flocks, the possession of which would also have conferred some social status. As others who have used these records have shown, the theft of sheep and cattle was overwhelmingly the most frequent charge heard before the border gaol delivery sessions.[123] Just under 83 per cent of the cases recorded were for theft alone or for theft and receipt of stolen goods and chattels. Sheep far outnumbered other stolen items, which were only rarely coins or everyday objects. Studies of areas further south suggest larceny accounted for half this rate, a difference made even more remarkable when one considers that a large number of the remaining cases from the far north combined charges of theft with other offences.[124] Taking all types of cases together, offences tried at gaol delivery in the far north look less like the deviant acts of low-status miscreants, harvest-time quarrels among field labourers or drunken brawls among rowdy tavern patrons and much more like the calculated livestock rustling of prominent yeomen. In this regard the prospect for future analysis of the gaol delivery evidence with other sources (such as the common pleas) to consider the extent to which livestock represented a form of currency as well as moveable property across the mixed landscapes of the marches is alluring. What is unknown is how far livestock may have served as security for financial debts, or even possibly a unit of account of the principal debt itself, and so to what degree reported animal thefts might represent forcible interest collection or loan recovery. While these latter points remain speculative, what is clear is that the preponderance of animal theft offences suggests gaol delivery evidence can serve for our purposes as a credible indicator of local tensions especially among the higher peasantry. It also points, in part, to a regional raiding culture, which has already been raised and to which we shall return in a cross-border context in the next chapter.[125]

The gaol delivery data tend to confirm the observation that war led to a reduction in local conflict, while truce led to an increase (see the offence dates plotted in Figures 9, 10 and 15). Concerning trends set

---

[122] A proportion suggested by the general impression of the evidence and confirmed by sample counts made of defendants tried in particular deliveries (JUST 3/199 rots 23, 23d, 30, 30d).

[123] Summerson, 'Crime and Society', 111–24; Neville, 'Gaol Delivery', 45–60.

[124] The present study tallies thefts alone, plus thefts with receipt of stolen goods, to account for 2,129 cases out of a total of 2,568 (see Armstrong, 'Local Conflict', 134nn, 191nn). By contrast, Hanawalt (*Crime and Conflict*, 65–75) finds larceny comprising 38.7 per cent of felonies in her early fourteenth-century sample from southern counties.

[125] See above, pp. 189–91.

Part III

against war, Figure 9 shows a drop in the number of offences in the wartime periods of 1400–2 and 1433–6, the latter being most telling as it comes in a period when the records are nearly complete. However, because of the dearth of records, the effects of the warfare of 1415–20 are hard to assess, and the same can be said for warfare in the 1440s and 1450s. Where it is possible to do so, looking at years of truce agreements plotted against the gaol delivery offences in Figure 15, we see an increase in offences in the truce years of 1420, 1424, 1429 and 1438. These graphs would suggest that, for the yeomen who were the predominant offenders mentioned in the gaol delivery sessions, war with Scotland tended to decrease numbers of offences, while truce tended to raise them.

Turning to the gaol delivery offences displayed in Figure 10, we can see that this pattern varied by county. For example, while both Northumberland and Westmorland peaked in 1438, Cumberland's peak came a year before the truce (but still following after the years of major conflict) in 1437. It is also apparent, more generally, that Westmorland's gaol delivery data plot quite differently from those of its neighbours. Notably, that county does not show the same dramatic peak of offences in 1429 that is found in Cumberland and Northumberland. Conversely, there are spikes in 1409 and 1420–1, which its neighbours do not match. This may indicate that proximity to the border meant that Cumberland and Northumberland had more in common with each other with respect to patterns of local conflict than they did with their small neighbour.

The manifestations of local conflict which are illustrated by both the king's bench evidence recording levels of court activity and the gaol delivery evidence recording dates of offences suggest that some relationship existed between Anglo-Scottish warfare and local tensions, at least before mid-century. No clear explanation exists as to why such a relationship should disappear thereafter. There is no comparable analysis of fourteenth-century legal records, but, if the patterns found in the early part of the fifteenth century were a continuation of older trends established during a time of more intense warfare, then perhaps, by mid-century, the more sporadic nature of Anglo-Scottish war was making it a less important factor in influencing local conflict. Moreover, the English domestic political turmoil of the 1450s and 1460s may have crystallised this change and made domestic political upheaval a more important driver of activity in court.

VIOLENT OFFENCES

The surviving court records allow for an analysis of particular details of offences, and the gaol delivery evidence can help in an assessment of the

Patterns of Conflict

incidence of violence in local conflict. Theft indictments in the marches were nearly always worded in a manner ('*furtive furatus fuit*') which conceals whether overt force was involved, and so theft will be excluded from this analysis.[126] Offences which involved a charge of assault, rape, kidnapping, homicide or lying in wait will be included (and of course such offences might accompany a separate offence of theft).[127] The 1430s and 1440s produced the bulk of these felonies. This observation becomes even more pertinent when compared with the decline for all offences after 1438 evident in Figure 9.[128] Also, of a total of twenty-one cases where suspects were accused of lying in wait (all of which, curiously, were from Northumberland), eleven occurred in the 1440s alone.[129]

By contrast, if we take only homicides, we find that these were recorded at a low rate in the border gaol deliveries. The sessions from all three counties reveal eighty-two killings committed between 1395 and 1459. This represents just over 3 per cent of proceedings, compared with Maddern's figure of just under 7 per cent in East Anglia in 1422–42.[130] Thus, homicide forms a smaller proportion of offences recorded among the border peasantry than it does elsewhere in England. Summerson has reasonably suggested that a low number of recorded homicides may have resulted from the border economy, which featured a lower density of population and, where pastoralism predominated, fewer communal agricultural tasks. This produced less social friction. He has also proposed that the threat of retaliation from kinsmen or lords of a potential victim acted to restrain this type of violence, a point to which we shall return in a subsequent chapter.[131] Moreover, although homicide was a difficult offence to conceal, it is not beyond reason that some slayings went unreported to judicial officials, especially if the victims' relatives were able to obtain satisfaction by extra-judicial, customary means. All these possibilities aside, it remains very difficult to give a convincing answer to why homicides among the border peasantry

---

[126] Despite not using the adjective '*felonice*', such thefts were tried as felony, and convicts were hanged. A much smaller proportion of robbery accusations ('*felonice depredavit fuit*') were recorded (sixty-six cases where this was the only offence) and, for simplicity, these are also excluded here.

[127] On the counting of multiple offences, see note 147 below.

[128] Presented decennially, the numbers of such offences are as follows: 1400–9, 17; 1410–19, 8; 1420–9, 27; 1430–9, 31; 1440–9, 38; 1450–9, 7. These are drawn from JUST 3/191, 199, 208, 211, 213.

[129] JUST 3/191 rot. 52; JUST 3/199 rot. 18; JUST 3/208 rots 20d, 22, 23, 30; JUST 3/211 rots 28d, 29, 30d, 31, 32, 33d, 34d, 36d, 37; JUST 3/213 rots 14d, 15.

[130] Maddern, *Violence and Social Order*, 50 (table 2.6 giving 6.8 per cent). The present survey is of 2,568 offences (including multiple offences for a given suspect). Hanawalt (*Crime and Conflict*, 96–101, 168–77) gives a figure of 18 per cent.

[131] See below, p. 304. Summerson ('Crime and Society', 118–19) found 27 Cbl. suspects accused of killing in a sample of 522 suspects in nineteen gaol deliveries from the period 1435–57.

Part III

should form a lower proportion of felonies than they did among their southern peers. Still, we can say that there is no sign of homicide numbers dropping in the 1440s when the total number of gaol delivery cases begins to decline.[132] The impact of the agrarian crisis of 1438–40 on both the arable and pastoral sectors may be one explanation for the relative increase in non-theft violent offences appearing in the 1440s, homicides among them.[133]

The gaol delivery evidence also shows differences by county. Figure 10 displays the data in this way, and it is clear that Westmorland produced the distribution which is least like the combined distribution for all three counties shown in Figure 9, with relatively few offences recorded between the peaks in 1420–1 and 1438. This small county also produced only 12 per cent of the offences recorded for all three counties. However, it was the location of a disproportionately high level of violence, producing 22 per cent of the violent offences and 27 per cent of the homicides. Cumberland, though probably slightly under-represented (since this county missed more gaol delivery sessions than its neighbours between 1445 and 1457), produced 35 per cent of all offences but closely matched its smaller neighbour to the south, with 21 per cent of the violent offences and 27 per cent of the homicides. Finally, the much larger county of Northumberland produced a more proportionate 53 per cent of all offences, 57 per cent of violent offences, and 46 per cent of the homicides. Westmorland, though small, stands out among its neighbours as a county with a disproportionately high level of alleged violence.

The king's bench cases can be examined for allegations of violence, revealing information about disputes where the landed elite tended to be involved. Excluding allegations of theft (as we did for gaol delivery, as this did not necessarily mean violence), and of course setting aside trespass *vi et armis* on its own (which could be a legal fiction), we find a steady rate of fewer than ten new cases per decade.[134] However, when homicides in king's bench are isolated, our findings become noteworthy. Thirty-two allegations of homicide in our period outnumbered other violent offences, and this became even more pronounced during the reign of

---

[132] Presented decennially, the numbers of homicides are as follows: 1400–9, 11; 1410–19, 1; 1420–9, 17; 1430–9, 23; 1440–9, 20; 1450–9, 5. These are drawn from JUST 3/191, 199, 208, 211, 213.

[133] This resulted in difficulties in rent collection and was linked with failed harvests and mortality: A.J. Pollard, 'The North-Eastern Economy and the Agrarian Crisis of 1438–40', *Northern History*, 25 (1989), 88–105.

[134] For *vi et armis*, see above, p. 200. Presented decennially, the numbers of cases alleging assault, mayhem, riot, homicide or lying in wait are as follows: 1400–9, 6; 1410–19, 7; 1420–9, 2; 1430–9, 6; 1440–9, 7; 1450–9, 2; 1460–9, 4; 1470–9, 3; 1480–9, 3; 1490–4, 8. These are drawn from KB 9 and KB 27.

Patterns of Conflict

Edward IV, when killing was overwhelmingly the most common allegation among new violent offences, almost to the total exclusion of others. This situation would only change a few years into the reign of Henry VII, when other violent allegations began again to appear alongside homicides.[135] Of these homicide allegations, nineteen involved a member of the local gentry as slayers, abettors or the slain. From additional sources (including selected king's bench plea rolls from law terms other than Michaelmas, chancery petitions and rolls, gaol delivery rolls and council records) at least fifteen further homicides may be detected which probably or certainly involved landowners.[136]

These numbers for homicide in king's bench, a total of at least thirty killings directly involving the gentry between 1399 and 1494, stand in stark contrast to findings for England further south. For example, Carpenter's study of Warwickshire found no more than seven homicides among the gentry in the whole century.[137] Maddern, whose work on populous East Anglia in 1422–42 presents a high count of homicides appearing in king's bench (sixty-one cases), does not isolate those which involved the gentry; however, her case studies specifically identify only three killings at this social level. Her argument, reflecting the wider scholarly consensus, is that homicide within English landed society was rare and destabilising, and those who committed murder normally faced serious opprobrium and exclusion by their peers.[138] Cherry's examination of Devonshire identifies a number of lethal incidents during the well-known Courtenay–Bonville dispute; however, that affair reached its worst excesses in the early 1450s during the period of national tension between the dukes of York and Somerset when local conflicts involving noblemen escalated in various parts of the realm, and in the months

---

[135] Presented decennially, numbers (drawn from KB 9 and KB 27) of homicides alone are: 1400–9, 3; 1410–19, 3; 1420–9, 2; 1430–9, 4; 1440–9, 6; 1450–9, 1; 1460–9, 4; 1470–9, 3; 1480–9, 0; 1490–4, 6.

[136] For example: C 1/7/313; *CCR 1413–19*, 356; E 368/211m93; *CPR 1429–36*, 358 (see Summerson, *Medieval Carlisle*, ii, 409n 160); C 47/22/7m67; *CDS*, IV, 266; *CPR 1446–52*, 214; *CPR 1436–41*, 477; JUST 3/54/34 m. 4; JUST 3/199 rot. 16; JUST 3/211 rots 33, 34d, 35, 36, 36d, 47; JUST 3/213 rot. 14; *Select Cases in the Council of Henry VII*, ed. C.G. Bayne and W.H. Dunham (London, 1958), 22. The homicides recorded at KB 27/874 rot. 13 (Easter 1480), KB 27/875 rot. 8 (Trinity 1480), KB 27/906 rot. 4 (Hilary 1488), KB 27/907 rot. 7 (Easter 1488) and KB 27/908 rot. 10 (Trinity 1488) have already been noted.

[137] Carpenter, *Locality and Polity*, 365, 510–12, 570, 573, 578, 622. Payling (*Political Society*, 199–201, 202–3) relates just four killings arising from two gentry disputes in Notts. in the Lancastrian period. Coates, examining Notts., Derbys., Herts. and Essex in the Yorkist period, detects only seven killings in which the gentry were involved (Coates, 'Law Enforcement Policy', 132, 135, 156, 206, 235, 242–3, 255).

[138] Maddern, *Violence and Social Order*, 5–6, 28, 121–6, 171, 205, 223–4. See also Carpenter, *Locality and Polity*, 622; Payling, *Political Society*, 202–3. See also further discussion of the nature of violence below at pp. 297–306.

235

Part III

following the first battle of St Albans.[139] Even at the same time, within Pollard's study of the 'general collapse of law and order in Yorkshire in 1453 and 1454', there was only one death of note.[140] Although one preliminary survey of the period after 1461 suggests similarities in homicide numbers across the entire north (a point which cries out for further investigation), it nevertheless seems that, in the course of their disputes, the gentry of the border shires had a higher propensity to use serious, lethal violence than did their counterparts further south.[141] This conclusion must be squared with the observation just made that homicides among the border peasantry appear in relatively low proportions, a statistic which, on the surface, suggests that the border gentry were more violent than their social inferiors. To explain better this apparent inconsistency, it could well be argued that, if some low-status homicides in the marches went unreported to the judicial system, it would be far more difficult, and probably impossible, for the same to happen in high-status cases directly involving landowners. Thus, a high level of gentry homicides may indicate that the apparently low levels of peasant homicides were, in fact, unrepresentative of the true scale of lethal violence in the region, which was greater than that found elsewhere in England. This is a point that will prove important in later chapters on discord and concord.

THE BORDER LIBERTIES

Finally, legal records allow a close look at the notorious Northumberland liberties of Tynedale, Redesdale and Hexhamshire, which were regularly singled out in parliamentary petitions and other documents as law-breaking havens.[142] Historians have long been aware of the apparent problem of the liberties and have cited these private jurisdictions as a cause of turbulence. Macdonald, on the other hand, has been cautious regarding this explanation and points out that, in the later fourteenth century, Tynedale and Redesdale were not identified by contemporaries

---

[139] Cherry, 'Struggle for Power', 123, 126–7, 131, 134–7; Cherry, 'The Courtenay Earls of Devon', 87–90 (noting earlier violent confrontations in the county in 1384 and 1392).

[140] Pollard, *North-Eastern England*, 260 (noting the killing of Sir John Salvin), 261 (quote).

[141] Regarding evidence from the KB 9 files alone, Hayes ('Ancient Indictments', 30) found that homicides appeared at a rate of 17.5 per cent between 1461 and 1485 from Lancs., Yorks. and the three border counties. For the three counties alone between 1399 and 1494, I found fifteen homicides in the KB 9 files out of ninety-nine alleged offences (15 per cent). Although Hayes's analysis does not isolate homicides directly involving the gentry, her findings and mine would suggest are roughly consistent across Lancs., Yorks. and the border shires.

[142] See above, p. 179.

Patterns of Conflict

as significantly more unruly than other parts of the north.[143] If we combine the evidence from gaol delivery and king's bench, together with some surviving court rolls from the palatinate of Durham, we can evaluate the extent to which offenders and offences were linked to these liberties. A count of the number of occurrences per year in which Redesdale, Tynedale and Hexhamshire are mentioned in these records reveals that such occurrences were most frequent in the mid- to late 1420s and the mid-1430s (see Figure 16).[144] The majority of references appear between about 1415 and 1450, and there are few mentions outside these dates. The lack of gaol delivery rolls after 1459 and the relatively small number which survive before 1421 go a long way to explaining this, but we can make two observations. First, there is no clear relationship to be detected between reference to the liberties in the legal records and years of war or truce. Second, the bulk of references appears after the statutes of 1414 and 1421, which, as discussed earlier, introduced the common law into these franchises.[145] It would make sense that references would be few before this extension of jurisdiction and that a period of increased attention would follow if a concerted effort was made to exercise the law in these formerly autonomous lordships. Such a scenario seems to be suggested in the data.

Gaol delivery records concerning the location of offences shows that misdeeds were committed within the three liberties in only 43 out of the total of 1,285 offences tried in Northumberland only, a rate of 3.3 per cent.[146] Given the large amount of territory covered by these franchises, this rate seems unexpectedly low. Tynedale, the largest of the three liberties, is outstanding as the location of thirty of these offences, eleven of which date from the 1420s. However, the gaol delivery evidence suggests that a comparatively large number of suspects tried before the itinerant justices was indeed from the liberties; that is to say, at least 128 out of the total 3,603 accused suspects and their abettors are recorded from all three counties. If we consider the numbers of accused

---

[143] Macdonald, *Border Bloodshed*, 208–9. By contrast, see Storey, *Thomas Langley*, 140, 153; Powell, *Kingship, Law, and Society*, 265; Neville, *Violence, Custom and Law*, 110–11, 115.

[144] As noted earlier, offence date information normally appears in the gaol delivery rolls but not the king's bench plea rolls; where possible, offence dates have been used in this calculation in preference to the date of appearance in the court record. Presented decennially, the numbers of mentions are as follows: 1400–9, 4; 1410–19, 18; 1420–9, 46; 1430–9, 39; 1440–9, 24; 1450–9, 6; 1460–9, 1; 1470–9, 3; 1480–9, 0. These mentions are drawn from the relevant KB 27 and KB 9 records and from JUST 3/191, 199, 208, 211, 213; DURH 3/33 (chancery court enrolments); and DURH 19/1/1 (quarter sessions and gaol deliveries 1471–1473); the latter are printed in *Durham Quarter Sessions Rolls, 1471–1625*, ed. C.M. Fraser and K. Emsley (Durham, 1991), 39–65.

[145] See above, p. 179.

[146] Two further offences done in Tynedale appear in Cbl. cases: JUST 3/199 rots 27, 30.

237

Part III

from the liberties before Northumberland sessions alone (120 out of 1,753), this represents a rate of just below 7 per cent. Tynedale, again outstanding, accounted for seventy-eight of the accused, while Redesdale and Hexhamshire accounted for twenty-eight and twenty-two, respectively.[147] Numbers of accused suspects from Tynedale peaked significantly in the 1420s, that decade alone producing forty instances. By contrast, Redesdale and Hexhamshire had smaller peaks in the 1430s. The prominence of Tynedale in these numbers suggests the possibility either that this liberty was particularly disturbed or that it was subject to special attention by royal officials, or both, but the exact balance between the two is impossible to assess. Combined with the relatively low number of offences located within the liberties, these data may also indicate that the royal judicial system was primarily concerned with the pursuit of offenders from the liberties who had committed offences elsewhere in the county, rather than with handling accusations of offences done within them. The Northumberland liberties, and Tynedale in particular, were by this calculation indeed producing the offenders of whom the northern petitioners complained.

To summarise these findings, national political upheavals had various implications for court activity. For example, the years 1458 and 1461 showed surges of cases reflecting partisan use of king's bench by those whose fortunes aligned with the interests of the de facto rulers of the moment. Periods of political uncertainty, and even outright civil war, such as in 1460 and 1462–6, seem to have led to relatively low levels of activity, a phenomenon that has been observed elsewhere during the years of the most serious crises. A rise in the year 1467 suggests that a return to the courts by disputants meant a cooling of tensions, but renewed uncertainty in 1469–71 seems to have kept activity low once again, and the abrupt regime changes in 1483 and 1485 produced a similar effect. High levels of activity sometimes indicate a judicial drive and an assertion of crown authority through the exercise of royal justice. This seems to be what happened in 1449, 1455, and 1480–2. Judicial commissions, such as those of oyer and terminer, had a variable effect. That of 1449 generated a high level of court activity, but those of the mid-1410s and early 1460s did not. In all these broad patterns, the far north did not behave in a manner especially different from other parts of England.

---

[147] The data used in this analysis include the few relevant cases from the printed Durham sessions noted above. They also include multiple database record entries of the same individual for different offences, and multiple individuals entered for the same offence. The number of accused and abettors for Nbl. includes those tried at the sessions for Newcastle-upon-Tyne town. Individuals are identified as being resident in a liberty if this was stated explicitly or if their given place of residence was obviously located within a liberty.

Patterns of Conflict

Great lords also affected patterns of judicial activity in the same way that they did further south but, towards the end of our period, the border region begins to look different. During the 1460s the forfeiture of the Percys, Cliffords and Dacres does not appear to have disturbed the region far beyond the wider divisions generated by the Yorkist ascendancy. This did not exacerbate local conflict in the far north in the same way as it did in Yorkshire.[148] Neither is a direct effect of the earlier Percy eclipse (1405–16) detectable. The brief absence from the north of the fourth Percy earl and Gloucester on campaign in 1475 seems to have affected the timing of a dispute in Cumberland, and wider tensions between these magnates are also linked to serious violence in this decade. In Westmorland at this time, Sir William Parr's dominance may well have been the reason behind the near-total absence of new cases from Westmorland after 1477. We are left to speculate, but it seems probable that the knight attempted to manage local disputes himself or to pass them up to the royal council. This county's dearth of new cases lasted for a decade, and, from 1483 to 1487, it was joined in this regard by Cumberland and Northumberland. This lack of new cases does not suggest low levels of conflict but, rather, that disputants ventilated their disputes in other fora. From 1484, the council in the north was the obvious alternative route to royal justice. All the same, the later 1480s were marked by serious instability in the border counties. In the absence of records of the northern council, we are unable to see whether antagonists indeed brought their claims there, and a scenario in which local political society hesitated to go to law and pursued their disputes primarily out of the courts remains a possibility.

We can also discern effects of Anglo-Scottish war and truce on English judicial activity in the border region. It seems that the expected dynamic was for domestic conflict in the marches to be put aside during open war in the interests of collective defence. Before about mid-century, war seems to have discouraged conflict among English borderers, while the signing of a truce appears to have coincided with a return to pursuit of legal claims in king's bench. Likewise, during truce years, rises in offences tried at gaol delivery are detectable following lower levels during war. The implication of these findings is that war tended to postpone local conflict. However, from the 1450s onwards, war no longer restrained levels of activity in the law courts, and truces no longer escalated them, suggesting that in this regard the relative importance of domestic political upheavals – as opposed to Anglo-Scottish relations – was on the increase. The fact that both became intermixed for a time in the 1460s

---

[148] Ross, *Edward IV*, ch. 3.

Part III

notwithstanding, this serves as a counterpoint to assertions about the sensitivity of northern regions to the instability of truces and the 'chronic insecurity of the border' in the latter half of the century.[149]

With regard to violent offences, the most outstanding difference with areas further south is the relatively large number of homicides among the gentry. This finding suggests that the members of landed society here were not averse to the use of serious, lethal violence. Especially during the Yorkist period and the early years of Henry VII, homicide was the predominant violent offence to be alleged in king's bench, a situation that changed only in the later 1480s. Especially from the gaol delivery evidence, Westmorland stands out as exceptional, particularly in its disproportionate level of alleged violence, and its trends of offence dates. This is all the more remarkable given that Westmorland is not reputed as the most unruly of the border shires. By contrast, Northumberland, adjoining Scotland and containing the liberties which gave rise to petitions and complaints, does carry a reputation for unrest. This survey indicates that, following the extension of common law jurisdiction into the border liberties, offenders from these areas were given increased attention in the itinerant courts during the 1420s and 1430s.

It cannot be said that governmental structures were weak in the marches. This evidence demonstrates the regular use by local inhabitants of the royal judicial system by contrast to Storey's implications and to the findings of more recent surveys.[150] Still, the distance between Westminster and the marches meant that English kings did not have a regular, personal impact on affairs in the far north. Some change in this regard began under Edward IV, through his close relationship with the Parrs, and through Gloucester, and under the latter as Richard III, through the new council in the north which institutionalised royal intervention. Still, as we have seen, the use of the northern council by border litigants is difficult to assess, although its appearance may help to explain a temporary absence of cases from the older institution of king's bench.

War had some effect on the timing of local conflict in our period, but the more pertinent question is whether the military aspect of the frontier influenced the intensity and nature of violence in the borderlands. As we have seen, the English historiography assumes that the marches were exceptionally shaped by war and, consequently, that borderers themselves readily resorted to violence in local conflict.[151] At least among

---

[149] Pollard, *North-Eastern England,* 219. See above, p. 60.

[150] Storey quoted above, see p. 213. See also Hayes, 'Ancient Indictments', 25–6.

[151] See above, p. 15. These assertions draw heavily on petitions (*PROME*, January 1410, item 17; November 1411, item 39; April 1414, item 20; May 1421, item 22).

Patterns of Conflict

landowners, a relatively high occurrence of homicides points to a political society that found serious violence to be more acceptable than historians have found to be the case in areas further south. If war and raiding impeded the English royal judicial system, and the experience of war at the frontier did partly make the far north more violent than it might otherwise have been, this would help to explain the conclusion that the Northumberland liberties were in fact troublesome sources of offenders, even if perhaps less frequent locations of offences than has been supposed. Yet, if all this were so, then it is our findings for Westmorland that require elucidation. This county was located furthest from the frontier, and thus furthest from raids and invasions, and yet it exhibited a disproportionately large share of violent offences in gaol delivery evidence but also, exceptionally, almost no new activity in king's bench in the decade 1477–87. Low numbers of king's bench cases from this county might indicate the use of alternative judicial venues. Yet given Westmorland's location, little evidence for the use of royal justice, and relatively numerous allegations of violence, suggest that this county's inhabitants used accustomed practices, including violence and peacemaking, not as a result of violent life on the frontier so much as a result of deeper cultural patterns. In the light of the main conclusions of this chapter, there now come into focus two lines of enquiry. One is to assess more closely the use of violence and peacemaking in borderland disputes, which will be the object of the chapters on discord and concord. The other, to which we turn next, is to assess the nature and scope of cross-border activity and conflict.

8

CROSS-BORDER CONFLICT

For both wardeyns with the kyng were gone,

No wardeyne there, but husbandes by their owne.[1]

—John Hardyng's *Chronicle*

In order to continue to assess the effect of the frontier on local conflict, this chapter considers activities in the marches with a cross-border dimension. It examines behaviour that was ostensibly illicit, either because it violated the truce or because it occurred in cooperation with the enemy. We begin by looking at the first category, activity that was primarily in breach of the truce. Evidence suggests that low-level raiding across the border was a normal state of affairs. Recurrent truce violations comprised the substance of complaints at days of march, diplomatic exchanges, and some conciliar deliberations. For example, in 1433 the English council instructed a border knight to ensure that the east march inhabitants kept the truce and to reassure them that march days would be ordered shortly for redress. At the same time, two border barons were told not to attend parliament but to remain in the marches for the prevention of '*attemptats*' against the armistice.[2] By the 1470s, diplomatic exchanges cited Tynedale, Redesdale and Liddesdale as trouble spots on the border. The English east march warden complained to James III in 1473 of truce-breakings perpetrated by the Scottish 'liegis of Liddalisdale uppoun Inglismen'. The Scottish king rejoined by pointing out that his subjects were 'richt complaintewss of Inglismen duelland within Tindaile and Riddisdaile, quhilks daili makis depredacionis and herschippis

---

[1] *Chron. Hardyng*, 358.
[2] The knight was John Bertram, with Thomas, Lord Dacre, and William Neville, Lord Fauconberg (*PPC*, IV, 172–73, 174). The northern lords were also instructed not to attend parliament in February 1449 (ibid., VI, 65). See also similar orders in May 1452 (ibid., VI, 125–6, 127).

Cross-Border Conflict

[harryings]' upon them.[3] Later that year, a truce indenture included an item concerning certain Scottish rebels of Eskdale ['Esdale'] and their English associates, which has already been noted in connection with the history of the debatable land in the west. The truce commissioners agreed that the Englishmen involved were to be liable for redress no further than could be proved by border law.[4] Unfortunately, no further details on this matter survive, but another example of lesser border offences comes in 1477, when the English ambassador to Scotland was given instructions on the matter of the robbery, by Englishmen, of the tenants of the Scottish Lord Carlyle in Dumfriesshire. The ambassador was advised to say that the English west march warden would make reformation according to the law of the march.[5] The durability of march law and administration ensured that truces could sustain a significant barrage of *attemptats* without collapsing.

Truce violations also happened on a greater scale. The landed elite might make raids, known as *chevauchées*, which were war-like acts with normative elements shaped by the law of arms.[6] Examples include the Scottish raid by the earl of Douglas into Glendale in 1433 (in which the earl and a 'grete numbre' of Scots lifted more than 60 horses, 2,600 cattle, and 5,000 sheep, burning and slaying and taking prisoners along the way), the confrontations at Fullhope Lawe in 1399 and Piperdean in 1435, or the Magdalen's Day raid into Annandale in 1484 led by the earl of Douglas and duke of Albany.[7] Although the law of arms allowed and regulated plunder, the destruction of property and the ransoming of prisoners in open war between princes, truce suspended such hostilities (though it did not end the legal state of war).[8] Despite this prohibition, major acts of international violence such as these were part of Anglo-Scottish relations in truce time and, like the lesser raiding just described, were dealt with by the border courts and royal diplomacy. That even these war-like raids need not necessarily provoke a resumption of open war was made clear by the English privy council in 1433. It noted recent Scottish attacks, including Douglas's Glendale incursion, in which the invaders had made 'divers rodes [raids]' and taken many 'pondes [poinds,

---

[3] The warden was the earl of Northumberland. Only the king's reply of 13 July survives. It has sometimes been dated to 1475 (E 39/102/22; *CDS*, IV, 291, and 408–9, appendix 1, no. 24).

[4] E 39/52; *Foedera*, V, iii, 34–5. See above, pp. 61–3.

[5] BL: MS Cotton Vespasian, C XVI, fol. 127, printed in *Letters of the Kings of England*, ed. J.O. Halliwell-Phillipps, 2 vols (London, 1848), i, 147–8.

[6] See above, p. 184.

[7] *PPC*, IV, 169–72, 310; *Scotichronicon*, viii, 293–5; *Chron. Hardyng*, 355–7; *The Chronicle of Adam of Usk 1377–1421*, ed. C. Given-Wilson (Oxford, 1997), 47–8. For the Magdalen's Day raid, see N. Macdougall, *James III* (rev. edn, Edinburgh, 2009), 232–3.

[8] Keen, 'Treason Trials', 94–5; Keen, *Laws of War*, 104–18, 120 and, on ransom, 156–85.

243

Part III

distraints] prayes [spoils] and prisoners and had them into Scotland *as though* it were open werre'.[9] As far as the council was concerned, the truce was still in effect.

There were some important means by which the landed elite invoked legitimacy for their truce-breaking. Major *chevauchées* happened in daylight, for this allowed for the display of heraldic insignia. Although the display of banners and standards could signal the legal resumption of hostilities, armigerous borderers seem to have shown their heraldic ensigns without hesitation.[10] For instance, in 1408, the east march warden claimed that breaches of the truce were escalating to the point of open war, and one such affront was doubtless the foray into Jedforest by Sir Robert Umfraville and his nephew Gilbert, displaying the eighteen-year-old's banner for the first time on what, it appears, was a coming-of-age raid.[11] In another case, already noted, when Douglas of Drumlanrig complained of the raid led by the English knights Robert Tilliol and Thomas Lucy into his Eskdale lands in 1424, he alleged that the attackers had come against the truce by full *chevauchée* in daytime with standards displayed, and not as thieves in the night.[12] These examples show that, although such war-like *attemptats* contravened the truce, and thus broke march law, the use of customary acts like the display of banners followed the law of arms. Such an appeal to the legitimacy of a different code of behaviour provided a normative dimension for this violence.

Cross-border conflict might place elite residences, including towers and castles discussed in an earlier chapter, in the line of attack. Siege warfare was also shaped by the law of arms, not least in regard to the firing of cannon to signal the opening of hostilities (rather than the display of banners), and the handling of a sack or surrender. Full-scale sieges were major military undertakings, and there are a number of examples in our period, not all arising from Anglo-Scottish conflict but rather in the course of domestic political strife.[13] Attacks on fortified sites could, however, comprise something less than full-scale siege. For

---

[9] *PPC*, IV, 169–72 (emphasis added); *DSL*, s.vv. 'poind', 'pray'.

[10] Banners displayed by knights banneret and other captains of war leading their own retinues could be considered a breach of truce. In contrast, the display of pennons carried by lesser knights was less provocative (Keen, *Laws of War*, 107–8, 112–13).

[11] The English warden was Prince John of Lancaster, who wrote, '*et ensi la guerre est semblable a comenser*' (Chrimes, 'Letters of John of Lancaster', no. 13). Hardyng himself served in Umfraville's retinue. Although *Chron. Hardyng* (367) gives the year of this raid as 11 Henry IV (1409–10), the raid has been re-dated to 1408: 'Umfraville, Sir Robert (d. 1437)', in *Oxford DNB*, LV, 883–5, by H.R.T. Summerson.

[12] '*par playne chivauche de jour od estandars desployetz ... ascune foytz par larrouns ... ublantz de nuyt*': *PPC*, III, 353–4. See above, p. 190.

[13] Keen, 'Treason Trials', 96 (firing cannon). See above, p. 81.

Cross-Border Conflict

instance, during wartime in 1401, John Middleton and his mother Christiane lost their stronghold of Bewcastle in northern Cumberland to the Scots 'from default of watch and good governance'. Both mother and son were made prisoners and were despoiled and robbed.[14] Two years earlier, Sir Thomas Grey had lost his castle of Wark-on-Tweed. While he was away at the extraordinary parliament of 1399 for the deposition of Richard II, an opportunistic Scottish raiding force led by the earl of Dunbar and the sons of the earl of Douglas captured Grey's castle, plundered his goods, burned his houses, beat down his castle walls, and held his children and 'people' for a ransom of £1,000. This attack occurred in breach of the truce of 1398, and it was used as a pretext for the invasion of Scotland the following year by Henry IV.[15] Wark was again assaulted in 1419, by a Scottish force of two dozen which seized the stronghold at night during wartime. As was noted earlier, this incident ended with the Sir Robert Ogle's retaking of the castle by deception, and the decapitation of the erstwhile invaders.[16] In these examples of smaller sieges, the use of guns is not recorded, which implies that the conventional declaration of war by cannon-fire was not involved. It seems that these attacks were more informal, underlining the risk to border strongholds from less numerous and less well-armed forces, sometimes operating by night. What is more, events like this could prompt a retaliatory response from across the border, coordinated with local assistance. King's bench records reveal what appears to have been a Scottish raid into Northumberland soon after Ogle's recapture of Wark. Four Northumbrian yeomen were accused of convening and conspiring in Scotland on 6 September 1419 with 'Andrea Karre' and other Scots to the number of 400 men, at 'Werk'.[17] Presumably identified here are the castle of Wark-on-Tweed and Andrew Kerr, the Roxburghshire laird of Altonburn and Cessford.[18] This large force launched a major raid, by night, allegedly riding deep into lower Coquetdale, lifting more than 500 cattle and 3,000 sheep, worth 1,000 marks. The timing of this incident suggests strongly a connection with the episode at Wark that summer. The leadership of this night-time incursion by Kerr indicates that war-like,

---

[14] They later regained their castle and were pardoned for their negligence (*CDS*, IV, no. 585, p. 121).

[15] Grey's pardon can be found at *CPR 1399–1401*, 287.   [16] *Scotichronicon*, viii, 112–13.

[17] The raiders went as far as Swarland and Framlington. The accused were William Colman of 'Ouresgare' [Overgrass beside Swarland?], Richard Atkynson of Newton-on-the-Moor, Thomas Swan of Biddlestone ['Bitillesden'] and Thomas Stavard lately of 'Werk'. Thomas Hesilrigge was the only specified victim (KB 9/1056 m. 23; KB 27/694 *rex* rot. 18d; KB 27/698 *rex* rot. 14; KB 27/710 *rex* rot. 16).

[18] For Kerr, see *The Douglas Book*, ed. W. Fraser, 4 vols (Edinburgh, 1885), III, 373, 431, 434–5; *HMC, 14th Report*, appendix, part III, nos 4, 5, 6, 34, 44, pp. 9–10, 19, 22.

245

Part III

chivalric conflict across the border was not always clearly set apart from lesser illicit activities.

LESSER ILLICIT ACTIVITY

Turning now from breaches of the truce, which could be done on a large scale and with a degree of normative legitimacy, to lesser cross-border misdeeds, we can find evidence that local society considered the latter to be illicit and worthy of punishment or redress. In the absence of surviving evidence of the days of march or domestic warden courts, the light that is cast on border-related cases comes mostly from the court records which featured in the preceding chapter. In addition, a few other sources from both sides of the border will not be neglected where they are informative. Given the nature of the sources which survive, it is most often the element of collusion with the enemy that brings lesser offences to light.

In stark contrast to the northern gaol delivery rolls, which contain a reasonable amount of information relating to Scots and cross-border offences, the king's bench material relating to the same counties yields relatively little on the topic. Only a handful of king's bench cases in this survey even mention Scots.[19] Thus, in the following analysis, references to material from king's bench refers almost exclusively to two cases. The first concerns the results of an inquisition at Newcastle on 21 September 1419, which produced accusations against a number of Redesdale residents.[20] This followed the statute of 1414, which extended common law jurisdiction into Tynedale and Hexhamshire, but did no more than enjoin the officers of Redesdale to cooperate with the king's officers in dispensing justice.[21] It is notable that the commissioners did not include the lord of Redesdale, Sir Gilbert Umfraville, or his uncle, Sir Robert. The gentry jurors seem, therefore, to have used this very general commission to pressure the Umfravilles into dealing with march offenders within their liberty.[22] The second king's bench case, from 1420, concerns allegations against the Northumberland gentleman, Nicholas Turpyn of Whitchester, who was pursued by his opponents for a variety of

---

[19] One indictment from 1409 mentioned Scots, including the son of George Dunbar, earl of March, sheltered in Westminster (KB 9/198 m. 28). Durham's court of pleas (DURH 13/227 m. 4) heard indictments in 1455 and 1456 against Robert Killyngworth, gentleman of Killyngworth (Nbl.), John Heppell of Ogle (Nbl.), yeoman, and six Durham men, including three Scots.

[20] See above, p. 213. The commission was dated 11 February 1419 (*CPR 1416–22*, 205). Only two of four commissioners sat (Richard Norton and Sir Robert Lisle). Nicholas Turpyn was among the jurors (KB 9/1056 m. 23; KB 27/694 *rex* rot. 18d; KB 27/698 *rex* rot. 14; KB 27/710 *rex* rot. 16).

[21] *PROME*, April 1414, item 20; *SR*, II, 177–8.

[22] Judicial process on these indictments continued until 1441: KB 27/722 *rex* rot. 14.

Cross-Border Conflict

wrongdoings, among them abetting English-resident Scots in illicit activities.[23] Nearly all the alleged culprits in both these cases were of non-landed status, the social level that was characteristic of defendants in the gaol delivery records. Another consequence of source survival, then, is that the bulk of our evidence for illicit cross-border activity is concerned with common borderers.[24]

The investigation of cross-border activity draws attention to problems of identity and allegiance. We have already noted the ambiguity attached to the term 'march' in this period. That ambiguity could extend to matters of identity, particularly for marchers who could not be sure of the side of the border on which they lived.[25] For instance, in the 1390s, the people of Teviotdale (the geographical name for the Scottish sheriffdom of Roxburgh) petitioned the English king and council, complaining that they suffered greatly through the default of the march warden, in robberies and slaughters done both by Scots and by the king's lieges, and asked for remedy to be ordained under an English sheriff of Roxburgh.[26] At the turn of the century, the English common law courts claimed authority over some Teviotdale inhabitants who were not called Scotsmen and who seem to have been in English allegiance.[27] Although Henry IV granted out some Teviotdale lands in 1400 before his invasion, by the following year, the English crown was not so ambitious as to claim control beyond the environs of Roxburgh and Jedburgh. Indeed, in 1401, the crown reimbursed the English warden for raids made into Teviotdale.[28] By early 1404, the Scottish crown reasserted its authority over this border dale, making a grant to John Turnbull of 'Cavelyne' (Crailing?) of wardship of lands in the barony of Cavers which had been forfeited by a Scot who had switched to English allegiance.[29] Turnbull's relatives appear to have worked for the overthrow of English control in the area. According to Walter Bower, the 'mediocres' of Teviotdale captured Jedburgh from English forces in May 1409. English records reveal that one of these Scottish middling men was a certain Thomas Turnbull, evidently a kinsman of John. In capturing the

---

[23] For the Turpyn case, see above, p. 213, and below, pp. 250–1, 280. [24] See above, p. 230.

[25] See above, p. 55. Ruddick, *English Identity*, 75–81, 245–8.

[26] SC 8/143/7139. The truce of 1386 noted that English east march warden had granted his protection to the inhabitants of Teviotdale, excluding Jedworth Forest (*Foedera*, III, iii, 205).

[27] John Pye and William Hert, both '*de Teuedale*', were pursued with others on an approver's appeal in 1399 and 1400 for non-specific felonies in Wml.: KB 27/554, *rex* rot. 19d; 558, *rex* rot. 24.

[28] E 404/16/695. On 25 May 1400 Henry IV granted Makerstoun in Teviotdale (Rox.) to his esquire Robert Harbottle (Alnwick Castle: Syon X.II.3, box 10, b). Robert Taillour and Thomas Treweman of 'Tewedale' were among the English archers defending Roxburgh Castle that year (*CDS*, IV, 118).

[29] John Bower had forfeited his Scottish lands: *Charter Chest of the Earldom of Wigtown, 1214–1681*, ed. F.J. Grant (Edinburgh, 1910), no. 231, p. 31.

247

Part III

fortress, Turnbull allegedly sought the help of an Englishman who was tried and acquitted at the Northumberland gaol delivery of 1411.[30] The same session convicted a notorious English 'traitor, thief, highwayman and depopulator of fields' called William Davyson, indicted for many offences including attempting to sell Roxburgh Castle to the Scots.[31] Lines of national allegiance and authority in Teviotdale in the early years of the century were by no means clear, and, as a consequence, cross-border activity posed problems for both realms.[32] As we shall see shortly, the parts of the sheriffdom to the south-east of Roxburgh continued to prove permeable as the century progressed.

Even in areas of clear English or Scottish control, some aliens lived permanently on the opposite side of the frontier.[33] Numbers of such march inhabitants were large enough to be singled out in the truce of 1398. It was recorded that, by the 'commoune vois' on both sides, cross-border dwellers (even those received into the faith of the opposite kingdom) were seen as the 'principale cause of distroublance of the quiet of both the reaumes'. Provision was made for their removal from the marches, to the north of Edinburgh in Scotland and to the south of the Tyne in England. Total enforcement would, however, have been a thorny prospect, and the measure was probably intended merely as additional leverage for officials in the pursuit of suspected offenders.[34] This pronouncement notwithstanding, on several occasions throughout our period, English border gentry and magnates employed in their personal forces Scots who were presumably regular residents in England.[35] Substantial numbers of Scots resident in England were prosecuted in the gaol delivery sessions. For example, Alan Donne, tried and hanged for a small theft perpetrated in Northumberland in October 1403, was described as being a former ('*quondam*') Scot, presumably having sometime transferred his faith to English allegiance.[36] Other accused Scots included Martin Caverhill, a Northumberland shepherd, and Robert

---

[30] The Englishman was Robert Kendall from Bamburgh (JUST 3/191 rot. 51d; *Scotichronicon*, viii, 72–3). For the demolition of Jedburgh Castle, see *ER*, IV, 115, 117.

[31] JUST 3/191 rot. 51: '*cognitus proditor latro[cinius] et incidiator viarum et depopulator agrorum*'. The other charges against Davyson were mostly for thefts, including selling a stolen horse to a Scot called Simon Bouer.

[32] For the previous century, see Brown, 'Teviotdale in the Fourteenth Century', 234–5.

[33] Bennett, 'Women (and Men) on the Move'. Noted above, p. 64.

[34] *Foedera*, III, iv, 150–1, 152.

[35] Sir Robert Ogle's force at the siege of Bothal in 1410 allegedly included Scots. See Hodgson, *Northumberland*, II, i, 382–3; ibid., II, ii, no. 3, pp. 170–1; *HOP*, III, 859–62. Similarly, during the Percy–Neville disturbances in Yorks. in 1453, three English-resident Scots were among the accused Percy supporters (KB 9/149/1/6 m. 8). See Booth, 'Landed Society', 50; Griffiths, 'Local Rivalries', 589–632.

[36] JUST 3/191 rot. 47.

Cross-Border Conflict

Johnson, from Hawksdale in Cumberland.[37] On separate occasions in the 1420s two Scottish servants stole sheep from their English masters, one from the esquire John Harbottle, and the other from Andrew Burell of Lanton in Glendale (probably a minor gentleman).[38] Harbottle's servant, who had lived at Mindrum, an English village right near the Roxburghshire border, was hanged as a known and notorious thief.[39] Burell's servant was received by an English yeoman, but he was dead before he could be brought to court.[40]

Scots permanently resident south of the border were also involved in more serious misdeeds in England, notably homicides. One such Scot, living in Westmorland, was among the receivers of an alleged killer in 1443.[41] A number of these homicides reveal further links among Scottish aliens with English gentry, often as servants or tenants. In a Northumberland affray in 1428, the accused party included twenty-four Scots, all of whom appear to have been the yeomen tenants of an English esquire.[42] In the late 1430s the arrest of 'a Scot called Ainislee', a servant of an English knight (and perhaps a relative of the Ainslie lairds of Dolphinston, Roxburghshire),[43] led to the death of William Cawode, the English east march warden's bailiff. Ainislee had been seized by Cawode, and the knight, one Sir Ralph Bulmer of the bishopric of Durham, later broke his Scottish servant out of custody and 'murdred and slowh' Cawode.[44] Although Bulmer was indicted, Cawode's mother claimed the law was not proceeding and asked the king for remedy.[45]

---

[37] Caverhill, 1425 (JUST 3/199 rot. 17d); Johnson, 1404 (JUST 3/191 rot. 57d).

[38] Possibly related to the Burells of Howtel: JUST 3/54/19 m. 12 (John Burell de Hovtell, gentleman, 1438); *CPR 1401–5*, 249; *CDS*, IV, 173; *CPR 1422–9*, 274; *CPR 1452–61*, 228; *CPR 1461–7*, 388.

[39] The accused was Thomas Anderson, who stole twenty-four sheep in 1423 (JUST 3/199 rot. 17d). It appears that the victim was the same John Harbottle, esq., who was a trustee of William Heron of Ford, esq., in 1427 and was a commissioner on a Nbl. inquest in 1431 (*CPR 1429–36*, 131; *CPR, 1436–41*, 258–9).

[40] Richard Wer stole ten sheep in 1428 (JUST 3/208 rot. 25) and was received by William Brandlyng of Kilham.

[41] JUST 3/211 rot. 49d: John Atkynson. The victim was Robert Atkynson Dikson, slain at Great Asby.

[42] This was John Maners of Etal. The accused Scots were all also from Etal (KB 27/672 rots 60, 60d, 60(a), 70).

[43] For the case of English yeoman Walter Ainslie of Biddlestone ['Anesley of Bedylsden'] in upper Coquetdale, hanged for theft of a horse at Morpeth in 1448, see JUST 3/211 rot. 34; JUST 3/54/33 m. 2. For the Ainslies of Dolphinston, see *Scotts of Buccleuch*, II, 25; *HMC, 14th Report*, appendix, part III, nos 6, 17, pp. 9–14.

[44] Cawode was the bailiff of the duke of Norfolk as east march warden in 1437–8 (C 47/22/7 m. 67; *CDS*, IV, 266).

[45] Neville cites this case twice, once dating it correctly (*Violence, Custom and Law*, 145) and once mistakenly placing it in the 1390s (ibid., 87). Confusion evidently stems from conflating the wardens Thomas Mowbray, earl of Nottingham and duke of Norfolk (east march warden,

Part III

Another homicide case involving Scots resident in England confounded the justices of gaol delivery. Alexander Mason, a Scot lately of Heton in Northumberland, was appealed in the Northumberland session of 1441 by Katherine Grey for killing her husband with a dagger wound in the chest on 20 September 1440. The widow did not pursue her appeal, but the jury for the king's suit against Mason found him guilty. Before he could be hanged, the jurors told the court that his victim, Laurence Grey, had also been a Scotsman and had been given to traversing the border. For the next several years his case was suspended while the justices sought advisement, and Mason remained in gaol or out on mainprise. This case, in which the victim was neither an English subject nor even continuously resident within the realm, brought into question whether an offence done by one alien to another within England could be tried at common law. No decision was ever returned on the matter and nothing suggests that the case was referred to the courts of march law. Still, a solution was reached in 1449 when Mason was pardoned on condition that he swear allegiance to the king of England. It would seem that Mason was well connected to the local English gentry, two of whom stood as his mainpernors and may also have been influential in securing his reprieve. The jury's information about Laurence Grey's proclivity to move back and forth across the border made more ambiguous the victim's status within England, and ultimately assisted Mason's case, perhaps a further sign of local influence in his favour.[46]

Claims like those made about Grey, of regular cross-border travel by aliens in England, were rare, but they did feature in the indictments against the gentleman Nicholas Turpyn and his followers. The main accusation against the Turpyn party was the killing of the Englishman Walter Michelson in June 1420, and so this is another English homicide involving Scots.[47] The Scotsmen Robert Raa, a shepherd, and William Softlawe, a 'dyker', were accused with others as principals and named

---

1389–91), and John Mowbray, duke of Norfolk (east march warden, 1437–8). The hand and vernacular language of the petition strongly suggest the later date. For Bulmer, see *Thirty-Third Annual Report of the Deputy Keeper of the Public Records* (1872), app. no. 2, p. 146.

[46] JUST 3/211 rot. 28d; *CPR 1446–52*, 28. The widow Katherine Grey's pledges at law were Edward Heron and Robert [S]wynhowe. Alexander Mason's mainpernors were John Collingwood of Duddo and Roger Burell of Howtel. On aliens, see Ruddick, *English Identity*, 108–16; K. Kim, *Aliens in Medieval Law* (Cambridge, 2000).

[47] See the Turpyn case above, pp. 213, 246–7, and below, p. 280. It appears at KB 9/213 mm. 58, 59, KB 9/216/2 mm. 4, 5; KB 27/646 *rex* rots 25, 25d, 25(a); KB 27/674 *rex* rots 3, 8d; KB 27/682 *rex* rot. 17d; KB 27/694 *rex* rot. 18d; KB 27/698 *rex* rot. 14; KB 27/702 *rex* rot. 15d; KB 27/710 *rex* rot. 16; KB 27/722 *rex* rot. 14. Powell, *Kingship, Law, and Society*, 251, briefly notes the Michelson killing and describes the offenders as 'Scottish raiders'.

Cross-Border Conflict

among Turpyn's servants, from Whitchester in southern Northumberland. Turpyn allegedly received other Scots of the Softelawe and Raa *cognomina* who had committed various thefts[48] and who were accused of riding back and forth across the border, divulging English secrets continually over a decade.[49] If credible, these accusations show that Turpyn, like other English border gentry, did have connections with Scotsmen resident in England and, furthermore, that it was at least plausible that he endorsed or directed their cross-border activities.[50] Surely, some of these Scottish aliens dwelling in England entered originally as fugitives from royal justice. In Scottish sources we can find glimpses of this process, like the case of the traitor James Hog, who escaped across the border before facing trial in the justice ayre held at Dunbar in 1456.[51] Other fugitives to England were recorded in the Annandale ayres of 1459 and 1465.[52] In 1446, the English east march warden, Lord Poynings, directed one of his officers to capture and detain a large number of Scots 'who had invaded the march' and take surety for their appearance in the warden court.[53]

There is, thus, evidence for a complicated picture of national identity, allegiance and residence among aliens involved in illicit activities in the borderlands, but what is really instructive about the subject of an illicit raiding culture in the marches is information concerning more *temporary* movement across the border, in either direction. There are plenty of cases of Scots, resident in Scotland, who crossed the border to commit offences in England, among which livestock thefts were frequent.[54] For example, at different times, two men from Annandale crossed into England and caused trouble. One of these men, John Shorte, went south and was hanged at Appleby in Westmorland in 1454 for stealing a saddle.[55] The other, a 'thefe' called John Colthird, went east, and came

---

[48] Turpyn purportedly received a Scot called David Softlawe of Whitchester, who had stolen two horses on 20 July 1409 at West Matfen (Nbl.) (KB 9/213 m. 59).

[49] Adam Softlawe, a Scot of Whitchester, allegedly stole a horse and armour in October 1414 and rode into Scotland treasonably adhering to the Scottish allegiance for a year before returning to England. Turpyn also allegedly received Richard Softlawe and his son Robert, and Thomas Raa, all Scots, who '*in Scociam equitasse et reuenisse contra ordinacionem dicti nuper regis consili sui diuersis scotis deuulgasse per decem annos continuantes prodicionem predictum*' (KB 9/213 m. 59).

[50] Turpyn's Scottish links are further illustrated by the claim (attributed to him in a proof of age) that he met George, earl of March at Gamelspath on the border in 1390 (*CIPM XIX 1405–13*, no. 1005, p. 370).

[51] Hog's unfortunate pledge, James Nisbet, was fined £10 and hanged (*ER*, VI, 184). Another flight to England was recorded in the Dunbar ayre of 1451 (ibid., V, 582).

[52] *ER*, VI, 554; ibid., VII, 312.

[53] The officer was Christopher Spencer (Alnwick Castle: Northumberland MSS, box 761, no. 22). In 1393, Adam Spenser had been issued with a similar directive (*CPR 1391–6*, 291).

[54] Thos. Johnson, Nbl., 1402 (JUST 3/191 rot. 48d); John Herdhose, Nbl., 1411 (JUST 3/191 rot. 51d).

[55] '*de Ananderdale in Scocia*', theft done at Stainmore (JUST 3/213 rot. 17).

251

Part III

to trial in 1432 for three livestock thefts in northern Northumberland, at Kilham and Yeavering in Glendale, and at Learmouth, near the Tweed. His victims, respectively, were Thomas Karr, relieved of twenty-seven animals worth £6; Robert Burell, who lost forty-seven animals worth £7; and John Paulyn, who lost twenty-four animals worth £13. Although Colthird was released on the grounds of an insufficient indictment, it is tempting to view the allegations against him as evidence of targeted, repeated livestock raids. One also wonders if, once his case was thrown out by the justices of gaol delivery, his alleged victims took their plaints to a day of march.[56]

Illustrations are to be found of Anglo-Scottish cooperation in illicit deeds for which Scots had crossed the border. Such was the case of the Englishman William Taylor, who joined with William Moscrop and other Scots in depredations committed at Wooler in northern Northumberland at Martinmas 1419.[57] More often, the evidence for cross-border contact of this sort relates to the disposal of goods (often wool).[58] But even more suggestive is the off-loading of stolen goods, an offence known in march law as 'outputting'.[59] Englishmen faced trial for stealing large numbers of animals and then crossing into Scotland to sell them.[60] An indictment was taken by the Northumberland inquisition of 1419 against John and Thomas Huntle, both yeomen of 'Sayntmaryshele' in Redesdale, for stealing £10 of livestock from the knight John Clavering in December 1417, and then treasonably fleeing across the border to Oxnam in Roxburghshire, conveying their booty to the Scots.[61] In similar cases the accused Scottish participants were actually named.[62] In a number of instances, all from Northumberland, Andrew Rutherford, John Walghop and different men of the Elwald *cognomen* were named as

---

[56] '*in comitatum de Anandirdale*' (JUST 3/208 rot. 26).   [57] JUST 3/199 rot. 19.

[58] In July 1439 one John Bwdyll of 'Nedirton' (Nbl.) treasonably delivered twelve stone of wool to Patrick Johnson, a Scot from Cockburnspath Castle ['Cowburnyschastell'] at 'Goldyngpoytt' (Nbl.). 'Nedirton' could be Netherton in upper Coquetdale, or Nedderton near Bedlington (JUST 3/211 rot. 27). For other examples, see (1441) JUST 3/211 rot. 29d and (1418) JUST 3/53/5 m. 20.

[59] Neville, 'Law of Treason', 29n 89.

[60] Laurence Nicolson of Humbelton ['Homildon'] in Nbl. stole twenty-four beasts from John de Hopis in November 1418 and treasonably fled into Scotland to sell the animals to the king's enemies. In the same session Nicolson was tried for theft of twenty-six beasts worth £4 from John Hepe, also of 'Homildon' in September 1415 (JUST 3/199 rot. 17d). A 'known thief and traitor' was hanged in Nbl. in 1407 for stealing and selling horses to Scots (JUST 3/191 rot. 49).

[61] KB 9/1056 m. 23; KB 27/694 *rex* rot. 18d; KB 27/698 *rex* rot. 14; KB 27/710 *rex* rot. 16.

[62] In November 1442, a shepherd called John Partus of Sharperton, in upper Coquetdale, allegedly stole two sheep at Kidland and treasonably sold the animals (belonging to Newminster Abbey) to a Scot called Alexander Dixon (JUST 3/211 rot. 31). A similar instance from 1407 named John Taillour, Scot (JUST 3/211 rot. 47d).

252

Cross-Border Conflict

the Scottish receivers of stolen English goods.[63] Scots almost certainly conveyed stolen goods into England with as much regularity, but specific evidence for this is thin. A lone clear example is that of the prominent Berwickshire laird Sir Alexander Hume of that ilk, accused of selling stolen livestock to 'Inglish men' against the truce in 1442. His opponent claimed that Hume held a 'garyson of refars [reivers]' which had raided more than two thousand animals in the Scottish east march.[64]

When Scots crossed the border to commit misdeeds, they often found local support from English abettors and receivers. Aid and adherence offered in this way to the king's enemies was, in some serious cases, maligned as high treason, on the basis of the statutes of 1352 and 1414.[65] A high-profile instance of such assistance involved John, prior of Hexham, who was accused in April 1408 of treasonably deserting his monastery and aiding traitors and Scottish invaders. He was pardoned three months later, but he did not set much of an example for the other residents of the liberty.[66] Not long after, in October 1408, an Englishman called Robert Hedle allegedly conducted a group of Scots, including a Robert Hunter, to raid cattle within Hexhamshire. His indictment did not allege treason. At trial two years later, the justices conceded the liberty's immunity, and he was released.[67] A number of other cases reveal Englishmen accused of receiving Scots who had crossed into England to plunder livestock.[68] Many of these Scots were from Roxburghshire and their receivers (one accused of treason) were from geographically proximate upper Coquetdale in northern Northumberland.[69] In the 1420s, at

---

[63] See the Elwalds discussed above as antecedents of this later Surname, p. 149. A father and son, both called William Raa, were tried for horse theft. The father, from Alnhammoor, was accused of selling his prey at 'Hertwaton' to Walghop (JUST 3/199 rot. 21). For Andrew Rutherford (in the same session), and Henry, John and Humphrey Elwald, see JUST 3/199 rot. 17, JUST 3/208 rot. 26, JUST 3/211 rot. 32d.

[64] DUL, DCM: Misc. Ch. 1087; *Coldingham*, no. 160, pp. 147–50.   [65] See above, pp. 182–3.

[66] He had received Scots and '*alios domini nostri regis ligeos falsos . . . et notorios proditores*', and helped them to invade the realm. He was deprived by the archbishop of York. (*Priory of Hexham*, ed. Raine, i, appendix, nos lxxii–lxxiii, pp. xciii–xciv). A link with the 1408 Percy rebellion is suggested (ibid., preface, p. clxxi; *CPR 1405–8*, 464).

[67] JUST 3/53/4 m. 1. For comment, see Neville, 'Law of Treason', 14.

[68] Two Scots from 'Eshdale' [*recte* Eskdale?], James and Matthew Taunce, burgled a house and stole a horse at 'Carewyk' in England in 1427 and were sheltered at 'Holdenhouse' in Tynedale by Richard Bell of Holdenhouse and Thomas Blount of Featherstonehaugh (JUST 3/208 rot. 30). Similarly, in 1403 Robert Refly allegedly received the Scot Robert Oliver, who stole twenty-four beasts worth £12 (JUST 3/191 rot. 47d).

[69] Such was the case against John Petegrew, yeoman of Biddlestone ['Betilsden'] in upper Coquetdale, accused of treasonably receiving Scots who had stolen oxen in England in June 1440 (JUST 3/211 rot. 29d). In 1445 a shepherd from Ryle on the River Aln was indicted for receiving Adam Wedall, a Scot from Bonjedward ['Bonegedworth'], knowing Weddall to have stolen a horse in England (JUST 3/211 rot. 32). For a similar affair involving an English Obilson, a Scottish Hunter

253

Part III

the sessions held for Newcastle town, men were tried and acquitted on indictments which included allegations of having received Scottish spies in time of war during 1413 and 1415. Some alleged treason specifically and others implied it.[70] Conversely, some prominent Scots were ready to welcome English malefactors north of the border. When the Roxburghshire laird Andrew Kerr of Altonburn and Cessford faced trial in 1456, the charges included the 'tresonabill in bryngyng of the Inglismen' who burned and harried the Scottish king's lieges in Roxburghshire.[71] At Kerr's second trial, for high treason in 1471, he was acquitted of charges, including treasonably communing with Englishmen and offering assistance to the English in battle the previous decade.[72]

Communing or trysting, like receiving, was an offence of high treason in England, and some indictments used the adherence clause from the statute of 1352 to make this accusation.[73] More specific march ordinances also forbade trysting with Scots (making it an offence under domestic march law, but distinct from march treason). Local officers were put under financial obligations to take such injunctions seriously.[74] The gaol delivery rolls record a number of cases of illegal convening with Scots, all occurring in Northumberland, and mostly along the Roxburghshire border. In almost every instance, trysting seems to have been the occasion for planning robbery and other offences within England, and it was not an activity confined to the peasantry, for Thomas Alder, gentleman of Mindrum, faced accusations of convening with Scots in 1422.[75] One yeoman was tried in 1432 for having met with certain Scots 'against the ordinance and proclamation of the march warden' but acquitted on an insufficient indictment.[76] Another case of this type might well relate to

and a burgled house at Linshiels in upper Coquetdale, see JUST 3/208 rot. 25d; and for still another involving oxen theft in lower Coquetdale, see JUST 3/211 rot. 32.

[70] The Newcastle town session of 1421 (where treason was alleged) appears at JUST 3/199 rot. 24, and the 1428 town session (where treason was not alleged) at JUST 3/208 rots 20, 20d.

[71] HMC, 14th Report, appendix, part III, no. 7, p. 10.

[72] HMC, 14th Report, appendix, part III, no. 54, pp. 27–28; RMS, II, no. 786, p. 168; Boardman, 'Politics and the Feud', 119–20; Brown, Black Douglases, 316–17.

[73] Neville, 'Law of Treason', 7, 13, 17.

[74] In 1490 the bailiff of Redesdale made a bond in £500 to execute his duties in capturing malefactors and allowing 'no conventicles or privy meetings' between Englishmen and Scotsmen (CDS, IV, no. 1556, p. 317).

[75] Alder convened with the Scots Robert and James Lokwod and stole forty cattle from Richard Heron, the Scots taking the booty across the border (JUST 3/208 rot. 34). On 11 October 1434, the yeoman Adam Tynedale from Hall Barns near Chipchase Castle met with three Scotsmen, David and Edward Nixon, and Matthew Croyser, and stole a horse (JUST 3/208 rot. 34). For similar instances, see JUST 3/199 rot. 17; JUST 3/199 rot. 23d; JUST 3/208 rot. 31; the latter two in upper and lower Coquetdale, respectively.

[76] David Fodirley of 'Baremore', indicted for meeting John Strange and other Scots in 1432 (JUST 3/208 rot. 26).

Cross-Border Conflict

Andrew Kerr of Altonburn and Cessford himself. In November 1434 an English yeoman named Thomas Chambirleyn from Pressen, just a few miles from the eastern Roxburghshire border, allegedly met with a Scot called Andrew 'Kar' (a variant spelling of Kerr), and drove (*'expulsit'*) to Andrew all the goods and chattels belonging to a man from Carham, right on the border.[77] Although it was not alleged in this example, a number of these trysting offences were construed as high treason.[78] Indictments from the Northumberland inquisition of 1419 offer examples of treasonable convening and conspiring with Scotsmen. The Northumbrian yeomen who were so indicted were 'Litill Gibbe Roderfordman' of Wark, who was the servant of Gilbert Rutherford,[79] and others from the north of the county, including Henry Rutour, lately of Ancroft,[80] and John Prendwyk, yeoman of Roxburgh, lately of Prendwick.[81] Whether singled out as treasonable or not, these accusations strongly suggest the regular occurrence of cross-border connivance in illicit activities, especially involving marchers living close to the frontier.

More dramatic than cattle raids or mischievous conventicles was cross-border kidnapping. This typically involved abduction in one country and detention in the other until a ransom was paid. Although there is no clear evidence for Scotsmen being abducted by Englishmen,[82] accusations of

---

[77] Kar was of unspecified social status. The victim was Thomas Tod of 'Karram', and his goods and chattels were valued at 100 s. (JUST 3/208 rot. 34). In 1429 the bishop of Durham had ordered the parishioners of Carham to cease using the parish church as a stable (*Register of Thomas Langley,* ed. Storey, iii, no. 811, pp. 153–4).

[78] Treason cases have already been noted concerning the castles of Jedburgh (JUST 3/191 rot. 51d) and of Roxburgh (JUST 3/191 rot. 51), and one warning of a trod (JUST 3/208 rot. 34d; JUST 3/54/16 m. 11), above, p. 190. See also treason alleged against John Gray Jr, yeoman, 1427 (JUST 3/199 rot. 17d); William Hogesson, 1431 (JUST 3/208 rot. 30); Robert Johnson of 'Edderslawe', yeoman, 1426 (JUST 3/208 rot. 35d); John Jay of Newcastle, 1419 (JUST 3/53/5 m. 1); and William Smart, 1417 (JUST 3/199 rot. 18).

[79] See above, p. 131. This man was accused of conspiring with two named Scots and others at Chillingham ['Cheuelyngham faldam'], on 8 December 1418, and stealing by night £8 of cattle from Sir Thomas Middleton, before fleeing into Scotland. He was named as *'Gilbertus seruiens Gilberti Roderford al[ias] dictus litill Gibbe Roderfordman de Werk'*. Whether this was Wark on Tweed or Wark in Tynedale was not specified. He was also called a *'cognitus et notarius proditor et latro [cinius] et consilii et secretorum regni Regis Angl[ie] prefatis Scotis deuulgator et expositor'*. Elsewhere in the indictment Rutherford was called a Scot (KB 9/1056 m. 23; see also KB 27/694 *rex* rot. 18d; KB 27/698 *rex* rot. 14; KB 27/710 *rex* rot. 16).

[80] He was accused of meeting with named Scots on 1 August 1419 at 'Yareford' to divulge the king's counsel and secrets and stirring the Scots to make *'diversas equitaciones'* into Nbl. to the destruction of the king's people.

[81] He was called a notorious traitor and conspirator, accused of convening with named Scots, stealing 120 animals worth £40 from victims at Glanton and Edlingham, and taking the plunder into Scotland on 8 November 1415.

[82] However, see the payment in salmon (worth £24) to James Lathis for his *'redempcione'* from England, by royal mandate, in 1456 (*ER,* VI, 128). Lathis may otherwise have been a pledge entered at a day of march.

Part III

participation with Scotsmen in the reverse scenario were consistently laid against Englishmen in both the fourteenth and fifteenth centuries, and the danger of capture by the Scots was mentioned in parliamentary petitions and declarations on the borders.[83] Kidnapping for ransom qualified as high treason under the statute of 1352, when construed as 'levying war' against the king.[84] Like cross-border livestock theft or trysting, such abductions involved breach of the truce, and so also constituted march treason, which could have been punished in the domestic warden courts.[85] Cases appearing in the English common law courts may also have come before the international days of march, which sought redress rather than punishment, although evidence does not survive which might demonstrate this. Some indentures of truce addressed ransom-takings directly. For example, the 1424 truce covered the taking of prisoners, and the 1473 indenture made explicit provision for the release and redress of all prisoners 'unlathfully' taken.[86]

One illustrative case arising from the Northumberland inquisition of 1419 illuminates cross-border kidnappings following on from illegal trysting. It concerned four yeomen who were 'known and notorious traitors and divulgers to the Scots of the counsel and secrets of the English king and people', called 'Lang John Homyll' of Hartburn, John Rutour Sr of 'Marelhirst', and two men from Redesdale, William Wardale of Stobbs and William Pottes. They were accused of convening and conspiring with Gilbert Rutherford and other Scots on 10 August 1419 at Gamelspath ['Kemylespath'] and Redeswyre, where the border met the heads of the Coquet and Rede rivers, and at many other locations in the east march in both England and Scotland. They and the Scots rode by night to diverse places in Northumberland, capturing the king's people and taking them into Scotland.[87] Further colourful evidence concerns a number of kidnappings also perpetrated in Northumberland.[88] The circumstances of a bond made in Redesdale in 1400 suggest such a ransom-taking.[89] Cases of this type were also handled in the gaol delivery

---

[83] *PROME*, April 1414, item 20; September 1429, item 43. See Neville, *Violence, Custom and Law*, 106–7, 110, 114, 129–30, 135.

[84] Neville, 'Law of Treason', 7; Keen, *Laws of War*, 156–85. Keen ('Treason Trials', 96–97, 99) discusses the charges against the earl of Northumberland in 1405 and against Ralph Grey in 1464.

[85] Except when the English wardens' powers over march treason were suspended from 1414 to 1449/1453. See above, p. 183.

[86] *Foedera*, IV, iv, 110; V, iii, 34.

[87] '*John Homyll alias dictus Lang John Homyll de Hertburn*' (KB 9/1056 m. 23; KB 27/694 *rex* rot. 18d; KB 27/698 *rex* rot. 14; KB 27/710 *rex* rot. 16).

[88] Several other cases involving kidnapping were found, but none involved abduction into Scotland. For example, see two from Cbl. in 1426 and 1442 (JUST 3/199 rot. 26d; JUST 3/211 rot. 42).

[89] See above, p. 157.

Cross-Border Conflict

sessions, and only one of these did not allege treason. This was against Gilbert Coll', a servant of the Northumberland esquire Sampson Harding. Together with a Scotsman called Robert Clyuere, Gilbert kidnapped Robert Johnson and carried him into Scotland to hold him for ransom.[90] Treason was mentioned in kidnapping cases from 1404,[91] 1419[92] and 1419–20.[93] In two other cases from 1410, Englishmen assisted Scots in carrying out treasonable kidnappings, and one was allegedly paid in advance for a share of the ransom money.[94] All of these incidents occurred between 1397 and 1420, but other sources suggest that cross-border kidnapping continued into the period for which our gaol delivery evidence does not survive.[95]

A final offence to be considered in this survey of illicit activities is homicide. We have already looked at a number of English homicides in which resident Scottish aliens were implicated, but the evidence for 'cross-border' killings – where the perpetrator or victim was temporarily in the opposite realm at the time – is surprisingly sparse. What information does survive amounts to only a few examples. The first is a case heard in Northumberland in 1442, concerning the lethal knifing of a 'Scotisman' near Morpeth. The accused was an English yeoman, and it is not clear if his victim was an English resident or if he had crossed the border.[96] The previous chapter noted the homicide of Richard Tweddall in Tynedale in 1476, and involved in this affair were two Roxburghshire Scots who do appear to have crossed into England. One was Richard Nevyn of Bamburgh, alias of Liddesdale, and this detail may suggest

---

[90] JUST 3/191 rot. 45 (31 December 1397): Johnson was from Prestwick in Ponteland. Harding was escheator for Nbl. in 1394 and a JP from 1397 (*CPR 1396–9*, 237; *LOE*, 102).

[91] The two accused kidnappers of William Emson (held in Scotland at a ransom of £24) were Thomas Raffell Sr and John Raffell, also tried for theft. They were found guilty and hanged (JUST 3/191 rot. 48).

[92] The yeoman Thomas Flecher of Ryal was indicted for convening in Redesdale in 1419 with Scots, including Nicholas Rutherford, and capturing six Englishmen together with two horses and goods to the value of 100 s. (JUST 3/199 rot. 23).

[93] The yeomen Richard Stokhalgh of Whitshields in Tynedale and John Smert of Haydon Bridge stole ten beasts from Thomas Dicson at Haydon Bridge in December 1419. They came back in February 1420 (this time with a group of Scots including John Bell Sr and Jr), kidnapped Dicson and held him in Scotland for five weeks (JUST 3/199 rot. 17).

[94] John Nicolson of Gunnerton in Tynedale treasonably convened with the Scots Thomas Grame and William Grame at 'Hedlewodde' and assisted them in kidnapping and ransoming William Tailliour in 1410 (JUST 3/191 rot. 51d). John Perysson treasonably kidnapped William of Heswell Jr, at Kirkharle, and sold him to Scots who ransomed him for £40 in 1410 (JUST 3/199 rot. 18).

[95] For a proof of age in Cbl. in 1490 a kidnapping by Scots in 1468–9 was recalled; this at least should indicate that the event was held to be a plausible recollection (*CIPM, I: 1–12 Henry VII*, nos 470–1, pp. 199–200).

[96] John Nicholson, yeoman, was acquitted of killing John Andrewson at Longhirst with a dagger known as a 'whynyard' (JUST 3/211 rot. 30; JUST 3/54/25 m. 13).

257

Part III

particular cross-border links with Sir Henry Percy of Bamburgh, the ringleader.[97] The scarcity of evidence for cross-border homicides is perhaps explained by the fact that these were the kind of incident with which the border courts would have been most concerned and, by the same token, were the least likely to appear in the English common law courts.[98] The third example shows that lethal violence could also erupt at the days of march themselves.[99] In late 1479 or early 1480 the English ambassadors to Scotland were instructed by Edward IV to inform themselves 'by the marchiers suche as knowe best the dealing of bothe sides' concerning Scottish allegations and 'considering that long before the said surmised charges, at a day of trewes, the Scottes murdred Robert Lisle, and toke Sir Henry Percy prisoner and many other gentilmen, in the presence and by auctoritee of the wardeynes lieutenaunt of Scotland'.[100] Other details on this incident are not forthcoming, and even Lisle and Percy are difficult to identify, although there is a strong possibility that this was Percy of Bamburgh.[101] Dating this incident to the 1470s would mean that the duke of Albany was the warden on the Scottish side, and among the charges laid against the duke in 1479 was the accusation that he had violated the truce by slaughter while he was warden.[102] So it is not an unreasonable possibility that Albany had by his 'auctoritee' condoned the killing of Lisle and the capture of the Englishmen.

---

[97] The other Scot was Robert Hyndmarte of Liddesdale (KB 27/861 *rex* rots 15, 19d; KB 9/343 mm. 34, 56, 70, 71).

[98] It should be noted that a case from 1453 (recorded in C 81/1461/2631–2, from a petition for pardon), highlighted by Neville, of a Cbl. man 'indicted in a border tribunal for the homicide of a Scotsman' (*Violence, Custom and Law*, 145) was not, in fact, concerned with the border courts. The killer was Richard Walker of Distington, alias of Moresby, and he was granted a pardon on grounds that in 'chaunce medley' he had fallen 'in handys' with Donkan Makynnan, manservant, killing him in self-defence, and that the indictment against him had been lost. No evidence other than his suggestive name identifies the slain man as Scottish. The relevant gaol delivery file gives Richard Walker of Distington, yeoman, indicted before the JPs for the murder and killing of '*Doncann Makeren manseruium*' in 1450 (JUST 3/11/21 mm. 1, 6).

[99] Regular procedure for days of march provided that 'all days of true be halden by both parties in sober and esy wise without spear bow harness or whip' (NRS: SP 6/20). The Scottish party was despoiled of £1,000 at a diet held at Reddenburn in January 1459, by one William Big and his accomplices (*RMS*, II, no. 677, p. 147).

[100] E 39/102/25, printed in *CDS*, IV, appendix 1, no. 28, pp. 412–14.

[101] William Lyle, esq., was involved with Percy of Bamburgh in the Tweddall killing of 1476. See above, p. 220. Other possibilities are Master Henry Percy and Sir Henry Percy, who purchased pasturage in Alnwick forest in the 1470s (although this Sir Henry may yet be Percy of Bamburgh): *Percy Bailiff's Rolls of the Fifteenth Century*, ed. J.C. Hodgson (Durham, 1921), 18. My analysis differs from that of Neville, *Violence, Custom and Law*, 160.

[102] Albany was accused of breaking the truce 'be slauchteris Reffis and hereschippis tresonabli committit contrare to the kingis hienes and to the comoune gud of his realme, the said Alexander being wardain in the sammyn boundis for the tyme': *RPS*, 1479/10/7.

Cross-Border Conflict

Frustratingly, no further evidence shows how the Lisle killing was handled at subsequent border tribunals.

AENEAS SYLVIUS PICCOLOMINI'S REPORT

We are fortunate to have a source available to us which illuminates the very area of the borderline that, in the evidence already presented, appears to have been especially permeable. This comes in the form of a first-hand account from a visitor to the marches, Aeneas Sylvius Piccolomini (the future Pope Pius II, 1458–64), who arrived in Scotland by sea on a diplomatic mission in late 1435. Sometime after the winter solstice (21 December), he decided to make his return journey overland through England. On his way south he spent a night in the east marches, and he recorded this and other aspects of his journey in his autobiographical 'commentaries', written later in life.[103] This account offers further insight into cross-border activities and the local attitudes associated with these affairs.

Travelling through England, Piccolomini was obliged to go secretly, disguised as a merchant.[104] In his memoirs, he recalled making a clandestine border crossing of the kind that required Anglo-Scottish cooperation. He crossed what was presumably the River Tweed in a small boat, near a point affected by the tide, travelling with two servants and a guide. They reached an unnamed large town ('*villam magnam*') about sunset and had dinner at a farmhouse with their host and the local priest. If the traveller was hoping to evade attention, this town was probably neither Berwick nor Norham, but perhaps a smaller place like Cornhill or Horncliffe.[105] Apparently, he became something of a novelty for the English villagers, who gathered for a meal which lasted until the second hour of the night ('*in secundam noctis horam*'). He relates how, at this stage in the evening, the locals prepared for an expected raid by the Scots, who were accustomed, when the river was at low tide, to cross and assault them by night (in patent breach of the truce). Interestingly, Piccolomini notes that all the men and youths or children ('*liberis*'), including his host

---

[103] For a Latin edition with Italian translation, see *Piccolomini,* ed. Totaro. For this visit, see ibid., book 1, cc. 4–6; I, 16–31. For an English translation, see Piccolomini, *Memoirs of a Renaissance Pope: The Commentaries of Pius II,* ed. L.C. Gabel and trans. F.A. Gragg (London, 1960), at 32–6.

[104] For the circumstances of Piccolomini's mission, see Nicholson, *Scotland,* 297. A vital analysis of Piccolomini's recollection is found in Goodman, 'Border Warfare and Hexhamshire', 54–5, and Goodman, 'Anglo-Scottish', 26–7.

[105] Horncliffe, between Norham and Berwick, was near the upstream limit of tidal flow, but I am not aware of a tower there. Further upstream, west of Norham, Cornhill is also a strong possibility, with its tower then owned by the Swinhowe family.

259

Part III

and the priest, excused themselves to take refuge in a tower a long way off. To the traveller's astonishment, and despite his appeals, the men could not be persuaded to take him or any of the women with them to the tower.[106] He was left behind with his servants and guide to spend the night with one hundred 'beautiful adolescent girls and matrons', who sat in a circle around the fire and stayed up cleaning hemp and chatting with the interpreter. The distinct gender roles in this story are immediately striking, and one wonders, as did Piccolomini, what their justification was and what the women thought of the arrangement.

If we can accept Piccolomini's report as untainted by dramatic literary exaggeration, this vignette may point us towards certain customs of cross-border raiding. Of particular note is the apparent gender segregation, and there are a number of possible explanations that might be ventured. First, it is conceivable that the villagers simply accepted the risks assumed by the women in remaining exposed, so that the latter could continue to work the hemp, generating its many useful products.[107] Second, the men may have left the women and foreign guests behind in order to keep them out of harm's way, because the tower complex was the expected target of raiding and they went there to defend it.[108] However, Piccolomini's claim that the men fled to the tower for fear of the Scots would seem to contradict this explanation: if the men were in fact running away to seek shelter, they would appear to be leaving the women precariously exposed to danger in the path of the expected raiders. But, if we consider a third explanation – that the men left the women because the women had nothing to fear, for it was the men themselves who were the expected target of the raiders – then we may be looking at fascinating evidence. A close reading of Piccolomini's own unclear explanation, '*Nihil enim his mali facturos hostes credunt, qui stuprum inter mala non ducunt*', suggests that the raiders may not have been expected to do the women any harm (presumably meaning rape, considering the word '*stuprum*').[109]

---

[106] On fortification and refuge see above, pp. 86 and 93. *Piccolomini*, ed. Totaro, I, 26: '*sacerdos et hospes cum liberis virisque omnibus, Aenea dimisso, abire festinantes dixerunt se ad turrem quamdam, longo spatio remotam, metu Scotorum fugere qui, fluvio maris reflexu decrescente, noctu transire praedarique soleant. Neque secum Aeneam multis orantem precibus quoquo pacto adducere voluerunt neque foeminarum quampiam, quamvis adolescentulae et matronae formosae complures essent.*'

[107] This first explanation and a variation on the second are suggested by Goodman, 'Border Warfare and Hexhamshire', 54–5, who also discusses Piccolomini's moral message of resisting the temptation of the women.

[108] Although livestock may have been the expected target and the men may conceivably have gone to bring animals within the tower's barmkin, Piccolomini's claim that he slept in the stable with cows and goats suggests otherwise (*Piccolomini*, ed. Totaro, I, 27).

[109] *Piccolomini*, ed. Totaro, I, 26: '*Nihil enim his mali facturos hostes credunt, qui stuprum inter mala non ducunt.*' The subjects and objects of this sentence are ambiguous. It has been translated as: 'For they think the enemy will do them no wrong – not counting outrage a wrong' (*Memoirs of a*

260

Cross-Border Conflict

It could be that Piccolomini's intended meaning was in fact to say that rape was improbable, because the enemies ('*hostes*') would not consider raping the women at all or harming them in any other way. If this means that the villagers thought that the women would not be molested by the raiders, their confidence may have been based on an unwritten rule, along the lines of the spontaneous cooperative arrangements which have been identified in social contexts, where opponents are aware of their shared interests and of the need to continue living alongside one another.[110]

If such an interpretation is valid, it suggests that a cooperative custom had evolved across the frontier, whereby male border raiders mutually acknowledged the terms of an agreement along the lines of 'we won't harm your women if you don't harm ours'.[111] In explaining this to the astonished and confused Piccolomini, the borderers may have told him that attacks on the women, including rape, were unlikely, as the women were shielded by the threat of tit-for-tat retaliation. How did the women feel about this? They apparently stayed up all night, comfortably conversing by firelight, clearly leaving themselves visible and audible to possible marauders. They seem not to have been greatly concerned for their own safety, although, later in the night, when a great clamour arose, as if the enemy were at hand, all the women scattered, soon returning with the interpreter to Piccolomini (hiding in the stable where he had been sleeping) to say that all was well and that those who came were friends, not enemies.[112] No matter what the 'real' meaning of his explanatory sentence, the important – and more certain – point remains that the women did not go to the tower.

It must be pointed out that the preceding argument goes against some evidence for border raiding in the sixteenth century. Meikle offers examples to show that border violence in the later Tudor period was not gender-specific, although she does note an absence of accusations of

---

Renaissance Pope, ed. Gabel and Gragg, 35). This faithful translation is no less vague than the Latin. It would seem unlikely that Piccolomini means that the women and men of his story did not reckon the sexual violence of rape to be a wrong. However, the sentence can be read in the following, alternative, way: 'For they [the men, or the men and women] believe the enemies will do them [the women] no wrong, because they [the enemies] do not reckon outrage among wrongs.'

[110] R. Axelrod, *The Evolution of Cooperation* (New York, 1984), 73–87, 145–69.

[111] For a similar custom among twentieth-century Bedouin tribes, see Black-Michaud, *Cohesive Force,* 199–200.

[112] Piccolomini, ed. Totaro, I, 28: '*Post medium autem noctis latrantibus canibus et anseribus strepentibus ingens clamor factus est, tumque omnes foeminae in diversum prolapsae, dux quoque itineris diffugit et quasi hostes adessent omnia tumultu complete … Nec mora reversae mulieres cum interprete nihil mali esse nuntiant, atque amicos non hostes venisse.*'

Part III

rape in the border courts in that period, and attributes this to the fact that rape did not fall under march law.[113] Certainly, in the fifteenth century the noms de guerre attributed to certain troublemakers in the marches are suggestive of a sexualised machismo: 'Out with ye swerd', 'Weykspere', 'Lusty John' and 'Wantoun Walter'.[114] An important element in Piccolomini's story is perhaps the significance of the tower. While attacks on women were considered taboo by some chivalric writers,[115] according to the law of arms, in the sack of a town following a siege women could be raped by the invaders.[116] If these customs of large-scale chivalric conflict influenced the conduct of violence among Piccolomini's villagers of the east march, it is conceivable that the women did not go to the tower at night because to do so would put them at risk of assault should it be taken; whereas, outside the tower they remained immune. Whatever Piccolomini's meaning, there seem to have been set patterns of behaviour in the face of raiding, which may suggest certain customary restraints observed by both sides.

Border raids were also influenced by environmental and economic factors, and Piccolomini offers further evidence touching on this aspect. One unquestionable part of his tale is that raiding happened at night. Certainly, in the sixteenth century, the illicit activities of common border 'thieves' – often involving livestock rustling – seem to have been nighttime events. Consequently, owing to changes in the length of the day, they also seem to have had a seasonal pattern. More than a century and a half later, in 1597, the English warden of the east march, Sir Robert Carey, observed that October and November were the favourite months for cattle raiding among the borderers: 'for then are the nightes longest, theyr horse hard at meat and will ride best, cattell strong and will drive furthest'. At this time of year, animals would be at their fattest, healthiest and most numerous, and so pickings would be generous. It may also be significant that Martinmas was the usual time of livestock slaughter.

---

[113] Meikle, 'Victims, Viragos and Vamps', 173–5, observes that victims may have been reluctant to admit that rape had occurred. Archbishop Gavin Dunbar did not list rape among the 'misdedis' perpetrated by the border thieves in his well-known 'monition of cursing' of 1525, printed in *Source Book of Scottish History,* ed. W.C. Dickinson et al. (2nd edn., 1958; repr., 1963), II, 100–3.

[114] A Scottish knight known as John Turnbull 'out with ye swerd', captured in 1400 (*CDS*, IV, 118); William Hedle otherwise called 'Weykspere' in 1498 (C 66/582/ m. 6d, also calendared in *CPR 1494–1509,* 160); 'Lustus' John Robsone, and 'Wantoun' Walter Dalglesch, recorded in the Jedburgh ayre of 1493 and the Selkirk ayre of 1495 (NRS: JC 1/1, fols 9v, 30v).

[115] See, for example, *The Tree of Battles of Honoré Bonet,* ed. G.W. Coopland (Liverpool, 1949), book IV, cc. 94, 102, pp. 184–5, 189.

[116] Keen, *Laws of War,* 121–2. John Hardyng wrote that, when Sir Robert Umfraville and his nephew raided Teviotdale in 1408, 'the wyves swere by seynt Rynyan and yelpe': see the unpublished MS version of Hardyng's chronicle, quoted in 'Umfraville, Sir Robert (d. 1437)', in *Oxford DNB,* LV, 883–5, by H.R.T Summerson.

Cross-Border Conflict

Animals which could not be kept alive over the winter on scarce fodder were butchered in early November, and their meat was salted down into 'marts'. At this time in particular, no doubt, raiders knew that fat animals driven away could not be stolen back if they were slaughtered quickly, and a store of salt meat in the larder would be a valuable commodity over the coming months. The relatively dry autumn ground was also an important factor, for the boggy border fells and laws would become more difficult for hooves to traverse as winter rainfall accumulated and animals weakened.[117] Thus, one would expect Piccolomini, travelling through the marches about Christmas 1435, to have arrived during the raiding season, although after the peak months. His description of habitual border raids by night at this time suggests that something resembling the patterns observed by Carey at the end of the next century already obtained in the 1430s.

The seasonality of raiding in the marches is borne out by the data gathered from the English gaol delivery records. While only a small proportion of these cases relate to cross-border offences, as observed in the preceding chapter, the theft of sheep and cattle was overwhelmingly the most frequent charge heard in these courts. A tally of all offence dates, by month, shows that the last five months of the year, from August until December, were the most unsettled. During this period the average monthly number of offences was 305, more than double the rate of 151 offences per month for the rest of the year. The month with the fewest offences was April (90), and the month with the most was November (479).[118] This overall configuration is matched when the fifty-seven cases involving Scots from this larger sample are considered alone. Of those cases involving Scots in some capacity, November was again the busiest month, with ten offences.[119] These data would, then, suggest that offences perpetrated in the English marches, mostly consisting of livestock theft, had a seasonal pattern that rose in autumn and peaked in November, while the early months of the year were much quieter. In this regard the pattern would appear to match well with the observations made by Carey about the seasonality of border livestock

---

[117] Tough, *Last Years*, 47–8.
[118] The sample of 2,583 dated offences tried at gaol delivery is from the data set used in the preceding chapter. The higher total figure here exceeds that of 2,568 because of the addition of a small number of offences occurring before 1395, from cases in the rolls JUST 3/191, 199, 208, 211, 213, and DURH 19/1/1. See above, p. 231; Armstrong, 'Local Conflict', 134nn, 191nn (including a full description and month-by-month frequency).
[119] Monthly frequency for gaol delivery offences involving Scots: January, 4 offences; February, 3; March, 1; April, 1; May, 4; June, 4; July, 2; August, 8; September, 7; October, 7; November, 10; December, 6.

Part III

rustling in the later Tudor era. That said, it also matches well with the seasonal pattern of offences detected in the southern counties of England in the early fourteenth century.[120] Thus, any assertion about the distinctiveness of such activities in the far north must be made cautiously. Clearly, environment and economy helped to shape unlawful deeds in aggregate, some of which individually can be classified as instances of lesser border raiding.[121]

A 'RAIDING CULTURE'

To what extent does all this evidence point to the existence of routine patterns of cross-border raiding? It is apparent that the frontier was porous and that lesser illicit cross-border activity did appear to pose a problem detectable in court records. The pertinent question is whether the surviving evidence is just the visible tip of the iceberg, and whether all this amounts to a 'raiding culture'. The impression given by the sources is that what has survived on record represents a proportion of a wider phenomenon, about which we can say certain things.

It appears that, while the English common law was competent to deal with border-related offences, these were generally handled in the local itinerant courts of gaol delivery, not before king's bench in the halls of Westminster. While Neville has suggested a 'jockeying for jurisdictional privilege' between the courts of march law and common law within England during the fifteenth century, this near-total absence of border cases from king's bench tells against any such sense of jurisdictional jealousy.[122] King's bench gave its direct attention to cross-border offences just twice, in the war-disturbed later 1410s, a period also when the statute of truces of 1414 severely curtailed the powers of the warden courts. As had been the case since the statute of 1352, allegations of high treason were a means by which local juries of presentment could ensure that border-related matters came before the common law courts and, from 1414 to mid-century, that allegations of the truce-breaking that constituted march treason were also used for this purpose.[123] Even

---

[120] Hanawalt found that 45 per cent of the annual total of larceny offences were committed in the period between September and November, with a peak in November (Hanawalt, *Crime and Conflict*, 68–9, 99–100).

[121] On the impact of season, environment, and geography on patterns of raiding in other cultures, see Black-Michaud, *Cohesive Force*, 197–8; Boehm, *Blood Revenge*, 175–80; J.L. Ruffini, 'Disputing over Livestock in Sardinia', in L. Nader and H.F. Todd (eds), *The Disputing Process: Law in Ten Societies* (New York, 1978), 209–46.

[122] Neville, *Violence, Custom and Law*, 41, quote from 145.

[123] See above, p. 183; Neville, *Violence, Custom and Law*, 97–8, 106, 114, 125–6, 137; Neville, 'Law of Treason', 14–20.

Cross-Border Conflict

without records of the wardens' tribunals or the truce days, it is clear that inhabitants of the marches used a complex mixture of legal systems and courts to further their own disputes and to address the illicit activities of other borderers. The findings of this chapter then reinforce the conclusions drawn earlier about the interaction of different frameworks of justice in the far north, chiefly that of royal justice and border justice. This was less about jurisdictional rivalries than about a local society ready and able to accommodate and use different and evolving systems of law.

Most border-related offences amounted to something more than one-off opportunistic acts that might be dismissed as simple 'crime'. They revolved principally around the theft of livestock, sometimes on a large scale, and involved associated deeds like trysting, either to plan in advance or to sell goods on once they had been stolen. Fewer in number, but still apparent, were more serious incidents of kidnapping and homicide. In this regard, elements of a nuanced routine of raiding are detectable. To the extent that it appears to have been habituated and familiar among the participants suggests that it may be meaningfully understood as a raiding 'culture'. The bulk of this evidence suggests that common borderers were more likely than their social superiors to establish and maintain direct personal cross-border connections necessary for these activities.[124] The English gentry do not seem to have been accused of cross-border misdeeds very often. If they were, perhaps their more serious cases would be taken to the march courts for punishment and redress. But the gentry's involvement at arm's length is visible (as noted above in the case against Nicholas Turpyn in 1420), and it appears that the peasants they recruited into their own networks of service were sometimes doing their masters' bidding when engaged on suspicious business.[125] In some cases, gentry employed resident-alien Scots directly. It may be that the majority of the border incidents discussed above were, in fact, a function of such bonds between lesser lords and their men. A crucial aspect of this raiding culture was that some parts of the border were more troublesome than others. The overwhelming majority of cross-border offences detectable in England happened in the east and middle marches, which meant Northumberland and its adjoining liberties. More specifically, within Northumberland, certain areas stand out. The borderline running south from Carham to the Cheviot, and west from the Cheviot to Redeswyre, at the head of the Rede, can be

---

[124] This offers further support to a point observed by Goodman ('Anglo-Scottish', 29) about cross-border economic contacts being of particular significance to common marchers.

[125] See above, pp. 246–7, 250–1; and see also the Sandford of Askham links with lesser families, at pp. 123, 156, and below, p. 296.

Part III

identified as particularly permeable. Cross-border communication along the Carham–Cheviot stretch of the frontier, running through very habitable countryside, would have been achieved with ease, and indeed there are to be found a number of cross-border offences and offenders.[126] On this stretch of the border was Reddenburn, a meeting-place frequently used for diplomacy in the thirteenth century, but largely ignored thereafter when the English pale extended further north. From the 1420s onwards, it again became a regular site for days of march and greater Anglo-Scottish diets.[127] Although north-west of this line was Roxburgh Castle, still an English-held bastion until 1460, it was within Scottish-controlled Roxburghshire (or Teviotdale) in our period.[128] In eastern Roxburghshire was the regality of Sprouston, where the Scottish Kerrs were the dominant local landholders.[129] Men called Andrew Kerr appeared in a number of border incidents, and, if the name refers to only one man (or even father and son), the laird of Altonburn and Cessford, he seems to have had influence in both realms. From this corner of Roxburghshire, those choosing to cross the border could also travel south-east to Redeswyre and Gamelspath, respectively the heads of the Rede and Coquet rivers, into the liberty of Redesdale. It was in this area, Redesdale and upper Coquetdale, that many illicit border trysts were held. It seems that, if the problems of national allegiance faced by the people of Roxburghshire during the two decades around 1400 slowly receded, the eastern corner of the sheriffdom remained very permeable to illicit cross-border activity well into the fifteenth century.

The conclusion that lesser illicit activity was especially focused on the boundary between eastern Roxburghshire and northern Northumberland partly concurs with the findings concerning the Northumberland liberties in the preceding chapter. If this was the county with the greatest extent of unlawful cross-border activity, this should have increased the turbulence of the border liberties about which complaints were made, and for which we have actual evidence in relation to offenders. Yet the majority of misdeeds were not recorded within these liberties but in upper Coquetdale and the area around the Cheviot. Of course, this may

---

[126] Unfortunately, the Durham records do not survive to illuminate Norhamshire, further north-east.

[127] For example, see the meetings at Reddenburn in 1426 (*PPC*, III, 205–6), 1433 (*PPC*, IV, 350–352a), 1458 (NRS: SP 6/20), 1473 (*Foedera*, V, iii, 34–5).

[128] Truces provided for the open victualling of English castles in Scottish territory: *Foedera*, III, iii, 205 (1386); III, iv, 151 (1398). However, in 1400, the English captain of Roxburgh, Richard, Lord Grey, was obliged to raid south towards Jedburgh in order to supply his garrison (*CDS*, IV, 119; discussed in Goodman, 'Defence of Northumberland', 165).

[129] See above, note 17; Goodman, 'Anglo-Scottish', 26–7.

Cross-Border Conflict

simply reflect greater use of the king's courts in these areas which were under the direct jurisdiction of the king's officers (rather than the franchise courts of the various liberties). This may suggest that what evidence survives with mention of Tynedale, Redesdale and Hexhamshire rather under-represents the situation. We can at least say that the relatively less turbulent appearance of the western end of the border, which was also subject to direct royal jurisdiction, implies that there was indeed a higher incidence of cross-border activity at the eastern end.[130]

The raiding culture identified here involved not only cross-border offences which were illicit for collusion with the enemy but also patterned group raiding (as in livestock rustling) that was illicit for violating the truce. The latter may also have entailed normative aspects derived from spontaneous cooperative arrangements, which suggests that the participants did not consider their behaviour to be entirely illegitimate. In fact, although the landed elite appear to have had indirect links to the lesser misdeeds that came before the English itinerant courts, their direct involvement in truce-breaking *attemptats* and *chevauchées* often invoked chivalric norms derived from the law of arms. Although a raid might constitute a breach of the truce and march law, and even march treason, a standard displayed in daylight invoked a legitimacy which was unavailable to common borderers acting alone. But the line was by no means clear, for the landed elite also perpetrated less formalised attacks on residences. We have seen good evidence that a Scottish laird like Andrew Kerr was implicated in the same sort of night-time raiding and illicit deeds as his social inferiors. The same would be true of the unknown English gentleman who owned the tower to which Piccolomini's village men-folk retreated in the night.

What evidence there is for a cross-border raiding culture is not spread evenly enough across the period to tell us whether this phenomenon was growing or receding over time. What information is available, especially from legal records, indicates that serious border-related offences were a regular part of life in the marches from the very beginning of the fifteenth century. One of the lines of enquiry brought into focus at the end of the previous chapter was what effect cross-border conflict had on violence in the region. If a detectable raiding culture contributed to an increased propensity to use violence in this local society, its direct effects were not spread widely. Some borderers, close to the frontier, were regularly involved in raiding which, we should expect, made them more familiar and even comfortable with violent behaviour. But this

[130] See above, pp. 236–8.

Part III

expectation should by no means apply to all or even most of the inhabitants of the marches towards Scotland. If northern Northumberland was the focal point of so much border-related activity, it was not, as we saw in the previous chapter, producing the largest amount of violence of the three English border counties. Rather, Westmorland, far from the boundary of eastern Roxburghshire, appears to have been most violent. So these findings do not suggest that it was the effects of the military frontier that made the far north of England more violent than further south. Rather, they support the argument that broader cultural patterns across the region, especially with regard to the management of conflict, were what made the difference.

CONCLUSION AT CHAPTERS 7 AND 8

This chapter and the previous one have shown a number of ways in which the far north's uneasy and turbulent reputation was, in fact, deserved, and not merely a matter of rhetoric or literary trope. As indicated by court activity in king's bench and offence dates in cases at gaol delivery, for a time patterns of conflict were in part shaped by the effects of war and truce. There is evidence for what might be described as a cross-border raiding culture, and various reminders that one function of elite residences was to be places of security and refuge. Court records show that troublemakers from the border liberties did come before the machinery of the common law as it was extended into these franchises and that, among the gentry of the region, the use of violence in the course of disputes appears to have been intense, particularly with regard to the number of recorded homicides.

For the general question about the far north and differences with areas further south, these broad findings do suggest that the marches were distinctive when compared with what is known about other parts of England. All the same, qualifications and gradations in these points must not be overlooked. The apparent effects of war on litigation in king's bench are no longer traceable from about mid-century onwards, when the effects of national political upheavals come to the fore. The evidence for cross-border raiding tends to be confined to a particular area of concentration, where northern Northumberland adjoined eastern Roxburghshire. The greatest evidence for a high intensity of gentry violence comes from furthest away from the border, in Westmorland. All this suggests a need for caution with how far differentiating aspects of the region are explained by the existence of the border with Scotland orientated towards military defence. Moreover, by no means were governmental structures weak in the far north, and there is a general similarity with rest of England regarding overall patterns of litigation and regarding the manner in which magnates (and kings) could steer local disputes among landowners. We have also seen in these chapters further evidence for the simultaneous operation of systems of border justice and royal justice, and indications that different venues for royal justice, such as the council in the north when first introduced in the 1480s, were readily adopted by landowners. There is also further evidence for Westmorland as the most intriguing county of the marches. Earlier it was noted for its strong sense of gentry kin-consciousness (alongside northern Northumberland); here it stands out again, this time for its disproportionately high levels of violence. The picture emerging is of the marches as a region with certain distinctive features visible through the prism of conflict, but whose distinctiveness was not wholly, or even primarily, driven by proximity to the frontier. Broader cultural patterns appear to be at work, and thus in the next two chapters we turn directly to the theme of the culture of conflict, to explore wider norms of disputing related to 'feud' as they appear in the border counties.

9

DISCORD

> In euery shire with Iakkes and Salades clene
>
> Myssereule doth ryse and maketh neyghbours werre.[1]
>
> —John Hardyng's *Chronicle*

This chapter and the one that follows focus on accustomed practices of conflict management in the far north. We have already seen the simultaneous function and vibrancy of the systems of royal justice and border justice in the marches, and in the latter case observed how it emphasised immediacy of action as much as redress and reparation. Here the intention is to look specifically at the extent to which practice and usage in the course of conflict reflected a wider normative system of disputing other than that provided by the king's law, a system that drew on a similar logic as did march law.[2] In this way specific concern for the type of dispute known as 'feud' comes to the foreground of attention. As we have observed, feud, like raiding and kin-based social organisation, has been assumed to be an essential characteristic of a turbulent march society. The conceptual framework provided at the outset of this book comes into sharp focus here,[3] and it will be helpful to summarise it briefly again: conflict is understood as an overarching category of social tension into which, among other phenomena, falls disputing. Conflict can also be viewed as a fundamental frame in which social relationships are created, tested and shattered, thus defining the very groups which participate in it. A specific dispute between parties can be pursued (or 'processed') using a variety of methods, and the episodes occurring in the course of a dispute draw deeper relationships of conflict to the surface. Once in the open, these relationships can be used, changed or put away again. Feud is a type

---

[1] C. L. Kingsford, 'Extracts from the First Version of Hardyng's Chronicle', *EHR*, 27 (1912), 749.

[2] For 'accustomed practices', see above, pp. 188, 193 and 196.

[3] See above, p. 25. Some European comparisons with England are examined at pp. 168–72.

Discord

of dispute which relies heavily on customary practices of conflict management. We have noted that attempts to construct and wield a general model of feud have proved difficult, and some historians have adopted a fruitful approach to the topic that starts with a working definition, and then looks for related 'feud-like' elements, such as words or processes. Taking that lead, the following assumptions about feud, derived from a wide scholarship on the subject, are offered for the purposes of this study.[4] To put it one way, feud is a relationship of hostility between two groups, stemming from a desire to seek redress by vengeance for some perceived wrong and involving (at least) the threat of reciprocal violence. This hostility, however, also holds the potential to be transformed into a lasting, peaceful relationship.

An amplification of these assumptions illustrates the dispute processes which might be deemed feud-like and which will inform our investigation of accustomed practices of disputing in the northern marches. The importance of emotion is signalled by the relationship of hostility which,[5] although it may begin between individual disputants, often becomes a relationship between opposing groups, usually of roughly balanced power and status, clustering around these principals.[6] The members of these 'support groups' share collective responsibility and liability for the actions of their companions. Of the bonds by which these supporters are recruited, kinship is often seen as the most important, for, although more recent work complicates this picture considerably, strong kinship ties have long been assumed to be a feature of 'primitive' societies where feud is strong and governmental authority is weak. We have already seen that the structures of government were not weak in the far north, but we have also observed that kinship was a strong social force and that attitudes and obligations associated with it overlapped with those of friendship and lordship.[7] A further feud-like element is vengeance, or the forceful taking of redress for a wrong (typically a violent injury), and this is

---

[4] See above, p. 34.

[5] For example, see the 'lengthy mutual hostility' noted in Evans-Pritchard, *The Nuer*, 150. In his distinction between 'customary vengeance' and feud, Halsall, 'Violence and Society', 22, suggests that customary vengeance could be a very short-term phenomenon.

[6] On balanced groups, see Black-Michaud, *Cohesive Force*, 119–207; Boehm, *Blood Revenge*, 167, 189, 224–5, 232, 236–7; White, 'Feuding and Peace-Making', 249–63; Smail, 'Hatred as a Social Institution', 112–13, 118, 120.

[7] See above, p. 23 and Chapter 5. If kinship has been assumed to be the essential social grouping in feuding societies (Bloch, *Feudal Society*, 125–8), it is now understood that kinship can hardly be considered in isolation: Geary, 'Living with Conflicts', 136–9; Wormald, *Lords and Men*, 79–90, esp. 83; Miller, *Bloodtaking*, 139–78, 198; Hyams, *Rancor and Reconciliation*, 4, 7, 9, 23; R.V. Gould, 'Revenge as Sanction and Solidarity Display: An Analysis of Vendettas in Nineteenth-Century Corsica', *American Sociological Review*, 56 (2000), 682, 684, 699.

Part III

essential to many characterisations of feud.[8] The principle of reciprocity implies the potential for a cycle of violent retaliation over time. It also allows for acts of peace to be countered with further acts of violence, and acts of violence with acts of peace,[9] sometimes involving attempts at 'score-keeping'[10] and involving the possibility of iteration ad infinitum.[11] These episodes of violence and peacemaking can call dormant relationships out into the open, especially as support groups are marshalled and enemies are identified.[12] Finally, all of this behaviour is typically hedged in by norms which limit and validate actions and choices, especially marking reasonable and licit violence off from unreasonable chaos. Such norms may remain unwritten, as customary practices, or they may be expressed in written form as law.[13] We have already considered common law and march law in our period of interest but, in shaping normative conduct, to these should also be added the influence of the church and its laws and practices, and of chivalry and its laws and practices, both of which were part of the pan-European experience.[14] This chapter and the next explore wider norms of disputing related to feud as they appear in the border counties. The question is not just about whether the culture of conflict management in the far north was different from further south; given the wider scholarship just reviewed, it is also about how we understand the problem of conflict in late medieval English sources. Thus our focus is on how far practices of violence and peacemaking in the marches offer signs of a feud-like culture of enmity[15] or, put more generally, of a normative system of disputing beyond that which was dominated by the framework of royal justice and familiar extra-judicial practices (such as arbitration) which were intermeshed with that system. The goal is to understand better conflict in the border counties, chiefly through processes of discord and concord and their associated social

---

[8] Hyams takes desire to avenge injury as his starting point for the whole concept: *Rancor and Reconciliation,* ix, 8.

[9] Hyams, *Rancor and Reconciliation,* 9, 16–21, discussing Axelrod, *Evolution of Cooperation,* for which see above, p. 261.

[10] Roberts, *Order and Dispute,* 201; Boehm, *Blood Revenge,* chs 6–8, 138, 173, 218–19; Miller, *Bloodtaking,* 179–81, and 283 on an 'economy of honour'; Black-Michaud, *Cohesive Force,* 31, 36, 63, 78–81, 110–11.

[11] On the theoretical 'interminability' of feud, see Black-Michaud, *Cohesive Force,* 46–50; Boehm, *Blood Revenge,* 191, 199–201, 203, 206, 218–21.

[12] Geary, 'Living with Conflicts', 139; Miller, *Bloodtaking,* 170–220; Halsall, 'Violence and Society', 19–20; Gould, 'Revenge as Sanction and Solidarity Display', 699.

[13] A point well observed for Scotland: Wormald, 'Bloodfeud, Kindred and Government', 54–97; Brown, *Bloodfeud in Scotland,* esp. ch. 9. For England in an earlier period, see Hyams, *Rancor and Reconciliation,* 7, 11, 19, 78–110.

[14] See p. 38.   [15] See p. 35; Hyams, *Rancor and Reconciliation.*

Discord

relationships and language. By extension, it is also to raise questions about conflict in the rest of England.

The present chapter is concerned as much with relationships of hostility, the gathering of supporters and the invocation of legitimacy as it is with actual episodes of violent disputing. The layout of discussion is, first, to begin by examining choice of language and matters of emotion as they were deployed in hostile relationships, for their implications locally and throughout the kingdom. Second, the ties through which disputants found supporters in processes of discord will be examined. Finally, we turn to acts of violence, as defined earlier.[16] Thus far in this analysis the English marches have appeared to be more violent than areas further south. This has been identified as especially the case for Westmorland in relation to quantities and proportions of recorded violent offences. At the same time, we have determined that the effects of cross-border raiding were concentrated in territory close to the frontier line itself.[17] Now we shall investigate the nature of violence in particular disputes, especially certain elements which appear to be feud-like. In this regard the concept of formulaic or 'strategic' violence, that which is kept within a set of norms and targeted to achieve particular goals, is relevant.[18] Throughout, we are looking at processes of discord which, it will be argued, were shaped in part by the frameworks of royal justice, and in part by accustomed practices.

LANGUAGE AND SOCIAL EMOTION

This first section of this chapter pursues an argument which, while being based predominantly upon sources concerning the far north, is not in itself intended to advance any further claims for the distinctiveness of the region from the rest of England. In fact, within this discussion of discord, this section does the opposite. It examines the terminology of conflict in a number of source types, in the documentation generated by the common law but also in a wider range of less formal records. The point to be made here is that the language used to describe conflict and its associated emotions and motivations helps to illuminate how relationships between adversaries were understood, in the far north in the first instance, but also with obvious implications for how such language ought to be examined throughout England.

---

[16] See pp. 28 and 200.   [17] See pp. 234 and 240–1.

[18] Halsall, 'Violence and Society', 17–18, 22, 29 (on 18 he credits C.J. Wickham with the term 'strategic' violence in this sense). Cf. Zmora, *State and Nobility*, 34 (on 'structured conflict').

Part III

The evidence examined for this purpose requires comment. The use of legal records raises the well-known issue of their standardised and formulaic nature, especially in the choice of writ or statute used by a party in pursuit of a claim in court. The precise forms of common law writs served as tools to initiate legal action, and thus with the advice of lawyers litigants were obliged to describe actual events by choosing from among a set of predetermined routes. As a consequence, descriptions of violent events in legal records frequently followed a 'common form'.[19] It was typical throughout England for formulaic terms and phrasings with very specific legal meanings in common law (like 'with force and arms' or 'against the peace') to be sprinkled in personal documents and chancery petitions, an indication of the pervasive influence of the royal judicial system.[20] What is more, correspondence might also contain such phrasings or contain copies of legal documents.[21] In such a way Robert Warcop of Warcop in Westmorland wrote to Sir Robert Plumpton at an unknown date to apologise for his man Umfrey Bell, who had 'trespased to a seruant' of Plumpton's.[22] As a result there is a valid concern that the language examined here could be expected to show little more than the ways in which the common law dominated landowners' thoughts and expressions. However, the evidence assembled in what follows results not from a strict concentration of attention on the wording of common law writs and statute law (such as the specific mechanism of allegations of trespass *vi et armis* which once led historians astray).[23] Rather, it is drawn from a wider base of materials including arbitration documents, chancery petitions, king's bench indictments and plea rolls, and rolls of gaol delivery, as well as a range of non-legal sources. The analysis presented in this section was first developed in my doctoral thesis in an exercise comparing English and Scottish evidence,[24] in part drawing inspiration from work which had shown how publicly acknowledged hatreds served as markers of disputes for medieval antagonists who harnessed courts and

---

[19] Carpenter, *Locality and Polity*, 705–9, quote at 705.

[20] Maddern, *Violence and Social Order*, 22, 68. This is also evident in chancery petitions from the border counties (e.g., C 1/5/57, C 1/6/158, and other examples below). See also, for instance, *CCR 1468–76*, no. 1317, p. 365.

[21] For example: *Paston Letters*, ed. Davis, i, no. 2 (dealing with canon law), 342, pp. 2–4, 559–60; ii, nos. 678, 737, 766, pp. 289–90, 369, 402–6; *Stonor Letters*, nos 16, 71–2, 79–80, 82–3, 91, 182, 220, 332, pp. 99, 151–4, 161–75, 185, 280, 315, 418.

[22] *Plumpton Letters*, no. 98, p. 102. See also letters by Sir William Plumpton's attorney: ibid., nos 27–9, pp. 50–4.

[23] Baker, *Introduction to English Legal History*, 71–5. See above, pp. 199–201.

[24] Armstrong, 'Local Conflict', 263–71.

274

Discord

their records for this purpose in continental contexts.[25] Since then such an approach has been further reinforced by work on felony, anger and the common law in the thirteenth and fourteenth centuries in England. That work in part examines the language of anger as it appears in English legal records (chiefly coroners' rolls and plea rolls) and also in an array of non-legal cultural texts to identify the wider resonances of the language of anger and felony.[26] Of particular importance here is the observation that 'felony' was layered with a specific meaning as a strict category of offence, and yet also with wider contextual meanings, closely associated with malice, and deliberateness and intent.[27] The interplay of these meanings surely went in both directions: from wider contextual meanings inwards to the formulae of the common law, and also from common law terminology outwards to other less formal contexts.[28] In what follows, which is of course concerned with understanding fifteenth-century England from the perspective of the border shires, the point is to explore how language concerning social emotion penetrated into a number of cultural areas, including that of the common law, and shaped what formulaic terms and phrasings were available for the description of discord. In the northern marches, as throughout the rest of the kingdom, the regular basket of terms used to describe conflict included words like 'debate', 'variance', 'strife', 'discord' and 'controversy'. All conveyed hostility, fighting and an absence of harmony and were often used in conjunction with the more legalistic terms 'quarrel', 'action' or 'cause'.[29] In his *Chronicle* Hardyng wrote of 'suche mysreule contecte and eke debate' when exhorting Henry VI to address local turbulence.[30] From here we resume at ground reached

---

[25] Bartlett, 'Mortal Enmities'; Smail, 'Hatred as a Social Institution'; Smail, *Consumption of Justice*, ch. 2; Smail, 'Faction and Feud in Fourteenth-Century Marseille'. See also p. 171.

[26] E. P. Kamali, 'The Devil's Daughter of Hell Fire: Anger's Role in Medieval English Felony Cases', *Law and History Review*, 35 (2017), 155–200; E.P. Kamali, *Felony and the Guilty Mind in Medieval England* (Cambridge, 2019), esp. chs 1–4.

[27] The idea of 'malice aforethought' will be discussed below at pp. 285–90. E. P. Kamali, '*Felonia Felonice Facta:* Felony and Intentionality in Medieval England', *Criminal Law and Philosophy*, 9 (2015), 397–421, at 400–1, 417–18.

[28] On the influence of the law and legal documentation in literary contexts, see the chapters by Holsinger, Steiner and Grady in E. Steiner and C. Barrington, (eds), *The Letter of the Law: Legal Practice and Literary Production in Medieval England* (Cornell, 2002). For a study of themes related to feud in literature, see M. Cichon, *Violence and Vengeance in Middle Welsh and Middle English Narrative: Owein and Ywain and Gawain* (Lewiston, 2009).

[29] For example, see *CCR 1476–85*, no. 129, p. 38; *Cata. Deeds*, iv, 327 (A 8559); CAC, Kendal: WD/Ry/Box 92/nos 91, 92. Latin was seldom used beyond the courts, which employed more specific legal language, such as '*transgressio*'. For an example of Latin/vernacular hybrid, see '*omnimodis accionibus causis querelis debatis & demandis*' (DUL, DCM: Loc. XXVIII, 26).

[30] Kingsford, 'Extracts from the First Version of Hardyng's Chronicle', 749, see also contekoure/s (746, 749). *MED*, s.v. 'contekour' (a quarreller).

275

Part III

in an earlier chapter where the importance of language to a descriptive concept of feud was observed, and also build upon the notion that language helped 'to constitute and shape behaviour as much as passively record it'.[31] In other words, to an extent, language provided the conceptual apparatus within which social activities took place. Attention is thus merited to the words used to describe particular disputes and relationships for what they express of the frameworks by which conflict was understood and of the norms invoked to address it.[32]

The Latin word *guerra* was sometimes used to describe conflict between private parties in the marches. Such was the case in 1465 when the monks of Durham used this word to label the antagonism between the supporters of the Scottish clerks John Hume and Patrick Hume in their dispute over Coldingham in Berwickshire.[33] Scottish historians have tended to translate *guerra* as 'feud'.[34] They have good reason to do so, for late medieval chivalric treatises on the laws of war drew a distinction between *bellum* and *guerra*, usually understood, respectively, as 'public' and 'private' war, and the latter referred to a dispute between nobles in which certain rules applied.[35] There is a related question of whether 'private' war is an appropriate term applied to a mode of conflict that was shaped by law, but that need not detain us.[36] For our purposes what matters is that the use of *guerras* in this example suggests not only that the English monks expected the Scottish adversaries to behave according to acknowledged rules of conduct, as in war, but furthermore that the same monks writing in the vernacular about the same matter noted the 'grete warre and trewbill among certeyn lordes of Scotland as it is said … and in especiall the maliciouse purpose' of the parties concerned.[37] The Englishmen avoided the vernacular term 'fede' and

---

[31] Knights et al., 'Commonwealth', 661. See above, pp. 34–5.

[32] For a related approach to a different topic, see C. Fletcher, 'What Makes a Political Language? Key Terms, Profit and Damage in the Common Petition of the English Parliament, 1343–1422', in J. Dumolyn, J. Haemers, H.R. Oliva Herrer and V. Challet (eds), *The Voices of the People in Late Medieval Europe: Communication and Popular Politics* (Turnhout, 2014), 91–106.

[33] '*propter guerras ibidem noviter exortas*'; '*propter guerras de nouo inter certos dominos regni Scocie*' (DUL, DCM: Reg. IV, fols 162v–163v; *Coldingham*, 196–201); '*propter guerras in regno Scociae noviter subortas*' (Reg. IV, fol. 165r; see also *Coldingham*, 201–6). For context, see Dobson, 'Last English Monks', 1–25.

[34] For example, H.L. MacQueen, 'Survival and Success: the Kennedys of Dunure', in S.I. Boardman and A. Ross (eds), *The Exercise of Power in Medieval Scotland* (Dublin, 2003), 85; S.I. Boardman, 'The Campbells and Charter Lordship in Medieval Argyll', in ibid., 104.

[35] Keen, *Laws of War*, 104, 108–9; Kaminsky, 'The Noble Feud', 55, 74; Bartlett, 'Mortal Enmities', 4–5, 15. On *guerrae* and a definition of seigneurial war, see Firnhaber-Baker, *Violence and the State*, 18–20.

[36] For a critique, see Zmora, *The Feud*, 15.

[37] DUL, DCM: Reg. IV, fols 164r–v; *Coldingham*, 203.

Discord

selected instead 'warre'.[38] This was much in the same sense that Malory deployed the term in his Arthurian retellings at roughly the same time, a sense that can also be detected in disputes from other parts of the realm.[39] A similar usage is also reflected in Hardyng's *Chronicle*, where the author writes of 'neyghbours werre' and uses this terminology as a way to describe violent local strife, as might occur within a shire.[40]

The word 'feud' itself, or 'fede' in Middle English and Scots, is rare in our period.[41] It does occur, however, in late medieval vernacular literature, especially from Scotland and in Scottish legislation of the fifteenth century.[42] In the Anglo-Scottish borders specifically, the earliest use of the word to be found is not before 1453, arising in the context of an indenture between two Roxburghshire landowners, which recorded the potential 'fedis and maugreis' (feuds and malgrés, or malices) which they or their men might incur.[43] This usage suggests the sense of a publicly acknowledged relationship, a state of hostility between groups, which fits our own working definition. In the English marches, the earliest use of 'feud' I have located comes from 1528 and, even then, like the Durham monks' use of *guerras* in 1465, describes a Scottish dispute.[44] The evidence, rather, suggests that 'feud', perhaps like *guerra*, was a term that was especially familiar north of the border.

Words that might be understood to convey emotion were also used to describe disputes. Such 'emotional' language can be valued for what it reveals, not only about the relationship between parties in conflict but also about the motivation behind particular confrontations. By the same token, emotional language used to signal a relationship or to explain a

---

[38] On the Latin word *faidus*, more typical than *guerra* in an earlier period, see Wallace-Hadrill, 'Bloodfeud of the Franks', 461; Halsall, 'Violence and Society', 19, 28. To what extent the development of a European law of arms in the late middle ages caused *faidus* to be supplanted by *guerra* is worth further investigation.

[39] *Malory, Works*, ed. Vinaver, 689 ('the grettist mortall warre that ever was'). See also *PROME*, November 1439, item 31: a Shropshire petitioner complained that his opponent had continually 'made werre unto the saide John, as in lyggyng often tymes in awaite to slee hym'; Carpenter, *Locality and Polity*, 581 (an example from 1494); *Stonor Letters*, no. 190, p. 287 ('opyne warre').

[40] Kingsford, 'Extracts from the First Version of Hardyng's Chronicle', 744, 746 (linked with 'grete malyuolence'), 749.

[41] The origins of the word are in the Frankish '*faithu*', and Old English '*fæhðe*'. See *OED*, s.v. 'feud'; *MED* and *DSL*, s.v. 'fede'.

[42] See works cited in Armstrong, 'Local Conflict', 264, and on legislation, see Armstrong, 'Justice Ayre', 36.

[43] Andrew Kerr of Altonburn to Robert Colville of Oxnam (*HMC, 14th Report*, appendix, part III, 9); *DSL*, s.v. 'malgré' (also meaning spite and enmity). See also *Malory, Works*, ed. Vinaver, 687, 689, 696 ('magré'); Cichon, *Violence and Vengeance*, 202 ('mawgré').

[44] *Letters and Papers, Foreign and Domestic, of the Reign of Henry VIII, 1509–1547*, ed. J.S. Brewer et al. (London, 1862–1910; addenda, London, 1929–32), IV, ii, no. 4134, pp. 1827–9. On feud in the marches, see Goodman, 'Introduction', in Tuck and Goodman (eds), *War and Border Societies*, 10.

Part III

motivation for action may serve to legitimate those same relationships and behaviours. This relies on everyone involved understanding the language used and the meanings invoked.[45] Surviving evidence suggests that certain words in the Anglo-Scottish marches, as elsewhere in medieval Europe, were invested with special significance. For example, 'enmity', adopted into the vernacular from '*inimicitia*', refers both to the emotion of hatred and to a state of mutual hostility. Just as the state of relations between friends ('*amici*') is that of friendship ('*amicitia*', a word of course closely related to '*amor*', or love), the state of relations between enemies ('*inimici*') may be understood as 'enemyship'.[46] Indeed, 'mortal' or 'capital' enmity was a legal concept, widely adopted into European cultures from at least the twelfth century. It denoted 'an objective and public relationship' with emotional and moral imperatives, characterised by rules and ritual.[47] As already noted earlier, one set of studies by Smail concerning late medieval Marseille has illuminated the way in which, in an urban context, publicly acknowledged enmities could function as a social institution. Such 'hatreds' shaped the legal behaviour of parties seeking justice in and out of court, and they could also form the basis of political associations.[48]

References to mortal enmity and, indeed, to mortal enemies are detectable in sources relevant to this investigation. Although vernacular literature has already been mentioned, our aim is not to examine language deployed in literary writing, instructive as that task can be for understanding 'accepted patterns of behaviour'.[49] Nevertheless, even if we confine our efforts to examples of historical writing, it becomes apparent that English audiences would have encountered such ideas. Hardyng's *Chronicle*, for instance, speaks of 'mortall fooes'[50] and 'mortall enemyes'.[51] The existence

---

[45] Rosenwein (ed.), *Anger's Past*; Hyams, *Rancor and Reconciliation*, 34–68; L. Abu-Lughod and C.A. Lutz, 'Introduction: Emotion, Discourse and the Politics of Everyday Life', in L. Abu-Lughod and C.A. Lutz (eds), *Language and the Politics of Emotion* (Cambridge, 1990), 1–23; White, 'The Politics of Anger', 145.

[46] Hyams, *Rancor and Reconciliation*, 22; Geary, 'Living with Conflicts', 144.

[47] Bartlett, 'Mortal Enmities', 1, 5–8, 12–15, quote from 12. See also A. Musin, 'Le droit de vengeance et son déclin dans les Pays-Bas (XIVe–XVIe siècles)', *Krypton*, 5-6 (2015), 9–16; Gauvard, '*De grace espécial*', ii, 686; Hyams, *Rancor and Reconciliation*, 57–9, 209.

[48] See p. 171; Smail, *Consumption of Justice*, ch. 2; Smail, 'Faction and Feud in Fourteenth-Century Marseille'. See also the sense of 'unfriendship' or 'unkinship' in Smail, 'Hatred as a Social Institution', 90.

[49] Cichon, *Violence and Vengeance*, 219 (quote). Malory's 'The Vengeance of Sir Gawain' (*Malory, Works*, ed. Vinaver, 685–700) is replete with such language ('I am thy mortall foo', 688; 'ever to be my mortall foo', 696). More generally on law, society and literature, see Steiner and Barrington, (eds), *The Letter of the Law*, introduction.

[50] *Chron. Hardyng*, 104 (quote); also 234 'mortall fo'.

[51] *Chron. Hardyng*, 271 (quote); also 140 'enemie moost mortall'.

Discord

of a state of enmity between adversaries, sometimes described as 'cruell enmitee', also features in his narrative account, which is very much the product of a northern author with direct experience of life in the marches.[52] And yet this was no regional oddity. A comparable terminology may also be detected in the *English Chronicle*, which is not a 'northern' source. That text too mentions 'mortall and extreme enemyes' and variations on the theme.[53] Although it does not feature in studies of late medieval landed society, equivalent language is also to be found in other English contexts, such as in disputes in London in 1390 and Norwich in 1485.[54] It is evident with reference to princely relations and diplomacy,[55] although not confined to princes alone,[56] for it featured in regard to the sour relationship between English merchants and the Hanse in 1435.[57] A particularly colourful illustration of such language in diplomatic exchange arises from the English embassy sent to Scotland in 1430 to discuss a marriage between Henry VI and a daughter of James I. The ambassadors' instructions from the council were to seek a peace prior to any nuptials, for:

it ne were in any wyse convenable the Kyng to stande in mortal ennemytee and werre with him whos doughter he had receyved and taken to wyf and madd him as by that meene his fader [and otherwise] it were not accordyng to the seuretee of the Kyng person to felawship by wey of matrimonie with her whos fader were his mortel adversarie and ennemye.[58]

What counts most for present purposes is that enmities are to be found in disputes in the northern marches and in sources that might be expected to reveal comparable findings elsewhere in England. Here, much as Smail makes clear for Marseille, hatred was part of a 'language of

---

[52] *Chron. Hardyng*, 429 (quote); also 422, 'drede none enmytee'; 400, 'compassed enmyte'; 219, 'drede of enmyte'; and 107, 'thei shuld espie emong the enemytee / by their frendes ... shuld let hym witte, there malice to vnderstande'.

[53] *English Chron.*, 84 (quote); also 72, 'a mortall debate and a variaunce bitwene ... theyre mortal enemy'; 91, 'oure mortall enemyes, the whyche by theyre venymous malice haue'.

[54] *PROME*, November 1390, item 36; ibid., November 1391, items 34–5; ibid., November 1485, item 61.

[55] The duke of Gloucester wrote in 1440 of the 'naturel were' between the dukes of Orleans and Burgundy, 'for the murdre of thair faders, and a capital enmyte like to have endured for ever': J. Stevenson, (ed.), *Letters and Papers Illustrative of the Wars of the English in France during the Reign of Henry the Sixth,* 2 vols in 3 (London, 1864), II, ii, 445. See also Keen, 'Treason Trials', 97; *PROME,* October 1383, item 4; ibid., April 1463, item 8; ibid., October 1472, first roll, item 8; ibid., October 1472 (1474–5), third roll, items 7, 10, 43.

[56] See Chapter 6. A '*maxima inimicia*' has already been noted, from English Gascony.

[57] In 1435 English merchants complained that the Hanseatic towns had put them out of their protection as their 'mortal enemyes' (*PROME,* October 1435, item 27). For context, see E.E. Power and M.M. Postan (eds), *Studies in English Trade in the Fifteenth Century* (London, 1933), 117.

[58] *PPC,* iv, 19–27, at 23.

279

Part III

emotions' which was used 'to characterise social bonds and social divisions' motivating active legal confrontations.[59] In 1398 a Newcastle jury found three men guilty of the several livestock thefts for which they had been indicted, but allowed the men the sanctuary of the town's Carmelite friary. The offenders alleged that they had been in that sanctuary but that by '*suos inimicos manu forti*', and against their will, they had been returned to the custody of the Newcastle gaoler, William Page. With this account the jurors concurred but found that the prisoners had evaded gaol in the first place. Here the identities of the '*inimicos*' remained unspecified, but the general narrative of the existence and action of enemies was clearly accepted.[60] A richer illustration comes from a case between the gentlemen Nicholas Turpyn of Whitchester and Thomas Whitley of Tynemouth, two Northumberland coroners concerned in the death of a minor border official. It would seem that in June 1420 one of Turpyn's servants killed the former bailiff of the east march who had served under John, duke of Bedford. Hatred featured as part of the claims made during the course of the dispute, for Turpyn petitioned the king to allege that he had been wrongly indicted in the affair by his '*enemys mortelx*'; the petition was directed to the council for a decision and copied into the plea roll recording the case.[61] Another example comes in reference to the cross-border dispute over the priory of Coldingham in the mid-1460s. In addition to the '*guerras*' just mentioned, a declaration by a Durham monk cited enduring '*inimicicias capitales*' among the inhabitants of both realms as one of his reasons for not crossing into Scotland to execute papal letters against his opponents in the affair.[62] Such occurrences suggest that hostile relationships defined by mortal enmities were not merely the colourful conceit of chroniclers seeking to build a narrative of events but useful descriptions of a category of social discord.

One expected consequence of such inimical relationships was revenge. Like enmities, 'vengeaunce' was part of the vocabulary of Hardyng's historical writing.[63] Similar usage is to be found in the *English Chronicle*, colourfully in the record there of the Yorkist manifesto of June 1460

---

[59] Smail, *Consumption of Justice*, 90–1.

[60] JUST 3/184 rot. 15. One of the offending prisoners was Robert de Hall.

[61] See pp. 213, 246–7, and 250–1. The dead bailiff was Walter Michelson. By June 1421 the council had decided in Turpyn's favour. In 1424 Whitley was removed from office on account of being 'too sick' (KB 9/213 mm. 58, 59; KB 9/216/2 mm. 4, 5; KB 27/646 *rex* rots 25, 25d, quote from rot. 25(a); *CCR 1419–22*, 152, 212, 247; *CCR 1422–9*, 90). See p. 141 for Turpyn and the Redes.

[62] '*propter . . . inimicicias capitales inter utriusque regni incolas continue durantes*' (DUL, DCM: Reg. IV, fols 162v–163v; *Coldingham*, 196–201). This language was nothing new: Reginald of Durham wrote of '*mortales adversarios*' in Teviotdale in the twelfth century (*Reginaldi Monachi Dunelmensis*, ed. J. Raine (1835), 290).

[63] *Chron. Hardyng*, 12, 19, 48, 56 'malicious . . . vengeaunce', 84n, 173, 176, 397; and 40 'reuenge'.

Discord

('shewe the largenesse of theyre vyolence and malyce as vengeably as they can')[64] and elsewhere in the text.[65] Parliamentary legislation concerning false appeals and indictments noted that men took such wrongful actions motivated by *'malice, enmyte, et vengeaunce'* (1419, 1420, 1421, 1439) or *'pur lour singuler vengeaunce, et nient do droit'* (1429).[66] Although 'vengeance' is not to be found mentioned in such explicit terms elsewhere in our present source base, it was not unknown among Englishmen in law courts elsewhere.[67] Words similar to enmity might also signal the feud-like status of a dispute, by drawing open attention to emotion (and thus to the associated behaviours which it might motivate, chiefly violent action): 'rancor', 'malice', 'odium' and 'ire' fit the bill.[68] In sources relating to local conflict in the marches, such words are most evident in quarrels among great magnates. This was the level of society most likely to be influenced by international and chivalric concepts. In 1405 Christiana Dunbar, countess of March, at that time in English allegiance with her husband, Earl George, wrote to Henry IV for aid. She made plain that the Dunbars bore great enmity (*'nous portons graunt enemyte'*) for the death of Sir Henry 'Hotpsur' Percy at the battle of Shrewsbury and that Percy's followers wished for Dunbar and his men to be dead and for the king's consent to act upon the malice in their hearts (*'pour alors faire la malice qui est forme en leurs coers'*).[69] The aftermath of Shrewsbury also led to tension between the earls of Northumberland and Westmorland, and similar language was used to describe their dispute.[70] Just as with mortal enmity, there are examples to be found of the language of 'jnvy and ill will' motivating 'grete hurtz and harmz', from among the local gentry in the marches, at a social level which also participated in European chivalric culture but whose direct continental

---

[64] *English Chron.*, 85.

[65] *English Chron.*, 86, 'dredyng the malyce ... of the forseyde Erll ... lest he wolde exercyse his vengeaunce'; 100, 'redy forto go with hym into the north to venge the dethe of the noble Duke Richard, hys fadre'.

[66] *PROME*, October 1419, item 17; ibid., December 1420, item 24 (*'par malice enmitee vengeaunce et pur covetise'*); ibid., May 1421, item 30; ibid., September 1429, item 50; ibid., November 1439, item 48. See also *'graund et outrageous vengeance'*, in Cambs.: ibid., September 1429, item 37.

[67] See the suit between Englishmen in northern France in 1426 recording one party's *'mal content et pensa comment il s'en vengeroit'*, cited earlier at p. 171.

[68] They are to be found in *Chron. Hardyng*, 57, 95, 107 and 104 'they wer full odyous, passyng yrefull, and full malicious ... they slewe theim all, through crueltee and hate'. 'Malice' appears to be more evident in the *English Chron.*, 23, 68, 76, 77, 79, 97, 86, 91.

[69] BL: MS Cotton Vespasian, F VII, fol. 96, no. 2, printed in J. Pinkerton, *The History of Scotland*, 2 vols (London, 1797), i, appendix, 450. I wish to acknowledge Anik Beaudoin, Paul Huggins and Yann Dahhaoui for their help with this text in 2006. Violence erupted (in Lincolnshire) in 1407 between Dunbar's men and their English enemies: *Select Cases*, ed. Sayles, no. 43, pp. 187–9.

[70] *PROME*, January 1404, item 18.

Part III

contacts may have been more limited than those of great lords.[71] Illustrative of this are two chancery petitions from the mid-1410s made by a Westmorland esquire, complaining that his opponents, acting out of '*lours ditz malice*', had attacked his house, loudly threatening to slay him, and had pursued him as far as London to accomplish their goal.[72] In these cases 'malice' conveys a sense of anger or hatred and, like enmity, heralds the relationship between the parties. Of course, its usage was not exclusively to signal personal hatreds, for it is also familiar from the language of international martial confrontation, as in exhortations to '*resiste le malice*' of '*les Enemys descoce*'.[73] In this context malice and wickedness have recently been placed in the context of wider 'discourse of abuse' against enemies.[74] However, the examples cited here show how it was applied in interpersonal confrontations among landowners. It also occurred before the municipal courts at York in an entry certifying English birth.[75] A cognate word, 'ire', occurs in a letter sent by the prior of Durham across the border to a Scottish laird in 1442, asking him to intervene in a dispute between two other Scottish landowners, that lest 'the fyre of ire kyndild betwixt thaym grow to fer [too bold], as yhe hafe begun yhe will labour to staunch'.[76] The colourful imagery of the heart and fire sometimes used with these words explained the intense motivation of the parties and signalled the special status of the dispute.[77]

Comparable emotional language can be found at an even lower social level. Two trials for homicide at gaol delivery, one heard in 1406 in Cumberland[78] and one heard in 1411 in Northumberland,[79] show a

---

[71] From a dispute of 1472 in Cumberland (CAC, Carlisle: D/HGB/1/221A).

[72] The esquire was John Helton of Burton and his adversaries were Thomas Warcop of Sandford, and Richard Wharton. C 1/6/282 (the first petition): '*lours ditz malice les ditz malfesours a celle tempe hautement disant et clamantz que le dit suppliant seront tue en quel lieu qil seront troue et ycelle malice et manasse vncore maliceousment continuont de iour en autr*'; C 1/6/196 (the petition delivered in London by Helton in person): '*coment lez ditz malefesours enchaserount et ensuerount le dit suppliant del sa meason suisdit tanque a londres pur luy avoir tuee*'. Both petitions are datable to 1413–17; for comment, see Storey, 'Disorders in Lancastrian Westmorland', 71–3.

[73] Chrimes, 'Letters of John of Lancaster', at 21; see also 26.

[74] Ruddick, *English Identity*, 143–50, quote from 148.

[75] Certification for a York resident who 'was notyd and diffamyd of the chylder of iniquite be veray malesse, that he shud be a Skotte and no Ynglysman': *York Civic Records*, i, 17.

[76] DUL, DCM: Reg. Parv. II, fols 154r–v, printed in *Coldingham*, pp. 136–8, no. 152.

[77] Armstrong, 'The Fyre of Ire Kindild'.

[78] JUST 3/191 rot. 58; Cbl. session of 7 August 1406; William Sharpp, 'tailour', for the felonious killing at Wetheral ['Wedrehill'] of Thomas de Pebels on 26 January 1405. The jurors said that Thomas '*ex odio antiquo quod habuit erga prefatum Willelmum cum quodam arma vocato carlelax quod habuit in manibus suis in eundem Willelmum insultum fecit*'.

[79] JUST 3/191 rots 52–52d; Nbl. session of 27 August 1411; John Smyth of Ovington ['Owyngton', near Prudhoe] for the felonious killing at Ovington of Nicholas Taliour on 20 June 1406. The jurors said that Nicholas '*ex odio antiquo quod habuit erga predictam Johannem cum quodam arma vocato*

Discord

striking use of the Latin '*odium*'. In both cases the accused man (one almost certainly of yeoman status, the other a craftsman) was indicted for felonious killing and pleaded not guilty. The trial juries offered the standard self-defence narrative to explain the killing, so that the men were remanded to prison, later to obtain pardons. However, both juries added the extraordinary detail that the dead assailants had made their attacks '*ex odio antiquo*' – out of old hatred – which suggests that the jury believed that the story of the assault, and the plea of self-defence, became more credible, even legitimate, when placed in the context of an ongoing dispute motivated by old enmity (perhaps even 'old feud'). But one wonders why they bothered, for it was quite normal in common law courts to distinguish between pardonable and serious homicide.[80] It is possible, however, that the actual events behind these cases looked very little like self-defence. It is tempting to explain these extra words as an effort to shoehorn a known feud into the rigid judicial system, in order to achieve a pardon for a revenge killing that was held as licit in local eyes, or at least considered worthy of extra-curial compromise rather than hanging. At the very minimum, they show that local juries were prepared to recognise the existence of old hatreds causing lethal violence and to use this itinerant court as a means to put a state of hostility on open record.[81] Although these two occurrences are the only examples of this type detected in the marches in our period, a wider context in which to understand them may be identified. The records of the city of York reveal comparable phraseology in a proclamation of 1476 ahead of the visit of the duke of Gloucester and the earl of Northumberland which ordered 'that no man make nor pike any quarrel for any olde rancour, malice, matier or cause heretofore doone'.[82] In 1482 Gloucester sent his treasurer's servant before the mayor of York to be punished for having 'of olde rancour and evil will' sheltered an offender.[83] And more to the point of this present section, neither was this an exclusively 'northern' phenomenon. Similar cases of old rancour have been noted elsewhere in

---

    dagger extracto quod habuit in membris suis in eundem Johannem insultum fecit'. A pardon (1412) is recorded in *CPR 1408–13*, 498.

[80] T.A. Green, *Verdict According to Conscience: Perspectives on the English Criminal Trial Jury, 1200–1800* (Chicago, 1985), 30.

[81] See above, pp. 177, 191–3. On *odium*, see Hyams, 'Feud in Medieval England', 6n 15; Hyams, *Rancor and Reconciliation*, 193–4, 247. Cf. Smail, 'Hatred as a Social Institution', 102–3. I appreciate having discussed these cases with Neil Coates in 2006.

[82] *York Civic Records,* i, 2–3.

[83] *York Civic Records,* i, 54. A royal letter later that same year was received in support of John Eglesfield, who had been unjustly punished 'thrugh the malice and evill wille' of his opponent (ibid., 49).

283

Part III

the fourteenth and fifteenth centuries.[84] Furthermore, language of this sort, concerning a London craftsman's 'firy heet and brennyng rancour' and his 'grete ire' against another man, was recorded by the Merchant Taylors' Company in 1492.[85] It also helps to illuminate the English ordinances for war in France set under Richard II and Henry V. Among these regulations was the provision that no man shall 'make no debat, nor contek, for eny hate of tyme past, ne for tyme to come, for the which hate if any man be dede for such contek or debate, he or they [that be implicated in the death, shall be hanged]'.[86] Even if the intention in this last example was to punish homicides motivated by enmity, it seems English armies, cities, magnates and kings were aware of and willing to recognise the existence of such hatreds, which look very much like those expressed by the local juries in the marches in 1406 and 1411. To reiterate the point, these examples are put forward to suggest that, in both the far north and also by extension in a wider national setting, the language of social emotion in connection with disputes served to mark out hostile relationships which carried some degree of legitimate social status. This language, of anger and hatred especially, resonated as much with the technical terminology of the common law as with wider non-legal cultural contexts.[87] These were terms associated with feud that have been identified in studies of various other European jurisdictions (including Scotland), readily used in a range of English sources.[88] In pointing out such usage, the immediate claim, therefore, is not that the far north was distinctive from the rest of England in this particular regard. Rather, such terminology in the region suggests feud-like customs at work. By extension, that the same terminology calls for renewed consideration when it appears elsewhere in England.

This discussion of language and social emotion merits further comment on malicious motivation for homicide in order to advance our

---

[84] J.M. Kaye, 'The Early History of Murder and Manslaughter' (parts 1 and 2), *Law Quarterly Review*, 83 (1967), 365–95, 569–601, at 376–7 (including a case from 1397); Green, 'Societal Concepts of Criminal Liability for Homicide', 690 (case from 1310), 692 (case from 1409). W.G. Hoskins, *The Midland Peasant: The Economic and Social History of a Leicestershire Village* (London, 1957), 78 quotes from a similar case (1336). See also Kamali, 'The Devil's Daughter of Hell Fire', 159, 188.

[85] *The Merchant Taylors' Company of London: Court Minutes 1486–1493*, ed. M. Davies (Stamford, 2000), 217.

[86] A. Curry, 'The Military Ordinances of Henry V: Texts and Contexts', in C. Given-Wilson, A. Kettle and L. Scales (eds), *War, Government and Aristocracy in the British Isles, c. 1150–1500* (Woodbridge, 2008), concordance 'i', 242.

[87] See in particular the work of Kamali, introduced above, p. 275.

[88] See above, pp. 32–5, 170–2 and 270–3. For examples from other jurisdictions, see Boardman, 'Politics and the Feud'; Netterstrøm, 'Feud in Late Medieval and Early Modern Denmark'; Zmora, *State and Nobility*; Kaminsky, 'The Noble Feud'; Bartlett, 'Mortal Enmities'; Smail, 'Hatred as a Social Institution'.

Discord

understanding of all this evidence and its wider implications. It points down an exciting path first cut by Maitland, regarding legislation on the classification of homicide in France (1356), Scotland (1369, 1373, 1469) and England (1390). All these statutes were informed by biblical text, isolated the issue of premeditated assault by ambush and 'malice aforethought' as defining characteristics of the most serious types of killing, and were concerned with restricting the availability of pardons for such offences.[89] For England, much of the history of the law of homicide has turned on the statute of 1390, which set out that no pardons should be allowed *'pur murdre mort de homme occys par agait assaut ou malice purpense treson ou rape de femme'*.[90] It seems clear enough that the statute was a statement of ambition for good justice; it was passed at a point in the reign of Richard II when the king wished to promise a new start for his rule. Parliament received petitions complaining about pardons granted for felonies which lords obtained for their followers. Thus the provision of a new law which set out severely to restrict the categories of homicide for which pardon might be obtained was part of a wider determination for better justice.[91] It also brought England up to date with contemporary claims made for access to pardons in France and Scotland.[92] As regards the law of homicide, the established view of this statute is that it was an expansive and comprehensive statement of different types of killing that were to be non-pardonable.[93] The ancient word 'murder' has been shown to have arisen as a term of art during the preceding decade, reintroduced by the peace commission of 1380 into indictments to denote 'secret or stealthy killing', and re-emphasised in 1390.[94] (Only in the sixteenth century would murder assume its lasting English legal meaning, alongside manslaughter, as one of two categories

---

[89] The wider implications of this legislation in all three realms merit a comparative investigation that cannot be allowed here. F.W. Maitland, 'Early History of Malice Aforethought', in *The Collected Papers of Frederic William Maitland*, ed. H.A.L. Fisher, 3 vols (Cambridge, 1911), i, 304–28. By the sixteenth century, Scottish indictments directly linked serious homicides to 'old feud': W.D.H. Sellar, 'Forethocht Felony, Malice Aforethought and the Classification of Homicide', in Gordon and Fergus (eds), *Legal History in the Making*, 43–59.

[90] Quoted in Green, *Verdict According to Conscience*, 75n 29; see also 30 for simple, culpable, excusable and justifiable homicide.

[91] Harriss, *Shaping the Nation*, 468, 474–5. See also Kaye, 'The Early History of Murder', 365–95, at 378; Green, *Verdict According to Conscience*, 33, 73–5.

[92] Armstrong, 'The Justice Ayre', 27. I argue that supplemental information as to wounds, cruelty and secrecy in Scottish homicide cases was useful to assist with setting fines and compensation paid through the system of pardon. Scotland in the 1490s seems to have had two main categories of homicide: *interfectio* and *precogitata felonia*.

[93] Kaye, 'The Early History of Murder', 395; Maddern, *Violence and Social Order*, 120.

[94] Kaye, 'The Early History of Murder', 377, 379, 386–7.

285

Part III

of culpable homicide.[95]) Our present interest is chiefly in the significance of the language of emotion used in relation to homicide in common law, such as the statutory term *malice purpense* and its variants, including *malicia precogitata*. Scholarly discussion has focused upon how many categories of culpable homicide were already recognised by 1390 and how many operated in practice in its aftermath, and upon the extent to which the phrasing *ex malicia precogitata* in indictments denoted deliberateness or actual premeditation.[96] Some have argued that it could refer to true premeditation but that 'everything depended upon context',[97] and even the holder of the strictest view in favour of 'deliberateness' also acknowledges that *malicia precogitata* was relevant to motive.[98] It has been shown that the two main categories of culpable homicide which operated after 1380 and into the early decades of the fifteenth century were identified by the terms '*felonice interfecit*' and '*felonice interfecit et murdravit*' and that the actual specification of malice aforethought was rare.[99] In summary, a wide range of phrases was available to litigants and clerks to ascribe to killings the characteristics of culpable homicide which might be used 'for further effect' in crafting allegations.[100] It is also clear that despite the legislation, pardons were widely available to offenders, and above all significant power rested with the self-informing trial jury which had the crucial role of applying the law and exercising leniency through returning verdicts of acquittal.[101]

It is worth considering the '*murdre mort de homme occys par agait assaut ou malice purpense*' of the 1390 statute and attitudes to homicide in a wider register than the technical legal sense just observed. The view from the church is instructive. Whereas in the later middle ages the common law classification of homicide was concerned more with the different types of *actus reus* than gradations of *mens rea*, the canonists of the period took the opposite approach.[102] In canon law a wide variety of types of homicide existed. They were primarily divided into spiritual and corporeal homicide, but were then further subdivided into numerous categories and

---

[95] For a recent treatment of homicide in sixteenth and seventeenth centuries, see Kesselring, *Making Murder Public,* esp. 19–32; T.A. Green, 'The Jury and the English Law of Homicide, 1200–1600', *Michigan Law Review,* 74 (1976), 413–99, at 472.

[96] Kaye, 'The Early History of Murder', 386–7, 388–9, 389–90, 394–5; Green, 'Societal Concepts of Criminal Liability for Homicide', 691–4; Maddern, *Violence and Social Order,* 89–90, 119–20.

[97] Green, 'Societal Concepts of Criminal Liability for Homicide', 691 (quote); Green, 'The Jury and the English Law of Homicide', 463n 182.

[98] Kaye, 'The Early History of Murder', 376 (see also 372, 374).

[99] Kaye, 'The Early History of Murder', 389–90, 394–5.

[100] Maddern, *Violence and Social Order,* 90, 120.   [101] Green, *Verdict According to Conscience,* 22–7.

[102] Kaye, 'The Early History of Murder', 367–8. And now see Kamali, '*Felonia Felonice Facta*', 403, 418–19; Kamali, 'The Devil's Daughter of Hell Fire', esp. 196.

Discord

corresponding degrees of guilt. Churchmen of c. 1400 were concerned especially with the problem of intent, and they explained the motivation for offences in terms of sin, such as *ira* and wrath.[103] One treatise, a spiritual dialogue written early in the fifteenth century, has much to say on the topic and has been used to underpin ideas relevant to all of England in the period. This text, *Dives and Pauper*, examines the ten commandments, and its commentary on *non occides* is the fulsome work of a friar asserting a moral framework for the fifth commandment.[104] In the work the character Pauper notes that 'sumtyme manslaute is done be hate & enmyte. As whan a man is slayn maliciouslych of his enmye.'[105] In several other instances, this text reveals a similar variety of terms for homicide to that encountered with the technical language of the common law, and a strong view on hate and vengeance as motives for killing. For example, three manners of wrongful killing are described by Pauper, one including a man 'slayn be enmyte & hate & cruelte, for to han venchance'.[106] And further on revenge, Pauper warns that 'venchancys comounly folwyn euery murde, for murde may nout ben hyd but [night] & day it askith venchance'.[107] Furthermore, in a discussion of temporal punishment, the author draws attention to the biblical passage Exodus 21:14 relating to the consequences for killing by ambush or lying in wait, one of the categories of homicide set out in 1390 as '*mort de homme occys par agait*'.[108] The passage sets out the divine command that no sanctuary should be had for a man who kills his neighbour by lying in wait for him. Maitland noted the significance of Exodus 21:14 to the cross-national legislation restricting pardons for homicide in the fourteenth century, and its place as a text of canon law.[109] Indeed, for the author of *Dives and Pauper* this, not parliamentary statute, was the relevant context in which to discuss punishment for killing by ambush.

The author of *Dives and Pauper* in his discussion of homicide acknowledges wrath and hate motivating some killings but sees such motivation

---

[103] J. Shaw, 'Corporeal and Spiritual Homicide, the Sin of Wrath, and the "Parson's Tale"', *Traditio*, 38 (1982), 281–300, at 283–4, 285–6, 293–7.

[104] *Dives and Pauper,* ed. Barnum, II, xxv, identifying the author as a friar employed in a magnate household. The text is also examined in Maddern, *Violence and Social Order*, 75ff.

[105] *Dives and Pauper,* ed. Barnum, I, ii, 36, where it is also stated that 'to slay a man 'for hate, wretthe & enmyte or for fals couetyse, it is alwey vnleful'. Prayer without devotion is said to include 'whan men preyn [against] charite, as for to han venchance of her enmyys' (21).

[106] *Dives and Pauper,* ed. Barnum, I, ii, 13.

[107] *Dives and Pauper,* ed. Barnum, I, ii, 32. See also wrath and hate (1, 38), malice (30, 33, 46–7, 53), vengeance (15, 30, 35, 36–7, 53) and cruelty (18, 35, 38).

[108] *Dives and Pauper,* ed. Barnum, I, ii, 33. On ambush, see Kaye, 'The Early History of Murder', 379, 388. See above, p. 233.

[109] Maitland, 'Early History of Malice Aforethought', 325–6.

Part III

as illegitimate. The author's acknowledgement of these motives served at once to condemn them and to confirm that they actually existed. In examining when homicide may be justifiable, the author makes an express comparison between just killing and just war, noting St Augustine's doctrine that (together with right cause and right authority) war must be fought for the right intent (*animus*) to be legitimate.[110] But he also recognises that not all wars are just, as not all killings are just. There is an ambiguity in this discussion. Here the author of *Dives and Pauper* makes reference to two sorts of law ordained by God, observing that there is 'the lawe of swerd & of cheualrye to bryngyn hem to pes with the swerd that wil nout obeyyn to the pes by the lawe of charite & of resoun'.[111] The former is legitimate only under certain conditions: battle should be undertaken 'for non malyce for to ben venchyd ne for non cruelte & lykynge to schadyn blood'.[112] Thus it seems for the author there are two possible modes of justice, the law of the sword and chivalry, and the law of charity and reason.[113] Both could be used to deliver God's will, but the latter was the first resort, and what counted was rightful intent and motivation in either case. Although malice, enmity and vengeance were nevertheless wrongful motivations for killing, the author recognised them as real enough.

So, all this is to propose that these ideas were relevant to how motivations for killing were understood in fifteenth-century England. In this regard the *malice purpense* of the 1390 statute might be understood as relevant not only to bare questions of intent but also, depending on context, to whether the action of killing arose from an openly acknowledged enmity between offender and victim. One term might capture multiple shades of meaning. It is of course possible that the use of phrases like *ex malicia precogitata* or *ex odio antiquo* constituted merely a 'ritualistic assertion' to indicate deliberateness or to assist in a claim of self-defence.[114] But from the brief review undertaken here these phrases look more like part of a grammar of social emotions for communicating the attributes of conflict, for signalling their importance to interested parties and, ultimately, for navigating towards a satisfactory outcome. This may be especially relevant to understanding the examples of feud-like 'old rancour' arising from beyond the marches in York, which were noted above and were not

---

[110] *Dives and Pauper,* ed. Barnum, I, ii, 55. [111] *Dives and Pauper,* ed. Barnum, I, ii, 54.

[112] *Dives and Pauper,* ed. Barnum, I, ii, 55.

[113] Chivalry was thus a set of practices which participated in the language of malice and enmity. It was not the source of this framework of ideas. Indeed, what look like open enmities are apparent in the Old Testament, as in Deuteronomy 19:4, 6, 11 (*odium*).

[114] Green, 'The Jury and the English Law of Homicide', 454 (quote); Green, 'Societal Concepts of Criminal Liability for Homicide', 691.

Discord

simply used to mechanise self-defence claims in court. Considering such usage in an England-wide context helps us to understand the terminology used in legal cases in the far northern counties. The statute of 1390, much like *Dives and Pauper*, asserted that various categories of homicide were illegitimate and unpardonable. But their identification – '*murdre*' (secret killing), killing by ambush (or assault) and killing '*par . . . malice purpense*' – acknowledged and confirmed their existence. Strictly, we might expect that the law of 1390 meant that no pardons were to be had for such cases in our period. Yet throughout the far north in the fifteenth century, there was a strong propensity to pardon or acquit what were formally non-pardonable homicides identified by premediated malice. This can be seen in the gaol delivery rolls, in which just two cases gave the particulars '*felonice et ex malicia precogitata interfecit*'; both ended with pardons for the accused.[115] Another case specifying '*felonice et ex malicia precognita murdravit et interfecit*' ended with an acquittal,[116] and a fourth with a more elaborate allegation was thrown out on grounds of insufficiency.[117] In the king's bench indictments and plea rolls sampled here, such terminology appears in connection with the *Causa de Heron*[118] and with the revenge killing of Giles Thornton, which will be discussed below.[119] Certain other homicide cases, including the Turpyn–Whitley affair mentioned above,[120] specified premeditated felony or assault even if they did not deploy the term malice.[121] None of these cases, many of them high-profile affairs, can be shown to have resulted in a conviction.[122] Moreover, a number of pardons relating to other disputes may be found which specify allegations of malice aforethought or malice of one's enemies.[123] It is here, in the application of the law in practice, that a contrast emerges with parts of England further south, where the conviction rate for *all* homicides was notably higher.

---

[115] JUST 3/191 rot. 53; JUST 3/191 rot. 55d.   [116] JUST 3/211 rot. 50.

[117] JUST 3/199 rot. 18: '*ex malicia sua precogitata et armata potencia congregatis sibi diversis aliis viris in insidiis iacuerunt ad verbandum siue ad interficiendum*'.

[118] KB 27/678 *rex* rot. 29d; KB 27/681 *rex* rot. 4: '*felonice et proditorie interficiendum et murdrandum . . . ex malicia precogitata felonice et proditorie*'. The case progressed to reconciliation out of court.

[119] KB 9/345 m. 9: '*ex eorum falsa malicia precogitata vi et armis . . . felonice interficiendum et murdrandum*'. The case appears to have reached compromise out of court.

[120] KB 27/646 *rex* rot. 25: '*felonice murdrarunt et interfecerunt . . . ex felonia sua precogitata*'. See also KB 9/213 m. 59; KB 9/216/2 m. 5. The royal council ordered the case to be discarded.

[121] KB 27/742 rot. 26 (the appeal by Agnes, widow of John Salkeld, a case which remained unresolved for some five decades, KB 27/933 *rex* rot. 14); KB 27/861 *rex* rot. 15 (released on a signet letter). See also a similar case (albeit from Middlesex, KB 27/917 rot. 37) concerning the killing of Thomas Pennington, a member of Henry VII's household and brother of Sir John Pennington of Muncaster; this ended in acquittal.

[122] See also the killing of Robert Robynson at Carlisle in 1494: KB 9/402 m. 94: '*ex malicia precogitata*'; KB 27/933 rots 10, 55l; outcome unknown.

[123] *CPR 1408–13*, 217, 289; *CDS*, IV, 161; *CPR 1436–41*, 545, and the related case at JUST 3/191 rot. 62.

289

Part III

While that comfortably aligns with the conclusions drawn in an earlier chapter,[124] it need not impede the wider argument of this section, which is about language and terminology rather than verdicts.

Thus we may expand upon existing conclusions about legal language and homicide law relevant to all of England. Whereas some have rightly emphasised the role of context in the use of particular terminology, and the wide scope of the jury to describe the sort of act which had been committed,[125] we might add to this the expectation that local juries recognised social emotions (hatred, enmity, malice) shaping conflictual relationships and directing behaviours, even validating them. In turn, this was also part of a wider discourse of sin, shaped to some extent by the spiritual advice of friars and parish priests.[126] The evidence surveyed here for language and social emotion suggests that 'mortal enmity' and related words signalled, across levels of social status from the yeomanry upwards, gravely violent and feud-like disputes enjoying a degree of legitimacy. Thus the parson of Workington petitioned the chancellor in 1402 about the menace of his violent foes, led by a Cumberland esquire who had attacked him in his church, and of their malice which grew '*plus habundant de iour en autre*' until they had waited at Egremont '*en fourme de guerre giseront sur le haute chemyn en agait*' to kill or maim him, from which ambush he had only narrowly managed to flee. Not only was this framed with information relevant to an accusation of felony, but the reference to growing malice also signalled a special enmity.[127] For disputants themselves, and for the jurors often involved in the shaping of allegations, giving mention of hatred, enmity or malice could communicate the gravity of a dispute to wider audiences and, at the very least, turn the mechanisms of the king's judicial system into a formal record of such social particulars. It would seem that, through a resonant vocabulary, a customary framework other than that of the king's justice was invoked with such language. And finally, to reiterate once more, the claim of this section to find feud-like elements in disputing language in the marches is not for the distinctiveness of the region. Indeed, the wider context in which this language is considered suggests that this was more than a local

---

[124] See above, pp. 177–8. Maddern, *Violence and Social Order,* 117, 133, notes a one-third rate of death sentences for homicide cases at gaol delivery in East Anglia.

[125] Green, 'Societal Concepts of Criminal Liability for Homicide', 691; Maddern, *Violence and Social Order,* 90; Kamali, 'The Devil's Daughter of Hell Fire', 196–200.

[126] See also 'dedly wrath' in the writings of John Myrc, who produced instructional texts for parish priests c. 1380–1420: *Mirk's Festial. Part I: A Collection of Homilies,* ed. T. Erbe (London, 1905), 130, 154, 285.

[127] C 1/3/39: '*et la malice le dit Ric Orfevre et les autres*'. The original attack against the parson and his servants in his church was made on 21 July 1401. For Orfevre, see *CPR 1396–9,* 366; *CPR 1399–1401,* 222.

Discord

or regional variation. So it may be that a renewed investigation of conflict in other English localities is required with this interpretation in mind.[128]

THE SUPPORT GROUP

In this section and the final one we resume examination of the general question about whether and how patterns of behaviour in the far north were distinctive, in some respects, from the rest of England. In the course of conflict, the pool of potential supporters which disputants might call upon comprised existing and new networks of relationships. These were chiefly those of lordship, kinship and friendship. Certain generalisations can be made about the support groups around lesser landowners. First, throughout the kingdom, a landed disputant's following of household men, servants and tenants comprised the most dependable body of supporters in the use of violence.[129] Evidence like Elizabeth Crackenthorpe's appeal against her husband's killers in 1438–9, and her later complaint that her own tenants were being harassed, suggests that the bulk of the support group was similarly composed in the English marches.[130] Second, looking up the ladder of lordship, the direct involvement of magnates in violence among the English gentry was rare throughout the realm,[131] and the border counties show no exception in this regard.[132] Third, throughout England, disputes among relatives were normal and sometimes violent, for it was often a disputed inheritance that set off bitter rivalries.[133] In the marches such intra-kin discords are equally evident.[134]

---

[128] See pp. 2, 24, 38–40, 169, 315, 334.

[129] Carpenter, *Locality and Polity*, 283, 335, 377, 379, 706; Maddern, *Violence and Social Order*, 121; Payling, *Political Society*, 199–201.

[130] KB 27/711 rot. 36d; KB 27/714 rot. 36; *CPR 1436–41*, 273. See also the Thornburghs' house assault on John Lancaster, threatening his two servants (SC 8/24/1174); Thomas Baty's complaint of attacks against his men and servants (*CPR 1436–41*, 576); and Henry Bellingham's complaint against Thomas Parr's menial men (C 1/10/83).

[131] Harriss, 'Political Society', 51; Carpenter, *Locality and Polity*, 357, 457, 625; Castor, 'Walter Blount', 31–2.

[132] See the role of the earl of Northumberland in the *Causa de Heron* (Armstrong, 'Violence and Peacemaking', 66). For more active, but still indirect, involvement, see the role of Dacre (lord of Gilsland), implicated as a receiver in the livestock raids against Sir John Lancaster of Rydal in 1421 (SC 8/24/1174); the role of Salisbury in the 1430s (C 1/24/227; Rowling, 'John Clyborne's Appeal', 182–3; C 1/10/291; Storey, 'Disorders in Lancastrian Westmorland', 79; Storey, *House of Lancaster*, 122); the role of Gloucester and Percy in violence in Nbl. in the 1470s (see Chapter 7 and p. 305 below); and the well-known role of Egremont in the 1450s (SC 8/29/1446; *PROME*, March 1453, appendix, no. 28; Griffiths, 'Local Rivalries', 592, 603).

[133] Carpenter, *Locality and Polity*, 261, 358, 393, 514, 620; Saul, *Scenes From Provincial Life*, 85.

[134] The best illustration is the dispute between the brothers Sir Robert Ogle and Sir John Bertram in 1409 (see above, pp. 126–7; Hodgson, *Northumberland*, II, i, 382–3; ibid. II, ii, no. 3, pp. 170–1; *HOP*, III, 859–62). Another may be found in C 1/5/57 (Heron of Bockenfield *v.* Heron of Meldon).

291

Part III

We have seen already that some border gentry kin groups could contain not only numerous landed branches but also wider members of mixed status.[135] The related issue of wider kin participation in violent disputing requires some examination. We have already noted that in general although distant kin were sometimes drawn in for support, disputes among the English gentry are better known for involving supporters drawn from ties of lordship and from local networks of friends than from more distant kinsmen. Indeed, ties to kin, friends and lords are more often underscored for their role in the limitation of violence than its perpetration (where lesser tenants provided muscle).[136] However, in the marches, there is plenty of evidence to demonstrate gentry kin groups operating together in local violence.[137] For example, a royal commission to arrest two opposing groups of peace-breakers in Westmorland in 1398 reveals one party consisting of three Threlkelds and three Beethams, and the other of two Lancasters.[138] Similarly, in the late 1480s an inheritance dispute in Cumberland led to a serious sequence of lethal violence between various members of the Musgrave, Colville and Martindale families.[139] Both cases suggest that brothers, sons and fathers were involved, rather than more distant cousins, and so, while on the extreme of what might be expected elsewhere in England, they are not that extraordinary. More outstanding is a homicide in Northumberland in 1451, in which no fewer than six minor gentlemen of the Ussher family, all living close to each other, were accused and later acquitted.[140] The most senior member of family, Roger Ussher, gentleman of Acomb and Styford, had also procured a pardon for another killing nearby in 1440.[141]

---

[135] See above, pp. 126–30, 140, 149, 162.

[136] See above, pp. 130 and 160. However, see kinsmen acting in violence in Lincoln in 1411 (*CPR 1408–13*, 317).

[137] See the Bellinghams and Fenwicks noted earlier, in Chapter 5. For other examples, see Cardew, 'Anglo-Scottish', 88, citing a Nbl. case from 1500 involving the Delavals (KB 8/3/part II); a Wml. case from 1496 concerning gentle members of the Lancaster family in the killing of John Threlkeld (KB 9/411 m. 39); and a Wml. case from 1499 concerning Layburn esquires and gentlemen in a riotous assault (KB 9/421 mm. 9–10).

[138] *CPR 1396–9*, 503, apparently linked to *CCR 1399–1402*, 88.

[139] The dispute followed the death in 1479 of William Colville (alias Tilliol), owner of Hayton Castle, leaving two daughters as co-heirs (C 140/71/no. 54; *CPR 1476–85*, 545–6; *CFR 1471–85*, nos 513, 526, 558; KB 9/389 mm. 15, 16; John Denton, *An Accompt of the Most Considerable Estates and Families in the County of Cumberland, by John Denton of Cardew*, ed. R.S. Ferguson (CWAAS, tract ser., 2, 1887), 153–4; *Select Cases*, ed. Bayne and Dunham, 22. See above, pp. 215–216.

[140] JUST 3/213 rot. 14: the victim was William Eryngton, killed at Newton Hall near Corbridge. The accused Usshers were Roger Sr, of Acomb, father of Roger Jr and John, both of Styford, and also John, of Broomhaugh, Simon ('del Lee'), and Robert (of Styford). One John Ussher was attorney for Thomas, Lord Dacre, in 1436 (E 179/240/269 m. 2d).

[141] For the death of John Kylne, 'sawere' of Corbridge, dated 9 November 1440 (*CPR 1436–41*, 477).

Discord

Even more exceptional by standards of what might be expected further south are cases where groups of gentle kinsmen, all apparently living under the same roof, acted together.[142] In this way, three Herons of Meldon[143] and five Crasters of Preston[144] stand out in cases from Northumberland. The most colourful example, however, comes from Westmorland. In 1421 the knight John Lancaster of Rydal[145] incurred the wrath of the Thornburgh family as he played the suitor to Dame Katherine, the widow of Sir Roland Thornburgh.[146] A petition by Lancaster himself recounted that, while visiting Dame Katherine at Maulds Meaburn, he had upset the plot of the five sons of William Thornburgh, who, by '*lour malice*', had concealed swords and Carlisle axes under their beds in order to kill him in the privy chamber as he slept. Following his escape, the Thornburghs brought forty men to assault his house, menacing two of his servants, driving off his animals and later obstructing a session of the peace.[147]

Still wider groups of kinsmen in acts of violence are to be found. Earlier some apparent 'Surnames' of mixed status were identified, with both gentle and common members,[148] and here there is further evidence to suggest that such members would have quite comfortably acknowledged their shared kinship despite differences in social status, and joined together in perpetrating violence. Some indictments show common and landed men sharing a surname implicated together in violent offences,

[142] The Hores of Solihull, however, are an example of a minor gentry family engaged in various violent affairs in Warwickshire: Carpenter, *Locality and Polity*, 396, 456.

[143] The esquire Thomas and the gentlemen Nicholas and Edward, involved in thefts of livestock from the abbot of Newminster in 1450 (JUST 3/54/34 m. 8; JUST 3/211 rot. 34d).

[144] Edmund (or Edward) Sr, Edmund (or Edward) Jr, Robert, John and Richard 'Crawecestre' accused of abetting William Benlee (alias 'Cok of Benley') in the killing of John Tesedale at Embleton in 1445 (KB 9/252/1 m. 11; KB 9/253 mm. 73,74). Another case against these same men appeared in 1446 (KB 27/738 rot. 53d; KB 27/741 *rex* rot. 8d; KB 27/742 rot. 30; KB 27/754 rot. 32; KB 27/794 rot. 24d).

[145] Lancaster's biography is given in *HOP*, III, 546–8. He is not to be confused with John Lancaster of Brampton, mentioned below, p. 300, who was dead by 28 October 1424 (*CFR 1422–30*, 82). Lancaster of Rydal was also a Clifford tenant (1422) and retainer (1408): *CIPM XXI 1418–22*, no. 958, pp. 347–9; NUL: Bainbrigg MS. 1, mm. 1a, 1b.

[146] Thornburgh's biography in *HOP*, IV, 587–8, suggests that Dame Katherine, before marrying Thornburgh (d. c. 1420), was already the widow of Sir William Threlkeld. At the time of Threlkeld's death in December 1408, his daughter Margaret was then the first wife of Sir John Lancaster of Rydal (*CIPM XIX 1405–13*, nos 508–11, p. 187). See also *CCR 1409–13*, 20; W. Jackson, 'The Threlkelds of Threlkeld, Yanwath, and Crosby Ravensworth', *TCWAAS*, o.s., 9 (1888), 298–317, pedigree.

[147] SC 8/24/1174, abstracted in *PROME*, December 1421, appendix, no. 1; printed in *RP*, IV, 163–4. For the role of Hugh Salkeld, see *HOP*, IV, 292; CAC, Carlisle: D/Lons/BM 95. Accommodation was achieved between Sir John and the Thornburghs, who acquiesced to his marriage to Dame Katherine (*HOP*, IV, 587; *HOP*, III, 548).

[148] See above, pp. 140, 149, 162.

293

Part III

very exceptional by standards detected elsewhere in England. This strongly suggests a wider kin group of more distant relations acting together.[149] One such illustration comes from 1465, when the gentleman John Ridley and the yeoman Thomas Ridley, both of Walltown in Tynedale, led a party to kidnap a man in the bishopric of Durham. They robbed him of money and two of his horses and took him into Hexhamshire. The offenders were probably kinsmen of Nicholas Ridley, JP in Northumberland.[150] Across the Pennines in the same year, the widow of Thomas Thornburgh of Westmorland appealed several men for her husband's death. She accused not only the gentlemen Thomas and Geoffrey Wharton of Wharton, but also the Wharton yeomen Oliver, of Ravenstonedale; James and Richard, of Raisgill Hall; Christopher, of Longdale, and his son Miles; and Roland, clerk of Croglin in Cumberland.[151] A similar example from 1462, for an unspecified trespass, implicated mixed-status Moresbys from Westmorland and Cumberland.[152] Examples such as these would suggest that the meaningful ties of kinship for gentry in the marches could stretch beyond the immediate family and extended to non-gentle relatives sharing the same surname.

Other disputes from the marches also show explicit use of kinship and friendship language to describe the support group. Throughout England the terms 'affinity' and 'alliance' could refer to the wider following of an important man, especially in peaceful circumstances. Kin and friends could form a component of this network.[153] Similar phrasing can be found in

---

[149] See above, p. 128.

[150] DURH 19/1/1 rot. 4d, published in *Durham Quarter Sessions Rolls*, ed. Fraser and Emsley, 64–5. The victim, taken at Witton in Weardale on 20 November 1465, was Ralph Eure, perhaps a relative of Sir William Eure. The Ridleys were accused alongside Richard Heryngton, yeoman of Coklawe in Hexhamshire, in which liberty they led Eure to 'Lynnelford'. Nicholas Ridley was special commissioner in Nbl. (1455), a JP for the county (1461, 1463, 1489), a border commissioner (1485) and bailiff of Tynedale in 1491 (*CPR 1452–61*, 299; *CPR 1461–71*, 561; *CPR 1485–94*, 336, 495; *CDS*, IV, 310). For two other Ridleys, see *CPR 1408–13*, 119; *CCR 1413–19*, 298.

[151] KB 27/818 rot. 41d. 'Langdale' and 'Raysegilhall'.

[152] KB 27/806 rot. 16d. The plaintiff was William Tilliol, esq. Accused were Chistopher Moresby and Robert Moresby, respectively, esquire and gentleman of Winderwath ['Wynanderwath'] in Wml., the yeomen John and George Moresby of the same place, and Hugh Moresby of Culgaith ['Colegarth'], just across the county boundary in Cbl. Three Machels of Crackenthorpe in Wml. were also accused: John Machel Sr, gentleman, his namesake John Jr, gentleman, and Thomas Machel, gentleman. This was evidently part of the inheritance dispute concerning Scaleby Castle in Cbl. (see above, p. 215). See also Richard Moresby, clerk, a feofee of Sir Christopher Moresby (*CPR 1429–36*, 116).

[153] Lander, 'Family, "Friends", and Politics', equates friends with the non-kin members of the magnate affinity, defining friends broadly as 'interest groups working together to provide mutual support and advantages' (28). His argument that 'blood relationships and marital connections did not create strong bonds of mutual interest and political support' (35) only accentuates the importance of a mixture of kin, friends and allies in the far-northern support group.

Discord

Northumberland, in the lethal *Causa de Heron* of 1428–31. Here the principals of the two opposing groups were the esquires William Heron of Ford and John Maners of Etal. Surviving documents make repeated references to the 'kyn alyance and frends', and in one instance the 'cosyns', of both parties.[154] This phrasing, while not well known in an English context, suggests similarities with conventional listings of supporters observed in Flanders and Scotland.[155] A close examination of court records shows more precisely to whom this language referred. Although only his bastard son was present to fight at Etal in January 1428, after the attack John Maners was able to rely on the support of no fewer than nine relatives from among the Northumbrian gentry who were accused of acting as receivers or who supported him in other capacities. These included cadet branches of the Maners family, as well as his gentle affinal kin.[156]

There are further occasions when kinship language in the marches suggests a wider kin network, beyond the immediate nuclear family involved in violent disputes. A complainant from Westmorland about 1403–6 alleged violence and threats from the undersheriff and his extended kindred ('*la graunde parantee*') and the other malefactors of their alliance in the same country ('*les autres malfesours de lour alliance en mesme la pays*').[157] In 1416 a complaint to the chancellor alleged an opposing party to be of great alliance affinity and cousinage in Cumberland ('*de si graunde aliaunce affinite et cosinage deins le dit countee*').[158] Another petitioner, Thomas Baty of Brougham in Wesmtorland, complained in 1441–2 that his violent adversaries, the gentlemen Alexander and Thomas Fetherstonhaugh (father and son of Whitfield in South Tynedale), were 'ryght myghty of kyn and alie with in the seide counte'. He identified their kin and allies as several gentle Salkelds and Lancasters.[159] Baty later wrote of

---

[154] DUL, DCM: Loc. V, 44, 45, 46, 48, 51, 52, 52d, 53; 'cosyns' is used in 52.

[155] J. Braekevelt, F. Buylaert, J. Dumolyn and J. Haemers, 'The Politics of Factional Conflict in Late Medieval Flanders', *Historical Research*, 85 (2012), 13–31, at 19; Wormald, *Lords and Men*, 90. For friends and cousins, see Payling, *Political Society*, 202–5.

[156] Armstrong, 'Violence and Peacemaking', 60–1.

[157] SC 8/23/1108. The petition by Sir Robert Leyburn against Thomas Warcop of Lammerside concerned Warcop's role in the abduction of Margaret Sandford, the heir-apparent of Leyburn's own wife. Leyburn also claimed that he and '*autre dez parantz de dite Margaret*' were menaced daily (*LOS*, 150; *HOP*, IV, 298–9).

[158] C 1/6/296. Thomas Skelton's trustees made this complaint against his female cousins and their husbands. See also *CCR 1413–19*, 333; *CPR 1416–22*, 6, 54; *CPR 1422–9*, 290.

[159] C 1/10/291. Baty accused Hugh Salkeld of Rosgill the elder, esq., Roger Lancaster, Richard Lancaster, William Lancaster of Hartsop and John Hutton of Penrith, all of whom were 'ryght nye kyn and alie' to Alexander and Thomas Featherstonehaugh. Baty's opponents had raided his livestock and forced him to submit to a bond. See also Storey, 'Disorders in Lancastrian Westmorland', 79; F.W. Ragg, 'Shap and Rosgill and Some of the Early Owners', *TCWAAS*, n.s., 14 (1914), 1–62, at 25, 48–53, 62; *CPR 1436–41*, 576. See below, p. 314.

Part III

the 'kyn and aliance' of Hugh Salkeld of Rosgill, esquire, numbering more than one hundred persons, who had raided his livestock and 'ofte tyme lyen in awaite armed and harnesed as in land of werre to murdre and slee' Baty and 'his seruantz and wellwillers'. In a recent attack, his adversaries had driven off one hundred of his cattle to the mountains, and they were 'so grete allyed and kynned' that Baty could have no recourse against them.[160]

The use of written contracts of lordship allowed some gentry in the marches to secure support from other kin groups to which they had no blood relations, in a manner that would be quite unexpected elsewhere in the realm. The Westmorland esquire Thomas Sandford of Askham, whom we have already met, provides some examples of formal bonds facilitating this process, including those in the form of monetary contracts framed to evade legal restrictions on livery.[161] A few of his bonds with the local yeomanry can be seen as attempts to build up support in the context of violent disputes, as when he retained his yeoman tenant William Bradley of Knipe in 1468. Bradley promised to bring 'his frends and all þat he may caus and streyn' to 'take trew and fayyfull part' with Sandford, who, in turn, agreed to be 'gud and tender maister' to his new man.[162] In 1477 Sandford and his son entered into another bond, this time with Thomas Wylkynson of nearby Butterwick and his son William, probably also Sandford's tenants. Here the Sandfords promised to 'take parte and mayntene' the Wylkynsons in a property dispute and to be 'tendyr maysters' to them, in exchange for having the rule and governance of the land in question.[163] The Sandford bonds appear to be exceptional, for nothing comparable has been found from Cumberland or Northumberland, or elsewhere in Westmorland. Yet they do indicate that such contractual arrangements between minor landowners and groups of inter-related peasant tenants were possible in the region. In summary, the role of kinship and contracts of lordship in the course of

---

[160] C 1/121/51; *HOP*, IV, 292. Baty accused Hugh Salkeld of Rosgill, esq., and John, William, Thomas, Roger, Richard and Hugh Salkeld, all gentlemen of Rosgill; Robert (and his brother whose name is obscured), James and Gilbert Lancaster, all gentlemen of Sockbridge; and John Lancaster of Helton Flecket, Richard Lancaster of Yanwath, Roger Lancaster of Dacre, and Roland Cliburn of Bampton Cundale, all gentlemen. He also named Hugh Forster and William Threlkeld. The dispute seems to have concerned the lease to Reagill Grange held from Shap Abbey.

[161] See above, pp. 123–4 (Sandford-Yate), 156 (Sandford-Nobles), and below, p. 331 (Sandford-Walkers).

[162] CAC, Carlisle: D/Lons/L5/1/3/69, formerly AS 63. Printed in Jones and Walker, 'Private Indentures', no. 149, pp. 173–4. For the Sandford of Askham manors, see *HOP*, IV, 299–300.

[163] CAC, Carlisle: D/Lons/L5/1/3/83, formerly AS 76. The dispute was over Heltondale, which was in the 'maynour off Robyn Wylkynson'. For Sandford's other transactions with the Wilkinsons in 1478, see D/Lons/L5/1/3/87, 88, 89, formerly AS 78, 79, 80.

Discord

discord shows that the wider kin and subordinate kin groups recruited through bonds played a significant role in the northern marches.

THE NATURE OF VIOLENCE

The nature, purpose and intensity of violent episodes is essential to an understanding of discord. For this purpose the concept of 'strategic' violence has already been noted above, by which we mean acts that are constrained and directed by accepted norms. Unlike the deviant behaviour of a sociopath, this refers to violence typically wielded with open displays of power and claims to validity, against carefully chosen targets. It might involve a raid to destroy property or harass tenants, or an armed assault with large numbers against an opponent's house. The point was to make a very public statement of one's purpose and right to be there, with no attempt to conceal the act as one would a furtive or illicit misdeed. By this means, the perpetrator hoped to force an adversary to back down or to consider compromise and, even more importantly, to force others to take sides or to assist in achieving a compromise.[164]

Disputes among the gentry throughout England could involve serious violence, but, more typically, while 'strategic' violence often accompanied litigation (like prosaic acts of close-breaking), severe violence of any type (whether strategic or not) was rare, very disruptive, and used only in the last resort. The tool of choice to pressure an antagonist to compromise was litigation, rather than overt force.[165] However, in the northern marches there is evidence for intense and feud-like violence which suggests that these generalisations do not apply in the same measure. Serious violence was not used in extreme, last-resort cases. Rather, it seems that those who participated were comfortable with it and knew what to expect from rivals. In many cases it seems that the use of the royal judicial system was a secondary resort for disputants, who viewed intense violence as a practical tool for disputing.

As further south, adversaries in the northern marches could offer minimal displays of force, such as the forcible entries against Sir William

---

[164] Some have viewed this as a signal of a desire or need for the rearticulation of relationships (Geary, 'Living with Conflicts', 146–8; Halsall, 'Violence and Society', 17, 22, 29). House assault and Anglo-Saxon 'hamsocn': see Pollock and Maitland, *History of English Law*, II, 493; Hyams, *Rancor and Reconciliation*, 85n 60, 210–11.

[165] Maddern, *Violence and Social Order*, 5–6, 14, 27, 170–1, 223–4, 227; Bennett, *Community, Class and Careerism*, 220–3; Powell, *Kingship, Law, and Society*, 96–9; Carpenter, *Locality and Polity*, 185, 430–2, 571, 622–3; Walker, *Lancastrian Affinity*, 5; S.J. Payling, 'Inheritance and Local Politics in the Later Middle Ages: The Case of Ralph, Lord Cromwell, and the Heriz Inheritance', *Nottingham Medieval Studies*, 30 (1986), 94–5; Payling, *Political Society*, 188, 202; Harriss, 'Political Society', 50–1.

Part III

Legh's fish weirs in 1438 that were observed in an earlier chapter. Like social emotion, such overt destructive acts asserted legitimate claims and invoked customary norms. This might announce a change in relationship, directing and transforming a dispute and its meanings, in this case, the legal claims over the fish weirs and other property.[166] In other ways, too, violent behaviour canalised into set forms. Certainly, symbolic acts of violence not just in the north are well known.[167] Sporting violence has been dismissed as a sign of the unruly and aggressive dispositions of borderers.[168] Yet popular sporting practices can be found concentrating the serious tensions of local disputes, as occurred in Westmorland in 1473 when Sir Thomas Curwen's tenant was 'sore hurt att þe foteball' by the servant of Thomas Salkeld. This was catalogued as one of many violent incidents between the parties.[169] Far from wild aggression, this example shows sporting activity as a focal point for group violence, steering wider tensions into customary forms. Parliament had sought to ban ball games since the fourteenth century and to promote archery instead (with the intention of encouraging military preparedness),[170] but football can be found as a focal point for group violence elsewhere in the fifteenth-century north, not only in the marches.[171] Like the duels and tournaments in the marches in the early part of the century or the customary practices which could shape border raiding, the evidence for some violence being directed into sport suggests a local society that was amenable to the use of force not in an unrestrained manner but within certain accepted boundaries.[172]

Northumberland offers a different illustration of violence channelled into a customary system, albeit in a judicial context, but unlike England further south. Jurors in the thirteenth century attested to the 'custom of the county', by which a killer or thief might be decapitated if he was taken immediately after his misdeed and confessed to the coroner before suffering any constraint.[173] In one case the custom was used to

---

[166] See p. 229; Phythian-Adams, 'Rituals of Personal Confrontation', 76–89; Thiery, 'Plowshares and Swords', 201–22.
[167] J. Bossy, *Christianity in the West 1400–1700* (Oxford, 1985), 44, on Shrovetide football and other carnival games; Maddern, *Violence and Social Order,* esp. chs 3 and 4; Carpenter, *Locality and Polity,* 383; Castor, 'Walter Blount', 31.
[168] Cardew, 'Anglo-Scottish', 322; Rae, *Administration of the Scottish Frontier,* 11.
[169] CAC, Carlisle: D/Lons/L5/1/33/SH 25.
[170] *SR,* II, 57, 163; *PROME,* January 1410, item 65; ibid., January 1478, item 29.
[171] For Durham and Yorkshire, see P.L. Larson, 'Local Law Courts in Late Medieval Durham', in Britnell and Liddy (eds), *North-East England,* 97–110, at 105; Hayes, 'Ancient Indictments', 42.
[172] See above, pp. 193–5.
[173] This was an even more summary procedure than trial upon 'record'. See above, p. 177n 48. On customs of a *patria* or *pays,* see P. Brand, 'Law and Custom in the English Thirteenth Century

Discord

take revenge for a slain kinsman, and this would bear comparison with analogous provisions concerning accusations made by sergeants (known as '*surdit de sergaunt*') against red-handed robbers north of the border in Galloway.[174] The custom may well explain a pardon issued in 1401 to William Selby, the gaoler of Newcastle.[175] His year-old offence was to have entered by night the church of St. Andrew in Newcastle and murdered William Forster (alias William Patonson), who was accused of having stolen a horse. Selby allegedly dragged the thief out of the church and beheaded him outside the cemetery. What would otherwise appear as a vicious and unpardonable homicide could be explained if the accused had confessed and then fled in a desperate attempt to claim sanctuary and avoid this local custom of violence, which the gaoler sought to exact, perhaps more out of personal motive than official duty.[176]

Serious 'strategic' violence could also be done in revenge for a wrong, which might involve violent injury, impediment of office or rights, or damage to property or subordinates and, consequently, to honour and reputation.[177] Even so it was not haphazard. At its most feud-like, vengeance might take the form of a pre-planned attack. Such assaults were typically executed with overwhelming superiority of numbers, as is illustrated by the ambush and 'premeditated assault' carried out by Sir John Clifford and more than twenty adherents who had waited for the arrival from the south of John de Coupland, killing him and Nicholas Bagot at Bolton Moor, Northumberland, in 1363.[178]

Common Law', in P. Andersen and M. Münster-Swendsen (eds), *Custom: The Development and Use of a Legal Concept in the Middle Ages* (Copenhagen, 2009), 18–19.

[174] See the Nbl. eyre roll from 1256 (JUST 1/642 rot. 13 recording that a violent malefactor had been decapitated at Alnwick following the 'custom of the county'), cited in Neville, *Violence, Custom and Law*, 7n 39). The eyre of 1293 revealed a couple examples of this practice (including the revenge case): JUST 1/651 rots 4, 4d, 21d, 24, 33, cited in Fraser, 'Northumberland Eyre', 21–2, 27; N.M. Hurnard, *The King's Pardon for Homicide before A.D. 1307* (Oxford, 1969), 127, 310; Hyams, *Rancor and Reconciliation*, 249, 284–6. On '*surdit de sergaunt*' in Galloway, and parallels with serjeants of the peace found in Wales and northern England in the thirteenth century, see W.C. Dickinson, 'Surdit de Sergaunt', *SHR*, 39 (1960), 170–5; H.L. MacQueen, 'The Laws of Galloway: A Preliminary Survey', in R.D. Oram and G.P. Stell (eds), *Galloway: Land and Lordship* (Edinburgh, 1991), 133–4; *PROME*, Documents Relating to the Parliaments of Edward I: Roll 12, appendix, no. 288; Petition 3 no. 71.

[175] *CPR 1399–1401*, 465.

[176] On sanctuary generally, see S. McSheffrey, *Seeking Sanctuary: Crime, Mercy and Politics in English Courts, 1400–1550* (Oxford, 2017).

[177] On honour, see P.C. Maddern, 'Honour among the Pastons: Gender and Integrity in Fifteenth-Century English Provincial Society', *Journal of Medieval History*, 14 (1988), 357–71; Algazi, 'Social Use of Private War', 257, 260–2, 265, 272; Geary, 'Living with Conflicts', 157; White, '*Pactum . . . Legem Vincit*', 286; Miller, *Bloodtaking*, 181, 185, 193, 200, 207, 247, 269, 271, 277, 283, 301–2.

[178] *CIM III 1348–77*, 195.

Part III

Destructive plundering might focus on assaults on tenants and servants or on property. Here the principal opponent's own person was not necessarily the desired target.[179] This is shown in the complaint by the esquire John Lancaster of Brampton in Westmorland that, in 1415, William Blenkinsop, esquire, had brought some two hundred soldiers from Carlisle to trample down his wheat.[180] In response, Blenkinsop complained that Lancaster and a local knight, Sir William Sandford, had assembled a party of two hundred men 'armed and arrayed in the manner of war with raised lances, iron bonnets and other manner of arms' and led them to Blenkinsop's residence at Colby Laithes, intending to kill or maim him, and there attacked and wounded his servants, wasted forty acres of crops, and killed two hundred of his livestock.[181] The latter attack occurred on 9 September 1415, a timing which further suggests that this episode was not haphazard but that both assault and counter-assault here played out at the time of the Agincourt campaign, while one significant marcher baron was overseas. It also followed a summer of heightened cross-border tensions which, it may have been hoped by some, would give cover for aggressive action.[182] Although these are noteworthy incidents, none was markedly different from the sort of attacks which could, from time to time, occur further south in defence of honour and reputation.[183]

All the same the Lancaster–Blenkinsop affair also shows severe, personal violence targeted in great force at antagonists. Further examples include the assault by numerous gentry against Robert Brisco on the Caldew bridge beside Carlisle in 1400[184] and the slaying of John Bates near Hexham in 1448, in which latter case Sir Robert Ogle and his sons

---

[179] For example, see SC 8/24/1174 (above, p. 293); C 1/10/291, C 1/121/51 (above, pp. 295–6); C 1/48/13 (above, p. 219); JUST 3/208 rot. 27d (the attack on Crookham in the *Causa de Heron*). For similar patterns in Germany, see Algazi, 'Social Use of Private War', 253–73, and in Scotland, see M.H. Brown, 'Scotland Tamed? Kings and Magnates in Late Medieval Scotland: A Review of Recent Work', *Innes Review*, 45 (1994), 120–46, at 127, 131, 143–4.

[180] C 1/6/213. Lancaster of Brampton, also a tenant of the Parrs in Strickland Roger within the manor of Kendal (*CIPM XIX 1405–13*, nos 446, 667, pp. 162–4, 240–1), claimed the soldiers came '*en le gise de guerre si come eux voillont avoir chivache en Escoce en temps de gurre*'. A barely legible sentence in the damaged document begins '*Et le dit Wardayn oue deux centz autre*', thus implicating the warden directly. If this was Thomas, Lord Dacre (see E 404/30/151; *Rot. Scot.*, II, 210–11, 226; *CDS*, V, 285; *PPC*, II, 155–8, 165, 78), he had an interest in nearby Orton and Hoffe (*CIPM XVI 1384–92*, nos 837–8, pp. 324–5; *CIPM XVII 1391–9*, no. 1323, p. 515; *CIPM XXI 1418–22*, no. 958, pp. 347–9).

[181] C 1/6/278: '*armez et arraie en maner de guerre oue lancez leuez chapelles de ferre et autres maners darmes*'. See also *CCR 1413–19*, 294, 298, 449.

[182] See above, p. 212. [183] Maddern, *Violence and Social Order*, 170–1, 223–4.

[184] E 159/177 *recorda* Hilary rot. 13; *CCR 1396–9*, 520; *CCR 1399–1402*, 100, 105; Summerson, *Medieval Carlisle*, ii, 399.

Discord

were implicated with others.[185] Blenkinsop's own enemies attacked him at his residence, something that was not unheard of elsewhere in the realm, but was always exceptional and seldom conducted with the lethal intent.[186] By contrast, overt and large-scale house assaults were a recurrent feature of violent disputing in the northern marches.[187] Not least among these was the attack by Sir Thomas Parr of Kendal about 1446 on Henry Bellingham's house at Burneside, with a great 'multitude of pople', intending to pull or burn it down and kill his men and servants. Parr failed and left himself vulnerable to be waylaid by Robert and Thomas Bellingham and three others as he travelled to parliament in March 1446.[188]

A well-documented inheritance dispute from Westmorland in the 1430s illustrates how a matter that might be found anywhere in England expanded into serious and strategic feud-like violence which was unusual further south, involving multiple gentry kin groups, themselves interlinked by marriage. A male entail set out by Sir John Lancaster of Rydal and his wife Dame Katherine disregarded a settlement in favour of his four daughters by his first marriage, and their prominent husbands.[189] One of these daughters married Robert Crackenthorpe, esquire, who complained

[185] The other accused gentry were Robert Musgrave of Ryal ['Ryell'] and William Horsley of Norham, and, in the same session, John Trewick son of John Trewick of Trewick was accused with the Ogles of thefts done the day after the killing (JUST 3/211 rots 35, 36, 36d). See Sir Robert Ogle's outlawry and the granting away of his goods in February 1449 (*CPR 1446–52*, 214), and his evident restoration to favour by April (*CDS*, V, 298). See also the related pardon of William Bidmore in July (*CPR 1446–52*, 282).

[186] For example: Powell, *Kingship, Law, and Society*, 208–10; Carpenter, *Locality and Polity*, 365 (a residence), 455 (a parish church); Castor, 'Walter Blount', 31; Cherry, 'Struggle for Power', 131; Cherry, 'The Courtenay Earls of Devon', 77. The duke of Norfolk's siege of Caister Castle in 1469 did not seek the death of the occupants, and it occurred at a time of national crisis (*Paston Letters*, ed. Davis, i, nos. 201–5, 241–5, 334–5, pp. 338–47, 401–2, 546–8, ii, no. 786, pp. 431–2). For lethal intent, see T. Turville-Petre, 'A Nottinghamshire Dispute: English Documents of 1438–42', *Nottingham Medieval Studies*, 57 (2013), 171–94, at 182–5.

[187] See above p. 215 (attack on Scaleby); *CPR 1389–92*, 340 (attack on Seghill); *CCR 1447–54*, 470, 467–8 (attack on Dalemain); C 1/7/256 (attack on Brampton); Armstrong, 'Violence and Peacemaking', 57–8 (attack on Etal and housebreaking at Crookham).

[188] C 1/10/83; SC 8/27/1347; SC 8/27/1348; *PROME*, February 1445, item 41, appendix no. 6; ibid., February 1449, appendix no. 20. See above, p. 213 and below, p. 316.

[189] Sir John Lancaster's daughters by Margaret Threlkeld were Christiana (wife of Sir Robert Harrington), Elizabeth (wife of Robert Crackenthorpe, esquire), Margaret (wife of Sir Matthew Whitfield) and Isabel (wife of Thomas Fleming, esq.) (CAC, Kendal: WD/Ry/Box 92/nos 73, 79, 81, 90). Storey (*House of Lancaster*, 119–20) mistakenly follows Nicolson and Burn (*History and Antiquities*, i, 387) in assuming that Sir John, the widower of Margaret Threlkeld, died in 1422 and that his son and namesake married Dame Katherine. The biography in *HOP*, III, 546–8, correctly finds only one Sir John (d. 1434). See the pardon of February 1435 for the entail made by Dame Katherine and Sir John (see p. 127). See also *Records Relating to the Barony of Kendale*, ed. W. Farrer and J.F. Curwen (CWAAS, Record Ser., vols 4–6, 1923, 1924, 1926), II, 23.

301

Part III

to chancery that Sir John had instigated trouble against him. His complaint was that Dame Katherine's relatives William Thornburgh and Sir Henry Threlkeld had threatened the jurors of a peace session held by Crackenthorpe at Appleby in March 1433. Afterwards, Thornburgh and his son of another household, together with Sir John's nephew and a party of thirty, set an ambush for him as he returned home, which he managed to evade.[190] Then, in the autumn, Dame Katherine again prompted her Threlkeld and Thornburgh relations into violence. They made a house assault against John Cliburn of Cliburn, and withdrew upon the arrival of Crackenthorpe and other JPs, only still later to attack Cliburn and his son-in-law, taking Cliburn prisoner.[191] Violent confrontation seems to have continued, and Sir John Lancaster was dead by June 1434.[192] Turbulence subsided, but only for a time before August 1438 when the Lancasters and Thornburghs slew Robert and William Crackenthorpe at Brampton.[193] The following year saw a further killing and assaults and a royal commission to inquire into complaints by Robert Crackenthorpe's widow Elizabeth that the Lancasters and Thornburghs continued to harass her and threaten her friends, well-wishers and tenants.[194] Not before 1442–3

---

[190] C 1/12/192, 193, 194. William Thornburgh of Meaburn, the father of Oliver, was perhaps the brother of Sir Roland, Dame Katherine's first husband. Sir Henry Threlkeld was the husband of Dame Katherine and Sir Roland's daughter Margaret. See William Thornburgh's grant to Sir Henry Threlkeld in 1435 (CAC, Kendal: WD/Ry/Box 92/no. 85). See Sir John, Dame Katherine and John Crackenthorpe, concerning two-thirds of the Clifford manor of Brougham (*CIPM XXI 1418–22*, no. 958, pp. 347–9).

[191] C 1/24/227. The attackers were William and Sir Henry Threlkeld, William Thornburgh, Thomas Musgrave and Thomas Warcop. The son-in-law was John Burrell, merchant of Appleby. The house assault was ceased by the arrival of the JPs Sir Christopher Moresby, Hugh Salkeld and Robert Crackenthorpe.

[192] He was first presumed dead on 12 November 1433 (*CFR 1430–7*, 165, 167). The summons to council of Thomas, Lord Clifford, in early 1434 was probably connected to this (*PPC*, IV, 203). For comment, see F.W. Ragg, 'De Lancaster', *TCWAAS*, n.s., 10 (1910), 395–494; Ragg, 'Cliburn Hervy and Cliburn Tailbois; Part II', *TCWAAS*, n.s., 28 (1928), 179–274; Ragg, 'De Threlkeld', *TCWAAS*, n.s., 23 (1923), 154–205; M.A. Rowling, 'John Clybborne's Appeal to the Earl of Salisbury', *TCWAAS*, n.s., 63 (1963), 178–83; Storey, 'Disorders in Lancastrian Westmorland', 69–80; Storey, *House of Lancaster*, 119–20.

[193] C 139/92/35a, 35b; *CPR 1441–6*, 191. At Hilary term 1439 Robert's widow Elizabeth appealed as principals in her husband's killing the gentlemen William Thornburgh lately of Selside, William's brother Roland, Oliver Thornburgh lately of Selside, John Lancaster of Howgill and two yeomen, William Toppyng of Reagill and Thomas Derby of Maulds Meaburn. She also appealed a further thirty-eight accessories, including Dame Katherine Lancaster, John Lancaster of Howgill's brother Christopher, the brothers Leonard and Edward Thornburgh, William Derwentwater of Maulds Meaburn and George Warwick of Warwick in Cbl., all gentlemen; and the yeomen John, Thomas and Robert Thornburgh, the sons of Walter Thornburgh of Orton, and John Derby of Maulds Meaburn (KB 27/711 rot. 36d; KB 27/714 rots 36, 82; *CCR 1435–41*, 354).

[194] JUST 3/211 rot. 47 (printed in Ragg, 'Cliburn Hervy', no. 17, pp. 254–5): the gentlemen Roland Cliburn of Bampton Cundale and Geoffrey Threlkeld of Paterdale were acquitted at gaol delivery in 1440 of having killed William Walker of Crackenthorpe with an arrow at

Discord

did the accused Thornburghs obtain pardons, having 'agreed' with Elizabeth Crackenthorpe, and, in the latter year, Sir John's four daughters obtained the disputed lands.[195] Over at least a decade this case involved repeated episodes of serious, feud-like violence among the local gentry. Though most of our information comes from the parties' use of the royal judicial system, especially appeals to the chancellor, unlike in other parts of England courts were of secondary importance to the threat and use of deadly force in this dispute.[196]

Such grievous violence in the far north also involved peasants.[197] There are a large number of homicides at the social level of the yeomanry that stand out for recording a large group of slayers and abettors, often using war-like weapons, which suggests that these were organised and pre-planned attacks conducted with a number of supporters.[198] One of three yeomen implicated in the death in May 1411 of John Dent of Sowerby in Westmorland was John Helbeck. Not long after this, a local group, including four related Dents, abetted another man in slaying Helbeck at nearby Brough with a 'Carlisle axe'. Both widows made private appeals, and these cases were considered serious enough to come into king's bench. They disappear after 1415, perhaps following a local compromise.[199] Similar cases show groups of apparent kinsmen, like the five Stevensons from Rothbury in Northumberland who allegedly lay in wait to kill John Ruture in 1449, even if they managed only to beat and wound their intended victim.[200]

Some of these examples reveal apparent acts of feud-like revenge, which suggest that those who participated knew what to expect from their enemies. Of course, similar instances of vengeance have been found in the rest of England, but, like serious violence more generally,

---

Crackenthorpe on 10 February 1439. The commission on Elizabeth's complaint was issued 11 March 1439 (*CPR 1436–41*, 273).

[195] *CPR 1441–6*, 64, 191 (William, Roland and Oliver Thornburgh secured pardons); CAC, Kendal: WD/Ry/Box 92/no. 90).

[196] This issue is discussed above, p. 235. On gentry attitudes to killing in other localities, see Maddern, *Violence and Social Order*, 5–6, 28, 121–6, 171, 205, 223–4; Carpenter, *Locality and Polity*, 622; Payling, *Political Society*, 202–3.

[197] We have already noted landowners' links with peasant kin-groups. See above, pp. 157–8, 158n 239 and 162.

[198] See discussion of homicides above, pp. 233, 249 and 257. For Wml. (JUST 3/191 rots 63d, 65; JUST 3/199 rot. 32d; JUST 3/208 rots 48d, 50; JUST 3/211 rots 49d, 50, 50d); for Cbl. (JUST 3/191 rots 54d, 55d; JUST 3/208 rots 42d, 43d); and for Nbl. (JUST 3/213 rot. 14).

[199] KB 9/201/4 mm. 23, 24; KB 27/602 *rex* rot. 19, rot. 57; KB 27/606 *rex* rots 3, 3d, 7d, 8d; KB 27/610 *rex* rot. 12d; KB 27/618 *rex* rot. 17d. For one John Dent on 3 April 1411, see CAC, Carlisle: D/Mus/2/8 box 31/no 78.

[200] JUST 3/211 rot. 36d. See also cases from Wml. (JUST 3/208 rot. 49) and Nbl. (JUST 3/211 rot. 34d).

303

Part III

these are very irregular and likely to occur only at times of wider political upheaval.[201] An earlier chapter suggested that, if a relatively low rate of homicides among the border peasantry (especially yeomen) was due to such cases going unreported to officials, this was because the victims' kin and friends were gaining satisfaction beyond the courts.[202] Of course, the point is speculative, but one direct means of doing this would be through taking revenge. Taken as a whole, there seems to be more evidence in the far north of England for feud-like violence than was normal in the rest of the kingdom.

Attempts to restrain the resort to violence in Westmorland are instructive. Evidence suggests that while the threat of retaliation constrained some violent acts, this did not deter it wholesale, for men expected their adversaries to seek redress by force.[203] Two indentures, both attempting to resolve disputes which had led to killings, prescribed local banishment for the offenders and speak to the rules of vengeance. In a case from 1498, one man was to 'forbear' the towns of Appleby and Crosby Garrett for his lifetime and Great Asby for seven years. The document set out that if he 'happyn to come within the seid townes duryng the seid space[,] he to be at his juparty and perell'.[204] Four years later, a similar award banished three men, providing that 'thay shal neuer com within Westmerland but at there perell and jopardie and if thay doo it shalbe lefull to the said [party] to take there avantage at the said three persons or any of them'.[205] Both of these documents reveal disputants accepting circumstances in which retaliatory violence was to be licit, even 'lawful'. Vengeance was also accounted for in the violent Northumberland dispute, known as the *Causa de Heron*, between the esquires William Heron of Ford and John Maners of Etal.[206] In negotiations between the parties following the killing of Heron and his yeoman

---

[201] Carpenter, *Locality and Polity*, 108, 510–12, 589, 612; Payling, *Political Society*, 199.

[202] See above, pp. 233 and 236.

[203] Some have argued that the threat of retaliation was primarily a deterrent to violence: S.J. Payling, 'Murder, Motive and Punishment in Fifteenth-Century England: Two Gentry Case Studies', *EHR*, 113 (1998), 16; Payling, 'Inheritance and Local Politics', 90; Summerson, 'Crime and Society', 118. By contrast, see White, 'Feuding and Peacemaking', 259; Armstrong, 'Violence and Peacemaking', 63.

[204] The banished man was John Atkynson, servant of John Wharton, esq. The opposing party consisted of Robertsons and Richardsons with connections to Queen's College, Oxford (CRO D/Mus/2/box 38/no. A31).

[205] The principals were Edward Musgrave, esq., and Robert Warcop of Warcop. Those banished were the Musgrave men John Walker and his son Robert, and Gerrard Collen (CRO D/Mus/2/box 38/no. A33). This provision would go seem to go well beyond some thirteenth-century cases where a disputant was banished for a period on pain of summary execution should he return sooner (Hyams, *Rancor and Reconciliation*, 209–10).

[206] Armstrong, 'Violence and Peacemaking', 62–3.

304

Discord

servant in 1428, John Maners asked that surety be made that 'no bodyly harme shall be done' to his kin and friends by the children and friends of William Heron, 'for þe sayd deth'. Indeed, possibly in recognition of the threat of renewed violence, the Heron party insisted early on that John Maners and his associates were not to dwell for seven years in any place north of York that was subject to the king of England.[207]

Several cases among the gentry of Northumberland in the 1470s all appear to be linked and suggest a coherent sequence of violent revenge not just threatened but actually taken. The killings in Northumberland of Henry Carr in 1474, and of Richard Tweddall in 1476, have already been remarked on.[208] Carr was slain by five Fenwick gentlemen, and Tweddall by eleven gentry leading a force of two hundred men, and, in both cases, the accused ringleaders are linked to the fourth earl of Northumberland. The esquire Giles Thornton of Witton was among those accused in the latter case.[209] Subsequent violence strongly points to retaliation against Percy's associates. In July 1477 Giles Thornton was viciously slain at Windsor in Berkshire by the direction of his own brother-in-law, Sir George Lumley, an adherent of the duke of Gloucester.[210] The connection to Gloucester suggests that this violence occurred in the context of continued unease between the duke and Percy during the 1470s. At the same time, related tensions existed between the Thorntons and Lumleys over the manor of Witton (held of Percy).[211] By May 1478, Thornton's widow had remarried another Henry Carr, and there is evidence for an attempted reconciliation.[212]

---

[207] DUL, DCM: Loc. V, 44, 47, 51.   [208] See pp. 129, 141 and 219–20.

[209] Thornton's residence was known more fully as Witton-by-the-Water. KB 9/343 mm. 70, 71; KB 27/861 rex rot. 15. The other accused gentry were Sir Henry Percy of Bamburgh and Thomas Cramlington of Newsham, gentleman (*CFR 1461–71*, 70, 80). In the coroner's indictment Edward Carre was among those accused as principals.

[210] KB 9/345 mm. 8, 9; *CFR 1471–85*, no. 405, p. 136. The accused killers were Thomas Lumley of Westminster, esq., and a group of Westminster yeomen. The prior of St George's chapel, Windsor, held the advowson of Simonburn parish, Nbl. (*CPR 1476–85*, 260). Sir George (designated in court as 'of Witton-by-the-Water') was the son and heir-apparent of Thomas, second Lord Lumley. His wife was Elizabeth, daughter and heiress of Roger Thornton, esq., who died in 1471 (*CFR 1471–85*, no. 1, p. 1). See also *GEC*, VIII, 274; *HOP*, IV, 596–8.

[211] Witton-by-the-Water was within the Percy barony of Beanley and is today known as Netherwitton, on the Font. Giles Thornton's grandfather had purchased it decades earlier. NA, Woodhorn: SANT/BEQ/18/4/19 (formerly ZAN/John Hodgson collection/MS Notebook M15A35 "S"), nos 2–3, p. 66, also p. 69; NA, Woodhorn: ZSW 2/61; *CPR 1405–8*, 138; *CPR 1429–36*, 55; *CPR 1461–7*, 541; *CPR 1467–77*, 317; *CFR 1471–85*, nos 1, 667, pp. 1, 236; *CIPM XXIII 1427–32*, no. 378, p. 197; *Register of Thomas Langley*, ed. Storey, iii, 164–7.

[212] *CCR 1476–85*, no. 378, p. 110. In 1478 it was not local violence which appears to have claimed the lives of more than ten Northumbrian gentry (*CFR 1471–85*, nos 449, 450, p. 151), but rather outbreak of disease (*Six Town Chronicles of England*, ed. R. Flenley (Oxford, 1911), 184). The speculative comment in Armstrong, 'Local Conflict', 294, should be disregarded.

305

Part III

Actual examples of revenge are also evident among those beneath the gentry,[213] and one final illustration will suffice.[214] This followed the judicial duel for treason which Robert Dodd of North Tynedale fought against his accuser, Robert del Hall, in the late 1390s, as discussed earlier.[215] The details of the accusation are obscure, but there is some suggestive evidence that Hall himself may have been implicated in a homicide at about the same time.[216] In the course of the duel Hall was slain. The king granted his forfeited goods to his widow, Mary, and to one Thomas Heysham, who was perhaps Mary's father or brother. However, sometime before May 1399, Heysham was ambushed and killed in North Tynedale, by unknown attackers who also took his goods and money. The killing prompted a swift royal inquest into the incident, and the earl of Northumberland was closely involved.[217] Although no surviving source identifies the malefactors, the likely candidates would be members of the Hall family offended by the joint grant of goods to Heysham, or possibly some of the Dodds still pursuing the dead Robert Hall's associates.

This survey brings us part way towards an assessment of the relative role of accustomed practices in conflict management in the northern marches. The evidence gathered strongly suggests that a customary framework of violent disputing, with certain feud-like aspects, obtained in the region. Some of these aspects, it is suggested, may not have been particular to the far north. This is so with the language of conflict, where 'enmity', 'malice' and equivalent words resonated beyond the strict terminology of the common law to describe a hostile relationship between contending parties. This appealed to the special status of the dispute and alluded to an acknowledged (but not specifically stated) set of rules to which all concerned should adhere. The subsidiary point made in

---

[213] For two early sixteenth-century cases demonstrating the group liability of English kinsmen following killings in Cumberland and Durham, see *Sanctuarium Dunelmense*, ed. Raine, 36, 41.

[214] See also the Nbl. cases between the Blyths and Smyths (JUST 3/211 rots 33d, 34d) and between the Hynemers, Laveroks and Rodoms (JUST 3/199 rots 18, 18d; JUST 3/54/19 m. 10; JUST 3/54/33 m. 1; JUST 3/199 rot. 20; JUST 3/208 rots 25d, 27; JUST 3/211 rots 26d, 27, 28d, 29d, 31d, 35). For gentle Rodoms, see *CCR 1413–19*, 322, *CCR 1419–22*, 99; *CDS*, IV, 183.

[215] See above, pp. 159 and 184.

[216] Robert de Halle was among those (including Robert Featherstonehaugh) absolved in April 1397 from excommunication for homicide (the killing of a tenant of Hexham liberty): *A Calendar of the Register of Robert Waldby, Archbishop of York, 1397*, ed. D.M. Smith (York, 1974), 4.

[217] Those commissioned on 12 May 1399 were the earl of Northumberland, his son 'Hotspur', John Fenwick, John Widdrington, John and William Mitford and William Carnaby. A confirmation by Henry IV, issued only six weeks into his reign, of the earlier grant to Mary Hall, points to further Percy influence in the matter (*CPR 1396–9*, 507, 584; *CPR 1399–1401*, 119; *Foedera*, III, iv, 167).

Discord

that regard is that such language, not just in the marches but across late medieval England, deserves fresh examination with these implications in mind: the result may be that a feud-like customary framework of disputing had similar vitality in other English localities, too.[218] What is more, and this time by contrast to the rest of England, we also find the evident importance of kinship networks in disputants' support groups, and not just kin confined to the nuclear family but spread more widely, and sometimes across status levels.

Although in some regards violent acts in the marches resembled what has been identified as typical of gentry affrays in other parts of England (physical assaults and intimidation of tenants and servants, destruction of crops and property, violent sporting incidents), it is the degree and intensity of violence that was remarkable. Lethal force was more often than rarely directed at principal adversaries, in the form of a house assault or an ambush with overwhelming numbers, and with the involvement of wider kin, sometimes of sub-gentry status.[219] All this could also be done according to custom, for there is strong evidence to show that revenge was considered to be a legitimate recourse for an injured party and that it was expected and carried out, sometimes provoking a cycle of retaliation. Such serious violence is detectable not just among the gentry but also in the lower levels of society. Above all, this does not appear to be random aggression but strategic violence structured with elements intended to signal its legitimacy. These findings suggest that a framework of accustomed practices partly influenced violent discord in the marches, a normative system of disputing beyond that which was dominated by the framework of royal justice. This is something that would be unexpected elsewhere in the realm given the current state of understanding. They also suggest that the acceptable boundaries for the use of violence in the far north were in fact lower than has been detected in other parts of England. The concurrent function of different frameworks of conflict management may well help to explain why violence in the English far north has so often been considered exceptional.[220] The other half of this equation, the making of peace, now needs to be considered before more extended conclusions can be drawn.

---

[218] See below, esp. pp. 339–40, for further development of these implications.

[219] On the number of homicides see above, pp. 234–6 and 240.

[220] See above, pp. 36–40, 195–7, 240–1, 264–8. See also Hayes, 'Ancient Indictments', 45, speaking of violence in the marches as well as Durham, Yorkshire and Lancashire.

10

CONCORD

> Whan Goddes Sone also was bore,
> He sende Hise anglis doun therfore,
> Whom the schepherdes herden singe,
> Pes to the men of welwillinge
> In erthe be among ous here.
> So for to speke in this matiere
> After the lawe of charité,
> Ther schal no dedly werre be.[1]
>
> —Gower, *Confessio Amantis*

This chapter continues an investigation of accustomed practices of conflict management in the far north, chiefly in the making of peace by compromise – or the other side of feud. It continues to pursue the question of how far a normative framework of disputing other than that of royal justice and its usual out-of-court practices is detectable, recalling that the system of border justice was itself heavily concerned with processes of reparation and conversant with broader frameworks of justice familiar in other parts of Europe, including Scotland. As a type of dispute heavily reliant on customary practices, feud remains in the forefront of attention, as do the feud-like elements of compromises. As we have seen, dispute resolution by arbitration is a well-studied feature of late medieval conflict,[2] and the evidence for it in the border counties will be surveyed, as will be the role of supporters and peacemakers. We shall then turn to the attempted resolution of violent disputes, to investigate the objectives of peacemaking in serious conflict. In drawing comparisons with the rest

---

[1] John Gower, *Confessio Amantis,* ed. R. A. Peck, and trans. A. Galloway, vol. 2 (Kalamazoo, MI, 2013), Book 3, lines 2255–62, consulted at TEAMS Middle English Text Series (METS), https://d.lib.rochester.edu/teams/publication/peck-gower-confessio-amantis-volume-2; accessed 1 July 2019.

[2] See above, p. 39.

Concord

of England, the general question about the distinctiveness of the far north in all this remains to the fore. All the same, in tracing accustomed practices of conflict management, our analysis moreover will reconsider the view, relevant to all of England, that genuine efforts at pacification were primarily concerned to restore a pre-existing orderly state of affairs. Discord was not simply a matter of order upset; concord was not simply the settlement of disputes or the quelling of disorder. Instead, peace-making's potential to construct social relationships will be explored, especially with regard to the feud-like elements of ceremonial reconciliation, compensation and the exchange of formal contracts.[3] The extent to which these processes reveal a customary normative framework of disputing is crucial to the final assessment of the normative balance of conflict management in the marches.

LOVE AND LAW

The topic of arbitration has already been touched on at various stages, but it is now time to develop it at greater length.[4] As is well known, arbitration was the major tool for compromise between adversaries throughout England. Defined simply as a resolution formally arranged between disputants by a third party, arbitration featured in Roman and canon law, and, throughout medieval Europe, it was closely associated with the concept of love, in the sense of amicable public agreement. Arbitration (love) and adjudication (law) were complementary processes by which disputants might achieve their objectives, but arbitration could comprehend a range of issues flexibly, addressing much more than a specific point of law. Frequently, courts assigned a day to disputing parties who undertook to reach a compromise out of court, the well-known '*die amoris*', or 'loveday'.[5] Studies have shown that arbitration and lovedays continued to go hand in hand with litigation in late medieval England, notwithstanding the elaborate and rapidly expanding legal system. Landowners, who regularly used litigation to pressure an opponent to compromise through arbitration, might look to a 'good lord' whose duties included ensuring that disputes among his followers were settled amicably before even reaching the courts.[6]

---

[3] See above, pp. 25–7.   [4] See above, pp. 26, 39–40, 169, 181, 185 and 217.

[5] Clanchy, 'Law and Love in the Middle Ages', 47, 59, 65; J.W. Spargo, 'Chaucer's Love-days', *Speculum*, 15 (1940), 36–56; J.W. Bennett, 'The Medieval Loveday', *Speculum*, 33 (1958), 351–70; Cheyette, '*Suum Cuique Tribuere*', 287–99; White, '*Pactum ... Legem Vincit*', 281–308; White, 'Feuding and Peace-Making', 195–263; Kuehn, *Law, Family, and Women*, 19–74.

[6] Powell, 'Arbitration and the Law', 57 ('hand in hand'); Powell, 'Settlement of Disputes', 39; Powell, *Kingship, Law, and Society*, 54–5, 62–4, 91–107; Clanchy, 'Law, Government and Society

309

Part III

In the border counties, thirty-five references to arbitration or other compromise settlements are identifiable, with evidence of a further nineteen actual determinations or awards. More than half of these occurred in Westmorland. Of all thirty-five references, fifteen related to violent disputes, and only one to a homicide.[7] Local arbitration could be overseen by the justices of assize, as was made explicit in a bond from 1413 whereby a dispute over five acres of land near Bampton, Westmorland, was submitted to *'lordinance agarde et arbitrement'* of three local esquires, with the provision that if unsuccessful the parties were to abide the award of the justices at the next session.[8] A similar role was given to one of 'the kyngys justys' in a Cumberland arbitration from 1422.[9] The term in England for the arbitrator who acted as umpire was *'nonpar'* or *'noumpere'*. In at least one case from Northumberland (the *Causa de Heron*, 1428–31) an umpire was designated, and the arbitrators assigned on each party's behalf were called 'dayers', a variation on the northern English and Scots word 'daysman' denoting this role.[10] Historians have tended to emphasise the connection between in-court litigation and out-of-court arbitration, but, although the survey of legal records in the present study is not exhaustive, few of the surviving awards can be clearly matched with court cases.[11] This suggests that arbitration was a regular first stop in disputing in the English marches, and, while royal justices could be involved in the process, it was also possible for the judicial system to be bypassed entirely, perhaps more often than was usual elsewhere in the realm. This point recalls the earlier suggestion that a low rate of recorded homicides among the peasantry of the far north may

in Medieval England', 73–8; Carpenter, 'Law, Justice and Landowners', 205–37; Carpenter, *Locality and Polity*, 624; Rawcliffe, 'The Great Lord as Peacekeeper', 34–54; J.T. Rosenthal, 'Feuds and Private Peace-making: A Fifteenth-Century Example', *Nottingham Medieval Studies*, 14 (1970), 84–90; I.D. Rowney, 'Arbitration in Gentry Disputes in the Later Middle Ages', *History*, 67 (1982), 367–76. This is only a selection; see the literature surveyed in J. Biancalana, 'The Legal Framework of Arbitration in Fifteenth-Century England', *American Journal of Legal History*, 47 (2005), 347–82; M.D. Myers, 'The Failure of Conflict Resolution and the Limits of Arbitration in King's Lynn, 1405–1416', in D. Biggs, S.D. Michalove and A.C. Reeves (eds), *Traditions and Transformations in Late Medieval England* (Leiden, 2002), 81–108.

7 The phrasing 'ordynaunce dome and awarde' was typical of such determinations (CAC, Whitehaven: D/Stan/1/21).

8 Sir Christopher Curwen *v.* John Cliburn, esq. The parties were to meet in the church of Bampton, a loveday in all but name (CAC, Carlisle: D/Lons/BM 95).

9 Berdesay *v.* Rybton, 1422 (CAC, Kendal: WD/Ry/Box 92/no. 77). On arbitration by justices of assize, see Ives, *Common Lawyers*, 127, 130.

10 *OED*, and *DSL*, s.vv. 'umpire', 'daysman'. For 'dayesmen' in Yorkshire, see Stapleton (ed.), *Plumpton Correspondence*, 82. See Powell, 'Settlement of Disputes', 29, 33; Rawcliffe, 'Great Lord as Peacekeeper', 40.

11 Powell, 'Arbitration and the Law', 57; Powell, 'Settlement of Disputes', 38–9; Payling, *Political Society*, 213, Carpenter, *Locality and Polity*, 364.

310

Concord

indicate that extra-judicial means of redress and resolution might be prominent in such cases.[12]

The surviving evidence of arbitration is far too meagre to offer much reinforcement to the supposition that lethal disputes among common borderers frequently went to arbitration without coming into the royal judicial system, but what is available does suggest as much. Throughout England, the gentry played an important role in regulating strife among the peasantry, through the peace sessions as much as through arbitration and command of their own tenants.[13] In the far north, the Sandfords of Askham in Westmorland furnish several examples of gentry arbitrating for yeomen in disputes which were sometimes violent.[14] In some of these cases Thomas Sandford acted alone;[15] once he acted with another knight;[16] and, at other times, he led a panel of yeomen arbitrators.[17] While not out of the ordinary in what might be expected to be found elsewhere in England, these examples show 'treaties and agreements' led by the gentry to address violent disputes among common borderers.[18] Unfortunately, these occur in a period without surviving gaol delivery and peace session records, so whether these cases also came before the king's justices in Westmorland cannot be assessed.

Throughout England the gentry were frequently ready to make peace among their social equals,[19] and this can also be observed in the marches. The process could involve both lay and religious members of local families.[20] Even violent disputes were capable of being moved to peace

---

[12] See above, pp. 234–6 and 299–304.

[13] Harriss, 'Political Society', 51–2; Rowney, 'Arbitration in Gentry Disputes', 369; Carpenter, *Locality and Polity*, 616.

[14] Thomas Sandford was only placed on the Wml. bench in January 1471, during the readeption. He was removed in the next commission, of May 1474 (*CPR 1467–77*, 634–5).

[15] Sandford for Yate (four men of this name) *v.* Laghorn, Hoghson, Noble and Laghorn, 1475 (CAC, Carlisle: D/Lons/L5/1/3/76, 77); Sandford for Noble (four men of this name) and others, 1477 (CAC, Carlisle: D/Lons/L5/1/3/81, formerly AS 72).

[16] Sandford and Sir Thomas Curwen for Gybson *v.* Bakstar, 1469 (CAC, Carlisle: D/Lons/L5/1/3/70, formerly AS 64). Curwen was a JP for Cbl. at this time, although not for Wml. (*CPR 1461–7*, 561–2).

[17] Sandford and others (yeomen) for Colynson *v.* Wilkynson, 1465 (CAC, Carlisle: D/Lons/L5/1/3/67, formerly AS 62); Sandford and other (yeomen) 'tretours' for Airey and Colperthwaite *v.* Ayra, 1467, rendering 'trete and agrementz' (CAC, Carlisle: D/Lons/L5/1/3/68, formerly AS 62a).

[18] See also John Huddleston esq. for Stanley esq. *v.* Gybson (yeo.), 1459 (CAC, Whitehaven: D/Stan/1/21).

[19] Powell, 'Arbitration and the Law'; Powell, 'Settlement of Disputes'; Wright, *Derbyshire Gentry*, 122–4, 144–5; Bennett, *Community, Class and Careerism*, 238; Pollard, *North-Eastern England*, 113–18; Carpenter, *Locality and Polity*, 358, 397, 479–9, 492, 499, 513–16, 521, 602–3, 606, 609–10. Liddy, *Bishopric of Durham*, 148–151, considers arbitrations in the context of peace bonds.

[20] For gentle arbitrators joined by their relations among the clergy, see Berdesay *v.* Rybton, and Highmoore *v.* Berdesay, 1422 (CAC, Kendal: WD/Ry/Box 92/no. 77. See also C 1/4/88); Musgrave *v.* Threlkeld, 1445 (CAC, Kendal: WD/Ry/Box 92/nos 91–2); Pennington *v.*

Part III

by networks of gentry.[21] In some cases those who moved the parties to compromise were described more specifically, as in the Brisco–Denton affair in Cumberland where it was 'be labour and mediacones of þer frends and welewillers' that they agreed to submit their violent dispute to arbitration in 1470.[22] Similar language can be found in other cases, some apparently resulting in agreements before arbitration even became necessary.[23] Descriptions of principals' supporters in arbitrations and related processes show similarity with the rest of England in that references to 'friends' and 'kin' can be found,[24] even if, throughout England, the latter was uncommon and the former unlikely to have kinship connotations.[25] In one extraordinary cross-border example, the 'frendshipp' of a Scottish party from Berwickshire can be seen to include some minor gentry from Northumberland.[26] Yet this seems to be a one-off instance, and surviving descriptions of supporters in arbitrations stand out more for another reason. Reference was sometimes made in the English far north not just to immediate kinsmen but to the wider kin group.[27] This can be seen in Westmorland in 1447, when several landed Threlkelds and Thornburghs and 'other of thaire frendes and cosyns' put the 'vareaunces querels and debates ... longe tym hongeynge betwene' them to local arbitration.[28]

Lamplugh, 1465 (CAC, Whitehaven: D/Pen/Bundle 47/22); Southayk *v.* Blencow, 1472 (CAC, Carlisle: D/HGB/1/221A); Sandford *v.* Salkeld, 1472 (CAC, Carlisle: D/Lons/L5/1/3/75, formerly AS 68).

[21] For example, see Boynton, Fenwick, Errington *v.* Horsley, 1455 (NA, Woodhorn: ZSW/2/60).

[22] CAC, Carlisle: D/Lons/D 64.

[23] Musgrave–Wharton–Warcop. 1455 (CAC, Carlisle: D/Mus/2/box 38/no. A111); Fleming *v.* Fleming, 1485 (CAC, Kendal: WD/Ry/Box 92/no. 110); Musgrave *v.* Bell, 1485 (CAC, Carlisle: D/Mus/2/box 38/no. 21); Harbottle *v.* Bellingham, 1450 (Alnwick Castle: Syon X.II.1, box 3, b).

[24] In the Sandford arbitration for the yeomen, Gybson *v.* Bakstar, in 1469, one principal's 'chylder and all oder thayre appliaunce frendys and supportours' are mentioned (CAC, Carlisle: D/Lons/L5/1/3/70, formerly AS 64). Note also that all of the mediators and witnesses to the Musgrave–Wharton–Warcop agreement of 1455 were kinsmen of each of the three parties concerned (CAC, Carlisle: D/Mus/2/box 38/no. A111).

[25] For examples, see *Stonor Letters*, no. 108, p. 199; Spargo, 'Chaucer's Love-days', 52; S.J. Payling, 'Law and Arbitration in Nottinghamshire, 1399–1461', in J.T. Rosenthal and C. Richmond (eds), *People, Politics and Community in the Later Middle Ages* (Gloucester, 1987), 156; Payling, *Political Society*, 202–5.

[26] DUL, DCM: Reg. Parv. II, fols 154r–v; *Coldingham*, no. 152, at p. 137. This was the Anglo-Scottish dispute between Alexander and David Hume in 1442, over the bailiary of Coldingham Priory. Four witnesses at Durham on behalf of Alexander were George Hume (probably his brother, of Spott), Edmund Hay (probably a Scotsman), and two lesser Northumberland gentlemen, John Ogle (perhaps the son of Sir Robert, although possibly a Scottish Ogill of Papple) and 'Collyngwood' (perhaps John Collingwood of Duddo). For Collingwood of Duddo, see JUST 3/54/29 rot. 2; JUST 3/54/19 rot. 12.

[27] Such provision has been viewed as a hedge against the risk of a failed peace: Brown, *Bloodfeud in Scotland*, 57–8.

[28] The Thornburghs were William, Roland, Edward and Leonard. The Threlkelds were Sir Henry, Lancelot his son, William his brother, and his other sons. Despite these nuclear family members

312

Concord

An even clearer concern for the wider kindred in peacemaking in the marches appears in the *Causa de Heron*, when the esquire John Maners expressed apprehension about the terms of arbitration. Cautious that not all his supporters would accept the agreement in this deadly dispute, he claimed that 'no man may reule all his kynn frendes and allies and for an unreule word or dede done or said be the ferrest [boldest, proudest] of his kynn he might forfait his surte'.[29] It was not just the wider kin of Maners and Heron who were involved but also that of the prominent knights Robert Umfraville and Robert Ogle, who each championed one party in this dispute. By taking the lead from these men, the lesser disputants tapped into a wide network of potential supporters. Each knight called upon his own ties of friendship and kinship to bring together groups, including men from outside Northumberland, to act as mainpernors, pledges, mediators and arbitrators.[30] The result was two large support groups of kin and friends of mixed status, from humble servants up to the knightly elite. The point is well made by a draft document which states that the Maners party was 'to have gode lordship and maystership of the hyer estates and gode love and frenship of the lawe estates of the kyn alyance and frendes of Wm Heron swyer'.[31] Further south in England, the extended kinship element of these alliances would have been unfamiliar.

As was normal across England, smaller local disputes overlapped with greater regional ones, and, typically, it was not until greater confrontations were resolved that lesser quarrels stood a good chance at compromise, for many participants were involved in both.[32] Furthermore, the royal council was involved in directing a number of arbitrations.[33] Across England perhaps the most typical scenario was for a great lord to arbitrate for lesser men,[34] and such lords can be found both directly and

---

appearing in the deed, their *other* friends and cousins were included in its terms (CAC, Carlisle: D/Lons L5/1/50/15, formerly T 58, printed in Ragg 'De Threlkeld', 198–9).

[29] See above, pp. 295 and 304. *MED*, s.v. 'fer'. DUL, DCM: Loc. V, 48. For reference to the Maners 'frendship', see ibid., nos 47, 52.

[30] Armstrong, 'Violence and Peacemaking', 64–6.

[31] DUL, DCM: Loc. V, 52d. See above, p. 295.

[32] Greater magnate confrontations with local manifestations include the Neville inheritance dispute of the 1430s, the Percy–Neville rivalry of the 1450s and the Percy–Gloucester rivalry of the 1470s, all of which are noted above in Chapter 7.

[33] See Stapleton *v.* Beetham, 1438 (*CCR 1435–41*, 235, 237); Pennington *v.* Huddleston, 1474 (*CCR 1468–76*, no. 1317, p. 365). For the rest of England: C. Rawcliffe, 'Great Lord as Peacekeeper', 40. On the king as peacemaker, see Carpenter, *Locality and Polity*, 542–4; Rowney, 'Arbitration in Gentry Disputes', 373.

[34] Powell, *Kingship, Law, and Society*, 89–91; Pollard, *North-Eastern England*, 118–20; Wright, *Derbyshire Gentry*, 124–7; Carpenter, *Locality and Polity*, 9–10, 282, 354, 357, 382–3, 393, 429, 450, 628; Walker, *Political Culture*, 23; Payling, *Political Society*, 207–13.

Part III

indirectly involved in arbitrations in the marches. As in the rest of England, prelates were important arbitrators among both lay and religious disputants, a finding which attests to the influence of canon law in this procedure.[35] The prior of Durham was the only great figure to attempt a cross-border pacification in our period, and even a man as powerful and capable as Prior John Wessington was unable to achieve success.[36] The duke of Gloucester's council arbitrated in 1482,[37] and the earl of Northumberland had an indirect part in resolving the *Causa de Heron* in 1431.[38] There is also evidence for lords arbitrating in a partisan fashion.[39] Most outstanding in this regard is the role of Thomas, Lord Egremont, in two Cumberland arbitrations in the 1450s, which can hardly be viewed as an effort at keeping the peace.[40] Rather, the baron squandered an opportunity to gain the goodwill of a local esquire, Lancelot Threlkeld, and instead walked over his property claims in favour of members of the Percy Cockermouth affinity.[41] This was not the only instance in which Lord Egremont worked against Threlkeld.[42]

---

[35] An example is Redman for Curwen *v.* Salkeld, 1473 (CAC, Carlisle: D/Lons/L5/1/33/SH 25). The role of ecclesiastical peacemakers is well explored in Dobson, 'Politics and the Church', 1–17; see also references in Powell, 'Arbitration and the Law', 52n 27; Powell, 'Settlement of Disputes', 25n 18; L.B. Smith, 'Disputes and Settlements in Medieval Wales: The Role of Arbitration', *EHR,* 106 (1991), 835–60, at 843–6.

[36] Armstrong, 'Fyre of Ire Kindild', 73, 81.

[37] Gloucester for Hilton *v.* Musgrave, 1482 (CAC, Carlisle: D/Mus/2/3 box 25/no. 124). See also John Neville of Montague for Whitfield *v.* Salkeld, 1465 (*CCR 1461–8,* 330); Montague for Fenwick *v.* Fenwick heiresses, 1465 (Bodleian: Dodsworth MS, 45, fol. 43v (62); *Northumberland and Durham Deeds,* ed. Oliver, p. 60, no. 55).

[38] DUL, DCM: Loc. V, 45, 46, 53; *CPR 1436–41,* 258–9; *CCR 1435–41,* 300–2.

[39] C 1/10/291. See above, Chapter 9. The king asked the second earl of Northumberland to favour Thomas Ilderton, esq., in an arbitration against William Bertram, esq. (C. Monro (ed.), *Letters of Queen Margaret of Anjou and Bishop Beckington and Others* (1863), 68, no. 40). See also the earl of Salisbury in the dispute between William Stapleton, esq., and the earl's rival, Lord Clifford, in 1443 (CAC, Carlisle: D/Mus/2/2 box 22/no. 172). Salisbury had arbitrated for Stapleton in 1438 (*CCR 1435–41,* 235, 237–8; *CPR 1441–6,* 191) in the related matter of Stapleton *v.* Beetham (C 1/9/68; C 1/12/220; C 1/70/85). On arbitration for partisan ends, see Clanchy, 'Law and Love in the Middle Ages', 61, 64; Bennett, 'The Medieval Loveday', 359, 364; Rawcliffe, 'Great Lord as Peacekeeper', 49–51; Carpenter, *Locality and Polity,* 495–9, 588.

[40] Summerson, *Medieval Carlisle,* ii, 439–40; Booth, 'Landed Society', 48–50.

[41] Egremont for Alice Threlkeld *v.* Lancelot Threlkeld (1453), concerning lands of Threlkeld and Yanwath (CAC, Kendal: WD/Ry/Box 92/no. 93). Lancelot's dead father had been a Salisbury retainer (CAC, Carlisle: D/Lons/L5/1/50/12, formerly T 51). See Alice Threlkeld's power of attorney granted to Sir John Pennington (1453), and the settlement (1454) of Yanwath lands belonging to Thomas Pennington, esq., and his wife Alice, widow of Sir Henry Threlkeld (CAC, Carlisle: D/Lons/L5/1/50/16, formerly T 60; CAC, Kendal: WD/Ry/Box 92/no. 94). Both Sir John and Thomas Pennington were indicted for joining Egremont in the Heworth affray in 1453 (KB 9/149/1/11 m. 16). The Threlkelds were tenants of the Greystokes and Cliffords (Nicolson and Burn, *History and Antiquities,* i, 356).

[42] Lord Egremont's arbitration between Threlkeld and his yeoman tenant (1453) can also be seen as deliberate antagonism of the esquire (CAC, Carlisle: D/Lons/L5/1/50/17, formerly T 61).

Concord

In conclusion, arbitration involved various different social forms and inflections, and it was an important part of the processes of peacemaking in the marches. If there is a difference in the far north, it is with the involvement of the wider kin, a finding which fits with the role of such relations which we have seen in processes of discord.[43]

THE OBJECTIVES OF PEACEMAKING

We have observed that late medieval England is well understood to be a collection of overlapping and self-regulating local societies, where effective rule by landowners relied upon the interplay of private power and public authority with regard, not least, to the interaction between the use of the king's law and out-of-court arbitration.[44] In this historiography the two linchpins of dispute resolution are seen to have been landed society's collective instinct to maintain a 'delicate local equilibrium', and the willingness of great lords to intervene where necessary to re-establish the peace when it was upset by abnormal episodes of disorder.[45] Historians of political society note that the risk of failure in attempts at peacemaking was ever-present.[46] With regard to our evidence from the border counties, it was partly because of this very danger that violent disputes, and especially lethal ones involving a regularised feud-like relationship of hostility between acknowledged enemies, were of special concern in local society. Such cases might call for measures that went beyond the cooperative setting-aside of differences in favour of consensus, or forceful restraint imposed from above to restore the status quo. The latter is exemplified by Carpenter's favoured imagery of a great lord (or the king himself) stepping in to 'knock heads' together.[47] There is no doubt that such exertions of authority were respected by English

---

In 1450 Egremont made a more genuine attempt to arbitrate for yeomen linked to Broughton, Thwaites and Huddleston (*Cata. Deeds*, iv, 327).

[43] See above, pp. 291–7.

[44] See pp. 39–40, 169 and 180. Powell, *Kingship, Law, and Society*, chs 1 and 4; Carpenter, *Locality and Polity*, 2, 283, 364, 370, 615–44.

[45] Carpenter, *Locality and Polity*, 358 (quote), 397, 429, 478, 508, 514, 610–12; Powell, 'Settlement of Disputes', 42; Powell, *Kingship, Law, and Society*, 246; Maddern, *Violence and Social Order*, 13–16, 25, 233–4; Payling, *Political Society*, 214. See also Rowney, 'Arbitration in Gentry Disputes', 371; Dobson, 'Politics and the Church', 12–13; Walker, *Political Culture*, 19; R.W. Hoyle, 'Faction, Feud and Reconciliation amongst the Northern English Nobility, 1525–1569', *History*, 84 (1999), 613.

[46] Rowney, 'Arbitration in Gentry Disputes', 371–2; Powell, 'Settlement of Disputes', 28; Powell, *Kingship, Law, and Society*, 242; Myers, 'The Failure of Conflict Resolution', 81–108; Carpenter, *Locality and Polity*, 499, 535.

[47] Carpenter, *Locality and Polity*, 376, 393, 397, 475, 545–6, 625 (quote); also Powell, 'Settlement of Disputes', 32.

Part III

northerners as much as anybody, but the effects of this approach might anyway only last until a change of royal dynasty,[48] and it did not extinguish the desire for vengeance.[49] In the far north we have already seen that the reciprocal threat of retaliation was no wholesale deterrent to violence and that disputants accepted and acted upon the vengeful imperatives of feud and mortal enmity.[50] Especially for this reason, there were two elements to the making of genuine peace in seriously violent, feud-like cases. The first was a de-escalation from violence and a restoration of pre-existing relationships, at least to the extent that mediation and negotiation could occur between the antagonists.[51] But even if this led to agreement and compromise, the conflict was only returned to the very position which had proved to be unstable in the first place. Hence the second element of an effective and lasting peace was that the compromise achieved should transform the social fabric which shaped the conflicting groups and which had given rise to episodes of violence. Inter-group relationships were to be redefined and, in some instances, so too was group membership. Illustrative examples from the far north, and also some examples which will be pointed out for comparison from other parts of England, suggest that a framework of ideas helped direct these processes. Here language and ritual again became important in shaping the norms of peacemaking, in this case touching the expectation that widely acknowledged relationships of enmity should be transformed into those of amity.[52]

Much as can be found throughout England, the marches provide examples of the first component of peacemaking, the initial restoration of peaceable behaviour which enabled cooperation and dialogue to follow.[53] This could be achieved by various means. In two house assaults from Westmorland, one gentry victim later recounted that the attack was averted 'through tretyee of gode Gentilmen of the same cuntre',[54] and

---

[48] See above, p. 181; Carpenter, *Locality and Polity*, 557. For dispute resolution in Scotland understood as a means to restore the status quo, see Wormald, 'Bloodfeud, Kindred and Government', 74–5.

[49] On escalation and containment, see Boehm, *Blood Revenge*, 181–3, 207, 226.

[50] See above, pp. 233, 271, 299–304 and 304. See also a related point in Carpenter, *Locality and Polity*, 625, on the implicit sanction of 'mutually assured destruction'.

[51] As per comment by Powell, 'Settlement of Disputes', 35.

[52] The power of conflict to sustain social bonds is fundamental to Black-Michaud's *Cohesive Force*, 33–85, a point adapted by Geary for medieval France ('Living with Conflicts', 150, 154–5 159) (see above, pp. 26–7). See also White, '*Pactum ... Legem Vincit*', 303–5, 308. On new amity, see also Hyams, 'Homage and Feudalism', 28–9; Hyams, *Rancor and Reconciliation*, 12, 16, 199.

[53] See p. 174. On efforts (and failures) to guarantee parties would keep the peace in order to allow dialogue, see Powell, 'Settlement of Disputes', 35; Bennett, *Community, Class and Careerism*, 33; Carpenter, *Locality and Polity*, 502, 555–6.

[54] Sir Thomas Parr *v*. Henry Bellingham, c. 1441–3 (C 1/10/83); Storey, 'Disorders in Lancastrian Westmorland', 77.

Concord

another said that his house would have been incinerated if not for the *'bones gentz'* who persuaded his assailants to abandon their malice and extinguish the fire they were building – not a figurative fire but an actual one.[55] After 'talking down' violent disputants, negotiation required facilitation, as might be conducted by social equals. Adversaries' own peers could become conciliators in the preliminaries to compromise, in a manner evocative of that facilitated by the 'cross-cutting' or 'cross-link' social ties which have long been understood to be important to pacification.[56] The cooling-off necessary for negotiation could be bolstered by formal undertakings for good behaviour, such as peace bonds. For example, in 1477, the esquires John Widdrington of Chipchase in Northumberland, Richard Salkeld of Corby in Cumberland and Richard Huddleston of Millom in Cumberland entered a 200 mark bond to Edward IV that the latter Richard and three of his named relations were to keep the peace towards the abbot of Furness and his servants or tenants and that a concord was to be made to end the strife and discord between the parties.[57] The application of royal authority and financial obligations drew supporters to the principals' sides, creating social pressure for compromise.

In relation to the second, transformative, element of effective peace and concord, some of the language of peacemaking as used in the marches reveals more specific information about the norms and ideas at work in accustomed practices of disputing, especially relating to affairs that had become violent. One example of an arbitration from Westmorland proclaimed that 'rest and peas ful frendshipp gude lufe and trewe acorde be had and keped emonge the saide parties'. The single arbitrator here also set out the expectation that 'bothe the saide parties and ychon of thayme to obserue and kepe this myn awarde eftir the trewe menynge and entente of me ... with oute any ymaginacon ther in that may seime to the contrary ther of in any tyme to come', on pain for forfeiture of their mutual obligations.[58] In another case, brought to arbitration before the prior of Carlisle and a prominent knight 'be labour and mediacones' of the disputants' 'frends and

---

[55] *'sinoun que y feust treite par bones gentz de lesses lours ditz malice'*: John Helton *v.* Thomas Warcop et al., c. 1413–17 (C 1/6/282).

[56] Colson, 'Social Control and Vengeance', 203, 210–11 ('cross-cutting'); Gluckman, 'The Peace in the Feud', 6 ('cross-link'). See also Evans-Pritchard, *The Nuer*, 156–9, 171–6, and later comment by Black-Michaud, *Cohesive Force*, 64–6; Roberts, *Order and Dispute*, 56, 160; Miller, *Bloodtaking*, 265, 304; Wormald, 'Bloodfeud, Kindred and Government', 55–6; Carpenter, *Locality and Polity*, 376, 397, 436, 555; Hyams, *Rancor and Reconciliation*, 14–16.

[57] *CCR 1476–85*, no. 129, pp. 38–9; Cardew, 'Anglo-Scottish', 331.

[58] Threlkeld *v.* Thornbugh, 1447 (CAC, Carlisle: D/Lons L5/1/50/15, formerly T 58).

Part III

welewillers', the terms of the award were for the parties to become 'full frends and herty lufhers and frohensforth kepe the kings peas and no chalange compleint or fray make ... or procure to be done for any hurt greiuances offensez had or done to tham or ony of thame afore this tyme'.[59] Both of these illustrations demonstrate specific expectations that peace, once made, was to be observed for the future. A third example, in which a bond to submit to arbitration was followed by an agreement for marriage between the disputing families, laid down contingency plans that any future disagreements were to come before the same panel of arbitrators and two additional men.[60]

In other cases the point is taken further. On a few occasions, new amity was to be established not just for the future but also, and at first glance bizarrely, for the past. Thus the first item of one award was for the disputants to be 'full freends and gud and feithfull freendshipp shew aither too vther from þis daie foorþewart', and the last item was for them to be 'full frends from þis daie bakkwarde'.[61] In another instance parties were likewise to be 'full frends and full frenschip bere frome hensforthe for any cawse or thyng done or movyd betwene thame fro þe begynyng off þe werd to þe sate off þe day' (i.e., from the beginning of the world to the setting of the sun on the day) of the making of the award.[62] Such backward-looking arrangements for amity may seem odd. However, they become intelligible if they are viewed as attempts to eradicate all excuses for revenge that might potentially be summoned by the memory of previous grievances and justified by relationships of enmity. Such an intention emerges more explicitly in an award from 1482 in which both parties were to be 'full frinds and louers[,] and all maner rancours and vnkyndenesses clerly remitte and set apart'.[63] In a successful compromise in a feud-like dispute, the very threat of retaliation and the legitimacy of vengeance had to be extinguished by the creation of new relationships. However, such language was not peculiar to the marches. For example, it appeared in 1426 in connection with the arbitration by the archbishop of Canterbury for the bishop of

---

[59] Denton *v.* Brisco, 1470 (CAC, Carlisle: D/Lons/D 64).

[60] Lowther *v.* Lancaster, 1499 (CAC, Carlisle: D/Lons/LO 112, 114). For a similar case of provision for future disputes to be resubmitted to the same arbitrators, see Powell, *Kingship, Law, and Society*, 102.

[61] Pennington *v.* Lamplugh, 1465 (CAC, Whitehaven: D/Pen/Bundle 47/22).

[62] Curwen *v.* Salkeld, 1473 (CAC, Carlisle: D/Lons/L5/1/33/SH 25). See also similar phrasing in Musgrave *v.* Threlkeld, 1445 (CAC, Kendal: WD/Ry/Box 92/no. 91); Sandford *v.* Salkeld, 1472 (CAC, Carlisle: D/Lons/L5/1/3/75, formerly AS 68); Sandford *v.* Salkeld, 1477 (CAC, Carlisle: D/Lons/L5/1/3/82, formerly A 73).

[63] Hilton *v.* Musgrave, 1482 (CAC, Carlisle: D/Mus/2/3 box 25/no. 124).

Concord

Winchester and the duke of Gloucester,[64] in an award in Lancashire in 1484[65] and in the Courtenay–Bonville award of 1441, whereby the parties set aside all disputes 'from the beginning of the world until now'.[66] Such a measure served to change the rules of the relationship between the parties and, in the eyes of God for whom past, present and future coexisted, transformed their relations into amity.[67]

The vocabulary regularly appearing in such instruments of compromise was, so the preceding examples show, focused on love and friendship, or amity.[68] Of course, this is the obverse of the normative language of hostility, and the heart, '*cor*', also stands out as a vital notion, appearing in the words 'accord' and 'concord', which were used to describe what should replace strife and discord. This language also evokes the opposite of expressions of rancor and malice of heart observed earlier.[69] However, the Christian ideals of love and forgiveness were so pervasive that, on their own, they cannot be taken as anything more than the most general normative statements about harmonious relations.[70] While still other instances from the far north could be cited of peacemaking done so that the disputing parties were to 'stand trewe and faithfull frendes' to each other and other similar sentiments,[71] it would show only that the inhabitants of England's northern marches deployed language which flowed in the European mainstream of conceptions of compromise.[72] And, as some of the illustrations above show, this vocabulary was not particular to the border counties but was consistent throughout England.[73] All that said,

---

[64] *Chronicles of London,* ed. C.L. Kingsford (Oxford, 1905), 89. Gloucester undertook to be good lord to Winchester, 'and have him in love and affeccion as his kinsman and vncle' (91); they took each other by the hand, before the king, in token of good love and accord (94).

[65] *Register of Thomas Rotherham,* ed. Barker, no. 1620, pp. 201–2.

[66] Storey, *House of Lancaster,* 88.

[67] J. Coleman, *Ancient and Medieval Memories: Studies in the Reconstruction of the Past* (Cambridge, 1992), 96–100 (on St Augustine and time). I am grateful to Carl Watkins for this reference.

[68] Others have suggested various origins for the idea of love in peacemaking, including Matthew 5:44, 'Love your enemies', or Vergil, '*Omnia vincit amor et nos cedamus amori.*' It is also famously expressed in the maxim '*pactum legem vincit et amor iudicium*' from the *Leges Henrici Primi* and in the motto on the brooch worn by Chaucer's prioress: '*Amor vincit omnia.*' The last three are cited in Clanchy, 'Law and Love in the Middle Ages', 48, and the first is alluded to by Hyams, *Rancor and Reconciliation,* 45.

[69] See above, pp. 181 and 281–2.

[70] On accord and emendation and the imagery of harp chords, see *Dives and Pauper,* ed. Barnum, I, ii, 28–9.

[71] Musgrave *v.* Wharton, 1455 (CAC, Carlisle: D/Mus/2/box 38/no. A111).

[72] For example, see D.L. Smail, 'Common Violence: Vengeance and Inquisition in Fourteenth-Century Marseille', *Past & Present,* 151 (1996), 44–5; Kuehn, *Law, Family, and Women,* 51, 71, 73.

[73] J. Bossy, 'Practices of Satisfaction, 1215–1700', *Studies in Church History,* 40, (2004), 106–18; W.H. Campbell, 'Theologies of Reconciliation in Thirteenth-Century England', *Studies in Church History,* 40, (2004), 84–94; Rowney, 'Arbitration in Gentry Disputes', 371; Payling, *Political Society,* 202–4.

Part III

what the preceding examples show is that this vocabulary and phrase-ology of peace could take on a more definite significance in serious, violent disputes, when the second component of peacemaking came into focus as a goal of successful conciliation, for the transformation of old enmity into new amity through creating new social bonds and similar steps to extinguish the desire for revenge. Yet, all the same, historians of other English localities, commenting on arbitrations, have not given much weight to the intentions behind this sort of language. Rather, they suggest that conciliation in gentry disputes (whether through the forceful direction of social superiors or the auspices of social equals) was more typically a matter of 'expeditious and equitable settlement,'[74] sometimes only temporarily acceptable compromise,[75] or restoration of order and neutralisation of conflict,[76] all in a manner corresponding especially to the first component of peacemaking which concentrated on ceasing violence and establishing an armistice between antagonists. Where the language of new amity together with the provision for actually making it has been found, it has been understood to be exceptional.[77] Is this so because fewer disputes elsewhere in England were serious enough to call for the invocation of new amicable bonds and their creation? The subsidiary point to be made here is that in evaluating evidence from the border counties in light of what has been established for other parts of the kingdom, some differences are readily apparent (such as the role of wider kin noted above), but we soon come to the supposition that in order to answer a question like this in a satisfactory way, the relevant evidence from other parts of the kingdom would benefit from reconsideration.

RECONCILIATION CEREMONIES

To achieve the second element of peacemaking, social relationships could be redefined through various customary practices. Elaborate cere-monial reconciliations are one such practice and have been observed as part of peacemaking across medieval Europe, and in many other

---

[74] For example, Bennett, *Community, Class and Careerism*, 221.

[75] For example, Wright, *Derbyshire Gentry*, 122.

[76] For example, Carpenter, *Locality and Polity*, 376, 397, 433, 472–5, 538, and wider comment at 621–9.

[77] This element of peacemaking is recognised by Powell, who plays it down as an exceptional pattern among arbitrations in England. In the Bruyn–Gatacre award of 1427 he observes the provision by one party to secure a noble patron's good lordship for the other as such a new social tie: 'Settlement of Disputes', 36–7, 37–8, 40 ('new bonds of association between the disputants'); Powell, *Kingship, Law, and Society*, 101–2, 107.

320

Concord

societies. Although they have been observed in an English context, the evidence from the northern marches suggests they flourished there. The rituals involved in such ceremonies, held before onlookers, often reveal the influence of the church and were another assertion of legitimacy and an invocation of customary norms quite apart from those of royal justice. These rituals were the obverse of the declarations of hostile enmities discussed in the preceding chapter. Their purpose was to enact the redefinition of group relationships, and so publicly to transform old enemies into new friends.[78]

In some ways reconciliations were similar to the better-known and already mentioned lovedays associated with arbitration, for both contained elements of open ritual through which adversaries formally confronted each other.[79] However, an essential difference is that lovedays were normally the occasion, following preliminary negotiations and receipt of written submissions, on which arbitrators decided the terms of an award and delivered it.[80] For example, a typical loveday was the 'day of þe arbetracion' assigned to be held in the church of the Friars Minor in Carlisle on the first Monday in Lent, 1422.[81] In another case from the same decade the parties and arbitrators met to make an award in the chapel on the Tyne Bridge at Newcastle.[82] By contrast, as we shall see, reconciliation ceremonies were not the setting for the determination of an award but, rather, for acting out the terms of an award previously given. Reconciliation ceremonies also differed from lovedays in that they were likely to incorporate rituals of submission and humiliation, which involved formal acts done by the offending party to acknowledge the dominance of their opponents.[83]

Acts of submission and self-abasement were designed to eradicate enmity and its imperatives of vengeance and to facilitate forgiveness and the start of new amity. They illustrate the role of honour and status: for a pacification to be honourably accepted by the offended party, the offender must even the score of honour by openly humiliating himself in favour of his opponent. The goal was to offer honour to a hostile opponent rather than (at the most extreme) the blood of a would-be

---

[78] I make no attempt to imbue the terms 'ritual' and 'ceremony' with any conceptual meaning beyond ritual as a symbolic, replicated act, and ceremony as a sequence of such acts.

[79] Clanchy, 'Law and Love in the Middle Ages', 58–61, 59; Powell, 'Settlement of Disputes', 33–4.

[80] Powell, *Kingship, Law, and Society*, 105; Bennett, 'The Medieval Loveday', 351–70. Cf. Miller, *Bloodtaking*, 261.

[81] Berdesay *v.* Rybton, 1422 (CAC, Kendal: WD/Ry/Box 92/no. 77).

[82] Ogle *v.* Elmeden, 1425 (*CCR 1422–9*, 210).

[83] Armstrong, 'Violence and Peacemaking', 69–71, implicitly contends that submission ceremonies can be equated with reconciliation ceremonies. I now understand reconciliations to incorporate submissions, but not by necessity.

Part III

expiator.[84] Visual imagery and physical acts of humiliation were abundant in various medieval rituals. For example, homage itself involved postures of submission and other acts including hand-holding, oath-taking and kissing.[85] Chivalry and its law of arms embraced analogous ceremonies, for during wartime the townsmen might make their personal surrender in a siege by wearing a rope around the neck, a symbol of low-status hanging, or bearing a naked sword by the point, a symbol of high-status beheading.[86] The dubbing of knights of the Bath in peacetime involved an elaborate ritual sequence including the bearing of a scabbarded sword by the point, kneeling and the 'accolade', by which the king struck the squire in the neck.[87] Executions for treason also regularly featured degradation for the elite. Archbishop Scrope was led to his execution for his part in the Percy rebellion of 1405 wearing a linen shirt and a blue cloak over his shoulders.[88] Exposed undergarments, especially shirts of linen, were associated with lowly manual labourers, and southern gentlemen who submitted to Henry VI in 1451 wore this attire.[89] The latter case points to the link between submission and reconciliation. Recently, one scholar has convincingly argued that the origins of the homage ritual itself lie in ceremonies of peacemaking.[90]

While historians of late medieval England have noted acts of contrition and atonement as part of the peacemaking process, the essential distinction between lovedays and reconciliation ceremonies

---

[84] J. Bossy, 'Blood and Baptism: Kinship, Community and Christianity in Western Europe from the Fourteenth to the Seventeenth Centuries', *Studies in Church History,* 10 (1973), 129–43; White, 'Feuding and Peacemaking', 220–1, 240, 256. See also Hyams, *Rancor and Reconciliation,* 9, 203; Miller, *Bloodtaking,* 185, 212, 269–71, 277, 283, 355; Boehm, *Blood Revenge,* 134–6, 152.

[85] This was the oath of fidelity, or fealty. Acts of 'servile' homage, done by unfree men to their lords in earlier centuries, could involve wearing a noosed rope or halter around the neck or placing pennies on the head: Hyams, 'Homage and Feudalism', 14, 20, 21; Hyams, *Rancor and Reconciliation,* 202–6; J. Le Goff, 'The Symbolic Ritual of Vassalage', in J. Le Goff (ed.), *Time, Work and Culture in the Middle Ages,* trans. Arthur Goldhammer (Chicago, 1980), 237–87, at 240–3, 256, 262–3.

[86] The Calais garrison's surrender in 1347 has been cited as an example of such display: Keen, *Laws of War,* 122.

[87] Described in the early fifteenth-century account printed in A. Wagner, N. Barker and A. Payne, (eds), *Medieval Pageant: Writhe's Garter Book: The Ceremony of the Bath and the Earldom of Salisbury Roll* (London, 1993), appendix B, 68–74. I am grateful to Maurice Keen for having directed me to this source.

[88] Keen, 'Treason Trials', 87, 92, also discussing the degradations and executions of Andrew Harclay in 1323 (89), and Sir Ralph Grey, in 1464 (90–1).

[89] *CPR 1446–52,* 508. Sumptuary legislation prescribed attire for the lower orders: *PROME,* October 1363, items 25–32, at 31. I am grateful to Robin Netherton and Laura Hodges for helpful exchanges concerning linen.

[90] Hyams, 'Homage and Feudalism', 13–49.

Concord

has been missed, the two often being lumped together in discussions of arbitration.[91] In some cases, the two types of events were also lumped together by participants, such as the great Yorkist-Lancastrian loveday at London on 25 March 1458, which incorporated an elaborate staged reconciliation ceremony (and which only reinforced the solidarities of the rival groups).[92] A less well-known reconciliation ceremony, but one which stood on its own, occurred before parliament in 1404. On this occasion, 'kiss and make up' was quite literally the order of the day when, at the king's command, the disputing earls of Westmorland and Northumberland 'took one another's hands and kissed one another openly three times, in confirmation of the complete unity and concord between them'.[93] This was doubtless an adaptation of the 'kiss of peace', familiar to all present from the communion liturgy. It also featured in rituals of marriage and homage, whereby persons were admitted into new relationships of kinship and lordship.[94]

Moving from the national context to the English marches, the evidence shows that reconciliation ceremonies were employed in this region to a degree not evidenced in local studies further south.[95] One arbitration award from 1442, in a violent dispute between Sir John Pennington and John Broughton, esquire, made a specific provision concerning Pennington's supporter William Lowte, who had struck Broughton's supporter Christopher Copeland (both men almost certainly of yeoman status). Lord Harrington, the arbitrator, ordained that the next time that Copeland came into Furness he was 'to com to me that I may make hym to take þe said William by þe hande in tokenyng of

---

[91] However, see Rawcliffe, 'Great Lord as Peacekeeper', 41–3; B.A. Hanawalt, 'The Power of Word and Symbol: Conflict Resolution in Late Medieval London', in B.A. Hanawalt (ed.), 'Of Good and Ill Repute': Gender and Social Control in Medieval England (Oxford, 1998), 35–52, at 49.

[92] H.E. Maurer, 'Margaret of Anjou and the Loveday of 1458: A Reconsideration', in Biggs, Michalove and Reeves (eds), Traditions and Transformations, 109–24. See also Watts, Henry VI, 343–8; Carpenter, Wars of the Roses, 143.

[93] PROME, January 1404, item 18: the earls were to expel 'toutz malices et rancours de lour coers'. By the king's command, 'coment qe n'avoit nul poisant coer ne moleste entre eux, come ils disoient, entrepristeront lour maynes, et s'entrebaiserent trois foitz overtement, en affermance de pleine unitee et concorde parentre eux'. See also the duke of Gloucester and Cardinal Beaufort reconciled in parliament in 1426, with hands only: ibid., February 1426, item 13.

[94] Clanchy, 'Law and Love in the Middle Ages', 59; Le Goff, 'Symbolic Ritual of Vassalage', 239, 242–4, 252, 255–6, 266; Bossy, Christianity in the West, 21, 60, 71; Hyams, 'Homage and Feudalism', 25–6. See also Matthew 5:23–4, on forgiveness before communion.

[95] It may be that historians focused further south have simply missed these ceremonies, or dealt with them as 'arbitrations' generally, but the lack of emphasis on such events in the historiography at any rate tells of their relative unimportance in an English context. For acts of contrition, see Rawcliffe, 'Great Lord as Peacekeeper', 41–3 (also relying on some northern examples); Hanawalt, 'The Power of Word and Symbol', 49.

Part III

frendschep'.[96] The vital element here was the physical act of taking an opponent by the hand, in what amounted to a gesture of forgiveness and unity in the presence of the peacemaking lord or other onlookers. Such handholding is evocative of 'bodily' oaths which involved touching the gospels and sometimes (as seems very likely) embracing the other party.[97] Moreover, it was the offended Copeland who was given the initiative. He could choose never to come into Furness again and so avoid the ceremony altogether, but such self-imposed banishment was perhaps not very tempting. Either way, the award intended that these men should never meet again as enemies, but rather to 'stonde full and sadd frends'.[98] In yet another example, two enemies were linked in new amity through plans for an annual encounter. A knight was to receive a life annuity from his former opponent (an esquire), 'to be hadd in the manner of a fee by the hand', thus reinforcing their new tie with a predictable and personal act.[99] The role inversion of superior and inferior status here suggests a complexity facilitated by amicable relations rather than conventional upwards deference.

Still more elaborate conciliatory arrangements can be found in this region, involving submission and oath-taking. Some appear in another violent Cumbrian dispute at Ulpha arising in 1450 between two groups of apparent yeomen connected with the gentleman William Thwaites and the esquires John Huddleston and the same John Broughton just mentioned.[100] Lord Egremont's award in the affair required one yeoman to supplicate to Broughton for forgiveness at his hall, and, in preparation, he was to sue by 'a frend of his' to know 'at what tyme resonatle it may plese hym [Broughton] to come to his submission forseid'. Likewise, the same man was then to sue to William Thwaites, to come to the 'Hall of Thaytis, and ther to submit hym[self]' to Thwaites.[101] Egremont's award

---

[96] The award was made at Ulverston in Furness on 25 September 1442 (CAC, Whitehaven: D/Pen/Bundle 47/19). Pennington's seat was Muncaster in southern Cbl., and Broughton, presumably of Broughton-in-Furness just across the county border, served as MP for Cbl. in 1437 (*REM*, I, 329).

[97] For example, see 'bodely assurit by þe trowth off þayr bodys' (CAC, Kendal: WD/Ry/Box 92/ no. 77); 'bodily sworn' (ibid., nos 93, 94); 'bodily sworn' to stand award (CAC, Whitehaven: D/Pen/Bundle 47/22); discharges to be made 'auther by surety of hande or buke' (ibid., 47/19); 'bondone by the suertie of ather of thare handez' (ibid., 23/2). See also Jones and Walker, 'Private Indentures', 30, on the unexplained 'pledge of faith' in Neville of Westmorland bonds.

[98] In homage, the vassal's journey to the lord was part of the ritual: Le Goff, 'Symbolic Ritual of Vassalage', 273, and 241–2 for comments on hand-holding.

[99] Musgrave (esq.) *v.* Hilton (kt.), 1482 (CAC, Carlisle: D/Mus/2/3 box 25/no. 124).

[100] *Cata. Deeds*, iv, 327 (A 8559).

[101] The 'Hall of Thwaites' is probably the modern Hallthwaites. William Thwaites was an oath-taker for Cbl. in 1434 (*CPR 1429–36*, 383), but otherwise was very obscure. See also the commissioners Henry Thwaites (*CPR 1422–9*, 499) and John Thwaites (*CPR 1429–36*, 425, 535).

Concord

also laid down that a man from the second party was to make an exculpating oath: at Millom 'kyrk' on Good Friday next, he was to 'excuse hym opon a boke . . . that he was never gelty of sleying' a doe 'wilk wase said he shuld have slan in Ulpho'.[102] Other disputes in the marches featured similar oaths, not simply to disavow responsibility but actually to deny events.[103] One appears in the award by Thomas Sandford of Askham, from 1467. Here one yeoman was to swear an 'excusacion' by the dean's letters at the parish 'kirkes' of Kendal and Windermere that he took no goods from his opponent or his 'childer', except certain animals which he had already acknowledged. Furthermore, 'this said excusacion' was to be made at such day and time as the swearer 'kan be made swre to com and gang to þe said Kirkes both at þe lawe and by þe lawe'.[104] These look like openly acknowledged attempts to rewrite agreed accounts of recent events. Such efforts, sworn before witnesses, would require oath-taker and audience to hold a shared view of memory in which recollection itself was valued not for factual accuracy but for its exemplary purpose; in this way an ideal, communal version of the past was agreed so as to create the desired social outcome. Certain understandings of time and memory advocated by prominent writers made such editing out of empirical fact not only possible but a meaningful step towards redemption.[105] Yet there seems to be another advantage gained by such shared revisions. Much like backward-looking arrangements for amity just explored, the expulsion of violent offences from an agreed narrative would serve also to invalidate, and so obviate, any future acts of vengeance.

The most detailed account of peacemaking in the English marches comes from the other side of the Pennines, in the *Causa de Heron*. The first item of the award delivered in September 1430 by the umpire, Prior John Wessington of Durham, required John Maners and his son and 'thair kyn and frendes' to come to Newcastle on a day to be assigned before Midsummer next and to

---

[102] He was to swear in the presence of Huddleston (lord of Millom and doubtless the owner of the doe) or, in his absence, of the vicar and the parish. The award was given on Ash Wednesday (18 February 1450). Because of the ecclesiastical prohibition on oath-taking during Lent, Good Friday (3 April) may well have been selected as the next closest date on which this could be done.

[103] Exculpating oaths appear in the Pennington–Broughton award just mentioned, and in the *Causa de Heron*.

[104] CAC, Carlisle: D/Lons/L5/1/3/68, formerly AS 62a.

[105] See, for example, the discussion of Cistercian 'blanched' memory in Coleman, *Ancient and Medieval Memories*, 175–85, at 180. I am grateful to Carl Watkins for bringing this book to my attention.

Part III

'lawely submyt thaym wt wordes [*'and dedes' interlineated in draft*] of humblenes and of submission forto be appoynted be the sayd nompers the whilk persones sall be pesably and agreably [*'and thankfully' struck through in draft*] resseyued vnto gude loue and charite in fourme as the sayd nomperes ther sall appoynte and declar'.[106]

Maners undertook this obligation quite seriously and sought exact clarification from Wessington as to how many of his 'kynn' he should bring and 'what ... wordes or dedes of humbleness' he and his 'frendes' should do, quite probably reflecting a desire to get it right to the satisfaction of all concerned.[107] The ceremony itself, like some arbitrations and oaths we have noted, took place on holy ground, in this case in the church of St. Nicholas in Newcastle. While churches had an important role as focal points for social and business life, they were also supernaturally charged spaces which solemnised the actions taken within and offered the opportunity to demonstrate humility before God himself.[108] Not only was the location of the ceremony sacred but so, it seems, was the timing. It took place on Thursday in Whitsun Week, 24 May 1431. Having made the award in September, it seems significant that Wessington would choose to wait until the following May to hold the reconciliation. Pentecost (Whitsunday) celebrates the descent of the holy spirit to the earth, which occurred when the apostles were all with one accord in one place ('*erant omnes pariter in eodem loco*'). The emphasis on accord and salvation in the festival may have made it an important time for peacemaking.[109] It is also noteworthy that Whitsunday was the deadline given for all reparation payments in the Pennington–Broughton award of September 1442.[110]

When the time came, all the sons and sons-in-law of Sir Robert Ogle, John Maners and his associates in the affair, and all his 'kyn and frendes and all thase persons' that were with him at the death of William Heron, attended the ceremony in the presence of the priors of Durham, Guisborough and Tynemouth, and of the earl of Northumberland. A script for the proceedings was prepared in draft, and the event was to begin with John Maners and his son swearing an exculpating oath 'apon a boke' to Sir Robert Umfraville, Isabel Heron and 'all the childer of William

---

[106] DUL, DCM: Loc. V, 45, and the draft at 45*.

[107] DUL, DCM: Loc. V, 48. See Armstrong, 'Violence and Peacemaking', 64, 69–70. I no longer see this as a Scottish custom imported experimentally across the border, but rather something already well understood in the English marches.

[108] Le Goff, 'Symbolic Ritual of Vassalage', 273–5. On churches as social focal points, see Carpenter, 'General Introduction', in *CIPM XXII 1422–7*, 33.

[109] DUL, DCM: Loc. V, 45d (date endorsed). See Armstrong, 'Violence and Peacemaking', 70n 90, for further comment on the word *pariter* in the Vulgate (Acts 2:1) and on Pentecost.

[110] Pennington *v.* Broughton, 1442 (CAC, Whitehaven: D/Pen/Bundle 47/19).

Concord

Heron ... all kyn alyes frendes and servantʒ of [Heron and his servant Atkynson] alswell present as absent'. The oath allowed father and son to recite an agreed version of events and to declare that they 'sore hase repented and yit repentes' the deaths and that they 'er noght gilty of na maner of felony nor malyce purpensed aforsayd'.[111] They then asked their adversaries to be good and tender friends to them and that 'gode love and charite may ever bide amang us'. In response, the Heron party then admitted the Maners party 'to pece euer to endure'.[112] Unfortunately, no record survives of the required 'deeds' of humbleness, nor of how the Maners party came dressed, and whether swords, ropes, kneeling, hand-holding or kissing were involved. Yet what is clear is that this ceremony's rituals eliminated enmity and the legitimacy of revenge and initiated new bonds of love and peace.

How far can these ceremonial conciliations be understood as part of a normative framework of disputing in the English marches operating apart from royal justice? The clearest indications come from the two later Westmorland indentures introduced in the preceding chapter.[113] In the first of these examples, the servant of a local esquire was to 'come in to the kirk of' Kirkby Stephen on Sunday, 7 October 1498, 'and summytte hym to the [opposing party] and þare frendes accordyng as he shalbe appoynted'. That this was an important and regularised procedure is suggested by three further references in the document to the submission, twice calling it as 'the seid day of summyssion'.[114] Four years later a second indenture, on a different matter, provided that another offender was to make a 'lawly submission' to the widow of a victim 'for his deth *after the custume and maner of the countrey*'.[115] Here is an unambiguous statement that existing local customary practice comprehended and shaped conciliatory ritual submissions.

The evidence suggests that a repertoire of elements was well understood and incorporated, in various combinations, into the process of peacemaking in the marches. This is hardly to suggest that behind every

---

[111] On 'malyce purpensed', see above, pp. 285–6.

[112] DUL, DCM: Loc. V, 53 (see also 45d): to be 'gude souereyns [and in no. 45 as 'souerans'] and tendre frendes till vs'. After this, Maners related that he had endowed masses for Heron's soul, and then bonds were entered by both parties for the payment of all sums and the observance of the award.

[113] See p. 304.

[114] CAC, Carlisle: D/Mus/2/box 38/no. A31. The submission was to be done on 'the sonday þe vviith day of October next folowing the date herof' [the date being 29 September, Michaelmas]. Following the submission the servant was to begin a period of banishment.

[115] CAC, Carlisle: D/Mus/2/box 38/no. A33 (emphasis added). The submission was to be done 'at suche daie and place as the said lorde [Dacre] shal appoynte be twix this [11 October 1502] and the fest of Crystynmes next to com'.

Part III

arbitration and loveday lies an unrecorded reconciliation ceremony, or indeed that such practices were exclusive to the region.[116] Yet it seems a fair contention that when feud-like enmities came up for resolution, participants in the local societies of the marches could require the performance of certain customary acts to direct and transform the hostile relationship into a peaceful one. In this way, significant weight and social pressure was laid upon those involved to accept the peace that was being made and to mark a new beginning of friendship and amity. Here we see the intention to reinforce new bonds until, like glue, they stuck on their own, for what had to be overcome was the inertia of a support group's desire to preserve the very relationships which lent it cohesion. However, in line with practice further south, neither the power of the church nor the authority of greater men was ever very far removed from this process.[117]

COMPENSATION

Another means of redefining group relationships was gift exchange, such as that accomplished through the payment of redress for wrongs.[118] We have already seen that compensation payments were built into international march law.[119] Comparable reparations, in various forms, are also sometimes to be found further south in England, although not granted by common law but rather as a result of arbitration awards, and not always in remedy of violence but sometimes as a lump sum or annuity to compensate for the loss of lands.[120] The potential for compensation payments to create a positive reciprocal bond of exchange, fostering and reinforcing a new relationship of amity between donor and recipient, is what stands out for the present analysis.[121] Payments might take the form of endowment of masses for the souls of the dead, and other gifts made to the church. Such donations were partly compensation rendered

---

[116] See the 'lowly submyssion' (1492) recorded in *Merchant Taylors' Company of London,* ed. Davies, 210.

[117] On enforcement (in terms of maintaining peace among potentially dissatisfied parties), see Powell, 'Arbitration and the Law', 56–7; Payling, *Political Society,* 214.

[118] From some early medieval societies, law codes providing for reparations are all that survive to tell us about conflict. See Wallace-Hadrill, 'The Bloodfeud of the Franks', 459–87; Davies, 'Survival of the Bloodfeud in Medieval Wales', 338–57; P. Wormald, 'Giving God and King Their Due: Conflict and Its Regulation in the Early English State', in P. Wormald (ed.), *Legal Culture in the Early Medieval West: Law as Text, Image and Experience* (London, 1998), 333–57.

[119] See above, pp. 188–9.

[120] On reciprocity in English arbitration, see Powell, *Kingship, Law, and Society,* 102–7.

[121] Le Goff, 'Symbolic Ritual of Vassalage', 253; White, '*Pactum . . . legem vincit*', 302; Geary, 'Living with Conflicts', 156, and his important comments at 156n 88 on gifts becoming grounds for the resumption of conflict. See also Miller, *Bloodtaking,* 77–83, 182, 277, 302.

Concord

to the kin and partly reparations made directly to the victim in the hereafter. They can be found occasionally throughout England,[122] and it must be said that just one clear example comes from the northern marches, in the *Causa de Heron*.[123]

However, the vocabulary of compensation in the border counties points to the importance of this aspect of conflict management. 'Assythement', a word of Anglo-Saxon origin meaning compensation paid in redress of wrong, is pertinent. It is well attested north of the border in Middle Scots.[124] The principle of reciprocity in this type of compensation comes across in a letter from a Scottish knight to the prior of Durham in 1443. The knight stated that he was ready 'to mak asythe, & to hafe the same' over the issues in debate between him and his nephew.[125] The verb 'to assyth' was used in Northumbrian Middle English in the fifteenth century. The *Causa de Heron* produces a document in which the Heron party asked that John Maners and his friends 'pay and assyth' all the debts of the deceased William Heron.[126] The word appears again in a mediated accord between Bertram Harbottle and Nicholas Bellingham from 1450, in which Bellingham's new wife, a Harbottle widow, was to receive various lands 'in full allouance and assethe of hir dower'.[127] The use of the word *assyth* south of the border at least indicates a specific vocabulary of compensation in the English far north.

The English marches also reveal several dispute pacifications which suggest that the provision of reparations in the far north was on a greater scale and with an emphasis that did not reflect the norms of disputes further south.[128] In a number of cases, 'hurts' and 'strokes' were recompensed by separate payments made between contenders.

---

[122] See, for instance, Bruyn *v.* Gatacre, Salop., 1427 (Powell, *Kingship, Law, and Society*, 101–2, 243–4); and the endowments for the dead earl of Northumberland and Lord Clifford after the battle of St Albans, 1455 (*English Chron.*, 77). See also Rosenthal, 'Feuds and Private Peace-Making', 90.

[123] The number and location of masses to be funded for William Heron were a major subject of the negotiations. Of the compensation paid to the Heron party, only 100 s. was to be given for the soul of Heron's dead supporter, Robert Atkynson (DUL, DCM: Loc. V, 44, 45, 51–3).

[124] Harding, 'Rights, Wrongs and Remedies', 2–8. See also p. 191.

[125] *Coldingham*, no. 160, p. 149. Discussed in Armstrong, 'Fyre of Ire Kindild', 75.

[126] DUL, DCM: Loc. V, 51.

[127] Bellingham's wife was Dame Margery, the widow of Sir Robert Harbottle. Bellingham *v.* Harbottle, 1450 (Alnwick Castle: Syon X.II.1, box 3, b).

[128] For instance, in Notts. in 1459 two lethal gentry disputes came to arbitration. One of these, Hastings-Ferrers *v.* Pierpont (W. Dugdale, *Baronage of England*, 3 vols (London, 1675), I, 580), involved reparation payments, while another, Pierpont *v.* Plumpton, did not (Payling, *Political Society*, 200–1).

Part III

For instance, one award from Cumberland in 1442 assigned no fewer than eight separate payments, seven of which were either 'for a hurt' or 'for a stroke'. Four went from the first party to the second, and four went in the opposite direction. Payments varied in amounts from one quarter-mark up to six marks for a 'greuous' stroke, and one mark was paid to a landlord for an entry into the houses of an opponent's tenants against their will.[129] In the Ulpha dispute of 1450, one offender, Thomas Proctour, was to pay £10 each to William and Hugh Sadeler, for injuries received at the hands of him and his 'feloship'. In return, both Sadelers were to pay ten marks to Proctour for like injuries.[130] Of course, Proctour lost out financially in this exchange, but the idea of one net payment by him would have missed the point. This was not cold accounting but a provision for a meaningful series of personal exchanges. Purses of silver were not simply delivered by messenger with compliments; some cases show specific provision for further ceremony. In an award from January 1470, payments in 'full recompence and satisfacon' of 'all maner strok hurtez offensez or greuancez' were to be made in the chapel of St Mary's Priory, Carlisle, 'aboue þe high auter', on two separate feast days.[131] Likewise, reparations for hurts assigned in 1473 by the abbot of Shap were to be paid by even portions at Whitsunday and Martinmas, into his own 'handys or in myne absence to my prior in oure abbay of Schapp and yt to be receyuyd in lyke fourme'.[132] In the *Causa de Heron*, reparations were to be paid 'in hand' at the reconciliation ceremony in 1431, and then by instalments every Christmas Day until the year 1440.[133] These unconcealed exchanges were less about satisfying a blood-price than about enacting

---

[129] Pennington *v.* Broughton, 1442 (CAC, Whitehaven: D/Pen/Bundle 47/19). William Lowte paid Christopher Copeland 80 s. (6 marks); Nicol Joneson paid William Davidson 13 s. 4d (1 mark); Nicol Joneson and John Hobken each paid Richard Paylea 6 s. 8d (half a mark each); Christopher Thwayt and Christopher Hudson each paid 40d (a quarter-mark each). John Davidson paid Christopher Thwayt 26 s. 8d (2 marks); John Davidson paid Richard Gaythird 26 s. 8d (2 marks); Richard Paylea paid Christopher Hudson 20 s. (one and a half marks); Roland Kirkby paid Sir John Pennington 13 s. 4d (1 mark) for the unwanted entry. For Kirkby connected to the Cockermouth affinity in 1448, see *Cata. Deeds,* iii, 101 (A 4751).

[130] *Cata. Deeds,* iv, 327 (A 8559). See also similar payments made so that 'diuerse and gret hurtys' be 'corecte' and 'amendit', in Sandford *v.* Salkeld, 1477 (CAC, Carlisle: D/Lons/L5/1/3/82, formerly AS 73).

[131] Brisco *v.* Denton (CAC, Carlisle: D/Lons/D 64). Half to be paid at the feast of St John the Baptist (24 June 1470) and half at feast of the Circumcision (1 January 1471). On the role of the high alter for oath-takings and investitures, see Le Goff, 'Symbolic Ritual of Vassalage', 273–4.

[132] Curwen *v.* Salkeld, 1473 (CAC, Carlisle: D/Lons/L5/1/33/SH 25).

[133] DUL, DCM: Loc. V, 44, 45; Armstrong, 'Violence and Peacemaking', 68. Maners was to pay the Heron party 250 marks, in £20 and then ten-mark instalments. These were in fact not a great deal more than the legal expenses claimed by Heron's widow (£137 5 s. 3d).

330

Concord

and reinforcing new relationships over time. They were also a phenomenon that appears to have been more common in the far north than in other parts of England.[134]

CONTRACTS OF LORDSHIP AND KINSHIP

So far we have seen that, in the pacification of serious feud-like disputes in the border region, a normative element was that new amity should replace old enmity and its hostile imperatives. Various practices helped to facilitate this redefinition and transformation of group relationships, such as reconciliation ceremonies and gift exchange in the form of compensation. A final practice of this type was the use of written contracts to redraw the very boundaries of group membership.

In late medieval England generally, peacemaking is not viewed as a direct function of indentures of retainer, although these have been linked in the aftermath of a resolution.[135] In the English marches there are, however, a few examples where the creation of bond between lord and man appears to be a direct tool of pacification.[136] Most well known is the indenture of 28 July 1474 by which the duke of Gloucester retained the earl of Northumberland, and which divided their authority after a period of animosity. As we have seen, for a time at least, this bond seems to have achieved calm.[137] Of a much lesser order of significance is the Ulpha dispute of 1450, in which a yeoman submitting to an esquire was to ask him 'to be his gode master knawlegyng that he has fautit to hym and offendit his god mastership'.[138] Also, one of Thomas Sandford of Askham's bonds of lordship with local yeomen in Westmorland was related to the resolution of a violent dispute. In October 1470 Sandford took a bond in £40 from William and John Walker, sons of Henry Walker, and all his children, who undertook to be true men and servants to Sandford, and take part with him in peace and war during their lives. More specifically, the Walkers agreed that, if Henry or his children were ever proved to have been at the 'hetyng' (injuring) of Wyll Wylkynson or the breaking of his house or the houses of Wyll Nobyll or Sandy Yate,

---

[134] For the arrangement of compensation elsewhere, see Rawcliffe, 'Great Lord as Peacekeeper', 44–5; Powell, 'Settlement of Disputes', 21–43, at 28–30.

[135] Powell, 'Settlement of Disputes', 27–8; Castor, 'Walter Blount', 31–2.

[136] See also Sir Thomas Dacre retained by Salisbury in 1435 (Jones and Walker, 'Private Indentures', no. 120, p. 150), above p. 158.

[137] Alnwick Castle, Northumberland MSS (Syon House), Y. II, 28 (consulted via BL microfilm reel 358). See pp. 218 and 305.

[138] Cata. Deeds, iv, 327 (A 8559). The esquire was John Broughton. See above, pp. 324 and 330.

331

Part III

then they would abide Sandford's arbitration in the matter.[139] All these examples show lordship bonds used more directly in border pacifications than was common further south in England, and in a manner that suggests networks of lordship were being extended to encompass old enemies.

A more commonplace form of social contract was of course the indenture of marriage, linking two kin groups. So-called peace-weaving marriages are a well-known practice of feud-like disputing in many societies, including Scotland in this period and England in earlier centuries.[140] This was the bond that had the strongest potential for successfully redrawing the boundaries of group membership, for in part its procreative aspiration was to breed new members. Considering the means by which it was put into effect, through betrothal rituals and a religious rite taking place in the communal and sacred space of a church, and involving oaths, hand-holding, kissing and gift exchange, marriage bears consideration as a ceremony with potential to be used in reconciliation.[141] Nuptials are not normally associated with dispute resolution in English local society.[142] Marriage arrangements are viewed by historians of this period primarily as business ventures in which families vied to maintain and augment their landed estates. Magnates often facilitated espousals among members of their own affinities, and such bonds made between existing associates reinforced their political and social ties. Typically, trust was a major prerequisite for the intermarriage of English families, and this fact would have caused many to shy away from the idea of giving a son or daughter to a violent enemy as a means of conciliation.[143] However, in the far

---

[139] Henry Walker's other son Thomas sealed the document (CAC, Carlisle: D/Lons/L5/1/3/71, formerly D/Lons/MD/AS 65; Jones and Walker, 'Private Indentures', 174n 372). For 'hetyng', see *MED*, s.vv. 'hete', 'heste'.

[140] For Scotland, see Armstrong 'Fyre of Ire Kyndild', 78–9n 115 (citing Wormald, 'Bloodfeud, Kindred and Government', 74, and other studies). The term comes from Anglo-Saxon literature: J. Sklute, 'Freothuwebbe in Old English Poetry', in H. Damico and A.H. Olsen (eds), *New Readings on Women in Old English Literature* (Bloomington, 1990), 204–10. See also Miller, *Bloodtaking*, 367n 12; Black-Michaud, *Cohesive Force*, 67, 92, 228.

[141] E. Chénon, 'Recherches historiques sur quelques rites nuptiaux', *Nouvelle revue historique de droit français et étranger,* 36 (1912), 573–660; Clanchy, 'Law and Love in the Middle Ages', 59; Le Goff, 'Symbolic Ritual of Vassalage', 256–61, 275; Gauvard, '*De grace espécial*', ii, 776–8; Hyams, 'Homage and Feudalism', 29, 39; Hyams, *Rancor and Reconciliation*, 13, 74, 201. Of course, marriage negotiations are also a potential source of discord; see Dean, 'Marriage and Mutilation'.

[142] Rawcliffe, 'Great Lord as Peacekeeper', 36, identifies a marriage alliance directed by the bishop of Durham to resolve an inheritance dispute at the end of the fifteenth century concerning the Neville Lords Latimer.

[143] See above, p. 314; Carpenter, *Locality and Polity*, 99–120, 620; *Stonor Letters*, introduction, 23–4; Bennett, *Community, Class and Careerism*, 26–30; A.J. Pollard, 'The Richmondshire Community of Gentry during the Wars of the Roses', in Ross (ed.), *Patronage, Pedigree and Power*, 47–8; Pollard, *North-Eastern England*, 107–10.

Concord

north, there is strong evidence to show the use of peace-weaving marriages along the lines of Scottish practice. At the highest level of local society, Hoyle has identified nuptials used to heal rifts among the nobility in the sixteenth-century far north, arguing that 'marriage, it turns out, marks the end of enmity rather than the celebration of amity'.[144] His point should be taken further, for marriage could mark the end of enmity *by creating new amity* and redefining group membership.

In the English marches in our period, there are strong indications that marriage was used as a tool of reconciliation among the gentry in this way. Two unions associated with violent disputes noted in the preceding chapter show signs that they were done in attempts to secure compromise.[145] Another marriage, from 1468 in Westmorland, was to all appearances part of a pacification. The knight Lancelot Threlkeld of Yanwath and the esquire Hugh Lowther Sr agreed to a contract of 'espouselx' between their families before an unusually large number of witnesses[146] and following local tensions.[147] Strains between the Threlkelds and Lowthers seem to evaporate from this time, suggesting that a successful compromise had been arranged in connection with this marriage.[148] A further example concerns the families of Pennington and Huddleston in southern Cumberland, who fell into strife before August 1474 when their dispute was put to arbitration, and they gave bonds to the king to do no harm or malice to each other, their tenants or servants. Eight years later, a marriage was arranged between them, in

---

[144] Hoyle, 'Faction, Feud and Reconciliation', 613.

[145] Sir John Lancaster of Rydal and Margaret Threlkeld (c. 1400), see above, pp. 292n 138, 293n 146, 301n 189.; Henry Carre and Katherine, widow of Sir Giles Thornton (c. 1478) (see p. 305).

[146] Done at Penrith, 11 April 1468 (CAC, Kendal: WD/Hoth/BR vol. 2, 477–8). Hugh Lowther's son Hugh was contracted to marry Lancelot Threlkeld's daughter Anne. Lancelot Threlkeld had married Margaret, the young widow of John, Lord Clifford (k. 1461). The witnesses were Christoper Moresby, esq. (husband of Lancelot's other daughter Margaret); Mr Thomas Eglesfield, master of the church of Greystoke; John Crackenthorpe of Howgill; John Vaux; Thos Wyber ['Ioyber']; and Edward Thornburgh. For comment on the marriage, see Booth, 'Landed Society', 25, 101–2, where he suggests a link through Threlkeld to Clifford lawyers at Skipton.

[147] The Lowthers were closely connected by marriage to a third family in this equation, the Lancasters. In 1456 Hugh Lowther Jr was contracted to marry Mabel, daughter and heir of William Lancaster of Hartsop (CAC, Carlisle: D/Lons/LO 111), and she was perhaps dead by 1468. Threlkeld took legal action in 1467 against Hugh and Robert Lancaster of Sockbridge, including an accusation of close-breaking at nearby Yanwath (KB 27/826 rots 9, 16d). These tensions probably related to the Threlkelds' acquisition of half of Yanwath in the 1420s from Lancaster co-heiresses (CAC, Kendal: WD/Ry/Box 92/nos 79, 90; Jackson, 'Threlkelds of Threlkeld', 307; see also above, pp. 301–3).

[148] For example, joint service on the Cbl. peace commission of February 1471 (*CPR 1467–77*, 610).

Part III

October 1482. The following January, Pennington gave a bond in £300 to Huddleston to perform the terms of the 'divers' indentures and obligations made between them, 'towchyng the mariage'.[149] Again, this case strongly suggests that a contract of kinship was used to achieve compromise between violent parties. In this process, group-based hostilities became obsolete when the barriers between these groups were dissolved. Through such marriages, opposing parties transformed their enmities into new bonds of amity through the giving and receiving of daughters, sisters, sons and spouses into a new web of kinship.

We can now summarise the findings of this chapter, and draw these together with those of the last. As throughout England, arbitration was widely used in the far north. However, by contrast with southern England, arbitrations here are not readily connected with court activity, suggesting that dispute resolution may often have been handled without reference to the courts. Westmorland stands out once again, in this case with a disproportionate share of arbitrations, a finding that further suggests extra-judicial dispute processes were strongly expressed in that county. In the resolution of serious, feud-like disputes, more was required than the restoration of local equilibrium or the status quo. Following the temporary restoration of cooperation, more profound change was needed. New bonds of amity were to replace those of enmity. In many ways, the language of dispute resolution in the marches was the same as that used throughout England, altogether strongly influenced by Christian ideals of love and forgiveness. But the language of new amity took on a greater significance when serious violence had occurred, and, in a few cases, this language allows insight into the intention of eradicating the legitimacy of possible vengeance. This was done by cancelling the commonly acknowledged relationship of enmity, in which such acts might be valid, and transforming it into one of amity, a process facilitated by certain practices. Reconciliation ceremonies involved elaborate rituals to even the balance of honour and to redefine relationships between groups. The reciprocal exchange of compensation for injury reinforced these new ties. In some cases, group membership itself could be redefined through new contracts of lordship and kinship. Some of these practices can also be found further south in England and cry out for reconsideration and better understanding, but, in our evidence from the English far north, they appear to have been part of a wider repertoire of accustomed practices of

---

[149] *CCR 1468–76*, no. 1317, p. 365. Sir John Pennington's son and heir, John, was to marry Sir John Huddleston's daughter Mary (Bodleian: Dodsworth MS, 41, fol. 113d (36); CAC, Carlisle: D/Hud/5/1).

334

Concord

disputing. Used in combination, these various elements could be the most effective way to manage serious feud-like strife. This was not a foolproof approach, for even these methods risked failure and required care. It is in this light that we can see the relative importance of strong lordship as a coagulant to hold these awkward new arrangements together until they stuck. All parties were aware that attempted resolution was not necessarily the end of the road.

Taking this chapter and the preceding one together, with regard to both violent disputing and to the making of peace, we have found robust evidence for a framework of conflict management at work in the marches other than that provided by royal justice or border justice. This took the form of accustomed practices of disputing, including as much overt, targeted attacks and the taking of revenge as elaborate conciliations conducted before onlookers. These practices could be very feud-like, particularly in reference to the use of language to signal the special status of a hostile relationship and in the renovation of that relationship in amicable terms through all the means just examined. There is a resonance in all this with the logic at work in march law, itself as we have seen best understood in a wider European context, including that of Scotland.[150] With respect to what is known about the rest of England, all this seems abnormal. In the northern marches, we have found clear indications that accustomed practices provided a framework for disputing that operated in addition to that of royal justice and that some disputes could be very feud-like indeed. We have also found influences shaping customary practices, not least the pan-European frameworks of chivalry and of the church. The chivalric law of arms shaped licit violence and also reconciliation ceremonies. Of course, it had the greatest influence on the nobility across England, but the lesser landed elite also participated in chivalric culture, and this influenced feud-like disputing in the English marches as well. There is evidence even to suggest that this trickled down to non-gentle yeomen, when emotional words like '*odium*' were used to describe a disputant's motivation for a lethal attack. It is especially with regard to pacification that we can see at work the norms of conflict shaped by the church, a framework which long pre-dated the late medieval expansion of royal justice. This is evident not least in the role of canon law in the legal basis of arbitration, in the direction of prelates in the making of peace, and in the influence of the liturgy in the rituals and timing of reconciliation. All this points to a deep reservoir of norms

[150] See above, pp. 170–2 and 197.

Part III

influencing practices of conflict. The same influence was present throughout England, but it seems to have been acted upon more often in the far north than it was, as far as has been appreciated by existing studies, in localities further south. All this would indicate that an overarching framework of royal justice and the king's law, despite its aspirations, was not wholly effective in crowding these other norms out of the picture.

11

CONCLUSIONS

This book has examined the English far north largely through the prism of conflict and its management. The region presents some remarkable patterns of local conflict and social organisation, and indeed in many ways appears exceptional given what is known about the rest of England. However, the region's reputation for being an exception oversimplifies matters to the point of distortion. In terms of landscape and settlement, the area reveals significant variation, and any attempt to treat those features as if they described an exclusively upland, pastoral environment devoted to livestock rearing must be avoided. Regarding elite architecture, there too is much variation, and the tower 'style' of the region cannot be understood solely as a response to military pressure of the frontier. The frontier itself must be appreciated in terms of both rhetoric and reality. The rhetoric of peril was a useful political tool; in reality, the marches of the frontier formed an outward-facing gateway for the kingdom, well integrated with the rest of the realm in all senses governmentally, and also legally and diplomatically integrated with the counterpart marches of Scotland. Real peril was experienced from time to time, but not as an omnipresent threat.

In the border counties, strong expressions of kin-based solidarities have been found. Some of these are unexpected and not well understood, such as the double patronyms featuring particularly in Westmorland. Others carry plenty of expectations but have not previously been investigated in any depth in the fifteenth century, particularly the antecedents of the riding 'Surnames' detectable in a suggestive way closer to the border itself. The evidence is indicative that these latter groups were already in existence in the years around 1400, but without a relevant terminology to describe them, for the nomenclature of the Surnames is not found before the 1490s. Strong expressions of kinship ties in the marches, even strong enough to cross the boundary between gentry and commoner, appear to show some similarity with aspects of Scottish

Conclusions

society across the frontier. They seem to result not from the pressures of an armed border but, as far as the Surnames go at least, from a wider shared cultural heritage in the areas closest to the border itself. And that more unexpected expression of the strength of kinship in the region, the use of patronymics generally and of double patronyms specifically among some of the elite peasantry, especially in Westmorland, does not appear to have an Anglo-Scottish dimension but rather reveals similarities with other parts of the English kingdom (i.e., Cornwall and Cheshire), which merit further investigation. One of the consequences of the strength of kinship bonds in the far north comes in relation to ties of lordship. Whereas it is understood that, as further south, lordship linked land-owners great and small in a web of relations (which a capable king could harness effectively to enforce his rule), in the far north kinship solidarities might take priority ahead of lordship and cut across the strength of that informal mechanism of governance. This could be a strength for an effective lord who might appreciate the need to accommodate webs of kin relations among his followers, as did nobles like the Percy earls and gentry like the Sandfords of Askham on a much more modest scale.

In the first part of our period of study, war tended to discourage and postpone local conflict in the marches among English borderers, while the resumption of legal claims in court and a rise in local offending coincided with the sealing of Anglo-Scottish truces. But from mid-century onwards that relationship can no longer be detected in the records. This suggests that the importance of military circumstances in the marches, never of primary significance anyway, declined across the century and that the relative importance of domestic political upheavals, exacerbated to the point of disaster in the late 1450s, grew by compari-son. Throughout the century, the Westminster-based court of king's bench was used regularly by marcher litigants. However, these same litigants were ready to experiment with new judicial structures, and there are possible signs of a diversion of court activity to the council in the north when it was first established in the mid-1480s. However, the reign of Henry VII from about 1490 produced a return of northern legal business to king's bench (and to the patterns of previous decades by 1494). All this confirms that royal justice, either through common law or indeed the equity jurisdiction of the council, was an active tool in local conflict. In this regard the marches show strong continuities with the rest of the kingdom.

A 'raiding culture' may be identified in the marches throughout the fifteenth century, but all the same this was neither widespread nor a symptom of a militarised war zone. While the border liberties did indeed produce the offenders of which so many petitions complained, illicit

Conclusions

cross-border activities were concentrated especially in the far north of Northumberland. Patterns in the practice of raiding are detectable, such as the apparent influence of the law of arms, and with regard to gender, expectations of men's and women's roles appear to have excluded women as acceptable targets. Raiding was focused especially on the plunder of sheep and cattle and should be interpreted primarily in the context of wider expectations and limits of social behaviour concerning retaliation for injury and wrong. In the trod, march law included provision for sanctioned retaliatory violence across the border chiefly for the recovery of stolen livestock. In some ways this patterned raiding looks very different from the rest of England, and it could be complicated by the possibility of escape across the border into another kingdom. Yet in other ways there are continuities too, for example, in terms of seasonal patterns, in traces of livestock theft in other regions with a similar mix of pastoral and arable farming, and in that internal borders between royal and franchise jurisdictions occurred elsewhere in the realm.[1]

This brings us to the normative frameworks of conflict management that have been investigated: royal justice, border justice and accustomed practices shaping processes of discord and concord. Normative influences on conflict here are best understood in their wider European context, encompassing the form of dispute known as 'feud'. In the far north there was an overlap and accommodation between the norms with which we are familiar further south and what we may justly call feud-like modes of conflict. The idea that there was a consensus shared by self-policing English landowners across the country on the limits to the use of violence in the course of local disputing would now seem incomplete in light of these findings.[2] That consensus did not hold in the far north, and this was not due to proximity to the Scottish border. Indeed, the greatest volume of evidence for local turbulence and a high intensity of violence comes from Westmorland, the county in the marches which was furthest from the border itself. The point about consensus among landowners not holding here may also be made in relation to the expectations of kinship and lordship just noted. One might ask where, then, did feud-like practices of conflict come from if not from Scotland? Certainly, kinship patterns, so important to aspects of conflict, shared in this region a

---

[1] For example, Thornton, *Cheshire*, 7–9, 103–18, on franchise jurisdictions; Wright, *Derbyshire Gentry*, 140, on cattle-stealing in the High Peak linked especially with the Vernon family (on whom, see ibid., 7–9, 18–20). On farming landscapes, see above, pp. 103–6. On the border liberties, see above, pp. 178, 236–8 and 266.

[2] See above, p. 40.

339

Conclusions

common heritage with Scotland in some regards. But the point bears reiteration here that kinship must be seen with nuance: some Surnames close to the border had direct Scottish elements and features, but the double patronyms concentrated away from the border in Westmorland did not. Still more importantly, the point of signalling wider comparisons with conflict in places like France, Germany and Scandinavia has in part been to show that relying for explanation on the proximity of Scotland to the far north of England can be a distraction.[3] That explanation assumes that feud-like practices of conflict must have 'come from' an external source. Yet in how conflict was expressed, pursued and managed, there are similarities between this region and other parts of Europe (including Scotland) that are known for feud-like practices in the later middle ages. Such comparisons also serve to highlight this study's implications not just for understanding the marches but for understanding all of late medieval England: that feud may have been indigenous to the English kingdom, too. To assume feud-like behaviour was merely a cross-border import risks confirming the country further south as normal and the far north as exceptional. The point goes to the heart of what historians mean by 'England' and the norms which shaped English political society.

The first chapter raised for discussion the ways in which assessments of the governance of the English polity have been framed by a reliance on ideas of centralisation and the relationship between centre and locality, and centre and periphery. The conceptual tool introduced there, that the English kingdom may usefully be thought of as a cellular composite, without reference to a 'centre', is pertinent to the question of norms. Multiple normative frameworks do not require a single centre but, rather, fit better an England of porous and outward-looking units sitting between the local and national levels of interpretation. This abstraction has the benefit of matching the contemporary idea of a realm made up of a series of 'contreis'; it also helps to capture some of the complexity and variation revealed in the far north. Assessments of the late medieval English polity which encompass the king's dominions beyond the realm itself tend towards pessimistic or conditional readings of the robustness of this political entity.[4] One historian has made the case for 'a serious failure'

---

[3] See above, pp. 28–36, 168–72, 197, 276, 284, 315–20 and 320–8.

[4] See Armstrong, 'Centre, Periphery, Locality, Province', for comment on the work of R. Frame, R.R. Davies and S.G. Ellis, among others. The influential work of J. Brewer, *The Sinews of Power: War, Money, and the English State, 1688–1783* (London, 1989), which should be read with M.C. Carpenter, 'Henry VI and the Deskilling of the Royal Bureaucracy', in L. Clark (ed.), *The Fifteenth Century IX: English and Continental Perspectives* (Woodbridge, 2010), 1–37, partly builds upon the idea of a centralised medieval kingdom, with Westminster at 'the centre of the core' (Brewer,

Conclusions

of governance towards the provinces (defined as the shires distant from the capital plus the palatinates of Durham, Chester and Lancaster) and the dominions (chiefly Gascony, Wales and its marches, and Ireland) in the fifteenth century, resulting from the crown's overextended obligations for supervision and control of these areas.[5] One response to that view might be described as centripetal in nature: it downplays particularity and emphasises the degree to which provincial politics were closely enmeshed with 'central alignments'.[6] Another reply has been to deny that there was any such structural imbalance between centre and periphery, and instead to ascribe governmental upheaval and territorial contraction from 1450 to an entirely 'circumstantial deficit in royal authority'.[7] By implication in the latter analysis the natural trend was centrifugal, so that without effective royal authority (undeniably essential in a monarchical government which, for all its administrative sophistication, still depended upon the active will of one assertive figure), the crown could become endangered.[8] If political society's behavioural attitudes were upheld by the royal authority which provided the sole normative framework of governance in the polity, then this centrifugal logic has force. On the other hand, if the framework of norms that ran throughout the cellular composite of the kingdom was more complex and variable than this, then it is less persuasive. Such complexity is what has been examined in the preceding chapters – an accommodation between norms of royal justice, border justice and accustomed practices of disputing (which encompassed feud-like modes of conflict). If royal authority was not an exclusive framework for the management of conflict, in the halls of Westminster any such mixing of norms could well have appeared awkward at best, threatening and destabilising at worst. Yet within the regions themselves, and for the country as a whole, could such circumstances have indicated not inherent instability and failure but, rather, durability and robustness?

With attention to palatinates, lesser liberties or towns, recent forays towards a pluralist or even polyfocal England have tended to focus on

---

Sinews of Power, xvi). Ellis's appraisal of the failure of Tudor governance has already been noted above: Ellis, *Tudor Frontiers*, 33, 40–5, 48.

[5] R.A. Griffiths, 'The Provinces and the Dominions in the Age of the Wars of the Roses', in S.D. Michalove and A.C. Reeves (eds), *Estrangement, Enterprise and Education in Fifteenth-Century England* (Stroud, 1998), at 4 (quote), 5–6, 11–12, 24–5.

[6] Pollard, 'Provincial Politics', 76–7 (quote). See also Frame, *Political Development*, 202; Pollard, 'Use and Ornament', 64–66; Thornton, 'Fifteenth-Century Durham'; Liddy, *Bishopric of Durham*, 10–11, 24; Holford and Stringer, *Border Liberties*; Arvanigian, 'Henry V'.

[7] Harriss, *Shaping the Nation*, 539. See also Carpenter, *Locality and Polity*, 348 (on a 'rudderless' kingdom without royal leadership).

[8] Watts, *Henry VI*, 364.

Conclusions

institutional frameworks.[9] The focus of this book has not been primarily on the institutions of government but on local conflict and its management, and the social structures associated with these, especially those of kinship and lordship. This theme of analysis is appropriate given the turbulence and emphasis on kinship and lordship that has been so prominent in historiography of the northern marches. More widely it responds to the McFarlane-inspired new constitutional history, an approach which gives due regard to the attitudes and behaviours of the members of late medieval political society. One aspect of new constitutional history has been to concentrate attention on 'the largely unspoken assumptions of the politically aware'; to produce a socially derived understanding of the relationship between locality and centre, between landowners and their king, between law, justice and the security of landed property; and (as we have already noted) to discern the scope of the 'consensus' among the gentry on the legitimate use of violence in local politics.[10] A crucial tenet in this approach has been the notion of a unitary centre and of the prevailing universal authority of the king and royal justice.[11] That view reflects the historiographical assessment that those parts of the realm distant from Westminster were self-evidently peripheral, exceptional in their isolation from the centre of power, and subject therefore to looser supervision and certain exemptions from the ordinary framework of governance.[12] That work has developed in an invigorating way our understanding of late medieval England. Yet the analysis presented in the preceding chapters questions whether areas associated with (for example) apparently high levels of conflict should be seen as exceptional, not least with reference to the fairly constrained and limited effects in our period of the fact that the far north was a military frontier. Throughout this study runs the evidence for inter-linkages between our area of enquiry and the capital, and the question of the nature of those connections. Undeniably, there was a 'hub of national government' at Westminster,[13] but the present exercise queries the expectation of the exclusivity of royal justice as the sole

---

[9] Holford and Stringer, *Border Liberties*, 4, 7; T. Thornton, *The Channel Islands, 1370–1640: Between England and Normandy* (Woodbridge, 2012); C.D. Liddy, *War, Politics and Finance in Late Medieval English Towns: Bristol, York and the Crown, 1350–1400* (Woodbridge, 2005); 15–17; Liddy, *Bishopric of Durham*, 9, 17, 23; E. Hartrich, 'Charters and Inter-Urban Networks: England, 1439–1449', *EHR*, 132 (2017), 219–49.

[10] See above, pp. 39–40, 169, 180, 315. Carpenter, *Locality and Polity*, 3–10 (and quote from 5), 624; Powell, 'After "After McFarlane"'; Carpenter, 'Political and Constitutional History: Before and after McFarlane'.

[11] Well expressed in Castor, *Duchy of Lancaster*, 306.

[12] Carpenter, *Wars of the Roses*, 56; Carpenter, 'Political and Geographical Space', 126.

[13] Harriss, *Shaping the Nation*, 41.

Conclusions

normative framework shaping conflict in political society – an expectation which is reinforced by the view of government requiring a 'centre'.

It has been suggested by one historian that it was the Hundred Years' War which closed the door to York's role as a 'competing capital' during the reigns of Edward I, II and III, in favour of settled royal government at Westminster.[14] Still, there are indications that such devolved or decentralised thinking remained viable, and even gained vigour under the Yorkist kings. It was in the 1470s and 1480s that the council of the Prince of Wales was established for Wales and its marches, and in which the council in the north was erected for the northern parts.[15] These were the means to enhance uniform access to the conciliar authority of the crown; yet the council also offered a highly flexible jurisdiction which might accommodate local conventions, values and attitudes. The council in the north marked a revived relationship between royal government and its northern capital. To be sure, Edward IV also followed the traditional pattern of rule by proxy in areas he did not visit regularly, through the practical delegation of the exercise of personal authority to great magnates such as Gloucester and Northumberland. This became most explicit in the palatinate grant to Gloucester in January 1483, whereby the royal duke received all regalian property and power in Cumberland, the west march wardenship in heredity, a one-off grant of 10,000 marks, and palatine authority over all lands yet to be conquered in south-west Scotland.[16] This grant prepared the ground for another Scottish campaign, and it is striking that the platform for this enterprise was to be focused on *Carlisle-Solway*. This was more than an ill-conceived concession to pressure from a grasping royal brother (who, as duke and later as king himself, had a significant relationship with the north); it aimed to re-project into Scotland the military pale of the

---

[14] Ormrod, *Edward III*, 91, 94–8, also commenting on Richard II's 'alternative power bases' promoted after 1387. By contrast, see Carpenter, 'Deskilling of the Royal Bureaucracy', 4, 20, 22–3, 28–9, 31, for the 'failure of much of the bureaucratic system in central government under Henry VI' (1), a system whose very strength, in Carpenter's assessment, partly derived from the concentration of personnel in Westminster and London. See also Carpenter, 'War, Government and Governance', 5, 11, 22, on bureaucratic achievement from Edward I to Henry V, and the potential durability of that system against an 'extended crisis of monarchy' (22).

[15] Brooks, *Council of the North*; D.E. Lowe, 'Patronage and Politics: Edward IV, the Wydevills, and the Council of the Prince of Wales, 1471–83', *Bulletin of the Board of Celtic Studies*, 29 (1981), 545–73.

[16] *PROME*, January 1483, item 13; *RP*, vi, 204–5. Discussed in Horrox, *Richard III*, 71–2; Booth, 'Landed Society', 145, 169–71, 182, 237. More generally, see D.A.L. Morgan, 'The King's Affinity in the Polity of Yorkist England', *TRHS*, 5th Ser., 23 (1973), 1–25; also D.M. Palliser, 'Richard III and York', in R. Horrox (ed.), *Richard III and the North* (Hull, 1986), 51–81; R.B. Dobson, 'Richard III and the Church of York', in R.A. Griffiths and J. Sherborne (eds), *Kings and Nobles in the Later Middle Ages: A Tribute to Charles Ross* (Gloucester, 1986), 130–54.

Conclusions

fourteenth century.[17] It was a rearrangement of the English north-west that was never to be. Yet as an illustration of what was believed to be possible in fifteenth-century minds it is instructive. To that extent it bears consideration alongside another might-have-been: the detailed programme for a confederate division of the realm set out by Owain Glyndŵr, Earl Henry Percy, and Edmund Mortimer in the so-called tripartite indenture of 1405, the year in which Henry IV faced down his last full-scale domestic revolt. Glyndŵr's portion was to be an enlarged Wales with an eastern boundary running from the Severn to the source of the Trent to the Mersey. The line of demarcation between the proposed Mortimer and Percy portions from Oxfordshire to the Wash broadly followed that between the watersheds of the Thames, on the one hand, and the Nene and Ouse, on the other.[18] It is a surprising document, yes, but in the words of R.R. Davies, 'not beyond the ken of political dreamers'.[19]

At its widest the aim of this book has been to prompt new questions about the norms of local conflict and the governance of the realm. Royal justice and the overarching framework of the common law were not wholly effective in crowding out other norms in shaping the behaviour of landowners in the exercise of power in the far north. Nor is it certain that the common law was even the paramount framework to which members of political society looked, even as it guaranteed rights in the land which was the basis of political power. Yet how far the importance of kinship went in shaping political power in the northern shires beyond the marches, and so served as a complicating factor in the exercise of authority, is a question open to further investigation. The common law was undoubtedly important, but it was not the only set of norms at work in the exercise of local power, the use of force and the making of peace. All this is not to revert the understanding of fifteenth-century English politics back to Storey's interpretation of the Wars of the Roses as an

---

[17] This had last been achieved with the English adherence of George Dunbar, earl of March, who assisted Henry IV's Scottish invasion of 1400 and temporarily brought Annandale into English control. See Macdonald, *Border Bloodshed*, 137–8. Gloucester's palatinate grant of 1483 coincided with the diplomatic intrigues of James III's disaffected brother Alexander, duke of Albany (d. 1485).

[18] M. Livingston and J.K. Bollard (eds), *Owain Glyndŵr: A Casebook* (Liverpool, 2013), 113–15, 341–2. This volume includes a short essay (at 489–95) which appraises the dating, authenticity and probable authorship of the original document, now lost.

[19] Davies cited in Livingston and Bollard (eds), *Owain Glyndŵr*, 489. The Percy portion was to include Northumberland, Westmorland, Lancashire, Yorkshire, Lincolnshire, Nottinghamshire, Derbyshire, Staffordshire, Leicestershire, Northamptonshire, Warwickshire and Norfolk. Mortimer was to have 'totum residuum tocius Angliae integre' (at 114–15). Cumberland, the bishopric of Durham and Rutland were not assigned to the 'Percy' portion; it seems most probable that they were omitted unintentionally.

Conclusions

'escalation of private feuds',[20] without heed to wider structures of government and shared ideas about governance of the age. Certainly, for instance, long before c. 1400 the role of rulers was special, and any view of politics that implies kings occupied merely the highest rung of 'private' lordship or that kings and landowners did not share a mutual interest in good governance is flawed.[21] Rather, it is hoped this study points towards a more multifaceted (but more complete) understanding of the norms of governance at work in late medieval England. Whether it may prove helpful in addressing for the first time, or by way of fresh revisits, the evidence for local conflict in other parts of the kingdom is a matter for the future; I hope to have convinced readers of the need at least to test this proposition. In an article some years back I concluded by asking whether the features of a violent affair in northern Northumberland appeared to resemble patterns more familiar in a Scottish context because of the strong influence of a (bluntly described) 'Scottish' culture of conflict in the English marches or because 'greater scope should be given to the consideration of feud-like elements in disputes found elsewhere in late medieval England'.[22] I hope now to have ventured an answer to that question, and propose that the configurations and forms found at England's northern frontier are a sign of greater social complexity than has yet been appreciated in the region, and in the kingdom as a whole.

---

[20] Storey, *House of Lancaster,* 8–9, 17, 27 (quote).
[21] Watts, *Making of Polities,* 68–78, 89–91, 205–62, on the period before c. 1400.
[22] Armstrong, 'Violence and Peacemaking', 71.

BIBLIOGRAPHY

MANUSCRIPT SOURCES

Alnwick Castle, Northumberland

Northumberland MSS
Syon House MSS
X. II. 1
X. II. 3

Bodleian Library, Dept. of Special Collections and Western Manuscripts, Oxford

Dodsworth Collection   MSS 32, 41, 45

British Library (BL), London

Cottonian Collection   Vespasian C XVI, F VII

Duke of Northumberland's Collections of MSS (Syon House), microfilms 280–416

C. VI, 2a, b, c	Bailiff's Accounts, Northumberland (temp. Edward IV)
C. VI, 4a-f	Bailiff's Accounts, Northumberland (temp. Henry VII)
C. VIII, 1a-i	Views of Accounts
Y. II, 28	Percy Indenture

Cumbria Archive Centre (CAC), Carlisle

D/HGB	Blencow of Blencowe papers
D/Hud	Huddleston family of Hutton John
D/Lons	Lowther, earls of Lonsdale records
D/Mus	Musgrave papers

346

Bibliography

Cumbria Archive Centre (CAC), Kendal

WD/Hoth	Hothfield of Appleby Castle MSS
WD/Ry	Fleming of Rydal Hall

Cumbria Archive Centre (CAC), Whitehaven

D/Lec	Leconfield papers (Cockermouth Castle Muniments)
D/Pen	Pennington family records
D/Stan	Stanley of Dalegarth records

National Archives of the United Kingdom (Public Record Office), Kew

C 1	Chancery: Early Chancery Proceedings
C 47	Chancery: Scottish Documents in Chancery Miscellanea
C 66	Chancery: Patent Rolls
C 81	Chancery: Warrants for the Great Seal, Series 1
C 138–42	Chancery: Inquisitions *Post Mortem*
DL 29	Duchy of Lancaster: Accounts
DURH 3	Palatinate of Durham: Cursitor's Records
DURH 13	Palatinate of Durham: Judgement Rolls (incl. Plea and Gaol Delivery rolls)
DURH 19/1	Palatinate of Durham: Miscellanea
E 28	Exchequer: Council and Privy Seal Documents
E 39	Exchequer: Scottish Documents
E 101	Exchequer: Various Accounts
E 159	Exchequer: Memoranda Rolls
E 179	Exchequer: Subsidy Rolls, Particulars of Account
E 368	Exchequer: Memoranda Rolls
E 404	Exchequer: Writs and Warrants for Issues
JUST 1	Justices Itinerant: Assize Rolls
JUST 3	Justices Itinerant: Gaol Delivery Rolls
KB 8	King's Bench: Crown side: *Baga de Secretis*
KB 9	King's Bench: Ancient Indictments
KB 27	King's Bench: *Coram Rege* Rolls
MPF	Maps and plans, from records of the State Paper Office
PSO 1	Privy Seal Office: Signet and other Warrants for the Privy Seal, Series I
SC 1	Special Collections: Ancient Correspondence
SC 8	Special Collections: Ancient Petitions

National Records of Scotland (NRS), Edinburgh

AD 1	Crown Office Writs, Records of the Lord Advocate's Dept.
GD 6	Biel Muniments
GD 98	Douglas Collection

Bibliography

GD 150   Morton Papers
GD 224   Buccleuch Muniments
JC 1/1   High Court of Justiciary, court books – old series
RH 6   Register House Charters
SP 6   Treaties with England, 1328–1605

Newcastle University, Philip Robinson Library, Special Collections, Newcastle upon Tyne (NUL)

Bainbrigg Library of Appleby   Bainbrigg MS 1 (Crescentius MS, bound volume
Grammar School MSS   containing Clifford estate accounts, 1408)

Northumberland Archives (NA), Woodhorn

SANT   Society of Antiquaries of Newcastle-upon-Tyne (formerly ZAN)
ZHW   Hope-Wallace MSS
ZSW   Swinburne (Capheaton) MSS

University of Durham Library, Archives and Special Collections, Durham (DUL)

5 The College

Durham Cathedral Muniments (DCM)
Locelli   Loc. V
   Loc. XXV
   Loc. XXVIII
Miscellaneous Charters
Registrum III   Prior and chapter's letter-book, 1401–44
Registrum IV   Prior and chapter's letter-book, 1444–86
Registrum Parvum II   Prior's letter-book, 1407–45
Registrum Parvum III   Prior's letter-book, 1446–81

Palace Green

Church Commission deposit of Durham palatinate and bishopric estate records
CCB B/1–110   Financial and Audit Records to 1649

Family Collections

HNP   Howard of Naworth Papers (formerly MS C/201)

Bibliography

PRINTED SOURCES (INCLUDING REFERENCE WORKS AND DIGITAL RESOURCES)

Accounts of the Lord High Treasurer of Scotland, 1473–1498, ed. T. Dickson and J.B. Paul et al., 13 vols (Edinburgh, 1877–1978)

The Acts of the Lords Auditors of Causes and Complaints, 1466–1494, ed. T. Thomson (Edinburgh, 1839)

The Acts of the Lords of Council in Civil Causes, 1478–1495, ed. T. Thomson (Edinburgh, 1839)

The Acts of the Parliaments of Scotland, ed. T. Thomson and C. Innes, 12 vols (Edinburgh, 1814–75)

Amundesham, John, *Annales Monasterii S. Albani*, ed. H.T. Riley, 2 vols (London, 1870–1)

Ancient Petitions Relating to Northumberland, ed. C.M. Fraser, Surtees Society, 176 (Durham, 1966)

The Anglo-American Legal Tradition, ed. R.C. Palmer, E.K. Palmer and S. Jenks, consulted at http://aalt.law.uh.edu/aalt.html; accessed 1 July 2017.

Anglo-Scottish Relations, 1174–1328; Some Selected Documents, ed. E.L.G. Stones (London, 1965)

'Annales Ricardi Secundi et Henrici Quarti', in *Johannis de Trokelowe et Henrici de Blaneforde monachorum S Albani, necnon quorundam anonymorum, Chronica et Annales*, ed. H.T. Riley, Rolls Series (London, 1866)

The Armburgh Papers: The Brokholes Inheritance in Warwickshire, Hertfordshire and Essex c. 1417–c. 1453, ed. C. Carpenter (Woodbridge, 1998)

Bede, *Ecclesiastical History of the English People*, ed. L. Sherley-Price (rev. edn, London, 1990)

Bonet [or Bouvet], Honoré, *The Tree of Battles of Honoré Bonet*, ed. G.W. Coopland (Liverpool, 1949)

Borough Customs, ed. M. Bateson, Selden Society, 18, 21 (London, 1904–6)

British Library Harleian Manuscript 433, ed. R. Horrox and P. Hammond, 4 vols (Gloucester, 1979–83)

Calendar of Ancient Deeds, List and Index Society, 10 vols (1973–83).

Calendar of Border Papers, ed. J. Bain, 2 vols (Edinburgh, 1894–1896)

Calendar of the Charter Rolls Preserved in the Public Record Office, 6 vols (1903–27)

Calendar of the Close Rolls Preserved in the Public Record Office, 61 vols (1892–1963)

Calendar of Documents Relating to Scotland, ed. J. Bain, 5 vols (Edinburgh, 1881–88)

Calendar of Entries in the Papal Registers Relating to Great Britain and Ireland, ed. W.H. Bliss et al., 20 vols (London, 1893–2005)

Calendar of the Fine Rolls Preserved in the Public Record Office, 22 vols (1911–1962)

Calendar of Inquisitions Miscellaneous, 8 vols: I–VII (London, 1916–68); VIII (Woodbridge, 2003)

Calendar of Inquisitions Post Mortem, 26 vols: I–XX (London, 1904–95); XXI–XXVI (Woodbridge, 2002–9)

Calendar of Inquisitions Post Mortem: Series 2, Henry VII, 3 vols (London, 1898–1955)

Calendar of the Laing Charters, 854–1837, ed. J. Anderson (Edinburgh, 1899)

Calendar of the Patent Rolls Preserved in the Public Record Office, 55 vols (1891–1916)

A Calendar of the Register of Robert Waldby, Archbishop of York, 1397, ed. D.M. Smith (York, 1974)

Bibliography

Calendar of Scottish Supplications to Rome, 6 vols, ed. A.I. Dunlop et al.: I–III, Scottish History Society (Edinburgh, 1934–70); IV–V, University of Glasgow (Glasgow, 1983–97); VI, Scottish Record Society (Edinburgh, 2017).

Calendar of Signet Letters of Henry IV and Henry V (1399–1422), ed. J.L. Kirby (London, 1978)

Calendarium Inquisitionum Post Mortem Sive Escaetarum, ed. J. Caley and J. Bayley, 4 vols, Record Commission (London, 1806–28)

Carey, Robert, *The Memoirs of Robert Carey*, ed. F.H. Mares (Oxford, 1972)

Catalogue of Ancient Deeds, 6 vols (London, 1890–1915)

Charter Chest of the Earldom of Wigtown, 1214–1681, ed. F.J. Grant, Scottish Record Society, 36 (Edinburgh, 1910)

Charters and Other Documents Relating to the City of Edinburgh. A.D. 1143–1540, ed. J.D. Marwick, Scottish Burgh Records Society (Edinburgh, 1871)

Chronicles of London, ed. C.L. Kingsford (Oxford, 1905)

Cokayne, G.E., *The Complete Peerage*, ed. H.V. Gibbs et al., 14 vols (London, 1910–98)

Coldingham Correspondence. The Correspondence, Inventories, Account Rolls and Law Proceedings of the Priory of Coldingham, ed. J. Raine, Surtees Society, 12 (London, 1841)

Concilia Scotiae: Ecclesiae Scoticanae Statuta tam Provincilia quam Synodalia quae Supersunt MCCXXV–MDLIX, ed. J. Robertson, Bannatyne Club, 2 vols (Edinburgh, 1866)

The Crowland Chronicle Continuations 1459–1486, ed. N. Pronay and J. Cox (London, 1986)

Denton, John, *An Accompt of the Most Considerable Estates and Families in the County of Cumberland, by John Denton of Cardew*, ed. R.S. Ferguson, CWAAS, tract ser., 2 (1887)

Depositions and Other Ecclesiastical Proceedings from the Courts of Durham, ed. J. Raine, Surtees Society, 21 (London, 1845)

Dictionary of the Scots Language, Scottish Language Dictionaries (2001–), www.dsl.ac .uk; accessed 1 April 2016

Dives and Pauper, ed. P.H. Barnum, Early English Text Soc., 275, 280, 323, 2 vols in 3 (Oxford, 1976–2004)

The Douglas Book, ed. W. Fraser, 4 vols (Edinburgh, 1885)

Dugdale, William, *Baronage of England*, 3 vols (London, 1675)

The Duke of Norfolk's Deeds at Arundel Castle, ed. H. Warne, 2 vols (Chichester, 2006–2010)

Dunelmensis, Historiae, Scriptores Tres, ed. J. Raine, Surtees Society, 9 (1839)

Durham Quarter Sessions Rolls, 1471–1625, ed. C.M. Fraser and K. Emsley, Surtees Society, 199 (Durham, 1991)

An English Chronicle, 1377–1461, ed. W. Marx (Woodbridge, 2003)

English Suits before the Parlement of Paris, 1420–1436, ed. C.T. Allmand and C.A.J. Armstrong, Camden Society, 4th ser., 26 (Cambridge, 1982)

The Exchequer Rolls of Scotland, ed. J. Stuart et al., 23 vols (Edinburgh, 1878–1908)

Extent of the Lordship of Longdendale 1360, ed. J. Harrop. P. Booth and S. Harrop, Record Society of Lancashire and Cheshire (2005)

Bibliography

Foedera, Conventiones, Litterae etc., ed. T. Rymer, 10 vols (Hagae Comitis, 1745; reprint, Farnborough, 1967)

Fortescue, John, *The Governance of England*, ed. C. Plummer (Oxford, 1885)

De Laudibus Legum Angliae, ed. S. Chrimes (Cambridge, 1942)

Froissart, Jean, *The Chronicle of Froissart*, trans. J. Bourchier, Lord Berners, ed. W.-E. Henley, 6 vols (London, 1901–3)

The Online Froissart, ed. P. Ainsworth and G. Croenen, version 1.5 (Sheffield, 2013), www.hrionline.ac.uk/onlinefroissart; accessed 1 July 2014

The Gascon Rolls Project 1317–1468, ed. A. Curry, P. Morgan and P. Spence et al., www.gasconrolls.org; accessed 1 April 2016

Gower, John, *Confessio Amantis*, ed. R. A. Peck, trans. A. Galloway, vol. 2 (Kalamazoo, MI, 2013), consulted at TEAMS Middle English Text Series (METS), https://d.lib.rochester.edu/teams/publication/peck-gower-confessio-amantis-volume-2; accessed 1 July 2019

The Great Chronicle of London, ed. A.H. Thomas (London, 1938)

Hardyng, John, *The Chronicle of Iohn Hardyng*, ed. H. Ellis (London, 1812)

Historical Manuscripts Commission: Reports of the Royal Commission on Historical Manuscripts (1– , London, 1870–), *6th Report, Appendix*, part I (1877); *7th Report, Appendix,* part II (1879); *10th Report, Appendix*, part IV (1885); *12th Report, Appendix*, part VII (1890); *14th Report, Appendix*, part III (1894); *15th Report, Appendix*, part VIII (1897); *Report on Manuscripts in Various Collections*, 8 vols (1901–13); *Milne-Home Report* (1902)

The History and Antiquities of North Durham, ed. J. Raine (London, 1852)

A History of Northumberland. Issued under the Direction of the Northumberland County History Committee, 15 vols (Newcastle-upon-Tyne, 1893–1940)

History of Parliament: The House of Commons 1386–1421, 4 vols, ed. J.S. Roskell, L. Clark and C. Rawcliffe (Stroud, 1992)

History of Parliament: The House of Commons 1509–1558, 3 vols, ed. S.T. Bindoff (London, 1982)

Incerti Scriptoris Chronicon Angliae . . ., ed. J.A. Giles (London, 1848)

Kingsford, C.L., 'Extracts from the First Version of Hardyng's Chronicle', *EHR*, 27 (1912), 740–53

Kingsford's Stonor Letters and Papers, 1290–1483, ed. M. C. Carpenter (Cambridge, 1996)

The Lag Charters, 1400–1720, ed. A.L. Murray and P.J. Hamilton-Grierson, Scottish Record Society, 88 (Edinburgh, 1958)

Lannoy, Ghillebert, *Oeuvres de Ghillebert de Lannoy*, ed. C. Potvin and J.C. Houzeau (Louvain, 1878)

Le Bel, Jean, *Chronique de Jean le Bel*, ed. J. Viard and E. Déprez, 2 vols (Paris, 1904–5)

Leges Marchiarum or Border Laws, ed. W. Nicolson (London, 1705)

Leslie, John, *De origine, moribus & rebus gestis Scotorum libri decem . . .* (Rome, 1675)

Letters of the Kings of England, ed. J.O. Halliwell-Phillipps, 2 vols (London, 1848)

Letters and Papers, Foreign and Domestic, of the Reign of Henry VIII, 1509–1547, ed. J.S. Brewer et al. (London, 1862–1910; *Addenda*, London, 1929–32)

Letters and Papers Illustrative of the Wars of the English in France during the Reign of Henry the Sixth, ed. J. Stevenson, 2 vols in 3 (London, 1864)

Bibliography

Letters of Queen Margaret of Anjou and Bishop Beckington and Others, ed. C. Monro, Camden Society, 86 (London, 1863)

Liber Pluscardensis, ed. F.J.H. Skene, 2 vols (Edinburgh, 1877–80)

List of Escheators for England and Wales, ed. A.C. Wood, List and Index Society, 72 (London, 1971)

List of Sheriffs for England and Wales, ed. A. Hughes, Lists and Indexes, Public Record Office, 9 (London, 1898; reprint, New York, 1963)*Lower Ecclesiastical Jurisdiction in Late-Medieval England*, ed. L.R. Poos (Oxford, 2001)

Malory, Thomas, *Malory, Works*, ed. E. Vinaver (2nd edn, Oxford, 1971)

Melrose Liber. Liber Sancte Marie de Melros, ed. C. Innes, Bannatyne Club, 2 vols (Edinburgh, 1837)

The Merchant Taylors' Company of London: Court Minutes 1486–1493, ed. M. Davies (Stamford, 2000)

The Middle English Compendium (including *Middle English Dictionary*), ed. F. McSparran et al., University of Michigan (2006–), consulted at https://quod.lib.umich.edu/m/mec/index.html; accessed 1 January 2018

Montesquieu, Charles de Secondat, baron de, *The Spirit of Laws*, trans. T. Nugent, rev. J.V. Prichard (London, 1914)

Morton Register. Registrum Honoris de Morton, ed. T. Thomson, A. Macdonald and C. Innes, 2 vols (Edinburgh, 1853)

Myrc, John, *Mirk's Festial. Part I: A Collection of Homilies*, ed. T. Erbe (London, 1905)

National Archives of the United Kingdom. Online catalogue, *Discovery*, http://discovery.nationalarchives.gov.uk; accessed 9 September 2014

Nederman, C.J. (ed.), *Political Thought in Early Fourteenth-Century England: Treatises by Walter of Milemete, William of Pagula, and William of Ockham* (Turnhout, 2002)

Northern Petitions Illustrative of Life in Berwick, Cumbria and Durham in the Fourteenth Century, ed. C.M. Fraser (Durham, 1981)

Northumberland and Durham Deeds from the Dodsworth MSS, in Bodley's Library, Oxford, ed. A.M. Oliver, Newcastle-upon-Tyne Records Committee, 7 (Newcastle-upon-Tyne, 1929)

Oxford Dictionary of National Biography, ed. H.C.G. Matthew and B.H. Harrison (Oxford, 2004)

The Oxford English Dictionary (2nd edn, 1989, and Additions series, 1993–), consulted at *OED Online*, http://dictionary.oed.com; accessed 1 July 2017

Paris, Matthew, *Matthaei Parisiensis Chronica Majora*, ed. H.R. Luard, 7 vols, Rolls Ser. (London, 1872–83)

The Parliament Rolls of Medieval England, 1275–1504, ed. C. Given-Wilson, 16 vols (Woodbridge, 2005)

Paston Letters and Papers of the Fifteenth Century, ed. N. Davis, 2 vols (Oxford, 1971–6)

Le pèlerinage de l'âme de Guillaume de Deguileville, ed. J.J. Stürzinger, Roxburghe Club (London, 1895)

Percy Bailiff's Rolls of the Fifteenth Century, ed. J.C. Hodgson, Surtees Society, 134 (Durham, 1921)

Piccolomini, Aneas Sylvius, *Memoirs of a Renaissance Pope: The Commentaries of Pius II*, ed. L.C. Gabel and trans. F.A. Gragg (London, 1960)

Enea Silvio Piccolomini, Papa Pio II, I Commentarii, ed. and trans. L. Totaro, 2 vols (Milan, 1984)

Bibliography

The Place-Names of Cumberland, ed. A.M. Armstrong et al., English Place-Name Society, 3 vols (Cambridge, 1950–2)

Plumpton Correspondence, ed. T. Stapleton, Camden Society, 4 (London, 1839)

The Plumpton Letters and Papers, ed. J. Kirby, Camden Society, 5th Ser., 8 (Cambridge, 1996)

Political Poems and Songs Relating to English History, ed. T. Wright, 2 vols, Rolls Ser. (London, 1859–61)

The Poll Taxes of 1377, 1379, and 1381, ed. C.C. Fenwick, 3 vols (Oxford, 1998–2005)

The Priory of Hexham, ed. J. Raine, 2 vols, Surtees Society, 44, 46 (Durham, 1864–65)

'Private Indentures for Life Service in Peace and War 1278–1476', ed. M. Jones and S. Walker, in *Camden Miscellany XXXII*, Camden Society, 5th ser., 3 (London, 1994)

Proceedings and Ordinances of the Privy Council of England, ed. H. Nicolas, 7 vols (London, 1834–37)

The Pylgremage of the Sowle, ed. F. van Vorsselen (s.d.), consulted at http://pilgrim .grozny.nl; accessed 1 June 2016

Reaney, P.H., *A Dictionary of English Surnames*, corrections and additions by R.M. Wilson (3rd edn, London, 1991)

The Records of the Parliaments of Scotland to 1707, ed. K.M. Brown et al. (St Andrews, 2007–), www.rps.ac.uk; accessed 1 June 2016

Records Relating to the Barony of Kendale, ed. W. Farrer and J.F. Curwen, CWAAS, Record Ser., 4, 5 6 (1923–6)

Reginaldi Monachi Dunelmensis, ed. J. Raine, Surtees Society, 1 (London, 1835)

The Register and Records of Holm Cultram, ed. F. Grainger and W.C. Collingwood, CWAAS, Record ser., 7 (Kendal, 1929)

The Register of Richard Fox, Lord Bishop of Durham, 1494–1501, ed. M.P. Howden, Surtees Society, 147 (London, 1932)

The Register of Thomas Langley, Bishop of Durham, 1406–1437, ed. R.L. Storey, 6 vols (Durham, 1949–67)

The Register of Thomas Rotherham, Archbishop of York 1480–1500, ed. E.E. Barker, Canterbury and York Society, 69 (Torquay, 1976)

Registrum Magni Sigilli Regum Scotorum. Register of the Great Seal of Scotland, ed. J.M. Thomson et al., 11 vols (Edinburgh, 1882–1914). Scottish Record Society, reprint (Edinburgh, 1984)

Registrum Secreti Sigilli Regum Scotorum. Register of the Privy Seal of Scotland, ed. M. Livingstone et al., 8 vols (Edinburgh, 1908–82)

Reports of the Deputy Keeper of the Public Records (London, 1840–), *Thirty-third Annual Report*, Appendix (1872); *Forty-fourth Annual Report*, Appendix (1883); *Forty-fifth Annual Report*, Appendices 1–2 (1885)

Return of the Names of Every Member . . ., Part I: Parliaments of England, 1213–1702 (London, 1878)

Rotuli Parliamentorum . . ., ed. J. Strachey et al., Record Commission, 6 vols (London, 1767–77)

Rotuli Scotiae in Turri Londinensi . . ., ed. D. Macpherson et al., Record Commission, 2 vols (London, 1814–19)

Royal and Historical Letters during the Reign of Henry the Fourth, ed. F.C. Hingeston, 2 vols (London, 1860–4)

353

Bibliography

Sanctuarium Dunelmense et Sanctuarium Beverlacense, ed. J. Raine, Surtees Society, 5 (London, 1837)

Scotichronicon by Walter Bower in Latin and English, ed. D.E.R. Watt, 9 vols (Aberdeen, 1987–98)

The Scotts of Buccleuch, ed. W. Fraser, 2 vols (Edinburgh, 1878)

Select Cases in the Council of Henry VII, ed. C.G. Bayne and W.H. Dunham, Selden Society, 75 (London, 1958)

Select Cases in the Court of King's Bench under Richard II, Henry IV and Henry V, ed. G.O. Sayles, Selden Society, 88 (London, 1971)

Six Town Chronicles of England, ed. R. Flenley (Oxford, 1911)

Smyth, John, *The Lives of the Berkeleys . . . and Description of the Hundred of Berkeley,* ed. J. Maclean, 3 vols (Gloucester, 1883–5)

Source Book of Scottish History, ed. W.C. Dickinson et al. (2nd edn., 1958, repr. 1963)

Statute Rolls of the Parliament of Ireland, Reign of King Henry the Sixth, ed. H.F. Berry (Dublin, 1910)

Statutes of the Realm, ed. A. Luders et al., 11 vols in 12, Record Commission (London, 1810–28; republ., London, 1963)

Testamenta Karleolensia, ed. R.S. Ferguson, CWAAS, extra ser., 9 (Kendal, 1893)

Usk, Adam, *The Chronicle of Adam of Usk 1377–1421,* ed. C. Given-Wilson (Oxford, 1997)

Warkworth, John, *A Chronicle of the First Thirteen Years of the Reign of King Edward the Fourth,* ed. J.O. Halliwell-Phillips, Camden Society (London, 1839)

The Westminster Chronicle, 1381–1394, ed. L.C. Hector and B.F. Harvey (Oxford, 1982)

Year Books of Henry VI: 1 Henry VI, ed. C.H. Williams, Selden Soc., 50 (London, 1933)

York Civic Records, ed. A. Raine and D. Sutton, 9 vols, Yorkshire Archaeological Society, Record Ser., 98–138 (Wakefield, York and Leeds, 1939–78)

SECONDARY WORKS

Abulafia, D., and Berend, N. (eds), *Medieval Frontiers: Concepts and Practices* (Aldershot, 2002)

Abu-Lughod, L., and Lutz, C.A., 'Introduction: Emotion, Discourse and the Politics of Everyday Life', in L. Abu-Lughod and C.A. Lutz (eds), *Language and the Politics of Emotion* (Cambridge, 1990), 1–23

Acheson, E., *A Gentry Community: Leicestershire in the Fifteenth Century, c. 1422–c. 1485* (Cambridge, 1992)

Alban, J.R., 'English Coastal Defence: Some Fourteenth-Century Modifications within the System', in R.A. Griffiths (ed.), *Patronage, the Crown and the Provinces in Later Medieval England* (Gloucester, 1981), 57–78

Alcock, N., and Miles, D., *The Medieval Peasant House in Midland England* (Oxford, 2013)

Algazi, G., 'The Social Use of Private War: Some Late Medieval Views Reviewed', *Tel Aviver Jahrbuch für deutsche Geschichte,* 22 (1993), 253–73

'Pruning Peasants: Private War and Maintaining the Lords' Peace in Late Medieval Germany', in E. Cohen and M.B. de Jong (eds), *Medieval Transformations: Texts, Power and Gifts in Context* (Leiden, 2001), 245–74

Amussen, S.D., 'Punishment, Discipline and Power: The Social Meanings of Violence in Early Modern England', *Journal of British Studies,* 34 (1995), 1–34

Anderson, L., *A Kind of Wild Justice: Revenge in Shakespeare's Comedies* (Newark, 1987)

Bibliography

Andrew, D.T., 'The Code of Honour and Its Critics: The Opposition to Duelling in England, 1700–1850', *Social History*, 5 (1980), 409–34

Armstrong, R.B., *The History of Liddesdale, Eskdale, Ewesdale, Wauchopedale and the Debatable Land, Part 1* (Edinburgh, 1883)

Armstrong, J.W., 'Violence and Peacemaking in the English Marches towards Scotland, c. 1425–1440', in L. Clark (ed.), *The Fifteenth Century VI: Identity and Insurgency in the Late Middle Ages* (Woodbridge, 2006), 53–71

'Local Society and the Defence of the English Frontier in Fifteenth-Century Scotland: The War Measures of 1482', *Florilegium*, 25 (2008), 127–49

'The "Fyre of Ire Kyndild" in the Fifteenth-Century Scottish Marches', in S.A. Throop and P.R. Hyams (eds), *Vengeance in the Middle Ages: Emotion, Religion and Feud* (Farnham, 2010), 51–84

'The Justice Ayre in the Border Sheriffdoms, 1493–1498', *SHR*, 92 (2013), 1–37

'Concepts of Kinship in Lancastrian Westmorland', in B. Thompson and J. Watts (eds), *Political Society in Later Medieval England: A Festschrift for Christine Carpenter* (Woodbridge, 2015), 146–65

'Centre, Periphery, Locality, Province: England and Its Far North in the Fifteenth Century', in P. Crooks, D. Green and W.M. Ormrod (eds), *The Plantagenet Empire, 1259–1453: Proceedings of the 2014 Harlaxton Symposium* (Donington, 2016), 248–72

Arvanigian, M., 'A County Community or the Politics of the Nation? Border Service and Baronial Influence in the Palatinate of Durham, 1377–1413', *Historical Research*, 82 (2009), 41–61

'Henry V, Lancastrian Kingship and the Far North of England', in G. Dodd (ed.), *Henry V: New Interpretations* (Woodbridge, 2013), 77–101

Axelrod, R., *The Evolution of Cooperation* (New York, 1984)

Bain, J., 'The Grahams or Graemes of the Debateable Land', *Archaeological Journal*, 43 (1886), 116–123

Baker, J.H., *An Introduction to English Legal History* (3rd edn, London, 1990)

Barber, P., and Harper, T., *Magnificent Maps: Power, Propaganda and Art* (London, 2010)

Barker, J.R.V., *The Tournament in England, 1100–1400* (Woodbridge, 1986)

Barrow, G.W.S., 'The Anglo-Scottish Border', *Northern History*, 1 (1966), 21–42

'Northern English Society in the Twelfth and Thirteenth Centuries', *Northern History*, 4 (1969), 1–28

'The Pattern of Lordship and Feudal Settlement in Cumbria', *Journal of Medieval History*, 1 (1975), 117–38

'Lothian in the first War of Independence', *SHR*, 55 (1976), 151–71

'Frontier and Settlement: Which Influenced Which? England and Scotland, 1100–1300', in R.J. Bartlett and A. MacKay (eds), *Medieval Frontier Societies* (Oxford, 1989), 3–21

'The Anglo-Scottish Border: Growth and Structure in the Middle Ages', in W. Haubrichs and R. Schneider (eds), *Grenzen und Grenzregionen, Frontières et régions frontalières, Borders and Border Regions* (Saarbrücken, 1993), 197–212

The Kingdom of the Scots: Government, Church and Society from the Eleventh to the Fourteenth Century (Edinburgh, 2003)

Barry, T.B., 'The Last Frontier: Defence and Settlement in Late Medieval Ireland', in T.B. Barry, R. Frame and K. Simms (eds), *Colony and Frontier in Medieval Ireland: Essays Presented to J.F. Lydon* (London, 1995), 217–28

Bibliography

Bartlett, R.J., '"Mortal Enmities": The Legal Aspect of Hostility in the Middle Ages', in B.S. Tuten and T.L. Billado (eds), *Feud, Violence and Practice: Essays in Medieval Studies in Honor of Stephen D. White* (Farnham, 2010), 197–212

Bartlett, R.J., and MacKay, A. (eds), *Medieval Frontier Societies* (Oxford, 1989)

Bates, C.J., *The Border Holds of Northumberland* (Newcastle-upon-Tyne, 1891)

Bean, J.M.W., *The Estates of the Percy Family, 1416–1537* (Oxford, 1958)

'Henry IV and the Percies', *History*, 44 (1959), 212–27

Beck, P., 'Personal Naming among the Rural Populations in France at the End of the Middle Ages', in G.T. Beech, M. Bourin and P. Chareille (eds), *Personal Names Studies of Medieval Europe: Social Identity and Familial Structures* (Kalamazoo, MI, 2002), 143–56

Beckingsale, B.W., 'The Characteristics of the Tudor North', *Northern History*, 4 (1969), 67–83

Beech, G.T., Bourin, M., and Chareille, P. (eds), *Personal Names Studies of Medieval Europe: Social Identity and Familial Structures* (Kalamazoo, MI, 2002)

Bellamy, J.G., *The Law of Treason in England in the Later Middle Ages* (Cambridge, 1970)

Crime and Public Order in England in the Later Middle Ages (London, 1973)

Criminal Law and Society in Late Medieval and Tudor England (Gloucester, 1984)

Bastard Feudalism and the Law (London, 1989)

The Criminal Trial in Later Medieval England (Stroud, 1998)

Bennett, J.M., 'Spouses, Siblings and Surnames: Reconstructing Families from Medieval Village Court Rolls', *Journal of British Studies*, 23 (1983), 26–46

'Women (and Men) on the Move: Scots in the English North c. 1440', *Journal of British Studies*, 57 (2018), 1–28

Bennett, J.W., 'The Medieval Loveday', *Speculum*, 33 (1958), 351–70

Bennett, M.J., *Community, Class and Careerism: Cheshire and Lancashire Society in the Age of 'Sir Gawain and the Green Knight'* (Cambridge, 1983)

Berend, N., 'Medievalists and the Notion of the Frontier', *The Medieval History Journal*, 2 (1999), 55–72

Bernard, G.W., *The Power of the Early Tudor Nobility: A Study of the Fourth and Fifth Earls of Shrewsbury* (Brighton, 1985)

Biancalana, J., 'The Legal Framework of Arbitration in Fifteenth-Century England', *American Journal of Legal History*, 47 (2005), 347–82

Binns, A., 'Pre-Reformation Dedications to St Oswald in England and Scotland: A Gazetteer', in C. Stancliffe and E. Cambridge (eds), *Oswald: Northumbrian King to European Saint* (Stamford, 1995), 241–71

Black, A., *Political Thought in Europe, 1250–1450* (Cambridge, 1992)

Black-Michaud, J., *Cohesive Force: Feud in the Mediterranean and the Middle East* (Oxford, 1975)

Blatcher, M., *The Court of King's Bench, 1450–1550* (London, 1978)

Bloch, M., *Feudal Society*, trans. L.A. Manyon, foreword by M.M. Postan (London, 1961)

Blow, J., 'Nibley Green 1470: The Last Private Battle Fought in England', in C.M.D. Crowder (ed.), *English Society and Government in the Fifteenth Century* (Edinburgh, 1967), 87–111

Boardman, S.I., 'The Campbells and Charter Lordship in Medieval Argyll', in S.I. Boardman and A. Ross (eds), *The Exercise of Power in Medieval Scotland* (Dublin, 2003), 95–117

Bibliography

The Campbells, 1250–1500 (Edinburgh, 2006)

Boehm, C., *Blood Revenge: The Anthropology of Feuding in Montenegro and Other Tribal Societies* (Lawrence, KS, 1984)

Bohna, M.L., 'Political and Criminal Violence in Fifteenth-Century England', in R.W. Kaeuper (ed.), *Violence in Medieval Society* (Woodbridge, 2000), 91–104

Booker, S., *Cultural Exchange and Identity in Late Medieval Ireland: The English and Irish of the Four Obedient Shires Series* (Cambridge, 2018)

Booth, P.W.N., 'Richard Duke of Gloucester and the West March towards Scotland, 1470–1483', *Northern History*, 36 (2000), 233–46

'Men Behaving Badly? The West March towards Scotland and the Percy–Neville Feud', in L. Clark (ed.), *The Fifteenth Century III: Authority and Subversion* (Woodbridge, 2003), 95–116

Bossy, J., 'Blood and Baptism: Kinship, Community and Christianity in Western Europe from the Fourteenth to the Seventeenth Centuries', *Studies in Church History*, 10 (1973), 129–43

Christianity in the West 1400–1700 (Oxford, 1985)

'Practices of Satisfaction, 1215–1700', *Studies in Church History*, 40 (2004), 106–18

Braddick, M.J., 'State Formation and Social Change in Early Modern England: A Problem Stated and Approaches Suggested', *Social History*, 16 (1991), 1–17

State Formation in Early Modern England, c. 1550–1700 (Cambridge, 2000)

Bradley, P.J., 'Henry V's Scottish Policy: A Study in Realpolitik', in P.J. Bradley and J.S. Hamilton (eds), *Documenting the Past* (Woodbridge, 1989), 177–95

Bradshaw, B., and Morrill, J.S. (eds), *The British Problem, c. 1534–1707* (London, 1996)

Braekevelt, J., Buylaert, F., Dumolyn, J., and Haemers, J., 'The Politics of Factional Conflict in Late Medieval Flanders', *Historical Research*, 85 (2012), 13–31

Branch, J., *The Cartographic State: Maps, Territory and the Origins of Sovereignty* (Cambridge, 2014)

Brand, P., 'Law and Custom in the English Thirteenth Century Common Law', in P. Andersen and M. Münster-Swendsen (eds), *Custom: The Development and Use of a Legal Concept in the Middle Ages* (Copenhagen, 2009), 17–31

Braudel, F., *The Mediterranean and the Mediterranean World in the Age of Philip II*, trans. Siân Reynolds, 2 vols (London, 1972–3)

Brewer, J., *The Sinews of Power: War, Money, and the English State, 1688–1783* (London, 1989)

Briggs, C., 'Taxation, Warfare, and the Early Fourteenth Century "Crisis" in the North: Cumberland Lay Subsidies, 1332–1348', *Economic History Review*, 58 (2005), 639–72

Britnell, R.H., and Liddy, C.D. (eds), *North-East England in the Later Middle Ages* (Woodbridge, 2005)

Brooke, C., *From Alfred to Henry III: 871–1272* (London, 1961)

Brooks, C.W., *Lawyers, Litigation and English Society since 1450* (London, 1998)

Brooks, F.W., *The Council of the North* (rev. edn, London, 1966)

Brown, K.M., *Bloodfeud in Scotland 1573–1625: Violence, Justice and Politics in an Early Modern Society* (Glasgow, 1986)

Brown, M., *How I Killed Pluto and Why It Had It Coming* (New York, 2010)

Brown, M.H., 'Scotland Tamed? Kings and Magnates in Late Medieval Scotland: A Review of Recent Work', *Innes Review*, 45 (1994), 120–46

Bibliography

The Black Douglases (East Linton, 1998)

'War, Allegiance, and Community in the Anglo-Scottish Marches: Teviotdale in the Fourteenth Century', *Northern History*, 41 (2004), 219–38

'French Alliance or English Peace? Scotland and the Last Phase of the Hundred Years War, 1415–53', in L. Clark (ed.), *The Fifteenth Century VII: Conflicts, Consequences and the Crown in the Late Middle Ages* (Woodbridge, 2007), 81–99

Bannockburn: The Scottish War and the British Isles, 1307–1323 (Edinburgh, 2008)

Disunited Kingdoms: Peoples and Politics in the British Isles, 1280–1460 (Harlow, 2013)

Brown, R.A., *English Castles* (London, 1976)

Brown, W.C., and Górecki, P. (eds), *Conflict in Medieval Europe: Changing Perspectives on Society and Culture* (Aldershot, 2003)

Bruce, M.P., and Terrell, K.H. (eds), *The Anglo-Scottish Border and the Shaping of Identity, 1300–1600* (New York, 2012)

Brunner, O., *Land and Lordship: Structures of Governance in Medieval Austria*, trans. H. Kaminsky and J.V.H. Melton (Philadelphia, 1992)

Burckhardt, J., *The Civilization of the Renaissance in Italy*, trans. S.G.C. Middlemore (5th edn, London, 1904)

Burgess, G. (ed.), *The New British History: Founding a Modern State 1603–1715* (London, 1999)

Burns, R.I., 'The Significance of the Frontier in Middle Ages', in R.J. Bartlett and A. MacKay (eds), *Medieval Frontier Societies* (Oxford, 1989), 307–30

Burt, C., *Edward I and the Governance of England, 1272–1307* (Cambridge, 2013)

Bush, M.L., 'The Problem of the Far North: A Study of the Crisis of 1537 and Its Consequences', *Northern History*, 6 (1971), 40–63

Campbell, W.H., 'Theologies of Reconciliation in Thirteenth-Century England', *Studies in Church History*, 40 (2004), 84–94

Carpenter, M.C., 'Law, Justice and Landowners in Late Medieval England', *LHR*, 1 (1983), 205–37

'The Fifteenth-Century English Gentry and Their Estates', in M.C.E. Jones (ed.), *Gentry and Lesser Nobility in Late Medieval Europe* (Gloucester, 1986), 36-60

Locality and Polity: A Study in Warwickshire Landed Society, 1401–1499 (Cambridge, 1992)

'Gentry and Community in Medieval England', *Journal of British Studies*, 33 (1994), 340–80

'Political and Constitutional History: Before and after McFarlane', in R.H. Britnell and A.J. Pollard (eds), *The McFarlane Legacy: Studies in Late Medieval Politics and Society* (New York, 1995), 175–206

'The Stonors and Their Circle in the Fifteenth Century', in R.E. Archer and S. Walker (eds), *Rulers and Ruled in Late Medieval England* (London, 1995), 175–200

The Wars of the Roses: Politics and the Constitution in England, c. 1437–1509 (Cambridge, 1997)

'General Introduction', in *CIPM XXII* (Woodbridge, 2003), 1–42

'Introduction: Political Culture, Politics and Cultural History', in L. Clark and M.C. Carpenter (eds), *The Fifteenth Century IV: Political Culture in Late Medieval Britain* (Woodbridge, 2004), 1–19

'War, Government and Governance in England in the Later Middle Ages', in L. Clark (ed.), *The Fifteenth Century VII: Conflicts, Consequences and the Crown in the Late Middle Ages* (Woodbridge, 2007), 1–22

Bibliography

'Political and Geographical Space: The Geopolitics of Medieval England', in B.A. Kümin (ed.), *Political Space in Pre-industrial Europe* (Farnham, 2009), 117–33

'Henry VI and the Deskilling of the Royal Bureaucracy', in L. Clark (ed.), *The Fifteenth Century IX: English and Continental Perspectives* (Woodbridge, 2010), 1–37

'Bastard Feudalism in Fourteenth-Century Warwickshire', Dugdale Society Occasional Papers, 52 (Stratford-upon-Avon, 2016)

Carroll, S., 'The Peace in the Feud in Sixteenth- and Seventeenth-Century France', *Past & Present*, 178 (2003), 74–115

Blood and Violence in Early Modern France (Oxford, 2006)

'Introduction', in S. Carroll (ed.), *Cultures of Violence: Interpersonal Violence in Historical Perspective* (Basingstoke, 2007), 1–43

Castor, H. R., '"Walter Blount is gone to serve Traytours": The Sack of Elvaston and the Politics of the North Midlands in 1454', *Midland History*, 19 (1994), 21–39

The King, the Crown, and the Duchy of Lancaster (Oxford, 2000)

Challett, V., '*Tuchins* and "*Brigands de Bois*": Peasant Communities and Self-Defence Movements in Normandy during the Hundred Years War', in L. Clark (ed.), *The Fifteenth Century IX: English and Continental Perspectives* (Woodbridge, 2010), 85–99

Champion, M., *Medieval Graffiti: The Lost Voices of England's Churches* (London, 2015)

Charlton, E., *The Memorials of North Tynedale and Its Four Surnames* (Newcastle-upon-Tyne, 1870)

Chénon, E., 'Recherches historiques sur quelques rites nuptiaux', *Nouvelle revue historique de droit français et étranger*, 36 (1912), 573–660

Cherry, M., 'The Courtenay Earls of Devon: The Formation and Disintegration of a Late-Medieval Aristocratic Affinity', *Southern History*, 1 (1979), 71–97

'The Struggle for Power in Mid-Fifteenth Century Devonshire', in R.A. Griffiths (ed.), *Patronage, the Crown and the Provinces in Later Medieval England* (Gloucester, 1981), 123–44

Cheyette, F.L., '*Suum cuique tribuere*', *French Historical Studies*, 6 (1970), 287–99

Chrimes, S.B., 'Some Letters of John of Lancaster as Warden of the East Marches towards Scotland', *Speculum*, 14 (1939), 3–27

Churchill, W.S., *The Story of the Malakand Field Force: An Episode of Frontier War* (2nd edn, London, 1899)

Cichon, M., *Violence and Vengeance in Middle Welsh and Middle English Narrative: Owein and Ywain and Gawain* (Lewiston, 2009)

Clanchy, M.T., 'Law, Government and Society in Medieval England', *History*, 59 (1974), 73–8

'Law and Love in the Middle Ages', in J. Bossy (ed.), *Disputes and Settlements: Law and Human Relations in the West* (Cambridge, 1980), 47–67

Clayton, D.J., 'Peace Bonds and the Maintenance of Law and Order in Late Medieval England: The Example of Cheshire', *BIHR*, 58 (1985), 133–48

Cockburn, J.S., 'The Northern Assize Circuit', *Northern History*, 3 (1968), 118–30

Cohen, M., and Madeline, F. (eds), *Space in the Medieval West: Places, Territories and Imagined Geographies* (Farnham, 2013)

Bibliography

Cohn, S.K., 'Highlands and Lowlands in Late Medieval Tuscany', in D. Broun and M. MacGregor (eds), *Mìorun Mòr nan Gall, 'The Great Ill-Will of the Lowlander'? Lowland Perceptions of the Highlands, Medieval and Modern* (Glasgow, 2009), 110–27

Coleman, J., *Ancient and Medieval Memories: Studies in the Reconstruction of the Past* (Cambridge, 1992)

Collingwood, W.G., *The Book of Coniston* (Kendal, 1897)

Colson, E., 'Social Control and Vengeance in Plateau Tonga Society', *Africa*, 23 (1953), 199–212

Conzen, M.R.G., 'Alnwick, Northumberland: A Study in Town-Plan Analysis', *Transactions and Papers (Institute of British Geographers)*, 27 (London, 1960)

Coomans, T., 'Review of P.N. Noomen, *De stinzen in middeleeuws Friesland en hun bewoners*', *Speculum*, 86 (2011), 1105–6

Coss, P.R., 'Hilton, Lordship and the Culture of the Gentry', in C. Dyer, P.R. Coss and C. Wickham (eds), *Rodney Hilton's Middle Ages: An Exploration of Historical Themes* (Oxford, 2007), 34–52

Coster, W., *Family and Kinship in England, 1450–1800* (New York, 2001)

Coulson, C., 'Structural Symbolism in Medieval Castle Architecture', *Journal of the British Archaeological Association*, 132 (1979), 73–90

'Freedom to Crenellate by Licence: An Historiographical Revision', *Nottingham Medieval Studies*, 38 (1994), 86–137

Castles in Medieval Society: Fortresses in England, France, and Ireland in the Central Middle Ages (Oxford, 2003)

Creighton, O.H., *Designs upon the Land: Elite Landscapes of the Middle Ages* (Woodbridge, 2009)

Creighton, O.H., and Liddiard, R., 'Fighting Yesterday's Battle: Beyond War or Status in Castle Studies', *Medieval Archaeology*, 52 (2008), 161–9

Cressy, D., 'Kinship and Kin Interaction in Early Modern England', *Past & Present* 113 (1986), 38–69

Crooks, P., 'Factions, Feuds and Noble Power in Late Medieval Ireland, c. 1356–1496', *Irish Historical Studies*, 35 (2007), 425–54

'State of the Union: Perspectives on English Imperialism in the Late Middle Ages', *Past & Present*, 212 (2011), 3–42

Crowley, D.A., 'The Later History of Frankpledge', *BIHR*, 48 (1975), 1–15

Curry, A., *Agincourt: A New History* (Stroud, 2005)

'The Military Ordinances of Henry V: Texts and Contexts', in C. Given-Wilson, A. Kettle and L. Scales (eds), *War, Government and Aristocracy in the British Isles, c. 1150–1500* (Woodbridge, 2008), 214–49

Curry, A., Bell, A.R., King, A., and Simpkin, D., 'New Regime, New Army? Henry IV's Scottish Expedition of 1400', *EHR*, 125 (2010), 1382–413

Curta, F. (ed.), *Borders, Barriers, and Ethnogenesis: Frontiers in Late Antiquity and the Middle Ages* (Turnhout, 2005)

Curwen, J.F., 'Penrith Castle. Some Suggestions and Notes from the Patent Rolls ...', *TCWAAS*, 18 (1918), 174–88

Dauphant, L., *Le Royaume des Quatre Rivières: l'espace politique français (1380–1515)* (Seyssel, 2012)

Davidson, P., *The Idea of North* (London, 2005)

Bibliography

Davies, R.R., 'The Survival of the Bloodfeud in Medieval Wales', *History*, 54 (1969), 338–57

'The Law of the March', *Welsh History Review*, 5 (1971), 1–30

Lordship and Society in the March of Wales, 1282–1400 (Oxford, 1978)

'Kings, Lords and Liberties in the March of Wales, 1066–1272', *TRHS*, 5th ser., 29 (1979), 41–61

(ed.), *The British Isles, 1100–1500: Comparisons, Contrasts, and Connections* (Edinburgh, 1988)

Domination and Conquest: The Experience of Ireland, Scotland and Wales, 1100–1300 (Cambridge, 1990)

'The Peoples of Britain and Ireland 1100–1400 I. Identities', *TRHS*, 6th ser., 4 (1994), 1–20

'The Peoples of Britain and Ireland 1100–1400 II. Names, Boundaries and Regnal Solidarities', *TRHS*, 6th ser., 5 (1995), 1–20

'The Peoples of Britain and Ireland 1100–1400 III. Laws and Customs', *TRHS*, 6th ser., 6 (1996), 1–23

The First English Empire: Power and Identities in the British Isles 1093–1343 (Oxford, 2000)

'The Medieval State: The Tyranny of a Concept?', *Journal of Historical Sociology*, 16 (2003), 280–300

Lords and Lordship in the British Isles in the Late Middle Ages, ed. B. Smith (Oxford, 2009)

Dean, T., 'Marriage and Mutilation: Vendetta in Late Medieval Italy', *Past & Present*, 157 (1997), 3–36

Crime in Medieval Europe, 1200–1550 (London, 2001)

'Violence, Vendetta and Peacemaking in Late Medieval Bologna', *Criminal Justice History*, 17 (2002), 1–17

Dendy, F.W., 'The Heton–Fenwick–Denton Line of Descent', *Archaeologia Aeliana*, 3rd ser., 14 (1917), 173–90

Dewald, J., *The European Nobility, 1400–1800* (Cambridge, 1996)

Dickinson, W.C., 'Surdit de Sergaunt', *SHR*, 39 (1960), 170–5

Dixon, P., 'Towerhouses, Pelehouses and Border Society', *Archaeological Journal*, 136 (1979), 240–52

'Border Towers: A Cartographic Approach', in J. Ashbee and J.M. Luxford (eds), *Newcastle and Northumberland: Roman and Medieval Architecture and Art* (Leeds, 2013), 248–65

Dobson, R.B., 'Richard Bell, Prior of Durham (1464–78) and Bishop of Carlisle (1478–95)', *TCWAAS*, n.s., 65 (1965), 182–221

'The Last English Monks on Scottish Soil: The Severance of Coldingham Priory from the Monastery of Durham, 1461–78', *SHR*, 46 (1967), 1–25

Durham Priory 1400–1450 (London, 1973)

'Cathedral Chapters and Cathedral Cities: York, Durham and Carlisle in the Fifteenth Century', *Northern History*, 19 (1983), 15–44

'Richard III and the Church of York', in R.A. Griffiths and J. Sherborne (eds), *Kings and Nobles in the Later Middle Ages. A Tribute to Charles Ross* (Gloucester, 1986), 130–54

Bibliography

'Politics and the Church in the Fifteenth-Century North', in A.J. Pollard (ed.), *The North of England in the Age of Richard III* (Stroud, 1996), 1–17

'The Northern Province in the Later Middle Ages', *Northern History*, 42 (2005), 49–60

Dockray, K., 'Richard III and the Yorkshire Gentry, c. 1471–1485', in P.W. Hammond (ed.), *Richard III: Loyalty, Lordship and Law* (London, 1986), 38–57

Dodds, B., *Peasants and Production in the Medieval North-East: The Evidence from Tithes, 1270–1536* (Woodbridge, 2007)

Donagan, B., 'Codes and Conduct in the English Civil War', *Past & Present*, 118 (1988), 65–95

Donnelly, J., 'An Open Port: The Berwick Export Trade, 1311–1373', *SHR*, 78 (1999), 145–69

Duffy, P.M., 'The Nature of the Medieval Frontier in Ireland', *Studia Hibernica*, 22–3 (1982–3), 21–38

Duffy, S., and Foran, S. (eds), *The English Isles: Cultural Transmission and Political Conflict in Britain and Ireland, 1100–1500* (Dublin, 2013)

Dunham, W.H., *Lord Hastings' Indentured Retainers 1461–1483* (New Haven, 1955)

Dunlop, D., 'The "Redresses and Reparacons of Attemptates": Alexander Legh's Instructions from Edward IV, March–April 1475', *Historical Research*, 63 (1990), 340–53

Dunning, R.W., 'Thomas, Lord Dacre and the West March towards Scotland, 1435', *BIHR* 41 (1968), 95–9

Eadie, G., 'Identifying Functions in Castles: A Study of Tower Houses in Ireland', in R. Oram (ed.), *A House That Thieves Might Knock At: Proceedings of the 2010 Stirling and 2011 Dundee Conferences* (Donington, 2015), 2–18

Eales, R., and Tyas, S. (eds), *Family and Dynasty in Late Medieval England: Proceedings of the 1997 Harlaxton Symposium* (Donington, 2003)

Edwards, J.G., 'The Parliamentary Committee of 1398', *EHR*, 40 (1925), 321–33

Elias, N., *The Court Society*, trans. E. Jephcott (Oxford, 1983)

The Civilizing Process, trans. E. Jephcott, 2 vols (Oxford, 1994)

Eliott of Stobs, Dowager Lady D.F.A., and Eliott, A.F.A.B., *The Elliots: The Story of a Border Clan* (Chatham, 1974; repr., Chippenham, 1986)

Elliot, G.F.S., *The Border Elliots and the Family of Minto* (Edinburgh, 1897)

Ellis, S.G., 'Crown, Community and Government in the English Territories, 1450–1575', *History*, 71 (1986), 187–204

Reform and Revival: English Government in Ireland, 1470–1534 (Woodbridge, 1986)

'A Border Baron and the Tudor State: The Rise and Fall of Lord Dacre of the North', *Historical Journal*, 35 (1992), 253–77

Tudor Frontiers and Noble Power: The Making of the British State (Oxford, 1995)

'A Crisis of the Aristocracy? Frontiers and Noble Power in the Early Tudor State', in J.A. Guy (ed.), *The Tudor Monarchy* (London, 1997), 330–40

Ireland in the Age of the Tudors, 1447–1603 (London, 1998)

'Civilizing Northumberland: Representations of Englishness in the Tudor State', *Journal of Historical Sociology*, 12 (1999), 103–27

'The English State and Its Frontiers in the British Isles, 1300–1600', in D.J. Power and N. Standen (eds), *Frontiers in Question: Eurasian Borderlands, 700–1700* (Basingstoke, 1999), 153–81

Bibliography

'Tudor Frontiers in History and Historiography', in S.G. Ellis and R. Esser (eds), *Frontiers and the Writing of History, 1500–1850* (Hannover-Laatzen, 2006), 73–93

'Civilizing the Natives: State Formation and the Tudor Monarchy, c. 1400–1603', in S.G. Ellis and L. Klusáková (eds), *Imagining Frontiers, Contesting Identities* (Pisa, 2007), 77–92

'Region and Frontier in the English State: The English Far North, 1296–1603', in S.G. Ellis and R. Esser (eds), *Frontiers, Regions and Identities in Europe* (Pisa, 2009), 77–100

Defending English Ground: War and Peace in Meath and Northumberland, 1460–1542 (Oxford, 2015)

Ellis, S.G., and Esser, R. (eds), *Frontiers and the Writing of History, 1500–1850* (Hannover-Laatzen, 2006)

Ellis, S.G., and Klusáková, L. (eds), *Imagining Frontiers, Contesting Identities* (Pisa, 2007)

Ellis, S.G., and Esser, R., with Berdah, J.-F., and Řezník, M. (eds), *Frontiers, Regions and Identities in Europe* (Pisa, 2009)

Emery, A., *Greater Medieval Houses of England and Wales: 1300–1500, Volume 1: Northern England* (Cambridge, 1996)

'Late-Medieval Houses as an Expression of Social Status', *Historical Research*, 78 (2005), 140–61

'Introductory Reflections after Greater Medieval Houses of England and Wales', in M. Airs and P.S. Barnwell (eds), *The Medieval Great House* (Donington, 2011), 1–30

Etty, C., 'A Tudor Solution to the "Problem of the North"? Government and the Marches towards Scotland, 1509–1529', *Northern History*, 39 (2002), 209–26

'Neighbours from Hell? Living with Tynedale and Redesdale, 1489–1547', in M. Prestwich (ed.), *Liberties and Identities in the Medieval British Isles* (Woodbridge, 2008), 120–40

Evans-Pritchard, E.E., *The Nuer* (Oxford, 1940)

Faith, R.J., 'Peasant Families and Inheritance Customs in Medieval England', *Agricultural History Review*, 14 (1966), 77–95

Fawcett R., and Oram, R.D., *Melrose Abbey* (Stroud, 2004)

Febvre, L., 'The Problem of Frontiers and the Natural Bounds of States', in L. Febvre, *A Geographical Introduction to History*, trans. E.G. Mountford and J.H. Paxton (London, 1932), 296–314

'*Frontière*: The Word and the Concept', in L. Febvre, *A New Kind of History: From the Writings of Lucien Febvre*, trans. K. Folca, ed. P. Burke (London, 1973), 208–18

Finch, A.J., 'The Nature of Violence in the Middle Ages: An Alternative Perspective', *Historical Research*, 70 (1997), 249–68

Firnhaber-Baker, J., 'Seigneurial War and Royal Power in Later Medieval Southern France', *Past & Present*, 208 (2010), 37–76

'Techniques of Seigneurial War in the Fourteenth Century', *Journal of Medieval History*, 36 (2010), 90–103

'*Jura in medio*: The Settlement of Seigneurial Disputes in Later Medieval Languedoc', *French History*, 26 (2012), 441–59

Violence and the State in Languedoc, 1250–1400 (Cambridge, 2014)

Bibliography

Fleming, P., *Family and Household in Medieval England* (Basingstoke, 2001)

Fletcher, C., 'What Makes a Political Language? Key Terms, Profit and Damage in the Common Petition of the English Parliament, 1343–1422', in J. Dumolyn, J. Haemers, H.R. Oliva Herrer and V. Challet (eds), *The Voices of the People in Late Medieval Europe: Communication and Popular Politics* (Turnhout, 2014), 91–106

Fletcher, J., *Violence and Civilization: An Introduction to the Work of Norbert Elias* (Cambridge, 1997)

Ford, C.J., 'Piracy or Policy: The Crisis in the Channel, 1400–1403', *TRHS*, 5th ser., 29 (1979), 63–78

Forrest, I., 'English Provincial Constitutions and Inquisition into Lollardy', in M.C. Flannery and K.L. Walter (eds), *The Culture of Inquisition in Medieval England* (Woodbridge, 2013), 45–59

Fox, C., *The Personality of Britain* (Cardiff, 1932)

Frame, R., *English Lordship in Ireland, 1318–1361* (Oxford, 1982)

   The Political Development of the British Isles, 1100–1400 (Oxford, 1990)

   Ireland and Britain, 1170–1450 (London, 1998)

Fraser, C.M., 'The Northumberland Eyre of 1293', *Northern History*, 36 (2000), 17–32

   'The Economic Growth of Newcastle upon Tyne, 1150–1536', in D. Newton and A.J. Pollard (eds), *Newcastle and Gateshead before 1700* (Chichester, 2009), 41–64

Gaskill, M., *Crime and Mentalities in Early Modern England* (Cambridge, 2000)

   'New Directions in the History of Crime and the Law in Early Modern England', *Criminal Justice History*, 17 (2002) 147–69.

Gatrell, V.A.C., Lenman, B., and Parker, G. (eds), *Crime and the Law: The Social History of Crime in Western Europe since 1500* (London, 1980)

Gauvard, C., '*De Grace Especial': Crime, État et Société en France à la fin du Moyen Âge*, 2 vols (Paris, 1991)

   'La justice pénale du roi de France à la fin du Moyen Âge', in X. Rousseau and R. Lévy (eds), *Le pénal dans tous ses états: justice, états et sociétés en Europe: XIIe–XXe siècles* (Brussels, 1997), 81–112.

Geary, P.J., 'Living with Conflicts in Stateless France: A Typology of Conflict Management Mechanisms, 1050–1200', in P.J. Geary, *Living with the Dead in the Middle Ages* (Ithaca, 1994), 125–60

Genet, J.-P., 'Scotland in the Later Middle Ages: A Province or a Foreign Kingdom of the English?', in H. Skoda, P. Lantschner and R.L.J. Shaw (eds), *Contact and Exchange in Later Medieval Europe: Essays in Honour of Malcolm Vale* (Woodbridge, 2012), 127–43

Given-Wilson, C., *The English Nobility in the Late Middle Ages* (London, 1987)

Gluckman, M., 'The Peace in the Feud', *Past & Present*, 7 (1955), 1–14

Godfrey, A.M., *Civil Justice in Renaissance Scotland: The Origins of a Central Court* (Leiden, 2009)

   'Rethinking the Justice of the Feud in Sixteenth-Century Scotland', in S. Boardman and J. Goodare (eds), *Kings, Lord and Men in Scotland and Britain, 1300–1625: Essays in Honour of Jenny Wormald* (Edinburgh, 2014), 136–54

Goodall, J., *The English Castle, 1066–1650* (Newhaven, 2011)

Bibliography

'The Early Development of Alnwick Castle, c. 1100–1400', in J. Ashbee and J.M. Luxford (eds), *Newcastle and Northumberland: Roman and Medieval Architecture and Art* (Leeds, 2013), 232–47

Goodman, A., 'Responses to Requests in Yorkshire for Military Service under Henry V', *Northern History*, 17 (1981), 240–52

The Wars of the Roses: Military Activity and English Society, 1452–97 (London, 1981; republ., 2002)

'The Anglo-Scottish Marches in the Fifteenth Century: A Frontier Society?', in R.A. Mason (ed.), *Scotland and England, 1286–1815* (Edinburgh, 1987), 18–33

'Religion and Warfare in the Anglo-Scottish Marches', in R.J. Bartlett and A. MacKay (eds), *Medieval Frontier Societies* (Oxford, 1989), 245–66

'Introduction', in J.A. Tuck and A. Goodman (eds), *War and Border Societies in the Middle Ages* (London, 1992), 1–29

'The Defence of Northumberland: A Preliminary Survey', in M. Strickland (ed.), *Armies, Chivalry and Warfare in Medieval Britain and France* (Stamford, 1998), 161–72

The Wars of the Roses: Military Activity and English Society, 1452–97 (London, 2002)

'Border Warfare and Hexhamshire in the Later Middle Ages', *Hexham Historian*, 13 (2003), 50–65

'Anglo-Scottish Relations in the Later Fourteenth Century: Alienation or Acculturation?', in A. King and M.A. Penman (eds), *England and Scotland in the Fourteenth Century: New Perspectives* (Woodbridge, 2007), 236–53

Gorski, R., *The Fourteenth-Century Sheriff* (Woodbridge, 2003)

Gould, R.V., 'Revenge as Sanction and Solidarity Display: An Analysis of Vendettas in Nineteenth-Century Corsica', *American Sociological Review*, 56 (2000), 682–704

Gouldesbrough, P., *Formulary of Old Scots Legal Documents* (Edinburgh, 1985)

Graham, T.H.B., 'The Barony of Liddel and Its Occupants', *TCWAAS*, n.s., 11 (1911), 55–83

'The Debatable Land', *TCWAAS*, n.s., 12 (1912), 33–58

'The Debatable Land, Part II', *TCWAAS*, n.s., 14 (1914), 132–57

Grant, A., 'Murder Will Out: Kingship, Kinship and Killing in Medieval Scotland', in S. Boardman and J. Goodare (eds), *Kings, Lord and Men in Scotland and Britain, 1300–1625: Essays in Honour of Jenny Wormald* (Edinburgh, 2014), 193–226

Grant, A., and Stringer, K.J., 'Introduction: The Enigma of British History', in A. Grant and K.J. Stringer (eds), *Uniting the Kingdom? The Making of British History* (London, 1996), 3–11

Gray, H.L., *English Field Systems* (Cambridge, MA, 1915)

'Incomes from Land in England in 1436', *EHR*, 49 (1934), 607–39

Gray, J., 'Lawlessness on the Frontier: The Anglo-Scottish Borderlands in the Fourteenth to Sixteenth Century', *History and Anthropology*, 12 (2001), 381–408

Green, R.F., 'Violence in the Early Robin Hood Poems', in M.D. Meyerson, D. Thiery and O. Falk (eds), *A Great Effusion of Blood? Interpreting Medieval Violence* (Toronto, 2004), 268–86

Bibliography

Green, T.A., 'Societal Concepts of Criminal Liability for Homicide in Medieval England', *Speculum* 47 (1972), 669–94

'The Jury and the English Law of Homicide, 1200–1600', *Michigan Law Review*, 74 (1976), 413–99

Verdict According to Conscience: Perspectives on the English Criminal Trial Jury, 1200–1800 (Chicago, 1985)

Griffiths, R.A., 'Wales and the Marches in the Fifteenth Century', in S.B. Chrimes, C.D. Ross and R.A. Griffiths (eds), *Fifteenth-Century England 1399–1509* (Manchester, 1972), 145–72

'Patronage, Politics and the Principality of Wales, 1413–1461', in H. Hearder and H.R. Loyn (eds), *British Government and Administration: Studies Presented to S.B. Chrimes* (Cardiff, 1974), 69–86

The Reign of King Henry VI (Berkeley, 1981)

'The English Realm and Dominions and the King's Subjects in the Later Middle Ages', in R.A. Griffiths, *King and Country: England and Wales in the Fifteenth Century* (London, 1989), 33–54

'Local Rivalries and National Politics: The Percies, the Nevilles, and the Duke of Exeter, 1452–55', in R.A. Griffiths, *King and Country: England and Wales in the Fifteenth Century* (London, 1989), 321–64

'The Provinces and the Dominions in the Age of the Wars of the Roses', in S.D. Michalove and A.C. Reeves (eds), *Estrangement, Enterprise and Education in Fifteenth-Century England* (Stroud, 1998), 1–25

'Crossing the Frontiers of the English Realm in the Fifteenth Century', in H. Pryce and J. Watts (eds), *Power and Identity in the Middle Ages: Essays in Memory of Rees Davies* (Oxford, 2007), 211–25

Hopkins, T., and Howell, R. (eds), *Gwent County History, Volume II: The Age of the Marcher Lords, c. 1070–1536* (Cardiff, 2008)

Grohse, I.P., *Frontiers for Peace in the Medieval North: The Norwegian-Scottish Frontier c. 1260–1470* (Leiden, 2017)

Groundwater, A., *The Scottish Middle March, 1573–1625: Power, Kinship, Allegiance* (Woodbridge, 2010)

Grundy, J., McCombie, G., Ryder, P., Welfare, H., and Pevsner, N., *Northumberland* (Harmondsworth, 1992)

Guarini, E.F., 'Center and Periphery', in J. Kirshner (ed.), *The Origins of the State in Italy: 1300–1600* (Chicago, 1996), 74–96

Guenée, B., *Tribunaux et Gens de Justice dans le Bailliage de Senlis à la fin du Moyen Âge* (Paris, 1963)

Gunn, S.J., *Early Tudor Government* (Basingstoke, 1995)

Guy, J.A., 'The Development of Equitable Jurisdictions, 1450–1550', in E.W. Ives and A.H. Manchester (eds), *Law, Litigants and the Legal Profession* (London, 1983), 80–6

Haas, J. (ed.), *The Anthropology of War* (Cambridge, 1990)

Halsall, G., 'Violence and Society in the Early Medieval West: An Introductory Survey', in G. Halsall (ed.), *Violence and Society in the Early Medieval West* (Woodbridge, 1998), 1–45

Hämäläinen, P., and Truett, S., 'On Borderlands', *Journal of American History*, 98 (2011), 338–61

Bibliography

Hamil, F.C., 'The King's Approvers: A Chapter in the History of English Criminal Law', *Speculum* 11 (1936), 238–58

Hanawalt, B.A., *Crime and Conflict in English Communities, 1300–1348* (Cambridge, MA, 1979)

'The Power of Word and Symbol: Conflict Resolution in Late Medieval London', in B.A. Hanawalt (ed.), *'Of Good and Ill Repute': Gender and Social Control in Medieval England* (Oxford, 1988), 35–52

Harding, A., *A Social History of English Law* (Harmondsworth, 1966; repr. Gloucester, MA, 1973)

Harding, A., *Medieval Law and the Foundations of the State* (Oxford, 2002)

'Rights, Wrongs and Remedies in Late Medieval English and Scots Law', *Miscellany IV*, Stair Society (Edinburgh, 2002), 1–8

Harriss, G.L., 'Introduction', in K.B. McFarlane, *England in the Fifteenth Century: Collected Essays* (London, 1981), ix–xxvii.

'Political Society and the Growth of Government in Late Medieval England', *Past & Present*, 138 (1993), 28–57

Shaping the Nation: England 1360–1461 (Oxford, 2005)

Hartrich, E., 'Charters and Inter-Urban Networks: England, 1439–1449', *EHR*, 132 (2017), 219–49

Hartshorne, C.H., *Feudal and Military Antiquities of Northumberland and the Scottish Borders* (London, 1858)

Hastings, M., *The Court of Common Pleas in Fifteenth Century England* (Ithaca, 1947)

Hatcher, J., *Rural Economy and Society in the Duchy of Cornwall, 1300–1500* (Cambridge, 1970)

Hay, D., 'England, Scotland and Europe: The Problem of the Frontier', *TRHS*, 5th ser., 25 (1975), 77–91

Hayes, R.C.E., '"Ancient Indictments" for the North of England, 1461–1509', in A.J. Pollard (ed.), *The North of England in the Age of Richard III* (Stroud, 1996), 19–45

Hedley, W.P., 'The Medieval Forests of Northumberland', *Archaeologia Aeliana*, 4th ser., 28 (1950), 96–104

Northumberland Families, 2 vols (Newcastle-upon-Tyne, 1968–70)

Heers, J., *Family Clans in the Middle Ages* (Amsterdam, 1977)

Herbert, A., 'Herefordshire, 1413–61: Some Aspects of Society and Public Order', in R.A. Griffiths (ed.), *Patronage, the Crown and the Provinces in Later Medieval England* (Gloucester, 1981), 103–122

Hermans, T., 'Tower Houses in the Netherlands', in R. Oram (ed.), *A House That Thieves Might Knock At: Proceedings of the 2010 Stirling and 2011 Dundee Conferences* (Donington, 2015), 47–61

Herrup, C.B., *The Common Peace: Participation and the Criminal Law in Seventeenth-Century England* (Cambridge, 1987)

Hicks, M., 'Dynastic Change and Northern Society: The Career of the Fourth Earl of Northumberland, 1470–89', *Northern History*, 14 (1978), 78–107

'Descent, Partition and Extinction: The "Warwick Inheritance" [1471–75]', *BIHR*, 52 (1979), 116–28

'The 1468 Statute of Livery', *Historical Research*, 61 (1991), 15–28

Bastard Feudalism (London, 1995)

Bibliography

'Cement or Solvent? Kinship and Politics in Late Medieval England: The Case of the Nevilles', *History,* 83 (1998), 31–46

(ed.), *The Fifteenth-Century Inquisitions Post Mortem: A Companion* (Woodbridge, 2012)

Higham, N.J., *A Frontier Landscape: The North West in the Middle Ages* (Macclesfield, 2004)

Hindle, S., *The State and Social Change in Early Modern England, 1550–1640* (Basingstoke, 2000)

Hodgkin, T., *The Wardens of the Northern Marches* (London, 1908)

Hodgson, J., *A History of Northumberland,* 3 vols in 7 (Newcastle-upon-Tyne, 1820–58)

Holden, B., *Lords of the Central Marches: English Aristocracy and Frontier Society, 1087–1265* (Oxford, 2008)

Holford, M.L., and Stringer, K.J., *Border Liberties and Loyalties in North-East England, c. 1200–c. 1400* (Edinburgh, 2010)

Horrox, R. (ed.), *Richard III and the North* (Hull, 1986)

Richard III: A Study of Service (Cambridge, 1989)

'Local and National Politics in Fifteenth-Century England', *Journal of Medieval History,* 18 (1992), 391–403

Hoskins, W.G., *The Midland Peasant: The Economic and Social History of a Leicestershire Village* (London, 1957)

Houlbrooke, R.A., *The English Family 1450–1700* (Harlow, 1984)

Housley, N., *The Later Crusades* (Oxford, 1992)

Hoyle, R.W., 'The First Earl of Cumberland: A Reputation Reassessed', *Northern History,* 22 (1986), 63–94

'The Earl, the Archbishop and the Council: The Affray at Fulford, May 1504', in R. Archer and S. Walker (eds), *Rulers and Ruled in Late Medieval England* (London, 1995), 239–56

'Faction, Feud and Reconciliation amongst the Northern English Nobility, 1525–1569', *History,* 84 (1999), 590–613

Hudson, J.G.H., 'Introduction: Customs, Laws, and the Interpretation of Medieval Law', in P. Andersen and M. Münster-Swendsen (eds), *Custom: The Development and Use of a Legal Concept in the Middle Ages* (Copenhagen, 2009), 1–16

'Feud, Vengeance and Violence in England from the Tenth to the Twelfth Centuries', in B.S. Tuten and T.L. Billado (eds), *Feud, Violence and Practice: Essays in Medieval Studies in Honor of Stephen D. White* (Farnham, 2010), 29–53

Huizinga, J., *The Autumn of the Middle Ages,* trans. R.J. Payton and U. Mammitzsch (Chicago, 1996)

Hunnisett, R.F., *The Medieval Coroner* (Cambridge, 1961)

Hunter Blair, C.H., 'The Sheriffs of Northumberland, Part III, the Sheriffs of Norham', *Archaeologia Aeliana,* 4th ser., 21 (1943), 72–89

'The Wardens and Deputy Wardens of the Marches of England towards Scotland in Northumberland', *Archaeologia Aeliana,* 4th ser., 28 (1950), 18–95

Hurnard, N.M., *The King's Pardon for Homicide before A.D. 1307* (Oxford, 1969)

Hurtado, A.L., 'Parkmanizing the Spanish Borderlands: Bolton, Turner, and the Historians' World', *Western Historical Quarterly,* 26 (1995), 149–67

Bibliography

Hyams, P.R., 'Feud in Medieval England', *Haskins Society Journal*, 3 (1992 for 1991), 1–21

'Feud and the State in Late Anglo-Saxon England', *Journal of British Studies*, 40 (2001), 1–43

'Homage and Feudalism: A Judicious Separation', in N. Fryde (ed.), *Die Gegenwart des Feudalismus* (Göttingen, 2003), 13–49

Rancor and Reconciliation in Medieval England (Ithaca, 2003)

Hyde, M., and Pevsner, N., *Cumbria: Cumberland, Westmorland and Furness* (New Haven, 2010)

Ibbetson, D., 'Custom in Medieval Law', in A. Perreau-Saussine and J.B. Murphy (eds), *The Nature of Customary Law: Legal, Historical and Philosophical Perspectives* (Cambridge, 2007), 151–75

Ives, E.W., *The Common Lawyers of Pre-Reformation England* (Cambridge, 1983)

Jack, S.M., 'The "Debatable Lands", Terra Nullius, and Natural Law in the Sixteenth Century', *Northern History*, 41 (2004), 289–300

Jackson, M.J., *Castles of Cumbria* (Carlisle, 1990)

Jackson, W., 'The Threlkelds of Threlkeld, Yanwath, and Crosby Ravensworth', *TCWAAS*, o.s., 9 (1888), 298–317

Jalland, P., 'The Influence of the Aristocracy on Shire Elections in the North of England, 1450–70', *Speculum*, 47 (1972), 483–507

James, M.E., *Change and Continuity in the Tudor North: The Rise of Thomas, First Lord Wharton* (York, 1965)

'The murder at Cocklodge, 28 April 1489', *Durham University Journal*, 57 (1965), 80–7

A Tudor Magnate and the Tudor State: Henry Fifth Earl of Northumberland (York, 1966)

'The First Earl of Cumberland (1493–1542) and the Decline of Northern Feudalism', *Northern History*, 1 (1966), 43–69

Family, Lineage and Civil Society: A Study of Society, Politics and Mentality in the Durham Region, 1500–1640 (Oxford, 1974)

Society, Politics and Culture: Studies in Early Modern England (Cambridge, 1986)

James, S.E., 'Sir Thomas Parr (1407–1461)', *TCWAAS*, n.s., 81 (1981), 15–25

'Sir William Parr of Kendal: Part I, 1434–1471', *TCWAAS*, n.s., 93 (1993), 99–114

'Sir William Parr of Kendal: Part II, 1471–1483', *TCWAAS*, n.s., 94 (1994), 106–20

'Sir John Parr of Kendal, 1437–1477', *TCWAAS*, n.s., 96 (1996), 71–86

'Henry VII and *Prerogativa Regis*: The Case of Mabel Dacre', *TCWAAS*, n.s., 99 (1999), 177–84

Jamroziak, E.M., *Survival and Success on Medieval Borders: Cistercian Houses in Medieval Scotland and Pomerania from the Twelfth to the Late Fourteenth Century* (Turnhout, 2011)

Jamroziak, E.M., and Stöber, K. (eds), *Monasteries on the Borders of Medieval Europe: Conflict and Cultural Interaction* (Turnhout, 2013)

Jewell, H.M., 'North and South: The Antiquity of the Great Divide', *Northern History*, 27 (1991), 1–25

The North-South Divide: The Origins of Northern Consciousness in England (Manchester, 1994)

Bibliography

Johnson, P., *Cathedrals of England, Scotland and Wales* (London, 1990)

Jolliffe, J.E.A., 'Northumbrian Institutions', *EHR*, 41 (1926), 1–42

Jones, W.R., 'The Image of the Barbarian in Medieval Europe', *Comparative Studies in Society and History*, 13 (1971), 376–407

Jordan, J., 'Rethinking Disputes and Settlements: How Historians Can Use Legal Anthropology', in S. Cummins and L. Kounine (eds), *Cultures of Conflict Resolution in Early Modern Europe* (London, 2016), 17–50

Justice, S., *Writing and Rebellion: England in 1381* (Berkeley, 1994)

Kadens, E., 'Order within Law, Variety within Custom: The Character of the Medieval Merchant Law', *Chicago Journal of International Law*, 5 (2004), 39–65

    'Custom's Two Bodies', in K.L. Jansen, G. Geltner, A.E. Lester (eds), *Center and Periphery: Studies on Power in the Medieval World in Honor of William Chester Jordan* (Leiden, 2013), 239–48

Kaeuper, R.W., *War, Justice and Public Order: England and France in the Later Middle Ages* (Oxford, 1988)

    Chivalry and Violence in Medieval Europe (Oxford, 1999)

    'Chivalry and the "Civilizing Process"', in R.W. Kaeuper (ed.), *Violence in Medieval Society* (Woodbridge, 2000), 21–35

    'Debating Law, Justice and Constitutionalism', in R.W. Kaeuper (ed.), *Law, Governance and Justice: New Views on Medieval Constitutionalism* (Leiden, 2013), 1–14

Kamali, E.P., '*Felonia Felonice Facta*: Felony and Intentionality in Medieval England', *Criminal Law and Philosophy*, 9 (2015), 397–421

    'The Devil's Daughter of Hell Fire: Anger's Role in Medieval English Felony Cases', *Law and History Review*, 35 (2017), 155–200

    Felony and the Guilty Mind in Medieval England (Cambridge, 2019)

Kaminsky, H., 'The Noble Feud in the Later Middle Ages', *Past & Present*, 177 (2002), 55–83

Kapelle, W.E., *The Norman Conquest of the North: The Region and Its Transformation, 1000–1135* (Chapel Hill, 1979)

Kaye, J., *Economy and Nature in the Fourteenth Century: Money, Market Exchange, and the Emergence of Scientific Thought* (Cambridge, 1998)

Kaye, J.M., 'The Early History of Murder and Manslaughter', Parts 1 & 2, *Law Quarterly Review*, 83 (1967), 365–95, 569–601

Kearney, H., *The British Isles: A History of Four Nations* (Cambridge, 1989)

Keen, M.H., 'Treason Trials under the Law of Arms', *TRHS*, 5th ser., 12 (1962), 85–103

    The Laws of War in the Late Middle Ages (London, 1965)

    Chivalry (New Haven, 1984)

    'The Jurisdiction and Origins of the Constable's Court', in J. Gillingham and J.C. Holt (eds), *War and Government in the Middle Ages* (Cambridge, 1984), 159–69

Kermode, J., 'Northern Towns', in D. Palliser (ed.), *The Cambridge Urban History of Britain, Volume I: 600–1540* (Cambridge, 2000), 657–79

Kesselring, K.J., *Making Murder Public: Homicide in Early Modern England, 1480–1680* (Oxford, 2019)

Kim, K., *Aliens in Medieval Law: The Origins of Modern Citizenship* (Cambridge, 2000)

Bibliography

King, A., 'Englishmen, Scots and Marchers: National and Local Identities in Thomas Gray's *Scalacronica*', *Northern History*, 36 (2000), 217–32

'"They have the Hertes of the People by North": Northumberland, the Percies and Henry IV, 1399–1408', in G. Dodd and D. Biggs (eds), *Henry IV: The Establishment of the Regime, 1399–1406* (Woodbridge, 2003), 139–59

'Best of Enemies: Were the Fourteenth-Century Anglo-Scottish Marches a "Frontier Society"?', in A. King and M.A. Penman (eds), *England and Scotland in the Fourteenth Century: New Perspectives* (Woodbridge, 2007), 116–35

'Fortresses and Fashion Statements: Gentry Castles in Fourteenth-Century Northumberland', *Journal of Medieval History*, 33 (2007), 372–97

'The Anglo-Scottish Marches and the Perception of "the North" in Fifteenth-Century England', *Northern History*, 49 (2012), 37–50

King, A., and Penman, M.A. (eds), *England and Scotland in the Fourteenth Century: New Perspectives* (Woodbridge, 2007)

King, A., and Simpkin, D. (eds), *England and Scotland at War, c. 1296–c. 1513* (Leiden, 2012)

Knight, S., and Ohlgren, T.H. (eds), *Robin Hood and Other Outlaw Tales* (Kalamazoo, MI, 1997)

Knights, M., et al., 'Towards a Social and Cultural History of Keywords and Concepts', *History of Political Thought*, 31 (2010), 427–48

'Commonwealth: The Social, Cultural and Conceptual Contexts of an Early Modern Keyword', *Historical Journal*, 54 (2011), 659–87

Kuehn, T., *Law, Family, and Women: Toward a Legal Anthropology of Renaissance Italy* (London, 1991)

Kümin, B. (ed.), *Political Space in Pre-industrial Europe* (Farnham, 2009)

Lander, J.R., 'Family, "Friends", and Politics in Fifteenth-Century England', in R.A. Griffiths and J. Sherborne (eds), *Kings and Nobles in the Later Middle Ages. A Tribute to Charles Ross* (Gloucester, 1986), 27–40

English Justices of the Peace 1461–1509 (Gloucester, 1989)

Lapsley, G.T., 'The Problem of the North: A Study in English Border History', *American Historical Review*, 5 (1900), 440–66

Larson, P.L., 'Local Law Courts in Late Medieval Durham', in R.H. Britnell and C.D. Liddy (eds), *North-East England in the Later Middle Ages* (Woodbridge, 2005), 97–110

Lattimore, O., *Studies in Frontier History: Collected Papers, 1928–58* (Paris, 1962)

Lavezzo, K., *Angels on the Edge of the World: Geography, Literature and English Community, 1000–1534* (Ithaca, 2006)

Le Goff, J., 'The Symbolic Ritual of Vassalage', in J. Le Goff, *Time, Work and Culture in the Middle Ages*, trans. Arthur Goldhammer (Chicago, 1980), 237–87

Le Patourel, J., 'Is Northern History a Subject?', *Northern History*, 12 (1976), 1–15

Leroy, C., and de La Rivière, D., *Cathédrales et basiliques de Bretagne* (Paris, 2009)

Liddy, C.D., *War, Politics and Finance in Late Medieval English Towns: Bristol, York and the Crown, 1350–1400* (Woodbridge, 2005)

The Bishopric of Durham in the Late Middle Ages: Lordship, Community and the Cult of St Cuthbert (Woodbridge, 2008)

Lieberman, M., *The Medieval March of Wales: The Creation and Perception of a Frontier, 1066–1283* (Cambridge, 2010)

371

Bibliography

Livingston, M., and Bollard, J.K. (eds), *Owain Glyndŵr: A Casebook* (Liverpool, 2013)

Lomas, R.A., 'Developments in Land Tenure on the Prior of Durham's Estate in the Later Middle Ages', *Northern History*, 13 (1977), 27–43

North-East England in the Middle Ages (Edinburgh, 1992)

'The Impact of Border Warfare: The Scots and South Tweedside, c. 1290–c. 1520', *SHR* 75 (1996), 143–67

Lott, B., 'Seigneurial Hierarchy and Medieval Buildings in Westmorland', in G. Meirion-Jones, E. Impey and M.C.E. Jones, (eds), *The Seigneurial Residence in Western Europe AD c. 800–1600* (Oxford, 2002), 101–11.

Lourie, E., 'A Society Organised for War: Medieval Spain', *Past & Present*, 35 (1966), 54–76

Lowe, D.E., 'Patronage and Politics: Edward IV, the Wydevills, and the Council of the Prince of Wales, 1471–83', *Bulletin of the Board of Celtic Studies*, 29 (1981), 545–73

Luckett, D.A., 'Crown Office and Licensed Retinues in the Reign of Henry VII', in R.E. Archer and S. Walker (eds), *Rulers and Ruled in Late Medieval England* (London, 1995), 223–38

Lydon, J.F., 'The Problem of the Frontier in Medieval Ireland', *Topic*, 13 (1967), 5–22

MacCannell, D., '"Dark Corners of the Land"? A New Approach to Regional Factors in the Civil Wars of England and Wales', *Cultural and Social History*, 7 (2010), 171–89

Macdonald, A., 'Calendar of Deeds in the Laing Charters Relating to Northumberland', *Archaeologia Aeliana*, 4th ser., 28 (1950), 105–31

Macdonald, A.J., 'Approaches to Conflict on the Anglo-Scottish Borders in the Late Fourteenth Century', in A.I. Macinnes et al. (eds), *Ships, Guns and Bibles in the North Sea and Baltic States, c. 1350–c. 1700* (East Linton, 2000), 47–64

Border Bloodshed: Scotland, England and France at War 1369–1403 (East Linton, 2000)

'Kings of the Wild Frontier? The Earls of Dunbar or March, c. 1070–1435', in S.I. Boardman and A. Ross (eds), *The Exercise of Power in Medieval Scotland* (Dublin, 2003), 139–58

'John Hardyng, Northumbrian Identity and the Scots', in R.H. Britnell and C.D. Liddy (eds), *North-East England in the Later Middle Ages* (Woodbridge, 2005), 29–42

'Courage, Fear and the Experience of the Later Medieval Scottish Soldier', *SHR* 92 (2013), 179–206

'Trickery, Mockery and the Scottish Way of War', *Proceedings of the Society of Antiquaries of Scotland,* 143 (2013), 319–37

Macdougall, N., *James III* (rev. edn, Edinburgh, 2009)

MacGregor, M., 'Gaelic Barbarity and Scottish Identity in the Later Middle Ages', in D. Broun and M. MacGregor (eds), *Mìorun Mòr nan Gall, 'The Great Ill-Will of the Lowlander'? Lowland Perceptions of the Highlands, Medieval and Modern* (Glasgow, 2009), 7–48

Macinnes, A. I., 'Making the Plantations British, 1603–38', in S.G. Ellis and R. Esser (eds), *Frontiers and the Writing of History, 1500–1850* (Hannover-Laatzen, 2006), 95–125

Bibliography

Macinnes, A.I., and Ohlmeyer, J. (eds), *The Stuart Kingdoms in the Seventeenth Century: Awkward Neighbours* (Dublin, 2002)

MacInnes, I.A., '"To Be Annexed Forever to the English crown": The English Occupation of Southern Scotland c. 1334–1337', in A. King and D. Simpkin (eds), *England and Scotland at War, c. 1296–c. 1513* (Leiden, 2012), 183–202

Scotland's Second War of Independence, 1332–1357 (Woodbridge, 2016)

Mack, J.L., *The Border Line* (Edinburgh, 1926)

MacKenzie, W.M., 'The Debateable Land', *SHR*, 30 (1951), 109–25

Mackinder, H.J., *Britain and the British Seas* (London, 1902)

MacQueen, H.L., 'The Laws of Galloway: A Preliminary Survey', in R.D. Oram and G.P. Stell (eds), *Galloway: Land and Lordship* (Edinburgh, 1991), 131–43

'Survival and Success: The Kennedys of Dunure', in S.I. Boardman and A. Ross (eds), *The Exercise of Power in Medieval Scotland* (Dublin, 2003), 67–94

'Some Notes on Wrang and Unlaw', *Miscellany V*, Stair Society (Edinburgh, 2005), 13–26

Maddern, P.C., 'Honour among the Pastons: Gender and Integrity in Fifteenth-Century English Provincial Society', *Journal of Medieval History*, 14 (1988), 357–71

Violence and Social Order: East Anglia 1422–1442 (Oxford, 1992)

'"Best Trusted Friends": Concepts and Practices of Friendship among Fifteen Century Norfolk Gentry', in N. Rogers (ed.), *England in the Fifteenth Century: Proceedings of the 1992 Harlaxton Symposium* (Stamford, 1994), 100–17

Maginn, C., 'English Marcher Lineages in South Dublin in the Late Middle Ages', *Irish Historical Studies*, 34 (2004), 113–36

Maitland, F.W., *The Collected Papers of Frederic William Maitland*, ed. H.A.L. Fisher, 3 vols (Cambridge, 1911)

Mann, M., *The Sources of Social Power*, 3 vols (Cambridge, 1986–2012)

Maurer, H.E., 'Margaret of Anjou and the Loveday of 1458: A Reconsideration', in D. Biggs, S.D. Michalove and A.C. Reeves (eds), *Traditions and Transformations in Late Medieval England* (Leiden, 2002), 109–24

McDonnell, J., 'The Role of Transhumance in Northern England', *Northern History*, 24 (1988), 1–17

'Upland Pennine Hamlets', *Northern History*, 26 (1990), 20–39

McFarlane, K.B., *The Nobility of Later Medieval England: The Ford Lectures for 1953 and Related Studies*, ed. J.P. Cooper (Oxford, 1973)

'Service, Maintenance, and Politics', in K.B. McFarlane, *The Nobility of Later Medieval England: The Ford Lectures for 1953 and Related Studies*, ed. J.P. Cooper (Oxford, 1973), 102–21

'Bastard Feudalism', in K.B. McFarlane, *England in the Fifteenth Century: Collected Essays* (London, 1981), 23–43

England in the Fifteenth Century: Collected Essays (London, 1981)

McGladdery, C., *James II* (rev. edn, Edinburgh, 2015)

McIntosh, M.K., 'Finding Language for Misconduct: Jurors in Fifteenth-Century Local Courts', in B.A. Hanawalt and D. Wallace (eds), *Bodies and Disciplines: Intersections of Literature and History in Fifteenth-Century England* (Minneapolis, 1996), 87–122

Bibliography

Controlling Misbehavior in England, 1370–1600 (Cambridge, 1998)

McKean, C., 'A Suggested Chronology for the Scottish Medieval Country Seat', in M. Airs and P.S. Barnwell (eds), *The Medieval Great House* (Donington, 2011), 61–80

'A Taxonomy of Towers: A Reconnaissance of the Difficulties in Scotland', in R. Oram (ed.), *A House That Thieves Might Knock At: Proceedings of the 2010 Stirling and 2011 Dundee Conferences* (Donington, 2015), 92–114

McKelvie, G., 'The Livery Act of 1429', in L. Clark (ed.), *The Fifteenth Century XIV: Essays Presented to Michael Hicks* (Woodbridge, 2015), 55–65

'Henry VII's Letter to Carlisle in 1498: His Concerns about Retaining in a Border Fortress', *Northern History*, 54 (2017), 149–66

McKinley, R., *The Surnames of Lancashire* (London, 1981)

McNiven, P., 'The Scottish Policy of the Percies and the Strategy of the Rebellion of 1403', *BJRL*, 62 (1979), 498–530

McSheffrey, S., *Seeking Sanctuary: Crime, Mercy and Politics in English Courts, 1400–1550* (Oxford, 2017)

Mears, N., 'Courts, Courtiers and Culture in Tudor England', *Historical Journal*, 46 (2003), 703–22

Meikle, M.M., 'Northumberland Divided: Anatomy of a Sixteenth-Century Blood-feud', *Archaeologia Aeliana*, 5th ser., 20 (1992), 79–89

'Victims, Viragos and Vamps: Women of the Sixteenth-Century Anglo-Scottish Frontier', in J.C. Appleby and P. Dalton (eds), *Government, Religion and Society in Northern England, 1000–1700* (Stroud, 1997), 172–84

A British Frontier? Lairds and Gentlemen in the Eastern Borders, 1540–1603 (East Linton, 2004)

Mertes, K., *The English Noble Household, 1250–1600* (Oxford, 1988)

Metcalfe, W.C., *A Book of Knights Banneret, Knights of the Bath, and Knights Bachelor* (London, 1885)

Midmer, R., *English Medieval Monasteries 1066–1540: A Summary* (London, 1979)

Miller, E., 'Farming in Northern England during the Twelfth and Thirteenth Centuries', *Northern History*, 11 (1976 for 1975), 1–16

Miller, W.I., *Bloodtaking and Peacemaking: Feud, Law and Society in Saga Iceland* (Chicago, 1990)

Moor, C., 'Crackenthorpe of Newbiggin', *TCWAAS*, n.s., 33 (1933), 43–97

Moreno, E.M., 'The Creation of a Medieval Frontier: Islam and Christianity in the Iberian Peninsula, Eighth to Eleventh Centuries', in D.J. Power and N. Standen (eds), *Frontiers in Question: Eurasian Borderlands, 700–1700* (Basingstoke, 1999), 32–54

Morgan, D.A.L., 'The King's Affinity in the Polity of Yorkist England', *TRHS*, 5th Ser., 23 (1973), 1–25

Morgan, P., *War and Society in Medieval Cheshire, 1277–1403* (Manchester, 1987)

'Wild Wales: Civilizing the Welsh from the Sixteenth to the Nineteenth Centuries', in P. Burke, B. Harrison and P. Slack (eds), *Civil Histories: Essays Presented to Sir Keith Thomas* (Oxford, 2000), 265–83

Morris, W.A., *The Frankpledge System* (New York, 1910)

Muir, E., *Mad Blood Stirring: Vendetta in Renaissance Italy* (Baltimore, 1993)

Bibliography

Musin, A., 'Le droit de vengeance et son déclin dans les Pays-Bas (XIVe–XVIe siècles)', *Krypton. Identità, potere, rappresentazioni*, 5–6 (2015), 9–16

Musson, A.J., 'Turning King's Evidence: The Prosecution of Crime in Late Medieval England', *Oxford Journal of Legal Studies*, 19 (1999), 467–79

Musson, A., and Ormrod, W.M., *The Evolution of English Justice: Law, Politics and Society in the Fourteenth Century* (Basingstoke, 1999)

Myers, M.D., 'The Failure of Conflict Resolution and the Limits of Arbitration in King's Lynn, 1405–1416', in D. Biggs, S.D. Michalove and A.C. Reeves (eds), *Traditions and Transformations in Late Medieval England* (Leiden, 2002), 81–108.

Nader, L., and Todd, H.F. (eds), *The Disputing Process* (New York, 1978)

Neilson, G., *Trial by Combat* (Glasgow, 1890)

'The March Laws', ed. T.I. Rae, in *Miscellany I*, Stair Society (Edinburgh, 1971)

Netterstrøm, J.B., 'Feud, Protection and Serfdom in Late Medieval and Early Modern Denmark (c. 1400–1600)', in P. Freedman and M. Bourin (eds), *Forms of Servitude in Northern and Central Europe: Decline, Resistance and Expansion* (Turnhout, 2005), 369–84

'Feud in Late Medieval and Early Modern Denmark', in J.B. Netterstrøm and B. Poulsen (eds), *Feud in Medieval and Early Modern Europe* (Aarhus, 2007), 175–87

'Introduction: The Study of Feud in Medieval and Early Modern History', in J.B. Netterstrøm and B. Poulsen (eds), *Feud in Medieval and Early Modern Europe* (Aarhus, 2007), 9–67

Netterstrøm, J.B., and Poulsen, B. (eds), *Feud in Medieval and Early Modern Europe* (Aarhus, 2007)

Newton, R., 'The Decay of the Borders: Tudor Northumberland in Transition', in C.W. Chalklin and M.A. Havinden (eds), *Rural Change and Urban Growth, 1500–1800: Essays in English Regional History in Honour of W.G. Hoskins* (London, 1974), 2–31

Neville, C.J., 'Gaol Delivery in the Border Counties, 1439–1459', *Northern History*, 19 (1983), 45–60

'Border Law in Late Medieval England', *JLH*, 9 (1988), 335–56

'The Law of Treason in the English Border Counties in the Later Middle Ages', *LHR*, 9 (1991), 1–30

'Keeping the Peace on the Northern Marches in the Later Middle Ages', *EHR*, 109 (1994), 461–78

'War, Crime and Local Communities in the North of England in the Later Middle Ages', in J. Drendel (ed.), *La société rurale et les institutions gouvernementales au Moyen Âge* (Montreal, 1995), 189–201

'Local Sentiment and the "National" Enemy in Northern England in the Later Middle Ages', *Journal of British Studies*, 35 (1996), 419–37

Violence, Custom and Law: The Anglo-Scottish Border Lands in the Later Middle Ages (Edinburgh, 1998)

'Scottish Influences on the Medieval Laws of the Anglo-Scottish Marches,' *SHR*, 81 (2002), 161–85

Bibliography

'Remembering the Legal Past: Anglo-Scottish Border Law and Practice in the Later Middle Ages', in R.H. Britnell and C.D. Liddy (eds), *North-East England in the Later Middle Ages* (Woodbridge, 2005), 43–56

'Arbitration and Anglo-Scottish Border Law in the Later Middle Ages', in M. Prestwich (ed.), *Liberties and Identities in the Medieval British Isles* (Woodbridge, 2008), 37–55

Nicholson, R.G., *Edward III and the Scots: The Formative Years of a Military Career, 1327–1335* (Oxford, 1965)

Scotland: The Later Middle Ages (Edinburgh, 1974)

Nicolson, W., and Burn, R., *The History and Antiquities of the Counties of Westmorland and Cumberland*, 2 vols (London, 1777)

Noomen, P.N., *De stinzen in middeleeuws Friesland en hun bewoners* (Hilversum, 2009)

Northumberland National Park Authority, 'Alwinton, Northumberland: An Archaeological and Historical Study of a Border Township', in *Northumberland National Park Historic Village Atlas* (2004), www.dartmoor.gov.uk; accessed 1 October 2015

O'Byrne, E., and Ní Ghradaigh, J. (eds), *The March in the Islands of the Medieval West* (Leiden, 2012)

Oram, R.D., 'Dividing the Spoils: War, Schism and Religious Patronage on the Anglo-Scottish Border, c. 1332–c. 1400', in A. King and M.A. Penman (eds), *England and Scotland in the Fourteenth Century: New Perspectives* (Woodbridge, 2007), 136–56

'The Greater House in Late Medieval Scotland: Courtyards and Towers c. 1300–c. 1400' in M. Airs and P.S. Barnwell (eds), *The Medieval Great House* (Donington, 2011), 43–60

'Introduction: Houses That Thieves Might Knock At', in R. Oram (ed.), *A House That Thieves Might Knock At: Proceedings of the 2010 Stirling and 2011 Dundee Conferences* (Donington, 2015), ix–xv

Ormrod, W.M., *The Reign of Edward III: Crown and Political Society in England 1327–1377* (London, 1990)

'Competing Capitals? York and London in the Fourteenth Century', in S.R. Jones, R. Marks and A.J. Minnis (eds), *Courts and Regions in Medieval Europe* (York, 2000), 75–98

'Parliament, Political Economy and State Formation in Later Medieval England', in P. Hoppenbrouwers, A. Janse and R. Stein (eds), *Power and Persuasion: Essays on the Art of State Building in Honour of W.P. Blockmans* (Turnhout, 2010), 123–39

Otway-Ruthven, J., 'The Request of the Irish for English Law, 1277–80', *Irish Historical Studies*, 6 (1949), 261–70

Padel, O., 'Names in *-kin* in Medieval Wales', in D. Hooke and D. Postles (eds), *Names, Time and Place: Essays in Memory of Richard McKinley* (Amersham, 2003), 117–26

Palliser, D.M., 'Richard III and York', in R. Horrox (ed.), *Richard III and the North* (Hull, 1986), 51–81

Towns and Local Communities in Medieval and Early Modern England (Aldershot, 2006)

Bibliography

Palmer, P., 'At the Sign of the Head: The Currency of Beheading in Early Modern Ireland', in S. Carroll (ed.), *Cultures of Violence: Interpersonal Violence in Historical Perspective* (Basingstoke, 2007), 129–55

Parker, F.H.M., 'Inglewood Forest', *TCWAAS*, n.s., 5 (1905), 35–61; 11 (1911), 1–37

Payling, S.J., 'Inheritance and Local Politics in the Later Middle Ages: The Case of Ralph, Lord Cromwell, and the Heriz Inheritance', *Nottingham Medieval Studies*, 30 (1986), 67–95.

'Law and Arbitration in Nottinghamshire, 1399–1461', in J.T. Rosenthal and C. Richmond (eds), *People, Politics and Community in the Later Middle Ages* (Gloucester, 1987), 140–60

Political Society in Lancastrian England: The Greater Gentry of Nottinghamshire (Oxford, 1991)

'Murder, Motive and Punishment in Fifteenth-Century England: Two Gentry Case Studies', *EHR*, 113 (1998), 1–17

Pease, H., *The Lord Wardens of the Marches of England and Scotland* (London, 1913)

Peters, E.M., 'Introduction: The Reordering of Law and the Illicit', in R.M. Karras, J. Kaye and E.A. Matter (eds), *Law and the Illicit in Medieval Europe* (Philadelphia, 2008), 1–14.

Petit-Dutaillis, C., *Documents nouveaux sur les moeurs populaires et le droit de vengeance dans les Pays-Bas* (Paris, 1908)

Peverley, S., 'Anglo-Scottish Relations in John Hardyng's Chronicle', in M. Bruce and K.H. Terrell (eds), *The Anglo-Scottish Border and the Shaping of Identity, 1300–1600* (New York, 2012), 69–86

Pevsner, N., *Cumberland and Westmorland* (London, 1967; repr., 1973)

Phythian-Adams, C., 'Rituals of Personal Confrontation in Late Medieval England', *BJRL*, 73 (1991), 65–90

Societies, Cultures and Kinship, 1580–1850: Cultural Provinces and English Local History (Leicester, 1993)

'Frontier Valleys', in J. Thirsk (ed.), *The English Rural Landscape* (Oxford, 2000), 236–62

Pihlajamäki, H., 'Comparative Contexts in Legal History: Are We All Comparatists Now?', in M. Adams and D. Heirbaut (eds), *The Method and Culture of Comparative Law: Essays in Honour of Mark Van Hoecke* (Oxford, 2014), 121–32

Pinkerton, J., *The History of Scotland*, 2 vols (London, 1797)

Pocock, J.G.A., 'British History: A Plea for a New Subject', *Journal of Modern History*, 47 (1975), 601–28

Pollard, A.J., 'The Northern Retainers of Richard Nevill, Earl of Salisbury', *Northern History*, 11 (1975), 52–69

'The Richmondshire Community of Gentry during the Wars of the Roses', in C.D. Ross (ed.), *Patronage, Pedigree and Power in Later Medieval England* (Gloucester, 1979), 37–59

'The North-Eastern Economy and the Agrarian Crisis of 1438–40', *Northern History*, 25 (1989), 88–105

North-Eastern England during the Wars of the Roses (Oxford, 1990)

'The Crown and the County Palatine of Durham, 1437–94', in A.J. Pollard (ed.), *The North of England in the Age of Richard III* (Stroud, 1996), 67–88

Bibliography

'Introduction', in A.J. Pollard (ed.), *The North of England in the Age of Richard III* (Stroud, 1996), ix–xx

'The Characteristics of the Fifteenth-Century North', in J.C. Appleby and P. Dalton (eds), *Government, Religion and Society in Northern England, 1000–1700* (Stroud, 1997), 131–43

'Provincial Politics in Lancastrian England: The Challenge to Bishop Langley's Liberty in 1433', in K. Dockray and P. Fleming (eds), *People, Places and Perspectives: Essays on Later Medieval & Early Tudor England in Honour of Ralph A. Griffiths* (Stroud, 2005), 69–78

'Use and Ornament: Late-Twentieth-Century Historians on the Late Medieval North-East', *Northern History*, 42 (2005), 61–74

Pollock, F., and Maitland, F.W., *History of English Law*, 2 vols (2nd edn, Cambridge, 1898)

Pollock, L.A., 'Anger and the Negotiation of Relationships in Early Modern England', *Historical Journal*, 47 (2004), 567–90

Post, J.B., 'Equitable Resorts before 1450', in E.W. Ives and A.H. Manchester (eds), *Law, Litigants and the Legal Profession* (London, 1983), 68–79.

'The Evidential Value of Approvers' Appeals: The Case of William Rose, 1389', *Law and History Review*, 3 (1985), 91–100

'Crime in Later Medieval England: Some Historiographical Limitations', *Continuity and Change*, 2 (1987), 211–24

Postles, D., *The Surnames of Leicestershire and Rutland* (Oxford, 1998)

'Defining the "North": Some Linguistic Evidence', *Northern History*, 38 (2001), 27–46.

The North through Its Names: A Phenomenology of Medieval and Early-Modern Northern England (Oxford, 2007)

Powell, E., 'Arbitration and the Law in England in the Late Middle Ages', *TRHS*, 5th ser., 33 (1983), 49–68

'Settlement of Disputes by Arbitration in Fifteenth-Century England', *Law and History Review*, 2 (1984), 21–43

Kingship, Law, and Society: Criminal Justice in the Reign of Henry V (Oxford, 1989)

'After "After McFarlane": The Poverty of Patronage and the Case for Constitutional History', in D.J. Clayton, R.G. Davies and P. McNiven (eds), *Trade, Devotion and Governance: Papers in Later Medieval History* (Stroud, 1994), 1–16

Power, D.J., 'French and Norman Frontiers in the Central Middle Ages', in D.J. Power and N. Standen (eds), *Frontiers in Question: Eurasian Borderlands, 700–1700* (Basingstoke, 1999), 105–27

Power, D.J., and Standen, N. (eds), *Frontiers in Question: Eurasian Borderlands, 700–1700* (Basingstoke, 1999)

Power, E.E., and Postan, M.M. (eds), *Studies in English Trade in the Fifteenth Century* (London, 1933)

Prestwich, M., '"*Tam infra libertates quam extra*": Liberties and Military Recruitment', in M. Prestwich (ed.), *Liberties and Identities in the Medieval British Isles* (Woodbridge, 2008), 111–19

Prevenier, W., 'The Two Faces of Pardon Jurisdiction in the Burgundian Netherlands: A Royal Road to Social Cohesion and an Effectual Instrument of Princely Clientelism', in P. Hoppenbrouwers, A. Janse and R. Stein (eds),

Bibliography

Power and Persuasion: Essays on the Art of State Building in Honour of W.P. Blockmans (Turnhout, 2010), 177–95

Pugh, T.B., and Ross, C.D., 'The English Baronage and the Income Tax of 1436', *BIHR*, 26 (1953), 1–28

Radulescu, R., *The Gentry Context for Malory's Morte Darthur* (Woodbridge, 2003)

Radulescu, R., and Truelove, A. (eds), *Gentry Culture in Late Medieval England* (Manchester, 2005)

Rae, T.I., *The Administration of the Scottish Frontier, 1513–1603* (Edinburgh, 1966)

Ragg, F.W., 'The Feoffees of the Cliffords from 1283–1482', *TCWAAS*, n.s., 8 (1908), 253–330

'De Lancaster', *TCWAAS*, n.s., 10 (1910), 395–494

'De Culwen', *TCWAAS*, n.s., 14 (1914), 343–432

'Shap and Rosgill and Some of the Early Owners', *TCWAAS*, n.s., 14 (1914), 1–62

'De Cundal, Bampton Cundal and Butterwick', *TCWAAS*, n.s., 22 (1922), 281–328

'De Threlkeld', *TCWAAS*, n.s., 23 (1923), 154–205

'Cliburn Hervy and Cliburn Tailbois; Part II', *TCWAAS*, n.s., 28 (1928), 179–274

Rawcliffe, C., 'The Great Lord as Peacekeeper: Arbitration by English Noblemen and Their Councils in the Later Middle Ages', in J.A. Guy and H.G. Beale (eds), *Law and Social Change in British Society* (London, 1984), 34–54

'Parliament and the Settlement of Disputes by Arbitration in the Later Middle Ages', *Parliamentary History*, 9 (1990), 316–42.

Reaney, P.H., *The Origin of English Surnames* (London, 1967; repr., 1991)

Redmonds, G., *Yorkshire, West Riding* (Chichester, 1973)

Reed, J. (ed.), *The Border Ballads* (London, 1973)

'The Ballad and the Source: Some Literary Reflections on *The Battle of Otterburn*', in J.A. Tuck and A. Goodman (eds), *War and Border Societies in the Middle Ages* (London, 1992), 94–123

Reid, R.C., 'Gillesbie Tower', *TDGNHAS*, 18 (1934 for 1931–3), 376–8

'The Border Grahams, Their Origin and Distribution', *TDGNHAS*, 37 (1961), 85–107

'The Office of Warden of the Marches: Its Origin and Early History', *EHR*, 32 (1917), 479–96

The King's Council in the North (London, 1921)

Reinle, C., 'Peasants' Feuds in Late Medieval Bavaria (Fourteenth–Fifteenth Century)', in J.B. Netterstrøm and B. Poulsen (eds), *Feud in Medieval and Early Modern Europe* (Aarhus, 2007), 161–74

'"Fehde" und gewaltsame Selbsthilfe in England und im römisch-deutschen Reich', in R. Lieberwirth and H. Lück (eds), *Akten des 36. Deutschen Rechtshistorikertages* (Baden-Baden, 2008), 1–34

Reynolds, S., *Kingdoms and Communities in Western Europe, 900–1300* (Oxford, 1984)

Ridpath, G., *The Border History of England and Scotland* (London, 1776)

Roberts, B.K., and Wrathmell, S., *Region and Place: A Study of English Rural Settlement* (London, 2002)

Roberts, S., *Order and Dispute: An Introduction to Legal Anthropology* (Oxford, 1979)

Bibliography

'The Study of Dispute: Anthropological Perspectives', in J. Bossy (ed.), *Disputes and Settlements: Law and Human Relations in the West* (Cambridge, 1980), 1–24

Robson, R., *The English Highland Clans: Tudor Responses to a Mediaeval Problem* (Edinburgh, 1989)

Rock, V., 'Shadow Royals? The Political Use of the Extended Family of Lady Margaret Beaufort', in R. Eales and S. Tyas (eds), *Family and Dynasty in Late Medieval England* (Donington, 2003), 193–210

Rokkan, S., 'Territories, Centres and Peripheries: Towards a Geoethnic-Geoeconomic-Geopolitical Model of Differentiation within Western Europe', in J. Gottmann (ed.), *Centre and Periphery: Spatial Variation in Politics* (London, 1980), 163–204

Rollason, D., 'St Oswald in Post-Conquest England', in C. Stancliffe and E. Cambridge (eds), *Oswald: Northumbrian King to European Saint* (Stamford, 1995), 164–77

Rosenthal, J.T., 'Feuds and Private Peace-making: A Fifteenth-Century Example', *Nottingham Medieval Studies*, 14 (1970), 84–90

Rosenwein, B.H. (ed.), *Anger's Past: The Social Uses of an Emotion in the Middle Ages* (Ithaca, 1998)

Ross, C.D., *Richard III* (London, 1981)

Edward IV (London, 1983)

Rouland, N., *Legal Anthropology* (London, 1994)

Rowling, M.A., 'John Clybborne's Appeal to the Earl of Salisbury', *TCWAAS*, n.s., 63 (1963), 178–83

Rowney, I.D., 'Arbitration in Gentry Disputes in the Later Middle Ages', *History*, 67 (1982), 367–76

Ruddick, A., *English Identity and Political Culture in the Fourteenth Century* (Cambridge, 2013)

Ruffini, J.L., 'Disputing over Livestock in Sardinia', in L. Nader and H.F. Todd (eds), *The Disputing Process: Law in Ten Societies* (New York, 1978), 209–46

Russell, F.H., *The Just War in the Middle Ages* (Cambridge, 1975)

Russell, M.J., 'I Trial by Battle and the Writ of Right', *JLH*, 1 (1980), 111–34

'II Trial by Battle and the Appeals of Felony', *JLH*, 1 (1980), 135–64

Ryder, P.F., and Birch, J., 'Hellifield Peel: A North Yorkshire Tower House', *Yorkshire Archaeological Society Transactions*, 55 (1983), 73–94

Sabean, D.W., Teuscher, S., and Mathieu, J. (eds), *Kinship in Europe: Approaches to Long-Term Development (1300–1900)* (New York, 2007)

Sahlins, P., *Boundaries: The Making of France and Spain in the Pyrenees* (Berkeley, 1989)

Sanderson, M.H.B., *Scottish Rural Society in the Sixteenth Century* (Edinburgh, 1982)

Saul, N., *Scenes from Provincial Life: Knightly Families in Sussex 1280–1400* (Oxford, 1986)

Sawyer, P., 'The Bloodfeud in Fact and Fiction', *Acta Jutlandica*, 63 (1987), 27–38

Scafi, A., 'Defining *Mappaemundi*', in P.D.A. Harvey (ed.), *The Hereford World Map: Medieval World Maps and Their Context* (London, 2006), 345–54

Scales, L., 'The Empire in Translation: English Perspectives on Imperium and Emperors, 1220–1440', in P. Crooks, D. Green and W.M. Ormrod (eds), *The Plantagenet Empire, 1259–1453: Proceedings of the 2014 Harlaxton Symposium, Harlaxton Medieval Studies* (Donington, 2016), 49–71

Bibliography

Schofield, R.S., 'The Geographical Distribution of Wealth in England, 1334–1649', *Economic History Review*, 18 (1965), 483–510

Schultz, J.M., *National Identity and the Anglo-Scottish Borderlands, 1552–1652* (Woodbridge, 2019)

Schwerhoff, G., 'Criminalized Violence and the Process of Civilization: A Reappraisal', *Crime, Histoire & Sociétés/Crime, History & Societies*, 6 (2002), 103–26

Scofield, C.L., *The Life and Reign of Edward the Fourth*, 2 vols (London, 1923)

Scott, W., *Minstrelsy of the Scottish Border*, 3 vols (London, 1802–3)

The Border Antiquities of England and Scotland, 2 vols (London, 1814)

Scott, W.W, 'The March Laws Reconsidered', in A. Grant and K.J. Stringer (eds), *Medieval Scotland* (Edinburgh, 1993), 114–30

Sellar, W.D.H., 'Courtesy, Battle and the Brieve of Right, 1368: A Story Continued', *Miscellany II*, Stair Society (Edinburgh, 1984), 1–12

'Forethocht Felony, Malice Aforethought and the Classification of Homicide', in W.M. Gordon and T.D. Fergus (eds), *Legal History in the Making: Proceedings of the Ninth British Legal History Conference* (London, 1991), 43–59

Sharpe, J.A., 'The History of Crime in Late Medieval and Early Modern England: A Review of the Field', *Social History*, 7 (1982), 187–203

Crime in Early Modern England 1550–1800 (2nd edn, London, 1999)

Sharpe, J.A., and Dickinson, J.R., 'Revisiting the "Violence We Have Lost"', *EHR*, 131 (2016), 293–323

Shaw, J., 'Corporeal and Spiritual Homicide, the Sin of Wrath, and the "Parson's Tale"', *Traditio*, 38 (1982), 281–300

Sheehan, J.J., 'The Problem of Sovereignty in European History', *American Historical Review*, 111 (2006), 1–15

Sherlock, R., 'The Evolution of the Irish Tower House, 1400–1650', in R. Oram (ed.), *A House That Thieves Might Knock At: Proceedings of the 2010 Stirling and 2011 Dundee Conferences* (Donington, 2015), 258–69

Simpson, W.D., *Further Notes on Dunstanburgh Castle* (Gateshead, 1949)

Sisam, K., *Fourteenth Century Verse and Prose* (Oxford, 1970)

Sklute, J., '*Freothuwebbe* in Old English Poetry', in H. Damico and A.H. Olsen (eds), *New Readings on Women in Old English Literature* (Bloomington, 1990), 204–10

Skoda, H., *Medieval Violence: Physical Brutality in Northern France 1270–1330* (Oxford, 2013)

Smail, D.L., 'Common Violence: Vengeance and Inquisition in Fourteenth-Century Marseille', *Past and Present*, 151 (1996), 28–59

[Review article] 'Factions and Vengeance in Renaissance Italy', *Comparative Studies in Society and History*, 38 (1996), 781–9

'Hatred as a Social Institution in Medieval Society', *Speculum*, 76 (2001), 90–126

The Consumption of Justice: Emotions, Publicity, and Legal Culture in Marseille, 1264–1423 (Ithaca, 2003)

'Faction and Feud in Fourteenth-Century Marseille', in J.B. Netterstrøm and B. Poulsen (eds), *Feud in Medieval and Early Modern Europe* (Aarhus, 2007), 113–33

'Violence and Predation in Late Medieval Mediterranean Europe', *Comparative Studies in Society and History*, 54 (2012), 7–34

Bibliography

Smith, B. (ed.), *Ireland and the English World in the Late Middle Ages: Essays in Honour of Robin Frame* (Basingstoke, 2009)

'Late Medieval Ireland and the English Connection: Waterford and Bristol, c. 1360–1460', *Journal of British Studies*, 50 (2011), 546–65.

Crisis and Survival in Late Medieval Ireland: The English of Louth and Their Neighbours, 1330–1450 (Oxford, 2013)

Smith, L.B., 'Disputes and Settlements in Medieval Wales: The Role of Arbitration', *EHR*, 106 (1991), 835–60

Smith, R.M. (ed.), *Land, Kinship and Life-Cycle* (Cambridge, 1984)

Smout, T.C., *Nature Contested: Environmental History in Scotland and Northern England since 1600* (Edinburgh, 2000)

Spargo, J.W., 'Chaucer's Love-Days', *Speculum*, 15 (1940), 36–56

Spence, R.T., 'The Pacification of the Cumberland Borders, 1593–1628', *Northern History*, 13 (1977), 59–160

'The Graham Clans and Lands on the Eve of the Jacobean Pacification', *TCWAAS*, n.s., 80 (1980), 79–102

Spencer, D., 'Royal Castles and Coastal Defence in the Late Fourteenth Century', *Nottingham Medieval Studies*, 61 (2017), 147–70

Stancliffe, C., 'Oswald, "Most Holy and Most Victorious King of the Northumbrians"', in C. Stancliffe and E. Cambridge (eds), *Oswald: Northumbrian King to European Saint* (Stamford, 1995), 33–83

Steiner, E., and Barrington, C. (eds), *The Letter of the Law: Legal Practice and Literary Production in Medieval England* (Ithaca, 2002)

Stell, G., 'Foundations of a Castle Culture: Pre-1603', in A. Dakin, M. Glendinning and A. MacKechnie (eds), *Scotland's Castle Culture* (Edinburgh, 2011), 3–34

Stevenson, K., *Chivalry and Knighthood in Scotland, 1424–1513* (Woodbridge, 2006)

Stone, L., *The Family, Sex and Marriage in England, 1500–1800* (London, 1977)

Storey, R.L., 'Disorders in Lancastrian Westmorland: Some Early Chancery Proceedings', *TCWAAS*, n.s., 53 (1953), 69–80

'The Wardens of the Marches of England towards Scotland 1377–1489', *EHR*, 72 (1957), 593–615

Thomas Langley and the Bishopric of Durham 1406–1437 (London, 1961)

The End of the House of Lancaster (London, 1966; rev. 2nd edn, 1999)

'The North of England', in S.B. Chrimes, C.D. Ross and R.A. Griffiths (eds), *Fifteenth-Century England 1399–1509* (Manchester, 1972), 129–44

Stringer, K.J., 'North-East England and Scotland in the Middle Ages', *Innes Review*, 44 (1993), 88–99

Stringer, K.J., and Winchester, A.J.L. (eds), *Northern England and Southern Scotland in the Central Middle Ages* (Woodbridge, 2017)

Suggett, R., 'Living like a Lord: Greater Houses and Social Emulation in Late-Medieval Wales', in M. Airs and P.S. Barnwell (eds), *The Medieval Great House* (Donington, 2011), 81–95

Summerson, H.R.T., 'Crime and Society in Medieval Cumberland', *TCWAAS*, n.s., 82 (1982), 111–24.

'The Early Development of the Laws of the Anglo-Scottish Marches, 1249–1448', in W.M. Gordon and T.D. Fergus (eds), *Legal History in the Making: Proceedings of the Ninth British Legal History Conference* (London, 1991), 29–42

Bibliography

Medieval Carlisle, 2 vols (Kendal, 1993)

'Carlisle and the English West March in the Later Middle Ages', in A.J. Pollard (ed.), *The North of England in the Age of Richard III* (Stroud, 1996), 89–113

'Peacekeepers and Lawbreakers in Medieval Northumberland, c. 1200–c. 1500', in M. Prestwich (ed.), *Liberties and Identities in the Medieval British Isles* (Woodbridge, 2008), 56–76

Taylor, C., 'Henry V, Flower of Chivalry', in G. Dodd (ed.), *Henry V: New Interpretations* (Woodbridge, 2013), 217–47

Teuscher, S., 'Politics of Kinship in the City of Bern at the End of the Middle Ages', in D.W. Sabean, S. Teuscher and J. Mathieu (eds), *Kinship in Europe: Approaches to Long-Term Development (1300–1900)* (New York, 2007), 76–90

Thiery, D.E., 'Plowshares and Swords: Clerical Involvement in Acts of Violence and Peacemaking in Late Medieval England, c. 1400–1536', *Albion*, 36 (2004), 201–22

Polluting the Sacred: Violence, Faith and the 'Civilizing' of Parishioners in Late Medieval England (Leiden, 2009)

Thirsk, J. (ed.), *The Agrarian History of England and Wales, Volume IV: 1500–1640* (Cambridge, 1967)

Thompson, M.W., *The Decline of the Castle* (Cambridge, 1987)

Thornton, T., '"The Enemy or Stranger, That Shall Invade Their Countrey": Identity and Community in the English North', in B. Taithe and T. Thornton (eds), *War: Identities in Conflict 1300–2000* (Stroud, 1998), 57–70

Cheshire and the Tudor State 1480–1560 (Woodbridge, 2000)

'Fifteenth-Century Durham and the Problem of Provincial Liberties in England and the Wider Territories of the English Crown', *TRHS*, 6th ser., 11 (2001), 83–100

The Channel Islands, 1370–1640: Between England and Normandy (Woodbridge, 2012)

Tilly, C., 'Reflections on the History of European State-Making', in C. Tilly (ed.), *The Formation of National States in Western Europe* (Princeton, 1975), 3–83

Todd, J.M., 'The West March on the Anglo-Scottish Border in the Twelfth Century, and the Origins of the Western Debatable Land', *Northern History*, 43 (2006), 11–19

Tough, D.L.W., *The Last Years of a Frontier* (Oxford, 1928)

Trevelyan, G.M., *English Social History* (London, 1994)

Tuck, J.A., 'Richard II and the Border Magnates', *Northern History*, 3 (1968), 27–52

'Northumbrian Society in the Fourteenth Century', *Northern History*, 6 (1971), 22–39

'War and Society in the Medieval North', *Northern History*, 11 (1985), 33–52

'The Emergence of a Northern Nobility, 1250–1400', *Northern History*, 22 (1986), 1–17

'The Northern Borders', in E. Miller (ed.), *The Agrarian History of England and Wales, Volume III: 1348–1500* (Cambridge, 1991), 34–41, 175–81, 587–95

'The Percies and the Community of Northumberland in the Later Fourteenth Century', in J.A. Tuck and A. Goodman (eds), *War and Border Societies in the Middle Ages* (London, 1992), 178–95

Bibliography

'A Medieval Tax Haven: Berwick upon Tweed and the English Crown, 1333–1461', in R.H. Britnell and J. Hatcher (eds), *Progress and Problems in Medieval England: Essays in Honour of Edward Miller* (Cambridge, 1996), 148–67

Tuck, J.A., and Goodman, A. (eds), *War and Border Societies in the Middle Ages* (London, 1992)

Tucker, P., 'Historians' Expectations of the Medieval Legal Records', in A. Musson (ed.), *Expectations of the Law in the Middle Ages* (Woodbridge, 2001), 191–202

Turner, F.J., 'The Significance of the Frontier in American History', in F.J. Turner, *The Frontier in American History* (New York, 1920), 1–38

Turville-Petre, T., 'A Nottinghamshire Dispute: English Documents of 1438–42', *Nottingham Medieval Studies*, 57 (2013), 171–94

Tyerman, C., *England and the Crusades 1095–1588* (Chicago, 1988)

van Dijk, C., *John Gower and the Limits of the Law* (Woodbridge, 2013)

Volckart, O., 'The Economics of Feuding in Late Medieval Germany', *Explorations in Economic History*, 41 (2004), 282–99

Wagner, A., Barker, N., and Payne, A. (eds), *Medieval Pageant: Writhe's Garter Book: The Ceremony of the Bath and the Earldom of Salisbury Roll* (London, 1993)

Walker, S., *The Lancastrian Affinity 1361–1399* (Oxford, 1990)

Political Culture in Later Medieval England, ed. M.J. Braddick (Manchester, 2006)

Wallace-Hadrill, J.M., 'The Bloodfeud of the Franks', *BJRL*, 41 (1959), 459–87

Walter, G., *Crime, Gender and Social Order in Early Modern England* (Cambridge, 2003)

Ward, R., *The World of the Medieval Shipmaster: Law, Business and the Sea, c. 1350–c. 1450* (Woodbridge, 2009)

Warner, M.W., and Lacey, K., 'Neville vs. Percy: A Precedence Dispute circa 1442', *Historical Research*, 69 (1996), 211–17

Waters, K. A., 'The Earls of Desmond and the Irish of South-Western Munster', *Journal of Medieval History*, 32 (2006), 54–68

Watkins, A., 'Landowners and Their Estates in the Forest of Arden in the Fifteenth Century', *Agricultural History Review*, 45 (1997), 18–33

Watts, J.L., *Henry VI and the Politics of Kingship* (Cambridge, 1996)

The Making of Polities: Europe 1300–1500 (Cambridge, 2009)

(ed.), *The End of the Middle Ages? England in the Fifteenth and Sixteenth Centuries* (Stroud, 1998)

Wedgwood, J.C., *Biographies of Members of the Commons House 1439–1509* (London, 1936)

Weiss, M., 'A Power in the North? The Percies in the Fifteenth Century', *Historical Journal*, 19 (1976), 501–9

Wells-Furby, B., 'The Origin of the 'Name and Arms' Clause and the Development of the Lineage Culture in Fourteenth-Century England', *Nottingham Medieval Studies*, 59 (2015), 77–111

Wheatley, A., *The Idea of the Castle in Medieval England* (Woodbridge, 2004)

White, S.D., '"*Pactum . . . Legem Vincit et Amor Judicium*": The Settlement of Disputes by Compromise in Eleventh-Century Western France', *American Journal of Legal History*, 22 (1978), 281–308

'Feuding and Peace-Making in the Touraine around the Year 1100', *Traditio*, 42 (1986), 195–263

Bibliography

'Clothild's Revenge: Politics, Kinship and Ideology in the Merovingian Blood-feud', in S.K. Cohn and S.A. Epstein (eds), *Portraits of Medieval and Renaissance Living, Essays in Memory of David Herlihy* (Michigan, 1996), 107–30

'The Politics of Anger', in B.H. Rosenwein (ed.), *Anger's Past: The Social Uses of an Emotion in the Middle Ages* (Ithaca, 1998), 127–52

Whittingham, A.B., *Bury St Edmunds Abbey, Suffolk* (London, 2012)

Williams, G., *Renewal and Reformation: Wales c. 1415–1642* (Oxford, 1993)

Wilson, J. (ed.), *The Victoria History of the County of Cumberland*, 2 vols (Westminster, 1901-1905)

Wilson, P.H., 'Social Militarization in Eighteenth Century Germany', *German History*, 18 (2000), 1–39

Winchester, A.J.L., *Landscape and Society in Medieval Cumbria* (Edinburgh, 1987)

The Harvest of the Hills: Rural Life in Northern England and the Scottish Borders 1400–1700 (Edinburgh, 2000)

'Hill Farming Landscapes of Medieval Northern England', in D. Hooke (ed.), *Landscape: The Richest Historical Record* (Amesbury, 2000), 75–84

Wood, D., *Medieval Economic Thought* (Cambridge, 2002)

Wood, J.C., 'Conceptualizing Cultures of Violence and Cultural Change', in S. Carroll (ed.), *Cultures of Violence: Interpersonal Violence in Historical Perspective* (Basingstoke, 2007), 79–96

Wood, M., *The English Medieval House* (London, 1983)

Wordsworth, W., *A Description of the Scenery of the Lakes in the North of England* (London, 1823)

Wormald, J.M., 'Bloodfeud, Kindred and Government in Early Modern Scotland', *Past & Present*, 87 (1980), 54–97

Lords and Men in Scotland: Bonds of Manrent 1442–1603 (Edinburgh, 1985)

Wormald, P., 'Giving God and King Their Due: Conflict and Its Regulation in the Early English State', in P. Wormald, *Legal Culture in the Early Medieval West: Law as Text, Image and Experience* (London, 1998), 333–57

Wright, S.M., *The Derbyshire Gentry in the Fifteenth Century* (Chesterfield, 1983)

Yorath, D.M., 'Sir Christopher Moresby of Scaleby and Windermere, c. 1441–99', *Northern History*, 53 (2016), 173–88

Young, A., 'The North and Anglo-Scottish Relations in the Thirteenth Century', in J.C. Appleby and P. Dalton (eds), *Government, Religion and Society in Northern England, 1000–1700* (Stroud, 1997), 77–89

Zmora, H., *State and Nobility in Early Modern Germany: The Knightly Feud in Franconia, 1440–1567* (Cambridge, 1997)

The Feud in Early Modern Germany (Cambridge, 2011)

UNPUBLISHED DISSERTATIONS AND THESES

Armstrong, J.W., 'Local Conflict in the Anglo-Scottish Borderlands, c. 1399–1488', PhD thesis, University of Cambridge (2007)

Boardman, S.I., 'Politics and the Feud in Late Medieval Scotland', PhD thesis, University of St Andrews (1989)

Bibliography

Booth, P.W.N., 'Landed Society in Cumberland and Westmorland, c. 1440–1485: The Politics of the Wars of the Roses', PhD thesis, University of Leicester (1998)

Brochard, T., 'The "Civilizing" of the Far North of Scotland, 1560–1640', PhD thesis, University of Aberdeen (2010)

Cardew, A., 'A Study of Society on the Anglo-Scottish Border 1455–1502', PhD thesis, University of St Andrews (1974)

Coates, N.J., 'The Law Enforcement Policy of Edward IV and Its Impact, with Special Reference to Nottinghamshire and Derbyshire, Hertfordshire and Essex 1461–83', PhD thesis, University of Cambridge (2005)

Gollancz, M.E.H.J., 'The System of Gaol Delivery Rolls of the Fifteenth Century', MA thesis, University of London (1936)

Johnson, T., 'Law, Space, and Local Knowledge in Late-Medieval England', PhD thesis, Birkbeck, University of London (2014)

Lott, B., 'Medieval Buildings in Westmorland', PhD thesis, University of Nottingham (1995)

Marsh, J.P., 'Landed Society in the Far North-West of England, 1332–1461', PhD thesis, University of Lancaster (2001)

O'Grady, O.J.T., 'The Setting and Practice of Open-Air Judicial Assemblies in Medieval Scotland: A Multidisciplinary Study', PhD thesis, University of Glasgow (2008)

Westervelt, T.M., 'William Lord Hastings and the Governance of Edward IV, with Special Reference to the Second Reign (1471–83)', PhD thesis, University of Cambridge (2001)

Woodger [now Clark], L.S., 'Henry Bourgchier, Earl of Essex, and His Family, 1408–83', DPhil thesis, University of Oxford (1974)

INDEX

acculturation, 18–19, 50
accustomed practices. *See* conflict
adjudication of conflict, 26, 223, 309
administration of justice, 45, 180–1
  border diets, 186–7
  border justice, 167, 181–97
  common law, 174
  cross-border homicide, 191–3
  days of march, 185–6
  equity, 174
  France, 170–1
  German-speaking lands, 170
  justices of the peace, 175–6
  liberties and franchises, 178–80, 196
  private appeal of felony, 177–8
  royal justice, 167, 169–70, 172–81
  Scotland, 171–2
  sheriff's tourn, 176–7
  sheriffs, 172–4
  treason, 182–5, 196
  truce-breaking, 187–91
  trust, 188–9
Afghanistan, comparison with northern
    marches, 3–4, 94
Agincourt, Battle of (1415), 68, 110, 300
agriculture, 45, 104–6
  cereal agriculture, 101–3
  diverse forms of productivity, 98–100
  hill farming, 98
aid and adherence, cross-border, 60, 114, 183,
    253–4
Alnwick, 69, 88–9
  Alnwick Abbey, 85
  Anwick Castle, 67, 78, 84, 147
  sieges, 81
Anglo-Scottish marches defined
  borders, marches as, 19–22
  east, west and middle marches, 58–9, 67
  frontiers, marches as, 19–22, 49–53

geographical area, 3
late medieval perception, 64–5
legal history of the marches, 16–17
unique nature, 51, 57
Welsh or Irish marches compared, 51–3
annuities, grants of, 120, 324, 328
antiquarian societies, 13
appeal of felony, private, 177–8
arbitration, 26, 39, 45, 169–70, 272, 309,
    334–6
  compensation, 328
  extra-judicial arbitration, 39, 272, 311, 334
  justices of assize, 310
  King's justices, 310
  kinsmen, 311–13, 333
  lovedays, 309
  peace-makers, 311–15
  umpires, 310
Arthuret, 61–3
assize, courts of, 71, 175–6, 201, 211, 310
assythement, 172, 329

Bamburgh, 69, 78
  sieges, 81
'bastard feudalism', 1–2, 9, 82, 120
Berwick, 69, 88
  Berwick Castle, 91
  sieges, 81
  trade, 63
bloodfeud. *See* feud
border justice, 16, 197, 268; *see also* arbitration;
    redress
  codification, 181–2
  King's role, 196
  liberties and franchises, 182
  offence of treason
    high treason, 183
    march treason, 183
  reparation, 308

387

Index

border justice (cont.)
  royal justice compared, 45, 167, 196, 265,
    270, 308, 335, 339, 341
  wardenial jurisdiction, 182
border magnates
  England, 8; see also Nevilles of Raby, earls of
    Westmorland; Percy earls of
    Northumberland
  Scotland, 60; see also Douglas family, earls of
    Angus (Red Douglases); Douglas family,
    earls of Douglas (Black Douglases);
    Dunbar family, earls of March
border raiding and defence, 5, 7, 36, 74, 338
  cross-border offences
    jurisdiction, 264–5
  Piccolomini's report, 259–60
    environmental and economic factors,
      262–4
    gender segregation, 260–2
border violence, 4–5, 15–16
  cross-border conflict, 249–50
  degree and intensity, 307
  homicides, 233–6
  landed elite, 234
  law, 40
  liberties and franchises, 240
  patterns of conflict, 232–3
  peasants, 303
  severe violence, 297, 300–1
  strategic violence, 297
  vengeance, 299–300
borderland towers. See towers and castles
Bourchier, Henry, Lord Bourchier (earl of
  Essex), 110, 178
Bower, Walter (abbot and chronicler)., 4–6, 247
  classification of buildings, 78
Braudel, F., 97–8
Brisco–Denton affair, 217–19, 300–1, 312
'British' history, approaches
  archipelagic approach, 20
  British Isles approach, 21
  English world approach, 21
Brunner, O., 32–3
by-names, 131–2
  patronymic by-names, 133, 136

canon law. See ecclesiastical law
Cardew, A., 17
Carlisle, 12, 88
  Carlisle Castle, 45, 91
  cathedral, 87, 115
  sieges, 81
  St Mary's Priory, 330
  trade, 63–4
Carpenter, C., 2, 105, 209, 235, 315

castles. See towers and castles
castra, 78–80
Causa de Heron (1428–31), 289, 295, 304, 310,
  313–14, 325, 329–30
cellular England, 42, 340–1. See also 'centre',
  'periphery' and 'locality'
centralisation of the English state, 2, 40–4,
  340–1
'centre', 'periphery' and 'locality'
  agglomeration, England as an, 42
  centre–locality model, 42
  centre–periphery model, 42–3, 51, 105,
    340–1
cereal agriculture, 102–3
ceremonial reconciliations. See reconciliation
  ceremonies
Chancery, court of, 44, 174–5, 213, 219, 235,
  274, 282
chevauchées, 243–4, 267
chivalry, 46, 188, 272, 288
  duels of chivalry, 184–5, 193–4
  international codes of chivalry, 38
  law of arms, 184–5, 193–4, 267, 322, 335
  shaping normative conduct, 272
Clifford family, 112–13, 122, 173–4, 176, 194–5,
  212, 216, 220, 239
cognomina, 131–4, 139, 145, 251; see also kinship;
  naming customs and practices
  kinship solidarity, 160–1
Coldingham, 115–16
  Coldingham Priory, 60, 116, 280
collaboration between the nobility and the
  gentry, 2, 10. See also cooperation
  between King and nobility
common law, 37, 39, 167, 344
  common law norms, 37
  'monotheism', 37
  royal justice, 172–81
  universal authority, 44
common pleas, court of, 139, 174, 195,
  202, 231
communing or trysting, 254–5, 265
compensation for injury; see also arbitration;
  assythement; peace-makers and
  peacemaking; redress; reparation
  cross-border homicide, 191–3
  restitution of plundered goods, 188
compromise, peace by, 45, 181, 297, 308
  supporters and peacemakers, role of, 308
conflict, 105, 339–40; see also arbitration; border
  violence; conflict management; cross-
  border conflict; vengeance culture
  accustomed practices, 45, 163, 185, 188, 193,
    196–7, 241, 306–7, 317, 334–5, 339
  concept of, 25–6

388

Index

crime, 29
  informal dispute resolution, 2, 45
  negotiation, 26
  socially constructive nature, 25–7
  violence, 27–9
  war, 29–30
conflict management, 26–7, 308–9; *see also*
    adjudication of conflict; arbitration;
    peace-makers and peacemaking
  contractual arrangements
    indenture of marriage, 332–4
    lordship, 296–7, 331–2
    support groups, 162
  continuity and stability, 10–13
  cooperation between King and nobility, 2,
    6–11. *See also* collaboration between the
    nobility and the gentry; conflict
    management; peace-makers and
    peacemaking
coram rege pleas, 199, 212, 215–16
council in the north, 175, 223–4, 239–40
courts. *See* Chancery, court of; common pleas,
    court of; gaol delivery, courts and rolls;
    King's bench, court of; manorial courts;
    warden courts
crime, 29
criminal law, 29
cross-border conflict; *see also* conflict
  abettors and receivers, 253–4
  communing or trysting, 254–5
  cooperation in illicit deeds, 252–4
  cross-border dwellers, 248–52
  cross-border kidnapping, 255–7
  homicide, 257–9
  identity and allegiance, 247–9, 251–2
  lesser illicit activity, 246–7
  siege warfare, 244–6
  truce violations, 242–4
    legitimising truce-breaking, 244
  violent offences, 249–50
cross-border homicide, 257–9
  administration of justice, 191–3
  compensation for injury, 191–3
cross-border kidnapping, 255–7
cross-border relations and diplomacy, 17–19, 59,
    63, 187, 196, 243, 266, 279
crown charges of felony, 199
crown charges of trespass, 199

Dacre family, 45, 111–13, 117, 122, 126,
    146, 149, 157–8, 162, 190, 212,
    216–17, 239
debatable land, 55–7, 59
  mapmaking and cartography, 65–6
  western debatable land, 60–3, 243

dispute/disputing. *See* conflict; conflict
    management
double patronyms, 133–6, 163–4, 337–8, 340
  kinship solidarity, 160–1
Douglas family, earls of Angus (Red Douglases),
    60, 152
Douglas family, earls of Douglas (Black
    Douglases), 60, 116
duels and tournaments, 193–4, 298. *See also*
    judicial duels
Dunbar family, earls of March, 60, 125, 245, 281
Dunstanburgh, 69, 78
Durham, bishopric and palatinate of, 12, 58, 96,
    104, 142, 145, 178, 237
Durham Priory, prior and monks of, 115–17,
    168, 282, 314, 326, 329

ecclesiastical architecture, 87
ecclesiastical law, 38, 309
  arbitration, 335
  common law, relationship with, 41
  homicide, 287
    actus reus and *mens rea*, 286
    spiritual and corporeal homicide, 286–8
  peacemaking, 314
  shaping normative conduct, 272
Edward III, 57, 180
Edward IV, 60, 113–14, 120, 180, 215, 220
  rule by proxy, 220, 343
  second reign, 224
Elias, N., 30
emotional language; *see also* language and
    terminology
  enemyship, 278
  enmity, 278
    mortal enmity, 278–80
  friendship, 278
  legitimising relationships and behaviours,
    278
  lower social levels, 282–4
  vengeance, 280–2
endowment of younger sons, 126
English crown land, 111
English Reformation, acts of supremacy and
    uniformity, 41
entail. *See* settlements in tail male
equity, 174, 338
extra-judicial arbitration. *See* arbitration

Fast Castle, 78
Febvre, L., 19
feud, 3–4, 33, 45
  assertion and defence of noble rights,
    mechanism for, 32
  concept of, 31–5, 270–1

389

Index

feud (cont.)
France, 170–1
French monarchism compared, 32
German-speaking lands, 170
negative connotations, 32
peaceful equilibrium in 'stateless' societies, mechanism for, 32
Scotland, 171–2
various types, 33–4
feud-like disputes
direct involvement of magnates, 291
norms limiting and validating actions and choices, 272
support groups, 271, 291
vengeance
principle of reciprocity, 271–2
fluidity of Anglo-Scottish frontier, 60–3
force, use of. *See* use of force
fortalicii, 79–80
Fortescue, John (chief justice), 42, 124
France, 26, 30–1, 54
administration of justice, 170
classification of homicide, 285
feud, 170
royal grace, 33, 171
frontier rhetoric, 92–4, 116, 180
frontier society concept, 18–19, 50–1, 74
frontiers; *see also* Anglo-Scottish marches
defined
concept of, 53–4
ambiguity of frontiers, 52, 55–8, 247
linear frontiers, 50–1
zonal frontiers, 50–1

gaol delivery, courts and rolls, 201, 210–16
gentry lordships
Huddlestons of Millom, 113
Ogle family, 114
Parrs of Kendal, 113
Tailboys family, 114
Umfraville family, 113–14
Germany, 30–1
feud, 33
Gluckman, M., 32
'good lordship', 120
Goodman, A., 17, 19
governance, 6–13, 39–40, 105
common law, 37
cooperation between King and nobility, 2, 10, 25, 31
ecclesiastical law, 38
extra-judicial arbitration, 39
march law, 38
merchant laws and customs, 38
view from Westminster, 38, 343

governmental structures, strength of, 23–5, 31–5, 119, 240–1, 268
Greystoke family, 45, 112, 147, 224

habitation. *See* human settlement and agriculture
Hardyng, John (chronicler), 6, 64, 181
feud, concept of, 276–8
identification of buildings, 78
inventory of marches, 71–2
maps and mapping, 72
surnames, 137, 161
vengeance, concept of, 280
Henry IV, 78, 111, 115, 211, 245, 247, 344
Henry V, 201
Henry VI, 216–17, 275, 279, 322
Henry VII, 138, 150, 173, 180, 223, 235, 240, 338
Heron, William. *See Causa de Heron* (1428–31)
Hexhamshire, 55, 115, 179, 236, 238, 246, 267
homicide, 233–6; *see also* language and terminology
classification of homicide, 284–91
actus reus and *mens rea*, 286
England, 285–91
France, 285
malice aforethought, 285
murder, 285
cross-border homicide, 191–3, 257–9
ecclesiastical law, 286–8
Homildon Hill, Battle of (1402), 59
human settlement and agriculture, 45, 69, 74–5, 100
agriculture, 98–100
cereal agriculture, 101–3
castellated habitations, 81–2
diversity of, 103–5
habitation, 45, 69, 75, 106
human habitation, 100–2
castellated habitations, 81–2
nucleated villages, 101–3
Hundred Years War, 343
Hyams, P.R., 35

identity and allegiance, 247–8, 251–2
cross-border dwellers, 248–51
Imperial Diet (1495) (Germany), 31
indentures of marriage (and peacemaking function), 279, 318, 332–4
indentures of retainer, 120
Crown control through licensing, 121, 124, 162, 296
exemption of certain kin relationships, 122–3
good lordship, 120–1
manrent, 123–4
military service, 121–2

390

Index

peacemaking function, 331–6
wardens of the march, 120–2
inheritance disputes, 80, 224, 291–2, 301–3
   See also conflict
international codes of chivalry, 38, 193
international frameworks of maritime and
   merchant laws and customs, 38
international laws of war, 38
inventories of sites in Northumberland
   Hardyng, John (chronicler), 71–2
   Nomina castrorum et fortaliciorum infra comitatum
      Northumbriae (1415), 68–71
   Northumberland 'holdis and towneshyppes'
      (1509), 49–71
Irish marches, 11, 51, 53, 185

James III of Scotland, 187, 242
James, M., 22, 31
judicial duels, 139, 193–5
   cross-border duelling, 185, 194–5
   duel of chivalry compared, 193
   march treason, 183–4, 306
justices of the peace, 175–6

Kendal, 36, 102, 110–11, 325
   Parr family, 113–14
King's bench, court of, 2, 174, 199–201, 225,
   264, 338; *see also* Westminster, view
   from
   private litigation, 174, 199
kinship, 17, 45, 124–5; *see also* surnames
   Anglo-Scottish marches, 136
   bonds between local families
      Anglo-Scottish marches, 157–60
      Northumberland, 156–7
      Westmorland, 156
   distant kinship ties, 128–30
      affinity and alliance, 294–6
   English kinship, 136, 156, 291–5
   extended kinship, 125
      participation in violent disputing, 291–4
   horizontal kinship ties, 126–8
   kinship among the gentry, 292–3
      Fenwicks, 128–30
   kinship solidarity, 160
      cognomina, 160–1
      double patronyms, 160–1
   Scottish kinship; *see* surnames
   strength of sociopolitical structures, 23–5, 40,
      119, 338
   uplands and lowlands compared, 125–6, 130
   vertical kinship ties, 125–6
   wide kinship grouping, 136
      bonds between local families, 157–60
knightly feud, 33

Lancaster, duchy of, 58
Lancaster, family of Rydal, 127, 155, 293, 301
Lancaster, Prince John (duke of Bedford), 78,
   91, 111, 140
landowners, 45, 163
   absentee lordship, 117
   Bourchier, Henry, Lord Bourchier (earl of
      Essex), 110–11
   diversity, 117–18
   English crown, 111
   gentry families, 113–14
   lesser nobility, 111–12
   Nevilles of Raby, earls of Westmorland,
      109–10
   Percy earls of Northumberland, 109
   religious houses, 114–16
   sub-baronial landowners, 112–13
landscape, 74–5, 93–105; *see also* human
   settlement and agriculture
   perceived remoteness, 92–5
language and terminology; *see also* emotional
   language
   anger and felony, 275–6
   borderland towers, 76–81, 105
   borderlands conflict, 276–7
   compensation, 329
   compromise, 319–20
   conflict and associated emotions and
      motivations, 273–91, 306
   feud, 34
   kinship and friendship, 294–6
   legal records, 273–6
   malice, 280–2
   marches and borderlands, 55–7, 105
   surname, 137–9, 146, 161, 163, 337
   violence, crime and war, 28–31
Lannoy, Ghillebert de, 65–6
Lattimore, O., 19
law of arms
   attacks on women, 262
   border raiding and defence, 339
   chevauchées, 243–4, 267
   chivalry, 184–5, 322, 335
   judicial duels, 193–4
   plunder, 243
   siege warfare, 244–6
'lawlessness', 6–15, 25
Le Bel, Jean (chronicler), 93
Leges Marchiarum (1249), 57, 67
Levyn rebels, 61–3
liberties and franchises, 3, 37, 43, 58
   administration of justice, 178–80, 196
   cross-border raiding, 266
   franchise lordships
      jurisdictional autonomy, 13

391

Index

liberties and franchises (cont.)
  patterns of conflict, 236–9
    Anglo-Scottish war and truce,
      239–40
    violent offences, 240
  privileged jurisdictions, 14
Liddesdale, 149, 151
linear frontiers, 50–1
livery. *See* indentures of retainer
livestock rustling, 144, 159, 170, 231, 251, 256,
  262–3, 267, 280, 339
long peace, 15
lord–man bonds, 121, 162; *see also* indentures of
  retainer
  legislation and proclamations, 120
lordship, role of, 45, 163
  continuity and stability, 11–13
  Ireland, 14
  liberties and franchises, 13–15
  'overmighty subject', 8–11
  support groups
    written contracts, 296–7
lovedays; *see also* arbitration
  reconciliation ceremonies compared, 321

Macdonald, A.J., 15, 194, 236
malice, 34, 36, 54, 275, 279nn 52 and 53, 280–3,
  285–6, 288–90, 293, 306, 317, 319, 333
Malory, Thomas (writer), 5, 54, 277
manorial courts, 38
manrent, 123–4
mapmaking and cartography, 65–73
  renaissance cartography, 65–8
march days, 182–3, 185–7, 242, 246, 256, 258,
  266
  judicial duels, 193
march law, 38, 45, 167
  border justice, 181–97
  days of march, 185–6
  days of truce, 185–6
  Leges Marchiarum (1249), 57, 67
  wardens, 9, 16
marches. *See* Anglo-Scottish marches
  defined
marriage. *See* indentures of marriage
McFarlane, K.B., 1, 4, 9, 82
mediation, 26, 316
Melrose Abbey, 116

naming customs and practices, 130–1; *see also*
  kinship; patronymic naming patterns;
  surnames
  hereditary surnames
    by-names, 131
    cognomina, 131–2

national politics and local conflict, relationship
  between, 45
Neville, C.J., 16
Nevilles of Middleham, 9–11, 110, 112
Nevilles of Raby, earls of Westmorland, 8–11, 110
  indentures of retainer, 121
Newcastle-upon-Tyne, 59, 88, 177
  trade, 64
*Nomina castrorum et fortaliciorum infra comitatum
  Northumbriae* (1415), 68–71, 80
north, concept of, 3, 9, 49–57

Oswald, saint, 168, 195
oyer and *terminer* commissions, 175, 210–11, 213,
  230, 238

palatinates, 14, 43
  governance, 341–3
patronymic naming patterns, 132, 134–6; *see also*
  surnames
  by-names, 131, 133, 136
  double patronyms, 133–6, 160–1, 163–4,
    337–8, 340
patterns of conflict, 199–201
  Anglo-Scottish war and truce, 224–32
    liberties and franchises, 239–40
  Brisco–Denton affair, 217–19
  court records
    gaol delivery rolls, 201, 210–16
    King's bench records, 201–10, 216–24
  Cumberland, 218–19
  French campaigns, 212–13
  Henry IV, 211–12
  impact of national political struggles,
    214–16
  liberties and franchises, 236–41
  Northumberland, 219–20
  Readeption of Henry VI, 217
  Richard II, 210–11
  violent offences, 232–3
    homicides, 233–6
    landed elite, 234
    liberties and franchises, 240
  Westmorland, 220–2
peace-makers and peacemaking
  de-escalation from violence, 316–17
  gentry, 311
  lords, 314
  objectives
    maintaining equilibrium, 315
    re-establishing the peace, 315
  prelates, 314
  religious members of local families, 311
  transformation of the social fabric, 316–19
    ceremonial reconciliations, 320–8

Index

contracts of lordship and kinship, 331–4
   gift-exchange/compensation, 328–31
   wider kindred, 312–13
perception of northerners, 5–6, 64–5
Percy earls of Northumberland, 8–11, 109
   indentures of retainer, 121
   Percy, Henry (Hotspur), 56
   Percy rebellions in 1403, 1405 and 1408, 211
Percy–Neville disputes (1453–4), 214
petition by 'poures liges' of Cumberland, Westmorland and Northumberland (1415), 91
Piccolomini, Aeneas Silvius (Pius II)
   cross-border raiding, report on, 259–60
   environmental and economic factors, 262–4
   gender segregation, 260–2
plundering, 5, 64, 141, 243, 253, 299–300, 339;
   See also border raiding and defence
Pocock, J.G.A., 20
Pollard, A.J., 12, 236
population distribution, 8, 18, 100, 117, 233
private power, 2, 24–5, 83, 169, 180, 315
   and public power, 25
private war, 30, 35, 37, 276
public authority, 169
   and private power, 2, 169–70, 180, 315
'public order', 29, 169

receiving, 149, 253–4
reciprocity, principle of
   compensation, 328–9
   king, nobility and gentry, relationship between, 39
   vengeance, 271–2, 316
reconciliation ceremonies
   contrition and atonement, 322–3
   England, 320–3
   handholding, 324
   lovedays compared, 321
   oath-taking, 324–5
   submission and humiliation, 321–2, 325–7
Redesdale, 69, 113–14, 136, 138–9, 178–80, 236, 238, 266
redress, 29, 63, 168, 187, 246, 265, 311; *see also* march days; reconciliation ceremonies; vengeance culture
   breaches of the truce, 183
   compensation, 172, 186, 188, 191, 270, 328–31
   cross-border homicide, 191–3
   injury, of, 170
   trod, 189–91
religious houses
   cross-border links within landed society, 116–17
   landowners, 114–16

towers and castles
   status and aspirations, 86–7
   remoteness leading to 'lawlessness', 6–13
reparation, 187–8, 192, 196, 270, 308, 326, 328–30. *See also* compensation for injury; reconciliation ceremonies; redress,
retaining. *See* indentures of retainer
Richard III
   council in the north, 175, 223, 240
   usurpation, 111, 210, 222
rights in land, 2, 24, 35, 39
Roxburgh, 78
   Roxburgh Castle, 112, 114, 248, 266
royal council, 174–5, 182, 222–4, 239; *see also* council in the north
   arbitrations, 313
royal justice, 37, 39–40, 45, 180–1, 270, 339, 344
   administration of justice, 169
   border justice compared, 45, 167, 196, 265, 270, 308, 335, 339, 341
   courts, 174–5
   justices of the peace, 175–6
   liberties and franchises, 178–80
   private appeal of felony, 177–8
   sheriff's tourn, 176–7
   sheriffs, 172–4

Sandford, family of Askham, 121, 123, 143, 156, 162–3, 217, 296, 300, 311–12, 318, 325, 330–1
Sark, Battle of (1448), 59, 61
self-policing, 39, 41, 169, 339
settlements in tail male, 125–7
shared cultural values, habits and pursuits, 18, 20. *See also* acculturation
sheriffs' powers and duties, 172–4
sheriff's tourn, 176–7
siege warfare, 244–6
social cohesion, 27, 328
social militarisation, 19
Storey, R.L., 2, 213, 240, 344
structures of landed society, 8–11
sub-baronial landowners, 112–13
surnames, 22–3, 25, 96–7; *see also* kinship; patronymic naming patterns
   Anglo-Scottish marches, 161–3
   Charltons, 139–40
   English surnames with Scottish dimensions
      Armstrongs, 151–2
      Bells, 146–9
      Elwalds, 149–51
      Grahams, 152–5
      Halls, 145–6

393

Index

surnames (cont.)
Fenwicks, 139
geographical clusters, 162
Hedleys, 142–3
mixed status, 293–4
Obilson/Oblisson/Olbison, 144
origins of, 22
Redes, 140–2
term, use of and meaning, 137–9, 161, 163, 337
symbolic acts of violence
duels and tournaments, 298
sporting violence, 298

towers and castles, 57–9, 87–93, 337
architecture, 75
classification, 76–7
contemporary usage, 77–82
defence, 81–2
Ireland, 89–90
military function, 75
status and aspiration, 75, 82–6
religious houses, 86–7
terminology, 75–89
trade
maritime trade, 64–5
overland, 63–4
treason
administration of justice, 196
high treason, 183
march treason, 183–5
Treasons, Great Statute of (1352), 31, 183, 253–4, 256, 264
Treaty of Edinburgh-Northampton (1328), 5
Treaty of York (1237), 51, 57, 59, 63, 67
trod, 189–91
truce indentures, 67, 189–91
Anglo-Scottish truces (1484, 1488 and 1497), 64–5, 224–32, 338
liberties and franchises, 239–40
debatable lands, 56–7, 243

truce violations, 242–4
legitimsing truce violations, 244
Turner, F.J., 19, 52
Turpyn, Nicholas, 141, 147, 159, 213, 230, 246–7, 250–1, 265, 280, 289
turris, 79, 81, 88
Tynedale, 13, 55, 57, 69, 109, 136, 138–9, 179, 236–8, 246, 267
petition for autonomy, 179

'unitary kingdom' of England, 36–9
bureaucratic centralisation, 40–1
institutional uniformity, 40–1

vengeance culture, 23, 34–7, 45, 168, 196, 303–6
pardons, 298–9
premeditation, 299–300
principle of reciprocity, 271–2, 316
violence; *See also* border violence; conflict; cross-border conflict; force, use of; language and terminology; symbolic acts of violence
violent offences. *See* border violence

warden courts, 59, 182–5, 187, 223, 246, 251, 256, 264
wardens of the march, 9–10, 53
authority, 58
indentures of retainer, 120–2
Wark, 111, 245–6
Wark Castle, 28
Wars of the Roses, 5, 344
wealth distribution, 8, 113, 118
Weber, M., 24–5
Welsh marches, 11, 51, 53, 185
Westminster, view from, 38, 343
Whethamstede, John (abbot), 5
Wilkinson family, 143–4, 149, 156

York, 12, 55, 59, 282–3, 288

zonal frontiers, 50–1

394

Lightning Source UK Ltd.
Milton Keynes UK
UKHW031015101120
373118UK00006B/57